Paddy McCallum

WORLD CIVILIZATIONS

A COMPARATIVE STUDY

ROBERT J. WALKER

OXFORD
UNIVERSITY PRESS

OXFORD
UNIVERSITY PRESS

70 Wynford Drive, Don Mills, Ontario M3C 1J9
www.oupcan.com

Oxford New York
Athens Auckland Bangkok Bogotá Buenos Aires
Calcutta Cape Town Chennai Dar es Salaam
Delhi Florence Hong Kong Istanbul Karachi
Kuala Lumpur Madrid Melbourne Mexico City
Mumbai Nairobi Paris São Paulo Singapore
Tapei Tokyo Toronto Warsaw

and associated companies in
Berlin Ibadan

OXFORD is a trade mark of Oxford University Press

Canadian Cataloguing in Publication Data

Walker, Robert J. (Robert John), 1941-
  World Civilizations: a comparative study

For use in Ontario.
Includes index.
ISBN 0-19-541290-7

1. Comparative civilization. 2. Civilization, Ancient.
3. Civilization, Medieval. I. Title.

CB69.2.W34 1997a   909.07   C97-930009-6

Editors: Monica Schwalbe, Lana Kong, Judith Dawson
Design: Brett Miller
Layout: Gail Nina
Illustrations: VISUTronX
Photo Research: Patricia Buckley Editorial Services
Cover illustration: Tom Owen Edmunds / The Image Bank
Printed in Canada by Friesens

This book is printed on permanent (acid-free) paper. ∞

2 3 4 5 6—03 02 01 00 99

ACKNOWLEDGEMENTS

The publisher wishes to thank the following people for their
contribution in reviewing the manuscript:

Doug Gordon
Department Head, History and Contemporary Studies
Oakridge Secondary School
London, Ontario

Bayne MacMillan
Tantramar High School
Sackville, New Brunswick

Jim Petrie, Director
Global Education Centre
Fredericton, New Brunswick

Rob Sandhu
David Thompson Secondary School
Vancouver, British Columbia

Peter Spitzer
History teacher
Ancaster High and Vocational School
Ancaster, Ontario

Greg Young
Silverthorn Collegiate Institute
Etobicoke, Ontario

CONTENTS

Introduction

HUMANITY BEFORE CIVILIZATION

As humans, we have always been intrigued by the mystery of our origins. In our study of the beginnings of human life, we have tried to find answers to many perplexing questions. Did modern humans develop from one common ancestor? What stages did humankind pass through in its evolution? What brought early humans to the dawn of civilization?

To answer these questions, we must study the development of humankind over millions of years. The evidence for our investigation has been scattered and is often open to question or debate. Nevertheless, in the last few centuries, scholars have created theories to answer some of these questions. Over time, new evidence has proven many of these theories to be incorrect. As we uncover more evidence and apply the resources of modern technology to our search, no doubt other theories will be refuted as well. Each day, in fact, we are challenging and replacing theories about the nature of humanity before civilization, and adding pieces to the puzzle of this fascinating period of human history.

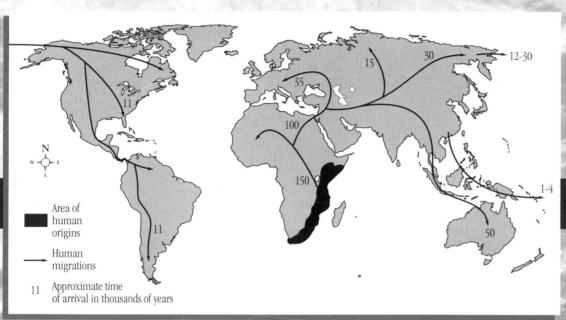

Area of
human
origins

Human
migrations

11 Approximate time
of arrival in thousands of years

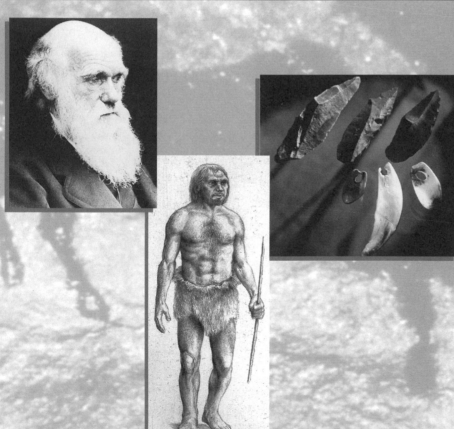

THE ORIGIN OF HUMANS

Figure 1-1
A reconstruction of Australopithecus afarensis

Ethiopia: Haddar, 1992—

"We need a skull. We really must have a complete cranium." That goal, which I underscored in my journal one night shortly after we arrived at Hadar, was on everyone's mind as we set up camp in the baking wilderness of Ethiopia's Afar region....

On February 26 Bob Walter and I visited colleagues working in another section of Hadar. When we returned, Bill Kimbel greeted us near the dining tent.

"Well, the hits keep coming," he said.

Yoel, sitting at a table, smiled broadly.

"I found a skull," he said simply. As he listed the various parts of the skull he had recovered, I could feel my heart racing. He had the occipital bone, a major chunk of palate with teeth, many fragments of the cranial vault, a canine tooth—and the face. He had most of a very large, rugged-looking skull—no doubt a male *afarensis!*

1993

Bill, Yoel, and I arranged a special trip back to Ethiopia early in 1993 to work solely on the reconstruction of the skull for a month. We spent long days examining the fragments in a tiny interior lab at the museum. We peered through microscopes and with sharpened needles picked away the grains of sediment that time had cemented to the skull fragments. Bill and Yoel then put the pieces together, and finally we could stare into the eyes of this magnificent face.

In 1974, the paleoanthropologist Donald Johanson had uncovered a fossilized skeleton in the parched earth at Hadar in Ethiopia. It was the most complete skeleton ever found of the human ancestor later named *Australopithecus afarensis*. But the team had not found a skull. The skull was the key to unlocking the major characteristics of this new species, believed to be the common ancestor of all later hominids (humanlike creatures), including

modern humans. In 1992, Johanson's team made their remarkable discovery. They found the critical skull fragments.

Reconstructing the skull from the fragments was a painstaking but rewarding task. Johanson and the paleoanthropologist Yoel Rak, who had originally discovered the skull fragments, worked with others to create a plaster cast. Then a team of scientists at the University of Zurich in Switzerland used computerized mirror imaging and stereo-lithography to create a more complete plastic model. At his studio in Denver, artist John Gurche applied the final touches to create a close representation of the original face. We now have a picture of what this human ancestor from more than 3.5 million years ago looked like.

Why is a discovery like that of the *afarensis* skull, and the reconstructive work that followed, so important to our understanding of our human ancestors? How has modern technology helped to provide a clearer picture of our distant past?

UNLOCKING THE SECRETS OF THE PAST

THE NATURE OF HISTORY

History is the study of change over time. The task of historians is to gather information from a particular time period when a significant change or development took place. In their research, they try to answer two important questions: *Why* did this change take place? and, *What effects* did this change have on the people who experienced it?

True historians are cautious about jumping to conclusions too quickly. Before they express a theory or viewpoint, they must follow a detailed process. To begin with, they must gather as much data as possible from a wide variety of sources. These sources may include physical remains of plants and animals, or ***artifacts*** (human-made objects) such as tools, shards of pottery, or ruined buildings. Other vital sources are written records, including both ***primary documents***, written by people of the period, and ***secondary accounts***, written about past events. Then the historians must care-

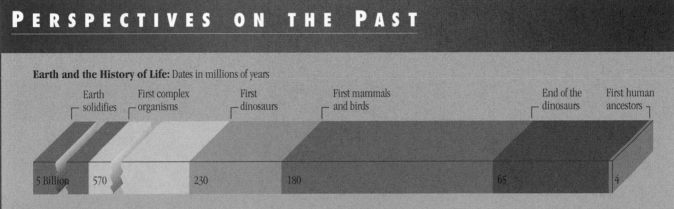

PERSPECTIVES ON THE PAST

Earth and the History of Life: Dates in millions of years

| Earth solidifies | First complex organisms | First dinosaurs | First mammals and birds | End of the dinosaurs | First human ancestors |

| 5 Billion | 570 | 230 | 180 | 65 | 4 |

Figure 1-2 *Human history in perspective*

Think back millions of years. What was the environment like on the earth? When did our first human ancestors walk the planet? What did they look like and how did they live?

We still do not have complete answers to these questions. What we do know, however, is that the study of our origins can be both an exhilarating and a humbling experience.

You may be surprised to discover that human history is just a blink of time in the history of the earth. Our planet is billions of years old. Dinosaurs roamed the earth until 65 million years ago. According to the most recent evidence, the earliest known human ancestors

first appeared only a little over four million years ago.

Although we have inhabited the planet for only a very short time, relatively, the story of humanity's survival and evolution is remarkable. Our human ancestors developed while the earth was going through radical climatic and environmental changes. They survived through four ice ages (each lasting between 50 000 and 100 000 years), when the world's climate cooled and huge ice sheets covered much of the earth's northern hemisphere. Our first human ancestors appeared in Africa, far from the great ice fields. As you will see, it was finally one species, known as *Homo sapiens,* that survived and went on to establish the first civilizations on earth.

fully analyze the data. Is the material reliable? Is it relevant to the issue under investigation? Which facts are most important? Which can be ignored?

Since historians are almost never able to unearth *all* of the facts in their investigations, they must fill in the missing pieces by speculation and interpretation. In other words, historians must make educated guesses. For example, how did humans first learn to grow grains? We may never know for certain, but we can speculate that when early humans gathered wild grains, some seeds fell on the ground and sprouted, giving people the idea of planting the seeds and growing their own crops.

Finally, the historian tries to reconstruct the past as accurately as possible. This reconstruction always involves some bias on the part of historians because they base their theories or possible explanations on their particular interpretations of the evidence. This blend of fact and opinion makes history both controversial and dynamic. Viewpoints are constantly being challenged, and exciting new discoveries are still being made.

Collecting the data is an extremely important stage in the historical process. To create a complete picture of a particular time period, the historian must gather material related to political, economic, social, and often geographic or environmental developments. Political developments concern the operation and decisions of the government. Economic developments include the ways in which the people survived or made a living. Social developments relate to people's homes and to their culture—art, architecture, and music, for example. Geographic developments include the ways in

which the environment changed or affected human actions and conditions. To truly understand what a society was like, the historian must collect political, economic, and social data relating to people of all classes within that society.

Historians studying modern history have the advantage of volumes of text material written by people who lived during a particular period or experienced a significant historical change. The farther back we go in our investigations, however, the more difficult the gathering of historical data becomes. Historians sometimes find themselves investigating a period that has no written records or has written records that cannot be translated. The lack of primary documents is one of the main

reasons why the study of humanity before civilization has been so difficult, and why theories about the period are constantly being challenged. Fortunately, historians researching ancient history have the assistance of various field specialists who act as detectives, helping to gather the evidence to reconstruct the past.

DETECTIVES OF THE PAST

Archaeology is the study of the material remains of the past. Without this science and the work of archaeologists, we would know very little about ancient humans. **Archaeologists** are specialists in the study of early humans and early civilizations because we have few, if any, written records from this era. To understand this

Figure 1-3

Donald Johanson (far left) displays the complete collection of hominid fossils found in deposits exposed along the ravines and tributary valleys of the Hadar River

INNOVATIONS
Determining the Date of Archaeological Finds

How are archaeological finds dated? How has new technology improved these methods?

Radiocarbon or carbon-14 dating is used as a way to determine the age of a find. Physicist Willard F. Libby of the University of Chicago discovered this method in 1948. Carbon 14 or C-14 is an unstable or radioactive form of carbon that has eight neutrons, rather than the six associated with ordinary carbon or carbon 12. All forms of life have organic molecules containing carbon atoms, and have about the same ratio of C-14 atoms to other carbon atoms in their tissues. When an organism dies, the C-14 begins to decay. In radiocarbon dating, the fewer the C-14 atoms, the older the organism.

When it decays, living matter gives off faint radioactive emissions. In Libby's radiocarbon dating technique, instruments such as a radiation detector and counter or a particle detector and counter record these emissions. The decay rate is used to figure out the proportion of C-14 atoms in the sample being dated.

The rate of decay is steady. The half-life of C-14 is about 5730 years. In other words, in 5730 years, half of the C-14 will have decayed. The next quarter decays after another 5730 years. After 50 000 years, there is little measurable C-14 left. Therefore, radiocarbon dating works well for dating relatively recent objects from the distant past.

To date older materials, however, other techniques are needed. For example, thorium decay and transformations can be used to date items between 100 000 and 500 000 years old. In rocks, the decay of potassium 40 to argon 40 can be used to date specimens from 500 000 years old to millions of years old. The decay of rubidium to strontium can be used to date archaeological finds into the billions of years.

Archaeologists have other methods as well. Sometimes, for example, they measure the amount of surface decomposition on certain stone tools or the amount of thermoluminescence visible when ancient pottery is heated.

During the 1980s, Derek York of the University of Toronto developed a new dating technology using lasers. This method made it possible to get an accurate date from a single microscopic crystal of volcanic mineral.

---

early period in our history, we depend on physical remains.

Excavations at archaeological sites have yielded many types of physical evidence. They include artifacts, such as ancient stone implements and pottery, as well as organic materials, such as animal and human bones or their fossilized remains. *Fossils* are the recognizable remains, or the impressions left by them, of a plant or animal preserved in the earth's crust.

Archaeologists study the finds at various sites to unravel some of the mysteries surrounding how humans lived. They are assisted in their detective work by other closely associated scientists called anthropologists, paleontologists, and paleoanthropologists. *Anthropologists* are scientists who study the origin, development, distribution, social habits, and culture of humans. A *paleontologist* examines the fossil remains of animal and plant life to understand past geological periods. A *paleoanthropologist* combines the work of both these scientists.

The discovery of fossil bones has helped the study of human origins immensely. While archaeologists have found stone implements and pottery in the acidic soils of tropical forests, they have not found plant or animal remains there because organic material decays very quickly. They have made their most important discoveries, therefore, at sites where the soil has preserved plant and animal material. These sites have usually been located in hot, dry regions, such as deserts, cold, dry areas, such as the Arctic, and some special environments, such as peat bogs. In peat bogs, acids cause bones to decay but the peat and moisture preserve the flesh.

The oldest human fossil remains have been found in Africa, where archaeologists are fairly certain the first humans lived.

From there, our ancestors spread along the seaward fringes of Europe and Asia and onto islands that were possibly once linked to the mainland, such as Java and Sumatra. It was not until late in the fourth ice age that humans entered the western hemisphere.

Through careful excavation at archaeological sites and painstaking analysis of fossil bones, scientists have concluded that human culture developed in three main stages. We can define human culture as the way people lived, including, for example, their arts, beliefs, inventions, traditions, language, and homes. During the earliest stage of human development, our ancestors lived in the open. In the second stage, humans learned to use fire, which provided the warmth and light they needed for living in rock shelters at the mouth of caves. During the third developmental stage, humans learned to farm and live in villages.

REFLECT AND ANALYZE

1. What stages does a historian go through before formulating a theory about the past? Why does history always involve some degree of bias?

2. Why is the study of early humans especially difficult and controversial?

3. What evidence do we have that the earliest humans lived in Africa?

4. Imagine that you are the paleoanthropologist working on an excavation site, and a team member has just unearthed the remains of an early human skeleton. Create a list of questions that you would ask about this find in order to learn as much as possible about it.

HUMAN EVOLUTION

THE THEORY OF EVOLUTION

Evolution as a theory suggests that the great variety of plant and animal life on earth developed gradually through natural processes. Although such an idea had been suggested as early as the sixteenth century, the great English biologist Charles Darwin (1809–1882) gave the theory prominence. The most important of Darwin's works is *On the Origin of Species by Means of Natural Selection*, first published in 1859.

In 1831, Darwin had accepted an appointment as an unpaid naturalist on the exploring ship *Beagle*. Over the course of a five-year round-the-world voyage, Darwin examined geological formations, collected fossils, and studied plants and animals. These investigations led him to doubt that divine creation had brought all species of living things into existence at one moment. His doubts challenged the traditional theory of creationism held for centuries in the western world. According to creationism, based on a literal interpretation of the Book of Genesis in the Bible, God created the earth and all living things in their ultimate forms.

Darwin's theory of evolution, on the other hand, was based on the idea that species changed or adapted over time in response to their environment. Darwin observed that members of a single species vary greatly in shape, size, colour, and strength. Most of these variations, he believed, could be inherited. He also noticed that the population of a species tended to remain the same size, even though parents usually produced more than two offspring. Therefore, he concluded, there had to be competition for survival. In the struggle for survival, his theory stated, organisms with characteristics less well suited to their environments likely died without producing young. Those organisms with more useful characteristics survived and reproduced, passing on these variations to their offspring. As descendants developed other favourable variations, they passed on these characteristics as well. As a result, Darwin argued, organisms with more helpful characteristics survived the struggle for existence. Others died out. He called this process ***natural selection***.

Natural selection had other effects as

Figure 1-4

Charles Darwin, photographed in 1869

well, Darwin believed. Many newly developed organisms remained in their old habitats and crowded older forms out of existence. Other new organisms made their way into new surroundings, prospered, and kept on adapting. Therefore, there was a steady succession of new species best suited to an environment at a particular time. A modern extension of Darwin's theory, known as neo-Darwinism, suggests that evolution proceeded rapidly at some points in history, but very slowly at others, resulting in long periods of little change.

Charles Darwin never professed that his writings provided proof of evolution or of the origin of species. They only proposed the theory and suggested that evolution might help to explain a number of mysterious facts about plants and animals. Two later scientific developments have given the theory its credibility. First, the science of genetics helped to explain the variations in each species and how these variations are passed on. Second, evidence gathered from fossil remains in recent years supports Darwin's ideas. Gaps in the theory still remain, however, and we do not have a complete record of human evolution.

Followers of the theory of evolution and believers in divine creation have not always found common ground on the questions surrounding the origins of species. Do the two viewpoints necessarily cancel each other out? All religions have creation stories. All the civilizations presented in this book developed creation stories to

PERSPECTIVES ON THE PAST

The Theory of Evolution Versus the Theory of Creation: The Scopes "Monkey Trial"

Why did this famous trial come about in 1925? Who won this case? Do you think that the theory of evolution necessarily disproves divine creation?

Figure 1-5
The Scopes trial. Clarence Darrow is in the centre of the photo

One of the great challenges to the theory of evolution came in the United States in 1925. Darwin's theory of evolution had existed for decades, but a strong movement arose against it in the 1920s because some people were concerned that fundamentalist protestantism was crumbling. Because the theory of evolution seemed to undermine beliefs in Christian ideas and values, the state of Tennessee passed a law prohibiting the teaching of Darwin's ideas.

In 1925, the American Civil Liberties Union convinced John Scopes, a high school biology teacher in Tennessee, to test the state law. The American Civil Liberties Union believed that the law threatened the First Amendment of the Constitution of the United States, which guaranteed freedom of speech.

Clarence Darrow, one of the greatest criminal lawyers of the era, defended Scopes. William Jennings Bryan, a popular political leader, argued the case in favour of the literal or fundamentalist interpretation of creation.

Many people followed the trial with keen interest. In particular, members of the American Civil Liberties Union looked upon it as a test case. If the jury decided to uphold the Tennessee law, other states might follow Tennessee's example and prohibit the teaching of Darwin's theory.

John Scopes was found guilty and fined a hundred dollars. He had broken a law that had been duly and legally passed by the legislature of the state of Tennessee. The verdict had a surprising outcome, however. Although Scopes lost the case, the negative publicity that much of the media gave the state of Tennessee awarded the American Civil Liberties Union a moral victory.

explain their origins. As these stories represent the spiritual beliefs of a people or culture, they are certainly valid. Some people believe that creation stories are not intended to be taken literally, and therefore they do not conflict with the theory of evolution.

REFLECT AND ANALYZE

1. How did Charles Darwin become interested in evolution?

2. What did Darwin mean by "the process of natural selection"?

3. Why was Darwin's theory considered revolutionary?

4. Working with a partner, imagine that you are the prosecutor and your partner is the defendant in the famous Scopes trial. Create key arguments for your side of the case and then role-play the scene. Would the same arguments still be valid today?

THE PHYSICAL EVOLUTION OF HUMANS

Evolution traces human development through several stages or species from the first humanlike beings to modern humans. Although we still do not know exactly when the evolution of humans and apes diverged or who our common ancestor is, we do know that **hominids** (humanlike creatures) began to appear over four million years ago. Hominids are distinguished from apes most notably by their bipedalism (their ability to walk on two feet) and by their larger brain size. All hominids are members of the human family tree.

Bipedalism was an important development. Walking on two feet left the hands free to perform many different tasks, including carrying young over long distances and making tools and weapons. What prompted the first hominids to begin walking on two feet? We can still only speculate. One theory, still unproven, is that a climate change transformed eastern and southern African forests into dry, open grasslands. This terrain might have favoured the survival of apes that could walk upright. The gradual increase in brain size was a second important development. The larger brain, associated with increased intelligence, is a crucial part of what we believe makes us human.

ARDIPITHECUS RAMIDUS

Our understanding of human evolution is constantly changing. For example, as recently as 1994 at Aramis, Ethiopia, people unearthed fossils of a previously unknown species dating from 4.4 million years ago. This humanlike creature walked the earth nearly half a million years earlier than the oldest human ancestor identified to that point. This exciting discovery led to the identification of a new genus called *Ardipithecus ramidus*. *Ramidus* has many chimplike as well as human features, but its position on the human family tree is still not certain. The mystery of this early hominid has still to be solved.

THE AUSTRALOPITHECINES

In 1995, Maeve Leakey of the National Museums of Kenya discovered some of the oldest representatives of a widely studied human genus, the australopithecines. She and her team located pieces of a bipedal hominid, 4.1 million years old, which she named *Australopithecus anamensis*. She made the discovery at Kanapoi, near Lake Turkana in Kenya. *Australopithecus anamensis* is an early species, with very pronounced apelike teeth. Some scientists suggest that this species may have given rise to *Australopithecus afarensis*.

At the beginning of this chapter, you read about one of the most important *Australopithecus* discoveries—a discovery that strongly suggests our origins lie in Africa. In 1974, at Hadar, Ethiopia, Donald Johanson and his team unearthed a set of fossilized bones of a female hominid approximately 3.18 million years old. They nicknamed their discovery "Lucy" after the Beatles song "Lucy in the Sky With Diamonds," which was popular at the time. These fossilized bones led to the identification, in 1978, of *Australopithecus afarensis*, a species that may have survived almost unchanged for 900 000 years. In Lucy's species, Johanson believed that he had found the earliest common ancestor of all later hominids.

In 1975, the Johanson team discovered the fossils of at least thirteen other *afarensis* individuals at a nearby site. These hominids, called the "First Family," are estimated to be 3.2 million years old. The sizes of their bones vary. Johanson explained this fact by theorizing that the males were much larger than the females. Critics argued that the variation in bone size actually meant that the bones belonged

Figure 1-6
A theatrical re-enactment of what Lucy may have looked like

Leakey discovered the footprints of two ancient hominids in volcanic ash left from an eruption 3.5 million years ago at Laetoli in Tanzania. Her discovery further supported the view that ancient hominids walked upright. The prints demonstrate a humanlike stride: a strong stroke with the heel and a push off with the big toe to propel the body forward. Paleontologists studying the evidence from the site suggest that the two sets of footprints are those of a man and a woman.

Donald Johanson believed that the footprints belonged to ancestors of Lucy, and therefore the *Australopithecus afarensis* species. Others believed the footprints belonged to a species called *Australopithecus africanus*, which lived in the southern part of Africa approximately 2.5 to 3 million years ago. There were two *africanus* lines. One, called the *Australopithecus robustus*, died out about a million years ago. A second line branched off to become the *Homo habilis*. Johanson's critics believed that *afarensis* was nothing more than an East African version of *Australopithecus africanus*. It was not a distinct species, as Johanson claimed.

In 1992, Johanson's team found the much-sought-after *afarensis* skull. Over three million years old, the skull helped to clarify Lucy's place on the human family tree. When scientists examined the skulls of the two species, *Australopithecus africanus* and *Australopithecus afarensis*, they found clear differences. Johanson concluded that *afarensis* was therefore a distinct species.

What has all of the scientific investigation told us about the characteristics and times of the australopithecines? The Johanson skull indicated that *afarensis* characteristically had a jutting jaw, heavy brow, flaring cheeks, and strong muscles. Their brain was about one-third the size of a modern human brain, probably exceeding 500 cm^3. They had long, powerful forearms, curved fingers and toes, upward-tilting shoulders, and were completely bipedal. Males were larger and heavier than females.

Afarensis likely travelled in groups, possibly of 25 to 30 members. Pollen evidence suggests that they lived in forests of juniper and olive trees. They walked relatively upright on two feet, but also

to at least two distinct species. They also believed that one of these other creatures—rather than Lucy—might be the earliest common ancestor of modern humans.

In 1978, anthropologist Mary D.

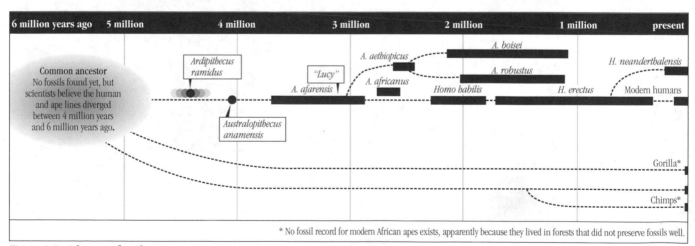

Figure 1-7 *A human family tree*

	EARLIEST ANCESTORS **2.5–4.4 MILLION YEARS AGO**	**HOMO ERECTUS** **2 MILLION YEARS AGO**
ENVIRONMENTAL DEVELOPMENTS	• *Ardipithecus ramidus*, 4.4 million years ago; possibly live in forests or on grasslands; scientists are not certain • *Australopithecus anamensis*, 4.1 million years ago • *Australopithecus afarensis* ("Lucy"), 3.18 million years ago; live in forests • *Australopithecus africanus*, 3 million years ago • *Homo habilis,* 2.5 million years ago	**THE PALEOLITHIC AGE (OLD STONE AGE)** • cold climate; glacial coverage of Europe, Asia, and North America forms four times through four ice ages • ice fields of Antarctica stretch over wide regions of the southern hemisphere • first ice age—2 000 000 years ago (the Gunz or Nebraska Ice Sheet) • only the central areas of the earth's surface remain warm enough to support human life • second ice age—1 250 000 years ago (the Mindel or Kansan Ice Sheet) • third ice age—500 000 years ago (the Riis or Illinois Ice Sheet)
PHYSICAL DEVELOPMENTS	• *Ardipithecus ramidus*, chimplike and human features; possibly walk on two legs, but evidence is not conclusive • *Australopithecus anamensis*, apelike teeth; walk on two legs (bipedal) • *Australopithecus afarensis,* completely bipedal; jutting jaw; heavy brow; flaring cheeks; strong muscles; long, powerful forearms; curved fingers and toes; upward-tilting shoulders; brain about one-third the size of a modern human • *Australopithecus africanus*, hips, legs, and feet more like humans than apes; brain about the size of a gorilla's; massive jaw • *Homo habilis*, larger brain size than predecessors; teeth formation similar to modern humans	• walk upright like humans • low-vaulted braincase, long and broad at the base • massive eyebrow ridges • high bony crests at the neckline • larger brains than those of the australopithecines
TECHNOLOGICAL/ECONOMIC DEVELOPMENTS	• *Ardipithecus ramidus*, very little is yet known about this hominid, discovered in late 1994 • *Australopithecus anamensis*, little is yet known • *Australopithecus afarensis*, no stone tools or weapons; travel in groups of 25 to 30 members • *Australopithecus africanus*, meat-eaters, probably scavenged carrion; relied on small prey such as reptiles and rodents • *Homo habilis*, first hominids to fashion stone tools	• survive by hunting wild animals and gathering plants for food • use tools made of stone, bone, and wood • spears and clubs are used as weapons • live in shallow dug-out pits covered with brush or hides, or in caves under rock ledges • learn to make fire • learn how to use language

HOMO SAPIENS 230 000–450 000 YEARS AGO	MODERN HUMANS – HOMO SAPIENS SAPIENS 40 000 YEARS AGO
THE PALEOLITHIC AGE (OLD STONE AGE) • Neanderthals • fourth ice age—100 000 years ago (the Würm or Wisconsin Ice Sheet)	**THE PALEOLITHIC AGE (OLD STONE AGE)** • fourth ice age begins to melt • Paleolithic Age ends as the climate warms (12 000 years ago) **THE MESOLITHIC AGE (MIDDLE STONE AGE)** • forests begin to develop • stretches of grassland and desert appear in some areas • Mesolithic Age ends (10 000 years ago) **THE NEOLITHIC AGE (NEW STONE AGE)** • the climate continues to grow warmer • additional new plants, such as wild barley, wheat, vegetables, and fruits, begin to appear • Neolithic Age ends (about 7 000 years ago)
• broad noses • thick eyebrow ridges • low foreheads • skull slopes back low over the brain • face juts forward • cheekbones angle to the side • short limbs • stocky bodies	• height equal to modern northwestern Europeans • high foreheads • curving noses • large jaws • small teeth
• hunters and gatherers • co-operate in groups to hunt large prey and take care of weak and sick members • may have had a form of religion; bury their dead • develop more sophisticated tools, e.g., hand axe to fit the thumb and fingers and flaked blades	• begin to hunt smaller animals, such as wild pigs and deer, and to fish in the lakes and rivers • some gatherers settle down into permanent homes • cave paintings indicate the development of art • grow their own food; domesticate animals • settle in large groups, forming villages • artisans make products such as pottery; trade begins • religion begins as humans search for answers to the mysteries of life • governments develop and begin making laws; earliest civilizations are formed

climbed trees, probably in search of fruits and nuts. They may also have climbed trees to sleep, or to escape predators. Our *afarensis* ancestors were more likely to be preyed on than to prey, scientists guess. Lacking stone tools or weapons, they could only hurl rocks when threatened.

REFLECT AND ANALYZE

1. Why was it so difficult for Johanson to get *Australopithecus afarensis* accepted as a separate species in the human family tree?

2. What have we learned about the characteristics and times of australopithecines from the body of scientific evidence to date?

3. What evidence do we have that our understanding of human evolution is far from complete?

THE STONE AGE

The descendants of the australopithecines lived in the period called the Stone Age. We call the period this because most of the artifacts found from this time are made of stone. Humans who lived in the Stone Age are generally classified into a group or genus called *Homo*. *Homo* was divided into two successive and overlapping species— *Homo erectus* and *Homo sapiens*. Most experts divide the Stone Age into three stages: the Paleolithic or Old Stone Age (2 million BCE–10 000 BCE), the Mesolithic or Middle Stone Age (10 000 BCE–8000 BCE), and the Neolithic or New Stone Age (8000 BCE–5000 BCE). What characteristics are associated with each of these stages? What significant developments took place in each stage? How did our human ancestors develop and live in each era?

HOMO HABILIS

Historians believe *Homo habilis*, or "handy man," flourished in Africa about 2.5 million years ago. *Homo habilis* were the first hominids to develop and use stone tools—proof of their ingenuity and creative ability. A fragmentary *habilis* skull found near the Olduvai Gorge in Tanzania may have had a cranial capacity of about 725 cm³. The brain size and the presence of humanlike teeth suggest that *Homo habilis* might have been our human ancestor.

Many scientists believe that *Homo habilis* bridges the evolutionary gap between *Australopithecus* and *Homo*. Yet, the sequence of human ascent is still uncertain. In 1972, Richard Leakey unearthed the remains of a very humanlike skull in Kenya that dates back 2.5 million years. His discovery suggests that a form of *Homo* might have coexisted with the australopithecines.

HOMO ERECTUS

Homo erectus first appeared about 2 million years ago. Their species name refers to the fact that they could walk completely upright, like modern humans. Only a few dozen skulls of this species have been found, notably in Africa, Java, and China. The *Homo erectus* skull shape differed from ours. Individuals had a low-vaulted braincase that was long and broad at the base. They had massive eyebrow ridges and high, bony crests at the neckline. Their brains ranged in size from 850 to 1400 cm³, and were larger than those of the australopithecines.

The first specimens were found in Java in 1891 and 1892 CE. Called Java Man, they are about 700 000 years old. Their teeth are very much like those of *Homo habilis* of eastern Africa, suggesting that *Homo erectus* might have evolved from this African species.

In 1984, on the west shore of Kenya's Lake Turkana, Richard Leakey and Alan Walker discovered the most complete

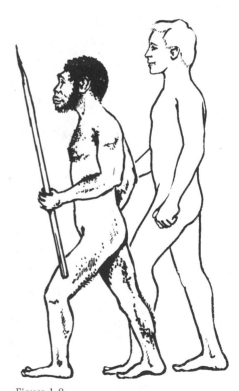

Figure 1-8
Homo erectus *compared with modern human*

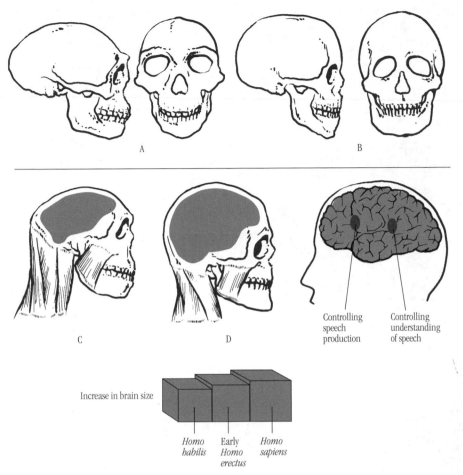

A   B

C   D

Controlling speech production   Controlling understanding of speech

Increase in brain size

Homo habilis | Early Homo erectus | Homo sapiens

Figure 1-9

Comparing the Homo erectus *skull (A, C) with that of a modern human (B, D).* Homo erectus *had heavy brow ridges and heavy neck and jaw muscles, while modern people have larger brain cases. Presumably, as the brain increased in size, its internal structure changed, particularly in regard to the speech centres.*

Homo erectus skeleton ever found. It was a skeleton of a 12-year-old boy dating from 1.6 million years ago.

These early human ancestors probably survived by hunting wild animals and gathering plants for food. With their increasing skills, they made tools of stone, bone, and wood.

Homo erectus was the first species to use fire and the first to migrate into Europe and Asia from Africa. As we will see later, the use of fire was a very significant development.

HOMO SAPIENS

The species name, *Homo sapiens*, means "man who thinks"—an appropriate title for the species that formulated the spoken language and developed more sophisticated tools. The most ancient *Homo sapiens* find was discovered in Hungary in 1965, in a Mindel deposit dating from about 450 000 to 400 000 years ago. (Mindel is the name given to the second of the four European glacial periods of the Stone Age.) The find consisted of a single occipital bone from the base of the braincase. Although the bone has a crest at the neckline, its shape is quite similar to that of the occipital bone in modern humans.

Other remains of *Homo sapiens* have been found in England, Germany, and France. These bones date from approximately 250 000 years ago, the period between the third and fourth ice ages. The skull shape of *Homo sapiens* differs from that of *Homo erectus*, although the cranial capacity of the two is similar.

There are two types of *Homo sapiens*: the Neanderthals, or *Homo sapiens neanderthalis*, and the *Homo sapiens sapiens*, whose earliest members have been traced to the Levant (the countries bordering on the East Mediterranean), the Near East, and the Balkans. By 40 000 BCE, they were well established in western Europe, where they are generally called Cro-Magnons.

NEANDERTHALS

Located in Europe, Neanderthals first appeared about 230 000 years ago and disappeared approximately 30 000 years ago. Quarry workers in Düsseldorf first discovered the remains of these people in the Neander Valley of Germany in 1856. More finds have since been located primarily in Belgium, France, and other parts of Europe. At the turn of the century, the bones of as many as 80 Neanderthals were discovered in a cave in the Croatian village of Krapina.

From central Europe, the Neanderthals travelled east into central Asia, even migrating south into the Middle East. Their

Figure 1-10

A Neanderthal hunter

Figure 1-11

A museum model of a Cro-Magnon man blowing pigment onto a cave wall, to create a painting like that shown in Figure 1-13

total population at any one time probably numbered fewer than 100 000. During the 200 000 years in which the Neanderthals flourished, anatomically modern humans (*Homo sapiens sapiens*) were evolving in Africa and possibly in the Middle East.

Where did the Neanderthals come from? Scientists wonder whether they were one of our direct ancestors or whether they were a separate species, driven to extinction by modern humans. Many scientists believe that the Neanderthals descended from the species *Homo erectus*, which migrated into Europe from Africa through western Asia between 700 000 and a million years ago.

During the classical Neanderthal period, considered to be about 130 000 years ago, the Neanderthals were formidable hunters and gatherers. They hunted small rhinoceroses and other large animals such as elk, bison, and even mammoths.

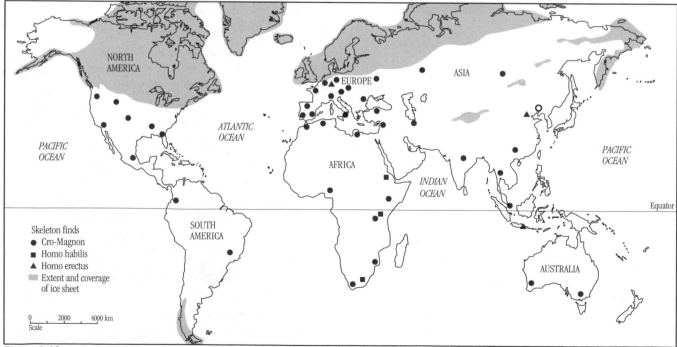

Figure 1-12

Skeletal find locations: Homo habilis, Homo erectus *and Cro-Magnon*

They gathered edible plants, shellfish, and small reptiles.

Characteristically, their faces were accentuated by broad noses and thick eyebrow ridges over their eyes. They had low foreheads and lacked the strong chin of modern humans. Their skull sloped back low over their brain. Their face jutted forward beneath the eyes, making the cheekbones angle to the side rather than to the front. Their limbs were short and their bodies were stocky.

For a Neanderthal, life was hard and dangerous. Life expectancy was short. Of six Neanderthal skeletons found in a cave near Shanidar, Iraq, the oldest person lived about 45 years. Most Neanderthals didn't survive their thirties.

One of the most intriguing questions about this species remains unanswered.

Why did the Neanderthals disappear? Perhaps they were conquered and destroyed by modern humans. Perhaps later arrivals brought deadly new diseases that wiped them out. Perhaps the Neanderthals inbred with modern humans. Other scientists suggest that they may have simply died out because they were unable to compete with modern humans.

HOMO SAPIENS SAPIENS

About 40 000 years ago, modern humans moved into Europe armed with the skills to make clothing, better shelters, and more efficient hearths. Nineteenth-century scientists named these newcomers the Cro-Magnon people after the French rock-shelter where three anatomically modern skeletons were discovered in 1868. Cro-Magnons were *Homo sapiens* who evolved

in Africa and slowly pushed their way into Europe. They developed the ability to endure colder climates, even climates as cold as those found in Iceland or Greenland.

Cro-Magnon people were about as tall as modern northwestern Europeans. Men were about 180 cm tall. Women were about 160 cm tall. Cro-Magnons also had many of the same facial and cranial features as modern northwestern Europeans. They had high foreheads, curving noses, large jaws, and small teeth. Eventually, their successors moved into Asia. About 30 000 years ago, they crossed the Bering Strait after the retreat of the ice and entered the Americas. Others reached Australia. With this migration, our modern human ancestors (*Homo sapiens sapiens*) spread throughout the world.

THROUGH THEIR EYES
Cave Drawings

Stone Age cave drawings are some of the earliest known forms of human art. What inspired early humans to create them? What can the drawings tell us about the lives and beliefs of the people who drew them?

These delicate cave drawings of bison, horses, rhinos, lions, and bears are among 300 found in the Vallon-Pont-d'Arc of France. The black and red figures have been created with soot, ochre, and blood. Archaeologists believe that the drawings may have been the focus of some tribal initiation rites 20 000 years ago.

Figure 1-13
Cave drawings from France

These works of art were created by Cro-Magnons, *(Homo sapiens sapiens)*. The Cro-Magnons had evolved in Africa 100 000 years earlier and had slowly pushed their way into Europe about 35 000 years ago, replacing the Neanderthals. The Cro-Magnons were the first of our ancestors to demonstrate artistic ability.

Art in this early period may have played an important social role. Drawings such as these might have been part of some initiation ceremony or ritual associated with hunting. The animals on the walls may represent the prey or the qualities sought by human hunters. Curiously, human figures seldom appear in the drawings, and when they do they are not rendered as finely or as realistically as the animals are. Perhaps drawing the animals in a lifelike way gave the artist some sense of power or mastery over them. The Cro-Magnons may have intended the "gallery of beasts" as a place for hunters to bond with one another and for young hunters to become part of their tribe.

REFLECT AND ANALYZE

1. In a chart or using labelled drawings, compare the distinguishing physical characteristics of Neanderthals and *Homo sapiens sapiens.*

2. What do you think probably caused the disappearance of Neanderthals some 30 000 years ago? Support your point of view.

3. Research other examples of early cave drawings. What do you find most remarkable about this art? What purposes do you think the drawings served? Try creating a cave drawing of your own.

Figure 1-14

A Neanderthal family buries one of its members: a reconstruction of a find at Shanidar Cave in Iraq

CULTURAL EVOLUTION IN THE STONE AGE

For thousands of years, there was no significant change in the cultural development of the human species. During the Stone Age, however, and particularly from about 35 000 years ago, remarkable technological, artistic, and cultural advances occurred. These developments are often called the "Great Leap Forward." It was during this period that humans showed their first signs of conscious planning, forethought, and creativity. They deliberately thought about making changes to their environment, and planned how they could produce these changes.

SOCIAL ORGANIZATION

One of the most significant developments was social organization. The people of the Stone Age lived in small groups or bands. Each band likely hunted and gathered within a region that it identified as its own home territory. That territory might have ranged over a distance of 16 to 80 km, depending on the size of the band and the availability of food.

People also began to live in the same place for relatively long periods, creating homes. For protection against the elements, they dug shallow pits and covered them with brush or hides. Sometimes they camped under rock ledges. Contrary to popular belief, they did not often live in caves. Caves were usually too cold and dark, and the smoke from campfires tended to linger, filling the lungs of the occupants and stinging their eyes. Therefore, people during the Stone Age used caves mainly during emergencies, such as storms, or when seeking refuge from large animals.

THEN AND NOW
The Tasaday of Mindanao

The scientific community has called the Tasaday of Mindanao "modern Stone Age people." Is this label appropriate? What ideas and images do people associate with the term "Stone Age"?

The Tasaday have kept alive the ways of their ancestors to an astounding degree. What can we learn from the Tasaday and from other aboriginal people who have protected their traditional ways of life?

In 1967, in the dense tropical forest of Mindanao, an island in the Philippines, a local hunter discovered a band of people who had never had contact with the outside world. The 24 men, women, and children were living just as their ancestors had lived thousands of years earlier. They had thrived independently of the outside world for all that time.

These people are the Tasaday. They live in the mountainsides of Mindanao in natural limestone caves. Some people believe that these caves may have served as the homes of the Tasaday for as long as 1000 years. Their ancestors had chosen to stay in one location because of a band ancestor's religious dream. In the dream, the ancestor had been told that remaining in one location would bring good health to the band. To leave the caves would only bring illness.

The Tasaday are food gatherers. They depend on the forest for food and clothing. Each day, the men and women go out in search of their food for the day. Their diet consists primarily of wild yam roots, berries, and bananas. They supplement these foods with crabs, frogs, tadpoles, and small fish, caught in cone-shaped cups made of twisted orchid leaves. Tasaday tools are made of bamboo and stone. Their clothing is created from orchid leaves and vines.

The Tasaday, who have mastered fire, use it to cook food and keep themselves warm. They have a spoken language but no written one. They neither have nor need a system for telling time or counting.

The Tasaday consider their discovery in 1967 to be a stroke of good luck. Their ancestor's dream had also spoken of the arrival of strangers who would bring them good fortune. The Philippine government has made the forest where the Tasaday live a protected area so that these people can continue to live in peace.

Cro-Magnons, who lived in the northern regions, built huts for part of the year. They made the walls and roof from animal skins held up by wooden posts, and then piled stones on the bottom to secure the posts in the ground.

Neanderthals were quite social. They organized group hunts, finding that cooperation helped them to capture large prey. Anthropologists also have evidence to suggest that Neanderthals took care of the weak and sick members within their community and that they buried their dead. Were they the first people to have a sense of religion—a belief, perhaps, in an afterlife?

We can't be sure, but the Neanderthals certainly had greater mental resources than their earlier human ancestors, and perhaps had the capacity for abstract thought.

The Cro-Magnons also lived in communities and survived through interaction. Like the Neanderthals, they found that cooperation with others improved their chances for survival. We can find evidence of this social interaction in fossil finds. For example, we know that Cro-Magnons traded stone tools over long distances. We also know that their settlements had housing for up to 40 or 50 individuals. Finally, like the Neanderthals, the Cro-Magnons collaborated to hunt and kill mammoths and woolly rhinoceroses.

HUNTING

Hunting may be described as the first specialized skill. Our earliest ancestors probably caught small prey, such as rodents, and ate carrion (dead meat) from larger animals. The Neanderthals, however, who were primarily hunters, learned to capture big game. To catch birds and smaller, fast-running animals, they used traps. To catch larger animals, such as rhinoceroses and elephants, they took advantage of the natural landscape in one of two possible ways.

The first way was to use pitfalls. A pitfall was a large hole covered by branches, leaves, and dirt. When the animal ran across the pitfall, it crashed through the covering, falling to the floor of the pit. The hunters then moved in and speared the animal over and over again until it bled to death.

The second way that the Neanderthals trapped larger prey was to use bogs and deep stream banks. They would surround and drive heavy animals into these swampy mudholes. As the heavy animal sank into the mud, the Neanderthals probably attacked it at close range with wooden spears topped by sharp stone points. In 1948 CE, one such wooden spear, approximately 2 m long, was discovered among the bones of a fossil elephant in a German bog. The Neanderthals' habit of thrusting their spears at their prey, rather than throwing them, put the hunters in greater danger and probably resulted in many injuries.

TOOL-MAKING

At first glance, we might think that Stone Age tools and weapons required only limited skill and technology. In fact, they represent a high level of craftsmanship and ingenuity. The earliest tools and weapons were made of stone; those of later periods were made of bone and wood as well. For their stone implements, the people preferred to use either flint or obsidian, a black volcanic glass. Both materials were hard but easy to shape. Some Stone Age tools and weapons were made of quartz or basalt, but these rocks were difficult to shape and could shatter easily.

The earliest tools were choppers and chopping tools. Choppers were stones that were chipped on only one face. Chopping tools were chipped on both sides to form a cutting edge.

Hand axes were the next implement created. These all-purpose tools were trimmed on both faces. Axe-crafters shaped the stone into an almond-shaped tool, pointed at one end and rounded at the other. Early in the Stone Age, they shaped the axes by striking the stone core with a hammerstone. Later, they flaked the rock to create sharper instruments. Flaking involved the careful chipping away of stone pieces from the original rock. If the toolmaker was skilful, the tool needed little refinishing.

Eventually, more efficient flake tools replaced hand axes. As their toolmaking skills developed, the people began to make side scrapers, points, and burins, using the same flaking technique. A burin is a narrow chisel used to cut notches and grooves in wood and bone. The people made it by striking a very small chip off the tip of a prepared flake.

Neanderthals developed a high level of expertise in toolmaking. They often travelled great distances in search of just the right piece of flint. After they found a suitable source, they had to remove or knap the flint from the core rock, a delicate process

Figure 1-15
Neanderthal blades and personal decorations, excavated in France

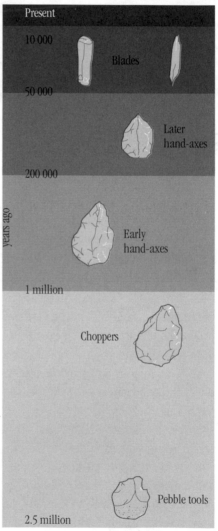

Figure 1-16
This chart shows when some of the different kinds of stone tools were made.

that took a great deal of skill. Learning this skill—knapping the flint unbroken—would have taken years.

During the classic Neanderthal period, toolmakers notched a hand axe to fit the thumb and the fingers. This new type of handle gave the user a more secure grip. They also skilfully fashioned pieces of flint into knives, scrapers, points, and blades. Neanderthals used different types of edges for cutting, butchering, scraping, and defleshing.

During the late Mesolithic Age, toolmaking improved even more. Finer blades and projectile weapons appeared. The people designed new implements for specialized purposes. For example, they created stone sickles and grinding stones to help them prepare wild grain for meals.

By about 40 000 years ago, when modern humans moved into Europe, they had learned to use the environment to their advantage, fashioning tools from stone, bone, horn, ivory, and wood. Their technology had advanced to the point where they could produce beads, ornaments, needles, fishing hooks, and—most importantly—bows and arrows. These better weapons allowed humans to become the hunters rather than the hunted.

SPEECH

Could early *Homo sapiens* speak? Scientists have long argued about whether Neanderthals had the anatomical equipment for speech. Voice boxes and vocal tracts do not fossilize, but the hyoid bone at the back of the tongue does. In modern humans, the voice box hangs from this very tiny bone.

In 1983 CE, an intact hyoid bone was discovered in a Neanderthal skeleton, 60 000 years old, excavated from a cave in Israel. When scientists examined this find closely, they could not distinguish it from a modern hyoid bone. Therefore, we can conclude that Neanderthals could speak, if only in a rudimentary fashion.

Language probably developed when humans first began to make different kinds of noises to mean different things. A certain type of grunt might have meant that someone was happy. A loud cry might have signalled danger. A soft cry might have been a plea for sympathy or compassion. A whimper might have indicated fear or loneliness.

Gradually, people developed a rudimentary language. Whether that language was sophisticated enough to store and pass on information and make sense of the world, we do not know. Christopher Stringer, a paleoanthropologist at the Natural Museum in London, believes that Stone Age humans may not have had a language as complex as ours, with past, present, and future tenses, but they could talk to each other.

Spoken language was an important development of the Stone Age. Language allowed people to work more closely together and to share their cultural knowledge.

USE OF FIRE

Prehistoric hunters and gatherers knew about fire hundreds of thousands of years before they learned how to make it themselves. Natural fires were a part of their world. Bolts of lightning struck trees, creating fires. Volcanoes erupted and spewed out burning coals. Piles of dry leaves and brush sometimes burst suddenly into flame. Paleolithic peoples first learned how to use these natural fires. They gathered embers, kindled them at campsites, and even carried them from one location to another. They used fire to keep their shelters warm, cook their food, and scare away wild animals.

Homo erectus learned how to make and control fire as early as 1.4 million years ago. They made fire by rubbing one stick back and forth against another, or by turning a stick rapidly in a hole in a dry log.

Evidence shows that Neanderthals had fire to keep them warm. Some cave floors where remains have been found consist almost entirely of compressed layers of ash, many metres thick. Hearths were simple. They resembled campfires rather than the more efficient rock-lined fireplaces of later humans.

Learning how to create fire revolutionized the lives of our ancestors, even though the full impact of this achievement was not felt for thousands of years. First, fire allowed humans to spread farther into the colder temperate regions of Europe and Asia. As they began to cook their food—a much faster process than eating it raw—they had more time to pursue other activities. Fire was also useful for hunting. They used it to harden the points of wooden spears so that the weapons could pierce the skin of a rhinoceros. Thus hunters had greater success and the food supply increased. Finally, Stone Age humans used fire for defence. They threw burning sticks at animals to drive them away from people's shelters.

THE NEOLITHIC REVOLUTION

THE NATURE OF THE REVOLUTION

During the Neolithic Age, people changed from being hunters and gatherers to being food producers. We call this transformation the Neolithic revolution.

Most scholars believe that Middle Eastern people were the first to discover that they could plant the seed from wild grain. How did they make such a discovery? We can picture a possible scene. . . .With the end of the last ice age, the climate has warmed and become wetter, allowing grains to grow. A woman who has gathered some wild rice grains from her home territory accidentally spills some of the seed on her way back to camp. Weeks later, she notices tiny shoots coming from the ground. Months later, she observes that the tiny shoots have grown into tall stalks bear-ing the same grains of rice that she spilled. She shares this discovery with her band, and they create the first planned crop.

During the same period, the Stone Age people began to domesticate animals such as dogs, cattle, pigs, sheep, and goats as another ready source of food. This important change may also have taken place by accident. Perhaps hunters built fences to close in a herd of wild animals. After killing one animal, they may have saved the rest for later. As the captured animals slowly lost their fear of people, they became domesticated. Hunters then became herders. They trained dogs—the first tamed animals—to help keep these herds under control.

THE EFFECTS OF THE REVOLUTION

The change to a food-producing economy had enormous impact on the lives of humans. The advent of agriculture increased the food supply dramatically, making it possible for larger groups of people to live together in one area. Therefore, permanent communities or villages began to develop.

The earliest known village is Jericho, which archaeologists date back to 8000 BCE. Another early village site was Catal Hüyük in southern Turkey, which prospered between 6500 BCE and 5700 BCE. Archaeologists have discovered that the Neolithic residents of Catal Hüyük lived in houses of sun-dried bricks with flat roofs made of mud-covered reeds. One of the unusual features of these homes was that they had no door. To help protect themselves against attack, residents entered their houses by ladder through a hole in the roof. Floors were covered with carpets of rushes and sleeping platforms were draped with mats.

A fairly steady food supply allowed Neolithic villagers to spend more time at activities other than farming. One of the most important new skills that they learned

Figure 1-17
The excavated walls of Jericho, the earliest known village

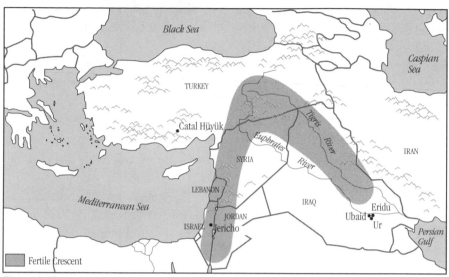

Figure 1-18

The "fertile crescent" in the Middle East, containing the earliest known agricultural sites

other goods from metal. Lumps of copper, lead, silver, and gold, found lying on the ground, they hammered into various shapes. These activities gave rise to a new group of craftspeople or artisans such as potters, jewellers, metal workers, carpenters, and weavers. In turn, these artisans helped to promote the development of trade as they became interested in exchanging their wares for food supplies. Trade led to new methods of transportation as Neolithic people began to think about better ways to transport their wares.

Settled communities also brought about the beginnings of government. Usually a single chief or leader was responsible for maintaining order in the village and ensuring that the property of all of the residents was secure. Most historians believe that the early chiefs filled a religious role as well as a political one, serving as priests as well as rulers. Their main religious responsibility was probably to offer up prayers on behalf of the entire village, asking the gods to protect the harvest and the community.

was how to make pottery. They made it from a mixture of clay, straw, and dung (animal waste). The straw kept the pottery from cracking when heated, and the dung gave the vessels extra strength. To build up a pot, people wound coils of the clay mixture in a circle and smoothed the sides. They then placed the pot in a trench, covered it with branches and straw, and set the kindling on fire. This early version of a kiln baked the pottery at a high temperature.

People of the Neolithic Age also learned how to make baskets, and how to weave cloth on a loom, an important invention of the age. They fashioned jewellery, eating utensils, weapons, and

Figure 1-19

The relative amount of land needed to feed individuals obtaining food in different ways

1 Hunter-gatherer: 10 km²
2 Dry-farmer: 0.5 km²
3 Irrigation farmer 0.1 km²

REFLECT AND ANALYZE

1. What was the Neolithic revolution and what were its most significant effects?

2. Why is trade an especially important development?

3. Compare life in a Neolithic village to the life of Neanderthal or early Cro-Magnon people.

CIVILIZATION

The word "civilization" comes from the Latin word *civis*, which means "citizen" or someone who lives in a city. By 5000 BCE, the effects of the Neolithic revolution had led to what we can describe as the earliest civilizations. People lived in permanent towns and cities. In the highly organized societies that began to develop, the people had a sophisticated knowledge of farming, trade, government, law, art, and science.

Some scholars have tried to identify very specific requirements or criteria that a society must meet in order to be considered a civilization. For example, some historians believe that literacy must be present before a group is civilized. In other words, the people must have a written language. Other historians believe that technology is the key factor. To them, a true civilization is one in which the people have developed the knowledge and expertise to build structures of stone or brick that are intended to last into the future. Still other scholars believe that specialization of labour or the presence of a diversity of artisans identifies a society as civilized.

It is difficult to find a satisfactory "civilization test." If one element is missing or relatively underdeveloped, does that mean a people are not civilized? The safest approach may be to say that a civilization should demonstrate most of the essential features that historians have noted, but not necessarily all.

The first civilizations developed in at least six distinct locations. For a very long period of time, they existed independently of one another. The oldest civilization was Mesopotamia, followed closely by ancient Egypt. A third, which flourished in India, overlapped with one on the Mediterranean island of Crete. Another developed in China. In the western hemisphere, civilization first appeared in Central America.

Why did civilization begin in these particular regions? If we examine where the societies were located and what characteristics they had in common, we come to an interesting conclusion. All were located in the northern hemisphere in a moderate climatic zone—away from the coldest and hottest areas of the earth. Four of these civilizations were in river valleys with rich soil. The other two civilizations arose in areas where the climate and vegetation used to be quite different. The western Asia was milder and wetter than it is now, and the northwest corner of India was a forest rather than the desert it is today. Generally, therefore, the first civilizations developed in areas where agriculture could flourish and the population could grow rapidly.

knowledge of how our ancestors developed. It is an exciting and evolving branch of science.

Early humans were forced to struggle against an inhospitable environment in order to survive. Gradually, they developed the skills that would improve the quality of their lives. Very early on, they learned the importance of community and cooperation.

The Neolithic revolution changed humans from a society of hunters and gatherers to a society of farmers. The advent of agriculture was one of the most significant developments in human history. Agriculture allowed those conditions that we consider to be characteristic of the earliest civilizations.

REFLECT AND ANALYZE

1. What criteria do historians consider essential in a civilization?
2. Why is it so difficult to develop a test to determine whether a society is civilized?
3. Why did the earliest civilizations develop where they did?

LOOKING BACK

Modern humans have constantly searched for clues to solve the mystery of their origins. As we shall see, civilizations have created myths or legends to answer these questions. Scientists have followed the path of evolution in their search for answers. New archaeological finds are constantly supplying new evidence that reshapes our

MAKING CONNECTIONS

1. Computers, lasers, cat scans, and other products of modern technology are proving tremendously helpful in uncovering new knowledge about early humans. Investigate an example of how modern technology is being used in the study of ancient history, and prepare a report.

2. Religion was one of the important developments that marked the beginning of civilization. Explain why Neolithic people might have begun to think about religious issues.

3. Assume that you are a Neolithic chief. Explain how you would organize village activities. Are there still areas in the world where village government may follow the same principles?

4. The Neolithic revolution's most significant effect was the birth of agriculture. How important is agriculture in our society today?

DIGGING DEEPER

5. Investigate more fully the work of one of the archaeologists, paleoanthropologists, or anthropologists mentioned in this chapter. Include some background information in your report, as well as a description of his or her area of study and the contributions he or she has made to the study of humanity before civilization.

6. Conduct further research into the evolution of Stone Age tools. Create a collage of pictures or illustrations to demonstrate how the tools improved.

7. Stonehenge is one of the most famous Neolithic sites in the world today. Write a report about the mystery of Stonehenge. How was it constructed and why?

8. How has modern technology improved the dating of artifacts and fossils discovered at recent sites? Explore some of the different ways.

SKILL DEVELOPMENT: CREATING FOCUS QUESTIONS

Whenever you are examining a historical issue, or attempting to solve a problem, you will complete your task more easily if you create focus questions to guide your investigation. Focus questions can be used to direct, define, or even limit your investigation. There are many different types of focus questions. Some investigations might require the use of only one type. Other investigations might require the use of several types. Examine the types of focus questions and the examples provided.

Issue—The Neanderthals

TYPE OF FOCUS QUESTION	EXAMPLE
FACTUAL	In what locations have Neanderthal remains been located?
DEFINITIONAL	What are the characteristics that distinguish Neanderthals?
COMPARATIVE	How does the physical appearance of Neanderthals compare to that of *Homo erectus?*
CAUSATIVE	What caused the Neanderthals to disappear?
DECISION-MAKING	Were the Neanderthals our direct ancestors or a separate species driven to extinction by modern humans?
MORAL	Should the hunting methods employed by Neanderthals be considered inhumane?
SPECULATIVE	Have we yet to discover the true importance of Neanderthals in human evolution?

Applying the Skill

Draw a chart similar to the one above.

Create a series of focus questions to limit or define an investigation of the Neolithic revolution.

UNIT

1

Middle-Eastern Civilizations
3500 BCE – 395 CE

MESOPOTAMIA AND EGYPT

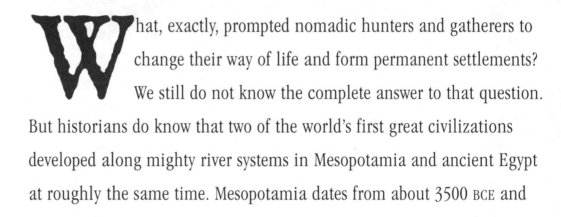

What, exactly, prompted nomadic hunters and gatherers to change their way of life and form permanent settlements? We still do not know the complete answer to that question. But historians do know that two of the world's first great civilizations developed along mighty river systems in Mesopotamia and ancient Egypt at roughly the same time. Mesopotamia dates from about 3500 BCE and ancient Egypt from about 3100 BCE.

The Mesopotamians drew their source of life from the Tigris-Euphrates river system in Asia, and the Egyptians from the Nile River in Africa. Peoples in both worlds learned to use the natural environment to their advantage by controlling the floodwaters of the rivers and working the rich soils along the banks. The availability of a constant food supply freed labour for other pursuits, and led to the development of thriving cities, magnificent temples, and powerful empires. These great civilizations laid the foundations for many others that followed.

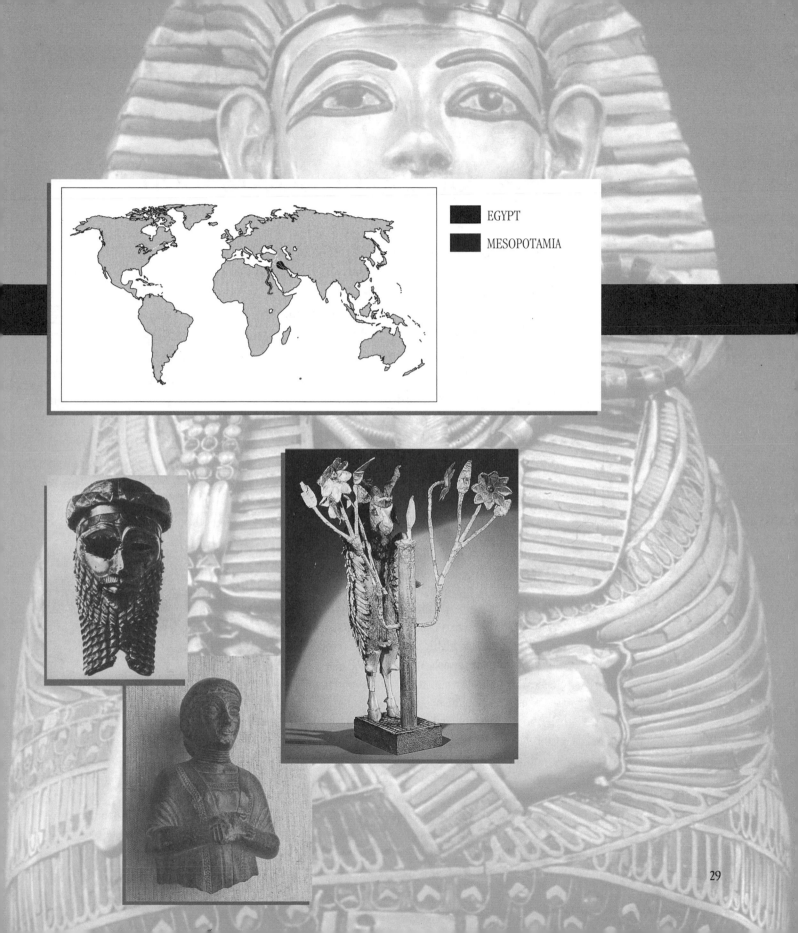

EGYPT

MESOPOTAMIA

MESOPOTAMIA:
Cradle of Civilization

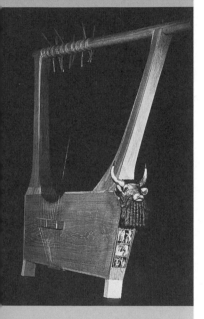

Figure 2-1
*Harp from a
Sumerian tomb*

In the Tigris-Euphrates valley of present-day Iraq lay the ancient Sumerian city-state of Ur. Between 1924 and 1934, an archaeological team led by Leonard Woolley conducted excavations that uncovered the ancient ruins. Among Woolley's findings was an incredible discovery. In the tomb of Queen Shub-Ad, the team discovered the remains of more than 60 female skeletons. Clothing remnants and jewellery indicated the likelihood that they had been women of the court. Nearby were the remains of soldiers with their spears, a harpist clutching his harp, and oxen still harnessed to wagons. The hands of most of the skeletons were raised towards their mouths. Little clay cups were scattered on the floor of the tomb. What could have happened here?

Those observing the scene speculated that the servants of the dead queen had followed the body into the tomb. There, they had taken poison so that their mistress would not go on to the afterlife alone. . . .

Ur was just one of the great city-states of Sumer, part of ancient Mesopotamia. Leonard Woolley's discovery points to some remarkable characteristics of the city and its people. During the period of Queen Shub-Ad's reign, Ur was the seat of a magnificent court and a highly sophisticated society with soldiers, court servants, musicians, and many others. The discovery also reveals an important aspect of Mesopotamian culture—a profound belief in an afterlife, and a desire to take some earthly belongings to the world after death.

For almost 3000 years, city-states and empires rose and fell in Mesopotamia. Among the empires were Sumer, Babylonia, Assyria, and Chaldea. Although periods of disunity and war mark the history of ancient Mesopotamia, the peoples of the region made many important contributions that other civilizations in the ancient world would build

upon. Today, we still consider Mesopotamia as a "cradle of civilization."

THE LAND BETWEEN THE RIVERS

Ancient Mesopotamia lay in what we know today as Iraq, northeast Syria, and part of southeast Turkey. It stretched from the Persian Gulf northwest through the valley of the Tigris and Euphrates rivers. The ancient Greeks were the first to call the region Mesopotamia. The Greek word *meso* means middle and *potamos* means river—thus it was "the land between the rivers." Mesopotamia was part of an area known as the Fertile Crescent which stretched in an arc from the Persian Gulf through northeast Syria to the Mediterranean Sea and was

Figure 2-2
Marsh scene in southern Iraq

the site of some of the world's first permanent farming villages.

Throughout its ancient history, Mesopotamia was home to different peoples and cultural groups. It lay at the crossroads of three continents: Africa, Asia, and Europe. Semitic, Asian, and Indo-European peoples all moved into the region at various periods. The mountains to the north and east were not high enough to isolate the area or protect it from invading or migrating peoples. Nomads living in the deserts to the west also attacked the river valley settlements periodically.

At first glance, the land and climate of the region hardly seem ideal for the development of a thriving civilization. The south was primarily a flat flood plain. Summers were very hot and dry; droughts could kill crops and cause famines. In spring, meltwaters from the nearby Zagros Mountains could cause flooding, and sudden downpours in winter could turn the plains to mud. The floods were unpredictable and posed a serious hazard to the river valley settlements. Sometimes floodwaters and sandbanks hindered travel and communication along the rivers as well.

The south had few natural resources such as minerals or forests and, except for clay, few building materials. Abundant fish and waterfowl lived in the marshes and rivers, however, and the silt deposited by the floodwaters was extremely fertile. As the people learned to control the flooding, drain the land, and irrigate the soil, the region produced excellent yields.

In the north, rainfall was more reliable and helped produce superb farmland. Because the banks and riverbeds of the Tigris and Euphrates are mostly rock in this area, rather than sand as they are in the south, the rivers run faster and rarely flood. Forests covering the foothills and mountains in this area teemed with animal life. Herds of wild cattle, gazelles, antelopes, and elephants roamed the plains, wild boars rooted through the valleys, and sheep

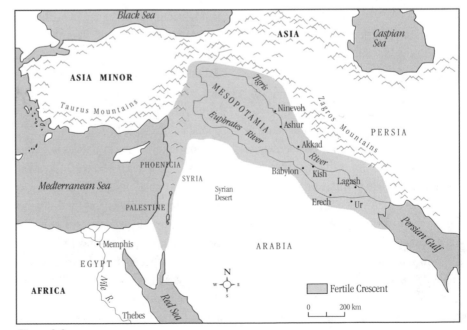

Figure 2-3
Mesopotamia. The shaded area is the Fertile Crescent

and goats grazed on the foothills of the mountains. The people of the north were also closer to the resources of the surrounding region, such as tin from the east and gold and silver from the west.

REFLECT AND ANALYZE

1. Referring to Figure 2.3, describe the location of Mesopotamia and the features of its surrounding area.

2. In a chart, outline the positive and negative features of the environment in southern Mesopotamia. Was the environment favourable to the development of a productive and secure civilization? Be prepared to defend your final position.

3. Was the environment of the north more favourable to the development of a productive civilization than the environment of the south? Explain your answer.

4. Suppose the area of Mesopotamia shown on the map in Figure 2.3 were to expand. In which direction do you think it would grow? Why? Draw a sketch map to illustrate your answer.

HISTORICAL OVERVIEW

Four main peoples dominated Mesopotamia in turn: the Sumerians, the Babylonians, the Assyrians, and the Chaldeans.

SUMER

The Sumerians came down to the banks of the Euphrates and Tigris rivers sometime around 3500 BCE from the mountains to the northeast. Their small farming communities eventually grew into the first great cities of the world. During the first thousand years of their history, the Sumerians lived in independent city-states, ruled by separate kings. Each *city-state*, which included the city and surrounding countryside, had its own government, laws, and military, and managed its own affairs independently from other city-states nearby.

The Sumerians considered Eridu, an ancient religious site in Sumer, to be the first city founded by their gods. By 3500 BCE, it had a population of about 4000. Over the next thousand years, other city-states developed, and several grew to be much larger than Eridu. Ur, for example, reached a population of 24 000 by 3000 BCE.

For centuries, the city-states of Sumer maintained their independence. On occasion, different city-states fought for control over land or irrigation rights, but these disputes did not develop into major wars as we understand the term. They were more like skirmishes that often continued only until one city succeeded in imposing its will over the other. As a result of these shifts in power, city-states in Sumer rose and fell. For example, as power declined in Kish, it rose in Erech. Finally, it shifted to Ur, and then to Lagash.

During times of conflict, the king of a Sumerian city-state acted as the head of the army, raising troops and training them. At first, these armies were quite small, consisting of the local men who were fit enough to wield an axe or throw a spear. Later, the Sumerians added wheeled chariots pulled by donkeys to their forces. (The Sumerians were the first people to develop and use the wheel.) The chariots held two men, a driver and a soldier who stood behind, equipped with a javelin to hurl at the enemy.

In about 2800 BCE, Etana of Kish managed to unite the city-states of Sumer, but his success was short-lived. After his death, the city-states vied again for control, leaving the weakened Sumerians ripe for conquest. Their wealth also made them attractive to outsiders. The Akkadians, Semitic mountain folk and desert nomads from the north, succeeded in overpowering the Sumerians. Sumer and Akkad were then united into the single empire known as the kingdom of Sumer, under Sargon of Akkad (2340 BCE–2305 BCE).

Sargon became known as Sargon the Great. He was a government official in Kish when he led a revolt to establish himself as king. As ruler, he attacked the Sumerian city-states to the south, capturing all of them, including the strongest, Ur. During his 35-year reign, he also invaded both Egypt and Ethiopia, extending his holdings from Palestine to the Persian Gulf and building the first true empire in history.

After the death of Sargon, Sumer fell into decline with only a brief resurgence during the reign of Naramsin (2291 BCE– 2255 BCE). Only the city-state of Ur continued to thrive, enjoying one last century of prosperity. During the reign of Ur-Nammu (2112 BCE–2094 BCE), Sumerian culture

Figure 2-4
This bronze mask may be a portrait of King Sargon

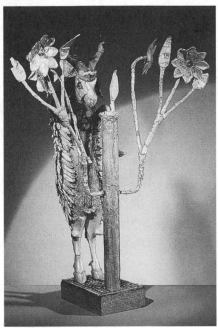

Figure 2-5
Inlaid statuette of a ram and a plant

Figure 2-6
The headdress of Queen Shub-ad, from the royal tomb of Ur

reached its peak. The Sumerians developed the first known form of writing, called **cuneiform**, made significant advances in scientific knowledge, created a vital mythology, and produced the first written literature. The *Epic of Gilgamesh,* which tells of a legendary Sumerian king who ruled Uruk around 2600 BCE, is the oldest known piece of literature in the world. All of these developments had a major influence on the later peoples of Mesopotamia. Although Ur finally fell captive to the Elamites from the east in approximately 2004 BCE, the Babylonians and the Assyrians adopted and spread many aspects of Sumerian culture.

PERSPECTIVES ON THE PAST
The Decline of Sumer

Why did the city-states of Sumer decline? Two viewpoints are given below. Does one seem more likely to you than the other? Why or why not? Is there a definitive answer to the question of why the city-states declined?

Viewpoint 1
Following the death of Sargon, waves of invaders fought for the best settled lands and the empire began to fall apart. Even though Sargon's grandson restored the empire to greatness for a short time, by about 2159 BCE Sumer had crumbled. It was unable to withstand the invasions.

Viewpoint 2
In an attempt to manage their environment, the Sumerians constructed hundreds of kilometres of canals to irrigate their fields. Unfortunately, these canals carried not only fertile silt to the fields, but also harmful salts that killed the plants. Eventually, the fields became so salty that nothing at all could be grown. Without an adequate food supply, the city-states of Sumer went into decline.

MESOPOTAMIA: A DEVELOPMENTAL TIMELINE

	SUMER **3500 BCE-1900 BCE**	**BABYLONIA** **1900 BCE-1300 BCE**
POLITICAL DEVELOPMENTS	• Sumerians move in from the north to take over Mesopotamia (3300 BCE) • Gilgamesh rules as King of Uruk (2600 BCE) • Sargon of Akkad claims the throne of Kish and establishes the Akkadian empire (2340 BCE) • Naramsin (grandson of Sargon) revitalizes the empire (2291 BCE) • mountain people of the northeast overthrow the Akkadian empire (2200 BCE) • resurgence of the city of Ur under Ur-Nammu (2112 BCE) • invasion of Ur by the Elamites from the east (2004 BCE)	• the Amorites (nomads from the west) establish their capital at Babylon (1900 BCE) • Hammurabi reigns as king of Babylon (1792 BCE) • the Empire of Babylon is destroyed by Indo-European invaders from Anatolia (Turkey) called the Hittites (1595 BCE) • Kassites from the east conquer the area and rule the valley until they are displaced by the Assyrians (1555 BCE)
CULTURAL DEVELOPMENTS	• cuneiform writing develops • invention of the potter's wheel aids the advent of pottery • a system of mathematics using a base of 60 is developed • a lunar calendar is developed • Sumerian culture reaches its peak; writing, science, mythology, and law are emphasized • the *Epic of Gilgamesh* becomes an important literary work	• Hammurabi's Law Code is developed • relief carvings of mythological and royal figures gain prominence
TECHNOLOGICAL/ECONOMIC DEVELOPMENTS	• the Bronze Age begins • a system of canals and irrigation ditches is designed to water the fields • oxen are harnessed to ploughs • the shoulder yoke for oxen is invented to make ploughing easier • the plough is redesigned to turn the soil rather than just scratch a furrow • a seed drill is added to the plough • the Sumerians develop wheeled carts and chariots • pulleys are created to raise water from wells • trade begins with Africa, Cyprus, Egypt, and Lebanon	• north–south river trade and trade with Arabia, India, Persia, and Asia Minor increase • the shekel, mina, and talent are introduced as currency; this is one of the first times money has been used

ASSYRIA
1300 BCE-609 BCE

- the Assyrians establish an independent kingdom in northern Mesopotamia with a capital at Ashur (1300 BCE)

- Ashurnasirpal rules, and the Assyrians become a people to be feared in the near east (884 BCE)

- Sargon II attacks the capital of Israel (722 BCE)

- Sennacherib (705 BCE) establishes the Assyrian capital at Nineveh and conquers Sidon in Phoenicia

- Esarhaddon (681 BCE) captures the Egyptian capital of Memphis

- Ashurbanipal (668 BCE) takes the Assyrian empire to its greatest heights

- the Chaldean people of Babylonia and the Medes people of Persia join forces to destroy Nineveh and the Assyrian empire (616 BCE)

- mythological and royal reliefs take on new importance

- Nineveh becomes the showplace of the ancient world

- library containing 22 000 clay tablets reflects new interest in science and mathematics

---

- the Assyrians learn to make iron from the Hittites

- Ashur and Nineveh become great northern trading centres

- efficient drainage and sewage systems are perfected

- Tiglath-pileser III establishes roads and a postal service for the empire (745 BCE)

CHALDEA
609 BCE - 530 BCE

- King Nebuchadnezzar rules Babylon (604 BCE)

- Jerusalem conquered, and its people led captive to Babylon (586 BCE)

- Belshazzar defends Babylon against the Medes and the Persians (539 BCE)

- the Hanging Gardens of Babylon are constructed

- interest is shown in astronomy and the development of a more efficient calendar

BABYLONIA

The decline of Sumer led to a shift in power northward, first to Babylonia and then to Assyria. The Babylonian period began when Semitic nomads from the west, the Amorites, established their kingdom at the city of Babylon. The city reached the height of its power during the time of the First Dynasty (ruling family), which lasted about 300 years. The most significant ruler of the First Dynasty was King Hammurabi (1792 BCE–1750 BCE), who created one of the world's first written codes of law. By conquering all of Sumer, Akkad to the north, and lands to the east and west, Hammurabi is also credited with establishing the empire of Babylonia. The Babylonians were great traders; their ships reached the distant shores of India and Africa, and their caravans travelled far into Persia and Asia Minor. The goods and ideas exchanged on these expeditions enriched both the Babylonians' culture and the cultures of those they met.

When Hammurabi died, he was succeeded by a number of weak kings who had difficulty holding the empire together. Wave after wave of Indo-European tribes invaded from the northern mountains. The Hittites invaded from Anatolia (Turkey) around 1595 BCE. Approximately 40 years later, the Kassites invaded Babylonia from the east, and established control over the valley. In about 1300 BCE, they were displaced by the powerful Assyrians.

ASSYRIA

The Assyrians took their name from their chief city of Ashur, located on the banks of the Tigris River in northern Mesopotamia. Ashur was an important trading centre on the east-west caravan routes between Meso-potamia and the surrounding lands. With economic influence, the Assyrians gained political influence as well. Long under the control of Babylon, the Assyrians had absorbed Babylonian culture, just as the Babylonians had absorbed Sumerian culture. Through a long succession of wars and conquests, the Assyrians came to dominate all of Mesopotamia.

The Assyrians were among the fiercest and most warlike people in the region, known for committing wartime atrocities against unarmed civilians and treating conquered armies with cruelty. Their enemies were shown no mercy, as the Assyrians often tortured and killed their captives. Between 1100 BCE and 600 BCE, Assyrian power spread throughout western Asia, as a number of warrior kings set out on a terrorizing path of conquest. Their efforts extended Assyrian influence west to the Mediterranean Sea and Egypt, south into Babylon, north into Syria, and east towards Persia.

Several factors contributed to this military success. Assyrian kings viewed professional armies as essential to conquest, and so they created large, skilled armies that were well organized into units of foot soldiers, charioteers, cavalry, and archers. Mercenaries, or hired foreign soldiers, were added to local armies, and officers were trained in combat strategies. The Assyrians had also learned the secret of making iron from the Hittites, and they used that knowledge to make arrows and lances of superior quality.

The Assyrian king Tiglath-pileser III (745 BCE–727 BCE) began the period of expansion by taking Damascus in Syria. After his death, a power struggle for succession continued until Sargon II (722 BCE–705 BCE) seized the throne. Sargon II made Israel an Assyrian province and brought the Israelites into his empire. His son Sennacherib (705 BCE–681 BCE) conquered Sidon in Phoenicia, and then Esarhaddon (681 BCE–668 BCE) conquered Egypt. But the greatest Assyrian empire builder of them all was Ashurbanipal (668 BCE–626 BCE). He succeeded in ruling more of the known world than any other ruler before him. Even more important, he managed to hold the empire intact throughout his entire reign.

Ashurbanipal treated all conquered peoples, both civilian and military, with great cruelty. He plundered his conquered

Figure 2-7 *King Ashurbanipal stabbing a lion*

Figure 2-8 *How the royal palace at Nineveh may have looked*

territories continuously to add to the richness of his own cities along the Tigris. His splendid palace at Nineveh was decorated with gold and ivory from Egypt, silver looted from Syria, lapis lazuli (a deep blue stone) from Persia, and the finest of Phoenician cedarwood.

Yet, with all his militarism and plunder, Ashurbanipal showed a keen interest in both science and mathematics. He constructed a garden and zoo at his palace, stocked from all parts of his empire, and established a library containing over 22 000 clay tablets that showed his special interest in science and mathematics.

At the peak of its power, the sprawling Assyrian empire spilled over the bounds of Mesopotamia, and a single ruler had great difficulty holding it together. As a result, the Assyrians began to experience serious attacks on their borders. At the same time, their conquered province of Babylonia, in southern Mesopotamia, struggled to gain its independence.

Shortly after the death of Ashurbanipal, the Babylonians and the foreign Medes united to overthrow Assyria. The capital, Nineveh, was captured and destroyed in 612 BCE. The Assyrians themselves, once so powerful, were killed or assimilated, and their empire disappeared.

CHALDEA

After the collapse of the Assyrian empire, Babylon once again became an important centre in Mesopotamia. The city had been prominent in the time of Hammurabi and had prospered once again in the 200 years

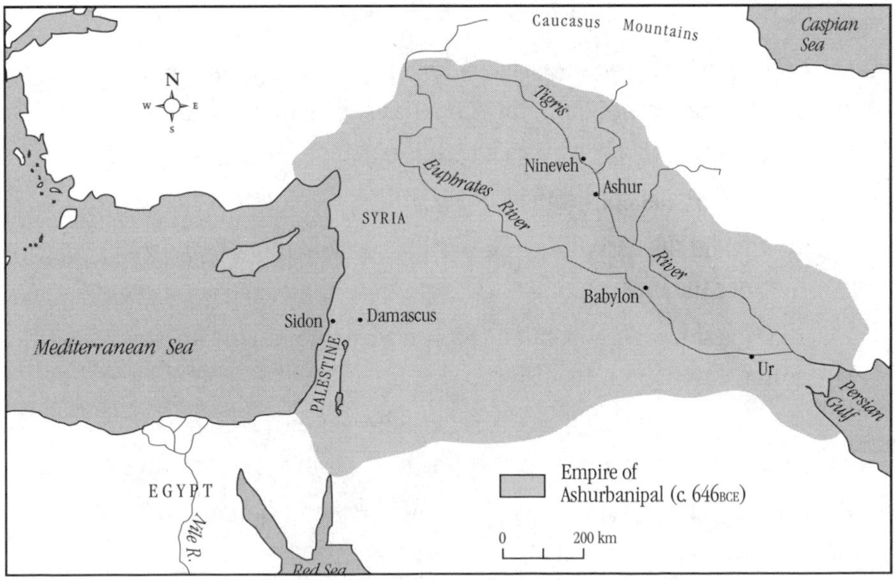

Figure 2-9 *The empire of King Ashurbanipal (circa 646 BCE)*

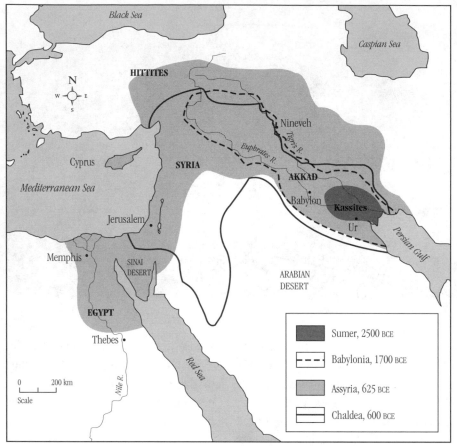

Figure 2-10
Ancient Mesopotamia: Sumer,
Babylonia, Assyria, Chaldea

oners. He only stopped his conquest of Egypt when he heard of his father's death and his own succession to the throne. Many historians, however, note that Nebuchadnezzar fought fewer battles than the Assyrian kings and should be remembered as a great builder rather than as a warrior.

Like many empires of Mesopotamia, the Chaldean empire fell to invaders. By 549 BCE, the Chaldeans were challenged by a new alliance of the Medes and the Persian king Cyrus (550 BCE–529 BCE). Babylon withstood a siege for several years, but ultimately the Chaldeans were no match for Cyrus of Persia. According to legend, one night he had his army dig a ditch around Babylon to divert the Euphrates River from its normal course. The invaders then marched into the city up the old river bed, and proceeded to kill Belshazzar, the Chaldean king, and his palace guards. The city itself was spared, but the Persians became the new rulers of a growing international world.

before the collapse of Assyria, but its glory was greatest during the 70 years after the destruction of Nineveh. During this period, it was ruled by the Chaldeans, a Semitic people who had settled in the fertile area of southern Babylonia near the Persian Gulf about 1000 BCE.

The Chaldean king Nebuchadnezzar (604 BCE–562 BCE) transformed Babylon into one of the most beautiful cities of the world. Nebuchadnezzar, as noted in the Bible, was a warrior king. He conquered Judah, captured and destroyed Jerusalem, and took many Jews back to Babylon as pris-

REFLECT AND ANALYZE

1. Outline at least two major achievements of each of the following peoples in Mesopotamia: the Sumerians, Babylonians, Assyrians, and Chaldeans. Explain why these achievements were important.

2. a) What factors contributed to the military strength of the Assyrians?

   b) Why did the Assyrian empire collapse? Which reason do you consider the most significant? Explain.

3. a) Suggest why Mesopotamia was invaded by so many different groups throughout its history.

   b) How do you think these invasions affected the development of Mesopotamian civilization? Outline both positive and negative effects.

4. Refer to the box on the next page. Write a short fictional account of a trader's visit to the Hanging Gardens of Babylon.

INNOVATIONS

The Hanging Gardens of Babylon—One of the Seven Wonders of the Ancient World

Why are the Hanging Gardens of Babylon considered one of the seven wonders of the ancient world? What do the palace and gardens reveal about the culture and economy of the ancient Chaldeans?

The new Babylon of Nebuchadnezzar was the showplace of the east. The king ordered the construction of enormous defensive walls, covered with reliefs of griffins and lions, to protect the city. The walls were so broad that two chariots could drive along the top side by side. Magnificent gates and great arched passageways flanked by towers marked the entrance to the city. The most famous of the gates, the Ishtar Gate, was decorated with glazed brick of many colours. Ishtar was the great goddess of fertility.

The Hanging Gardens, in the midst of the palace grounds, were the glory of the city. According to legend, Nebuchadnezzar built the gardens because of his deep love for his Median wife, Amyns, granddaughter of Cyaxares, king of Media. Amyns was troubled by her longing for the forested mountains of her homeland.

To ease her concern, Nebuchadnezzar ordered great hewn stones to be brought from the mountains of the plain. With the stones, his workers constructed a building with a series of vaulted terraces, one above the other. A moat flowed around the building and, inside, deep wells fed hydraulic pumps that raised water to a reservoir at the top of the structure. On each terrace, workers laid deep layers of rich soil for the gardens.

Moistened by the abundant water and warmed by the hot sun, the terrace gardens supported a profusion of flowers, vines, and flowering trees and shrubs. Beautifully decorated halls meandered through the terraces and housed the treasures of the empire. Visitors observed the finest fabrics of Phoenicia, silver from Asia Minor, and gold from Egypt. While reclining on divans and sipping the finest wines of Palestine, served to them by slaves, guests took in the beauty and scent of the magnificent Hanging Gardens.

Figure 2-11
The Hanging Gardens of Babylon

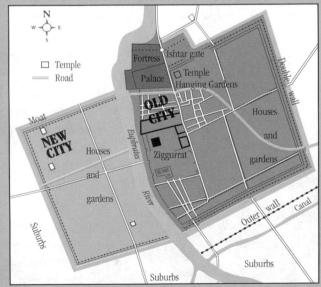

Figure 2-12
A plan of the city of Babylon

GOVERNMENT

In the early history of Sumer's city-states, free citizens elected an assembly to run the government. The assembly consisted of two houses: an upper house, which contained the wealthiest citizens, and a lower house, which contained soldiers. These elected members chose the judges, who were responsible for enforcing the laws, and selected the military leaders needed in time of war.

When wars between the city-states became more frequent and the threat of foreign invasion became a concern, the city-states recognized the need for strong leaders. The assembly then created the additional role of king.

The kings in the Sumerian city-states were called *lugals*. Most considered themselves to be living representatives of a particular god, sent by that god as a steward or servant. Thus, the system of government in Mesopotamia was a **theocracy**.

The lugal's major responsibility was to

Figure 2-13
Lugal Gudea of Lagash

provide for the defence of the city-state. In addition, he and his government officials supervised the development and maintenance of the irrigation works, which were essential to the economic survival of the city-state.

The Sumerian kings kept a tight rein on their people. What the lugal said was law, and the common people were expected to comply with his wishes. Some kings developed codes of law to guarantee that citizens maintained peace and order. Ur-Nammu in Ur, for example, established one of the most important legal codes in Sumer.

The earliest kings in Sumer were elected, but later, when the people began to consider the lugals as gods, the crown passed from father to son. This development marked the beginning of dynasties or hereditary monarchies in Mesopotamia.

Like the Sumerians, the Assyrians saw the importance of strong government, but they took a different approach. In Assyria, religious leaders had less political power than they had in Sumer. Assyrian kings derived their authority from the god Ashur, and acted as his representative, but there was a clear separation between government (state) and religion. Temples, palaces, and monuments in Assyria were built for the use of the king, not for the honour of a particular god. Yet the Assyrian king was still bound by religious customs. For five days each month, for example, he was required to fast and perform certain religious ceremonies. On the first day of each new year, he had to go without food and water until the new moon rose in the evening.

The Assyrian kings were among the most powerful leaders in all of Mesopotamia. Since they eventually ruled an empire that stretched from the Persian Gulf

to the Nile River, their far-reaching authority was almost a necessity. They acted as first judge in the land, supervisor of all canal construction in Assyria, and protector of all farmers and shepherds within their territory. In times of war or conquest, they were present for all military campaigns and took personal charge of the operation.

The Sumerians and Assyrians also approached governing their expanding empires somewhat differently. When one Sumerian city-state was conquered by another, it was forced to accept the conqueror as ruler. In most cases, the king appointed a governor, or *ensi*, to look after the smaller towns while he focused on the needs of the main centre.

The Assyrians devised a similar system, but on a grander scale because they had to control a much larger territory. They divided their empire into provinces and appointed officials to govern each one. These governors were responsible for collecting taxes, raising troops for the army, and enforcing the king's laws.

The Assyrians faced frequent rebellion from their subject peoples. One way they dealt with such rebellion was by resettlement: populations were forced from their lands and replaced by settlers from other parts of the empire. This policy kept conquered nationalities weak, and led to a mixing of peoples.

LAW AND JUSTICE

One of the Mesopotamians' most significant contributions to the advance of civilization was in the field of law. Both the Sumerians and the Babylonians developed law codes. Basically, the codes were an

THROUGH THEIR EYES

Hammurabi's Law Code

Figure 2-14
The Stela of Hammurabi

Hammurabi's law code was inscribed on an upright stone, or *stela*, that originally stood in Babylon's temple of Marduk, the chief god. In 1901, the French archaeologist Jean-Vincent Scheil discovered the stela at the site of ancient Susa. It is now located in the Louvre in Paris.

At the top of the stone, we see King Hammurabi receiving the symbols of authority, a rod and ring, from the god Marduk. Below this portrayal, cuneiform writing outlines the code. The following are some of Hammurabi's 282 laws.

Do you consider Hammurabi's laws fair and just or harsh and unjust? What are the main differences between this code of laws and our own today?

If a noble has stolen the young son of another noble, he shall be put to death.

If a noble destroys the eye of another noble, they shall destroy his eye.

If a noble has destroyed the eye of a commoner or broken the bone of a commoner, he shall pay one mina of silver.

If a noble has destroyed the eye of a noble's slave or broken the bone of a noble's slave, he shall pay one half the slave's value.

If a noble has committed robbery and has been caught, that noble shall be put to death.

If a robber is not caught, the man who has been robbed should make claim to the city and the governor in whose territory and district the crime was committed, and they shall make good to him his lost property.

If a noble has accused another noble and brought a charge of murder against him, but has not proved it, the accuser shall be put to death.

If a noble has come forward with false testimony concerning grain or money, he shall bear the penalty of that case.

If a man has given his boat to a boatman on hire, and if the boatman has been careless, has grounded the boat or destroyed it, the boatman shall give a boat to the owner in compensation.

If a builder has built a house for someone and has not made his work strong, with the result that the house he has built has collapsed and has killed the owner of the house, that builder shall be put to death.

If the collapse of the constructed house has caused the death of a son of the owner of the house, they shall put the son of that builder to death.

If a physician has performed a major operation on a noble with a bronze lancet and has caused the noble's death, or he has opened up the eye-socket of a noble and has destroyed the noble's eye, they shall cut off his hand.

If a son has struck his father, they shall cut off his hand.

attempt to collect, organize, and record all existing laws so that there would be one common code for all citizens of the empire.

The ruler of Ur, Ur-Nammu, developed an early code based on Sumerian tradition. It gave legal protection to peasants and commoners as well as to nobles, but the laws were applied differently to different classes of people. Nobles found guilty of committing a crime were treated more harshly since better behaviour was expected from them than from a commoner. Penalties usually took the form of fines or physical punishment.

Mesopotamia's most important legal legacy, however, is the law code established by Hammurabi, king of Babylonia. Hammurabi's code listed 282 different laws, organized under headings such as trade, family, labour, real estate, and personal property. The code distinguished between a minor crime and a major crime and it established some important legal principles. It asserted that the state is the authority responsible for enforcing the law, and it confirmed that social justice should be guaranteed to all citizens. It also promoted the idea that the punishment should fit the crime. The basic principle behind the code was "an eye for an eye and a tooth for a tooth." For example, if a house in Babylonia collapsed and killed the owner, the builder of the house would be put to death.

REFLECT AND ANALYZE

1. How did government evolve in ancient Sumeria?

2. Compare the power of a Sumerian king with that of an Assyrian king. Discuss the advantages and disadvantages of each system.

3. a) Why does a society need laws? What are the advantages of a written code of laws? On what do we base our laws?
   b) In groups, develop and record a code of ten basic laws for your class. Decide first on the principles that will inform your laws and the major issues the laws should deal with. Record and present your laws in an appropriate and creative format.

MESOPOTAMIA:
Society and Culture

The god Enki said to Ziusudra, the king of Shuruppak:

> *"Listen to my instruction:*
> *By our will a flood will sweep over the cities to destroy*
> *the seed of mankind*
> *And put an end to the rule of kings."*

The next forty lines are missing from the original text, but a later version has these lines:

> *"Tear down your house, forget your belongings,*
> *build a large ship and take with you the seed of all*
> *living creatures."*
> *Ziusudra began work the next day*
> *building a huge ship with seven decks*
> *sealed with bitumen.*
> *He then loaded on gold, silver,*
> *wild beasts and farm animals.*
> *He loaded on his family, relations*
> *and workmen and only then boarded up the hatch.*
> *Then came the powerful wind from all*
> *Directions and attacked the land at once.*
> *At the same time the flood swept the cities.*
> *After the flood had covered the land for seven days*
> *and seven nights*
> *And the huge boat had been tossed by the wind on*
> *the great waters,*
> *The sun-god, Utu, came out."*

SUMERIAN LEGEND
CLAY TABLET FROM NIPPUR

Figure 3-1
*A Sumerian god
and goddess*

Why do civilizations create **legends**? Often, legends help to explain a major event in a people's past or some mysterious aspect of their natural world. The Assyrian legend above, which suggests that a "great flood" took place in Mesopotamia, tries to address a mystery that dates from an early period in this civilization's history. For a short time, clay tablet accounts of kings and their reigns ceased to be produced. What had happened to these kings? What had happened to the people of these city-states? How can this gap in Mesopotamian history be explained?

One possible explanation was that the god Enki had brought a great flood upon the people. As floods were common in Mesopotamia, the legend made sense to the people, even though it did not explain why the wrath of the god was unleashed. Archaeologists, however, have found no evidence to prove that a great flood ever swept over the city-states of Mesopotamia. It is more likely that the legend is based on several smaller floods, rather than on a single catastrophe.

Can you think of other flood legends or stories associated with other civilizations and their religions? How do the legends compare?

RELIGION

GODS AND GODDESSES

The Mesopotamian people believed that their gods had the traits and appearances of human beings. In other words, their gods were **anthropomorphic**. Though immortal, they ate, drank, developed relationships, got married, and had children. They experienced and expressed human emotions such as anger, hate, jealousy, and love. When a flood struck the riverbank

Figure 3.2 *A Sumerian seal, showing the liberation of the sun god*

communities, it was not uncommon to believe that one of the gods was angry.

Religion in Mesopotamia was also **polytheistic**. That is, the people worshipped many different gods and goddesses. The Sumerians, for example, believed in over 3000 different deities. Each city-state also selected one of the gods as its personal patron, and the people believed the city belonged to that god.

As was the case in many other ancient civilizations, the main deities in Sumer were associated with aspects of nature. Four gods were considered superior to all others: Enlil, the god of air, whose city was Nippur; An, the god of heaven, whose city was Uruk; Enki, the god of earth and water, whose city was Eridu; and Ninhursag, the mother goddess of all living things, whose city was Lagash. Other important gods and goddesses were Utu, the sun god; Nannar, the moon god; and Innana, goddess of love.

In the Sumerian world view, the gods lived in the skies or heavens and ruled over the earth. Below the earth was a gloomy underworld where the dead were entombed. The god Enlil provided the universal laws that governed everything in the universe, though he broke one of the laws himself and was banished for a time to the under-

world. Enki provided all that made the earth rich, from the water in the rivers to the stalls for livestock. Humans were created from clay to serve the gods on earth and save them from the hard work of providing for their own food and shelter.

The Babylonians replaced many of the Sumerian gods with gods of their own, although their functions remained much the same. The goddess Ishtar, for example, replaced Innana, Marduk replaced Enlil, and Anu replaced An. The Babylonian

Figure 3.3 *An Assyrian priest with a whip used to chase away evil spirits*

pantheon also contained several lesser deities such as Apsu, god of fresh waters; Ti'amat, goddess of the sea; and Ea, the god of wisdom.

The Assyrians also recognized many of the same gods as the Sumerians, but worshipped as well a chief god, Ashur. Ashur was lord of heaven and earth and creator of the world. All of the Assyrian kings were closely associated with Ashur. One of the other most popular deities among the Assyrians was the mother goddess, Ishtar, the goddess of love

THEN AND NOW
The Temple-Towers of Sumer

What role did the temples have in Sumerian society? What determined their unique shape? Since little of the temples remain today, how do you think historians are able to reconstruct what they actually looked like?

Figure 3-4 *The ziggurat at Ur (then)*

Some of the most fascinating remains of Sumerian civilization are the magnificent terraced temples called ziggurats. The Sumerians built their mountain-shaped temples, with a shrine at the very top, to house the gods while they visited the land of mortals. The ziggurat was always the most important architectural structure in any Sumerian city. In plain view of all citizens, it served as a reminder that the people were under the watchful eye of their gods.

In all likelihood, the temples were first built to raise the shrine above the level of the floodwaters. Over the centuries the Sumerians built them larger and larger. The ziggurat at Uruk, for example, constructed on a terrace 12 m high, was one of the oldest, though not one of the highest. Some archaeologists believe that this temple would have taken 1500 men five years to construct, an

estimate that suggests Sumerian rulers could mobilize large numbers of people in the service of the gods.

The ziggurat at Ur, built by King Ur-Nammu in about 2110 BCE, was used for over 1500 years. Like most of these temples, it was constructed from thousands of sun-dried bricks. Burnt brick laid in bitumen mortar covered the entire outside. Rectangular at its base, the ziggurat measured 65 m by 45 m, and rose 30 m to the top of the shrine.

Construction likely took place in several stages. A staircase connected each section to the next. The final staircase rose to the shrine of Nanna, the city's god, situated at the pinnacle. There were no interior chambers.

Since the Sumerians intended the ziggurat to represent the far-off mountains where the gods lived, they might originally have planted trees on the terraces to more closely reflect the mountainous landscape.

Figure 3.5 shows the ziggurat of Ur that was exca-

Figure 3-5 *The ziggurat at Ur (reconstructed)*

vated by the team of English archaeologists led by Sir Leonard Woolley. Unfortunately, mud brick weathers badly, and little of theoriginal ziggurat remains today. The main structure is a reconstruction.

and fertility and the mistress of battle.

Although Mesopotamians believed that their gods lived in the heavens and in high places such as on the summits of mountains, they also believed that the deities came down to earth. To house them, they built high temples called **ziggurats**—terraced pyramids topped with a shrine—and dedicated these buildings to the gods' honour. Food was placed in the shrine daily for the gods to eat while they were in the temple.

RELIGIOUS BELIEFS AND PRACTICES

The Mesopotamian gods controlled all aspects of the human and natural world. They controlled the rains, the floods, the changing seasons, the fruitfulness of the harvest, and all other forces of nature. They could influence major human events, such as peace or war, and they could also affect events in individual lives, such as the success or failure of a business venture. They could bring good or ill fortune at will. The people were subject to the mysterious whims of the gods, but their religion also provided them with a sense of a universal order and explained some of the mysteries of life and the natural world.

The Sumerians, Babylonians, and Assyrians all created a strong **mythology** which told stories of the gods and their relationship to the world. This mythology also included tales of demons, who lived in the fearsome underworld and fought constant battles with the deities of good.

Since the gods and demons could bring good or ill fortune, the people were constantly on the lookout for omens of the future. Many consulted **oracles** or seers to interpret the signs of the gods. Liver divina-

tion was a popular method of interpretation because the liver was considered the seat of emotion and true knowledge. Priests sacrificed sheep and examined the lines, valleys, spots, and wrinkles on the liver to uncover the future.

Religious festivals were also frequent events in Mesopotamia. The new year's festival, which could last for as long as 12 days, was the most popular and sacred. Almost the entire population of a city gathered to witness the ritual renewal of the earth's fertility and to celebrate the marriage of the city's god to the city. Festivals were also held when a city won a war to celebrate the capture of the conquered city's treasure. Competitions, games, and short plays telling stories of the gods were often part of the festivities.

DEATH AND THE AFTERLIFE

The people of Mesopotamia feared death. They believed that, once they died, they entered a bleak underworld that was a land of no return. Some sources refer to it as a place with seven walls and no gates, where the dead would live forever, alone and in darkness. Therefore, it was important for

the dead to take their most treasured possessions along with them into the afterlife.

When a king died, the people's fear of death increased because they considered a ruler's death to be a bad omen for the future of the country. Mourning was officially observed throughout the land.

A deceased king being prepared for burial was sprinkled with perfumes, anointed with oils, and clad in his royal robes. He was then laid out in a huge rectangular stone chest, or sarcophagus, that had great rings inset in the sides so that cords or rods could be passed through to help move it. A lid was fixed in place with bronze bolts, and a curse label was attached to the outside to frighten away would-be grave robbers. Once the sarcophagus was buried along with a large treasure, usually inside the palace, sacrifices were made.

Leonard Woolley's discovery of the royal cemetery at Ur revealed that the Mesopotamians buried the servants of a dead king or queen in the tomb as well. The belief was that a royal person should not go on to the afterlife alone. In the later period, only statues of servants were buried in the tombs.

REFLECT AND ANALYZE

1. a) Construct a diagram or chart identifying the main gods and goddesses of Sumer and their functions.
   b) Explain how the Assyrian hierarchy of gods was different from that in Sumer.

2. Define the term "myth." What role did mythology play in the religion of the ancient Mesopotamians?

3. You are a citizen of Mesopotamia. Describe your relationship to your gods, the religious practices you follow, and your view of the afterlife.

4. Construct a three-dimensional model of a Sumerian ziggurat. Explain the stages in construction and the ways in which the building was used.

SOCIAL ORGANIZATION

In Mesopotamia, the kings were at the pinnacle of the social pyramid. They derived their power from their position as head of the government, either as divinely ordained humans, as the Sumerians believed, or as actual gods on earth, as the Assyrians believed. Among all of the peoples of Mesopotamia, the word of the king was law.

Priests and scribes formed the upper class or nobility of Mesopotamian society. The priests were influential because of the importance of religion. Sumerians, for example, accepted that the priests were the only direct link with the gods of their cities. Priests were also influential because they controlled the distribution of land to farmers and ran the schools where scribes were educated.

Scribes, the educated class, were able to read and write. The Mesopotamians were one of the first civilizations to develop a system of writing. This development, which made it possible to record knowledge, brought great prestige to those who were educated. The scribes, primarily the sons of the wealthy, worked either for the temple, the palace, the government, or the army. Others worked for merchants or set up their own businesses as public writers.

The merchants and artisans were the traders and craftspeople. They helped to develop Mesopotamian civilization by exchanging products and ideas throughout the territory and beyond. They traded up and down the Tigris and Euphrates rivers, and their caravans ventured even farther afield to Egypt, Cyprus, and Lebanon. The artisans of Mesopotamia pro-

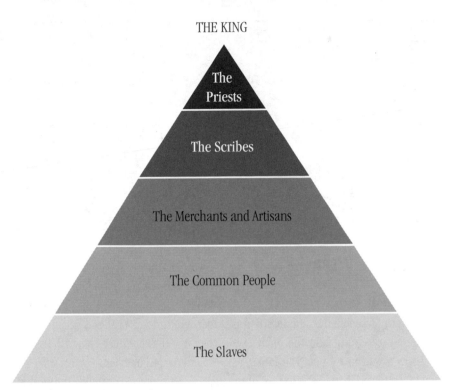

THE KING

The Priests

The Scribes

The Merchants and Artisans

The Common People

The Slaves

Figure 3.6 *The social pyramid—Mesopotamia*

duced varied products such as gold rings, statuettes inlaid with lapis lazuli, and intricate shell containers used for holding coloured cosmetics. The evolution of a distinct merchants and artisans class, which allowed for specialization in the economy, was possible in Mesopotamia because of the stable food supply. Many historians point to specialization in areas other than farming as evidence of a true civilization.

The common people, who made up the lower class, earned their living from the land as farmers. Close family ties were important. Although the husband was the head of the family, women in Mesopotamia enjoyed more rights than in most other ancient civilizations.

Slaves, who performed household labour and various chores, were at the bottom of the social pyramid and had no rights. They were identified by a single name only; when they lost their freedom, their family name was taken away. Masters owned their slaves outright, and any slave caught trying to escape was beaten, branded, and put in chains. If a slave was injured, the master received the compensation—not the slave.

In Mesopotamia, there were two types of slaves. The first group included prisoners captured in battles against foreign cities; they were given as slaves to the temple or sold by auction to wealthy citizens. The second group included debtors who sold themselves, or members of their family, into slavery for a number of years to pay off the debt. In general, most masters treated their slaves well, but the slaves were expected to work long and hard.

REFLECT AND ANALYZE

1. What groups made up the upper classes of Mesopotamian society? How did they earn their prestigious positions?

2. Why were the artisans and merchants important in Mesopotamian society?

3. Write a brief first-person account describing a day in the life of a Mesopotamian priest, scribe, merchant, farmer, or slave. Argue that you are vitally important to the fabric of your society.

EVERYDAY LIFE

THE FAMILY

Throughout Mesopotamia, the family was considered important and the birth of a child was a welcome event. The father, as head of the family, had unlimited authority over his children. In fact, legal documents of the period describe the father as "master" or "owner" of his children. Legally, he could deposit any of his children with a creditor as security for repayment of a debt. Parental respect was the focus of a child's upbringing.

Women in Mesopotamia had more rights than women living in many other lands at the time. They were highly respected, could own land and property, and could also set up their own businesses. However, they could not vote or rule, and were not considered equal to men. In upper-class families, women stayed in a separate part of the house.

Traditionally, parents arranged marriages for their sons and daughters when their children were still in their teens. During the engagement ceremony, the future husband poured perfume on the head of his future bride and brought her

presents. After that, she was considered a full member of her future husband's family. On the wedding day, the bride was delivered to her husband where he veiled her in the presence of witnesses and solemnly declared her to be his wife.

The newlyweds usually went to live in the household of the husband until he was old enough to set up a household of his own or, if the family was wealthy, until his father died and he was granted the estate. The bride brought with her a *shirqu* or dowry as well as a trousseau (clothing, linens, etc.),

both of which became the future property of her children. If the bride's father was rich enough, he gave her a gift of gold, silver, furniture, or slaves at the time of her engagement, and she was allowed to use this gift in any way she wished, including to set up her own business. This property remained hers even if her husband divorced her.

While ***monogamy*** was the rule among the people of Mesopotamia, some men took in secondary wives. The title "wife," however, was reserved for the legal wife alone. The secondary wives, sometimes referred to as concubines, were often members of the slave class and were tolerated within the household and society.

EDUCATION

At age eight or nine, boys of the wealthiest families began to attend school. Children from lower-class families were taught life skills at home. Boys learned a specific trade such as boat-building or brickmaking, and girls were trained as wives and mothers.

The school, constructed of brick with small windows near the roof, was called an

Figure 3-7 *A Sumerian school room*

edubba or "tablet house" because the children wrote school exercises on clay tablets. Sitting on rows of benches made of mud bricks, pupils learned writing, arithmetic, grammar, history, and geography. The students were called "sons," the teacher (who was a priest and scribe) was called "father," and his monitors were called "big brothers."

The school day ran from sunrise to sunset, and discipline was very strict. Students who did not do their work perfectly were punished. If they made mistakes, they had to smooth the work over and repeat the exercise. If the clay dried before they could make the corrections, the errors remained forever. Archaeologists have found many such tablets with the teacher's corrections marked on them.

URBAN AND RURAL LIVING

What was life like in a Sumerian city-state? What would you see if you took a walk around Ur, Kish, or Lagash? The city-states in Sumer were surrounded by thick, high walls of mud brick. Inside the walls were a few broad streets, public squares, and bustling marketplaces. The temple, the most sacred building, was always located in the centre and served as the focus of most activities including craft industries and religious ceremonies.

The homes of lower-class Sumerians would probably have seemed quite simple. They were constructed of sun-dried earthen-brown bricks. A typical home featured a low door and a few windows covered with wooden grilles high up on the walls. An outside staircase led to a flat roof where people often slept on hot nights.

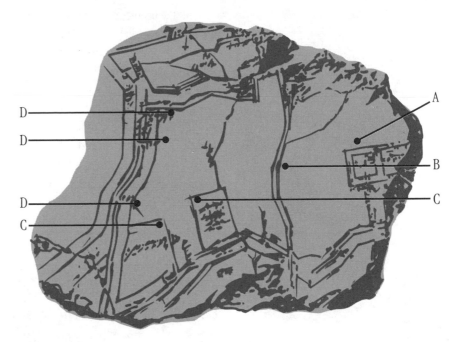

Figure 3-8
A map of the city of Nippur, showing (a) the ziggurat, (b) the canal, (c) the enclosure and gardens, and (d) the city gate

Inside was a single room, which was cool but poorly lighted. Decorations were limited to matting on the floor and woven blankets along the walls.

Wealthy urban Sumerians lived in more elaborate homes. We know more about their dwellings because they could afford to build with kiln-dried rather than sun-dried bricks. These more permanent materials have allowed archaeologists to determine more accurately what the homes were like.

A vestibule (passage) connected the home to the street. Off the vestibule was a large reception room for guests and a link to an open court, around which the house was built. The open court contained a well, an oven, and a grinding stone for making flour. Rooms for dining, sleeping, and leisure were located around the court.

In Assyria, the urban homes of the wealthy were similar to those in Sumer.

Assyrian homes, however, may have been better decorated, with wall paintings, hangings, and fine rugs. Each room had a niche for lamps and for storing personal belongings. For the very well-to-do, lavatories were constructed with asphalt floors and drains, a testimonial to the excellent technology of the Assyrians.

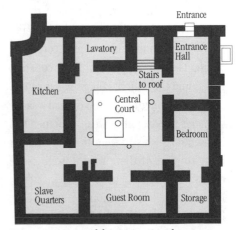

Figure 3-9 *A wealthy Sumerian home*

Figure 3-10
Sumerian woman of the wealthier classes

Compared to houses in the cities, the rural homes of tenant farmers throughout Mesopotamia were very simple. Built close to the irrigated fields, each one was linked to the nearest neighbour by a well-beaten footpath. Because stone was very scarce for construction, the earliest rural dwellings were simple reed huts covered in mud. Later, sun-dried mud bricks were used to build somewhat more permanent dwellings. While these homes, with their flat roofs, were small and cheap to construct, residents had to live with the constant threat that they might collapse at any time!

Management of the household was the woman's responsibility. Wealthy women had household slaves to help them with their daily routine. If there was no well in the courtyard, water had to be transported from the public well. In addition, grain had to be fetched from the granary, children had to be cared for, and food had to be prepared.

All the peoples of Mesopotamia shared a similar daily diet. Supper was the main meal of the day. In poorer homes, family members gathered on floor mats and ate with their fingers from an array of food set out in baskets and on pottery dishes. The wealthy usually dined at tables, eating from tableware that often included fine copper cups. A typical menu included staples such as baked fish, unleavened bread, goat's milk, dates, honey, grapes, and other fruit. The wealthy could afford to add lamb, chicken, and pork to their diet. The common drinks were beer and date wine.

Banquets and feasts were popular forms of entertainment among all classes of Mesopotamians. The wealthy served lavish spreads of duck, deer, and roasted wild pork on huge copper platters, along with side dishes of fresh fruit and vegetables and loaves of bread. Even poor families enjoyed opportunities to host a feast. For the main dish, they generally offered dried or fresh fish dressed up for the occasion with a mixture of onions, cucumbers, apples, spices, cheese, and eggs.

REFLECT AND ANALYZE

1. Why do we know more about the general living conditions of the wealthy Mesopotamians than we do about the poor?

2. Provide evidence that, in both design and materials, city and farm homes were products of the Mesopotamian environment.

3. What advantages and disadvantages can you see in the design of lower-class homes in both city and country?

4. Consider the status of women in ancient Mesopotamia. What are some of the positive and negative aspects of their lives?

5. Create a sketch or mural depicting a Mesopotamian wedding feast. Include a menu for the feast and pay attention to details such as clothing and decorations.

THE ECONOMY

AGRICULTURE

Little rain falls in [Mesopotamia], enough, however, to make the corn begin to sprout, after which the plant is nourished and the ears formed by means of irrigation from the river. For the river does not, as in Egypt, overflow the corn-lands of its own accord, but is spread over them by the hand, or by the help of engines [invention]. The whole of Babylonia is, like Egypt, intersected with canals. Of all the countries that we know there is none which is so fruitful in grain. It makes no pretention indeed of growing the fig, the olive, the vine, or any other tree of the kind; but in grain it is so fruitful as to yield commonly two hundred fold, and when the production is the greatest, even three hundred fold.

The Persian Wars
Herodotus
(Greek historian, fifth century BCE)

In this excerpt, the Greek historian Herodotus shows his amazement at the grain yields that farmers in Babylonia were able to produce, in spite of the environmental obstacles. The farmers had to control the floodwaters of the rivers and irrigate the lands to produce sizeable crop yields.

The fertile banks of the Tigris and Euphrates produced three main crops: barley, dates, and sesame seeds. The choice farming lands were located in the higher regions out of reach of the floodwaters, or else in areas that drained on their own.

The Sumerians' agricultural developments testify to their ingenuity. They were the first people to harness animals (oxen) to their ploughs. They then developed a shoulder-yoke for the oxen that made steering the plough easier. Next, they changed the shape of the plough so that it became a machine for turning the soil, not just one for scratching a furrow. The Sumerians were also the first people to add a seed drill to the plough.

But their most significant invention was the system of dams and canals that they developed to control the floodwaters and to irrigate their fields. Each city-state built a main canal that was fed by a dam on either the Tigris or Euphrates river. Feeder canals, constructed on a slant so that the water could flow easily, linked the main canal to ditches surrounding the city's fields. All channels, large and small, were controlled by gates regulated by removing or inserting clods of earth. Simply maintaining such an intricate network of canals required a great deal of time and effort.

Even a well-constructed canal system could not guarantee the farmers success. Flooding remained a constant concern. At any time, rushing floodwaters could dump soil into the canals, clogging them and destroying the fields. Even one clogged canal could mean disaster. Therefore, the government hired irrigators to help keep the large canals clear, and made each farmer responsible for maintaining his own small canals and cleaning them out regularly.

The importance of the irrigation works is illustrated in the message on this clay tablet, dating from 2000 BCE:

When you are about to cultivate your field, take care to open the irrigation works so that the water does not rise too high in it. When you have emptied it of water, watch the field's wet ground that it stays even; let no wandering ox trample it. Chase the prowlers and have it treated as settled land. Clear it with ten narrow axes weighing no more than two thirds of a pound each. Its stubble should be torn up by hand and tied in bundles; its narrow holes should be dragged and the field fenced. During the hot weather divide the field into parts. Let your tools hum with activity.

The fertile, rain-watered valleys in the northern areas of Mesopotamia did not need as much irrigation to grow grain and fruit. Yet the Assyrians also developed a system of irrigation. Like the regions farther south, farming land in Assyria was limited to a narrow band along the river banks. The people protected this valuable land by preventing cows, donkeys, and sheep from grazing on it. Instead, most farm animals were raised in enclosed pens. But on the rich grasslands of the northern mountain slopes, flocks of sheep grazed freely, and wool became an important industry in the region.

Agriculture was closely linked to the political and social organizations in Mesopotamia. The Sumerians, for example, believed that the land surrounding a particular city-state belonged to the god of that city-state. Since priests were the voice of the gods, the land was owned by the temples and the priests leased out the land to farmers.

Sumerian farmers were expected to return one-third of the proceeds from their harvest to the god of the city-state and one-third to the king to help finance the operation of the government. The final third was theirs to keep, even though the government still taxed them on their profit! In the period between 2500 BCE and 2360 BCE, priests levied higher taxes than usual and confiscated the land of any farmer who did not pay. These actions enraged the farmers.

Urukagina, king of Lagash, realized how unfair the system was. He took over the taxing powers of the priests and returned much of the land in his city-state to the farmers. Later, during the time of Hammurabi and the Babylonian empire, individuals were allowed to own a great deal of the land around the cities.

INDUSTRY

Abundant agricultural production in Mesopotamia meant that not all citizens had to farm: some could become craftspeople or artisans. Workrooms were located around and within the low walls of the ziggurats. Here, in various clusters, you could see tanners preparing animal skins for containers, military dress, and harnesses; potters spinning clay vessels on wheels; carpenters making agricultural tools, wagons, and ships; and weavers producing woollen textiles. There were also metalworkers, whose smiths worked in copper,

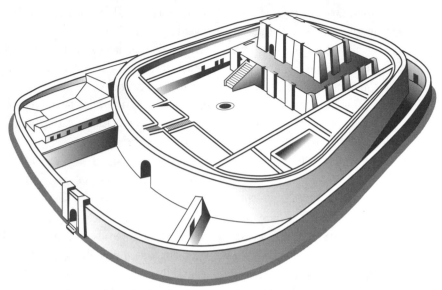

Figure 3-11 *The temple oval where industry and crafts developed*

gold, silver, and bronze, creating copper bowls, statues of gods and goddesses, tools for the fields, weapons, objects for the temples, and ornaments for the public.

Overseers supervised the various operations, monitoring the quality of each person's crafts. The temple scribes kept detailed records and accounts on clay tablets to guarantee that the industries were run efficiently.

TRADE

Small boats made of reeds and inflated goatskins, called *keleks*, carried goods up and down the Tigris and Euphrates rivers from one Sumerian city to another. But transport along the river was not always easy. Swift currents and sandbanks encountered on the trip downstream could cause the boats to capsize. Sometimes, the travellers had to dismantle the vessels and carry them back upstream.

Long ships, powered by square sails and oars, brought back building stone from Africa, copper from Cyprus, gold from Egypt, and cedar from Lebanon. In exchange, the Sumerians traded wool, cloth, jewellery, oil, and grains. Overland, caravans of donkeys set out in search of silver from the Taurus Mountains. Such ventures in trade netted an exchange in culture and ideas that further promoted the development of the civilized world.

The Babylonians were perhaps the greatest traders of all. The main trade routes of the ancient world met at the city of Babylon. While Babylonian ships traded down the river and along the coast of Arabia

INNOVATIONS
The First Use of Money

Why did the Babylonians decide to introduce coins as the unit of exchange in trade? How did the Babylonians determine the relative value of each coin? How is the value of our currency determined today?

When trading, the Sumerians used a barter system: that is, instead of using money, they traded goods for other goods. But the medium of exchange was grain. Therefore, if they were negotiating a trade deal, they would strike the final bargain by exchanging a volume of the product they hoped to purchase for an agreed-upon number of sacks of grain.

The Babylonians changed this practice by introducing one of the first uses of money in the ancient world. Although it was still based on grain, the Babylonian system was much more practical.

The Babylonians introduced a precious metal coin, most often of silver, called the *shekel*. The shekel weighed the same as 180 grains of barley, the most important grain product of the Mesopotamian economy. Another coin, the *mina*, was worth 60 shekels. Finally, a *talent* was worth 60 minas.

The most commonly used coin was the mina. With these coins in use, ships and caravans had a much lighter load since they no longer had to carry the heavy sacks of grain!

and India, Babylonian merchant caravans ventured far into Persia and Asia Minor.

Like the Sumerians and the Babylonians, the Assyrians were enthusiastic traders. Ashur and Nineveh became trading centres very early in their history, long before either was considered a prominent city. Caravans came to these centres from Babylonia to exchange manufactured goods for Assyrian raw materials such as stone, metal, and wool. In time, the small trading bazaars of these two cities became major market centres where people could purchase linens from Egypt, pearls from the Red Sea, and iron weapons from Anatolia (part of Turkey in western Asia).

Trading became very important to the economy of major Assyrian cities. A population of craftspeople grew in each centre, taking up residence in their own quarter of the city according to their specialty. They opened stalls on the streets to exchange their bronze, pottery, or woollen goods for imported products. Like the Sumerians, the Assyrians recorded all of their business transactions, but they simplified the system somewhat by using fewer signs and symbols.

REFLECT AND ANALYZE

1. What agricultural innovations did the Mesopotamians introduce? Explain how these innovations were used.

2. On a map, sketch Sumerian and Babylonian trade routes and label the products they exchanged with distant lands.

3. What role did religion and religious beliefs play in the economy of the Mesopotamians?

4. Evaluate the positive and negative effects these innovations might have had on Mesopotamian society:
    - shoulder yoke
    - money
    - irrigation canals
    - iron.

5. Role play a conversation between a Mesopotamian craftsperson, such as a tanner or carpenter, and a common farmer. The craftsperson argues that the specialization of labour is a positive development, while the farmer argues that it is not.

THE ARTS

WRITING

Iran, 1835

Henry Rawlinson stood staring up at the sheer face of the Behistun Rock, a 120-m cliff that contained ancient carvings praising the greatness of the Persian King, Darius I. In 450 BCE, Darius had ordered stone-cutters to climb the side of this mountain and carve out a testimony to his greatness in three languages. One was old Persian, a language Rawlinson could read. Another was cuneiform, the script of ancient Babylon.

Rawlinson wanted to copy the script from the monument so that he could compare the languages. Maybe the old Persian would help him to read the cuneiform, which linguists had been trying to decipher for centuries.

Viewing the script through binoculars didn't give Rawlinson enough clarity. The only way he could get closer was to climb halfway up the face of the wall to a narrow ledge. A ladder was raised to the ledge from the roadway far below. Carefully, Rawlinson climbed to the top rung as the ladder pressed against the steep cliff. Standing at the top, he leaned over, hanging on to a rope, and pressed pieces of wet paper onto the grooves of the inscription. As they dried, he carefully peeled them away and lowered them to the ground. Rawlinson had his inscriptions.

Once Henry Rawlinson had copies of the script, he was able to begin the work of deciphering cuneiform by comparing it to the old Persian text. He spent 12 years deciphering the text before he could begin translating.

Cuneiform was one of the earliest forms of writing and was based on picture signs. It first appeared in Sumer about 3000 BCE, and probably developed from the need to keep accurate records in trade and agriculture.

Until Rawlinson and others learned how to read cuneiform, historians didn't know that ancient Sumer had ever existed. They knew about the ancient Babylonians and Assyrians, from the Bible and other sources, and they knew that cuneiform

Figure 3-12
The Behistun Rock. The Great King Darius receives the submission of his enemies

tablets were the records left by these peoples. But it wasn't until they began to decipher the thousands of cuneiform texts found in Mesopotamia that they began to learn of an earlier civilization that predated all the others.

People wrote cuneiform on mud or clay tablets, inscribing the picture signs while the tablet was still wet. Rather than scratch the notations into the mud, scribes would jab the tablet with the end of a reed cut in the shape of a sharp triangle. The word cuneiform comes from the Latin word *cuneus*, meaning wedge. Once the wedge-shaped marks were made, the tablet was baked like a brick.

The earliest Sumerian cuneiform symbols were picture symbols or pictograms that represented concrete objects such as an ox or a shaft of grain. At first, they were written in columns and read downwards from right to left. As time passed, however, cuneiform evolved. Scribes rotated the symbols ninety degrees to make them easier to record and the symbols became more stylized. Eventually, the symbols came to represent not only objects, but abstract ideas as well. Symbols representing ideas are called ideograms. The Sumerians also abandoned the practice of writing from right to left because it tended to smudge the tablet. On tablets dating from later periods, the symbols were clearly recorded and read from left to right.

In the ancient world, the scribes were responsible for reading and writing. The early scribes were priests, but later they became a recognized professional group on their own, greatly respected by all classes of people. Rulers depended on them to record laws, and common people needed them to

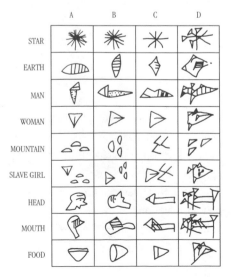

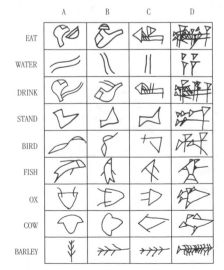

Figure 3-13 *The development of cuneiform writing*

Figure 3-14 *The oldest known medical text*

write letters and to read for them. Because of their education and social standing, scribes rose to positions of high government service in the ancient world. In Sumer, for example, they oversaw such government operations as the development and maintenance of the irrigation works.

Cuneiform spread from Sumer to the north, where it was adopted and developed by the Babylonians and Assyrians. Historians give part of the credit for the language's migration to Sumerian traders, who used this form of writing to maintain records of their sales and purchases.

LITERATURE

In long narrative poems or **epics**, the people of Mesopotamia preserved ancient legends and passed on religious teachings, accounts of disasters, and stories of their heroes. The earliest example of this literary form, and one of the oldest pieces of literature in the world, is the *Epic of Gilgamesh*.

This epic is the story of a heroic Sumerian king, Gilgamesh, who ruled around 2600 BCE. The story was likely passed down orally for many generations, and not recorded until long after its creation. Some historians suggest that the epic's tablet versions date from about 1700 BCE.

Gilgamesh, both admired and feared, was considered to be two-thirds god and one-third man. In the epic, Gilgamesh was often seen as brutal and quick to forget the feelings of others. For example, even though he protected his city with a solid defensive wall, he made the people work hard to construct it. Finally, the people asked the gods to send a heavenly being who could match the strength of Gilgamesh.

The gods sent a huge, hairy beast-like creature called Enkidu, who went to live in the hills near Uruk. Gilgamesh then sent a woman into the hills to tame Enkidu and bring him back to Uruk to live like a man. When Gilgamesh and Enkidu later came to battle, neither emerged a winner. Instead, they joined forces and set out on adventures together.

ART AND SCULPTURE

Sculpture was an important part of life in Mesopotamia. Almost everyone owned a small statue of one of the gods made of terra-cotta, gypsum, stone, or copper. Nearly all of the statues depict a figure standing quietly with hands clasped in prayer. Larger carvings were done for the temples.

Mosaics were often used to tell a story. One of the most famous mosaics is

THROUGH THEIR EYES
The Epic of Gilgamesh

Figure 3-15
Gilgamesh

In this extract from the *Epic of Gilgamesh*, Enkidu is describing to Gilgamesh a place he was forced to enter in a dream. What is this place? What does this extract tell us about how the Sumerians view the afterlife?

His was a vampire face, his foot was a lion's foot, his hand was an eagle's talon. He fell on me and his claws were in my hair, he held me fast and I smothered; then he transformed me so that my arms became wings covered with feathers. He turned his stare towards me, and he led me away to the palace of Irkalla, the Queen of Darkness, to the house from which none who enters ever returns, down the road from which there is no coming back.

'There is the house whose people sit in darkness; dust is their food and clay their meat. They are clothed like birds with wings for covering, they see no light, they sit in darkness.

…

In the house of dust which I entered were high priests and acolytes, priests of the incantation and of ecstasy; there were servers of the temple, and there was Etana, that king of Kish whom the eagle carried to heaven in the days of old. I saw also Samuqan, god of cattle, and there was Ereshkigal the Queen of the Underworld; and Belit-Sheri squatted in front of her, she who is recorder of the gods and keeps the book of death. She held a tablet from which she read. She raised her head, she saw me and spoke: "Who has brought this one here?"

Figure 3-16 *Stone carved Sumerian figure—Lugal of Gudea of Lagash*

Figure 3-17 *The Standard of Ur*

the Standard of Ur found by Leonard Woolley during his excavations of the royal tombs at Ur in 1922. A standard is a symbol of the power or authority of the king. In modern times, we often use a flag as a standard of king or country. The Standard of Ur consists of two small rectangular wooden panels inlaid with mother-of-pearl, mussel shells, and lapis lazuli. Each panel is 56 cm long and 28 cm wide. One side of each panel depicts scenes of war. The other side depicts scenes from a banquet or victory feast.

The mosaics of battle show soldiers bringing prisoners of war back to their king, some of the people riding in four-wheeled chariots. The depiction of these vehicles is the earliest evidence we have of the use of the wheel.

Relief carvings on buildings were an important art form in Babylonia and Assyria. In some cases, they depicted mythical animals or figures; in other cases, they portrayed an important king.

REFLECT AND ANALYZE

1. What important event unlocked the secret to the ancient language of cuneiform? Describe the method used to copy and decipher the script.

2. How did cuneiform evolve as a form of writing throughout the history of Mesopotamia?

3. Explain the importance of art and literature in the lives of the Mesopotamian peoples.

4. Using a flattened piece of plasticene as your clay tablet and a straw with a sliced bottom edge as your stylus, write a sentence in cuneiform. Use the pictograms in Figure 3.13 as a guide.

5. In groups, devise a job advertisement for a Mesopotamian scribe. Outline his or her qualifications and the ways in which the cuneiform script could be used.

6. Find modern retellings or translations of the *Epic of Gilamesh*. These can be the subject of dramatic readings.

THE SCIENCES

THE WHEEL

Mesopotamia's most important technological advance was the wheel, invented by the Sumerians. How did this discovery come about? We can only speculate. Perhaps an inventive citizen was watching a farmer struggling hopelessly with a heavy load, and suddenly got the idea that simply rolling a tree trunk beneath the burden would move it along more easily.

The wheel had a monumental impact from the first days of its discovery. By 3250 BCE, the Sumerians built wheeled wagons and chariots to replace the sleds that they had used previously. With an ox pulling a wagon, farmers transported three to four times the weight in crops and produce that they had been able to carry on sleds, on donkeys, or on their own backs.

The invention of the wheel had applications beyond the field of transportation. Pulleys, for example, made it easier to raise water from wells, facilitating the irrigation process. The potter's wheel marked the beginning of fine pottery, as it made shaping symmetrical vessels much easier.

METALLURGY

Historians have credited the Sumerians with the technological advance that gave rise to the Bronze Age, which began about 3000 BCE. Some recent discoveries in Thailand, however, suggest that the Bronze Age may have begun in eastern Asia.

Before the Bronze Age, dating from as early as 8000 BCE, copper had been the main metal used in western Asia. A soft metal, copper is fine for creating jewellery but poor for making weapons or tools. Most tools in this period were made of stone. For a long time, copper was processed by being hammered into shape. Then someone discovered how to smelt and cast copper by pouring it into moulds.

Bronze is an alloy composed of copper and tin. It is superior to copper because it is harder, more durable, and provides a sharper cutting edge. The Sumerians probably created bronze by accidentally smelting copper and tin together. The Sumerians traded with Egypt for supplies of copper, and with Anatolia and Armenia for tin. Bronze was an expensive metal to produce, but easier to cast than copper because it has a lower melting point. Bronze took over from stone as the chief material for tool-making, and was widely used in western Asia and Europe for about 2000 years. Then it was replaced by iron, which makes better tools and is more common, but is more difficult to process.

The Iron Age began in about 1200 BCE. The Hittites introduced iron into the Middle East, and the Assyrians were the first people in Mesopotamia to work with the new metal. The Hittites of Anatolia (Turkey) were descendants of waves of Indo-Europeans who had arrived in the Middle East approximately 2500 BCE. The Hittites learned how to extract the iron from the ore found in the mountains of their homeland. They found that the smelting process required a hotter fire than for bronze, and that the ore needed to be mixed with limestone. When the ore was poured into moulds, it hardened as cast iron, but was relatively weak. But if the cast iron was reheated, beaten or "wrought," and then cooled, it became stronger. This metal was called wrought iron. Trade and military conquests spread an awareness of iron and its value to the Assyrians in Mesopotamia.

MATHEMATICS

The Sumerians could count in tens and hundreds, but they preferred to use 60 as their arithmetical unit. Some mathematicians, who have tried to guess why the Sumerians preferred this system, note that 60 can be divided by all numbers up to six. Perhaps this base made their mathematical calculations easier.

Whatever the reason for the number 60, mathematics was extremely important to the Sumerians' political and economic systems. They used mathematics to help build canals, to keep accurate farm and trade records, and to tabulate taxes owed to the state. This mathematical system left us a legacy as well. From the Sumerians, we have received the 360-degree circle, the 60-minute hour, and the 60-second minute.

TIME

The ancient Mesopotamians believed that the stars controlled the forces of heaven. They named various groups of stars, gave them special meanings, and used these groups and their movements to predict the future. The signs of the zodiac that astrologers use today developed from this practice.

Astronomers studying the stars worked out a lunar calendar of 12 months. They divided their year into two seasons, *emesh* (summer) and *enten* (winter). Since the time lapse from one new moon to another is only 29¼ days, the lunar year of 12 months contained only 354 days—11¼ days short of the solar year. After three years, therefore, the calendar was 33¾ days out. As a result, an extra month was put into the calendar to bring it in line with the solar year. It was always the king's responsibility to decide when to add the extra month every three years, but he usually relied upon the advice of his astronomers.

Of all the Mesopotamian peoples, the Chaldeans took the greatest interest in the movements of the heavenly bodies. They believed that they needed detailed observation and measurement to develop a more accurate calendar so that they could plan agricultural operations more effectively.

The Chaldeans were convinced that events on earth were a reflection of, or related to, events in the sky. In particular, they relied on the stars for determining direction, whether on land or sea.

opment of a true civilization.

Consider the legacy. The first known form of writing was developed in Sumer and was used to record business transactions, farm yields, laws, myths, and legends. It was also used by the Assyrians to chronicle the history of their kings. Sumerian cuneiform writing evolved and remained the standard form for thousands of years. Laws and law codes, developed by Ur-Nammu and Hammurabi, were recorded to regulate human behaviour and served as models for later codes. The rulers of Mesopotamia, although not democratic, demonstrated the need for stable government, a principle that other civilizations would adopt as well. Finally, the innovations that Mesopotamians made in the fields of architecture and art, their invention of the wheel, and their extended use of iron would greatly affect the course of human history.

REFLECT AND ANALYZE

1. What contributions did the Mesopotamians make in the fields of mathematics and astronomy?

2. How were bronze and iron acquired by the Mesopotamians?

3. "The wheel was the greatest mechanical invention of all time." Defend or dispute this statement.

4. Some of the greatest innovations in human history have been achieved by accident. Research two such innovations and consider how our lives would be different without them.

LOOKING BACK

The people of Mesopotamia developed a magnificent and thriving civilization despite environmental obstacles. They learned to control the forces of nature and turn adversity to advantage. Throughout their history, they established and nurtured most of the basic components that historians consider essential to the devel-

EGYPT:
Land of the Pharaohs

Egypt: Valley of the Kings, 1995

D r. Kent Weeks, professor of Egyptology, and his team from the American University in Cairo have reached the central hall in the largest tomb ever found in Egypt. The giant crypt is located in the Valley of the Kings on the west side of the Nile near the Egyptian city of Luxor. The tomb was originally discovered by an English traveller in 1820, but was never explored. In the 1920s, its entrance was covered over with debris during the excavation of the tomb of King Tut close by. Dr. Weeks discovered the hidden entrance in 1987 by studying the diaries of the English traveller. Excavation work has been in progress ever since that exciting discovery.

What is in this tomb? Archaeologists believe that the tomb contains the remains of 50 sons of the pharaoh Ramses II. Ramses II, who lived well into his eighties, ruled Egypt from 1279 BCE to 1213 BCE and fathered more than 100 children. Sixty-seven rooms have been discovered in the mass tomb so far, but since none is smaller than 3 m square, Egyptologists believe that they may have been carved all at once, as part of a master design. The tomb contains a wealth of burial objects, inscriptions, and a statue of Osiris, the ancient Egyptian god of the underworld. The names of four of the sons have already been found inscribed on the walls and on objects in the tomb. Archaeologists have only brushed the surface of the knowledge and treasures the tomb may hold.

Figure 4-1
Ramses II

Egyptologists have toiled for centuries uncovering ancient ruins and artifacts, deciphering inscriptions, and restoring the monuments of this great civilization on the Nile. Khaemwese, the high priest of Memphis and the fourth son of Ramses II, was likely the first Egyptologist. In the thirteenth century BCE, the pharaohs who had built the pyramids had been dead for almost a thousand years. Khaemwese spent hours wandering around the pyramids and other ruins of the region, studying the mysteries surrounding his ancestors.

We are still trying to unravel those mysteries today. With every new archaeological discovery, historians raise new questions. For example, was Ramses II's tomb built gradually over the course of his reign? Was it built according to a master design? Were the pharaoh's sons buried in the tomb when they died, or were their bodies all brought there near the end of Ramses' reign? What more will this tomb tell us about ancient Egyptian civilization?

RED LAND, BLACK LAND

Civilization in Egypt began about 3100 BCE, not long after it began in Mesopotamia. Like Mesopotamia, Egypt developed around a great river system. Egyptian civilization had its humble beginnings as a scattering of villages and settlements stretching in a narrow strip along the mighty Nile River, the longest river in the world.

The land along the banks of the Nile was extremely fertile. The river flooded annually, depositing rich supplies of silt for surrounding fields. The flooding created a narrow ribbon of fertility that cut through the deserts in North Africa. To the Egyptians, therefore, the Nile was a lifeline. It provided water for both irrigation and

Figure 4-3 *The Nile valley near Aswan: desert cliffs rise up behind the cultivated land beside the river*

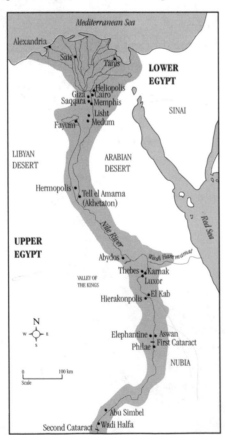

Figure 4.2 *Ancient Egypt*

drinking, silt for their fields, and a natural highway to link their communities.

The Nile was a friendlier river than either the Tigris or the Euphrates, and so life was more stable in ancient Egypt than in Mesopotamia. Sudden and disastrous floods like those in Mesopotamia happened rarely. The flooding of the Nile was more predictable. In fact, flooding was so predictable that Egyptians could set their agricultural calendar according to the river's schedule.

As ancient Egyptian civilization developed, it stretched from the mouth of the Nile on the Mediterranean Sea south to Elephantine, near the First Cataract of the Nile. Filled with granite rock, this cataract served as a natural border between Egypt and Nubia to the south.

The Egyptians called the region of rich silt soil along the banks of the Nile the *Kemet*, or Black Land. Beyond this fertile strip of land were the dead sands of the surrounding deserts, the Libyan Desert to the west and the Arabian Desert to the east. The Egyptians called these forbidding territories the *Deshret*, or the Red Land.

The desolate appearance of the Red

Land was somewhat deceiving. A treasure house of minerals lay beneath the shifting sands. The Arabian Desert was a source of gold and fine gems, including garnet, agate, and chalcedony. The desert lands farther east in the Sinai Peninsula provided copper for the manufacture of tools and weapons. The Libyan Desert in the west yielded valuable building materials such as granite, quartzite, flint, marble, and slate.

The Deshret was also valuable in other ways. In the Libyan Desert, running parallel to the Nile, were six oases (fertile areas) called **wadis**. Most were under Egyptian control. Two of these wadis became important suppliers of wine; another, the Wadi Natrun, was a source of natron, a salt used in the embalming of bodies. The deserts also acted as a buffer, shielding Egypt from invasions and, to some extent, insulating it from outside influences.

In addition to the sharp contrast between the Red Land and the Black Land, there were also major differences between the landscapes of the upper and lower regions of the Nile.

The landscape of Upper Egypt was marked by the Nile river valley, which ranged from 6 to 20 km wide. In this region, called the *ta-shema* or land of the shema-reed, the Nile flows from the high-lands in a single stream towards modern Cairo, cutting through a plateau of sand-stone in the south and limestone in the north, and creating a deep trench with cliffs on either side towering several hundred metres high. The people living in the Nile river valley could never forget how close they were to the desert. Its mountains and cliffs stood in clear view, reminding the Egyptians of their dependence on the Nile.

By contrast, in Lower Egypt, north of present-day Cairo, the Nile separates into different branches that veer northeast and northwest to the Mediterranean Sea, creating a fertile triangular plain. This area was called the *ta-mehu*, the land of the papyrus plant, or the Nile delta. In ancient times, the river emptied into the Mediterranean Sea from as many as seven different mouths, all abundant in ducks and geese, ibis and heron. Here, the land was black and flat, often swampy, but with extensive areas of ideal pasture land. The delta was more isolated and protected from land invasions than the valley of Upper Egypt, and the desert only encroached upon it at its margins. The outlet to the sea was also important for trade and cultural exchange. Trade routes stretched from Egypt through-out the Mediterranean region. Historians have evidence, for example, that Egyptians influenced early Minoan and Mycenean civilizations which led to ancient Greece.

Figure 4-4 *A pharaoh receives the double crown from the goddesses*

HISTORICAL OVERVIEW

The two regions of Upper Egypt and Lower Egypt began as separate kingdoms. The rulers of Upper Egypt wore a tall white crown, while the rulers of Lower Egypt wore a red crown. About 3100 BCE, political manoeuvring by powerful leaders in the north and south resulted in war between the two areas. The king of Upper Egypt triumphed, and the united kingdom emerged as a powerful civilization. This was the beginning of the Predynastic Period of ancient Egypt.

Later rulers of the united Egypt wore a double crown representing both regions, and used titles such as "Lord of the Two Lands" and "King of Upper and Lower Egypt" to remind the people that the land had once been divided into two distinct kingdoms. Following unification, two god-desses served to protect the king: Nekhbet of the south and Buto of the north.

The king of Upper Egypt who unified the country was Menes. He founded a new capital city, Memphis, 16 km south of modern Cairo. Here he built a temple to Ptah, chief god of Memphis, and con-structed administration buildings that served ancient Egypt for over 3500 years. Menes became the first of a long line of kings to rule ancient Egypt. He began the first Egyptian ***dynasty***—the first succes-

EGYPT: A DEVELOPMENTAL TIMELINE

	PREDYNASTIC PERIOD 3100 BCE-2650 BCE	OLD KINGDOM 2650 BCE-2134 BCE	MIDDLE KINGDOM 2040 BCE-1640 BCE
POLITICAL DEVELOPMENTS	• Menes unites Upper and Lower Egypt • Memphis becomes the capital of the united Egypt, the first nation state in the world	• pharaohs are seen as living gods • Egypt is divided into provinces, each headed by a governor **FIRST INTERMEDIATE PERIOD– 2134 BCE-2040 BCE** • local chieftains struggle for political power • Memphis falls into neglect	• pharaohs are threatened by the independence of local governors • Luxor gains prominence • Egypt recruits a standing army • Asians seize control of the delta region **SECOND INTERMEDIATE PERIOD– 1640 BCE-1550 BCE** • the Hyksos dominate Egypt
CULTURAL DEVELOPMENTS	• hieroglyphics are developed	• hieroglyphics improve	• foreign cultural influences increase • renewed interest in learning takes place • literature flourishes
TECHNOLOGICAL/ECONOMIC DEVELOPMENTS	• irrigation systems are developed	• Djoser builds the Step pyramid at Saqqara • Khufu builds the Great Pyramid at Giza • the pyramid of Chephren is built at Giza • the pyramid of Mycernius is built at Giza • the government begins to regulate farming and trade	• trade promoted with Palestine and Syria • workshops begin to produce fine crafts • Hyksos introduce horse-drawn chariot, copper arrowheads and daggers, curved-blade swords, compound bow

NEW KINGDOM 1550 BCE–1070 BCE	LATE DYNASTIC PERIOD 1070 BCE–332 BCE	GREEK PERIOD 332 BCE–48 BCE	ROMAN PERIOD 48 BCE–395 CE
• Thutmose I extends the empire into southwest Asia (1504–1492 BCE) • Hatshepsut becomes a powerful female pharaoh (1479–1457 BCE) • Thutmose III brings Palestine and Syria into the empire and re-establishes control over Nubia and Kush (1479–1425 BCE) • the army is developed into a highly organized fighting force • Ramses II rules as the empire of Egypt begins to crumble under pressure from the Hittites (1279–1213 BCE)	• a struggle for royal power sets in among priests and nobles of Egypt • General Piankhi of Nubia invades Egypt (728 BCE) • Ashurbanipal of Assyria invades Egypt (667 BCE) • the Saite kings begin a century of domination in Egypt (664 BCE) • the Persians dominate Egypt (525 BCE)	• Alexander the Great of Macedonia takes control of Egypt (332 BCE) • Ptolemy, the Macedonian governor of Egypt, becomes Ptolemy I (305 BCE) • Cleopatra VII becomes the last Ptolemy to rule Egypt (51 BCE)	• Cleopatra VII forms an alliance with Julius Caesar (48 BCE) • Cleopatra VII forms an alliance with Mark Antony (41 BCE) • Mark Antony is defeated by Octavian at the Battle of Actium (31 BCE) • Cleopatra VII commits suicide (30 BCE) • Egypt is ruled as a territory of Rome
• Hatshepsut promotes the arts in Egypt • Amenhotep IV (Akhenaton) carries out the Amarna Revolution, making the god Aton the only recognized god of Egypt (1352–1336 BCE) • Tutankhamen restores the old religion of Egypt (1336–1327 BCE) • Horemheb completely repudiates the religion of Akhenaton (1323–1295 BCE) • extensive monumental works are built at Thebes	• period of great temple building	• Alexandria becomes the most brilliant metropolis of the Greek-speaking world	
• Hatshepsut extends foreign trade into Punt (Somalia)			• the use of iron tools and weapons spreads • clear glass, terra-cotta lamps, the lathe, the split-nib pen, and the key are introduced • agriculture is improved by the introduction of the ox-drawn waterwheel and the threshing machine

sion of rulers who claimed their descent from a common ancestor.

The Predynastic Period lasted a little over 400 years. During this time, kings faced considerable internal opposition as they tried to secure their power. But it was during this period that the Egyptians began to develop essential irrigation systems along the Nile River, and created a system of writing called **hieroglyphics**.

THE OLD KINGDOM OR "THE AGE OF THE PYRAMIDS"

It was not until the beginning of the Old Kingdom in 2650 BCE that a powerful king finally created a central government strong enough to command the country. This king was Djoser. During his rule, Djoser ordered his people to build him an enormous tomb, the Step Pyramid at Saqqara. Rising to a height of 60 m in six giant steps, this pyramid was the first monumental stone building ever constructed in the world. The magnitude of this project—which involved moving massive amounts of stone, recruiting thousands of labourers, and feeding the workers—indicates how powerful Djoser was, and symbolizes the unlimited authority enjoyed by Egyptian rulers of the period.

From the Third to the Sixth Dynasties, the Egyptians considered the rulers of the Old Kingdom to be living gods. The kings, known as pharaohs, demonstrated an attitude of being more than earthly mortals by remaining distant or aloof from the general population they ruled. The images that remain of these early kings reflect severe features and suggest how aloof and powerful they must have been.

The great pyramids of the kings of the Fourth Dynasty, on the plateau of Giza high above Cairo, mark the zenith of the rulers'

Figure 4-5 *The Step Pyramid at Saqqara*

power and achievement. Today, we still marvel that a civilization could accomplish such feats. The famous pyramid of Khufu (Cheops) stands an impressive 146.6 m high. The other two famous pyramids, those of Khufu's son Chephren and his brother Mycerinus, were built by farmers, who could be recruited when the floodwaters of the Nile covered their fields. Historians often describe the Old Kingdom as "the age of the pyramids" because these monumental structures are one of the greatest achievements of the period.

The Old Kingdom also witnessed other important accomplishments. Hieroglyphics, the Egyptian form of picture writing, improved. More sophisticated engineering skills led to the construction of temples and elaborate tombs for the king or pharaoh. The Egyptians designed irrigation systems and improved farming. Trade became more regulated, and spread throughout the Mediterranean region, enriching Egypt with new inventions and goods, including the potter's wheel from Mesopotamia, timber

from Syria, and oil and wine from Crete. The foundations of organized government were laid when the rulers divided the state into provinces or districts, each with its own governor appointed by the pharaoh.

During this period, the king had a personal bodyguard but ancient Egypt had no standing army. When regions such as Libya or Nubia posed any potential threat to the kingdom, the governors of the various provinces raised troops to defend the empire. Once this temporary army completed a specific military campaign, it was either disbanded or assigned to some other state work project, such as building the pyramids at Giza.

By the Fifth Dynasty, the authority of the king had weakened. High priests and government officials vied for power. The pyramids of the kings of the Fifth and Sixth Dynasties are markedly smaller, reflecting the general impoverishment of Egypt. Towards the end of the Sixth Dynasty, the climate and the Nile River combined to bring about the end of the old **monarchy**.

With low rainfall and a series of weak floods from the Nile, Egypt suffered from famines.

After the death of Pepi II, who had risen to the throne as a boy and ruled for 94 years, the organization of the Old Kingdom failed. Egypt again separated into two distinct parts. Without a king strong enough to control the entire territory, the country entered a time of general disorder called the First Intermediate Period.

The First Intermediate Period lasted a very short time, certainly less than 100 years. Records are few and badly written, but historians think that many local chiefs competed for power, each declaring himself king and attempting to form his own dynasty. Meanwhile, the court at Memphis fell into a state of neglect. Governors no longer chose the traditional pattern of burial in the capital near their king, preferring instead to be buried in their own towns in tomb shafts built for family and friends.

THE MIDDLE KINGDOM OR "THE AGE OF THE NOBLES"

The Middle Kingdom, which began in 2040 BCE, was formed when one strong family from the region of Luxor re-established order and succeeded in claiming the throne. These kings of the Eleventh Dynasty, called either *Intef* or *Mentuhotep*, reunited Egypt, controlling its administration from a town called Itjtawy, rather than from Memphis. Although its actual location is unknown, Egyptologists think it was located in the region of the Fayum, south of Memphis. Egypt began to prosper once again. Trade links forged during the Old Kingdom were rebuilt with neighbours such as Syria and Palestine. Workshops started to produce fine crafts. As scholars began again to copy literary texts, the people's interest in learning was renewed.

Architecture, literature, and the arts flourished in this period.

Despite the new control established by pharaohs of the Middle Kingdom, local governors or nobles were still quite independent and posed a constant threat to the monarchy. Amenemhat I (1985 BCE-1955 BCE), first king of the Twelfth Dynasty, was murdered as a result of a conspiracy involving his own bodyguard. A strong ruler, Amenemhat I had managed to restore many of the traditions associated with the Old Kingdom and had conquered much of Nubia.

The powerful nobles of the Middle Kingdom maintained their own permanent armies. By the Twelfth Dynasty, pharaohs began to see the need for maintaining a standing army to preserve their own power. Therefore, after appointing army scribes, they raised and maintained a state army by setting recruitment quotas for each district within the kingdom.

The rulers of the Thirteenth Dynasty

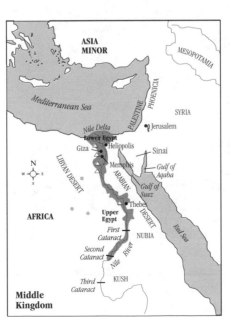

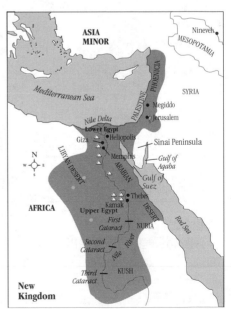

Figure 4-6 *Old, Middle, and New Kingdoms*

inherited a strong power base and an empire that had expanded its economic influence and political boundaries. But this dynasty was characterized by a series of short reigns and kings who gained little personal fame. Consequently, the authority of the throne weakened. At the same time, a great number of people from other countries settled in Egypt. Many of them were brought in from Asia as prisoners of war during the campaigns of the Twelfth Dynasty kings. These settlers gained power rapidly, establishing their base in the town of Avaris in the delta and seizing control about 1670 BCE.

During a Second Intermediate Period, Egypt was controlled by foreign rulers now often called the Hyksos kings. These kings were probably not all from one country, but were a mixture of races of non-Egyptian origin, many from Syria and Palestine. The Egyptians referred to them as the "rulers of foreign lands." It was the Greeks who later named these kings Hyksos.

While the Hyksos adopted many Egyptian traditions, they also introduced important innovations into Egypt. Their new technology included the horse-drawn chariot, copper arrowheads, daggers cast in one piece for greater strength, the scimitar or curved-blade sword, and the compound bow, built of several layers of tough springy wood for greater strength. In fact, the Hyksos had used these very innovations to conquer the Egyptians.

Eventually, a warlike family from Luxor rallied the forces of Upper Egypt and drove the Hyksos out, using the improved military technology that the Hyksos had introduced. The victorious generals from Luxor began the New Kingdom, one of the greatest periods in Egyptian civilization.

REFLECT AND ANALYZE

1. Define the term "nation." How did ancient Egypt become a powerful, united nation?

2. How did the people come to view the pharoahs during the period of the Old Kingdom? How did the pharoahs show their power?

3. a) What caused the decline of the Old Kingdom?
   b) What caused the decline of the Middle Kingdom?

4. Imagine you are an Egyptian noble during the Old or Middle Kingdom. Write a letter to a fellow noble explaining why you oppose the power of the pharoahs and how you could conspire to overthrow them.

THE NEW KINGDOM OR "THE AGE OF THE EMPIRE"

The New Kingdom emerged in 1550 BCE. During this period, Egypt became the ancient world's strongest empire and Luxor (Thebes) became a great city once again. The pharaohs of the New Kingdom seemed fearless, tireless, strong, and invincible in battle. They were determined that Egypt should never again fall into the hands of foreigners. Yet they were less aloof than rulers of old, and were always keen to advance the positions of worthy supporters. They protected their borders from foreign invasion by maintaining permanent garrisons in the towns and cities to the north.

The pharaohs of the New Kingdom increased the size of their standing armies and concentrated more on building the empire. Thutmose I (1504 BCE–1492 BCE) led a military force into southwestern Asia as far as the Euphrates River. Tribute flowed into the Egyptian treasury from the peoples he conquered, enriching the empire. Later rulers extended Egypt's territory even farther.

Thutmose III (1479 BCE–1425 BCE) became the greatest military leader of the New Kingdom, and the country reached the zenith of its power during his reign. He was determined to create a mighty Egyptian empire, and led his armies on military campaigns into Asia almost every year for more than two decades.

Through Thutmose III's conquests, Palestine and Syria became part of the empire. Egypt also re-established control over Kush and Nubia, both valuable sources of slaves, copper, gold, ivory, and ebony. The army took children of foreign princes back to Egypt to guarantee that the conquered territories would obey the pharaoh. Egyptian envoys and military posts, established in foreign cities, watched for any local activity that could threaten the growing power of Egypt. By the end of his reign, Thutmose III ruled the east: the Egyptian empire stretched as far as the Euphrates River and the Taurus Mountains.

During this period, innovations began to appear in the Egyptian military. Leather body armour covered with metal scales was introduced. Charioteers, the elite branch of the military, began to carry large shields, and both warrior and horse wore heavy blankets of quilted leather, lined with linen, to cover most of their backs. The armies became highly organized fighting forces. Slaves captured in the Asiatic and Nubian wars were often forced to serve in the Egyptian military. In the later period of the New Kingdom, armies included increasing numbers of hired foreign troops or mercenaries.

The coronation of Amenhotep IV (1352 BCE–1336 BCE), who called himself Akhenaton, marked a turning point in Egyptian power. Akhenaton turned his back on many of the old traditions of ancient Egypt. He built a new capital city at an isolated location near what is now Tell el Amarna, 280 km north of Thebes, and changed the nature of Egyptian religion by declaring that the people could only worship one god, the sun god Aton. Utterly preoccupied with religious matters, he neglected the Egyptian empire at a time when it was being threatened by the Hittite nation.

Akhenaton's religious reforms, known as the Amarna Revolution, led to an outpouring of art and sculpture that glorified the sun god Aton but angered many Egyptians. The ruler's immediate successors finally ended this religious unrest. King Tutankhaton (1336 BCE–1327 BCE) re-

PERSPECTIVES ON THE PAST
Personalities and Power

Hatshepsut
(1479 BCE–1457 BCE)

Was Hatshepsut the first great woman in history? Some historians claim she was. What do you think?

Hatshepsut was certainly one of the most outstanding pharaohs of ancient Egypt, achieving great power and influence during the New Kingdom. As was common in royal families, Hatshepsut originally married her half-brother, the pharaoh Thutmose II (1492 BCE–1479 BCE). When he died, the throne passed to his small son, Thutmose III (1479 BCE–1425 BCE). As the child's stepmother, Hatshepsut served for a period as regent and co-ruler. Then, in a bold move, she seized the throne for herself and gained the backing of several high court officials and priests. She ruled Egypt as pharaoh in her own right for 22 years. Because a pharaoh was by custom male, Hatshepsut dressed in men's clothes and attached a ceremonial beard to her chin. Statues usually depict her wearing the beard.

While ruling the nation, Hatshepsut ordered the construction of a temple in her honour at Deir El-Bahri. On the walls of the temple, reliefs tell of her birth as the daughter of the god Amon and of her right to rule Egypt. They also portray her being crowned during the reign of her father, Thutmose I, but this event was a fiction.

The reign of Hatshepsut was a peaceful period of efficient government, expanding foreign trade, and artistic

Figure 4-7
A sphinx bearing the face and features of Hatshepsut

rebirth. Carved on the walls of Hatshepsut's funeral temple is a record of a successful trading expedition sent south to Punt (in present-day Somalia), which opened up the possibility of trade in ivory, incense, ebony, and gold. New types of sculpture developed during her rule. A unique style of temple construction that employed terraces became popular; her cult temple at Deir El-Bahri was a fine example of this new architectural design.

Hatshepsut came to a mysterious end. During a revolt in the period of Thutmose III, she disappeared. Her statues, temples, and shrines were later mutilated, and her body was never found.

PERSPECTIVES ON THE PAST

Personalities and Power

Ramses II
(1279 BCE–1213 BCE)

What were the main accomplishments of Ramses II? Imagine that you could interview this famous pharaoh. What questions would you ask him? Do you think he deserves to be called "Ramses the Great"?

Figure 4-8
The face of Ramses II

The face of Ramses II, the most important ruler of the Nineteenth Dynasty, shows the large hooked nose that was typical of the Rameside kings. Ramses II ruled Egypt for 67 years and lived into his eighties. He was married to more than 90 wives and fathered over 100 children! Archaeologists excavating his tomb describe him as one of the most colourful figures of the ancient world.

Ramses II came to power at a time when the great empire was crumbling. His reign represents the final period of grandeur in ancient Egyptian civilization. Egypt's main enemy was the Hittite empire based in Anatolia. Ramses challenged the Hittites early in his reign by leading his army north to Kadesh, but they drove him back. While he fought valiantly to maintain the empire and considered himself a great warrior, evidence proves that he exaggerated his claims to bravery and valour. Even when he was driven back by the Hittites, Ramses II had inscriptions carved in temples all over Egypt stating that he had been victorious. In his vanity, he even had his name inscribed on monuments built by earlier pharaohs. Because of this desire to prove his magnificence to all future generations, many

scholars refer to him as "Ramses the Great."

When he attempted a second invasion of the Hittite empire, the attack ended in a stalemate. The two opponents made the first treaty of non-aggression in history: they simply agreed to not attack each other again and to help one another if attacked by another enemy.

Ramses launched an unprecedented building program of monuments and public buildings during his reign. In fact, he constructed more monuments than any other pharaoh, perhaps to ensure his own immortality. The buildings from his reign have left us with a magnificent legacy. Ramses made Thebes the first monumental capital city of history, adding to existing temples in the city and at Karnak, and building dozens of others. The two huge temples at Abu Simbel, cut in rock for the pharaoh and his wife, Nefertari, are stunning examples.

Figure 4-9
Colossal seated sandstone statues of Ramses II on the façade of the main temple at Abu Simbel

moved "Aton" from his name and became Tutankhamen. He restored the former state religion, allowing the worship of old deities as well as Aton. Horemheb (1323 BCE–1295 BCE), the last pharaoh of the Eighteenth Dynasty, completely rejected Akhenaton's religious beliefs.

The ultimate decline of the New Kingdom began in the Late Dynastic Period be-

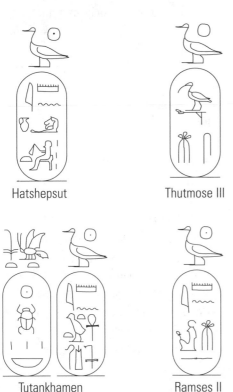

Figure 4-10
*Hieroglyphic representations of New
Kingdom rulers—Hatshepsut, Thutmose III,
Tutankhamen, Ramses II*

Hatshepsut

Thutmose III

Tutankhamen

Ramses II

tween 1070 BCE and 332 BCE, when bitter struggles for royal power increased among priests and nobles. Gradually, the empire broke up into a number of small states. The process accelerated rapidly after about 1070 BCE, following the end of the Twentieth Dynasty. When Egypt eventually lost its territory abroad, its weakness attracted invaders.

Over the next 700 years, more than ten different dynasties ruled Egypt, most formed by Nubian, Assyrian, or Persian rulers. In 728 BCE, a Nubian army officer, General Piankhi (Piy) invaded from the south and conquered the country. Although he returned to Nubia after his conquest and ruled Egypt from there, Piy had huge tem-

ples built and restored many ancient Egyptian traditions that had almost died out. After about 50 years, however, the Nubians were driven out by Assyrian invaders under the command of Ashurbanipal in 667 BCE. He established the Twenty-Sixth Dynasty and appointed Nekau, a prince of the western delta, to govern the delta region of Sais.

Order was only restored in Egypt under Nekau's son and successor Psamtek, who extended his rule over all of Egypt and became the first in a line of Saite kings that dominated Egypt for a century. Longing for former glories, the Saite kings revived ancient styles, turning to the Old Kingdom for inspiration. But their attempt to restore the past eventually failed, and the Assyrian empire fell to the Persians.

THE GREEK PERIOD

The Egyptians greatly resented Persian domination. Revolts and opposition to their presence marked much of the Persians' occupation over the next two centuries. In 332 BCE, however, the Macedonian armies of Alexander the Great conquered Persia and marched into Egypt, launching a period in Egyptian history when the people were ruled by Macedonians and administered in Greek. In fact, Greek became the language of government in Egypt for almost a thousand years.

Alexander ruled Egypt for only a few years before his death in 323 BCE. The Macedonian governor of Egypt at the time was Ptolemy, and in 305 BCE he declared himself Ptolemy I (305 BCE–282 BCE), king of Egypt. Over the next three centuries, a line of Ptolemies turned Alexandria into the most brilliant metropolis of the Greek-speaking world. Alexandria was a city founded by Alexander the Great

on the north end of the Nile delta.

The generations of Macedonian kings and their sister-wives, called Cleopatras, were kind but patronizing to the native Egyptians, and only one monarch, Cleopatra VII, took the time to learn the Egyptian language. Instead, the dynasty's rulers spread Greek culture from their capital at Alexandria. They built temples to Greek gods, developed Egypt's natural resources, and increased foreign trade. But the second and third centuries of Ptolemaic rule were marred by family strife and internal power struggles. The reign of this magnificent family line came to an end with the children of Ptolemy XII: two sons, both named Ptolemy, and a daughter, Cleopatra VII.

THE ROMAN PERIOD

When Cleopatra VII (51 BCE–30 BCE) and her brothers wrangled over the control of Egypt, their dispute drew Rome's attention. After ruling first with one brother and then with the other, Cleopatra finally established her own power by forming an alliance with two Roman leaders, first with Julius Caesar from 48 BCE–44 BCE and then with Mark Antony from 41 BCE–30 BCE.

Cleopatra's great ambitions came to an end in the civil wars fought among the Roman conquerors. In 31 BCE, Caesar's nephew Octavian defeated Mark Antony at the battle of Actium. When Octavian marched victorious into Egypt the following year and Mark Antony and Cleopatra committed suicide, the reign of the Ptolemies was over. Egypt then became a province of Rome.

After Egypt was absorbed into the Roman Empire, Greek continued as the language of government. Few emperors of Rome during the first three centuries

Figure 4-11 *A possible bust of Cleopatra*

visited Egypt or showed much interest in the area. A prefect was usually sent to rule on behalf of the Roman emperor, and native Egyptians were excluded from government positions. Roman law was also introduced into the country.

Roman culture brought many material changes to Egypt. The use of iron weapons and tools spread. Clear glass vessels, the terra-cotta lamp, the lathe, the split-nib reed pen, and the key were all introduced into Egypt. The introduction of the ox-drawn waterwheel and a wheel-drawn threshing machine changed agriculture as well.

Rome's control of Egypt gradually weakened after 395 CE when the Roman empire split into eastern and western parts. By 642 CE, the Muslims from Arabia had conquered Egypt.

pharaoh as Osiris, an indication that they thought of their ruler as being one with the great god of the dead.

The actual word **pharaoh** comes from the Egyptian word meaning "great house." Sometime between 1554 BCE and 1304 BCE, the ancient Egyptians chose to address their king as pharaoh to show their great respect. Rather than use the ruler's own name, subjects spoke instead of the palace or "great house."

The position of pharaoh passed to the eldest son of the king's chief wife. This distinction was important because many Egyptian kings had several other wives, called lesser wives. Some chief wives gave birth to daughters but not to sons, and several of those daughters claimed their right to the throne. At least four women ruled ancient Egypt.

THE BUREAUCRACY

All government administrators, ranging from personal staff to imperial officials, were subject to the approval of the pharaoh. The pharaoh's personal staff included a steward, who looked after the vast royal estates, a chamberlain, who was in charge of the daily affairs in the palace, and a first herald, who supervised the palace guard.

The highest-ranking official was the vizier, who served as the pharaoh's deputy in all the affairs of state. During the Old Kingdom, this office was usually held by a prince of royal blood, as were all important positions. The vizier had enormous responsibilities. He was in charge of almost all administrative affairs from collecting taxes to overseeing judges, scribes, and treasury officials. Eventually, the office got so complicated that, during the Eighteenth Dynasty, two

---

REFLECT AND ANALYZE

1. In a chart or on a timeline of your own design, identify the main accomplishments of the ancient Egyptians during
   a) the Old Kingdom
   b) the Middle Kingdom
   c) the New Kingdom.

2. What was the Amarna Revolution? Why do you think it angered many Egyptians?

3. Egypt became a powerful empire because of the strong leadership of the pharaohs. Do you agree or disagree with this statement? Explain your answer.

4. In which of ancient Egypt's major historical periods would you have preferred to live? Write a personal journal entry explaining your choice.

GOVERNMENT

THE PHARAOH

The ancient Egyptians looked upon their king or pharaoh as a god, a descendant of the great sun god Re. They also believed that Horus, the powerful sky god represented by a hawk, entered the pharaoh when he or she sat on the throne. After death, the people often referred to the

viziers were appointed, one for Lower Egypt and one for Upper Egypt. By this time, commoners could also apply for these positions.

Working under each vizier, an overseer of the treasury kept track of taxes and tribute. Since the government collected taxes from farmers in the form of crops, and taxes from skilled workers in the form of goods they produced, the pharaoh's treasuries and temples actually served as warehouses. Therefore, an overseer of the granaries and of cattle worked very closely with the overseer of the treasury.

Other high government officials included an army commander and the governors appointed to rule conquered territories within the empire. The governors also regulated the garrisons of Egyptian soldiers left behind to keep the conquered people in check.

Ancient Egypt was divided into 42 provinces called **nomes**. Each of these local areas was governed by an official

Figure 4-12 *Tomb wallpainting in Thebes depicting the punishment of a servant*

called a **nomarch**, appointed by the pharaoh. He was responsible for collecting the local taxes, maintaining law and order, raising troops, and organizing workers.

LAW AND JUSTICE

The ancient Egyptians did not look upon the law as a specialized area separate from their government. They had laws, they had punishments with varying degrees of severity, and they had tribunals or courts. Unlike the Mesopotamians, however, they did not develop extensive codes of law and did not view their laws as gifts from the gods.

The composition of a tribunal or court varied from case to case. In a village or town, the courts dealt with a wide variety of general matters, and local landowners were expected to sit in judgement

THROUGH THEIR EYES
Egyptian Justice

The following instructions from a pharaoh to his vizier outline some of the goals for justice in ancient Egypt. In your own words, describe the pharaoh's general advice. Which of the goals would be acceptable for judges in the Canadian judicial system today? Which would be unacceptable?

Do not judge inconsistently; the abomination of the divine king is partiality. Look upon him who is known to you in the same way as him who is unknown to you; him who is close to you in the same way as him who is far from you.

Do not send a petitioner away before listening to him. Dismiss him only after telling him why you are dismissing his case, because it is said that a petitioner would rather that you pay attention to what he says than win his case.

Do not be angry with any man without good cause; be angry only when there is good reason to be angry. Inspire fear of yourself so that men are afraid of you because a true magistrate is one of whom people are afraid. But the reputation of a magistrate comes from his giving justice. If people are too frightened of a magistrate, then there might be something unjust about him.

when called upon. Each nome or province had its own court as well, where high officials heard the more important cases. Priests, soldiers, or government officials presided over local courts. For very serious cases, such as treason, a special commission might be appointed to prosecute the case.

The administration of justice within the kingdom was mainly the responsibility of the vizier. He judged most capital or high court cases. Although the pharaoh was the supreme judge in ancient Egypt, he or she only intervened personally in cases involving crimes punishable by death.

Penalties for crimes often included harsh physical punishment that ranged from a beating (for failure to do one's duty) to death (for treason). If a person did not show up for communal work when summoned, he or she might be sentenced to a permanent work assignment in a state institution. If someone charged with a crime ran away and could not be caught, his or her family would be taken instead.

REFLECT AND ANALYZE

1. a) Provide evidence that the Egyptian pharoahs ruled with absolute power.
    b) Discuss the advantages and disadvantages of this system of government.

2. Write a job description for a vizier in ancient Egypt. Then imagine you have been offered the job. What are the advantages and disadvantages of this opportunity?

3. Bureaucracy became more complicated in the Middle Kingdom and the New Kingdom. Suggest reasons why this was so.

4. Compare similarities and differences in the forms of law and justice in Egypt and Mesopotamia.

EGYPT:
Society and Culture

I n the beginning, there was a formlessness, a primeval abyss—or chaos. Out of the waters of that chaos emerged a hillock of wet ground, and on this mound appeared Atum, the Creator. Atum produced the first divine couple, a pair of twins: Shu, the god of air, and his sister, Tefnut, the goddess of moisture.

Shu and Tefnut married and also gave birth to twins, Geb and his sister, Nut. Geb was the god of earth and Nut represented the heavens. Geb and Nut married, but Atum opposed the match. Atum ordered their father, Shu, to raise Nut into the sky away from Geb, dividing the heavens from the earth. The speckles on Nut's body became the stars.

In spite of their separation, Geb and Nut had several children, including Osiris, god of vegetation along the Nile, Isis, goddess of female fertility, Seth, god of the desert, and Nephthys, goddess of the dead. This group of deities made up the Ennead of ancient Egypt, or the original family of nine gods.

When Geb went to heaven, Osiris became pharaoh and took Isis as his queen. Jealous of his brother's position, Seth killed Osiris, cut his body into pieces, stuffed the pieces into a box, and set it afloat on the Nile. He then made himself pharaoh of Egypt.

Isis refused to accept her husband's death as final, and searched for his remains with the help of her sister, Nephthys. When Isis finally found the box, she put the body together and restored Osiris to life. Thereafter, he became the god of the afterlife.

At the same time, Horus, son of Osiris and Isis, overthrew Seth and became pharaoh himself.

Figure 5-1
Gods—Isis, Osiris, and Horus

There are different creation stories associated with ancient Egypt. Because these myths seem to conflict with one another, students of Egyptian religion often find sorting things out rather difficult. For example, the creation story above combines two of the traditional myths, the Ennead myth and the Osiris myth. Despite the sometimes mind-boggling complications, the myths can provide us with some interesting insights into Egyptian society and culture.

What basic questions does the creation myth above try to answer? What does it suggest about the relationships among the forces of nature, the gods, the pharaohs, and human beings? What does it tell us about the Egyptian view of life after death?

RELIGION

GODS AND GODDESSES

Religion was an integral part of Egyptian life. The ancient Egyptians believed that immortal beings influenced all aspects of nature and every human activity. Therefore, they worshipped many different deities. With a pantheon of more than 80 gods and goddesses, the Egyptians had one of the most **polytheistic** religions of any civilization. Yet they tolerated and even welcomed other beliefs. If visitors to the country could not find an Egyptian god or goddess to their liking, then the Egyptians allowed them to worship their own gods. In fact, they sometimes added these foreign deities to their own pantheon.

Many Egyptian gods were associated with the life-giving forces of nature. The main god was the sun god Re, whom the Egyptians relied upon for a good harvest. The most important goddess was Isis, who represented female fertility and was worshipped as a devoted mother and wife. Other important deities had associations with death and the afterlife. Osiris, for example, ruled over vegetation and the dead, and represented the constant renewal of life along the Nile. The god Anubis escorted the dead to the entrance of the afterworld, helped restore Osiris to life, and invented the elaborate Egyptian funeral rituals and burial practices. Figure 5.2 describes some of the other important gods and goddesses in the Egyptian pantheon.

Many deities were also associated with animals or pictured with human bodies and animal heads. A god or goddess took the form of the animal whose characteristics he or she embodied. For example, the Egyptians believed that a dog or cat repre-

Figure 5-2
Principle gods of the pantheon of ancient Egypt

Amon-Re
The sun god and chief god of the Egyptian pantheon. He is depicted with a double-plumed crown.

Shu
God of the air, who separated the earth and the sky. He sometimes had a solar disk on his head.

Tefnut
Goddess of moisture. She supported the sky with Shu and received the newly dawned sun each morning.

Geb
The earth god. Kings claimed to be descendants of Geb. The goose on his head symbolizes that Geb laid the cosmic egg containing the sun.

Nut
Goddess of the sky. The vase on her head represents the hieroglyphs of her name. Sometimes she was depicted as stretched across the horizon with stars forming her clothing.

Seth
God of the desert. He is portrayed as an imaginary animal resembling a donkey.

Nephthys
Goddess of the dead. She was thought to be skilled in magic.

Osiris
God of the earth, vegetation, and the dead. He was also associated with resurrection and was always portrayed as a mummy.

Isis
The mother goddess, goddess of female fertility, and protector of children.

Anubis
Guide of the afterlife, depicted with the head of a jackal. He presided over the embalming rituals and heard prayers on behalf of the dead.

Horus
God of the sky and lord of heaven, portrayed with the head of a falcon.

sented loyalty, a crocodile or serpent inspired fear, and a hawk or falcon represented swiftness. Horus, god of the sky and lord of heaven, was often pictured with the head of a falcon. Anubis had the head of a jackal, an animal that prowled at night and destroyed desert grave sites. Historians believe the Egyptians used the jackal in religious writings and symbols to stave off its anger.

Each Egyptian city and town worshipped its own god in addition to the major deities. One of the most important was Amon, a sun god worshipped by the people of Thebes. Amon was originally a tribal god, but his cult spread from Thebes until he was worshipped all over Egypt. He took over much of the prestige and mythology of the original Egyptian creation god, Atum, and was also identified with the sun god Re. In time, Amon-Re became the chief deity of Egypt. Other local deities included Ptah, the creator god of Memphis and inventor of the arts, Thoth, the god of wisdom and writing in Hermopolis, and Khnum, the creator god of Elephantine.

Egyptian households worshipped specific household gods as well as the state gods. A household god could be any god with whom the people felt a connection.

RELIGIOUS BELIEFS AND PRACTICES

The ancient Egyptians believed that the creator god, Khnum, fashioned infants on his potter's wheel and placed them in their mother's womb. But for each human moulded, Khnum also created a spiritual double called the *ka*. The ka remained in the heart until death, when spirit and body separated.

Another element also entered the body at birth and left it at death. This element, called *ba*, was like the personality or character of the individual. In Egyptian art, the ba often appears as a human-headed bird, sometimes along with a small lighted lamp. The ancient Egyptians believed that both the ka and the ba returned to the body of a person who died if the body was properly preserved and sustained in the tomb with food, drink, and earthly belongings. This remarkable belief in a spiritual life inspired the elaborate burial practices of the Egyptians.

Ancestor worship was another important part of Egyptian religion, and people took great care in maintaining the tombs of departed relatives. Many people also kept busts of their ancestors in the main room of the house, alongside the statues of household gods.

Priests of the major temples conducted daily religious services or rituals to honour the various state gods, but these ceremonies were closed to the general public. Instead, ordinary citizens worshipped at smaller local shrines, where they offered up prayers to their favourite gods, often acting as their own priests.

Religious festivals were important public events and tended to attract thousands of citizens. During a festival, a statue representing the god or goddess being honoured was carried in procession through the streets. The Festival of Osiris at Abydos, for example, re-enacted the betrayal and murder of Osiris by his brother Seth. It included several days of mourning, a funeral procession to the traditional site of Osiris' tomb, and a final return to the temple. The festivals were a welcome opportunity for people to celebrate and to honour their gods.

At different times in the history of ancient Egypt, citizens worshipped particular gods or rulers with added fervour. These *religious cults* arose for varied reasons, but the people never forgot the other gods in the pantheon or stopped worshipping them altogether. They simply devoted more of their attention to the cult favourite.

One famous religious cult was that of Amenophis I, the first ruler to be buried in the Valley of the Kings and the founder of a group of artisans located at Deir el-Medina. As worship of him spread beyond his burial temple, shrines sprang up in his honour at several locations on the west bank of the Nile. Amenophis I became the patron deity of crafters, an intermediary between humans and the other gods of the Egyptian pantheon.

During the period of the New Kingdom, oracles became an important part of religious belief and practice in Egypt. An oracle offered citizens a chance to communicate with their gods. The oracle was expected to answer a pressing question at hand or provide guidance for the future. While statues of the gods were carried through the streets, citizens would approach with a question. Whether the question was spoken or written on papyrus or ostracon (broken pottery), it had to be one that could be answered by a simple yes or no. The citizen would know the response when the statue of the god moved either forwards (for yes) or backwards (for no).

Superstition also had a part in Egyptian life. For example, the ancient Egyptians believed in the power of good luck charms. People wore amulets, like the *ankh*—the sign of life—to combat known and unknown forces of evil. They considered certain days of the week to be either good or bad, depending on the influence of the planets, and identified these days on their calendars. Dreams could foretell events to come, the Egyptians believed, and special books were written to explain their meaning and significance.

DEATH AND THE AFTERLIFE

Most of us know something about the fascinating burial practices of ancient Egypt. When we think of Egypt, we often think of mummies, great stone tombs, and elaborate burials. Can we conclude that the Egyptians were obsessed with death? In fact, almost the opposite is true. Egyptian burial practices were a way to ensure that the person who had died could continue to enjoy living in the world beyond.

For a person to pass on to the afterlife, the body had to be preserved in a recognizable form. During the Predynastic Period, corpses were covered with a skin or matting, and buried in shallow graves in the desert. Here, the hot, dry sand acted as a powerful dessicating agent. That is, it preserved the body by removing the moisture and preventing decay.

When burials became more elaborate and the Egyptians began to place corpses in burial chambers, they had to find a new way to preserve the bodies. Although evidence is scanty, historians believe that Egyptians first thought they could stop decomposition simply by keeping the corpse covered. Bodies discovered from the Old Kingdom, for example, had arms and legs tightly wrapped in linen bandages. Later evidence indicates that the Egyptians learned to remove the internal organs to prevent decay.

Yet there seems to have been no planned or consistent method of preserving a body during the Old Kingdom or the Middle Kingdom. Only in the New Kingdom did the Egyptians fully understand the basic requirements for preserving a corpse. This is when the embalming process called **mummification** began.

Among the more interesting objects found in tombs from the New Kingdom and later were *shabti* or **shawabto funerary figurines**. These small carved figures were placed in the tomb as deputies, so that they could carry out all of the deceased's agricultural duties in the afterlife. In later years, the Egyptians buried so many of these shabtis in each tomb that they enclosed them in special shawabti boxes. A box could contain as many as 401 figurines, one for each day of the calendar in an Egyptian year (365), as well as 36 overseers dressed in kilts and carrying whips.

By the time of the New Kingdom, the journey to the afterlife was associated with the story of Osiris, who had been restored to life from death and who stood as judge over the dead. If Osiris judged the deceased worthy, the person enjoyed rebirth in the

Figure 5-3 *Egyptian funerary figures: a thief is brought before judges*

Figure 5-4 *The Book of the Dead*

INNOVATIONS

The Egyptian Art of Mummification

For the wealthy, the Egyptians perfected the practice of mummification to give the soul the use of its body in the afterlife. The process was a fascinating mix of science and religion. What scientific knowledge did the Egyptians need to develop the process?

The mummification process was a long one. It took a total of 70 days from the time of death until the burial. When death occurred, the body was handed over to an embalmer.

Removing the Internal Organs

The embalmer removed the brain through the nostrils with a hook-like instrument and made an incision on the lower left side of the abdomen to extract the internal organs. The heart, considered by ancient Egyptians to be the seat of understanding, remained in the body.

The Drying Process

The corpse was then packed in mounds of dry natron, a natural salt with a high proportion of sodium bicarbonate. After about 40 days, the natron had absorbed the body fluids, preventing the body from decaying further. Rather than discarding the internal organs, the embalmer treated them with natron separately and kept them in a special cache.

Packing and Sealing the Body

After the drying period, the embalmer packed the cavity of the body with linen, sawdust, or even dry lichen, and plugged the eye sockets with linen pads or, in later periods, with artificial eyes. The embalming incision was closed and covered by a stone tablet or a plate of leather, metal, or wax that usually bore a representation of the Wedjat eye of Horus, a powerful protective amulet (charm). The embalmer then massaged the body with lotions and coated it with resin.

Wrapping the Mummy

Approximately 15 of the 70 days were spent bandaging the mummy. The process was time-consuming because the wrappings had to be tight to maintain the shape of the body. First the head, toes, fingers, and limbs were wrapped individually. Then, they were wrapped with the entire torso. While the torso was being wrapped, rolls and pads were inserted to round out the finished outline of the body. Before the final layers of bandages, a funeral mask was fitted over the head and shoulders so that the soul could identify the body when it returned to the burial chamber. The funeral mask was usually made of linen or papyrus stiffened with plaster, or with precious metals if the deceased was a member of royalty. Amulets were placed on the mummy and within the bandages to offer the person protection from evil spirits on the journey into the afterlife.

The embalmed internal organs were placed in four containers called canopic jars and came under the protection of four minor gods called the sons of Horus. The human-headed god, Imsety, guarded the liver; the baboon-headed god, Hapy, guarded the lungs; the jackal-headed god, Duamutef, guarded the stomach; and the falcon-headed god, Qebhsenuef, guarded the intestines. The jars themselves were protected by the four goddesses Isis, Nephthys, Neith, and Selket.

The Burial

For the tomb burial, the mummy was placed inside a coffin or series of coffins enclosed within a box called a *sarcophagus*. The sarcophagus, the canopic jars, and various belongings and objects associated with daily life were buried as well. The tombs of royalty usually included furniture and precious materials.

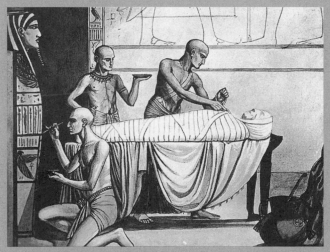

Figure 5-5 *The embalming process*

land of eternal contentment. But the soul might encounter many obstacles, such as evil spirits, on the way. Therefore, tombs included anything that might help the soul complete the journey. For example, spells written on a papyrus roll were often wrapped inside the bandages of the mummy or enclosed within tall wooden statues inside the tomb. The Egyptians called these rolls of spells *The Book of Coming Out Into the Day*, but they are better known as *The Book of the Dead*. They varied considerably in length, and the longer ones included beautiful painted pictures. While there were as many as two hundred spells in all, no single collection contained them all.

REFLECT AND ANALYZE

1. How did the gods and goddesses in ancient Egypt represent both natural and human characteristics? Give examples in your answer.

2. Explain the Egyptian idea of the spirit (the *ka* and *ba*).

3. Compare the Egyptian and Mesopotamian views of death and the afterlife. What preparations were made for the dead in each society?

4. Create labelled diagrams illustrating key stages in the mummification process and explain their significance.

MAGNIFICENT STONE TOMBS— THE PYRAMIDS

During the Old Kingdom, the Egyptians built the pyramids to house the bodies of their dead kings. The pyramids are the oldest and largest stone structures in the world. Today, the ruins of 35 major pyramids stand near the Nile River. The three largest pyramids at Giza rank as one of the seven wonders of the ancient world.

The first pyramids, constructed of limestone, were step pyramids. The most famous, the Saqqara Step Pyramid (see Figure 4.5 on p. 64), was built on a rocky plateau 3 km west of Memphis. It was buried by sand in antiquity, and remained hidden until its discovery in the 1920s. Later, in 1934, when archaeologists entered the burial chamber of the king, they found nothing but the foot of a mummy! The chamber had been rifled by tomb robbers thousands of years earlier.

Smooth-sided pyramids appeared in Egypt after 2600 BCE. One of the oldest, located at Medum, began as a step pyramid, but the steps were filled in with casing stones to provide smooth, sloping sides. Other pyramids were built during the Old and Middle Kingdoms at Abusir, Dahshur— near present-day Cairo—and at Hawara, Illahun, and Lisht. The remains of these pyramids are still impressive.

Sometimes smaller pyramids, constructed for the body of the queen, stood next to the king's pyramid. Egypt has at least 40 of these smaller pyramids. The king's relatives and officials were buried in smaller rectangular tombs called *mastabas*, which had sloping sides and flat roofs.

The Great Pyramid of Khufu (Cheops), pharaoh of the Fourth Dynasty, is one of the most impressive structures of all. It was built about 2600 BCE from more than two million stone blocks averaging 2.3 tonnes in weight, with the largest blocks weighing as much as 15 tonnes. Standing about 147 m high, the pyramid covers an area of approximately five hectares. Each side of the pyramid is equal to the length of about two football fields.

From the entrance, located on the north face, a corridor leads downwards at an angle of 25 degrees into the rock plateau beneath the pyramid. This low passage levels off and ends in a small, uncompleted chamber. The architect might originally have intended this room to be the king's burial chamber, since the burial chamber in other pyramids was often located underneath the structure rather than inside. The corridor continues beyond this chamber and then ends abruptly.

For some reason, Khufu must have changed his mind about the location of his burial chamber. A second passage cuts off from the descending corridor and branches upward, before levelling off into a chamber built right in the centre of the pyramid. Today, this room is called the Queen's Chamber although, in the second stage of design, it was likely intended as the king's burial chamber rather than the queen's.

Apparently, Khufu changed his mind about the location of his burial chamber for a third time, making interior modifications of the pyramid necessary once again. The final burial place is accessed through the Grand Gallery, the most magnificent corridor in any of the pyramids. The gallery walls are faced with polished limestone and are corbelled. That is, each section juts out about 7.5 cm beyond the course beneath to form a vaulted passage.

The king's burial chamber is lined entirely with pink granite blocks and the smooth walls have neither inscriptions nor paintings. The chamber still holds a sarcophagus that must have been put in place before the chamber was completed. On the north and south walls, two very small openings lead to shafts that open to the outside. Although we are still uncertain, these shafts might have been constructed to provide either ventilation for the chamber or a way out of the pyramid for Khufu's soul, since the Egyptians expected his soul to join the stars.

Five small rooms or compartments lie above the ceiling of the King's Chamber. The bottom four have flat roofs while the top one is pointed. These might have been constructed to absorb some of the enormous weight on the ceiling of the burial chamber.

To prevent grave robbers or vandals from entering the tomb, the builders took special precautions to seal it off. They inserted three huge granite stones in the heart of the pyramid to plug the bottom of the ascending corridor after the funeral of the pharaoh. How did they accomplish this unusual feat without trapping any workers inside? The builders likely stored these sealing blocks in the Grand Gallery during construction.

Once the pharaoh's coffin was placed inside his sarcophagus, a crew of workers probably levered the three stones into the lower end of the passageway. Then, in the dark, they may have lowered themselves through a narrow vertical shaft to the abandoned burial chamber below, walked

Figure 5-6 *The Great Pyramid at Giza*

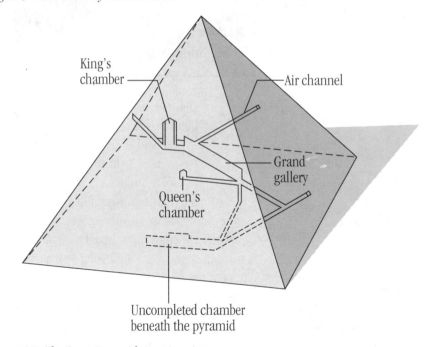

King's chamber — Air channel — Grand gallery — Queen's chamber — Uncompleted chamber beneath the pyramid

Figure 5-7 *The Great Pyramid: interior view*

up the descending corridor to the entrance of the pyramid, and stepped outside. The descending corridor was then blocked and the completed facing stone set in place to seal the pyramid.

THE VALLEY OF THE KINGS

During the New Kingdom, royal burials were in the Valley of the Kings, the royal necropolis (cemetery) of ancient Thebes. By the early twentieth century, archaeolo-

THEN AND NOW

The Discovery of the Tomb of Tutankhamen

One archaeologist believed that the Valley of the Kings still contained hidden secrets, despite the ravages of the grave robbers. Howard Carter was convinced that the tomb of the pharaoh Tutankhamen remained hidden in the valley.

Why was the day of Carter's discovery marked by both caution and suspense? Why is the discovery of Tutankhamen's tomb still considered one of the greatest archaeological discoveries of all time?

Tutankhamen had became pharaoh at age nine in about 1334 BCE, and ruled until his untimely death at age 18. The boy-king's funeral was held in the Valley of the Kings.

Later pharaohs destroyed or removed all monuments built by, or in honour of, Tutankhamen and other rulers who had at any time accepted Aton as Egypt's chief god. In the years that followed, archaeologists learned little about Tutankhamen.

In Carter's view, signs pointed to a yet undiscovered tomb. A cup bearing the name of the pharaoh had been found under a rock. A small mud-filled pit tomb containing pieces of gold foil with pictures and inscriptions of the pharaoh had been located. Finally, a selection of pottery jars used for funerary rites, bearing the seal of Tutankhamen, had also been discovered.

Carter began his personal search in 1914 after he found a financial backer, the British Earl of Carnarvon. Unfortunately, World War I interrupted the enterprise and work did not really begin until 1918. Carter needed Carnarvon's financial backing because the Egyptian government allowed only one archaeological team to work in the valley each year (to prevent rival archaeologists from tearing the necropolis apart), and charged a

Figure 5-8
Tutankhamen's coffin

very expensive fee. By 1923, this annual fee cost Carnarvon over half a million dollars in today's currency. He even considered abandoning the project.

In November 1923, Carter decided to make one last attempt to find the tomb. This time, he employed a crew to dig in the only remaining unexplored spot in the valley—beneath a group of huts used by the labourers who had built the nearby tomb of Ramses VI. Carter had considered this unexplored area an unlikely location because he had believed that officials of the necropolis would never have allowed structures to be built over the tomb of another pharaoh.

When the first hut was removed, the crew discovered a staircase. Sixteen steps led down to a doorway that contained the seals of a royal necropolis, the jackal god Anubis. Carter was jubilant. He sealed in the staircase and posted guards. Then he sent a cable to Carnarvon, informing the earl of the discovery and telling him that he would await his arrival before exploring further.

When Carnarvon arrived, the stairway was cleared again. The crew removed the door, revealing a rubble-filled passageway, 7.5 m long, ending in another sealed door. The corridor was cleared. What lay beyond?

Diary of Howard Carter

November 26, 1923

This was the day of days, the most wonderful that I have ever lived through. Lord Carnarvon, his daughter, and my assistant stood beside me as I drilled a small hole in the upper left-hand corner of the door.

Darkness and blank space, as far as an iron testing-rod could reach, showed that whatever lay beyond was empty. Widening the hole a little, I inserted the candle and peered in. At first I could see nothing, the hot air escaping from the chamber causing the candle flame to flicker, but presently, as my eyes grew accustomed to the light, details of the room within emerged slowly from the mist, strange animals, statues of gold—everywhere the glint of gold.

For the moment—an eternity it must have seemed for the others standing by—I was struck dumb with amazement and when Lord Carnarvon, unable to stand the suspense any longer, inquired anxiously, "Can you see anything?" it was all I could do to get out the words, "Yes, wonderful things...."

Tutankhamen's tomb was one of the few ancient Egyptian tombs to be discovered almost completely undamaged. The four rooms contained more than 5000 objects, including many beautiful carved and gold-covered items, notably the magnificent gold mask of Tut that covered the head and shoulders of the royal mummy. Other items included luxurious chests, thrones, chariots, swords, trumpets, statues, toys, and jars containing precious oils. Most items are now displayed in the Egyptian Museum in Cairo.

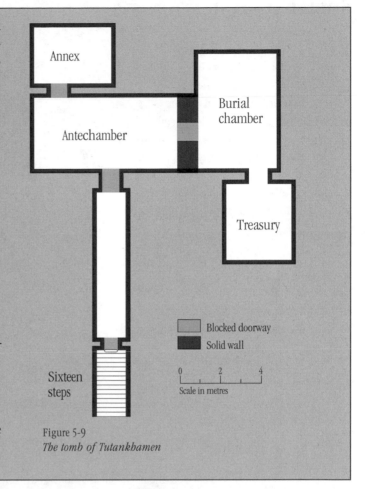

Figure 5-9
The tomb of Tutankhamen

gists had discovered over 30 tombs carved as corridors or chambers in the bedrock or rock walls of the valley. Unfortunately, professional grave robbers had stripped the tombs almost bare over the centuries, and the few objects left behind told archaeologists very little about ancient Egyptian civilization.

The tomb of Seti I, discovered in the Valley of the Kings in 1817, is the largest and most ornate. The carved and painted religious scenes and hieroglyphic texts that cover the walls deal mainly with the pharaoh's activities in the afterlife.

REFLECT AND ANALYZE

1. How did the Egyptians attempt to protect the tombs from grave robbers?

2. Compare the Egyptian pyramids with the ziggurats of Sumer or with the monuments of another civilization. Consider using diagrams, models, and charts in your answer.

3. Today, there is a great deal of controversy surrounding the opening of tombs to the public and the removal of objects for public display. Even the paintings on tomb walls have been damaged by the moisture from the bodies of thousands of visitors. Should the tombs be open to the public? Why or why not? Are we any different from the grave robbers of the past? Provide your answer in a short report.

SOCIAL ORGANIZATION

The pharaoh, as a living god, stood at the pinnacle of the social pyramid in ancient Egypt. The people viewed the pharaoh as the owner of all lands and citizens, the bestower of all public offices, the leader of all armies, and the high priest of all gods.

The nobles and military leaders held the highest positions in the bureaucracy or administrative departments of ancient Egypt. Important families controlled the most influential offices and passed these positions along to family members from generation to generation. A bureaucrat might oversee the property and storehouses of a god, serve as a steward to the pharaoh, or supervise engineering and construction works for the government.

The priests and scribes were the educated class of ancient Egypt. Although the pharaoh was high priest of every god, he or she could not be in all areas of the empire at once. Religious functions were therefore delegated to the priests.

Scribes were highly respected members of Egyptian society because of their ability to read and write the Egyptian script called hieroglyphics. Called the "white kilt class" because of their dress, they ranked among the more important officials of the kingdom. They collected taxes, kept records, wrote reports, educated the young, and organized rations for the army. Their role as teachers was one of their most important because education was highly valued. As most military leaders, government administrators, and high-ranking priests came from the ranks of the scribes, anyone hoping to move up the social ladder needed an education.

A wide variety of skilled craftspeople

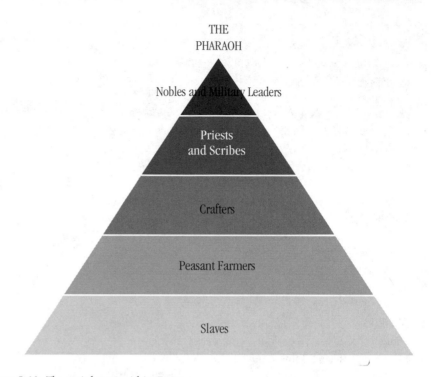

Figure 5-10 *The social pyramid in Egypt*

earned a living in ancient Egypt, including weavers, sandal-makers, mat-makers, incense moulders, potters, brick-makers, jewellers, carpenters, stonemasons, silversmiths, and goldsmiths. Some lived and worked in the cities while others were employed by the palace of a pharaoh or a wealthy noble. These craftspeople produced many of the goods that Egyptian traders carried into foreign territory.

The *fellahin* or peasant farmers were the common folk. They made up the majority of the population. We know very little about them, except that most were illiterate, and all were attached to the estate of the pharaoh, a temple, or a rich landowner. The pay they received was just enough to live by. If they were fortunate enough to be granted a plot of land to farm, they lost a large portion of any profit through rent and taxes.

Figure 5-11 *An Egyptian priest and a sacred scribe*

The fellahin might even have envied the slaves, who were on the bottom rung of the social ladder, because the fellahin were constantly plagued by duties and obligations owed to the state and their employers. Although free, the fellahin were targeted for *corvee duty*, in which they had to provide the labour for specific tasks such as maintaining the vital irrigation systems and constructing tombs, temples, and public buildings. It was nearly impossible to escape the corvee. If caught, runaways were classed as fugitives and sentenced to permanent service, spending time between jobs in prison. As well, their children inherited their status as state servants.

Slaves in ancient Egypt were prisoners of war brought back by the armies during the Middle Kingdom and later. Female and child slaves did household work for the wealthy. Male slaves were put to work as soldiers, farmers, or maintenance labourers around the household. Slaves in ancient Egypt could own property or rent land, and could even be set free if their master chose to do so.

added prestige within both their family and the community. A male child was most desired because sons had the responsibility of carrying out the funeral ceremonies for parents and providing their spirits with food and drink in the afterlife. If a couple was childless, they appealed to Hathor and Taweret, the main fertility and childbearing deities.

THE ROLE OF WOMEN

Women in ancient Egypt did not share equal rights with men. They could not hold office in government unless they belonged to the royal family. They could not choose professions such as carpentry and sculpting, and they probably could not become scribes. Most of the evidence that we have about the role of women in ancient Egypt comes from tomb paintings, which never show women doing heavy physical labour, writing, or creating works of art. However, they played a vital role in domestic life, and some women in royal and noble families rose to positions of great power. Female pharaohs such as Hatshepsut are evidence of this fact.

During the New Kingdom, the status of women improved as they gained property rights. If a daughter received an inheritance from her father, she could keep it after she married and leave it to anyone she wished. A wife was expected to tend to her husband's comfort, prepare his food, keep his house and clothing in order, and be a good mother to his children. But if the couple divorced, the woman's property rights were protected. She was entitled to one-third of the couple's assets at the time of the marriage breakdown. Obtaining a divorce was quite easy. One party in the marriage simply had to repudiate the other.

REFLECT AND ANALYZE

1. Which social classes served in the bureaucracy of ancient Egypt? Could craftspeople or farmers become bureaucrats? Why or why not?

2. Why were the scribes held in such high regard within Egyptian society? What roles did they have?

3. What was corvee duty? In your opinion, was corvee duty forced labour or a civic duty? Explain.

EVERYDAY LIFE

THE FAMILY

Egyptian boys customarily shaved their heads except for one long lock of hair that they braided on the side. This lock of hair was associated with boyhood and was traditionally cut off when a youth came of age. Coming of age, or entering manhood, occurred at about the same time a young Egyptian got married, often when he was 20 years of age or in his late teens. His bride was usually younger.

Marriage partners were selected from within the same social class and often within the same family. It was not uncommon for uncles to marry nieces, or cousins to marry cousins. Marriage between brothers and sisters did occur in ancient Egypt, but was not as common as many people believe. Parents arranged some marriages, and certainly couples needed their parents' approval, but many Egyptian marriages were based entirely on love.

A private legal contract was drawn up to establish each partner's rights to possessions. Once the man and woman agreed to this marriage settlement, they were considered married. No religious or civil ceremony took place, as we might expect, but family parties and festivities celebrated the event.

Since the family was so important in ancient Egypt, a new baby gave a couple

If a husband was cruel, and his wife divorced him, she kept the children and he was required to help support them.

Although **polygamy** (the practice of having more than one spouse at a time) was legal in Egypt, it was not very common. When a man did have two or more wives, the first wife received formal recognition as the head of the household.

EDUCATION

Early childhood education was left to parents. They taught children respect for their elders, but left them free to enjoy typical childhood activities such as playing with toys, participating in games and gymnastics, or fighting mock battles with stick weapons. The children of the wealthy also learned archery and horseback riding.

For both boys and girls, formal education was largely vocational. Girls stayed in the home with their mothers, aunts, and sisters, and learned the skills they needed to run a household. Boys were taught the skills for a particular occupation, usually their father's. Therefore, most became farmers. Children born into a family of tradespeople served an apprenticeship period in the family trade or craft, during which they were taught by their father or another close relative. If parents lacked skills in a craft but wanted their sons to do better, they placed the boys with master craftspeople. Young people who aspired to a profession, such as medicine, were placed with a doctor after they finished their basic schooling.

A formal education was essential to success because the key to advancement was the ability to read and write. Therefore, children of priests and administrators began attending a scribal school at about the age of five. Historians are not certain whether these schools were run by the temples, the state, private tutors, or all three. They also do not know whether female students could attend or not.

A student arrived at school with pen, ink, and *ostraca*, smooth fragments of broken pottery or stone used as slates. (Papyrus—strips of papyrus reed pressed together into sheets—was far too expensive to be used in education.) Students sat and listened to their instructors and repeated what they were taught. They took down dictation and spent long periods of time copying texts.

During the Middle Kingdom, the schools used a basic text called the *Kemyt*, which means "completion" in ancient Egyptian. This popular text was used for over a thousand years, probably because the language was quite simple and the vertical columns made the writing easier for young people to copy. The *Kemyt* presented model letters, useful phrases and expressions, and interesting pieces of advice for future scribes. Scribal schools also used an advanced text called the *Miscellanies*. It was a collection of short compositions in the form of letters, written on rolls of papyrus. The letters described how the country was administered and what life was like for the members of the upper middle class of Egyptian society.

The scribal school also offered a basic course in simple mathematics, literature, ethics, and history. Foreign languages grew in importance during the New Kingdom. Graduates from a scribal school either took a position with a master or attended a specialized school, where they learned the particular information and skills that they would need to work in the royal palace, a government department, the army, or a temple.

REFLECT AND ANALYZE

1. What was the curriculum offered in a scribal school? Why did the Egyptians consider these subjects important?

2. In your experience, how is classroom instruction today different from classroom instruction in ancient Egypt?

3. Discuss the role of women in ancient Egyptian society.

URBAN AND RURAL LIVING

CLOTHING AND COSMETICS

Many of us today will find the ancient Egyptians' attitudes to personal appearance fascinating. As discoveries of combs, mirrors, and razors testify, personal grooming was important to all classes of Egyptians. People washed at least twice a day because of the hot, dry, and dusty conditions. Many wore dark wigs, sometimes for protection against the sun and sometimes for special occasions. These wigs often held small cones of perfumed wax. Cosmetics were also widely used. Women wore red lip powder, painted their fingernails, outlined their eyes, and coloured their eyebrows with grey, black, or green paint. Men often wore as much make-up as

Figure 5-12 *A carving showing a princess having her hair dressed*

women, and both sexes used perfume.

Clothing ranged from the simple to the elegant. Women of the lower classes wore simple woven tunics. Farmers working in the fields wore a loincloth of white cotton or linen. If the weather was extremely warm, they may have worn nothing at all.

Elegant dress was limited more to the upper class. Many wealthy Egyptians wore white linen garments, woven from flax, and leather sandals. Women wore long straight dresses with shoulder straps, made of very fine material, and often added colourful shawls and capes. Men wore skirts that were drawn tight in the back and pleated in the front. Some also wore shirts, coats, or capes, and many completed their attire with coloured, shoulder-length headdresses. Both sexes wore necklaces, rings, and bracelets.

HOMES

The homes of the ancient Egyptians also reflected differences in social class. For the wealthy, the countryside offered an ideal retreat. In the less densely populated rural areas, they built large estates or villas. Each estate consisted of a main house surrounded by magnificent flower and vegetable gardens, and fruit and shade trees. It also included a variety of outbuildings, such as servants' quarters, kitchens, stables, workrooms, and storerooms. The entire compound was surrounded by a mud-brick wall.

Since stone was reserved for the building of temples, the walls of the main house were constructed of mud bricks. The roof was made of wooden beams covered with papyrus and clay. At the heart of the house was a central room, or living room, that people reached through an entrance hall and an antechamber. Bedrooms, storerooms, and the women's quarters were organized around this main room. Most villas contained a bathroom and toilet. A staircase led to the roof where the family spent a great deal of time during hot weather.

The interior brick walls were plastered with mud and painted with colourful scenes. Furnishings included wooden stools, chairs, beds, and chests. Wet mats placed on the floors helped cool the inside air. Light shone from candles and from lamps with wicks afloat in jars or hollowed-out stones filled with oil.

Town villas were smaller than those in the country and were usually occupied by an extended family. Their surrounding walls, which contained a single gate, tended to be higher, demonstrating a desire for security and privacy. While many of the city gardens were small, most still had shade trees and a pool.

Living conditions were quite different for the farmers and common people. Farmers in the countryside lived in humble dwellings of one or two rooms, similar in design to the large villas, but much smaller. Like the wealthier homes, these houses were built of mud bricks and palm trunks, and were surrounded by walls. Similarly, they contained a staircase to the roof where the family sought relief during the hot weather. Vents on the roof trapped cool breezes blowing from the north, and a spout attached to the house drained off any water.

In the cities, the common people lived in smaller homes that were built much closer together and had no gardens. A door from the street led into a small room that served as the father's workroom. A second room was divided into a bedroom and a kitchen. Steps led from the kitchen to the roof. Middle-class town homes were also narrow, but sometimes contained a second or third floor.

What did the ancient Egyptians eat? Wheat bread and beer made from barley were the main items on the menu of the common people. Fruit, vegetables, fish, milk, cheese, butter, ducks, and geese added variety. Wealthy Egyptians regularly ate beef, antelope, and gazelle and enjoyed fancy cakes and baked goods, often with a glass or two of grape, date, or palm wine. Food was prepared in clay ovens over charcoal or wood fires.

REFLECT AND ANALYZE

1. To what extent were Egyptian clothing and cosmetics:
    a) practical?
    b) a reflection of social class?

2. How do the attitudes of ancient Egyptians to clothing and cosmetics compare to our attitudes today?

3. Sketch and label a diagram of a typical rural villa in ancient Egypt.

4. Compare the living conditions of rural Egyptians with those living in towns or cities. Can you see any parallels with rural and urban living today?

THE ECONOMY

AGRICULTURE

Agriculture was the most important economic activity in ancient Egypt. In fact, the majority of the population took part in farming. Most farmers worked as labourers on large estates owned by the royal family, the temples, or wealthy landowners, but some were able to rent fields and control production themselves.

As payment for their efforts, labourers received a small portion of the crop, usually wheat or barley. This they used to feed their families. But since ancient Egypt had no monetary system, they also used these small payments of grain to trade or barter for other goods or services.

The agricultural cycle began with the annual flooding of the Nile, which took place in late August and September. The flooding left rich deposits of silt for planting and was critical to the survival of the Egyptian population. If the Nile flooded too little, the people could face famine. If the river flooded too much, the water could destroy the dykes and irrigation canals, and delay planting.

When the floodwaters drained, the agricultural year began in earnest. As water was vital, the farm labourers first repaired all damaged dykes and irrigation canals. They then redefined the boundary lines of the fields by replacing any dislodged field markers. This important task made sure that the tax assessors could correctly calculate what each landowner owed in taxes to the government.

October was the month for ploughing and planting. Hard soil was broken up manually with a hoe, but farmers generally used a wooden plough pulled by a pair of oxen or donkeys to prepare the soil for planting. Seeding often took place at the same time as ploughing. A young man or boy walked along in front of the plough spreading the seed, which was then dug under.

During the growing season, farmers had the backbreaking jobs of moving water

Figure 5-13 *A wall painting from a tomb of agricultural work in Egypt*

INNOVATIONS
The Shaduf

An important agricultural innovation from the New Kingdom of ancient Egypt was the *shaduf*. Before this invention, how did farm labourers transport water to the irrigation ditches? Why do you think this invention improved agricultural production in ancient Egypt?

The shaduf was designed to transport water from the irrigation ditches

Figure 5-14 *The shaduf*

to the fields, saving the farmers from some of the backbreaking labour.

The shaduf was a tall, upright post with a long cross-pole at the top that could swing freely in all directions. At one end of the pole was a water container, and at the other end was a heavy counterweight. The shaduf allowed a farmer, working alone, to raise water from the Nile and deposit it into a canal or irrigation ditch.

from the irrigation canals onto existing fields and developing new irrigation works for land farther away from the river. To build these new canal networks, they dug small ditches that were separated from the main canals by sluices.

One sure sign of the approaching harvest was the appearance of the tax assessor, who arrived to estimate the potential crop yield and calculate the amount of taxes the landowner owed. Soon after that visit, the men went to work in the fields, cutting the grain with their sickles and then carting it away in large baskets for threshing. Family members of farm labourers were allowed to glean or pick up any grain left on the ground when the crop was harvested. Sometimes the labourers would drop part of the yield on purpose for gleaners who came from very needy families.

While grain crops were the most important in ancient Egypt, farmers grew other crops as well. Irrigated gardens produced lettuce, beans, onions, figs, dates, grapes, melons, and cucumbers. Castor seeds and sesame seeds provided oil for

cooking and for skin lotions. The papyrus plant was grown to make paper, mats, baskets, footwear, and rope. Part of the date and grape crops were crushed to make wine—a very important industry in ancient Egypt. Many farms raised domestic animals such as cattle, ducks, geese, goats, and pigs for meat, and bred donkeys for beasts of burden.

INDUSTRY

Craftspeople operated small shops in the towns and cities, close to a pharaoh's palace, a wealthy noble's estate, or a temple. Taking advantage of resources and materials close at hand, they produced most of the manufactured goods for the home and export markets. Furniture-makers used local woods to make chairs and beds. Weavers used local flax to make linen and other textiles. Potters used local clay to produce bowls, vases, and plates, and brickmakers used mud from the banks of the Nile River to mould their bricks. Some products, such as rope, baskets, mats, and sheets of writing material, were made

from plants. Other urban craftspeople included carpenters, stonemasons, silversmiths, goldsmiths, boat-builders, and jewellers, who produced bracelets and pendants for the wealthy.

In rural areas, mining was an important industry. Egypt had rich supplies of minerals such as limestone, sandstone, and granite, which were used in the construction of pyramids and monuments. The Egyptians also mined for copper, gold, tin, and gems such as turquoises and amethysts.

TRADE

Trade played an important role in the Egyptian economy as far back as the Old Kingdom. Merchants working for the pharaoh or rich nobles began crossing the deserts by caravan, venturing up and down the Nile, and sailing to lands bordering the Aegean, Mediterranean, and Red seas. Their purpose was to exchange Egyptian goods for those of their neighbours. With them they took barley and wheat, wines from the eastern delta region, papyrus sheets, gold, and other minerals. In return, they acquired silver, iron, horses, cedar logs, ivory, leopard skins, copper, cattle, and spices.

Trading ventures brought the Egyptians into contact with people from Lebanon, Crete, Syria, Sumer, and other parts of Africa and Asia. But trade proved to be more than just an exchange of goods—it allowed for an exchange of ideas and a sharing of cultures. As people from different societies met, they enriched each other's civilizations.

Merchants travelled on the Nile by barge or by boat. The earliest boats were made of papyrus reeds and were moved by poles. Later boats were powered by oars.

Longer journeys became common when the Egyptians invented sails and began to rely on the wind for power. By about 3000 BCE, wooden planks were used to build ships.

PERSPECTIVES ON THE PAST

A Story of Cross-Cultural Exchange

Although Egypt was one of the largest and most powerful empires in the ancient Middle East, it was not the only civilization in the region. Two of the small but important civilizations that the Egyptians encountered were the Phoenicians and the Israelites.

How did these civilizations influence or affect the development of one another? In what ways have they shaped us today?

The Phoenicians

The Phoenicians came from the land of Canaan, a territory between ancient Egypt and Syria. Today, Canaan is made up of the countries of Lebanon, Israel, and Jordan. About 3000 BCE, Semitic groups known as the Canaanites migrated to this region from the Arabian Peninsula. The Phoenicians settled in the northern part of Canaan. Because they had limited space for farming, the Phoenicians turned to the sea to earn a living, and from their coastal cities they sailed throughout the Mediterranean.

Voyaging as far as England, they traded crops and handicrafts such as metal and glass ornaments, jewellery, vases, and weapons. They also transported Babylonian and Egyptian learning to parts of the Mediterranean world such as Greece. From Greece, these advances spread to Europe and served as a cornerstone of contemporary learning.

One of the most significant Phoenician developments was an alphabet of 22 letters, with each letter standing for a single consonant sound. The Greeks added vowel sounds and the Romans made even more changes later, transforming the Phoenician alphabet into the one we use today.

The Israelites

The Israelites or Hebrews were the ancestors of the Jewish people. Living in a land midway between the civilizations of ancient Egypt and Mesopotamia, they absorbed influences from both.

The early history of the Hebrew is told in the holy books known to the Jews as the Torah, and to Christians as the Old Testament of the Bible. The Bible tells how Abraham, a tribal leader, led his followers out of the land of Ur in Mesopotamia, in obedience to his god Yahweh. Yahweh promised that He would give Abraham's descendants a land of their own in Canaan. Historians think that Abraham's migration took place sometime around 1900 BCE.

Abraham's grandson Jacob, also known as Israel, gave his name to the followers of the god Yahweh. Thereafter, they were called Israelites. Jacob had 12 sons, each of whom became a leader of one of the 12 tribes of Israel. The youngest son, Joseph, led a tribe into Egypt, where they were enslaved until about 1230 BCE.

Moses, another important Israelite leader, led his people out of captivity in Egypt, and the Israelites wandered through the desert for 40 years, preparing to occupy the land of Palestine. During this period, Yahweh gave Moses stone tablets on which were carved the Ten Commandments.

After Moses led the Israelites to Canaan, they had to

fight a series of battles to establish themselves in their new land. Under the rule of their early kings, the Hebrew nation prospered. Saul became their first ruler in 1015 BCE. King David (1012 BCE–972 BCE), who replaced him, established a capital at Jerusalem, and united and strengthened the Hebrew nation. Solomon (973 BCE–933 BCE) built a beautiful temple in Jerusalem and earned great respect among the people of the Middle East. When Solomon died, his kingdom split into the kingdom of Israel in the north and the kingdom of Judah in the south. The kingdom of Israel lasted for 250 years until it was destroyed by the Assyrians in 722 BCE. In 586 BCE, Nebuchadnezzar destroyed the temple in Jerusalem, enslaving the Hebrews and destroying the kingdom of Judah.

The Hebrews were later freed by the Persians, and when some of them returned to Palestine, they began to rebuild their temple. Although Israel was no longer an independent state, Hebraic religious traditions had enormous influence on other religions such as Christianity and Islam.

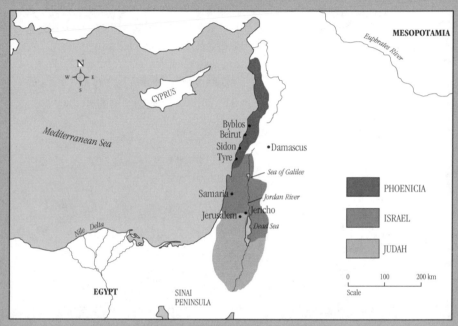

Figure 5-15 *Lands of the Phoenicians and Hebrews*

REFLECT AND ANALYZE

1. Develop a chart of the Egyptian agricultural cycle, identifying the activities associated with each stage.

2. What were the principal industries in ancient Egypt?

3. How can it be said that the entire economy of ancient Egypt was linked to the Nile River? Use a sketch diagram or a chart in your answer.

THE ARTS

Some of the most significant information that we have about life in ancient Egypt comes from the arts. Paintings, sculpture, architecture, and translations of writings offer a fascinating picture of daily life and beliefs.

WRITING

Hieroglyphics, developed by the Egyptians about 3000 BCE, were originally a collection of picture signs, possibly borrowed from the Mesopotamians. Each pictogram was designed to represent an entire word or idea. They were carved on stone monuments and painted on the walls and coffins of tombs. Scribes drew them on papyrus sheets, using reed pens and ink made from a mixture of vegetable dyes, water, and soot. Writing in hieroglyphics took considerable time and effort.

The nature of hieroglyphs evolved greatly over the centuries. Of the more than 700 signs in use during the New Kingdom, the vast majority represented sounds rather than objects. New and simpler versions of writing developed as well. A cursive form of writing called

Figure 5-16
Part of a hieroglyphic inscription

LITERATURE

Ancient Egyptian literature included adventure stories, fairy tales, poems, and love stories. Among the non-religious or **secular** works were popular collections of wise sayings that offered practical advice on how to succeed in life. One of the oldest books in the world, for example, written about 250 BCE, is called *Instructions of the Vizier Ptahhotep*. In it, Ptahhotep tells his son how to succeed as an official in the household of the pharaoh.

The following excerpts give us a sampling of his advice. Do you agree or disagree with his views?

Do not let your heart be puffed-up because of your knowledge. Do not be confident because you are a wise man. Take counsel with the ignorant as well as with the wise. . . .

If you, as a leader, have to decide on the conduct of a great many people, seek the most perfect manner of doing so, that

your own conduct may be blameless. . . .

Do not repeat slander; you should not hear it, for it is the result of hot temper. Repeat a matter seen, not what is heard. . . .

Be active while you live, doing more than is commanded. . . . Activity produces riches, but riches do not last when activity slackens.

PAINTING AND SCULPTURE

Many of ancient Egypt's finest paintings and other works of art were created for tombs and temples. Artists covered the walls with bright, imaginative scenes of daily life and guides to the afterlife. The Egyptians intended these images to present a perfect world so that the good life would continue forever. Egyptian art followed certain conventions established early in the Old Kingdom that remained unchanged for thousands of years. Representations of people, scenes, and objects in paintings aimed to reflect balance, harmony, and the

hieratic, much like our handwriting, allowed the Egyptian scribes to adapt the hieroglyphics to a pattern of lines. Another simpler version of the language, called **demotic**, developed in the late period of Egyptian history and became even more popular. This script was used for practical matters, such as record-keeping, because it was faster and simpler to write.

In 384 CE, the Christian Roman emperor Theodosius ratified a decree abolishing pagan rites in the temples of Egypt. The same decree also ended the writing and reading of hieroglyphics. For the next 1400 years, therefore, hieroglyphs remained little more than symbols or designs on the artifacts of an ancient civilization.

Figure 5-17 *An example of demotic writing on papyrus*

THEN AND NOW

Solving an Ancient Mystery: The Rosetta Stone

Figure 5-18 *The Rosetta Stone*

The mystery of Egyptian hieroglyphics puzzled linguists for centuries. How was this mystery solved? What doors would the discovery open for historians in their quest to understand Egyptian life and culture?

The Rosetta Stone, a black basalt stone measuring under a metre in width and a little over a metre in length, was the clue. Soldiers of Napoleon dug the stone up near the Rosetta branch of the Nile River in 1799. Later, the British captured this archaeological treasure, and it is now displayed in the British Museum.

The Rosetta Stone bears an inscription written in three different scripts. Today, we know that the inscription is a public record of honours given by the Egyptian priests to the Greek king, one of the Ptolemies, who ruled Egypt in 195 BCE. The top script is written in ancient Egyptian hieroglyphics, the middle script is written in demotic (the last cursive form of the Egyptian language), and the bottom script is written in upper-case Greek letters.

The French linguist Jean-François Champollion used the stone to decipher hieroglyphics and rediscover the Egyptian language. Born in southwest France in 1790, Champollion was a brilliant linguist and Egyptologist. He mastered a dozen languages, including Coptic, a language used by Egyptians between 300 CE and 1500 CE.

Patiently, Champollion compared the three sections of the stone. He then compared them to inscriptions from tombs and temples in Egypt. Slowly, he came to the conclusion that hieroglyphics were not just pictures representing whole or part words, but symbols that stood for sounds as well.

When he found the name of Ptolemy in the Greek section of the stone, he realized through his knowledge of Coptic that the Egyptians would have pronounced the name as *Ptolmys*. He compared this pronunciation to a cartouche (hieroglyphic inscription of a king's name) in the upper section of the stone, and to the inscription on a monument from Egypt.

Thanks to this painstaking work, Champollion discovered the hieroglyphic form of the names Ptolmys and Cleopatra in 1822. Comparing these two names, he concluded that he had found the hieroglyphs for three of the common sounds: *p, o,* and *l*. This humble beginning of discovering three sound values led to the discovery of 12.

As more and more cartouches were collected, dating from 300 BCE to 100 CE, Champollion's ability to decipher hieroglyphics increased. He moved farther and farther back in history until he was able to decipher the cartouches of Thutmose and Ramses.

Jean-François Champollion died in 1832 at the age of 42, but his contribution in unlocking some of the mysteries of ancient Egypt was monumental.

ideal. Images of old age, sickness, or imperfection rarely appeared. People were always portrayed in profile with the hips at a three-quarter turn and the shoulders shown at full width. Since the Egyptians believed that these scenes could come to life in the next world, tomb owners had themselves depicted as young and attractive in pleasant settings.

Egyptian sculpture tended to depict subjects such as religious festivals, military victories, and important people and gods. These works of art ranged in size from small statues, such as those found in the tomb of Tutankhamen and in temples, to colossal monuments, such as those carved to honour Ramses II. The small sculptures or figurines were created from wood, ivory, alabaster, bronze, gold, and turquoise. A favourite subject was cats, which the Egyptians considered sacred and valued for protecting grain supplies from mice. Large sculptures, such as the large stone sphinxes of the Old Kingdom which represented kings or gods, were made of limestone.

Most sculptures seem rather rigid because the figures look straight ahead and are seldom seen involved in any activity. The artists intended to capture the grandeur and ideal character of the subject for eternity—not to portray the person (often the pharaoh) in a life-like way. Thus the sculptures reflected some of the basic values and beliefs of Egyptian society.

ARCHITECTURE

Although we most often associate Egyptian architecture with the pyramids, the people in ancient Egypt also built magnificent limestone temples that were used for religious rites and funeral ceremonies. Typically, these temples had three main sections: a small shrine, a great hall, and an open courtyard with a monumental gateway. Ornamentation and design of the large hall often incorporated columns carved to look like palm trees or papyrus reeds.

One of the most magnificent examples of Egyptian temple architecture, and one of the greatest artifacts of the ancient world, is the temple at Karnak, dedicated to the god Amon and situated on the northern edge of Thebes. The pharaohs Seti I and Ramses II built the temple during the New Kingdom. Succeeding rulers added on to the structure, extending it to over two hectares in size. Large pillared gateways connected the ten additions to the original temple: six additions at the front and (as space ran out) four at the side.

Ramses II enlarged the temple at Karnak to demonstrate his vast wealth. Since the main purpose of the temple was to celebrate religious festivals, Ramses had a sacred lake built beside it to supply holy water.

Figure 5-19
The pillars of the temple of Karnak

REFLECT AND ANALYZE

1. How did the Egyptian system of hieroglyphics evolve over the centuries? Why did these changes take place?

2. What characteristics of Egyptian art show that they wanted to depict a perfect world? What was the purpose of this art?

3. Study an example of an Egyptian painting, noting the stance and proportion of the figures, the colours, and the scale. Then create your own illustration for a tomb painting, showing a scene from daily life. Keep in mind some of the basic goals and characteristics of painting in ancient Egypt.

THE SCIENCES

TECHNOLOGY

The ancient Egyptians showcased their technological expertise most dramatically in the construction of the pyramids. How did they quarry, transport, cut, hoist, and fit the huge stone blocks they needed to build the pyramids, without wheels or pulleys? How and where did they acquire the knowledge they needed to design and construct these monumental structures so precisely? Historians

PERSPECTIVES ON THE PAST
Building the Great Pyramids

How did the ancient Egyptians build the pyramids? The traditional theory suggests that construction took as long as 20 years, involved the labour of thousands, and incorporated four stages. Do you think that this traditional theory offers a believable account of how workers built these monumental structures? Why or why not? Investigate an alternative theory presented by Erich von Daniken in his 1968 book, *Chariots of the Gods*. Do you find his theory realistic?

During the first stage, or planning stage, the builders selected a site, levelled it, and determined the location of true north. The chosen site was on the west bank of the Nile since religion associated death with the setting sun.

It was above the flood level of the river, yet close enough to transport the large stone building blocks. The site was also close to the capital so that the pharaoh could keep an eye on progress. During levelling, workers removed sand and gravel down to the bedrock. They then surrounded the area with a low mud or brick wall and constructed a grid of shallow criss-cross trenches. Water was poured in to find its own level, and workers took depth measurements at several points. Then they drained the water away, levelled the area to the height of the markers, and filled it with rubble to complete the base.

The mining stage involved quarrying the limestone from nearby Giza or from the Tura Quarries across the Nile in the Arabian hills. Harder stone, such as dolerite

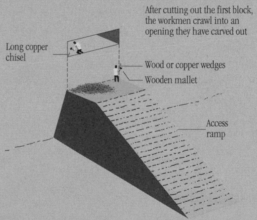

Figure 5-21 *The mining stage*
Limestone was mined by means of tunnelling. Copper chisels were likely used to cut the blocks away from the cliff on all sides except the bottom. Then, when almost free, the block was detached from the base using wedges and pulled down a ramp to the ground.

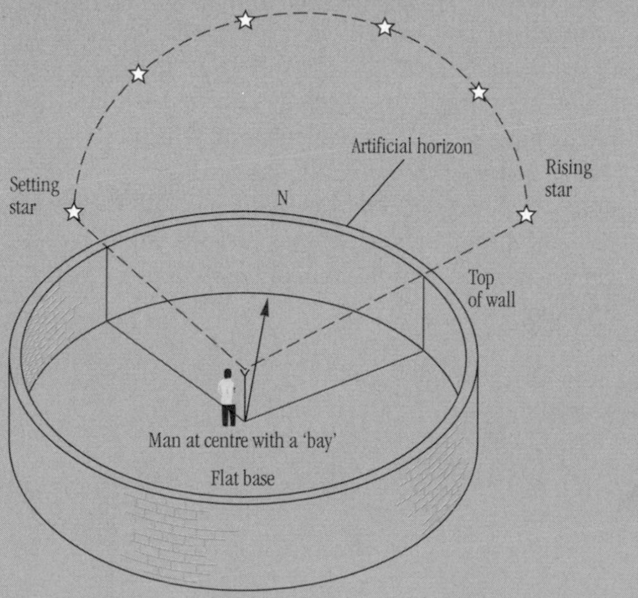

Figure 5-20 *The planning stage*
The pyramid was oriented with true north by taking a sighting on a star in the northern sky. A circular mud wall built on the site acted as an artificial horizon. A surveyor faced east from the centre and used a cleft stick or "bay" and located the precise spot where the star first rose. This spot was marked and later when the star set, a second spot was marked. Lines were drawn to the ground and extended to the centre of the circle. The angle was bisected to determine due north and south. Correct positioning was then determined since the ancient Egyptians had instruments to draw right angles.

and granite, came from as far away as Aswan and was more difficult to mine because of its consistency. It seems unlikely that the Egyptians could have cut this stone without tempered (hardened) copper chisels and saws.

During the third stage, the transportation stage, workers had to transport the stones, which weighed an average of 2.3 tonnes each, without the use of wheels or

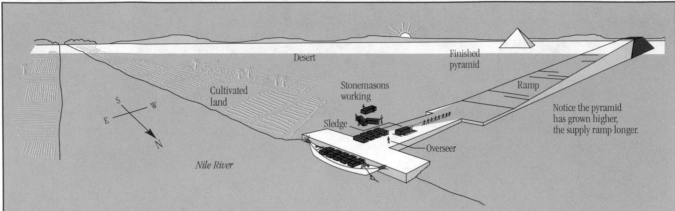

Figure 5-22 *Transporting the stone to the building site*
The most difficult aspect of the transportation stage was moving the large stones across land. Hundreds of workers would have been needed. Many men were required to pull a single sledge bearing even one of these massive stone blocks. Possibly a man at the front poured water on the ground to lubricate the track. A causeway may have linked the site to the Nile to make it easier for sledges to carry the huge stones to their destination and serve as a route for the pharaoh's funeral procession.

engines. According to this theory, the Egyptians brought them down the Nile in boats, taking some advantage, perhaps, of the annual flooding to float the stones up to the base of the site.

The final stage was the actual construction stage. About 400 stonemasons trimmed the stones to size. Since the pyramid was assembled from the base upwards, underground rooms and corridors were cut from the bedrock, according to the original plans. The workers then hauled the blocks for the first layer into place. To reach the higher levels, they constructed supply ramps made of brick and earth paved with wooden logs. Water was poured over the ramps to allow sledges to run more smoothly. Once they had placed the capstone at the top of the pyramid, they demolished the ramp level by level. As the ramp was coming down, stonemasons smoothed the face of the casing stones, the final outside row of stones laid at each level. The casing stones were fitted so precisely that, from a distance, the pyramid looked like a single white stone. Most of these stones are now gone, but a few are still in place at the bottom of the Great Pyramid.

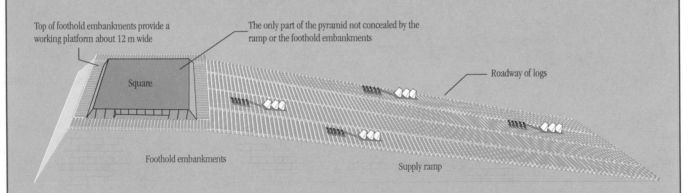

Figure 5-23 *Constructing the pyramid*
As the pyramid rose in height so too did the supply ramp. It would have been impossible to view the full pyramid during the stage of construction. The gradient of the ramp was maintained at a constant 1:12 ratio as the pyramid grew, so that sledges could still be pulled up the ramp and the blocks put into place. The supply ramp became higher and longer as new levels of stone were added.

have advanced various theories to explain how these great monuments were constructed. Many Egyptologists support one view of the process (see box on page 93). In more recent years, others have challenged this traditional theory with ideas of their own.

In 1974, for example, the French chemist Joseph Davidovits suggested that the ancient Egyptians might have known about a simple chemical process that would have allowed them to mould large stone blocks right at the building site. His theory is a genuine possibility because the Egyptians had access to all of the essential ingredients for producing an almost natural moulded rock: natron, the chemical used to make artificial stone, and the binders of aluminum and silicon.

MEDICINE

The practice of mummification taught the ancient Egyptians a great deal about dissection and human anatomy. Their physicians understood that injury to the brain could affect motor control and that the pulse was in some way connected with the heart. Egyptian doctors became the first to specialize in selected fields of medicine such as eye defects or stomach disorders. They developed ways to set broken bones, care for wounds, perform elementary surgery (as saw-cuts found on skulls indicate), and treat many illnesses common at the time, such as rheumatism, kidney stones, gallstones, and smallpox.

Yet the Egyptian approach to medicine was not entirely scientific. Prayers and incantations played an important part in all treatments, and doctors often chose them as their first weapon against disease and injury. Some remedies were selected entirely for their magical potential. For example, if a patient was suffering an injury to an internal organ, a plant leaf shaped like the organ might be selected as a cure.

Several papyrus scrolls surviving from the Middle and New Kingdoms give us more information about other unscientific treatments offered by physicians. Some of the ingredients used in prescriptions included blood, fat, bones, and the organs of various animals. One suggested remedy for various childhood illnesses required swallowing a skinned mouse whole. These prescriptions and other strange potions made from bats, bees, frogs, and vultures were accepted without question for centuries.

MATHEMATICS

The ancient Egyptians used a numerical system like ours with ten as the base. Seven different symbols—representing 1, 10, 100, 1000, 10 000, 100 000, and 1 000 000—were used to form any required number. For ex-

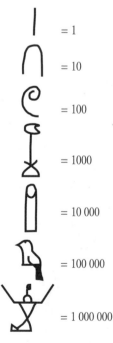

Figure 5-24
Ancient Egyptian number symbols

ample, the first two symbols, in various combinations, could represent all numerals between 1 and 99. For writing large numbers or recording dates, this numeral system became very cumbersome because so many symbols were required.

Although the ancient Egyptians understood geometry and could calculate the area of triangles, trapezoids, rectangles, and circles, their mathematics could be likened more to simple arithmetic. At the time, the Babylonians were ahead of the Egyptians in this science. The use of fractions seems to have presented particular problems.

TIME

The ancient Egyptians developed a calendar based on geographical observation that enabled them to date much of their history. Rather than use astronomical signs, they measured out the year according to the annual flooding of the Nile River. The flooding began around June 20, soon after the star Sirius reappeared on the eastern horizon after months of being out of sight.

The calendar itself is a distant ancestor of our own. It contained 365 days, which were divided into 12 months of 30 days each with an extra five days added at the end. These extra days were celebrated as the birthdays of the gods. Each day was divided into 24 hours, 12 for day and 12 for night.

The Egyptian calendar did not allow for smaller units of time such as the 60-minute hour or the 60-second minute. In fact, an Egyptian hour varied in length from season to season. Since a day-time hour was considered the twelfth part of the time from sunrise to sunset, day-time hours were longer than night-time hours in the summer, and shorter in the winter.

REFLECT AND ANALYZE

1. According to traditional theory, what problems did the ancient Egyptians have to overcome to construct the Great Pyramid at Giza?

2. What disadvantages can you see in the ancient Egyptian systems of measuring and recording time?

3. Why can we not describe ancient Egyptian medicine as a "pure science"? What similarities and differences can you see with modern medicine? Explain.

LOOKING BACK

In 1278 BCE, the Egyptians signed a peace treaty to end a costly war with the Hittites of Asia Minor. Egypt then entered into a long period of decline. Over time, the Egyptians lost their once mighty empire to invaders. Mycenaean Greeks, known to the Egyptians as "the people from the sea," swept into the delta in about 1100 BCE. Libyans and Nubians attacked from the deserts. Then, in turn, came the Assyrians, the Babylonians, the Persians, the Greeks, and the Romans.

Trade and commerce deteriorated. The flow of gold from Nubia was lost around 1100 BCE, and tribute from conquered lands ceased. As the treasury emptied, the pharaohs and their governments could not stop the empire's decline, and its glory passed.

Ancient Egypt, however, holds the record as the world's longest continuous civilization, and its legacy is impressive. When Upper Egypt united with Lower Egypt, the first nation in the world was born, and the concept of central government began.

Modern religions owe much to the ancient Egyptians as they were among the first to believe in a life after death. Modern science owes them a debt of gratitude as well. People in ancient Egypt were the first to develop a yearly calendar of 365 days. They created papyrus, one of the earliest forms of paper. They made careful studies of drugs, diseases, and medicines, and were the first to use geometry. Finally, Egyptian art and culture have fascinated other civilizations for centuries, and that fascination continues today.

MAKING CONNECTIONS

1. In groups, develop a list of the influences Mesopotamian and Egyptian civilizations have had on our society today. Identify specific examples of these influences around you wherever possible.

2. Create a bulletin-board display comparing Egyptian pyramids and Sumerian ziggurats. Consider purpose, method of construction, and materials used. Include an evaluation of each buildings' technological and architectural merits and its importance within the civilization.

3. How did religious beliefs shape the cultures of Mesopotamia and Egypt? In a short report, consider the influences of religion on government, law, art, and daily life in each civilization.

4. What practical advances did the Mesopotamians make in writing, mathematics, and architecture? How were these advances similar to achievements in ancient Egypt? How might you explain these similar advances in both civilizations?

5. Compare Hammurabi's law code with the Ten Commandments of Moses.

6. The civilizations of both Mesopotamia and ancient Egypt included large empires. What methods did these civilizations use to hold these empires together? Which civilization was more successful in maintaining a unified empire? Explain.

DIGGING DEEPER

7. Choose one of the following people and investigate further how he helped to unravel the mysteries of ancient Egypt and Mesopotamia.
   • Leonard Woolley
   • Howard Carter
   • Henry Rawlinson
   • Jean-François Champollion
   Write a short news report outlining the significance of this person's discovery and explain his interest in ancient Egypt or Mesopotamia.

8. Do some further research into the discovery of the tomb of Tutankhamen, Ramses II, the Royal Tombs at Ur, or another major archaeological find in ancient Egypt or Mesopotamia. Assemble a picture collage of some of the most significant artifacts discovered, or develop a portfolio of illustrations and descriptions.

9. On a large sheet of paper, design a plan for a Mesopotamian city. Refer to the plan of Babylon in Figure 2-12 on page 39 as a starting point. Include the following elements:
   - river
   - canals
   - a palace and gardens
   - temples
   - the city wall and moat
   - houses and gardens
   - roads and paths
   - farms

   Write or record on audiotape a guide to your city.

10. Do further research on the *Epic of Gilgamesh* or the *Egyptian Tales of Sinhue (Sinbad the Sailor)*. What truth might there be in these stories? What role did they serve? Stage short scenes from one of these tales for the class.

11. The people of ancient Egypt and Mesopotamia demonstrated genius in the field of science and technology. Support this statement in a short essay or seminar presentation.

12. Debate: The invention of writing and a system of keeping records is the most significant achievement to come out of ancient Egypt and Mesopotamia.

SKILL DEVELOPMENT: THE COMPARISON ORGANIZER

In studying different civilizations in history it can be helpful to make comparisons of their environments, attitudes, beliefs, values, and achievements. Making comparisons can help us to uncover some of the important patterns in time that have been observed over the course of human history.

To conduct an effective comparison, structure and organization are essential. Using a comparison organizer can provide the needed structure and organization.

Process

1. **Focus** your investigation. That is, clarify the purpose of the investigation by deciding exactly what it is that you wish to find out.

   For example: To what extent does the physical environment affect the development of civilization?

2. Establish the **parameters** of your comparison.

    For example: Do you want to compare two river-valley civilizations or one river-valley civilization and one land-based civilization?

3. Determine the **criteria** that will serve as the basis of the comparison. Develop 5 or 6 different criteria for comparison. Enter the criteria for comparison in the left-hand column of the comparison organizer.

CRITERIA	THE PHYSICAL ENVIRONMENT OF MESOPOTAMIA	THE PHYSICAL ENVIRONMENT OF EGYPT
ECONOMICS		
COMMUNICATION/ TRANSPORTATION		

4. Develop a **category** system within the main major topics or concepts identified as the criteria.

CRITERIA	THE PHYSICAL ENVIRONMENT OF MESOPOTAMIA	THE PHYSICAL ENVIRONMENT OF EGYPT
ECONOMICS Positive factors Negative factors Neutral factors		

5. Use the text as a basic resource to locate information for each of the cells in the comparison organizer where information is available. Consult other resources for additional information.

CRITERIA	THE PHYSICAL ENVIRONMENT OF MESOPOTAMIA	THE PHYSICAL ENVIRONMENT OF EGYPT
ECONOMICS Positive factors Negative factors Neutral factors	- silt deposits from the Tigris and Euphrates - unpredictable flooding	- silt deposits from the flooding of the Nile - predictable flooding
COMMUNICATION/ TRANSPORTATION Positive factors Negative factors Neutral factors	- use of the wheel	- prevailing north wind for travel up river - cataracts on the river

6. Evaluate or assess the information in your comparison organizer. What conclusions can you draw?

Applying the Skill

Extend the above organizer to include more criteria. Complete the research. Prepare a written report based on your conclusions.

OR

Select another aspect for comparison from the two civilizations in this unit. Complete a comparison organizer and write a report based on your conclusions.

UNIT 2

The Mediterranean World

1500 BCE - 450 CE

GREECE AND ROME

The two great ancient civilizations of the Mediterranean world were Greece and Rome. Greek civilization began on the Mediterranean island of Crete about a thousand years after the Egyptian civilization emerged. Roman civilization developed and flourished after the decline of Greece. From their humble beginnings as agricultural communities, both Greece and Rome grew to become great empires, spreading their ideas and culture over a vast territory and shaping later civilizations for centuries. Some of their accomplishments still influence the world today.

We remember Greece primarily for the early form of democracy that it practised, and for its great philosophers, artists, and writers. While the Romans preserved and built on Greek achievements, they eventually developed a distinctly Roman culture with its own form of government, laws, and customs. At its height, Rome was one of the largest and most impressive empires in recorded history.

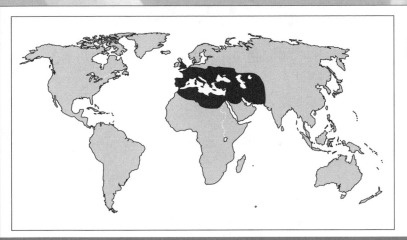

THE GREEK AND
ROMAN WORLD

GREECE:
Land of the Hellenes

Figure 6-1
A bust of Homer

H e drew the keen blade that hung by his side,
A sword both heavy and long. Then bracing himself
He charged at Achilles, ...
his sharp sword held high. And Achilles,
Seething with savage wrath, met the advance
With one of his own, protecting his chest with his intricate,
Exquisite shield . . . .
he scanned the form
Of his foe to find the spot where a spear was most likely
To pierce the firm flesh of Hector. He saw that his armor
Of bronze covered him all the way. . . .
But there where the collarbones separate neck
And shoulders, there at his throat, most fatal of targets,
Appeared a spot unprotected by bronze. So there,
As on him he charged, great Achilles drove in his spear,
And the point went through his soft neck and stuck out behind. . . .
Dying, he sprawled in the dust,
And shining Achilles exulted above him, vaunting. . .

Homer
The *Iliad*

The great poet Homer, whose works date from about 700 BCE, created some of the earliest Greek writings. His poems tell of people who lived in Greece 500 years before his time. The Greeks passed these stories down by word of mouth for centuries before Homer recorded them. In the lines above, from the famous poem called the *Iliad*, Homer writes about the legendary Trojan War in which Achilles, one of the Greek heroes, fought a great duel with Hector, the son of the king of Troy. The *Iliad* and the *Odyssey,* Homer's two great epics, inspired the Greek people by telling them of great deeds in their history and by praising heroic values—courage, glory, and valour. Not only do these poems represent some of the great literature of the period, but they also give us a fascinating glimpse into ancient Greek society.

LAND AND SEA

In the southeastern corner of Europe, between modern Greece and Turkey, lies the Aegean Sea. This island-filled arm of the Mediterranean was the heart of ancient Greece. Few of the people lived more than 70 km from its shores. Unlike the river valley societies of Egypt and Mesopotamia, Greek civilization was oriented to the sea.

More than 2000 islands dot the Aegean, the remnants of a submerged mountain system. While some islands were rocky and infertile, others had rich soils ideal for farming. The earliest Aegean civilization began on one of these fertile islands—Crete—and spread from there to other islands and to the Greek mainland. In ancient times, Greek cities dotted even Asia Minor (part of modern Turkey) on the eastern edge of the Aegean Sea.

Greece has nearly 3200 km of coastline, a remarkable length for such a small land area. Besides the islands, the Greek mainland has a long rocky coastline that is indented with deep fjords. These narrow inlets provided excellent harbours. Greeks sailed from island to island across the Aegean and around the whole rim of the Mediterranean sharing products and ideas. Sea travel had its dangers, however. Although distances from island to island across the Aegean are short, violent storms and strong prevailing winds can make navigation difficult. To sail safely beyond the islands to places farther east and south, such as Mesopotamia and Egypt, navigators needed to know the precise wind conditions.

Mainland Greece stretches from the Peloponnese peninsula in the south to the regions of Attica, Thessaly, and Macedonia in the north. The area has no major rivers, and only a few of the minor rivers flow all year round. Most are active only in the winter or after storms. At other times, they are little more than a trickle running across a bed of stone.

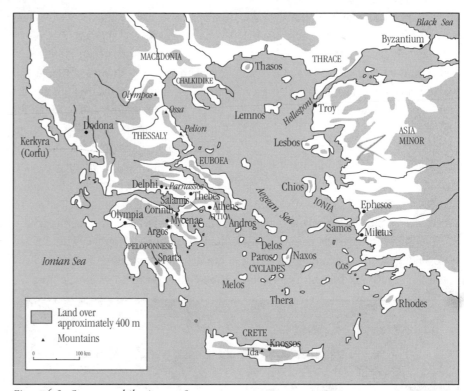

Figure 6-2 *Greece and the Aegean Sea*

The rugged landscape of the mainland is marked by mountains. As a result, the ancient Greeks could not cultivate even a fifth of this territory, and prized the small

Figure 6-3 *Mountainous Greek landscape*

amount of fertile land highly. On the narrow coastal plains and valleys—the only land suitable for farming—fig vines and olives thrived in the mild, wet winters and dry summers. The people also grew grain crops, such as barley, and put sheep and goats out to graze on the higher ground.

Like the sea, the mountains had a significant effect on the development of the ancient Greek world. While they made Greece a very difficult territory to conquer by land, they also acted as natural partitions among the Greek communities on the plains. Ancient Greece became a collection of separate, fiercely independent city-states, often at war with one another.

In ancient times, cedar, cypress, and pine covered the mountains of Greece. But the people cut most of the trees down to get timber for shipbuilding and charcoal for fuel. This deforestation led to erosion, which swept away precious soil, making it even more difficult to produce enough wheat for a growing population. Except for iron in Spartan Laconia and silver in Athenian mines at Laurium, Greece also had few mineral deposits. With limited farmland and few natural resources, many Greek city-states relied on foreign trade.

brought to light actual evidence of this ancient kingdom. His discovery of the palace of King Minos at Knossos was one of the most important archaeological finds of the century.

The palace Evans uncovered was like a huge maze, with over 800 interconnecting rooms grouped around the large central courtyard. While construction probably began about 2000 BCE, the palace was enlarged and rebuilt several times during the Minoan period. In some places, it rises to several storeys. Rooms seem to have had various purposes, suggesting that the palace served as a government centre, royal residence, temple, and storehouse. The west side housed the official quarters or state rooms, including a throne room and large storerooms. The huge jars found in these storerooms, originally for olive oil, wine, and grain, may represent taxes paid by the people to the king. The east side, which extends beyond a large courtyard, housed the domestic or living quarters.

The palace also included several architectural innovations well advanced for the time. The Minoans built light-wells or shafts in some of the rooms to create a brighter, more open atmosphere. They piped water into the palace, incorporated flush toilets and baths in the living quarters, and constructed an advanced drainage system. Indoor plumbing such as this did not become common again for 3600 years.

On the interior walls of the main rooms, colourful frescoes or wall paintings depicted scenes of nature and Minoan life. One room had an entire mural of dolphins. Other paintings show crowds watching lively dances or sports such as bull-leaping. In some of these frescoes, young men and

---

REFLECT AND ANALYZE

1. a) What geographic features might support communication and sharing of ideas in ancient Greece? Explain.

    b) What obstacles might geography present to the development of a large, united Greek state? (Consider at least three factors.)

2. You are a Greek living in Sparta on the Peloponnese peninsula. How do you think the geography of the area would affect your attitude to people living in Athens to the north or in another area of Greece?

3. Using an organizer, compare the geographic features of Greece with those of either ancient Egypt or Mesopotamia. What were the advantages and disadvantages of each area?

HISTORICAL OVERVIEW

THE MINOANS

The earliest centre of civilization associated with ancient Greece was located on the island of Crete. Here, a Bronze Age society flourished for over a thousand years, reaching its zenith between 2000 BCE and 1450 BCE. This was the Minoan civilization, named after a legendary ruler, King Minos. For centuries, the only information we had about this civilization came from the writings of the fifth-century BCE Greek historian Thucydides. Thucydides told of a King Minos of Crete who dominated a large part of the Aegean with his powerful navy. Tales of Minos and his navy had been Greek legends for centuries before Thucydides recorded them.

In 1900, the British archaeologist Arthur Evans began excavations on the north shore of Crete, at Knossos, and

Figure 6-4 *Bull-leaping – a fresco from the palace at Knossos*

women are grabbing the horns of a charging bull and vaulting over its back. The bull seems to have been sacred to the Minoans, and bull-leaping may have begun as a religious ritual. Other artifacts discovered at Knossos suggest that the Minoans worshipped a mother goddess or goddess of fertility, who often appears with snakes. As no battle scenes appear on the walls and few weapons were found in the excavations, historians believe that the Minoans were a peaceful people, more preoccupied with nature and life than with war.

Archaeologists also discovered at Knossos two clay tablets bearing different scripts, which they named Linear A and Linear B. The script called Linear B, finally decoded in 1952, probably replaced the earlier script, Linear A, which remains a mystery. Texts written in Linear B have also been found at several mainland locations in Greece. Their discovery suggests that Greeks from the mainland—possibly from the Mycenaean civilization that emerged in

about 1600 BCE—dominated Knossos in its final years.

Knossos was not the only Minoan centre on the island of Crete, but it was the most important. Sometime around 1450 BCE, most of the palace-centres were destroyed, although historians are not certain why. One theory, first proposed in 1939, suggested that the massive eruption of a volcano on the island of Thera destroyed the palaces. This theory also linked the sudden destruction of the Minoan civilization with the legend of the lost continent of Atlantis. Recently, however, historians have found flaws in this theory and now believe that invaders from the Greek mainland probably destroyed the palace-centres on the island.

THE MYCENAEANS

While Minoan palace-centres were flourishing on Crete, people on the Greek mainland were living in small, simple farming communities. Waves of invaders from the

north hindered their development. Indo-European peoples may have invaded the Greek mainland as early as 2500 BCE. Within 500 years, they had penetrated southern Greece, building fortress settlements on the fertile plains. Some of the early invaders spoke a language called Achaean, which became the basis of modern Greek.

These invaders seized Mycenae in the Peloponnese, the main centre on the Greek mainland at the time. With this city as their political centre, they built a wealthy and powerful civilization, known as Mycenaean, that flourished for about 500 years. Mycenaean culture dominated the Mediterranean between 1600 BCE and 1100 BCE.

Mycenaean kings ruled over their territories from fortified palaces and gained much of their wealth through trade and piracy. In the most famous of their expeditions, they attacked the city of Troy on the northwest corner of Asia Minor. Mycenaean minstrels passed down treasured songs and

GREECE: A DEVELOPMENTAL TIMELINE

	THE EARLY PERIOD 2000 BCE-800 BCE	THE EARLY CLASSICAL PERIOD 800 BCE-480 BCE
POLITICAL DEVELOPMENTS	**THE MINOAN PERIOD 2000 BCE– 1450 BCE** • kings ruled Minoan centres **THE MYCENAEAN PERIOD 1600 BCE–1100 BCE** • Achaean invaders enter the Greek mainland as early as 2500 BCE • the Achaeans seize Mycenae in the Peloponnese • the Trojan War begins circa 1250 BCE **THE DARK AGES 1100 BCE–800 BCE** • new raiding parties invade from the north • Greek-speaking people are dispersed all around the Aegean Sea	**THE RISE OF THE CITY-STATE AND THE AGE OF COLONIZATION 800 BCE–550 BCE** • the first Greek colony is established in the Bay of Naples (about 750 BCE) • Syracuse becomes the greatest of the Greek colonies • a second wave of Greek colonization begins (about 650 BCE) **THE AGE OF THE PERSIAN WARS 550 BCE–480 BCE** • Cyrus of Persia defeats Croesus of Lydia to make the Persians masters of the Greeks in Asia Minor (546 BCE) • the Ionian revolt led by the city-state of Miletus is crushed by the Persians (494 BCE) • the Athenians defeat the Persians at Marathon (490 BCE) • the Persians defeat the Spartans at Thermopylae (480 BCE) • the Athenians defeat the forces of Xerxes of Persia at the Battle of Salamis (480 BCE)
CULTURAL DEVELOPMENTS	• construction of the palace of Knossos begins (2000 BCE) • frescoes illustrate artistic ability of Minoans • Minoans develop a script, as noted on the writing tablets Linear A and Linear B • frescoed walls of the palace of Agamemnon depict scenes of hunting and war • the shaft graves at Mycenae contain valuable objects of gold and silver • Homer writes the *Iliad* and the *Odyssey* • invasion and dispersal result in the creation of different Greek dialects: Dorian, Aeolian, and Ionian • most of the cultural advances of the Mycenaeans are lost	• the Greeks adopt the Phoenician alphabet • the first Olympic Games are held (776 BCE) • Thales of Miletus develops the first two steps in the scientific method • Pythagoras of Samos, the great mathematician, discovers five geometric theorems • Acropolis is begun in Athens
TECHNOLOGICAL/ECONOMIC DEVELOPMENTS	• use of light-wells and advanced drainage system in Knossos demonstrate advanced technology • Minoans are a Bronze Age society • shaft graves are abandoned by the Mycenaeans in favour of beehive-shaped tombs called *tholos* tombs	• trade develops on the Mediterranean • metal currency comes into common use • metics (foreign craftspeople and traders) are welcomed to the mainland states • the Greeks learn how to use iron

CLASSICAL GREECE
480 BCE-338 BCE

- Athens develops the most democratic government of all the city-states
- Athens assumes leadership of the Delian League (478 BCE)
- the Peloponnesian War between Athens and Sparta breaks out (431 BCE -404 BCE)
- Pericles, the Athenian leader, defends Athens against the Spartans
- plague strikes Athens (430 BCE)
- Sparta emerges victorious over Athens (404 BCE)
- city-states struggle for power, opening the way for invasion from Macedonia

---

- Athens develops as a great cultural centre, enjoying a golden age in the century following the Persian Wars (480 BCE-380 BCE)
- the great Athenian playwrights Aeschylus, Sophocles, Euripides, and Aristophanes produce their works
- Athens is home to the great philosophers Socrates, Plato, and Aristotle
- Hippocrates, the father of medicine, is born on the island of Cos
- Greek art flourishes; sculptures depict the ideal human form; architecture develops the graceful Ionic style
- Herodus and Thucydides, the great Greek historians, produce their works

---

- Athens becomes a prosperous commercial city
- Greek traders exchange goods and ideas with Egyptians, Persians, and other societies in the Mediterranean region
- the Parthenon is built in Athens

THE HELLENISTIC AGE
338 BCE-27 BCE

- Philip II of Macedonia defeats the independent Greek city-states at Chaeronea (338 BCE)
- Alexander becomes king of Macedonia (336 BCE)
- Alexander begins his campaign of conquest into Egypt, Persia, Mesopotamia, and as far east as the Indus River in India (334 BCE)
- Alexander dies (323 BCE)
- Alexander's generals fight for control of his empire

- Greek, Persian, Indian, and Egyptian customs mix during the Hellenistic Age
- Euclid systematizes geometry
- Archimedes advances theoretical physics
- Aristarchus formulates view that the earth revolves around the sun

---

- Philip II builds a formidable army using the phalanx formation and cavalry
- Alexander the Great founds the port of Alexandria (332 BCE) and several other cities in his empire

PERSPECTIVES ON THE PAST

The Legend of the Minotaur

Legends are stories relating to a people's past, often telling of a great hero or historical event. Legends may be partly fact, or they may be all fiction.

What historical facts, if any, can we find in the legend of Theseus and the Minotaur?

A favourite legend of the Athenian Greeks told of Theseus and the Minotaur. This story linked King Minos of Crete with Theseus, one of the earliest and greatest kings of Athens.

The legend tells how King Minos angered the gods by failing to sacrifice a particularly strong bull. As a punishment, his wife gave birth to a monster called the Minotaur, who was part man and part bull, and fed on human flesh. Minos kept the Minotaur hidden away in a huge maze called the labyrinth.

One year, the eldest son of Minos journeyed to Athens to participate in the Athenian games. After he had won several prizes, he was murdered by those he had defeated. Enraged, Minos sent his powerful fleet to attack Athens, and forced the Athenian king, Aegeus, to agree to a terrible form of compensation. Every nine years, Aegeus had to send seven young men and seven young women to Crete. Minos imprisoned these young people in the labyrinth, where the Minotaur hunted them down and ate them.

When the time came to send the third group of unlucky Athenians to Crete, Theseus, the son of Aegeus, volunteered to go, claiming that he would slay the Minotaur. If he was successful, Theseus promised his father, he would change the colour of the returning ship's sails from black to white.

When he arrived in Crete, Theseus was led towards the labyrinth. His princely manner impressed Ariadne, the daughter of Minos, and she decided to do what she could to save him from the Minotaur. In the black of night, Ariadne drugged the guards and gave Theseus two swords, one long and one short. Then she led him to the entrance of the labyrinth and gave him a long coil of thread to help him find his way back through the maze.

Theseus tied one end of the thread near the entrance and made his way cautiously into the labyrinth. After some time, he stumbled on a pile of bones and knew that he had found the place where the Minotaur came to feed. He hid in a passageway and waited. Finally, he heard the roar of a wild beast and the hungry Minotaur appeared. The monster had a giant man's body, an enormous bull's head, and a lion's teeth.

Theseus leapt out of the passageway and attacked the Minotaur with the short sword, slicing the back sinews of the monster's knees. When the Minotaur fell on his back, Theseus plunged the long sword into his heart. Victorious, the Athenian prince cut off the creature's head and carried it under his arm as he followed the thread safely back to the entrance. Accompanied by Ariadne, Theseus brought the severed head to King Minos in his throne room.

Minos was so impressed by the young man's bravery that he freed the other imprisoned Athenians and guaranteed them safe passage home. The king also agreed that Ariadne could return to Athens with Theseus to become his wife.

But Theseus's triumph was short-lived. The return voyage to Athens was long and stormy. In one version of the legend, Ariadne became ill and died in the arms of Theseus on the island of Naxos. In another version, Theseus simply abandoned Ariadne on the island. In all versions of the story, however, as he approached home Theseus completely forgot his promise to his father—to change the colour of the sails to white.

As Aegeus paced the cliff tops, scouring the horizon for the first sight of his son's ship, he saw the black sails and assumed the worst. Broken-hearted, Aegeus threw himself to his death in the sea.

---

stories about a great Trojan War and other adventures from generation to generation. After the Greeks learned the art of writing from Phoenician merchants, the poet Homer wove many of these songs together to form two great epics, called the *Iliad* and the *Odyssey*. From these poems, written about 700 BCE, and from archaeological discoveries, we gain much of our knowledge of the Mycenaean age.

In 1876, the German archaeologist Heinrich Schliemann conducted excava-

PERSPECTIVES ON THE PAST

The Trojan War: Fact or Fiction?

For a long time, historians believed that the story of Troy and the Trojan War in Homer's poems was fiction rather than fact. What facts have been uncovered in the story? Why might the Greeks have preserved the story in this form?

The *Iliad* and the *Odyssey* spoke of a city called Troy that controlled the trade routes between the Aegean and Black seas and that rivalled Mycenae as a commercial centre. About 1250 BCE, the Mycenaeans banded together under the leadership of the king of Mycenae to attack Troy. According to Homer, the struggle began when Paris, a Trojan prince, kidnapped Helen, the wife of Menelaos, the king of Sparta. The Spartan king and his brother, King Agamemnon of Mycenae, enlisted the help of other Greek rulers to save Helen.

Perhaps the most famous story associated with the Trojan War is that of the Trojan horse. To make the Trojans think that they were giving up the conflict, the Greek warriors burned their tents and sailed away. Behind them on the shore, they left a large wooden horse. Hidden inside were Odysseus and other Greek warriors.

Curious about the horse, the Trojans pulled it into their place of assembly and considered what to do with it. Some wanted to destroy it right there. Others wanted to take it to the top of the rock on which their fortress stood and throw it down the precipice. Still others wanted to leave the wooden horse as an offering for the gods.

When the Trojans decided on this third course of action, and left the horse standing unharmed inside their gates, they sealed their doom. During the night, the Greek warriors concealed within the horse crept out and attacked the unwary Trojans, bringing death and destruction down on the city.

The long and devastasting Trojan War had raged for ten years before the Mycenaeans emerged victorious. In the end, they destroyed Troy and drove the Trojans into exile.

In 1871, Heinrich Schliemann excavated a site that he believed was the legendary city of Troy. He found the ruins of an ancient city, but discovered that nine different cities had been built on the same site over the centuries. Could one of the cities have been Troy in the period of the Trojan war? Later archaeological digs proved that a city on one level had been destroyed in battle around 1240 BCE, but it had been little more than a simple, fortified town. Had the Trojan War really been an epic battle?

---

tions at Mycenae, hoping to discover the legendary city spoken of in the *Iliad*. Schliemann had dreamed about this project most of his life. He wanted to prove that Homer's poems were based on actual places and events.

The Mycenae that he discovered stood atop an easily defended hill or acropolis on the edge of the Plain of Argos. It was more like a fortress than a city. The royal palace took up the greater part of the land inside the walls, while most of the people lived in villages in the surrounding countryside.

According to Homer, each Mycenaean city had its own king, but the king of Mycenae itself, Agamemnon, was the most important. Like all other Mycenaean royal residences, his palace was built around a central hall or *megaron* accessed from a courtyard. A large circular hearth occupied the centre of the hall, and it was surrounded by four pillars to support the roof. A hole in the roof allowed smoke to escape. The domestic quarters were located at the sides, while storage rooms and workshops, behind the great hall, were where almost

all necessities were manufactured. The interior walls were decorated with frescoes, many of which depicted scenes of war or hunting.

Among the most remarkable discoveries that Schliemann made at Mycenae were vertical burial shafts. He found these graves sunk deep into the ground and grouped inside a circular wall at the edge of the fortress. Many had been used as graves more than once. Inside these shaft graves and alongside the bodies lay exquisite objects of gold, silver, ivory, and pottery,

Figure 6-5
The lion gate to the citadel of Mycenae

Figure 6-6
The golden mask of Agamemnon

including a death-mask of finely beaten gold. Although Schliemann thought he had found the mask of Agamemnon himself, archaeologists now believe that this treasure predates the legendary king by about 300 years.

Because of the artistic style of the artifacts from the shaft graves, and the subject matter of the images on them, archaeologists believe that the objects date from the sixteenth century BCE. The artifacts also reveal a strong influence from the earlier Minoan civilization. The Mycenaeans adopted the Minoans' art of wall painting, their vase designs, style of dress, and form of writing (developing the Linear B script from the Minoan Linear A).

After the sixteenth century BCE, the Mycenaeans seem to have abandoned the shaft graves in favour of ingeniously constructed beehive-shaped vaults called *tholos* tombs. These tombs were massive chambers cut into hillsides with walls constructed of fine stone blocks carefully laid in rows, each row narrower than the one below it. Why did the Mycenaeans make this change? Perhaps, with the Mycenaean civilization near its zenith, the Minoan influence declined, or perhaps the ruling household in Mycenae decided on the new burial method. Unfortunately, these tombs were very visible, unlike the shaft graves that were cut into the ground, and grave robbers stole almost all the artifacts inside.

Beginning in the twelfth century BCE, many of the Mycenaean fortresses were destroyed and settlements were abandoned. Several factors may have led to the decline of this civilization: civil wars among the Mycenaean cities, outside invasion, drought and famine, or disease. Whatever the cause, all of the Mycenaean centres, except for Athens, fell. Mycenae itself was destroyed by 1100 BCE.

REFLECT AND ANALYZE

1. Describe the main achievements of the Minoan civilization.

2. What evidence do we have that the Minoan civilization directly influenced Mycenaean culture? What major differences are there between the two cultures?

3. What questions about the Minoan and Mycenaean civilizations remain unanswered? Do you think any of these questions will ever be resolved? Why or why not?

4. Create two frescoes on large sheets of paper—one depicting a scene from Minoan society and the other a scene from Mycenaean society.

THE DARK AGES

Following the collapse of the Mycenaean civilization, Greece entered a bleak period that lasted for 300 years (1100 BCE–800 BCE). Historians have named this period the Dark Ages in Greek history, partly because we know so little about these years. It was a time when new raiding parties arrived from the north, dispersing the Greek-speaking people all around the Aegean Sea.

The new invaders from the northwest, the Dorians, spoke a different dialect of Greek. To escape the Dorians' approach, mainland Greeks took refuge across the Aegean in Asia Minor. Refugees from Thessaly and Boeotia, speaking the Aeolian dialect of Greek, moved across to Lesbos and the adjacent mainland. People of central Greece and the Peloponnese, the former Achaeans, escaped to Ionia, or central Asia Minor, and became known as the Ionians.

The achievements of the Mycenaean civilization in construction, art, monument building, and writing were lost or forgotten. In their trek south, the invaders wiped out farming communities, drastically reducing the food supply. Famine struck, and the Greek population rapidly declined. One of the tougher Dorian tribes dominated most of the southern Peloponnese. From here, in about 900 BCE,

they spread out to settle Rhodes, Crete, and other islands in the Aegean.

THE RISE OF THE CITY-STATE AND THE AGE OF COLONIZATION

Despite the hardships of the Dark Ages, Greeks gradually developed small, secure, and independent communities. These communities formed the basis of the Greek city-state or *polis* (polis means "community of people"). Even at its largest, a polis rarely exceeded 20 000 people and was more like a town than a city. The two major exceptions were Athens, with its surrounding villages in Attica that covered about 2500 km², and Sparta, which came to control two-fifths of the Peloponnese.

By the middle of the eighth century BCE, the population of the Greek world was growing once again, and putting a strain on the available food supply. The Greeks needed to find additional land to grow

more food, and needed to resettle some of the people from the overcrowded city-states. Colonization, therefore, became essential. Various city-states launched a search for *apoikai* or "away homes." Their goal was to create colonies that would become self-sufficient, bound to the parent city only by trade.

The first Greek colony was established in about 750 BCE on the Bay of Naples. During the next century, Greek cities appeared on almost every fertile coastal plain in Sicily and southern Italy, and eventually in parts of northern Africa, Spain, and France. The greatest of the colonies was Syracuse in Sicily, the population of which grew to over 100 000 people by the fifth century BCE.

A second wave of colonization occurred about 650 BCE. During this period, the Greeks founded a chain of cities all around the Black Sea to give them access

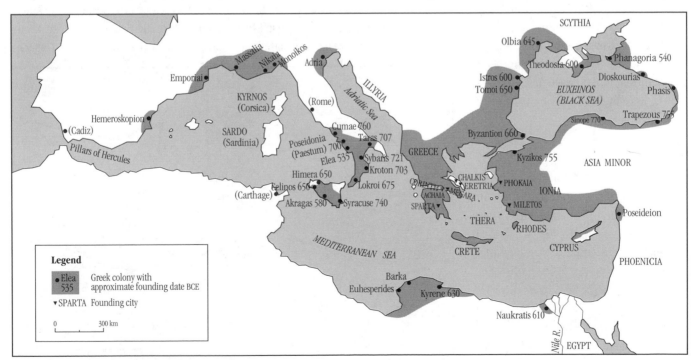

Figure 6-7 *Greek colonization—750 BCE–600 BCE*

to Crimean wheat. Greek galleys, called *triremes*, plied the waters of the Mediterranean as well, in search of timber.

Important developments marked this period of colonization in ancient Greece. Because of the upsurge in trade, metal currency came into common use. A new middle class emerged, made up of the people who made their living through commerce and industry rather than from the land. The Greeks learned how to use iron and, from the Phoenicians, adopted the alphabet that would be passed down to us by way of the Romans. Metics, foreign craftspeople and traders, were welcome in mainland city-states, although they did not enjoy the same rights as the native population. Some city-states began to specialize in particular products. Athens, for example, produced a great deal of pottery. During this period, as well, the first Olympic games were held (776 BCE) and Homer wrote his great literary works (700 BCE). Growth, exploration, trade, the exchange of ideas, the glorification of past heroes and exploits in Homer's poems—all of these factors played a crucial role in the development of Greek society. Ancient Greece was on the verge of its greatest period.

THE PERSIAN WARS

At the beginning of the fifth century BCE, the growing city-states faced a serious threat—invasion by the powerful eastern empire of Persia. Persia, the largest of all the near-eastern empires, stretched from Afghanistan in the east to the shores of the Mediterranean in the west. It was ruled by a powerful general, Cyrus the Great. In comparison, the Greek city-states were small, scattered units, weakened by fighting one another and ill-prepared to defend

themselves. Would they fall easy prey to a powerful and unified empire?

In 546 BCE, Cyrus, King of Persia, defeated Croesus of Lydia at Sardis, making the Persians masters of the Greeks living in Asia Minor. Rule by the Persians was not entirely unjust, but a basic Greek love of independence sparked a strong desire for freedom from foreign domination. In 499 BCE, therefore, the city-state of Miletus led the other Ionian city-states in a revolt. Although the Ionians gained the support of Athens, the Persians sacked Miletus and crushed the rebellion five years later. The Persians, however, did not forget the affront to their power.

Marathon

In 490 BCE, the Persians advanced across the Aegean as far as the Plains of Marathon, about 40 km northeast of Athens. The new Persian king, Darius, was determined to punish the Athenians for their role in the Ionian revolt and to expand his burgeoning empire. The battle of Marathon

was one of the most famous in the Persian Wars. Miltiades, the Athenian general, decided to march his army out to Marathon and set up camp at the southern end. He hoped to delay the battle until Sparta could send reinforcements.

Miltiades dispatched a professional runner, Pheidippides, to Sparta to seek help. Pheidippides ran the distance of 250 km in two days, then ran back to Marathon with the Spartans' response. He told the Athenians that the Spartans were anxious to help but, for religious reasons, could not come until after the next full moon. According to legend, Pheidippides collapsed and died after gasping out his message. His amazing feat made marathon running a popular sporting event.

The Persians heavily outnumbered the Athenians at Marathon, and the Greeks had neither cavalry nor archers. Nevertheless, the Athenians chose to attack. It was a risky decision, because defeat would leave Athens unprotected. Their plan was to take advantage of one of the Persians' key strategies.

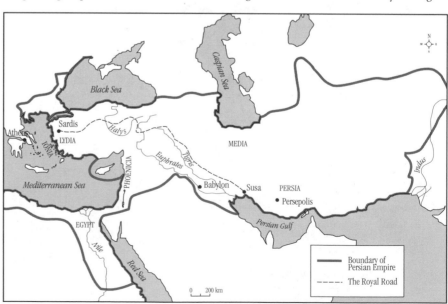

Figure 6-8 *The Persian empire at the beginning of the fifth century* BCE

Since the Persians placed their best troops in the centre of their formation, the Athenians would counter by strengthening the wings of their force.

The battle was long. As expected, the Persians broke through the weakened Athenian centre, but the Greeks defeated them on the wings. The Athenian troops then closed in on the Persian soldiers in the centre, trapping those who had broken through and driving them back to their ships.

The Persians who escaped sailed south, hoping to find Athens unprotected. But the Athenian army rushed back to the city from Marathon and reached it by evening, in time to force the Persians to abandon their plan and sail back to Asia. Today, visitors can still see the funeral mound for the 192 Athenian dead on the battleground at Marathon. Thousands of Persian soldiers perished in the battle. The Athenians saw their victory as a glorious event. A stone in the central marketplace of Athens reads: "The valour of these men will shine as a light imperishable forever."

Thermopylae

Realizing that the Persians would probably return, the Athenians, under Themistocles, took defensive precautions. Most importantly, they developed a strong navy, with a fleet of 200 ships. In 481 BCE, all Greek states that were prepared to resist the Persians held a congress at the Isthmus of Corinth. Sparta and Athens decided to share the leadership role. Although many states either turned down the invitation, or indicated that they did not intend to fight the Persians, the congress was still significant. It represented the first attempt the Greek states ever made to form a national league.

The concern of the Athenian leaders was well-founded. Xerxes, the son and successor of Darius, was determined to continue the assault against the Greek mainland. In May of 480 BCE, Xerxes set out from Sardis. His army, estimated at more than 180 000, was so large that the troops took weeks to cross the Hellespont. His fleet, supplied and manned mainly by subject peoples, consisted of over 1200 ships.

The Greeks chose a defensive position at Thermopylae, a narrow pass through which the Persians had to pass. The Greeks had about 7000 troops, mainly Peloponnesians, commanded by the Spartan king Leonidas, who had brought with him 300 of the finest Spartan soldiers. The Greeks hoped to hold the Persians at Thermopylae while attacking the Persian fleet north of the island of Euboea. After three days, however, the exhausted Greek fleet turned south and things began to go wrong on the mainland.

A Greek traitor led the Persian forces along a mountain path to the far end of the pass at Thermopylae. Seeing that his forces were being trapped, Leonidas ordered most of the army to leave. He and his Spartan contingent held the pass as long as possible, fighting valiantly, but all were killed. Not one Greek soldier survived the battle.

Salamis

The defeat at Thermopylae left Athens vulnerable. The city had to be evacuated, and most of the people escaped to Salamis, a large island off the coast of Athens. When the Persians burned the defences of Athens, Themistocles put all able-bodied men on ships and assembled the Greek fleet in the straits of Salamis. He was convinced that their best chance to defeat the Persians lay

in fighting the invaders in those narrow waters, which the Athenians knew so much better than the Persians did.

Themistocles dispatched a messenger to Xerxes with false information. The messenger told the Persian king that the Greek fleet was about to sail away. Furthermore, if Xerxes attacked the following day, the message continued, the Athenians would undoubtedly come over to the Persian side because they were disgusted with the cowardice displayed by the other Greek states.

Taken in by the message and eager for victory, Xerxes moved his fleet forward into the narrow gulf, leaving some ships to block both ends of the strait. Although outnumbered in the battle, the Greeks swiftly attacked the advancing Persian boats. There was mass confusion as the ships fought in the narrow confines of the strait, but while the Persians lost 200 ships, the Greeks lost only 40. According to legend, Xerxes was so confident his ships would win that he sat watching the battle on a throne placed on a hill overlooking the strait. The Persian army watched from the shore. Instead of a victory, they witnessed a crushing defeat.

The Persian Wars End

Following the Persian defeat at Salamis, Xerxes ordered the remnants of the fleet to withdraw to the Hellespont while he returned home. He left the army in Thessaly. The Persians fought their final battle with the Greeks in Boeotia near the small town of Plataea. Faced with poorly disciplined allied troops, the Spartan leader, Pausanias, had to retreat. But as the Persians pursued the Greeks, a single Spartan unit valiantly held off their attack and turned

THROUGH THEIR EYES

The Battle of Salamis

Here are two different Greek accounts of what took place at the Battle of Salamis. How do the two accounts differ? Are you more inclined to believe one than the other? If so, which one and why?

Figure 6-9 *The battle of Salamis*

Herodotus

The historian Herodotus was born about 484 BCE and came to live in Athens about 450 BCE. His *Histories* represent the first attempt to record history. Aged four at the time of the battle, he grew up hearing about the famous event. He based his account on the memories of Athenians living a generation after.

The Persians believed Themistocles and proceeded to put ashore on the islet of Psyttaleia. Then, about midnight, they moved their western wing in an encircling movement upon Salamis, while at the same time they also blocked the whole channel as far as Munychia.

These tactical moves were carried out in silence to prevent the enemy from being aware of what was going on; they occupied the whole night, so that none of the men had time for sleep.

The whole fleet now got under way, and in a moment the Persians were on them. The Greeks checked their way and began to go back astern and they were on the point of running aground when an Athenian ship drove ahead and rammed an enemy vessel. Seeing the two ships locked together, the rest of the Greek fleet hurried to the Athenian's assistance and the general action began. . . .

There is also a popular belief that a phantom shape of a woman appeared and, in a voice which could be heard by every man in the fleet, contemptuously cried out: "Fools, how much further do you propose to go astern?"

Aeschylus

The playwright Aeschylus was born in 525 BCE and lived most of his life in Athens. He fought both at Marathon and at Salamis. In his play *The Persians*, a Persian messenger tells the Queen of Persia of the Persian defeat.

When at last the sun's bright chariot rose, then we could hear them—singing; loud and strong rang back the echo from the island rocks, and with the sound came the first chill of fear. . . . Then trumpets over there set all on fire; then the sea foamed as the oars struck all together, and swiftly, there they were! The right wing first led on the ordered line, then all the rest came on, came out, and now was to be heard a mighty shouting: "On sons of the Greeks! Set free your country, set your children free, your wives, the temples of your country's gods, your fathers' tombs; now they are all at stake." And from our side the Persian battle-cry roared back the answer; and the time was come. Then ship on ship rammed with her beak of bronze; but first a Greek struck home; full on the quarter she struck and shattered a Phoenician's planks; then all along the line the fight was joined.... those Greek ships, skilfully handled, kept the outer station ringing us round and striking in, till ships turned turtle, and you could not see the water for blood and wreckage; and the dead were strewn thickly on all the beaches, all the reefs; and every ship in all the fleet of Asia in grim confusion fought to get away.

the tables. The last action of the war came in Ionia at Cape Mycale, where the Greeks destroyed what remained of the enemy's fleet. Against all odds, they had driven the mighty Persians out of Greece, and the city-states were free. However, Persia remained a force to be reckoned with for many years to come.

REFLECT AND ANALYZE

1. a) Why is the period after the fall of the Mycenaean civilization called the Dark Ages of ancient Greece?

    b) What major developments occurred between 800 BCE and 550 BCE, just before the Persian Wars?

2. Account for the outbreak of the Persian Wars. What were the major causes?

3. Using sketch diagrams, illustrate the strategies used by the Greeks and Persians in each of the following battles. Explain the victor's success in each case.
    a) Marathon
    b) Thermopylae
    c) Salamis Bay

4. What effects do you think victory in the Persian Wars would have on the development of ancient Greece? Support your answer.

5. During the Dark Ages and the early period of colonization, wandering minstrels played an important role in preserving the past and spreading news of current events. Compose a short minstrel's song from this period. It could tell of a sailor's adventure or of the Dorian invaders, for example.

CLASSICAL GREECE

The end of the Persian Wars marked the liberation of the Ionian city-states and the dawn of the greatest age in ancient Greek history. The single century from approximately 480 BCE to 380 BCE saw a phenomenal rush of achievements in the ancient Greek states. Many of these remarkable developments, although not all, stemmed from Athens. This golden age—often referred to as Classical Greece—developed partly because of contacts with the Egyptians and Persians that inspired a blossoming in the arts and sciences. Returning from the east, Greek travellers and merchants told of great temples, colourful wall paintings, and huge stone statues on the Nile. They brought back techniques for fine metal work, glass-making, and other crafts, and awakened in the Greeks a new curiosity about the world around them. This was a time of great thinkers, poets, and artists, so impressive in their accomplishments that some call this century "the age of the Greek miracle."

During the golden age of Classical Greece, Athens became a prosperous commercial city and great cultural centre. It was the principal polis of Attica, the greatest of the Ionian Greek cities, and had the most democratic government of all the city-states. Its leadership of the other Greek states grew with the control it wielded over the Delian League. The league was formed in 478 BCE to provide protection against any further attacks from the Persians, and encompassed 150 city-states at its peak. Members had to contribute men plus either ships or money to a common defence fund. Most city-states chose to contribute money, and Athens used the capital to build ships. According to the rules of the league, a member could not withdraw without the consent of all. When Naxos and Thasos tried to break away, they were crushed by Athens and forced to pay a heavy tribute.

The other great city-state—and the rival of Athens—was Sparta. Sparta was the principal polis of Laconia in the Peloponnese and the greatest of the Dorian city-states. It developed very differently from Athens. Although it was the only unwalled city in Greece, Sparta was the first polis to keep a standing army of professional soldiers, and became a highly militaristic state. Unlike democratic Athens, Sparta was ruled by a small group of powerful aristocrats.

Sparta had taken almost no part in the colonization movement between 800 BCE and 550 BCE. It had remained an agricultural state, leaving commercial ventures to other cities. Instead, Sparta had chosen to expand its power and holdings in the Peloponnese. In the seventh century BCE, after two long wars, it had conquered the Messenians in the west. By the middle of the sixth century BCE, Sparta dominated most of the Peloponnese.

Tensions between the two rival city-states increased when Athens tried to expand its empire in central Greece, threatening Sparta's power base. Athens also blocked some cities from trading at Athenian-controlled ports. States within the Delian League that opposed this oppression, and that resented Athenian interference in their affairs, sought an alternative. To solve their problems, they asked Sparta for help. The result was the outbreak of the great Peloponnesian War in 431 BCE. The 27-year struggle was costly and bitter.

THE PELOPONNESIAN WAR

At the outset of the war, Athens had a powerful navy and enough wealth in its coffers to mount a strong attack. Sparta, on the other hand, had a formidable land army of disciplined professional soldiers. The Athenians quickly dispatched their fleet to blockade the towns in the Peloponnese, while the Spartans marched their army into Attica, burning farms and villages.

The Athenian leader, Pericles, devised a strategy to defend Athens. He used his forces to guard the long walls that surrounded the city and that stretched as far as the port of Piraeus. He ordered all of the Attican people inside the walls for protection. According to his plan, the powerful Athenian navy would maintain the food supply through the protected port of Piraeus.

But the strategy had a fatal flaw, one that Pericles perhaps could not have foreseen. Too many people lived in confined quarters, often in badly ventilated huts, and hygiene deteriorated. A terrible plague struck the city in 430 BCE, killing one-third of the population, including the general

THROUGH THEIR EYES

Pericles' Funeral Oration

Thucydides, the fifth-century BCE Athenian historian, wrote an account of the Peloponnesian War in which he recalls a speech given by Pericles at the state funeral held in 430 BCE for the Athenian soldiers killed in the first year of the war.

What is Pericles trying to achieve with this speech? What does Pericles value in Athens and seem to find lacking in Sparta? How effectively do you think the speech achieves the Athenian leader's goals?

Figure 6-10
Pericles addressing the Athenians

Our constitution is named a democracy, because it is in the hands not of the few but of the many. But our laws secure equal justice for all in their private disputes, and our public opinion welcomes and honours talent in every branch of achievement, not for any sectional reason but on grounds of excellence alone. And as we give free play to all in our public life, so we carry the same spirit into our daily relations with one another....

Yet ours is no work-a-day city alone. No other provides so many recreations for the spirit—contests and sacrifices all the year round, and beauty in our public buildings to cheer the heart and delight the eye day by day. Moreover, the city is so large and powerful that all the wealth of the world flows in to her, so that our own Attic products seem no more homelike to us than the fruits of the labours of other nations.

Our military training too is different from our opponents'. The gates of our city are flung open to the world. We practice no periodical deportations, nor do we prevent our visitors from observing or discovering what an enemy might usefully apply to his own purposes. For our trust is not in the devices of material equipment, but in our own good spirits for battle.

So too with education. They [Sparta] toil from early

boyhood in a laborious pursuit after courage, while we, free to live and wander as we please, march out none the less to face the self-same dangers.... Indeed, if we choose to face danger with an easy mind rather than after a rigorous training, and to trust rather in native manliness than in state-made courage, the advantage lies with us; for we are spared all the weariness of practicing for future hardships, and when we find ourselves amongst them we are as brave as our plodding rivals. Here as elsewhere, then, the city sets an example, which is deserving of admiration.

We are lovers of beauty without extravagance, and lovers of wisdom without unmanliness. Wealth to us is not mere material for vainglory but an opportunity for achievement; and poverty we think is no disgrace to acknowledge but a real degradation to make no effort to overcome. Our citizens attend to both public and private duties, and do not allow absorption in their own various affairs to interfere with their knowledge of the city's. We differ from other states in regarding the man who holds aloof from public life not as "quiet" but as useless; we decide or debate, carefully and in person, all matters of policy, holding, not that words and deeds go ill together, but that acts are foredoomed to failure when undertaken undiscussed. For we are noted for being at once most adventurous in action and most reflective beforehand. Other men are bold in ignorance, while reflection will stop their onset. But

the bravest are surely those who have the clearest vision of what is before them, glory and danger alike, and yet notwithstanding go out to meet it. ...

In a word I claim that our city as a whole is an education to Greece, and that her members yield to none, man by man, for independence of spirit, many-sidedness of attainment, and complete self-reliance in limbs and brain.

This is no vainglorious phrase but actual fact, as the supremacy which our manners have won us bears testimony. No other city of the present day goes out to her ordeal greater than ever men dreamed; no other is so powerful that the invader feels no bitterness when he suffers at her hands, and her subjects no shame at the indignity of their dependence. Great indeed are the symbols and witnesses of our supremacy, at which posterity, as all mankind today, will be astonished. We need no Homer or other man of words to praise us; for such give pleasure for a moment, but the truth will put to shame their imaginings of our deeds. For our pioneers have forced a way into every sea and every land, establishing among all mankind, in punishment or beneficence, eternal memorials of their settlement.

Such then is the city, for whom, lest they should lose her, the men whom we celebrate died a soldier's death: and it is but natural that all of us who survive them should wish to spend ourselves in her service.

himself. Athens had been dealt a severe blow.

The war dragged on in a seesaw struggle with victories gained by one side and then the other. In 421 BCE, the two city-states agreed to a truce, but it was short-lived. Finally, Athens decided to strike a decisive blow. The Athenians attacked and captured the island of Melos, which wanted only to stay out of the struggle. All men of military age on the island were put to death and women and children were sold into slavery. The following year, the Athenian

forces set out to invade Syracuse on the island of Sicily. Their choice was deliberate. Not only was Syracuse closely allied with Corinth, a commercial enemy of Athens, but the city's defeat would also allow Athens to conquer the entire island of Sicily more easily.

The leader of the expedition to Syracuse was the Athenian general Alcibiades. The fleet assembled in 415 BCE for this invasion was one of the finest and most expensive ever mounted by a Greek city-state. Many Athenians had mixed feelings

about the huge cost in money and people, however. When the fleet failed again and again to penetrate the walls of Syracuse, there were grumblings at home, particularly from those who had questioned the wisdom of the attack. Other misfortunes plagued the expedition. Alcibiades was charged for a prank at a drinking party and fled to Sparta. When he finally returned, he lost a naval battle and was exiled again.

Eventually, the Athenian fleet was defeated in Syracuse harbour and the army was surrounded and forced to surrender.

The war lasted another ten years, but Athens could not recover.

The Spartans, who had formed an alliance with the Sicilians, next allied themselves with the Persians and grew even stronger on land and particularly on sea. When a combined Spartan and Persian fleet defeated the Athenian fleet at Aegospotami in 405 BCE, the power of Athens crumbled.

The following year, the Spartan fleet blockaded Athens, preventing the essential grain supply from reaching the city. Near starvation brought an end to the fighting. Sparta's allies wanted to destroy Athens and sell its citizens into slavery, but Sparta blocked the move. Instead, Athens was forced to surrender its empire and all of its fleet, except for 12 war galleys. The Spartans also tore down the city's long walls, but left Athens intact and free, partly in recognition of its service to the Greek states during the Persian Wars.

During the first half of the following century, various Greek city-states struggled incessantly for power. First Sparta prevailed as the chief polis of Greece. Then, for a time, Thebes was the strongest centre. But the most serious threat to the city-states was on the northern frontier in Macedonia.

dent Greek city-states, and made them part of the Macedonian realm. This conquest was only the first of Philip's ambitious imperial plans. He was also determined to conquer the whole Persian empire.

Philip's military strength rested on two factors—his ingenious use of the phalanx formation as the main unit in his military machine, and the strong support of a well-trained cavalry. In the phalanx formation, densely packed lines of foot soldiers armed with long lances created a formidable obstacle, even to armed cavalry.

But Philip II did not have the opportunity to fulfil his ambitions. In 336 BCE, he was assassinated by a member of his own bodyguard during his daughter's wedding celebration, and his 20-year-old son Alexander (356 BCE–323 BCE) was proclaimed king. Alexander had already proven his military prowess as leader of the cavalry in the great victory over the Greek city-states at Chaeronea.

Once in power, Alexander immediately set about consolidating his position. He had possible rivals murdered, and launched swift campaigns against Greek states to demonstrate his military strength. He ruthlessly put down an attempted revolt by Thebes, and used the city as an example to discourage other possible rebels. Under Alexander's orders, all of Thebes was destroyed, except for the temples, 6000 Thebans were executed, and the rest of the citizens were sold into slavery.

Alexander then set out to complete his father's original plans for expanding the empire. In 334 BCE, he crossed the Dardanelles with 50 000 men and began an 11-year campaign of conquest that took his armies into Egypt, Persia, Mesopotamia,

REFLECT AND ANALYZE

1. Why is the period 480 BCE to 380 BCE called the golden age of Classical Greece?

2. Outline the major reasons for the rivalry between Athens and Sparta that led to the Peloponnesian War.

3. At the beginning of the Peloponnesian War, Athens seemed certain of victory.
   a) What factors contributed to its defeat?
   b) Why might we say that all Greeks were losers in the Peloponnesian War?

4. Assume the role of a Spartan leader and compose a short speech in response to Pericles' funeral oration. Try to use some of the same persuasive techniques.

ALEXANDER THE GREAT AND THE HELLENISTIC AGE

The Macedonians lived in the north of the Greek peninsula, and spoke a dialect of Greek. Mostly farmers and shepherds, they had not achieved the same cultural glory as the Greeks to the south. In the fourth century BCE, however, several kings united the Macedonian people and transformed the state into a great military power. The most brilliant and ambitious king was Philip II (359 BCE–336 BCE). The discovery of rich gold deposits had provided the wealth Philip needed to assemble one of the greatest fighting forces the world had ever seen.

At the battle of Chaeronea near Thebes in 338 BCE, Philip II crushed the indepen-

and as far east as the Indus River in India.

In the first year of this campaign, Alexander won his first victory in Persia, and after several battles succeeded in conquering the mighty Persian empire. In 327 BCE, he continued eastwards and took a Greek army of 30 000 through the Khyber Pass into India. The following year, at the river Hydaspes, his troops confronted an even larger Indian force that included a company of 200 elephants. The elephants virtually immobilized Alexander's cavalry because the horses were terrified by the strange, huge animals.

The battle at Hydaspes dragged on for nearly eight hours. Alexander's forces worked to lure the flanks of the Indian cavalry away from the elephants, so that the Greeks could attack each separately. They also tried to use their phalanx formation to crush the Indian infantry and to attack the elephant drivers, in the hope that the beasts would then take flight. Both sides lost many men, but the victory finally went to Alexander.

Even though Alexander wanted to push even farther into the east, he turned back. His exhausted men were ready to mutiny, and his generals convinced him that it was time to return home. The Greek forces turned southwards down the Indus, along the northern coast of the Persian Gulf, and finally marched into Babylon. But the long campaign took its toll on Alexander. In 323 BCE, he died at the age of 33, perhaps of typhoid or malaria.

The period that begins with Alexander's conquests and ends around 27 BCE is called the ***Hellenistic Age***. Hellenistic civilization was a blend of eastern and western influences. Alexander welcomed both Greeks and Persians into his armies,

Figure 6-11 *The Macedonian Phalanx.*
The phalanx contained 16 rows of heavily armed foot soldiers, each equipped with a 4.5 m long lance. During battle, lances were extended forward from the front ranks. Those in the back ranks were held upright to deflect opposition missiles. Each soldier's shield guarded his own left side and the right side of the man beside him.

so the different cultures learned from one another and became more cosmopolitan in their outlook. Young conquered nobles were enlisted in the cavalry.

Alexander's huge empire, stretching from Greece to India, provided a broad base for the spread of Greek culture. Greek and Macedonian citizens settled in the new cities that were founded all along the route of Alexander's conquest. Greek scholars, artists, craftspeople, and soldiers eagerly ventured into the new territories, sparking a rich cultural exchange. Alexander intended to make Greek culture and language a unifying force in the empire, but he also respected the customs and laws of the people he had conquered. Wisely, he won the allegiance of former Persian officials by maintaining them to administer over the conquered lands.

Among the great accomplishments of the Hellenistic Age, several in the field of science and philosophy stand out. Euclid, for example, systematized geometry, Archimedes advanced theoretical physics, and Aristarchus formulated the view that

the earth moved around the sun—a view that his contemporaries did not accept. The ethical philosophy of stoicism was also developed in the Hellenistic Age. According to this philosophy, humans should be virtuous despite the pain or consequences, and people should always obey the laws of nature or Divine Reason, which ruled the universe and all people.

When Alexander died in 323 BCE, there was no heir apparent. For 40 years, his generals fought over the spoils of the empire. Finally, a pattern of large states emerged, each ruled by a king descended

Figure 6-12 *Alexander The Great*

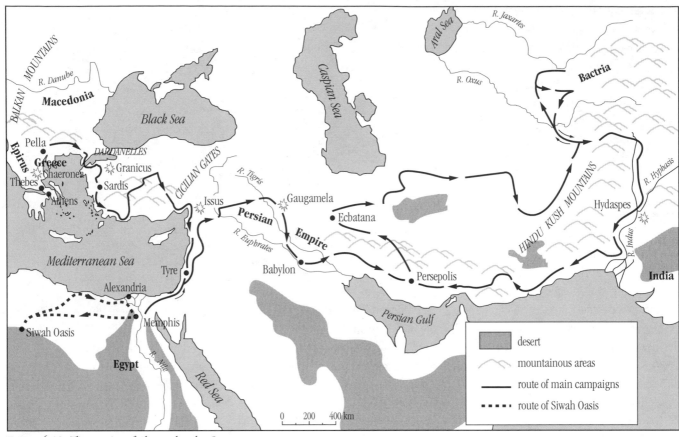

Figure 6-13 *The empire of Alexander the Great*

from one of Alexander's men. (One example was the Ptolemaic kingdom of Egypt.) On the Greek mainland, turmoil again marked the lives of the citizens. Peace was not restored until Rome conquered Greece in 27 BCE.

REFLECT AND ANALYZE

1. What advantages allowed Philip II to conquer the Greek city-states?

2. What are the most significant accomplishments associated with the Hellenistic Age?

3. Alexander of Macedon is often referred to as Alexander the Great. Does he deserve that title? Explain your answer.

4. People in the ancient world came to regard Alexander as a legendary figure, larger than life. One story tells of how Alexander solved the riddle of the Gordian knot. Investigate and report on this story.

GOVERNMENT

Although we often associate Greece with the first great democracy, this political system did not come about immediately.

EARLY FORMS OF GOVERNMENT

The development of ancient Greek government began in the Dark Ages with the emergence of the polis or city-state. Each Greek polis developed its own independent form of government and protected its individuality fiercely. The citizens of the polis generally included all adult males who were born in the state and who joined the army during wartime. Women and children, foreigners, and slaves had no share in political power. During this period, there was no nation state as we understand the term today. Across Greece, the only unifying forces were religion, language, and the Olympic Games.

Most early city-states were ruled by a monarch or a government headed by a king. In some city-states, the monarchy was hereditary. In others, such as Athens, the king was elected by a council of elders who assisted in the daily operation of the government. Although the people considered their king as chief priest, judge, and general, they never viewed him as a god. The rulers were regarded as one of the small community of people.

As city-states developed during the periods of colonization, kings gradually lost their power to the land-holding aristocrats. Many of the aristocrats profited from the growth in trade and, with their new economic power, they seized control of the city-state governments.

When the king of Athens lost much of his power, the position of **archon** was created. An archon was a land-holding aristocrat initially appointed to office for life. His responsibility was to supervise government administration. Later the number of archons was increased from one to three, and in about 682 BCE, it became the practice for a citizen assembly of landowners to elect the archons for a term of one year only.

THE AGE OF TYRANTS

Colonization and the expansion of trade also led to the rise of a middle class of wealthy merchants and artisans in many of the Greek city-states. While the new middle class wanted to expand trade routes, the aristocrats wanted instead to expand agricultural holdings. The feud between the two classes escalated as the merchants demanded greater influence in government. Since the lower classes also suffered from oppression by the aristocrats and had no political rights, they backed the merchants and artisans.

With money from trade, the new middle-class citizens could buy land and—more importantly—arms and armour. Before this time, only the wealthy aristocrats could afford weapons, and they therefore held the balance of military power. As the middle class bought arms, a new type of Greek warrior called the hoplite emerged. The hoplite was a foot soldier equipped with bronze body-armour, shield, helmet, and spear. With the hoplites as a power base, **tyrants** who championed the cause of the middle class were able to seize power.

Anyone who seized power unconstitutionally was called a tyrant. Although tyrants were common between 650 BCE and 550 BCE, before the Persian Wars, not every ruler was a tyrant. Many acquired their position of authority through legitimate means.

When tyrants seized power, they often managed to keep it in their family for two or three generations. Most tyrants were good administrators who encouraged naval development, promoted trade, and carried out public works projects. Because they seized power by force and because a few did govern harshly, however, the word "tyrant" is more commonly associated with its present meaning of cruel and unjust ruler.

THE RISE OF DEMOCRACY IN ATHENS

In some Greek city-states, reformers and tyrants played a key role in the transition

Figure 6-14 *A Greek hoplite*

from an aristocratic form of government to a democracy. In Athens, four men helped to bring about this transition: Draco, Solon, Pisistratus, and Cleisthenes.

When Draco was elected first archon for the year 621 BCE, Athens was deeply divided by class. Power was in the hands of the aristocrats, who owned the land. Commoners had no political rights, and Athens had no written code of laws to protect them from arbitrary and unjust rulings by their officials and judges. Draco's main contribution was to codify Athenian laws so that they would apply to all citizens. Although his code still favoured the interests of wealthy merchants and aristocrats over the farmers and the poor, it offered the common people more protection and pointed the way to universal legal rights.

Solon, an Athenian of noble birth who had gained wealth and prestige as a merchant, was first elected archon in 594 BCE. In Solon's time, farmers who had borrowed

Figure 6-15
A statue of Solon carved in 1898

seed from wealthier landowners when crops were poor were often sold into slavery if they could not repay the debt. Concerned for their plight, Solon cancelled the crippling debts and freed the farmers who had been forced into slavery.

Solon also changed the criteria for holding political office. All wealthy men, aristocrats or not, were now eligible for public office. Birth into an aristocratic family was no longer an essential requirement. This measure gave the landless a voice in the citizen assembly. Solon's other democratic reforms included increasing the number of archons from three to nine. The six additional archons, the *thesmothetai*, were given responsibility for enforcing Athenian law. In addition, Solon set up the Council of Four Hundred, which drafted legislation for the citizen assembly to vote

on. The council was composed of 100 citizens from each of the four traditional tribes of Athens.

After Solon left office, Athens was in turmoil. The aristocrats felt that he had gone too far. The farmers, on the other hand, felt that he had not gone far enough. Into this void stepped Pisistratus, a tyrant who seized power in 546 BCE with the backing of a mercenary army and the support of most of the nobility.

During his rule from 546 BCE to 527 BCE, Pisistratus instituted many significant political reforms. He drove many of the wealthy landowners out of the Attican peninsula and divided their lands up among the landless. He established a system of state loans for small farmers and encouraged the large-scale expansion of commerce. In the area of law, he created 30 circuit judges who superseded the authority of local aristocracies.

After the death of Pisistratus, his sons Hipparchus and Hippias ruled Athens with brutal force. Their harsh, unpopular policies led to the murder of Hipparchus in 514

BCE and the exile of Hippias in 510 BCE. After a successful coup d'état in 508 BCE, an ambitious noble named Cleisthenes consolidated his power and dominated Athenian politics for six years.

Cleisthenes made significant changes in the organization of the assembly. Originally, Athenians had been divided into four tribes based on clan ties and their location in Attica. Cleisthenes replaced this ancient system with a new arrangement based on ten tribes, each tribe including precincts or *demes* from different areas of Attica. This new division, which ensured that each tribe contained a cross-section of Athenian society, allowed for fairer representation of all classes of people within the assembly. Cleisthenes also gave all citizens membership in the assembly, regardless of whether or not they owned land. The assembly passed laws, served as a supreme court, and elected ten generals to run the armed forces.

In addition, Cleisthenes continued to reduce the influence of the powerful old noble families by changing the Council of

Figure 6-16 *Ostraka from Athens*

Four Hundred. He increased the size to 500 members, and ensured that 50 members from each tribe were chosen randomly each year by lot. The Council of Five Hundred proposed and administered laws, organized religious festivals, and controlled state finances, public works, shipping, and foreign affairs. The council also conducted routine business for the city when the assembly was not sitting.

Finally, Cleisthenes instituted measures to safeguard the citizens against the rise of tyrants or any people who sought to abuse their power. The conduct and expenditures of all officials, even the generals, were held accountable to the assembly. The practice of **ostracism** was also introduced. The assembly could vote into exile any men considered a threat to the city-state's democracy. If at least 6000 people scratched the names of the citizen they most distrusted on a shard of pottery or *ostraka,* then the citizen with the most votes cast against him had to leave Attica within ten days and remain in exile for ten years.

ATHENIAN DEMOCRACY ACHIEVED

By the golden age of Classical Greece in the fifth century BCE, a system of democracy, called **direct democracy**, had been established in Athens. Every adult male over the age of 18 could speak and propose resolutions in the assembly, vote directly on every piece of legislation, and stand for public office. The assembly was the most important government institution. It elected a number of executive officers, and met three or four times each month to debate and decide matters of domestic and foreign policy.

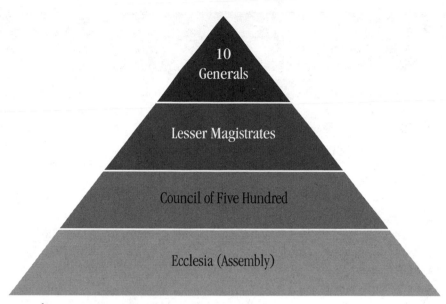

Figure 6-17 *Government in Athens*

The members of the Council of Five Hundred had to be over 30 years of age. As citizens could serve on the council only once in their lifetime, almost all citizens had the opportunity to take part. The council was organized into ten governing committees, of 50 members each, that rotated in office. This gave all of the committees an opportunity to govern, since each committee ruled for one-tenth of the year.

Originally, the Council of Five Hundred appointed the ten generals, or *strategos,* but eventually they were elected by the assembly and could be re-elected year after year. The generals replaced the nine archons, and were responsible for promoting domestic policy in Athens and directing military operations. In emergencies, the office of supreme commander rotated daily among the ten.

Pericles (in power 495 BCE–429 BCE), the famous general of the Peloponnesian wars, was a powerful figure in Athens for 30 years. Because he was elected one of the ten generals for 15 consecutive years, he had more influence than the other *strategos.*

Pericles was a major architect of the Athenian empire. In 454 BCE, he moved the treasury of the Delian Confederacy from Delos to Athens to increase Athenian naval development and expand foreign trade throughout the Mediterranean. He invited skilled foreigners to settle in Athens, adding to the wealth of the city. As a patron of the arts, he encouraged the development of art, literature, and philosophy.

Part of Pericles' success stemmed from his ability to win favour with large sectors of Athenian society. He gained the support of the poor by instituting a system of pay for military service so that they could afford to leave their farms or occupations and serve the state. He also increased his popularity by speaking out with great pride on the value of Athenian citizenship and by restricting the vote to those whose mother and father had both been born in Athens.

INNOVATIONS
Athenian Direct Democracy

The following scenario represents a typical meeting of the Athenian assembly.

Was the Athenian system of government truly democratic? Was it an efficient system of decision-making? How does it compare to the system of democracy used in Canada?

Shortly after dawn, the citizens of Athens gathered at the Pnyx, an open-air theatre on the sloping hillside. They were about to participate in a meeting of the Ecclesia or assembly, the most important government institution of their city. The crowd consisted entirely of adult males over the age of 18. Women, foreigners, and slaves were not allowed to join the gathering and had no vote. Although farmers from outlying areas sometimes found attending difficult, all citizens from the city itself were expected to be present and could be fined for shirking their duty.

The required quorum of 6000 was in attendance this morning. A herald called for silence and a priest offered prayers to open the meeting. The herald then asked if any citizen wished to speak. Cleon, an Athenian tradesperson, asked to be heard and was granted permission. Cleon stood on a raised rock platform and expressed to the assembly his concern over the state of the road leading into the city from the north. More taxes should be spent on repairing transport routes and less on supporting public games, he declared.

Some members of the assembly applauded; others booed or hissed. Cleon put forth a motion in support of his position, and a vote was taken by a show of hands. Clearly, those who supported the games outnumbered Cleon and his allies. There was no need for a more accurate or detailed count.

The assembly then turned to discuss a motion presented by the Council of Five Hundred. This was not unusual since it was the right of the council to prepare motions for the assembly. The council also conducted routine business for the city when the assembly was not sitting. At this meeting, the council called for funds to build a new athletic playing field. Since those in favour of the public games seemed to be carrying the day, the motion was greeted with enthusiasm. Several speakers spoke in support and only two in opposition before the motion was put to a successful vote.

Besides the generals, other officials played significant roles in the government of Athens. Treasurers were responsible for the administration of tribute coming in from the empire. Market controllers, grain wardens, and controllers of measures helped to manage domestic and foreign trade. Public servants, jurors, members of the council, military employees, and all magistrates received a small daily payment for their service to the state. This salary was an important innovation because it meant that even the poorest citizens could take some time away from their own work to serve in government. Only the generals and the treasurers did not receive a salary.

GOVERNMENT IN SPARTA

The Spartans' desire to develop a strong military state dominated all their other concerns. The only people who could be Spartan citizens were adult males whose parents were from citizen families. At any one time, therefore, Sparta never had more than 10 000 official citizens. The majority of people living in this city-state were helots—people who had been conquered by the Spartans and were forced to work as slaves. They had no political rights. Perhaps because the Spartans constantly feared a helot revolt, they valued order over liberty in the structure of their government.

The government, composed of four separate political elements, tried to strike a balance among monarchy, oligarchy, and democracy. When we examine the system closely, however, we can see that an *oligarchy*—government controlled by a very few—prevailed. There were two hereditary kings, one in charge of the military and the other in charge of government. A Council of Elders called the Gerousia advised the kings.

THROUGH THEIR EYES

Viewpoints on Government—Plato and Aristotle

Two of the great philosophers of ancient Greece, Plato (427 BCE–347 BCE) and Aristotle (384 BCE–323 BCE), expressed opinions about government and governing in their writings. Plato, in his book *The Republic,* outlines his plan for an ideal state. Aristotle, in *The Politics,* presents his opinions on the purpose of government and the most desirable kind of society.

According to Plato, who should rule the state? How does Aristotle feel about Plato's viewpoint? Which of these two philosophical viewpoints is closer to your own? Explain.

Suppose the following to be the state of affairs on board a ship.... The captain is larger and stronger than any of the crew, but a bit deaf and short-sighted, and doesn't know much about navigation. The crew are all quarrelling with each other about how to navigate this ship, each thinking he ought to be at the helm; they know no navigation and cannot say that anyone ever taught it them, or that they spent any time studying it; indeed they say it can't be taught and are ready to murder anyone who says it can. They spend all their time milling round the captain and trying to get him to give them the wheel. If one faction is more successful than another, their rivals may kill them and throw them overboard, lay out the honest captain with drugs or drink, take control of the ship, help themselves to what's on board, and behave as if they were on a drunken pleasure-cruise. Finally they reserve their admiration for the man who

knows how to lend a hand in controlling the captain by force or by fraud; they praise his seamanship and navigation and knowledge of the sea and condemn everyone else as useless. They have no idea that the true navigator must study the seasons of the year, the sky, the stars, the wind and other professional subjects, if he is to be really fit to control a ship.

The Republic
Plato

A difficulty arises when we turn to consider what body of persons should be sovereign in the polis.... Should the better sort of men have authority and be sovereign in all matters? In that case, the rest of the citizens will necessarily be debarred from honours, since they will not enjoy the honour of holding civil office. We speak of offices as honours; and when a single set of persons hold office permanently, the rest of the community must necessarily be debarred from all honours. ...the people at large should be sovereign rather than the few best—...There is this to be said for the Many. Each of them by himself may not be of a good quality; but when they all come together it is possible that they may surpass—collectively and as a body, although not individually—the quality of the few best.

The Politics
Aristotle

The council, which consisted of 28 aristocrats over the age of 60, prepared business for presentation to the Spartan assembly and acted as a law court for important cases.

The Assembly of Citizens, which included all male citizens over the age of 30, met each month outside the city. The council would explain and debate legislation before the assembly, and the citizens would then vote on the proposals. Unlike the Athenians, the Spartans voted by shouting. Decisions depended on whether those voting yes or those voting no shouted the louder! The assembly was intended to be a democratic body but, in reality, it had no voice in policy-making. Members could not propose policies or laws and had no right of debate. Furthermore, its decisions could be set aside. In essence, the assembly's role was to rubber-stamp the council's proposals.

In Sparta, a body of five Ephors or

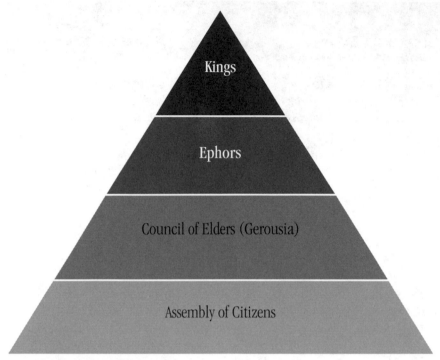

Figure 6-18 *Government in Sparta*

overseers, elected each year by the citizens, held the most power. The Ephors directed the affairs of state. They had the right to attend meetings of the council, and to summon the assembly and preside over its meetings. They could also arrest and prosecute the kings, if necessary, and decree punishment on any citizen.

REFLECT AND ANALYZE

1. Create a chart illustrating the various forms of government in Athens up to and including the establishment of democracy. With each form of government, describe the position and power of the following groups:
   a) aristocracy
   b) merchants
   c) farmers
   d) women.

2. What measures did the Athenians take to guard against the abuse of political power? How effective do you think these measures were?

3. Compare the government of Athens with that of Sparta, and assess the advantages and disadvantages of each system.

LAW AND JUSTICE

When the archons appointed Draco as a special administrator in 621 BCE, they gave him the responsibility of codifying the laws. That is, his task was to organize a set of laws and related punishments that would be fairer to all Athenians. Since only one of Draco's laws has survived, questions remain unanswered about his work. Did he actually complete the code? If he did complete it, did someone try to destroy his work? Did his code touch upon a broad spectrum of legal areas?

The one surviving law deals with homicide. Draco was determined to end private feuds and to give the victim's family a voice in deciding the outcome of the case. According to his law, a court had to determine whether a murder was accidental or intentional. If the verdict was accidental murder, the victim's family could grant a pardon to the accused. If the victim's family did not agree with the court's decision, however, the defendant could be banished from Attica.

Traditionally, historians have suggested that Draco's laws were so severe that even the most trivial offences warranted capital punishment. Some modern historians now believe that this interpretation may be inaccurate. Nevertheless, we have come to associate the word ***draconian*** with measures that are extremely severe or oppressive.

Surprisingly, perhaps, Athenians entrusted the daily maintenance of law and order to foreigners. They could not accept the idea of one Athenian policing another. Therefore, they enlisted foreign slaves drawn from Scythian tribesmen from the north who lived in tents near the Acropolis. These slaves formed a corps of archers that maintained public order when necessary.

One of the great innovations in the Greek justice system related to juries. First of all, the court was dominated by a panel of jurors rather than by a judge. But instead of a jury of 12, as we have today, a Greek jury varied in size from as few as 201 to as many as 1501. Bribery was next to impossible! The court selected the panel from 6000 Athenian citizens chosen for jury duty every year by lot. The jurors were paid a small fee for their trouble.

Although all types of cases were tried in the courts, there was no public prosecutor. Individual citizens had to prosecute others or defend themselves in all cases, even those involving theft, murder, and high treason. A citizen began the process by serving the accused with a summons in the presence of a witness. Then both the accused and the accuser appeared before a magistrate for a preliminary hearing, where a clerk recorded the evidence. The evidence, copies of laws, and any other related documents were then put in a box and sealed.

After an interval, the trial was held in front of the jury. A magistrate presided over the case, but the citizen-jurors always decided the verdict. Court proceedings were held in the open air, with benches for the jurors and a platform for speakers. Witnesses testified to the accuracy of the statements given by the accuser and the defendant at the preliminary hearing, and were not cross-examined. All statements from the sealed box were simply read aloud to the court. Both the accuser and the accused addressed the court in person. If one of them could afford to hire a gifted speech writer, he or she sometimes had the advantage. Jurors expressed their approval or disapproval throughout the trial by shouting, stamping, and groaning.

Even though these jurors had little knowledge of the law, the Athenians believed they were shrewd judges of character and could detect honesty or dishonesty. When the entire case was presented, the jury determined the verdict by a vote. Each juror dropped a mussel shell in one of two jars, one representing *guilty* and the other *not guilty*. If the accused was found guilty and the penalty was not defined by law, the jury held a second vote to decide the sentence. Sentences varied from fines, to loss of citizenship, to exile, and to death by hemlock (poison). The Athenians did not favour imprisonment because they did not have the means to keep people in jail very long.

REFLECT AND ANALYZE

1. What contribution did Draco make to the legal system in Athens?

2. How does the Athenians' legal system reflect the value they placed on direct democracy and equality?

3. Role-play a trial in ancient Athens. Choose the crime, the accuser, the defendant, the magistrate, and witnesses. The rest of the class is the jury and will decide the verdict.

GREECE:
Society and Culture

Figure 7-1
The head of Zeus

In the beginning, there was Chaos. Everything was in confusion and darkness. Out of Chaos there appeared night and depth (Erebos).

From the union of Chaos and Erebos came Eros or Love, the most important of all elements. Eros represented order, and created an ordered universe out of Chaos. Eros also performed the first marriage, uniting Uranus, the sky, with Gaea, the earth.

Gaea and Uranus had many different offspring. Gaea gave birth to monsters called the Hundred-Handed Children, and to huge one-eyed giants called the Cyclopes. Her most famous children were the 12 Titans or giants, in whose image human beings were later created.

Uranus did not prove to be an ideal father. Jealous of his children, and afraid that they might try to steal his power, he buried them alive in the earth. Horrified, Gaea plotted with Cronos, the youngest of the Titans, to overthrow Uranus. With his mother's help, Cronos wounded his father with a long, curved knife, and became supreme ruler.

Once in power, Cronos began to worry that he, too, might be overthrown as he had overthrown his father. As a safety measure, therefore, he released only the Titans from the earth, leaving the Hundred-Handed Children and the Cyclopes buried. He married one of his sisters, Rhea, and together they had 12 children. But to prevent his children from ever stealing his power, Cronos ate each child as it was born.

Overwhelmed with grief, Rhea was determined to save one child. When her last son, Zeus, was born, she fed Cronos a stone wrapped up in a cloth, and sent Zeus in secret to Mount Ida in Crete, where he was raised in a cave. When Zeus became a young man, he went to his father's court disguised as a page, and fed Cronos an emetic. This substance caused Cronos to regurgitate all 11 of his children—fully grown. Naturally, the other children were only too willing to help Zeus conquer their father, and a war began.

Zeus and his forces established their headquarters on a high mountain called Mount Olympus. His main allies were his brothers, Poseidon and Hades, and two Titans, Prometheus and Epimethus. Zeus also released the Cyclopes on condition that they help him fight Cronos. After ten years of war, Zeus was finally victorious and he divided the world among himself and his two brothers. Zeus became god of the sky and the upper world, Poseidon became god of the sea, and Hades became god of the underworld.

Hesiod, a Greek writer who lived in Boetia in the eighth century BCE, recorded this account of creation and the birth of the Greek gods. The ancient Greeks developed a vast and fascinating body of **mythology** to answer questions about their origins and to explain the nature of their world. How would you describe the behaviour of the gods in this creation myth? How does the myth explain the origins of the earth and human beings? How does it reflect aspects of human life and basic human emotions?

RELIGION

GODS AND GODDESSES

Greek myths still captivate many readers today. The stories offer us an intriguing picture of the Greek deities—gods and goddesses who quarrelled, fell in love, experienced jealousy, and played tricks on one another and on mortals. Like the gods of Mesopotamia and ancient Egypt, the gods of ancient Greece were **anthropomorphic**. They possessed human characteristics, both virtues and failings, and they played an important role in the everyday lives of mortals.

The Greeks believed their gods controlled everything from the movements of the stars and planets to the success or failure of a harvest. There were gods who ruled the sky, the sea, the earth, and the underworld; there were gods for marriage and childbirth, for music, hunting, and war; and there were gods for trades such as metalwork.

The Greeks believed that 12 brilliant and strong-willed gods, called the Olympians, lived on Mount Olympus in northern Greece. The chief Olympian was Zeus, god of the sky. The people celebrated the Olympians frequently at festivals and built many temples in their honour.

The 12 Olympian gods and goddesses were:

ZEUS	Sky god and the chief of the gods
HERA	Goddess of marriage and childbirth
POSEIDON	God of the sea and the earthquake
DEMETER	Earth mother and the goddess of fertility and crops
HESTIA	Goddess of the hearth
ATHENA	Goddess of wisdom and skills
APOLLO	Sun god and the god of music
ARTEMIS	Goddess of hunting and the moon
HERMES	Messenger of the gods
APHRODITE	Goddess of beauty and love
HEPHAESTOS	God of metalwork
ARES	God of war

Outside the Olympian circle, two important gods were Hades, the brother of Zeus and god of the underworld, and Dionysus, a late arrival in Greece who became the god of wine and drama. At festivals of Dionysus, which were often riotous affairs, people drank wine, dressed in costumes, and staged dramatic performances.

The ancient Greek pantheon included other lesser deities as well. For example, the people believed in the Muses, the Fates, and the Furies. The Muses, associated with the god Apollo, inspired artists, writers, and musicians. The Fates, three female deities, controlled the destinies of human beings. The Furies, born from the spilled blood of Uranus, enforced family law and avenged those who were killed by family members. Other lesser gods were associated with particular crafts and industries. Each Greek home customarily held particular gods in great esteem.

RELIGIOUS BELIEFS AND PRACTICES

The ancient Greeks tended to practise their religion individually. If a person wished to invoke the intervention of any of the gods, he or she would go to one of the many shrines, altars, or temples and say a prayer or leave a small gift. People might appeal to a god or goddess because of an illness, a bad harvest, an upcoming battle, or a joyous occasion such as a marriage or birth. They usually hoped for the god's blessing, but they sometimes sought to avoid a deity's punishment. A citizen offered up a prayer by standing alone with both arms outstretched towards the sky, and speaking out loud in a clear voice.

The Greeks called on their gods directly because they had no organized church, no powerful class of priests, and no established religious teachings and laws. There were some priests in ancient Greece, but they did not have much authority or influence. Some travelled around the country preaching to the poor. A record of their teachings, known as *The Book of Orpheus*, is as close as we have come to finding a sacred text in ancient Greece. Other priests presided over special rituals or acted as caretakers to a temple, but their mission was not to persuade others to live better lives. Once they performed a particular ceremonial duty, their responsibility ended.

THROUGH THEIR EYES

The Myth of Prometheus

How does the Greek myth of Prometheus portray the interaction of the gods with one another and with mortals? What questions about the origins and nature of human civilization does the myth attempt to answer?

The Greek poet Hesiod represents Prometheus as a troublemaker and a trickster. The Greek dramatist Aeschylus, in his *Prometheus Bound,* represents him as a tragic hero and a champion of humanity. After you read the story of Prometheus, decide which view is closer to your own. Why?

Prometheus was a member of the earliest race of gods called the Titans. During the war between the Titans and the Olympians, Prometheus did not join his siblings' rebellion, but he was also not ready to submit to Olympian laws. When the Olympians were victorious, Prometheus tricked Zeus during a sacrifice of a bull. In one half of the hide, Prometheus hid the bones of the bull under a rich layer of fat. In the other half, he hid the meat under the entrails. Then Prometheus had Zeus choose between the two halves. The one that Zeus did not choose would be given to humankind. Zeus chose

the half with the fat, but then looked closer and realized that Prometheus had tricked him. The Olympian flew into a rage and, in revenge against Prometheus and humankind, deprived the earth of fire.

To help mortals, Prometheus stole fire from the gods and returned it to earth once again, along with all art and civilization. The theft enraged Zeus so much that he considered how to punish Prometheus and humankind even more severely.

To punish mortals, Zeus created Pandora, the first woman of earth, and sent her down with a small casket to Epimetheus, the young brother of Prometheus. Although Prometheus warned his brother against Pandora, Epimetheus was enchanted and married her anyway. Pandora then opened the lid of the small casket and released evil, hard work, and disease into the world. Only hope was left inside, under the lid, as consolation.

To punish Prometheus, Zeus bound him to a remote peak in the Caucasus Mountains. He then sent an eagle to devour the Titan's liver every day. Every night, the liver grew back. Prometheus suffered this punishment for many centuries until the hero Heracles killed the eagle and set him free.

Perhaps one of the most intriguing Greek beliefs was in the power of oracles. According to the ancient Greeks, the gods spoke through certain priests or priestesses at particular shrines. People often consulted these oracles to find out answers to pressing questions. The most famous oracle was the oracle of Apollo at Delphi, where visitors came seeking the god's advice on various problems. Anyone could approach the oracle at Delphi. A famous story tells of how Croesus, king of Lydia, once consulted the oracle before a great battle. He was anxious for advice from Apollo because he planned to attack King Cyrus and the mighty Persians.

When Croesus entered the temple, he gazed upon the Pythia, the temple priestess, seated on her three-legged stool over a gaping chasm. Sulphurous gases emanated from the cleft beneath her stool, shrouding the priestess in a veil of mystery. She sat very still, seemingly in a trance.

Croesus posed his question. "Oh God Apollo, I humbly beseech your advice. Would it be wise for Lydia to attack Persia?"

The Pythia remained still for some time and then began to utter unintelligible responses. Only the priests of the temple could interpret these words from Apollo.

The priests presented Croesus with the god's answer. "The god Apollo has spoken,"

Figure 7-2 *The Pythia, Priestess of Apollo, utters a prophecy*

they said. "If you cross a river, you will destroy a great empire."

Croesus left Delphi full of confidence, ready to attack the Persian army. Apollo had spoken. Unluckily for the king of Lydia, he had misunderstood the oracle. After he crossed the river, he lost the battle with Cyrus and his own empire was destroyed.

The ancient Greeks also believed in omens, curses, and superstitions. For example, they often considered a thunderstorm, an earthquake, an eclipse—any rare natural occurrence—as a sign of good or bad luck. When misfortune befell a person, his or her first concern was often to find out which god had been offended. When people were about to drink a cup of wine, they would usually first pour a few drops on the floor as a libation to a particular god. The ancient Greeks also believed

profoundly in the significance of dreams and the mystical power of charms.

Festivals of all kinds were held frequently across Greece to honour the gods. They often involved sacred processions, religious ceremonies, carnivals, dancing and singing, and feasting and drinking. Competitions played an important part in festivals as well. Participants might compete in drama, oratory, music, or sports. In Athens, which held more than 60 annual festivals, the competitions were most often between individuals. In Sparta, however, which held about 30 festivals every year, competitions were always between groups.

The Panathenaea, held in honour of the patron-goddess Athena, was one of the most impressive religious festivals in Athens. A depiction of the main event, the

procession to the Acropolis, appears on the great Parthenon frieze, now housed in the British Museum. A monstrous wheeled ship headed the procession, carrying a sacred robe woven for the statue of the goddess and destined to be laid on her knees as an offering. Following the ship were girls carrying baskets of scent and jars of wine, boys bearing pitchers, old men waving olive branches, and sheep and cattle on their way to be sacrificed. Every fourth year, the festival took on added importance and was conducted on a grander scale.

DEATH AND THE AFTERLIFE

The ancient Greeks believed that the messenger god, Hermes, led the deceased to the River Styx, the great divide between the world of the living and the world of the dead. Here the boatman Charon waited to

THEN AND NOW
The Olympic Games

According to Greek mythology, how did the Olympic Games originate? What was their purpose? How do the ancient Olympic Games compare to the modern Olympic Games?

Oenomaus, the king of Olympia, had a beautiful daughter, Hippodamia. Any man who wanted to marry her had to compete in a chariot race with the king, who was the best charioteer in the land. If the young man was able to defeat the king, he would be allowed to marry the princess. If he lost the race, he would be put to death. Many men had tried to defeat Oenomaus, but all had lost their lives.

Pelops, the grandson of Zeus, wanted to marry Hippodamia and so he challenged Oenomaus to a race. With the help of the gods, he defeated and killed the king and made Hippodamia his wife.

To remember his victory, he ordered that athletic games be held every four years at Olympia in honour of Zeus.

The Ancient Games
The greatest festival in ancient Greece, open to all city-states, was the Olympic Games. Held every four years between 776 BCE and 396 CE, the games lasted five days and were part of a celebration to honour Zeus at Olympia, his most famous shrine.

Every fourth spring, heralds went out to the city-states, summoning the people to the Olympic festival. A sacred truce allowed the games to continue even in times of political crisis. All travellers to Olympia were guaranteed safe passage, regardless of conflicts or wars among the different city-states.

Only free-born Greek men and boys could enter the games. Women were not allowed to compete, and married women were banned from watching, under penalty of death. Competitors arrived at Olympia at least a month before the games, reported to the officials, and began their training.

The Program at Olympia

Day 1   Sacrifices, oaths, checking of athletes
Day 2
   Morning: Equestrian events
   Afternoon: The Pentathlon, a combined test in five
   events: quoits (a game in which the player
   throws a ring of stone or metal at a peg),
   sprint, wrestling, long jump, and javelin.
Day 3
   Morning: Religious observances
   Afternoon: Boys' events
Day 4
   Morning: Track events
   Afternoon: Wrestling, boxing, race in armour
Day 5   Banquet and sacrifices

On the final day, the stewards of the games proclaimed the winners and crowned them with a wreath of wild olive, cut from a sacred tree growing in the sanctuary. The victor often received a financial reward of some kind when he returned in triumph to his home polis. Sometimes he was allowed to marry the woman of his choice, perhaps someone from an important family with a large dowry. In other instances, Olympic heroes were freed from future taxes.

The Modern Olympic Games

The modern Olympic Games began in 1896 and have been held every four years since, except for once during World War I and twice during World War II. The spirit behind the modern games is much the same as it was in ancient Greece. The goal is to foster the development of a sound mind in a sound body and, on a grander scale, promote good relations among nations of the world. At times, however, the games have been the centre of political controversy and tragedy. At Munich, Germany, in 1972, Israeli athletes were murdered in the Olympic village by terrorists. In 1980, 62 nations boycotted the games in Moscow to protest the Soviet invasion of Afghanistan.

Winter games became part of the Olympic agenda in

1924. The summer and winter games used to be held in the same year, but after 1992 the system changed and they are now held two years apart. Greece is no longer the permanent host of the games. Cities of the world now apply to the International Olympic Committee to act as host, well in advance of a particular Olympic year. To bid successfully, a city must have the funds to build the required facilities. Cities often compete intensely to win the position of host because the games give the local economy an enormous boost.

The modern games feature many more events than the original games, and new events are still sometimes added. The summer Olympic Games include archery, boxing, canoeing, cycling, horseback riding, fencing, field hockey, gymnastics, handball, judo, rowing, shooting, and soccer—to name only some of the sports. The main track and field event is the Decathlon, which comes from the Greek words *deka* (ten) and *athlon* (contest). The athletes compete in ten different events involving running, jumping, and throwing. In the modern Pentathlon (*penta* means five), the athletes compete in fencing, riding, running, shooting, and swimming. Another famous event is the marathon race, which was created to honour the Greek runner, Pheidippides.

The Winter Olympics include such events as bobsledding, ice hockey, luge, skating, skiing, tobogganing, and the Biathlon (an event combining cross-country skiing and sharpshooting).

Figure 7-3 *Boxers at the Olympic games*

ferry the dead across the river into Hades (the underworld). A watchdog, Cerberus, stood at the entrance to the underworld and prevented any who entered from leaving again. Inside sat the judges of the dead, who assigned each ghost to its appropriate place. Though descriptions of the underworld vary in some details, Hades was generally seen as a dreary place where the dead led a shadowy and cheerless existence.

Most Greeks, therefore, tried to greet death with calm courage, but had little hope of future happiness. Most believed that any existence beyond the grave would offer few joys, and could never compare with the rich life of this world. Nevertheless, family members ensured that relatives received proper burial rites so that their souls could enter the afterlife.

The work of performing these essential rites fell to the women of the household. They washed the body, anointed it with oil, and wrapped it in a shroud. They then placed a coin in the mouth of the corpse to pay the fare demanded by Charon at the River Styx. Finally, they set a crown or wreath upon the deceased's head.

The body was then laid out on a couch for a single day so that relatives could gather to express their grief. On the following day, the body was carried to the tomb on a bier, transported either by pallbearers or by cart. Some families used the funeral as an occasion to display their wealth. At the most lavish funerals, families might hire professional mourners to fill out their ranks.

The Greeks believed that their dead belonged to a great community of souls that depended on the living for its well-being. Therefore, remembering the dead was very important. On appointed days, the departed received offerings of food and drink.

Those who sought happiness in the afterlife turned to the mysteries or mystery religions. The mysteries were secret rituals intended to purify the individual and ensure a happy afterlife. The most famous of these rituals was held each September at Eleusis, some 20 km west of Athens, where a cult honoured Dionysus, the god of wine, Demeter, the earth mother, and her daughter Persephone.

Only the initiated were allowed to be present at these secret rites. To be admitted, a candidate had to abstain from particular foods. When the day of celebration arrived, followers gathered outside Athens and bathed in the sea to be purified. Then they proceeded along the Sacred Way to Eleusis, clad in white, carrying pine torches to light their way. They sang hymns to Dionysus as they marched.

At Eleusis, the worshippers spent a day or two in ceremony. The final event took place in a darkened hall where mysterious visions were revealed in flashes of light. Because participants in these rites kept strict secrecy, the nature of these visions remains unknown.

REFLECT AND ANALYZE

1. Describe the role played by the gods and goddesses in the everyday lives of the ancient Greeks. Provide specific examples in your answer.

2. a) What role did priests play in ancient Greek religion?
   b) How does this role compare to the role of priests in ancient Egypt?

3. Assume the role of a Greek citizen. Write a journal entry describing one of the following events:
   a) a visit to the oracle at Delphi
   b) your attendance at the Olympic Games
   c) your participation in a religious festival such as the Panathenaea.

4. Research another ancient Greek myth. Report on the following:
   a) What does the myth reveal about ancient Greek beliefs and values?
   b) What relevance does the myth have for us today?

SOCIAL STRUCTURE

The social organization of the ancient Greek city-states changed throughout the course of their history. In the classical period, for example, the influence of the wealthy aristocrats gave way to the growing power of the middle class. There were important distinctions as well between the social structure in Athens and the social structure in Sparta.

ATHENS

As we have seen, citizenship in Athens was limited to adult males who had been born in the state. The body of citizens was made up of a small number of aristocrats who owned large country estates; a commercial and industrial class including craftspeople, shopkeepers, labourers, and sailors; and a large number of small landholders and farmers. Neither the wives and children of

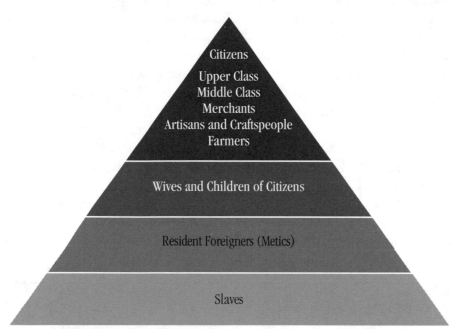

Figure 7-4 *The social pyramid—Athens*

citizens, nor the foreign residents (*metics*), had any political rights.

By definition, the metics included all immigrants from other Greek states, all descendants of immigrants, any children born of a citizen and a non-citizen, and any freed slaves. Many of them were merchants who handled the overseas trade and lived at Piraeus, the port of Athens. All metics were registered by the state.

No matter how long they lived in Athens, metics could not become citizens. They were required to pay a small annual tax, were forbidden to own a house or land, and were expected to serve in the military. If they became involved in lawsuits, they had to be represented by an Athenian.

Slaves came from "barbarian" countries such as Thrace, the coastlands of the Black Sea, Asia Minor, and the Levant. The Greeks used the term barbarian to refer to all peoples outside the Greek city-states who did not speak Greek or share Greek cus-

toms. Some slaves were the captives of war, and others were the victims of professional kidnappers. Two-thirds of the population of Athens owned slaves in the classical period. Upper-class citizens had as many as ten slaves working in the household or in the fields. Middle-class citizens usually had two. Even the business community used slaves for trade.

The Greeks considered slaves the property of their owners. For the most part, slaves were treated well. Those working in homes were frequently accepted as family members and given skilled, responsible jobs. Thieves and runaways, however, were whipped and branded. Slaves employed in the mines, where conditions were wretched, suffered the most.

We have very little evidence to give us insight into the actual population of a city-state. There are no reliable figures. Historians believe, however, that Athens at the time of Pericles had a population of

approximately 300 000. Some other typical city-states had populations about one-fifth the size, and many were even smaller. Today, we would think of them as towns rather than cities. Because the communities were small, every citizen could participate in public affairs and vote directly on all issues. The city centre was rarely more than a day's walk away.

SPARTA

In Sparta, the free citizens—adult males over the age of 30 who were born in Sparta—were called the Spartiates. They dedicated themselves to the state and to the military. Spartan boys were trained from an early age to become disciplined soldiers. Citizens did not work the land or engage in trade. The city's leaders discouraged citizens from amassing wealth in case money began to interfere with the people's dedication to the welfare of the state.

As in other Greek city-states, the wives and children of citizens had no legal or political status. Foreigners, called *perioikoi*, could engage in industry and trade, but they had no political rights, were heavily taxed, and were subject to military service.

The slaves or helots of Sparta were the original citizens of Lacedaemon in the Peloponnese. When the Spartans took over the region, they enslaved the people and set them to work tilling the land. When the Spartans conquered neighbouring Messenia, they enslaved those citizens as well. The Spartiates ruled the helots with an iron fist. Slaves were owned by the state, had no political rights, and had no hope of freedom. Because the helots eventually outnumbered the citizen population by a ratio of 20 to one, revolt became a

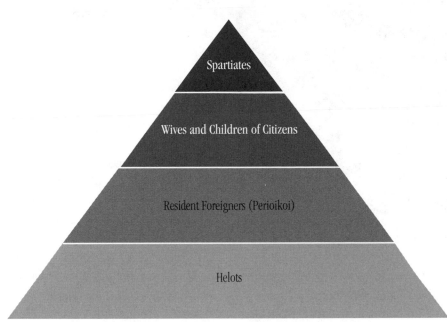

Figure 7-5 *The social pyramid—Sparta*

constant danger. This threat of an uprising helps to explain why Spartan society developed so differently from society in Athens. In Sparta, *eunomia* or order—not liberty—was paramount. To protect the society, the state established a permanent standing army of citizens and discouraged all foreign travellers and foreign ideas.

REFLECT AND ANALYZE

1. a) How did the ancient Greeks define citizenship?
   b) How does their definition compare with our definition of citizenship in Canada today?

2. Who were the non-citizens in Athens and Sparta, and how were they treated? With a partner, role-play an interview with a non-citizen in either Athens or Sparta. Discuss this person's rights, role in society, and his or her view of these circumstances.

3. Compare and contrast the social order in Athens and Sparta. Suggest reasons for the similarities and differences.

4. Individual freedom was an ideal of Athenian society. How, then, can you explain slavery in this city-state? In what other ways was individual freedom limited in ancient Athens?

EVERYDAY LIFE

How do we know about the everyday lives of the ancient Greeks? Certainly the surviving literary works of the period tell us a great deal. But another fascinating source—artifacts—provides us with a visual reconstruction of the past. The Athenians, in particular, were distinguished potters. They depicted many aspects of their daily life on their colourful vases, presenting vivid and intriguing details about childhood, education, marriage, work, and dress.

FAMILY LIFE

The Athenians liked to portray scenes from childhood on their pottery. Mothers were primarily responsible for raising the children since fathers were occupied with matters outside the home. Grandfathers, no longer involved in public life, sometimes took an active interest in the children as well, and the relationship between grandfather and grandson was often close. At the naming ceremony, held seven to ten days after birth, boys were often named after their grandfather.

Festivals including feasts and offerings to the gods marked important events in the lives of children. For example, the family usually gathered to celebrate the presentation of the newborn. Another festival took place when a child passed out of infancy. On this occasion, the family presented the infant with a miniature wine jug called a *chous*.

EDUCATION

Formal education began early in childhood and was offered only to boys. Since it was costly, schooling was also more accessible to the sons of the wealthy. A typical educa-

Figure 7-6 *Red-figured pelike (storage jar) showing a music lesson*

tion for an Athenian boy might have gone something like this. Cleon, the son of a wealthy landowner, began his schooling at the age of seven. His family had the choice of hiring a private tutor or sending the boy to a *grammatikos*, where he would be taught reading, writing, and arithmetic. The state required that all young males learn how to read and write. Cleon's parents chose to send him to a grammatikos.

The Athenians considered a well-rounded education essential for all citizens. This meant that Cleon not only had to do well in his studies at the *grammatikos,* but also had to develop himself physically and culturally. Since Greek poetry was sung to the accompaniment of a lyre, Cleon received music lessons from his school's *kitharistes* or music teacher. Cleon knew that a cultured man must be able to sing and play an instrument.

Coming from a wealthy family, Cleon was accompanied to the grammatikos by Ari, a slave-tutor or *pedagogue*, who was responsible for the boy's manners and morals. Ari observed Cleon as he learned how to write with a metal instrument on a tablet of soft wax, take dictation, and memorize and recite long passages from Homer's *Iliad* and *Odyssey*.

To develop his physical abilities, Cleon attended a *palaistra*, or athletic training ground, kept by a professional trainer. Here, he took part in boxing, wrestling, and pancreation, a sport that combined the two. On special occasions, Cleon visited one of the large *gymnasia* where many boys and men went to keep fit. The Athenians believed that physical exercise developed the character as well as the body.

When he turned 14, Cleon completed his elementary education. At this point, many boys became apprentices in a craft or trade, especially since higher education was expensive. But Cleon's parents encouraged their son to continue at one of the two great schools located outside the walls of Athens. The Academy was founded by the famous philosopher Plato, while the Lyceum was established by his pupil Aristotle. Cleon attended Aristotle's Lyceum for four years, studying moral philosophy, oratory, and rhetoric (the art of presenting an articulate and plausible argument).

Spartan education was quite different from schooling in Athens. The Spartan educational system developed from the reforms of the seventh-century BCE lawgiver, Lycurgus. Lycurgus himself is something of a mystery, but most of what we know about him and his reforms comes from the writings of the Greek historian Plutarch who lived in the second century BCE. According to Plutarch, Lycurgus believed that education should have only one purpose: to create an efficient garrison of hoplites to control the helots. Lycurgus abolished study and the practice of "the unnecessary and superfluous arts." The ideal educational system, he believed, would produce highly disciplined soldiers.

The tough regimen began early. Newborn babies were carefully inspected for any mental or physical weaknesses. If a defect was found, the infant might be left outdoors, to die from exposure. Some abandoned babies were picked up and raised as slaves. Plutarch writes that this practice of infanticide was based on the conviction that a life poorly equipped at the very beginning with health and strength was of no benefit to either itself or the state. Babies who passed inspection were raised in an environment designed to harden them. Infants ran about naked, exposed to the elements. They were taught not to whimper, to be absolutely obedient, and to endure pain or hardship without complaint.

Education was not entrusted to families or tutors. At the age of seven, Spartan boys were removed from their homes and sent to live in austere barracks, where they were subjected to rigid discipline. They went barefoot, wore only a single garment, and slept on a bed of thistledown and reeds. Their instruction emphasized physical exercise so that the boys would grow up to be good soldiers. They received training in

THROUGH THEIR EYES
Plato's *Republic*

In the following excerpt from *The Republic*, Plato describes the kind of education that he believes the leaders of a city-state should have. According to Plato, what were the essential characteristics of effective leaders? Are Plato's views on education well-suited for contemporary society? Explain.

Then our perfect guardian must have the following characteristics: a philosophic disposition, high spirits, speed, and strength. How are they to be brought up and educated? . . . . We've already arranged for their physical training and their education in literature and music . . . . We can then lay down that arithmetic shall be a subject for study by those who are to hold positions of responsibility in our state. Geometry is obviously useful in war. If a man knows geometry it will make all the difference to him when it comes to pitching camp or taking up a position. Then you must be sure to require the citizens of your ideal state not to neglect geometry.

a variety of sports, including running, wrestling, and a form of musical drill. They learned the laws of Sparta and memorized the poems of Homer. Little emphasis was placed on reading and writing.

At 18 years of age, Spartan males were drafted into the *Krypteia,* or secret corps. This draft marked a critical juncture in their military training, and served as a boundary between boyhood and manhood. For two years, they lived apart from the community in the country, where they were expected to survive by their wits. The experience was intended to train them in boldness and cunning. At 30, the Spartan man became a full citizen.

Marriage did not significantly change the life of a Spartan citizen. He continued to live in a barracks called a *Syssitia,* simple quarters without any decoration. The daily diet included cheese, pork, figs, bread, and wine.

MARRIAGE

When the time came to consider marriage, Greek parents negotiated a betrothal in much the same way as they would set up a business contract. The family of the bride had to provide a dowry of either money or valuables. In most cases, the higher the dowry, the more attractive the offer of marriage. The dowry was held in trust for the bride throughout her marriage. If her husband died or divorced her, the dowry could be used to contract a second marriage.

On the eve of the wedding, a bride usually sacrificed her toys to the virgin goddess, Artemis. On the wedding day itself, separate feasts were held in the homes of the bride and the groom. It was not until later in the evening that the couple met.

At the end of the day, the groom set out with his best man to fetch his bride in a simple mule-drawn country cart, and brought her back to his home. Upon arrival, he led his bride to the hearth where both knelt and bowed their heads. Family members then showered the couple with nuts and sweetmeats. This symbolic gesture, much like the tradition of throwing confetti or rice, was intended to bring the man and woman prosperity in their union.

On the following day, the relatives of both families gathered to celebrate the wedding at the home of the groom. The relatives of the bride brought gifts as well as the dowry chest. Sacrifices and prayers were offered before the couple sat down with family and friends to a light meal of sesame-seed cakes. Male and female guests were seated in separate parts of the room.

WOMEN IN ANCIENT GREECE

Women in Greek society had few rights and little freedom. Once a Greek woman married, she passed from her father's into her husband's keeping. Any possessions she had became the property of her husband, and in the eyes of the law she held no independent status. Even if her husband died, she reverted to the charge of her father or brother. If a marriage broke down, a husband could renounce his wife, but the wife could not do the same without the support of a government official. The condition of women did not improve significantly throughout the history of ancient Greece. In fact, the status

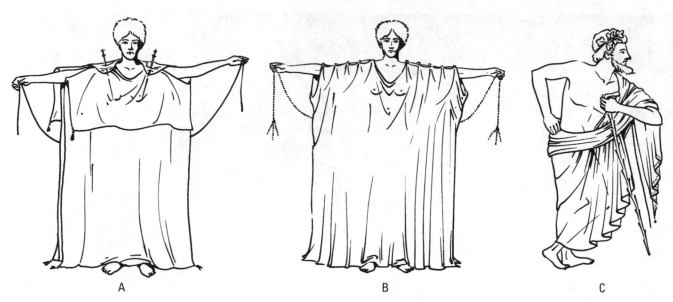

Figure 7-7 *Greek apparel*
A: The Peplos *Women used long pins to hold this woolen dress on their shoulders.*
B: The Chiton *The chiton, worn by both men and women, was made of linen and fastened at the shoulders with pins. It was most popular in the mid sixth century BCE.*
C: The Himation *This cloak is typical of the plain single garment worn by Athenian men in the fifth century BCE.*

of women during the fifth century BCE was lower than it had been in the eighth century BCE, the age of Homer.

Married women spent most of their time and energy on the management of household affairs. They oversaw the work of household slaves, handled finances, and attended to domestic activities such as spinning, weaving, and breadmaking. They lived in separate quarters, and did not eat with the men or participate socially when their husbands entertained guests. When women did appear in public to shop or to attend family events such as weddings or funerals, they were always accompanied by a slave or other attendant.

Women were excluded from most important civic activities, including military operations, politics, and the law. The only public role that they could aspire to was priestess. The idea of giving women the vote

would have met with the same support as one calling for the freedom of slaves.

Life for women in Sparta, however, was somewhat different. Spartan women could own property and took part in athletic competitions. As young girls, they received almost as rigorous a training as the boys. They, too, had to endure cold and hardship so that they would develop the strength and endurance to become the mothers of great warriors. A Spartan woman did not weep when her son or husband marched off to battle.

Despite the severe restrictions on their lives, some Greek women achieved lasting prominence. Sappho, for example, was a lyric poet born about 600 BCE on the island of Lesbos. Lyric verse is a shorter, more personal form of poetry than the epic. It dealt with feelings of love rather than themes of war. Sappho's poems were filled with intense

emotion. Many parents sent their daughters to Lesbos to be taught by Sappho. Although few of her poems survive, she is considered one of the greatest ancient poets.

Figure 7-8 *Statue of a Spartan girl maintaining her physical conditioning*

URBAN AND RURAL LIVING

In Athens, the *agora*, or marketplace, was located in the centre of the city and was the focus of Athenian life. Around this hot, dusty, noisy square stood the government buildings. Immediately to the west were the temples of Hephaistos and Apollo.

On the edge of the agora stood three arcades or *stoas*. This was the busiest part of the marketplace, where people conducted business and friends gathered to talk. Athenians strolled up and down among the arcades, stopping occasionally to discuss the weather, the next law to be debated at the assembly, or the coming athletic games. Learned men also used the stoas as places to gather and teach their followers.

The centre of the agora was a sea of activity. Flimsy stalls, hastily built and crowded together, conducted every kind of business imaginable. Country people brought their produce to the market to sell so that they could purchase other goods.

Onion sellers, spice merchants, garlic boys, wine merchants, book merchants, potters, hat merchants, and people selling food shouted out prices and competed for customers. Chaotic as it looked, the agora had a degree of organization. Barbers, bankers, money changers, and fishmongers, for example, set up shop along the north side, while merchants selling olive oil were located to the east. Free men seeking employment lingered along the west side, near the Temple of Hephaistos.

Beyond the bustle of the agora lay the residential streets of the city. Homes were quite stark in appearance. Built of unbaked brick with ceramic tile roofs, the homes had no windows opening onto the street. Builders made no attempt to decorate the outside of the house except to construct pillars that flanked the front door.

The distinguishing feature of the home was its central courtyard, hidden away from the street. The courtyard was surrounded by a verandah that provided shade in the summer and shelter from the winds in winter. The people of ancient Greece often conducted household business and took their meals in this favourite part of the house.

A series of rooms of varying size surrounded the courtyard. The male members of the household used one of the larger rooms, the *andron*, for dinner parties and entertaining. The andron was situated close to the front entrance so that guests would

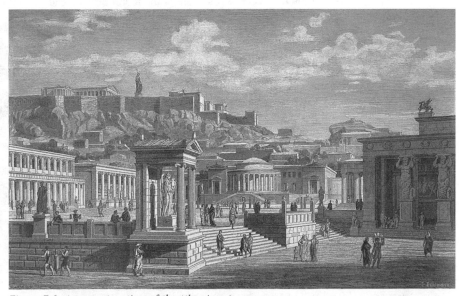

Figure 7-9 *A reconstruction of the Athenian Agora*

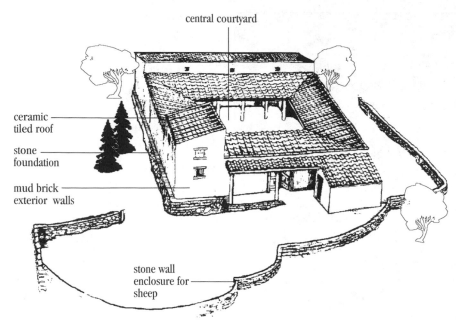

central courtyard

ceramic tiled roof

stone foundation

mud brick exterior walls

stone wall enclosure for sheep

Figure 7-10 *A country house south of Athens*

lay a small stool or table to hold the food and drink.

The symposion menu featured two elaborate courses. The first course offered a choice of poultry or fish, goat's cheese, and a variety of vegetables, including lentils, celery, and beans, accompanied by sauces. The second course featured grapes and other fruits, sweetmeats, figs, olives, and nuts. Fine wines from Chios and Rhodes, diluted with water, were served as drink, but not until the meal was completed and the tables tucked away. Lively discussion, singing, and the reading of poetry rounded out the evening.

On a typical day, most Greeks did not eat meat. The main dishes consisted of fish from the sea—fresh, salted, or dried— along with eggs and cheese. Milk, however, was considered fit only for animals or "barbarians." Olive oil and spices such as garlic were used in great supply to prepare savoury foods, and honey was used to sweeten dishes. The basic diet of working-class citizens included broth and barley-meal porridge.

not see the women of the house when they arrived.

The uncarpeted floors of the various rooms were made of beaten earth. Sunlight from open doorways provided light during the day, and oil-lamps lit the rooms at night. Only curtains covered the doorways, so houses must have been quite drafty. A charcoal brazier supplied heat.

Greek homes had no household drainage system. Slops were thrown into the streets, with only a warning cry to alert passersby! People generally bathed at small public bathhouses or at gymnasia.

Traditionally, men ate separately from women, even during formal dinner parties. When dining, men reclined on couches and propped themselves up on pillows to leave their right arm free. Although knives were used, people ate their food with their fingers or sometimes fashioned a spoon from a piece of bread. There were no forks.

Formal dinner parties with friends,

which the Greeks called *symposia,* were a popular form of recreation. After the andron was decorated with flowers and ivy, the host would place a garland for each of the male guests attending the late afternoon **symposion** on the couches set against the walls of the room. Beneath each couch

Figure 7-11 *A Greek symposion, painted on the rim of a flat wine cup such as the man in the centre is raising in a toast*

THE ECONOMY

AGRICULTURE

During the early history of ancient Greece, the city-states were able to produce enough food to feed their populations, even though the dry summers and thin soils made cultivating grain crops difficult. As populations grew, however, the land's low productivity became a problem. For example, Athens imported almost two-thirds of the grain it needed, notably from the Black Sea region of Russia.

After about 750 BCE, many of the city-states turned to colonization as an answer to their agricultural shortages. Supplied with imported grain, Greek city-states used their scarce arable land to grow crops that they could use for trade. The most important of these export crops were olives and wine grapes.

Olives grew freely throughout Greece. The trees were considered quite precious because they took 16 years or more to mature enough to produce a good harvest. When the trees were ready for harvesting in autumn, farmers hired workers from town to pick the berries by hand or shake them down with long sticks. The process was long and tedious. Once picked, the berries were placed in a circular trough and crushed by a circular stone wheel. A wooden lever then squeezed out the oil.

Some of the most famous wine grapes grown in ancient Greece came from the Aegean Islands of Chios and Thasos. Once pickers had harvested the fruit in September, they placed the grapes in a wine press with a low wall and a sloping floor. They then trampled the grapes until the juice trickled down the floor to a spout that drained into a jar. The juice was stored in these large jars and allowed to ferment into wine.

During the classical period, the Greeks tried to conserve the quality of the limited arable land. First, they practised a biennial system of farming, where they cultivated the land one year and left it fallow the next. Later, they practised a three-field system, where they sowed a different crop in each of two years and then left a field fallow in the third.

Two other Greek agricultural activities were stockbreeding and market gardening. Stockbreeding took place mostly on the plain of Thessaly, where large estates owned by aristocrats provided excellent grazing lands for horses and cattle. Outside of Thessaly, good grazing land was in short supply, although people in all parts of Greece pastured sheep and goats in the upland regions. Other domestic animals included donkeys and mules, which were bred for transportation, and pigs, which were raised for meat. In their market gardens, people grew fruit—notably figs—and vegetables such as peas, onions, cabbages, and lentils.

INDUSTRY

The bustling activity in the agora testified to the variety of industries and craftspeople in ancient Greece. These enterprises first began as small, private workshops of independent labourers, assisted by family or slaves. All city-states, for example, had their own potters, metalworkers, weavers, and shoemakers. These craftspeople handed down their expertise to family members from generation to generation. Within a workshop, apprentices worked with the master craftsperson and other assistants, practising the trade until they were prepared to set up on their own. The purpose of these workshops was to produce goods for the people living in the same city-state.

As the city-states grew in size, industry changed. The larger populations created a demand for new food sources, and people began to manufacture goods that could be traded or exchanged for food. In many city-states, industry became more specialized and more regulated. Corinth, for example, was noted for metalwork. Miletus was known for woollen textiles and furniture.

INNOVATIONS

Athenian Pottery: The Art of Everyday Life

In what ways did the design of pottery change throughout the history of ancient Greece? What made Athenian pottery so distinctive? Why is ancient Athenian pottery important historically?

Figure 7-12
Early geometric-designed vase

The artisans of the ancient Greek city-states produced pottery in all shapes and sizes. Most of it was intended for everyday use and included drinking cups, mixing bowls, and oiljars. Although all of the city-states produced their own pottery, Corinth and Athens were among the most important centres, exporting their wares to foreign markets. After the sixth century BCE, Athens became the dominant manufacturer.

Mainland Greek pottery dating from the late Dark Ages was simple, yet pleasing to the eye. The potters decorated the vessels with abstract patterns of lines, circles, and bands of colour. This style is now referred to as "geometric." Even when the artisans began to represent human figures in the eighth century BCE, they portrayed them in the same geometrical, abstract way.

The pottery industry flourished in Athens because extensive beds of fine potter's clay, containing a high iron content, were located quite near the city. When the pottery was fired in a kiln, the iron content gave it a rich reddish tinge, a distinctive quality of all pottery made in Athens.

Potters moulded vessels using hand-operated wheels. Once shaped, the pots, cups, and vases were kept in a damp room until ready for decorating. At the first stage of painting, the potters covered the surface with an ochre wash to heighten the colour of the clay. They then added a design to the pottery.

During the sixth century BCE, Athenian potters used the reddish colour of the clay as the background on their vases. They then added figures depicting events from mythology and everyday life in black. During the classical period, the reverse colours became more popular. Potters glazed the background black and added the figures in red. Black lines provided details.

No two pieces of pottery were ever alike; each was a work of art. Once the potters completed the decorating, they fired the painted pieces in a kiln to ensure a lasting finish.

Figure 7-13 *Sixth century black-figured vase showing a chariot race*

Megara was renowned for fine cloaks, and Athens became famous for fine painted pottery.

Workers involved in specialized crafts sometimes joined together in guilds or associations. They practised common religious rites and lived near each other in a separate quarter of the town. The metalworkers of Athens, for example, lived near the Temple of Hephaestos, god of smiths.

Two of the larger industries that developed in ancient Greece were mining and stone quarrying. The most common building material that the Greeks quarried on a large scale was limestone. They mined gold mainly at Mount Pangaeus in Thrace, and silver at Laurium in southeast Attica. The finest stones quarried were the marbles of Mount Pentelicus near Athens. The city-states often controlled mining operations, but sometimes they leased pits to private citizens. For example, Athens leased the silver mines at Laurium to a private operator.

Slaves working in the mines suffered appalling conditions. The shafts were extremely narrow, and the underground passages were so low that the slaves had to work on all fours or on their backs. They used hammers, chisels, and picks to hack at the rock. Oil lamps provided the only light and inadequate ventilation shafts brought in little fresh air. Here and there, pillars of rock were left to prop up the pits and reduce the chance of the roof collapsing—a constant danger.

TRADE

After the period of colonization, shipping became increasingly important to the city-states of ancient Greece. Athens, for example, built a fleet of merchant ships to help transport export products and bring back needed food supplies. To protect the merchant fleet and the harbour, Athens also built a great navy.

City-states with a natural port—such as Athens with Piraeus—enjoyed the most successful trade. Water transport, however, at times was very slow. Storms were a constant danger, particularly in winter, and chance encounters with pirates posed another threat.

Trade was a private enterprise. The owners of the merchant ships decided on their ports of destination, buying and selling wherever possible. Most of the Greek states used coins as their medium of exchange. The Mesopotamians and the Egyptians likely introduced the Greeks to the idea of coins as currency. Greek money was based on a system of weights, where the common unit was the drachma, which weighed between 4 and 7 grams. The drachma was divided into six obols. Higher units were the stater (two drachmae), the mina (100 drachmae), and the talent (60 minae).

All Athenian coins were made of silver mined at Laurium. They were stamped on one side with the head of Athena and on the other with an owl, the favourite bird of the goddess. Athenian coins acquired international status during the classical period.

There was a great deal of trade beyond the Greek world as well. Merchants sailed to every corner of the Mediterranean and even beyond the Strait of Gibraltar, where they traded with the Spanish tribes. They bought corn from the Black Sea, and perfumes and spices from the Levant. Some imports came to the Greek states by way of merchants from other countries. Tin, for example, originated in France or Britain, but likely came to the Greeks by way of the Carthaginians of North Africa. Similarly, agents brought the Greeks gems, ebony, and spices from India and silks from China.

During the classical period, Athens imported grain and timber, iron and copper, salt fish, hides, slaves, fine wines, drugs, paints and dyes, papyrus, and linen. At the same time, Athens exported pottery (often full of wine or oil), marble, silver, honey, arms, furniture, and books to other parts of the Greek world.

REFLECT AND ANALYZE

1. How did the ancient Greeks get the most out of their limited arable land?

2. a) How and why did the crafts and industries of Greek city-states begin to specialize?
    b) What effects do you think specialization had on the everyday life of the people?

3. Assess the strengths and weaknesses of the Greek economy. Include comparisons with another ancient civilization.

THE ARTS

The arts—sculpture, architecture, pottery, literature, and theatre—are often considered the crowning achievements of Greek civilization. Classical Greek art has had such a profound effect on western culture that we still see its influence everywhere around us today. What inspired this magnificent blossoming of Greek art?

One explanation is that Greek society allowed adult males the leisure time to follow artistic pursuits, and provided them with an education to develop their talents.

Another factor is that although they had a strong sense of independence, the Greek city-states (with the exception of Sparta) were open to outside influences and welcomed new ideas. The Greeks learned from their near-eastern neighbours and built on their accomplishments.

SCULPTURE

Sculptors in ancient Greece excelled in representing the human form. Modern civilizations observe the natural and realistic style of the Venus de Milo statue from the Hellenistic period, for example, and associate the sculpture with the genius of ancient Greek art. These early works of art had a great influence on later European Renaissance artists, such as Michelangelo.

Some of the earliest Greek sculptures—terra-cotta figurines dating from about 675 BCE—depicted people in awkward, rigid poses. These figures seem almost stiff or ritualistic in their stance. The hair looks unnatural, like a wig, and folds in clothing are merely suggested by a few simple lines or patterns. These early sculptures, however, inspired the production of larger marble figurines on the Aegean Islands of Naxos and Paros around 650 BCE. By the classical period, Greek sculpture had reached its zenith.

Artists in the classical period sought to represent the ideal human form—the most beautiful representation possible. The great philosopher Socrates described the goal of these sculptors when he said, "It is so difficult to find a perfect model that you combine the most beautiful details of several, and thus contrive to make the whole figure look beautiful." Rather than individual people, therefore, the sculptors created ideal types. They paid attention to

Figure 7-14 *An early Greek statue, from the seventh century* BCE

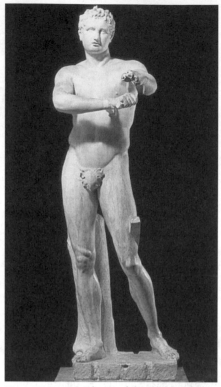

Figure 7-15 *A sculpture from the late fourth century* BCE *(a Roman copy of a lost Greek original)*

the accurate representation of natural movement and the details of appearance, but consistently sculpted the faces as dignified and serene. The male nude was the principal theme, with the gods—Apollo in particular—as favourite subjects. The artists also sculpted the female form to represent various goddesses.

During the Hellenistic period, the focus shifted from idealism to realism. Characteristically, the human faces on these sculptures displayed much greater emotion than those on earlier figures—in some cases, the features even looked contorted and strained. One of the most famous sculptures of the Hellenistic period, known as the "Laocoon," demonstrates this realism. The sculpture portrays a mythical

event of the Trojan War, when Apollo sent snakes to destroy Laocoon, the priest of

Figure 7-16 *The Laocoon*

Troy, for warning his fellow citizens about the Trojan horse. Far from serene, the faces of the figures reveal terror and agony.

Although the Greeks carved many of their sculptures out of stone, they also sculpted in bronze. The advent of bronze casting increased the artist's creative range because stone was brittle and broke easily. Bronze casting allowed the sculptor to depict the human form in a greater variety of poses.

ARCHITECTURE

Like sculpture, Greek architecture, particularly in the classical period, was concerned with harmony and unity—with a sense of the wholeness of things. Some of the most remarkable buildings constructed in ancient Greece were the temples. Temples consisted of a long hall with rows of columns on the outside supporting a low-peaked roof. A triangular piece was set in at the front and back above the columns, under the peak. This design is sometimes called post-and-lintel construction, because the vertical walls of columns (posts) held up the horizontal beams of the roof (lintels) at right angles. The Greeks did not use the arch in their buildings.

The columns that supported the weight of the structure were fluted with grooves so that they would look more pleasing when caught by the light. On the top of each column was a capital, a decorative crown that helped to support the weight of the roof. There were three different designs that reflected the three main styles of Greek architecture: Doric, Ionic, and Corinthian.

Symmetry and proportion were key principles in Greek architectural design. Ideally, that is, if you divided a symmetrical design in half with an imaginary line, each

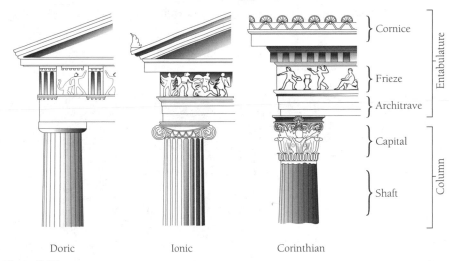

Doric   Ionic   Corinthian

Figure 7-17

Doric Capital The Doric style was plain, massive and dignified. This was the style most favoured by the Athenians of the fifth century BCE and was used in the construction of the Parthenon.

Ionic Capital The Ionic capital curled out on either side in volutes like a pair of ram's horns.

Corinthian Capital The later Corinthian style was rich and ornate. The capital was carved to represent a bunch of acanthus leaves.

half would appear to be the same as the other. In a proportional design, each part of the structure would also stand in pleasing relation to the next. If a column was be-tween 6 m and 9 m high, for example, its width at the top would be six-sevenths of its width at the bottom. If the column was between 12 m and 16 m high, the width at

Figure 7-18 *The Acropolis of Athens*

the top would be seven-eighths of the width at the bottom.

The decorated area between the top of the column and the roof, often carved of stone, is the ***frieze***. In an Ionic temple, the frieze might run continuously around the whole building. In a Doric temple, the frieze was a series of individual panels called *metopes*, separated by stone slabs. Each stone slab was decorated with three carved vertical lines.

THEN AND NOW

The Parthenon—Preserving a Cultural Treasure

Why is the Parthenon considered a cultural treasure? Should modern materials be used in the restoration? What alternatives might the restorers have? How can important historical buildings be protected from the ravages of time and the hazards of our modern environment?

The Athenians paid for the Parthenon and the other buildings of the Acropolis with money from the empire. Workers spent 15 years building the Parthenon, and completed it between 447 BCE and 432 BCE. Tourists visiting the site today are impressed by the Doric style of the temple with its plain columns—eight along each of the eastern and western sides and 17 along each of the southern and northern sides.

The interior frieze of the Parthenon, carved from Athenian marble, ran along all four sides high up on the walls. One of the greatest Greek artists, the sculptor Pheidias, planned the design and had his workers depict the great Panathenaea, the procession held every four years to honour Athena. Some of the frieze survives today, part in a museum on the Acropolis and part in the British Museum.

Pheidias also designed a towering statue of the warrior goddess, Athena Parthenos, for the centre of the temple. Likely over 10 m high, with Athena's flesh carved from ivory and her armour made of gold, the statue must have been dazzling. Ancient records indicate that over 1000 kg of gold went towards the creation of the armour.

The Parthenon—and the Acropolis in general—is one of the most valuable cultural treasures in the world. Over the centuries, it has endured damage by looters, warriors, souvenir-hunters, renovators, and an estimated 4.5 million tourists who file by it every year.

Figure 7-19
Work underway on the Parthenon

As a result, a team led by Manolis Korres and fellow antiquities experts has been working since 1986 to restore the Acropolis. The cost of restoration, estimated at close to $15 million, will be shared by the Greek government and the European Union. The total project will take more than ten years.

The team has stabilized the rock on which the entire Acropolis stands, and has reinforced the ruins with titanium rods. A protective roof made of thin metal may be added over some of the more delicate structures, and some fragile sculptures may be removed to museums and replaced with copies. Dislodged stones will be repositioned only if their original placement is obvious. Also, any stones that the members of the team add now can be taken off later if they find more original material or they change their minds. It is estimated that, before the restoration is completed, the team will have examined, discussed, and catalogued 70 000 pieces of the Acropolis that lie scattered among the ruins.

LITERATURE

Although many ancient Greek philosophers and dramatists made remarkable achievements, we could argue that no single writer had a greater influence than Homer, the epic poet from Chios. The *Iliad* and the *Odyssey*, written during the Dark Ages, helped to create a "national literature" for the ancient Greeks. As part of every Greek boy's education, the poems became a unifying force in Greek culture.

Epics were long poems telling stories of heroic deeds that often affected the fate of an entire city or people.

But not all poems dealt with major deeds or sought to glorify the past. The poet Hesiod, who lived just after Homer, produced a popular poem called *Works and Days* in which he detailed the daily life of the farmer in ancient Greece. Hesiod also wrote *Theogony*, an account of the creation of the universe and the history of the gods.

Another popular form of literature was lyric poetry. Lyric poems are shorter and more personal than epics, expressing feelings such as love. In ancient Greece, most of them were written to be sung, accompanied by the lyre. In addition to Sappho, the great lyric poets of the fifth century BCE included Pindar, whose poems often celebrated the victors of the Olympic Games. His poems were often performed in a procession for the athletes as they returned

THROUGH THEIR EYES

Homer's *Odyssey*

Homer's second epic poem, the *Odyssey*, is about the wanderings of Odysseus as he makes his way home after the Greek wars against Troy. Odysseus may have represented the travellers of Homer's times. With its fantastic adventures in foreign lands and its remarkable characters, the *Odyssey* captured the imagination of the Greeks.

On his homeward journey, Odysseus and his crew visit the land of the Cyclopes. One of these one-eyed giants imprisons Odysseus and his crew in a cave and proceeds to eat the sailors, two at a time, for breakfast and supper. But the resourceful Odysseus develops a plan and has it ready one night when the giant gets drunk.

Homer recounts the hero's plan of escape in this excerpt from the *Odyssey*.

What qualities does Odysseus display in the passage that would cause the Greeks to view him as a hero? What modern heroic stories do we have that are similar?

He toppled over and fell face upward on the floor, where he lay with his great neck twisted to one side, conquered, as all men are, by sleep. His drunkenness made him vomit, and a stream of wine mixed with morsels of men's flesh poured from his throat. I went at once and thrust our pole deep under the ashes of the fire to make it hot, and meanwhile gave a word of encouragement to all my men, to make sure that no

one should play the coward and leave me in the lurch. When the fierce glow from the olive stake warned me that it was about to catch alight in the flames, green as it was, I withdrew it from the fire and brought it over to the spot where my men were standing ready. Heaven now inspired them with a reckless courage. Seizing the olive pole, they drove its sharpened end into the Cyclops' eye, while I used my weight from above to twist it home, like a man boring a ship's timber with a drill which his mates below him twirl with a strap they hold at either end, so that it spins continuously. In much the same way we handled our pole with its red-hot point and twisted it in his eye till the blood boiled up round the burning wood. The fiery smoke from the blazing eyeball singed his lids and brow all round, and the very roots of his eye crackled in the heat. I was reminded of the loud hiss that comes from a great axe or adze when a smith plunges it into cold water—to temper it and give strength to the iron. That is how the Cyclops' eye hissed round the olive stake. He gave a dreadful shriek, which echoed round the rocky walls, and we backed away from him in terror, while he pulled the stake from his eye, streaming with blood. Then he hurled it away from him with frenzied hands and raised a great shout for the other Cyclopes who lived in neighbouring caves along the windy heights.

home in triumph. Even at dinner parties, guests often sang lyric poetry to musical accompaniment.

The fable is another literary form that we associate with ancient Greece. Fables are short, concise tales that use animal characters to convey a moral message. Many children today still read Aesop's fables, including such popular stories as "The Shepherd Boy and the Wolf," "The Fox and the Grapes," and "The Hare and the Tortoise"—a fable that teaches the value of keeping a steady course against seemingly insurmountable odds, even when progress seems slow. It is from Aesop that we have inherited our modern form of the fable.

No one knows the true identity of Aesop. During the fifth century BCE, the historian Herodotus claimed that Aesop was a slave who had lived a century earlier. Today, historians consider it more likely that the popular collection of fables was composed by a variety of anonymous authors.

THEATRE

The ancient Greeks also enjoyed drama. Productions of Greek tragedies and comedies attracted thousands of spectators to annual drama competitions. Greek theatre was an outdoor event. The site chosen for the construction of a theatre offered a sloping area where a natural auditorium could be built. The slope allowed for banked tiers of audience seats, an orchestra, and a stage. Among the more famous Greek theatres were the theatre of Dionysus on the southern slope of the Acropolis, the theatre at Delphi, and the theatre at Epidauros in the Peloponnese, which was possibly the finest of all.

Figure 7-20 *The theatre at Epidauros*

The circular area in the centre of the theatre was called the *orchestra,* a Greek word meaning dancing place. It was given this name because the 15 members of the Greek *chorus* recited and danced in this area during the performance of the play. Behind the orchestra was the stage, and behind the stage either a building or a tent where the actors changed and where properties were stored. The stage, which always represented either a temple or a palace, had a central door with additional doors opening to the sides. There was a painted backdrop, which never changed during the performance, and usually only one large prop. In Greek drama, properties were kept to a minimum because what was said was considered far more important than what was seen.

The chorus was an essential component of all Greek drama. In fact, the earliest plays may have started with only a chorus of men dancing in a ring, reciting a mythological story. Later, one of these men dressed up in robes to impersonate a particular character, and entered into dialogue, still in verse form, with the chorus. He was called the *Hypocrites* or Answerer.

The Hypocrites became the leading actor in the play. Eventually, a second and third actor were added, but productions never employed more than two or three performers. Playwrights wrote their dramas so that the leading actor never assumed more than one role; the other two actors portrayed all other characters. Actors wore masks made of linen, cork, or wood with highly exaggerated features, designed to be seen from the back of the theatre. When a performer switched masks, the audience knew that he was changing roles.

The tragedians Aeschylus, Sophocles, and Euripides, and the comedic playwright Aristophanes, were among the most famous Greek dramatists. Although each was a prolific writer, only a small number of their collected works survive today. Aeschylus (525 BCE–456 BCE) wrote about murder,

THROUGH THEIR EYES

A Scene from *The Ecclesiazusae*

The comedy *The Ecclesiazusae* (Women In Parliament) is one of eleven surviving plays of Aristophanes. It was produced in 393 BCE, at a time when Athens was in decline. The play tells of how the women of Athens, led by Praxagora, go to the assembly. In the scene that follows, Praxagora and the women are rehearsing what they will say in the assembly.

What complaints do Praxagora and the women have about the governing of Athens? What changes in Athens are being suggested by Praxagora? How would her suggestions be viewed in Canada today? Explain.

PRAXAGORA: . . . .I am a citizen as deeply involved
As any of you in this our country's fate,
And I am sadly stricken to behold
The darkness hurrying over our state.
For I behold the city lifting up
Base men to walk upon its broken face;
And if one day a man advocates wisdom,
The next ten times he leads you into disgrace.
And then you try another, only to find
One ten times worse. Ah, very hard it is
To counsel men so rash . . . your wits desert you,
Always suspecting those that most do love you,
Always smiling on those that smile to hurt you.
Once on a time we did not flock to assemblies— . . .
But now we bustle along, because the man
Whose palm takes money uses it to clap,
And he who gets no dole we hear fiercely railing
That those who got it deserve instant jailing.

FIRST WOMAN: By Aphrodite, isn't it a wonderful speech!

PRAXAGORA: . . . When we deliberated in the League
It was agreed that nothing else could save
The ruining state; but once the pact was signed,
It was the worst prick galling the state's flesh.
The sponsor of the vote took to his heels,
He had to. . . .
Wisdom's a babbler, and the biggest fool
The state's philosopher . . . for then we saw
A peep of safety flutter past; but now
Thrasybulos' advice is no longer asked.

FIRST WOMAN: This is a very clever fellow.

PRAXAGORA: That's right.
But you, people of Athens, are to blame.
You draw your doles out of the public store,
Yet each man's care for the state ends precisely
Where that salary ends; and so the city
Staggers shamefully, like Aisimos.
But trust my counsels and you may yet be saved,
For I propose this law: that we put at once
The city's entire rule in the women's hands.
Do they not manage households efficiently?

FIRST WOMAN: Hear, hear! by the Lord Zeus, speak on, my man!

revenge, divine justice, and the relationships between humans and gods. Sophocles (496 BCE–406 BCE) chose moral and religious beliefs as his themes, and considered how destiny affected the lives of individuals. Euripides (480 BCE–406 BCE) wrote of everyday life, and questioned the moral and religious beliefs of his contemporaries. In *Medea* and *The Trojan Women*, for example, he expressed sympathy for women. In their comedies, playwrights such as Aristophanes ridiculed people, ideas, and social customs.

One of the most significant events in Athens was the drama competition held in March called the City of Dionysia, dedicated to Dionysus. The four-day event opened with a procession, followed by sacrifices to the god at an altar set up in the middle of the orchestra. On each of the next three days, the playwrights selected for the competition presented their works.

Most citizens attended and came prepared to view several plays at a sitting, sometimes for ten hours a day. Most of the presentations were tragedies, but each day ended with a comedy. A panel of ten citizens judged the competition. At the end of the fourth day, a winner was determined by a vote.

REFLECT AND ANALYZE

1. How did sculpture evolve over the history of ancient Greece? In your answer, refer specifically to the photographs of sculptures on page 146.

2. What were the main features of Greek temple design? Find examples of these architectural features in buildings from your local community, and create a portfolio with captioned photographs noting the similarities.

3. Write and stage a short Greek drama using chorus and masks. Choose a theme for your comedy or tragedy from ancient Greek life, such as the role of women or the death of a hero.

4. Choose a modern movie, play, or television program and write a report on how it compares with ancient Greek drama.

THE SCIENCES

PHILOSOPHY— "THE LOVE OF WISDOM"

How can people find happiness? What makes some actions good and others bad? Is it better to obey the rules of society or to follow one's own judgement? How can we be certain about what we know? If you have ever asked yourself these questions, then you have ventured in the world of **philosophy**.

In Classical Greece, there was a great deal of debate over issues relating to personal conduct and morality. The people most involved in theses debates were called philosophers. While some philosophers were interested in morality, others focused on the world around them, hoping to discover the laws and principles that governed not only human behaviour, but also the physical universe. Following this quest for knowledge, they laid the foundations of modern science. Three of the most important Greek philosophers were Socrates, Plato, and Aristotle.

Socrates (470 BCE–399 BCE) lived during the height of Athenian power. He was a well-known figure in the streets of Athens, easily recognized by his rolling walk, snub nose, shaggy eyebrows, and bulging eyes. In his endless arguments with other citizens, Socrates questioned most of the ideas that were generally accepted during his lifetime. As a result, he managed to make many enemies among the leaders in Athens. The Delphic oracle proclaimed him one of the wisest men in all of Greece, but Socrates devoted himself to a search for someone who knew more than he did.

When examining issues, Socrates employed a question-and-answer method. He would pose a question and the student would respond. Socrates would then use his logic to expose the flaws in the answer, the gaps in the student's knowledge, and the still-unanswered parts of the question. This teaching method helped his students to clarify their thinking and sharpen their reasoning skills. Socrates believed it was his mission to expose ignorance and lead people to truth. He is reported to have said, "The life that is unexamined is not worth living."

Using this socratic approach, he cross-examined anyone who wished to discuss these issues with him and found none who could answer his searching questions. He charged no fee to those who would listen, and lived in a state of poverty. But he continued to engage men in the streets in conversation and to discuss the problems of existence with young people attracted by his ideas.

Socrates believed in an inner being or soul—a person's moral and intellectual character—and believed that the soul should strive for good. One of his central concerns was moral behaviour and what constituted a "good life." As a result, he cast doubt on the stories about the behaviour of the gods and questioned the motives behind people's actions. In time, people saw him as a destructive critic of many accepted beliefs, and questioned his loyalty to the state. When he debated the existence of so many gods and goddesses, the government charged him with atheism and sentenced him to death. He chose death by poison, and drank hemlock.

Although Socrates left no writings, he figures prominently in the works of his famous pupil, Plato (427 BCE–347 BCE).

One of Plato's main interests was politics. His book *The Republic*, which explores the ideal state or government, was the first book ever written on political science. Plato believed that a state could only achieve the good of all if every citizen adhered to the four basic virtues of truth, wisdom, courage, and moderation. In 388 BCE, Plato established the school called the Academy where he taught philosophy and science.

Aristotle (384 BCE–323 BCE) was a pupil of Plato's. For seven years he served in Macedonia as tutor to Alexander the Great. In 323 BCE, he established his own school called the Lyceum.

Although he was interested in the traditional areas of philosophy, Aristotle's primary interest was in biology. Rather than focusing on the ideal, as Plato had, Aristotle turned his attention to the observable world around him. He collected extensive samples of plants and animals, and began to classify them according to their characteristics, from the simplest to the most complex forms. His system of investigation is the basis of modern biology.

Aristotle also contributed to the field of science in another area. He built on the work of an earlier Greek scientist, Thales of Miletus (636 BCE–546 BCE), who had developed the first two steps in what we know today as the scientific method. Thales had identified collecting information as the first step in the scientific method. The second step was to develop a hypothesis or possible explanation based on the information collected. Aristotle added the third step, the idea of testing the hypothesis to see if it is correct. His works and interests extended into the fields of physics, astronomy, psychology, and metaphysics.

Figure 7-21 *The death of Socrates*

MATHEMATICS

Mathematics was widely studied and taught in ancient Greece. As well as a noted scientist, Thales of Miletus was one of the first mathematicians. He discovered five geometric theorems, including the theorem that the angles at the base of an isosceles triangle are equal. His knowledge of geometry helped to improve navigation.

Perhaps the most famous Greek mathematician of all was Pythagoras of Samos (582 BCE–500 BCE). Pythagoras studied the pattern of numbers, often by laying out pebbles on the sand. He worked out many different mathematical principles, including the intervals in a musical scale. But his most famous theorem concerned the right-angled triangle. He proved that where ACB is a right angle, the side AB squared equals the sum of AC squared and CB squared.

Several important mathematicians are associated with the Hellenistic Age as well. Euclid (365 BCE–300 BCE), the most famous, wrote 13 books of geometry that teachers were still using as textbooks a hundred years ago. His principles are still part of geometry studies today. The mathematician Archimedes (287 BCE–212 BCE) worked out the area of a circle by studying its diameter and circumference. He proved that the circumference of a circle is approximately 3.142 times the length of its diameter, and named this number *pi* after a Greek letter. Archimedes also discovered that an object weighed less in water than it did out of water. He calculated that the difference in the object's weight was exactly the same as the weight of the water the object displaced. History has it that Archimedes made this remarkable discovery quite by accident. Sinking down into a tub of water one day at the baths, he noticed that the water rose and spilled over the edge. He jumped gleefully out of the tub shouting, "Eureka!" To his delight, he had found the solution to a problem that had been puzzling him for some time.

Both Euclid and Archimedes were influenced by eastern thinkers. Archimedes studied in Egypt (Alexandria), and Euclid operated a school in that country. Alexandria was a noted research centre, famous for its library. Students travelled there to study literature, mathematics, astronomy, and medicine.

MEDICINE

Although they gained much of their early knowledge from the Egyptians, Greek doctors were famous throughout the world. But their practice of medicine included a great deal of spirituality. For example, in the shrine to Asclepius, the god of healing, patients lay in a corridor all night in the hope that the god would appear in the form of a snake and lick the diseased parts of their bodies. Many remedies seem to have worked, and grateful patients set up tablets displaying carved images of ears, eyes or whatever body parts might have caused them trouble.

During the fifth century BCE, approaches to medicine changed. Doctors abandoned some of their earlier notions about healing in favour of a more scientific approach. Doctors learned more about the use of herbs, drugs, and ointments, and began to study symptoms more carefully. They believed that diet, exercise, and the patient's comfort were all important components of the healing process.

Doctors did not need a licence or a medical degree. Instead, they were judged by their successes and failures. One doctor, Hippocrates (460 BCE–377 BCE), has been called the father of medicine. Born on the island of Cos in the south Aegean, Hippocrates founded a medical school there where he and his successors wrote a great deal about the treatment of illness and the responsibility of doctors. Hippocrates made important contributions to the diagnosis of illnesses such as quinsy and epilepsy. But he is more famous for his ideas about scientific methods and medical ethics. He

established a rigorous scientific approach to medicine, and set high standards of professional conduct for doctors. For centuries, the Hippocratic oath has served as a code of conduct for medical graduates.

ASTRONOMY

The ancient Greeks made significant advances in the field of astronomy and in the measurement of time. They knew, for example, that the earth was round and that the moon travelled around it. Aristarchus (310 BCE–230 BCE) formulated the view that the sun was the centre of the universe, not the earth, and that the earth travelled around the sun.

Greek astronomers came remarkably close in their reckoning of the length of the solar year. They calculated it to be 365 days, 5 hours, 55 minutes, and 12 seconds—only 6 minutes and 26 seconds longer than the true length. The astronomer Hipparchus (165 BCE–125 BCE) calculated that the moon took 29 days, 12 hours, 44 minutes, and 2.5 seconds to travel around the earth. He was less than a second out in his calculations.

The Greeks developed a luni-solar calendar that contained 354 days of 12 lunar months. Each month began with the new moon. To keep the calendar in agreement with the seasons, the Greeks added an extra month three times during every eight-year cycle. Therefore, three out of every eight years contained 13 months. In 432 BCE, the Athenians made another modification, adopting a system that added an extra month to seven of the years in a 19-year cycle.

REFLECT AND ANALYZE

1. Identify three major contributions of the ancient Greeks in each of the following fields, and explain their importance. How have these contributions affected our lives today?
   a) medicine
   b) mathematics
   c) astronomy

2. Compare Greek medical practices and accomplishments to those in ancient Egypt or in another ancient civilization.

3. To understand how Greek philosophers tackled fundamental questions, ask a partner: "What is a stone?" After your partner answers, ask another question to try to clarify the definition. Continue this process until you think you have a good definition for a stone. Then reverse roles, using another question. Share your experiences with other pairs.

LOOKING BACK

Although the ancient Greeks were few in number and their city-states small when compared to the mighty empires of Persia and Egypt, they had a profound influence on the development of later European civilizations. The Europeans considered ancient Greece the source of advanced civilization in the western world.

Western civilization has been built upon many of the important ideas, beliefs, and artistic techniques that the Greeks created and developed. Much of contemporary science, for example, stems from the efforts of the Greek philosophers to find order in the natural world and to develop human reason. The study of philosophy in colleges and universities often begins with the work of Socrates, Plato, and Aristotle.

Greek sculpture and literature remain a standard of excellence.

The ancient Greeks were the first civilization to emphasize the rights of the individual and to value individual freedom. Many people believe that this was their most important contribution of all. The Greeks did not view people as mere instruments of the gods, but as intelligent beings capable of great achievements. Over the centuries, people have turned to the writings of the ancient Greeks to help them

work out better ways to organize society. The Greek idea of democracy lies at the heart of most political systems in western society today.

Within the Mediterranean world, Hellenistic civilization built on the achievements of Greek civilization, bringing elements of Middle Eastern culture to the west. It also created the environment for the rise of an even more influential civilization—Rome.

ROME:
Republic to Empire

Figure 8-1
*A Roman legionary
soldier*

The emperor Augustus has more than 60 legions under arms. Over 30 legions protect the imperial frontier—a sizeable force, since each legion contains 5000 men. The legionaries are highly trained and disciplined. They regularly march long distances across rough country, carrying their weapons and a heavy pack. Each pack contains rations for two weeks, trenching tools, cooking pots, and the heavy stakes needed to build a camp near the battle site. A Roman legion always builds a camp before engaging the enemy in battle.

If a legionary disobeys orders, he may be flogged. If an entire company shows cowardice in battle, one man out of ten may be put to death. Absolute obedience is expected, and most legionaries are fiercely loyal to their companies.

Armour is kept as light as possible because legionaries fight on foot and must be quick and mobile. They wear a brass helmet with neck guards and cheek flaps, and a leather coat strengthened with plates of metal. As weapons, they carry a long javelin, a short stabbing sword in a wooden or leather sheath at their right side, and a knife in a sheath at their left side. A long shield with the edges turned back protects their bodies. In battle, they hurl the javelins at the enemy and then move in to attack with their swords.

Their lives are severe and demanding, and their pay is meagre. Yet the legionary is more than a skilled fighter. He is a surveyor, engineer, road-builder, and bridge-maker, ready to execute his skills wherever he is stationed.

The Romans were among the greatest empire-builders in recorded history. For two centuries, the Roman legions helped to maintain control over the vast empire. They guarded the distant borders, helped to build the extensive network of roads and bridges, kept trade routes open, and fought the wars that allowed the Romans to expand their territory. In many ways, the legions were the backbone of the empire. Yet, in the end, their support was not enough and the empire crumbled. The reasons why the Roman empire collapsed have fascinated historians for centuries. Why do great civilizations fall? What are the signs of stagnation and decline?

THE LAND OF THE ANCIENT ROMANS

The land of the ancient Romans, the Italian peninsula, was about three times as large as the homeland of the ancient Greeks. Shaped like a boot, the

north, helped to protect Rome from invasion, although mountain passes allowed people to cross into Europe. In contrast to the high peaks of Greece, however, the rugged Italian landscape did not prevent the Romans from unifying under a single ruler and creating a large empire.

Fertile land was located in three main areas on the peninsula. The first was the great northern plain, which was enriched by the fertile deposits from the Po River. In ancient times, the Apennine ridge, extending from the west coast to the east before its turn southwards, effectively cut off this plain from the rest of Italy. Until the time of Julius Caesar, therefore, the area was considered to be part of Gaul. The other main fertile areas were the plains of Latium and Campania on the west coast. Both were small areas, but their soil was enriched by phosphate from volcanoes, which were active until about 1000 BCE. As the population of the Roman empire increased, these fertile lands could not supply the growing demand for grain. Rome was more productive agriculturally than Greece, but like the Greeks, the Romans had to find colonies to supplement their food supply.

Figure 8-2
The landscape of the Apennine Mountains

peninsula juts approximately 960 km out into the Mediterranean Sea and averages 160 km in width. Despite 3200 km of coastline, good harbours were harder to find than in Greece. As most were located on the west coast, Rome was more westward-oriented than ancient Greece, which had been oriented more to the east. In spite of the peninsula's few good harbours, trade up and down the coast and across the Mediterranean was lively. Strategically located in the centre of the Mediterranean region, Romans could reach the Middle East, Greece, Spain, and North Africa easily by sea.

Most of the Italian peninsula is either hilly or mountainous, which made overland transportation and communication difficult. The main mountain chain, the Apennines, runs down the eastern length like a backbone. The Alps, the range in the

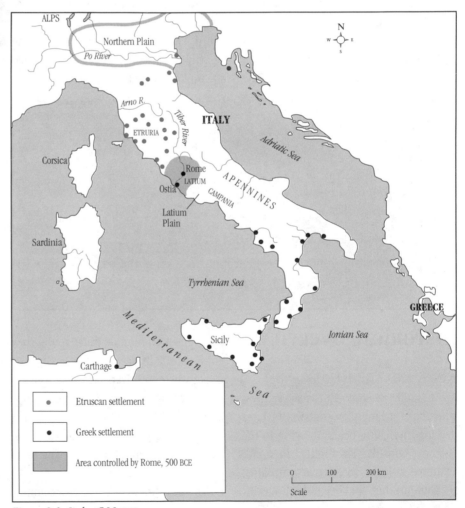

Figure 8-3 *Italy: 500 BCE*

The mountainous character of the peninsula also robbed it of many great rivers. The three main rivers were the Po, the Arno, and the Tiber. While the Po emptied into the Adriatic Sea to the east, the Arno and Tiber flowed into the Tyrrhenian Sea to the west. The Tiber River was particularly important because the city of Rome developed on its banks 24 km upstream from the sea. Rome came to control trade on the river and throughout the Mediterranean. The Romans built the port of Ostia at the mouth of the Tiber to accommodate ships too large to travel up the river to Rome.

Most of the Italian peninsula enjoys a Mediterranean climate with rainy winters and hot, dry summers. The river valley of the Po, however, has a continental climate with moderate winter snow, summer rain, and a wet spring and fall. The weather on the peninsula suited the production of wheat, olives, and grapes very well.

Among the resources available to the ancient Romans was building stone, including a workable yellowish limestone found around Rome. After the first century BCE, the Romans used marble from Carrara, although it was more difficult to work with. They also mixed a volcanic dust with water to make a type of concrete, which became an essential building material. Mineral deposits included copper from the Tuscany coast and iron from the island of Elba. The Romans imported tin and combined it with copper to make bronze. The heavily wooded Apennine slopes provided the timber needed for building ships.

pied the Italian peninsula—the Greeks and the Etruscans. Greek settlers had built towns in southern Italy and on the island of Sicily during the period of Greek colonization between 750 BCE and 500 BCE. The towns grew into prosperous city-states, and Greek culture in the colonies flourished. Famous Greeks such as Archimedes and Pythagoras, who lived in the Italian colonies, helped to make these cities centres of learning, trade, and commerce. The Greek presence in the Italian peninsula would have a profound influence on Roman culture.

The Etruscans occupied the plain just north of Rome in the region called Etruria. Historians are not certain where these people originated. They may have come from Asia Minor or they may even have been native to the peninsula. By 800 BCE, they had established a number of city-states ruled by kings (rather like the early Greek city-states), and had developed a highly sophisticated society. Wall paintings and rock carvings in their tombs depict scenes of lavish banquets, chariot races, musicians, and even gladiatorial combats. As they gained power, the Etruscans eventually expanded their territory to the north and advanced south towards Rome.

The Roman military organization was no match for the sophisticated Etruscan armies. Because the Etruscans enforced compulsory military service and training, their troops were organized and experienced. In contrast, the Romans summoned able-bodied men to defend the city only when necessary, and required the recruits to supply their own weapons. The richest Roman citizens served in the cavalry. The poorest, who could

REFLECT AND ANALYZE

1. What geographic features put Rome in a good position to
   a) establish control over the Italian peninsula?
   b) establish a large empire in the Mediterranean region?

2. What obstacles do you think the physical environment posed for the development of a large empire?

3. Compare and contrast the geographic features of the Italian peninsula with those of Greece.

HISTORICAL OVERVIEW

ROME AND THE ETRUSCANS

About 1200 BCE, Indo-European settlers, who spoke a language that would later develop into Latin, began arriving in the Italian peninsula. They settled in small, scattered villages on the central plains, took up farming, and began trading with their neighbours. Because the Tiber River interrupted one major trade route, they constructed a bridge, to allow passage, at a spot where the river narrowed. Villages sprang up near the bridge, and by approximately 800 BCE these villages had grown into a town on the slopes of the Palatine and Capitoline hills. The town was Rome.

As the Latins established their communities, two other influential groups occu-

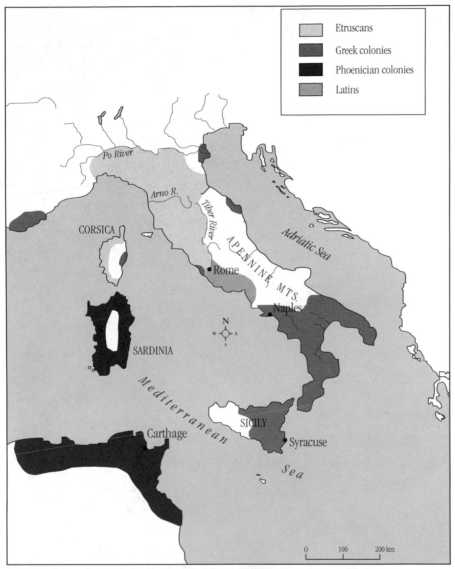

Figure 8-4 *Peoples in the Italian peninsula circa 500 BCE*

the people and scorned religion. In a popular uprising, the Romans overthrew Tarquin the Proud and declared their independence.

The period of Etruscan control, which lasted almost 100 years, had a major influence on the development of Rome. From the Etruscans, the Romans learned how to use the arch, how to build huge aqueducts to transport fresh water, and how to construct fine harbours, urban drainage systems, and walled cities. They also learned the skills of metal-working, and took advantage of the rich iron ore deposits on the island of Elba. Many of the Etruscans' religious beliefs became part of Roman life. The Romans also adopted the Etruscan alphabet. The Etruscans had taken their alphabet from the Greeks and the Romans changed it to fit their own Latin language. Later, this alphabet formed the basis of many written languages, including modern English, French, Italian, and Spanish.

By the end of the Etruscan period, the Romans had also accepted the principle of compulsory military service and had solidified their views of government. The way had been paved for the birth of the Roman republic.

not afford full armour, served as light-armed troops. In about 600 BCE, the better-trained Etruscan soldiers overpowered those of Rome.

The Etruscan family called Tarquin ruled Rome until 509 BCE, when rivalries within the family weakened the power of the king. The last Etruscan ruler was Tarquin the Proud (534 BCE-509 BCE), an oppressive king who opposed the wishes of

Figure 8-5 *Etruscans wining and dining—a picture from a tomb painting near Tarquinia*

ROME: A DEVELOPMENTAL TIMELINE

	ROME AND THE ETRUSCANS 1200 BCE-509 BCE	**THE REPUBLIC AND THE PUNIC WARS 509 BCE-146 BCE**
POLITICAL DEVELOPMENTS	• Indo-European people move into the Italian peninsula (circa 1200 BCE) • Rome founded (circa 800 BCE) • Etruscans establish city-states in Etruria and expand to take over Rome (800 BCE) • the Romans drive the Etruscan rulers out and establish a republic (509 BCE) • Greeks establish colonies in southern Italy (750 BCE–500 BCE)	• the Romans form the League of Italian Nations • Rome gains control over all of Italy (265 BCE) • the First Punic War is fought (264 BCE–241 BCE); Carthage surrenders and Rome gains control of Sicily • the Second Punic War is fought (218 BCE–202 BCE); Romans defeat the Carthaginian general Hannibal and Carthage surrenders its empire • the Third Punic War is fought (149 BCE–146 BCE); Carthage is crushed and North Africa becomes a province of Rome • Rome makes further imperial gains in Greece, Egypt, and Asia Minor
CULTURAL DEVELOPMENTS	• the Romans learn an alphabet from the Etruscans, which the Etruscans adopted from the Greeks • Romans adopt aspects of Etruscan religion and culture	• Law of the Twelve Tables is established (449 BCE) • plebeians (common people) gradually gain greater representation in government • first public combats of gladiators in Rome (264 BCE)
TECHNOLOGICAL/ECONOMIC DEVELOPMENTS	• Romans learn how to use the arch and build aqueducts to transport fresh water • Etruscans teach the Romans about metal-working	• earliest known paved streets appear in Rome (circa 170 BCE)

THE DECLINE OF THE REPUBLIC
146 BCE-31 BCE

- the size of the Roman "mob" increases greatly
- Tiberius Gracchus attempts to reform the system of land distribution (133 BCE)
- Gaius Gracchus attempts to reduce the power of the nobility in Rome (123 BCE)
- Gaius Marius reforms the Roman army to make the republic more secure
- Cornelius Sulla uses the army to seize power in Rome (82 BCE)
- Caesar, Pompey, and Crassus form a triumvirate (60 BCE)
- Caesar becomes dictator of the republic (49 BCE)
- Caesar is assassinated in the Roman Senate (44 BCE)
- Octavian defeats Antony at the battle of Actium (31 BCE) and becomes the emperor Augustus

- final years of the republic and early years of the empire are the golden age of Latin literature; notable writers include the poet Catullus (84 BCE–54 BCE), the orator Cicero (106 BCE–43 BCE), the historian Livy (59 BCE–17 BCE), and the poet Virgil (70 BCE–19 BCE)
- Roman sculptors adopt a realistic style, breaking away from the idealistic Greek classical style
- the Julian calendar is introduced (45 BCE)

- the Romans perfect the technology to build aqueducts to transport water to towns and cities throughout their territory
- the famous road known as the Appian Way, extending over 200 km, is completed (312 BCE)

THE EMPIRE AND THE PAX ROMANA
31 BCE-180 CE

- Augustus places the empire on a sound footing as *princeps*
- after Augustus a number of weak and unpopular emperors rule
- after the death of Nero, the army takes part in the selection of emperors
- the "Five Good Emperors" create a period of stability (96 CE–180 CE), the high point in imperial Rome
- the emperor Trajan expands the empire to its greatest extent

- Jesus Christ begins his teachings and is crucified for being portrayed as King of the Jews (30 CE)
- Christians are blamed for the great fire in Rome that many believe was started by the emperor Nero (64 CE)

- the Colosseum is constructed (75 CE–80 CE)
- the Romans construct thousands of kilometres of roads to link the empire

THE DECLINE AND FALL OF THE EMPIRE
180 CE-476 CE

- enemies of Rome in the north and the east begin to threaten the Roman frontier in the second century CE
- Diocletian decides to split the Roman empire into eastern and western sections (293 CE)
- Constantine becomes the sole emperor of the empire, and builds a new capital at Constantinople (324 CE–330 CE)
- the Vandals sack Rome, causing extensive damage (455 CE)
- Odoacer, a barbarian general, deposes the last Roman emperor in the west and proclaims himself king (476 CE)

- despite persecution, Christianity spreads throughout the empire
- Christianity becomes the official religion of Rome (395 CE)

- costs of maintaining the empire become a burden
- Diocletian increases taxes to raise more revenue but these stifle businesses
- inflation is high
- empire depends heavily on slave labour
- little new technological development

REFLECT AND ANALYZE

1. Why did the city of Rome develop where it did? What natural advantages did this location have?

2. What groups of people occupied the Italian peninsula and surrounding islands in 500 BCE? Which group had the greatest influence on the early development of Rome? Why?

3. The Phoenicians were a major trading power in the Mediterranean. What role do you speculate they might have played as Rome began to expand its influence in the region?

THE ROMAN REPUBLIC

Following the overthrow of Tarquin the Proud, the Romans were determined never again to be ruled by oppressive kings. Accordingly, they chose a form of government called a ***republic***. In a republic, the citizens elect representatives to run the government. In the early republic, however, only ***patricians***—members of noble families—could hold office. The Roman republic lasted for almost 500 years, a period marked by external pressures, social and political changes, and the expansion of Roman power and influence. During the republic, Rome became the leading power in the Mediterranean.

The Romans were fortunate that their region of the Italian peninsula had rich agricultural land, but they spent much of their early history defending it against attacks from envious neighbours. The Volscians, the Samnites, and the Sabines, as well as the other Etruscan city-states in the south, all mounted attacks against Rome. In 390 BCE, the Gauls from north of the Po River crossed the Alps and sacked Rome, but the Romans fought back and succeeded in pushing the Gauls out. Ul-timately, the Romans decided to take the offensive. They soon discovered that several other small states in the peninsula were willing to help them fight their aggressive neighbours.

As the Romans changed their ideas about defence, they significantly modified their military organization. Because the population had increased, they no longer needed to recruit all adult males whenever the city was threatened. Instead, they instituted a program of selective conscription among landowners. All citizens who owned land—farmers and nobles—had to undergo training and serve in the army. The Romans also introduced a system of pay (although quite low) for poorer citizens. This salary was important because soldiers had to feed, clothe, and arm themselves while fighting far from home in long military campaigns.

The Romans organized their troops into ***legions*** of 4000 to 5000 men each. Initially, they established four legions, each subdivided into smaller units called *cohorts* or companies. When a Roman company went into battle, it was arranged in three separate lines. In front were the *hasti* or young men, as yet unproven in battle, equipped with javelins and spears. In the second line were the *principes* or older men, carrying superior weapons and cylindrical shields. In the third line were the *triarii*, or veterans, who had previously proven their courage. The small companies could separate and manoeuvre quickly to attack the enemy from all sides.

If an enemy seriously threatened the security of the republic, the government increased the number of legions. Under the most serious circumstances, they sometimes recruited slaves into the ranks. But this rapid military expansion had drawbacks. Notably, because the newest recruits tended to be ill-trained, the Romans often suffered high casualty rates.

Early in the fifth century BCE, Rome established a League of Italian Nations and began to fight for control of the Italian peninsula. First, it annexed the southern part of Etruria. Then it conquered the central region and the Greek settlements of southern Italy. By 265 BCE, Rome controlled all of Italy.

Following each conquest, Rome made allies of its defeated enemies by adopting a policy of just treatment and leniency. Unlike other conquerors, such as the Egyptians and Persians, the Romans took only a portion of the conquered lands and allowed the conquered people to keep the rest. They also permitted the people to keep their own customs, local government, and laws, although the defeated regions had to acknowledge Roman leadership. Rome did not take slaves, and gave some people limited citizenship rights. These reasonable measures won Rome the loyalty of the people on the Italian peninsula.

Figure 8-6 *Hannibal*

THE PUNIC WARS

The Roman republic's first territorial interest outside of Italy was in Africa. The target was the Phoenician city of Carthage, a great naval power with outposts on the Mediterranean islands of Sicily and Sardinia. Rome desired Carthage for two reasons. First, Carthage controlled much of Sicily, an island rich in wheat that could provide the republic with a valuable source of grain. Second, the navy of Carthage posed a threat to the western coastal plains of Italy, and hindered trade along the west coast of the peninsula. Rivalry and suspicion eventually led to three lengthy conflicts called the Punic Wars, named after *punicus*, the Latin word for Phoenician.

The First Punic War (264 BCE–241 BCE) erupted when Rome violated a treaty with Carthage and invaded Sicily. The war continued sporadically for almost 23 years until Rome finally claimed victory. The Roman army fought effectively and valiantly on land, but Rome's naval forces fared badly during the early years against the powerful Carthaginian fleets. To improve their chances, the Romans redesigned their fleet so that the ships could hook onto the side of enemy boats and the troops could fight on the enemy's deck.

Although storms destroyed two Roman fleets during the war, wealthy Romans raised money to build another 200 ships. This fleet defeated Carthage off the western tip of Sicily in 241 BCE. At the end of the war, the Carthaginians agreed to pay Rome 3300 talents of silver and to surrender Sicily, where Rome founded its first province.

The Second Punic War (218 BCE–202

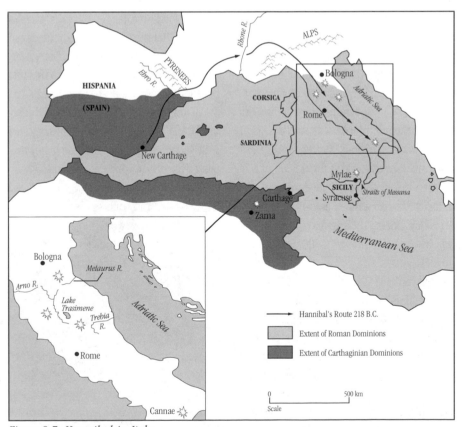

Figure 8-7 *Hannibal in Italy*

BCE) proved a far more serious threat to Rome. Once again, the Romans became suspicious of Carthage's growing influence in the western Mediterranean. The Carthaginian general in the First Punic War, Hamilcar Barca, had conquered parts of Spain. Hannibal, his son and commander of the armies in Spain, pressed even farther north on the Spanish coast, capturing one of the few remaining independent cities in 219 BCE. When Rome demanded that Hannibal surrender the city, he refused.

According to legend, Hamilcar had made the young Hannibal swear on a sacred altar that he would remain an enemy of Rome for life. Hannibal acted on his pledge and took the offensive against Rome, launching a sudden invasion of the Italian peninsula from the north. This move was completely unexpected—the Romans considered the towering Alps to be a natural defence barrier. However, Hannibal organized a force of 40 000 infantry and 8000 cavalry, and decided to use 60 elephants to transport the necessary military equipment through the mountain passes.

It was a perilous strategy, but Hannibal must have felt that the advantages of surprise would outweigh the dangers of the journey. After 15 days he descended into the Po valley. During the crossing of the Alps he had lost half his infantry, 2000 cavalry, and 40 elephants.

Nevertheless, Hannibal had astounding success against the Romans. Undaunted by his losses, he defeated the Roman troops at the Trebia River, opening the route to central Italy. To stop the advancing Carthaginian army, the Romans marched north. In 217 BCE, the two armies met on the shores of Lake Trasimene, and again Hannibal won the battle.

Figure 8-8 *The battle of Zama; 2nd Punic War 202 BCE*

With Hannibal approaching the city of Rome, the Romans turned to a military leader named Fabius. Fabius planned to trust the city's fortifications and wear Hannibal down by waiting him out. He believed that Hannibal lacked the equipment for a prolonged siege and that a delay in the battle would seriously reduce the Carthaginian food supply.

In the end, however, Fabius's methods were too slow for many impatient Romans, who were anxious to rid the peninsula of Hannibal and his army. In 216 BCE, a Roman army marched against Hannibal at Cannae and fell victim once again to the strategic genius of the Carthaginian leader. Although Rome had a larger infantry, Han-

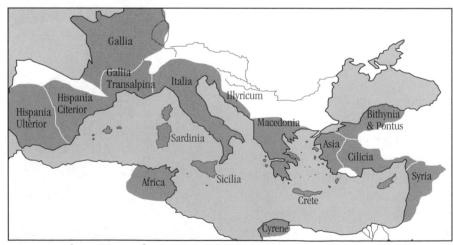

Figure 8-9 *The provinces of Rome circa 50 BCE*

nibal had a stronger cavalry and a plan to take advantage of this strength.

The general of Carthage positioned his infantry in a crescent-shaped formation that bulged out in the centre towards the Romans. On the wings, he placed his cavalry. As the Romans drove forward, they pushed Hannibal's infantry back in the centre, and thought the victory would be theirs. But the Carthaginian cavalry routed the Roman wings, swept in behind the Roman legions, and surrounded the troops in a vice-like grip. The defeat devastated Rome. More than 25 000 men were killed, and as word of Carthage's victory spread, many southern Italian towns, fearful for their future, surrendered to Hannibal.

Before launching an attack on Rome itself, Hannibal marched south for food and supplies. In this critical interval, the Romans were able to regroup and recover from their losses. When Hannibal began to prepare for the assault, he decided that his army was too small and that he should wait for reinforcements from his brother Hasdrubal.

In 207 BCE, Hasdrubal arrived in Italy with 30 000 men, and sent a messenger to inform Hannibal of their approach. The Romans intercepted the messenger, however, and when they learned the location of Hasdrubal's army, they crushed the reinforcement troops at the Metaurus River. Finally, after 11 years of war, the Romans had achieved a major victory. Hasdrubal was killed in the battle, and the Romans threw his severed head into Hannibal's camp as a sign that the tide was turning.

The Romans also began to win other battles elsewhere. They conquered Spain and invaded North Africa. Fearing an attack on his homeland, Hannibal decided to leave Italy in order to defend Carthage. In 202 BCE, just south of the city, his last stand came at the Battle of Zama.

At Zama, the Carthaginians outnumbered the Romans, but the Romans had the stronger cavalry. Hannibal feigned flight with part of his cavalry to draw the Roman horsemen into pursuit. Then the remainder of his cavalry and his infantry attacked the Roman foot soldiers. For a time, the strategy worked, but before Carthage could complete its rout, the Roman cavalry turned back to the battle. Zama was the only defeat Hannibal suffered in his military career.

Carthage asked for peace, surrendering its empire and its fleet. It agreed to pay 10 000 talents to Rome in 50 annual instalments as reparations for the war. Hannibal fled into exile and committed suicide.

Although the Carthaginians were forced into a crippling peace at the end of the Second Punic War, a third confrontation broke out half a century later. The Third Punic War (149 BCE–146 BCE) began when Carthage violated the peace treaty by building up its military strength once again. Furious, Rome decided that the city must be destroyed. The war ended in the complete defeat of Carthage. The Romans plundered, burned, and then ploughed the city under, sowing the ground with salt so that nothing would grow. Any people they did not kill, they sold into slavery. North Africa then became a province of Rome.

In the century that followed the Punic Wars, significant changes took place in the Mediterranean world. Rome became the unrivalled power in the western Mediterranean. Smaller states turned to it for alliances and for assistance in settling disputes. Sardinia, Corsica, Hispania (Spain) Ulterior and Hispania Citerior joined Sicily as Roman provinces. After becoming involved in diplomatic activity and fighting in the east, Rome expanded throughout the eastern Mediterranean, with territorial gains in Greece, Egypt, and Asia Minor. One of the earliest imperial gains following the Punic Wars was Macedonia which Rome linked with the remainder of Greece. In 133 BCE King Attalus of Pergamum bequeathed his kingdom to Rome and it became the province of Asia. In 120 BCE Transalpina Gaul (Gaul-across-the-Alps) was added. In 81 BCE Cisalpina Gaul (Gaul-this-side-of-the-Alps) became a province. Cilicia was added in 102 BCE and between 75 BCE and 64 BCE Rome acquired Bythinia and Pontus, Syria, Cyrene, and Crete.

REFLECT AND ANALYZE

1. Write a series of newspaper headlines announcing the major events in the Punic Wars and the expansion of the Roman republic.

2. If you had been a Roman centurion (commander of 100 men) at the battle of Cannae, what strategy would you have used to counter Hannibal's offensive?

3. Does Hannibal, the Carthaginian general, deserve to be remembered as one of the greatest military strategists of the ancient world? Support your point of view.

THE DECLINE OF THE ROMAN REPUBLIC

Ironically, the imperial success of the republic coincided with the beginning of its decline. While outside Rome the territories expanded, inside Rome the problems grew. A widening gulf between the wealthy and the poor led to serious social unrest and a vicious power struggle. In the republic, the Roman Senate represented the interests of the wealthy patrician families. The Assembly represented the interests of the common people, or **plebeians**.

Two leaders challenged the power of the Roman Senate in attempts to champion the cause of the landless poor. In 133 BCE, the tribune Tiberius Gracchus (162 BCE–133 BCE) tried to change the system of land distribution in Rome. He revived an ancient law of 367 BCE that limited the amount of land one family could own or rent. If enacted, this law would bring thousands of hectares of land into the public domain and restore the devastated farming class. To make the deal more acceptable to large landholders, Tiberius doubled the minimum limit and promised payment for any losses. Although the reform law passed the Assembly, the Senate decided to withhold the funds that the land commission needed to carry it out.

Tiberius then took an unprecedented step and sought elected office for a second term. Angered by his decision, the landowning Senate provoked a riot in the centre of the city. Tiberius and 300 of his followers were murdered.

Ten years later, Gaius Gracchus (153 BCE–121 BCE) tried to continue his brother's efforts to reduce the nobility's power by taking the control of the law courts away from the Senate. He also expressed his concern that the republic had stopped treating the defeated regions with leniency. He disapproved of measures that denied conquered peoples citizenship, that forced them to pay tribute to Rome, and that condemned some of their citizens to slavery. Instead, he proposed that Rome extend the rights of citizenship to its Latin allies. This plan alarmed many Romans, who feared having their influence overridden by outsiders. Both measures were greeted with the same response as the reforms of Tiberius ten years earlier. Rioting broke out again, and 3000 of Gaius Gracchus's followers were killed. Gaius himself committed suicide.

This violent reaction shows how determined the wealthy were to protect their privileged position within the republic. The riots and subsequent deaths of the two Gracchus brothers launched Rome into a period of political turmoil. For almost a hundred

PERSPECTIVES ON THE PAST

The Roman Mob

What caused a great gulf to grow between rich and poor in Rome? How did the politicians use "the mob" and keep it under control? What do you think the government of the day should have done to solve this serious social problem?

The Roman wars expanded the republic's territory throughout the Mediterranean region, but they also contributed to grave social problems within the capital itself. The new supply of grain from conquered regions created a surplus on the home market and forced the price down. Small farmers received so little for their crops that many went into debt and had to sell their lands.

While the farmers grew poorer, patricians and merchants grew richer on booty from the wars and profits made in trade. Many used their new-found wealth to buy up the small farms of the debt-ridden farmers and create vast estates called *latifundia*. Some landless farmers became tenants on these large properties but they had to compete with the thousands of war prisoners that Rome imported annually. These slaves became the empire's new source of cheap labour.

The landless poor drifted to Rome in search of some relief from their plight. Their numbers grew each year and they became a restless group, frustrated by their desperate condition and eager to listen to anyone who offered any hope. In the crowded slum tenements where they lived, in poorly constructed buildings that can best be described as firetraps, disease was a constant concern.

Politicians attempted to keep this "mob" under control and to win the people's support by offering them "bread and circuses." Some political candidates bought grain and distributed it to the poor at low prices. Others sponsored free entertainment such as chariot races and gladiatorial games.

years—filled with wars, plots, assassinations, and mass murders—various would-be leaders tried to seize power.

Control over the army became the key to success. Gaius Marius (155 BCE–86 BCE), a government leader and general, reformed the army of the republic. By removing the requirement that soldiers must own land to serve in the army, he opened the door for farm labourers and debtor farmers to enlist. He also made the army a full-time professional force. Soldiers were supplied with all their weapons and clothing, and were trained in a uniform manner.

These military reforms helped make the republic more secure, but they had serious consequences at home. Romans who signed up for a term of 16 (later 20) years in the military expected something in return for their services. Many of them were landless poor. They wanted a share in any military booty, and a piece of land from the grateful government when they retired from the army. When the government failed to provide these land grants, soldiers turned to their generals for support, transferring their loyalty from the state to their commanders. From then on, anyone who wanted to control Rome needed the support of the army.

A number of men seeking the leadership of the republic plunged Rome into turmoil. Often their drive for power was so great that they would use any means to achieve their goals. Most followed the same plan of attack. They gained command of a professional army, used it in an imperial cause to gain booty for themselves and their soldiers, and therefore won the army's undying loyalty. They then used the army to march into Rome and seize power.

Lucius Cornellius Sulla (138 BCE–78 BCE) was the first politician and general to use his army to take over Rome. Sulla was a rival of Gaius Marius. While Sulla was away fighting in Asia Minor, Gaius Marius killed many of Sulla's supporters and gained control of Rome. When Sulla returned to Rome at the head of his army in 82 BCE, he seized the city, executed his rival's supporters, and set himself up as a dictator. By Roman law, in an emergency, a dictator could hold office only for six months. But Sulla refused to accept this limit and ruled for several years.

When Sulla stepped down in 79 BCE, a new group of generals began fighting for control of Rome. The most illustrious was Julius Caesar (103 BCE–44 BCE). Caesar led his army to glory, conquering Gaul and raiding Britain. His military success made him a hero, and he used the opportunity to seize power. At first, in 60 BCE, Caesar ruled with two other successful and amibitious generals, Pompey and Crassus. Together, they completely disregarded the principles of the republic and formed a powerful *triumvirate*, or rule of three men. The triumvirate broke up when Crassus died in battle in 53 BCE. In the meantime, Pompey had become increasingly concerned with Caesar's growing popularity and had allied himself with the Roman Senate. In 49 BCE, with Pompey's support, the Senate ordered Caesar to disband his army. For a general, disbanding the army was tantamount to suicide—and Caesar refused.

Instead, he marched his soldiers towards Rome from Gaul but paused at the Rubicon River, the recognized southern boundary. A general could not legally cross the river without the permission of Rome. To cross without permission was treason and could lead to a civil war, but Caesar took the chance. He crossed, not knowing whether he would be treated as a hero or a traitor.

To Caesar's good fortune, the people in Rome welcomed him as a hero. After taking charge of the Senate, he became dictator of the republic and instituted many reforms designed both to strengthen Rome and to protect his own power. He gave people in provinces outside Italy the right to become citizens, ensuring their loyalty to Rome. He expanded the republic's holdings by establishing colonies in North Africa, France, Greece, and Spain, and sent unemployed Romans to settle in these areas. To secure the allegiance of the soldiers as well, he increased their pay.

Eventually, Caesar had himself appointed dictator for life. In public, he wore a purple gown and a laurel wreath, symbols of kingship in Rome. When conducting state business, he sat in a gilded chair and seldom bothered to stand when speaking to members of the Senate. Was he a megalomaniac—so full of his own sense of importance and so ambitious that he would go to any length to secure his power? Some in Rome began to think so.

Many members of the Senate feared Caesar's power and believed that he might declare himself king of Rome. This fear led to a conspiracy, led by Brutus and Cassius, to murder Caesar and save the republic. As Julius Caesar entered the Senate on March 15, 44 BCE—the fateful Ides of March—he was stabbed to death by the conspirators.

Following the murder, the assassins fell into disarray. Caesar's leading supporters, Mark Antony and Octavian, Caesar's nephew, gathered forces to avenge the murder. With their combined troops, they executed more than 2000 enemies in Rome and defeated the army of Brutus and Cassius at Philippi in Greece in 42 BCE.

Figure 8-10 *The assassination of Julius Caesar*

THE ROMAN EMPIRE AND THE *PAX ROMANA*

During his 45 years in power, Augustus (ruled 31 BCE–14 CE) never forgot the valuable lesson he learned from the fate of Caesar. Although he assumed supreme authority, Augustus always carefully avoided the appearance of grasping too much power. He accepted public offices and titles granted to him by the Senate, but did not flaunt his authority. To the people, the old laws and institutions of the republic seemed to remain in place. Though he ruled with absolute power, he preferred to be called *princeps* or first citizen rather than emperor.

During his reign, Augustus placed the Roman empire on a sound footing by introducing a number of key political and social reforms. He also established a sense of peace and security that led to a blossoming of Roman art and culture.

To protect himself and the empire, Augustus established a unit called the Praetorian Guard. Composed of nine cohorts of 500 men each, it acted essentially as a bodyguard for the emperor and his family. Members of the guard were given special treatment by the emperor, serving only 16 years and receiving three times the pay of a regular legionary. To avoid any impression of military dictatorship, he stationed the Praetorian Guard at various depots outside of Rome, but the troops were always at his call.

To administer the large Roman empire, Augustus decided to share control over the provinces with the Senate. He established a system whereby the Senate administered the settled provinces, but the emperor directed the newer frontier territories, where Roman legions were stationed.

Both Brutus and Cassius committed suicide following the defeat.

Octavian and Antony then decided to divide the Roman world, with each of them ruling a region. But Octavian recognized that this plan was only temporary—eventually there would be more conflict. He therefore began to prepare for battle while Antony, in Egypt, was preoccupied by the Ptolemy queen, Cleopatra. When the two leaders finally confronted each other at Actium in 31 BCE, the naval forces of Octavian defeated Antony and his army. Octavian became the first emperor of Rome, assuming complete power. He was given the title *Augustus*, which meant the "highest one." Although the Romans did not know it at the time, his rule marked the end of the 500-year-old republic—and the beginning of the Roman empire.

REFLECT AND ANALYZE

1. Both Tiberius Gracchus and Gaius Gracchus attempted to introduce political reform in Rome during the second century BCE. Why did they believe these reforms were necessary? Why did both efforts fail?

2. a) Identify the factors that contributed to the decline of the Roman republic.
   b) Which factor do you believe was the most significant? Support your view.

3. Imagine you are a citizen of Rome during the period of Julius Caesar's power. Write two letters to a friend expressing your views of Caesar—one dated on the day Caesar crossed the Rubicon River and marched into Rome, and the other on the day of his assassination.

Figure 8-11
The Emperor Augustus in battle dress

In this way, he kept firm control over the army.

Augustus instituted other measures as well to guarantee the security of the border areas. He tried to create buffer territories by allowing the kings in border regions to keep their thrones—as long as they maintained peace and prevented any foreign armies from invading Roman territory. He continued Caesar's policy of granting citizenship to people in the provinces. He also ordered a complete census or population survey, and introduced a more uniform tax system to promote equal and fair treatment of the provinces. He established a civil service, responsible to him, that governed the provinces justly. He awarded positions in the civil service on the basis of talent and merit, rather than class, and paid civil servants salaries for their work.

Augustus believed that the strength of the Roman empire lay in the simple and traditional values of the early Roman republic. Therefore, he encouraged devotion to family and religious duties. He levied a special tax on childless couples, for example, and promoted the observance of religious festivals in Rome. He also built and renovated many temples. Augustus claimed that he had found Rome built of sun-dried bricks and left it clothed in marble.

Several of the emperors who followed Augustus were his descendants. The Romans treated many of them with hostility, and two were notorious tyrants. Among the most notable were Tiberius, Caligula, and Nero. Tiberius (14 CE–37 CE) was unpopular because he tried to be economical and spent little money on public games. Caligula (37 CE–41 CE) was spiteful and even insane. He blatantly offended the Senate by behaviour such as having his favourite horse named as consul, and was assassinated by a member of the Praetorian Guard in 41 CE. Nero (54 CE–68 CE) was vain, cruel, and revengeful. Wary of any opposition, he ordered the assassination of scores of real or imagined

opponents. In 64 CE, a disastrous fire swept through Rome and many believed that it had been set by Nero himself.

After the death of Nero, the Senate and the army began to play a more active role in selecting the emperor, even though their involvement sometimes led to wars between Roman armies. Between 96 CE and 180 CE, during the era called the "Five Good Emperors," the Romans handled the problem of succession by having each emperor select a younger, capable colleague to train as a "Caesar," or successor. This period was the high point in imperial Rome. The emperors of the period—Nerva, Trajan, Hadrian, Antoninus Pius, and Marcus Aurelius—kept the Senate informed, consulted it regularly, and submitted legislation for its approval.

Trajan (97 CE–117 CE), the second of the "Five Good Emperors," was chosen by Nerva to become his successor. He had served as a military commander in Germany. A Spaniard by birth, Trajan was the first Roman emperor who was not of Italian origin.

Trajan was popular with the Senate because he sent them reports of his cam-

Figure 8-12 *The Emperor Trajan (97 CE–117 CE) and members of his court*

paigns and waited for their approval before signing any treaties. He was popular with the general public because he greatly increased Rome's wealth through military conquest, and spent large sums on building aqueducts, temples, and public baths.

Trajan was also popular with the army because of his extensive and successful military campaigns. To weaken hostile neighbouring Germanic tribes, Trajan led his armies across the Danube into Dacia (Romania), conquered the area, and relocated thousands of residents south of the Danube. He then moved colonists from eastern Roman provinces into Dacia. To reduce the threat posed in the east by the Parthians, Trajan annexed Armenia and Mesopotamia. During his reign, the boundaries of the Roman empire reached their greatest territorial extent. The empire stretched from the Atlantic Ocean to the Caspian Sea, and from Britain to Egypt.

The efforts of the "Five Good Emperors" resulted in almost a century of stability. Except for a few disturbances along the frontier, Europe and most of the Mediterranean enjoyed peace. The emperors kept taxes reasonably low and provided work. During the *Pax Romana* or the "Roman Peace," the civilization developed and flourished. Traders and merchants ventured as far as India and China, bringing back silks, fine dyes, and spices. From northern Europe, they brought animal furs, honey, and amber, which artisans used to make jewellery. Hundreds of cities were built throughout the territories, linked by an extensive network of paved roads. Latin became the common language throughout the empire, later forming the basis for what we know today as the Romance languages (French, Spanish, Italian, Portuguese, and Romanian).

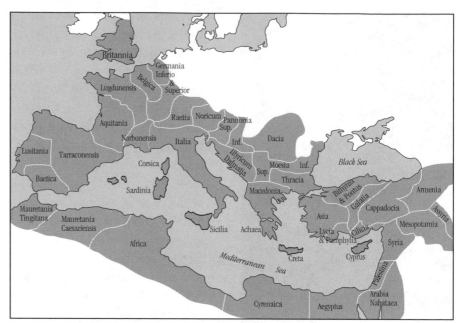

Figure 8-13 *The Roman provinces under Trajan*

REFLECT AND ANALYZE

1. "Unlike Julius Caesar, Augustus maintained absolute power without gaining a reputation for arrogance." Explain this statement.

2. How might Tiberius Gracchus or Gaius Gracchus have viewed the rule of Augustus? Present your opinions in a short editorial.

3. What reforms did Augustus introduce to bring peace and harmony to the Roman empire? Why do you think these reforms were effective?

4. Do further research into the reign of Nero or Caligula. How can you account for such abuse of power in the Roman government?

THE DECLINE AND FALL OF THE ROMAN EMPIRE

The decline of the great empire of Rome began in the second century CE when enemies to the north and east began crossing the borders and plundering Roman territory. The empire's frontier was so extensive that even the many Roman legions could not hold back an invasion that threatened several different border regions at one time.

From the east, the threat to the empire came from the Parthians, an Iranian people who controlled much of the old Persian empire and had extended their influence west to the Euphrates River. Since the Euphrates formed the eastern boundary of Roman Syria, the Romans were concerned. Trajan tried to weaken the Parthians by conquering Armenia and Mesopotamia. The emperor Hadrian (117 CE–138 CE) opted to create buffer zones between Roman and Parthian territory, ruled by kings friendly to Rome. Later, when the Parthians attempted to invade Armenia and Mesopotamia, the emperors Marcus Aurelius (161 CE–180 CE) and Septimius Severus (193 CE–211 CE) took the strongest stands of all, and repelled the Parthian invasions by force.

In 241 CE, the Sassanians took over the rule of Iran and Persia from the Parthians. They improved the political administration of the area, and extended religious freedom to groups persecuted by the Romans. The Sassanians also scored small military victories over the Romans in eastern provinces such as Syria-Palestine and Mesopotamia. Although the Sassanians were never capable of a full-scale invasion of the empire, they were a constant nuisance on the eastern frontier at a time when Rome faced serious internal problems.

By the time Diocletian (285 CE–305 CE) became emperor, many parts of the empire were in revolt. Diocletian led campaigns against the Franks and the Burgundians, who were raiding Roman territories across the Rhine, but he failed to suppress uprisings in Gaul and Britain. In 293 CE, Diocletian decided to divide the Roman empire along a line from the Danube River to Dalmatia. He believed that two sections and the presence of two leaders would make it easier to control such a vast area.

Diocletian chose to rule the eastern provinces and appointed Maximian to rule the western half of the empire. Each co-emperor, to be called Augustus, was to rule for 20 years. Each was to appoint an assistant, called a Caesar, who would be named as his successor. The two rulers would issue all laws jointly, and enforce them uniformly throughout the empire.

This new administrative arrangement had a direct impact on the city of Rome. Diocletian chose to rule the eastern provinces from Nicomedia in Asia Minor and Maximian ruled the western part of the empire from Milan in Italy. Therefore, Rome ceased to be either the capital of the empire or the centre of power. The once influential Roman Senate was reduced to little more than a city council. For the military, on the other hand, the division of the territories proved useful. The army reconquered Britain, suppressed an uprising in the African provinces, and preserved Egypt and Armenia in the east for the empire.

Despite its advantages, this administrative arrangement broke down when Diocletian and Maximian resigned as co-emperors in 305 CE. Instead of a smooth succession, seven rival Augusti vied for power. Constantine (306 CE–337 CE) de-feated his rivals in a civil war, and by 324 CE became the sole emperor of Rome. In 330 CE, he built a new eastern capital at the site of the Greek town of Byzantium at the entrance to the Black Sea. The town was renamed Constantinople, and later became the capital of the great Byzantine empire.

The next emperor, Theodosius (347 CE–395 CE), was the last to rule a united Roman empire. Germanic tribes from the west and Huns from the east—both called **barbarians** by the Romans—were constantly fighting and invading Roman territory. After Theodosius's death, the empire was again divided in two parts, each with its own ruler. Rome is said to have "fallen" in 476 CE, when Odoacer, a Germanic chief, captured Rome and forced the western emperor to step down. But, as we have seen, this was only the final blow during the long, slow decline of a once-mighty empire.

REFLECT AND ANALYZE

1. Where did the first breaches in the defence of the Roman empire occur? How did the Romans handle them?

2. Evaluate the effectiveness of the administrative changes that Diocletian introduced during his rule.

3. You are a Roman citizen in the second or third century CE, facing the growing problems of defending and administering the empire. What measures do you feel the imperial government should take? Support your views.

GOVERNMENT

The Romans had created and successfully administered one of the greatest empires in history for hundreds of years. Yet, by 476 CE, Rome had crumbled. How did the Romans govern such an extensive empire? In the end, why did the government fail?

GOVERNMENT IN THE REPUBLIC

During the republic, power was distributed among different individuals and governing bodies so that no one person could seize absolute control. The people elected representatives to public office although, in the early years of the republic, candidates came only from the upper classes. In fact, much

PERSPECTIVES ON THE PAST
The Decline and Fall of the Roman Empire

What caused the decline and fall of the Roman empire? Historians have debated this issue for centuries. Read the following viewpoints. Which factor do you think played the most significant role in the empire's decline? Why?

Viewpoint 1: Politics

Following the reign of Augustus, Rome was wracked by political strife and shaken by frequent disputes over succession. Several bloody civil wars broke out, with one imperial army pitted against another, each championing its leader of choice. Generals plotted intrigues and emperors were assassinated. Corruption ran rampant. This political upheaval led to a terrible drain on Roman resources and caused severe social unrest.

The problem worsened after Trajan became emperor. Because Trajan was a professional soldier from Spain, people believed that the position of emperor was no longer restricted to those of Italian background. More candidates therefore came forward, some from faraway places like Britain, Africa, and Syria.

The second and third centuries CE suffered the greatest number of civil wars. Between 235 CE and 284 CE, Roman armies nominated more than 50 different candidates for emperor! Almost all of them met violent ends.

The changes that the emperor Diocletian introduced to the administrative system did little more than increase rivalry and division, and led to the empire's eventual decline.

Viewpoint 2: Economics

Eventually, the expense of running a vast empire brought Rome to its knees. As costs increased, tax levels never seemed to supply the necessary revenue. Diocletian taxed the middle class particularly heavily. He imposed land taxes, property taxes, occupation taxes, and poll taxes. To the frustration of enterprising Romans, the high levels of taxation discouraged innovation and squelched new businesses. When tenants began

to flee their farms and businesspeople and workers started to abandon their occupations to escape the tax burden, the government passed measures ordering all to remain at their jobs. Further decrees required that sons follow the same trade as their fathers and therefore pay the same taxes—guaranteeing the state its revenue. The government was also forced to take over many kinds of businesses to keep them running, at even more expense to the empire.

The state compounded the revenue problems by printing more money, thus devaluing the currency. Severe inflation resulted. Prices shot up and stayed high until Diocletian succeeded temporarily in stabilizing the currency.

Another factor in the growing economic crisis was the Roman empire's failure to develop technologically. Why? For one reason, the people's heavy dependence on slave labour discouraged them from inventing new types of technology. The nature of Roman education also played a part. Instructors focused on teaching rhetorical or public speaking skills rather than on stimulating the students' curiosity and creativity. A third factor was poverty. Since the people in the frontier regions were too poor to purchase goods, the Romans felt little incentive to create new products for a non-existent market. Subsequently, trade declined between the provinces and with foreign nations.

Viewpoint 3: Defence

The continuing problem of defending the frontier against foreigners was the most important factor in the decline and fall of the Roman empire. As the government began to lose control of the army, its concern about external invasion increased.

Citizens of the empire were not as eager to serve in the military as they had been during the republic. For a time, emperors tried to encourage recruitment by promising men in the provinces citizenship if they enlisted. However, the emperor Caracalla (211 CE–217

CE) destroyed this incentive when he granted citizenship to all freeborn men within the empire. The once proud Roman army seemed to appeal only to criminals. Out of necessity, the government hired troops or mercenaries to maintain the numbers.

During the fourth century CE, attacks on the frontiers intensified. The Huns, a Mongolian nomadic people from Asia, began to invade western Europe, pushing other invaders out of their path as they pressed forward. Fighting on horseback, the Huns easily defeated the Germanic peoples they encountered. First, they displaced the East Goths, or Ostrogoths, north of the Black Sea. Then they conquered the West Goths or Visigoths. In 376 CE, the Visigoths petitioned the Romans for permission to cross the Danube, seeking refuge from the Huns in Thrace. Rather than face the likelihood that the Visigoths would occupy the area even without permission, the Romans granted the request.

Before long, the Visigoths in Thrace complained of poor treatment by Roman officials. When the emperor took no action, the Goths took up arms. In 378 CE, their cavalry defeated the Roman infantry at Adrianople.

The defeat at Adrianople was a significant one for Rome because the invaders had breached the Roman frontier. The following century brought many more defeats, and Germanic tribes flooded into the empire. In 396 CE, Alaric, prince of the Visigoths, ravaged Thrace and marched to the walls of Constantinople. In 406 CE, the Vandals, another German tribe, invaded Spain. Meanwhile, Britain fell to the Angles and the Saxons, and Gaul was taken by the Franks and the Alamanni.

In 410 CE, the Visigoths under Alaric sacked Rome, stealing many objects of value although damaging the city little. Eventually they settled in Spain, forcing the Vandals into North Africa where they built a powerful seafaring kingdom. From here, the Vandals could disrupt Rome's grain imports, and restrict communication between eastern and western sectors of the empire. In 455 CE, they raided Rome itself, and caused extensive damage.

Meanwhile, the Huns continued their westward migration under their leader, the feared Attila. In 451 CE, the Romans stopped them in Gaul at the battle of Troyes, and the Huns turned south into Italy. But Attila did not attack Rome. Disease and famine were ravaging his troops, and he allowed himself to be dissuaded by Pope Leo I.

The Huns, the most dreaded of invaders, had dealt a severe blow to the unity and power of the Roman empire. In 476 CE, a German chieftain, the Ostrogoth Odoacer, deposed the last Roman emperor in the west and proclaimed himself king. The western Roman empire had ended.

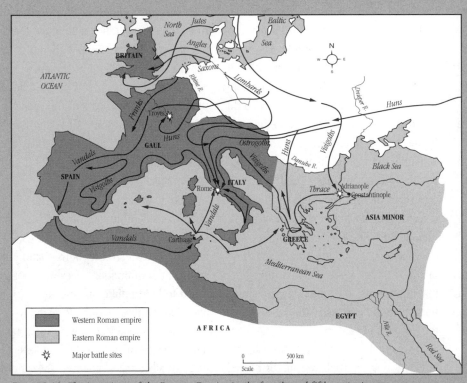

Figure 8-14 *The invasions of the Roman Empire in the fourth and fifth centuries CE*

of the republic's history is the story of the plebeians (farmers, merchants, labourers, and artisans) struggling for greater control over the government.

The early republic included three distinct governing bodies: the *Senate,* the *Assembly of Centuries,* and the *Assembly of Tribes.* The Senate was composed of 300 patrician men who served for life. They were the heads of the most wealthy and influential families in Rome, the families that had helped to drive out the Etruscan kings.

The Senate had extensive powers. It collected taxes, decided where to spend the money from the treasury, received foreign ambassadors, and ratified treaties and alliances with foreign powers. Each year, the Senate elected two **consuls**—magistrates or officials—from its membership. These two men held *imperium* or complete power for their term. They appointed new senators, enacted laws and decrees, supervised the business of government, called meetings of the assemblies, held elections, and commanded the armies.

However, the Romans placed definite checks on the consuls to prevent them from abusing their power. The two officials had to seek the advice and approval of the Senate on all matters, and the Senate administered all laws and decrees. While each consul could issue an edict, the other had the power to veto it. During times of peace, they alternated in office each month. During times of war, they alternated each day. Each consul could be elected for only one term, but when his term was completed, he remained a senator for life.

During the republic, the Romans disregarded this model only during a crisis. At such times, the Senate and the consuls

Figure 8-15 *The Roman Senate*

could appoint a **dictator**, who would exercise absolute power for a period of six months. During a crisis, they believed, it was unwise to alternate leaders. After six months, however, the dictator was required to step down.

The Assembly of Centuries represented the concerns of the army. The assembly included groups of voters called *centuries,* based on social class and wealth. The organization operated on the principle that a citizen's voting power should correspond to his worth as a soldier. Those who could afford armour and a horse, and could serve in the cavalry, should have more say in the assembly than those in the infantry. Accordingly, the centuries varied in size. A century of the wealthy might include 200 citizens while a century of the poor might include 20 000. Since each century had only one vote, the wealthiest men and those of highest rank controlled the decision-making process. The mass of the population, the plebeians, had little influence in the Assembly of Centuries.

A second assembly, the Assembly of Tribes, was organized by tribe or *curia.* This assembly, composed mainly of plebeians, represented the 35 tribes to which

Roman citizens belonged. Each curia was polled separately, and then a majority opinion was determined in a public meeting. The most important role of this assembly was to vote on legislation presented to it by the magistrates of Rome.

Since each member of a curia had one vote, this governing body operated somewhat more democratically than the Assembly of Centuries. As the population of the tribes varied considerably, however, tribes with a smaller number of people had an unfair advantage. Location also made the representation unequal. All voting had to take place in Rome, and the 31 tribes scattered throughout Italy often found it difficult to make the journey.

Thus, while the patrician class exercised considerable political power, the common people had very little real say in government and faced both social and political discrimination. They were not allowed to hold public office or marry into patrician families, and the Roman laws—unwritten and subject to wide interpretation—treated them harshly. The plebeians had two advantages, however: sheer numbers and an increasingly important presence in the military.

In 494 BCE, plebeian soldiers went on strike to demand political rights. As the plebeians had become vital to the armies of Rome by this time, the Senate granted them the right to form their own assembly, the *Concilium Plebis*. Like the Assembly of Tribes, it was organized by tribes and had the power to pass decrees—but only decrees that were binding on plebeians. In this way, Rome created one government for the patricians and one for the plebeians.

To protect the plebeians further, the Concilium Plebis gained the right to elect two **tribunes** (later ten) to speak out for the people's interests. In 449 BCE, the plebeians successfully demanded Rome's first written law code. Although the code still discriminated against the plebeians, its listing of laws and punishments protected all citizens from arbitrary arrest.

Over the next 200 years, the plebeians gradually gained more rights and an even stronger voice in making laws. In 445 BCE, the Canuleian Law was passed, removing the restriction on intermarriage between patricians and plebeians. In 447 BCE, a fourth assembly was created, called the *Comitia Tributa Populi*. This assembly, which included all free citizens of Rome organized by tribes, was intended to provide a means for determining the will of the people. The Comitia Tributa Populi did not replace any of the other assemblies. Instead, all four functioned with overlapping membership and purpose.

The tribunes helped the plebeians to improve their political status even further. They had the strict laws punishing debtors eased. They obtained veto power over any government action that threatened the rights of plebeians. In 367 BCE, a new law required that one of the two consuls be a plebeian. Eventually, the plebeians won the right to hold any public office. Since the Senate was open to all citizens who had served in public office, plebeians gained the right to membership there as well.

During the third century BCE, the people made further gains in the assemblies. After 287 BCE, the Comitia Tributa Populi could enact laws on its own and the Concilium Plebis could pass laws binding on all Romans.

Yet even these reforms did not guarantee equality for all citizens of the Roman republic. As the republic grew during the wars of expansion, a new class of wealthy plebeians emerged. These people had made their wealth through trade and industry. Many members of this new class intermarried with the patricians, and they were just as careful to guard their power and monopolize government offices as the patricians had been in the early years of the republic.

MAGISTRATES OF THE REPUBLIC

The two consuls chosen annually to administer the Roman laws were the most important officials or **magistrates** of the republic. Initially chosen by the Senate, the consuls were later elected by the Assembly of Centuries. Early in the history of the

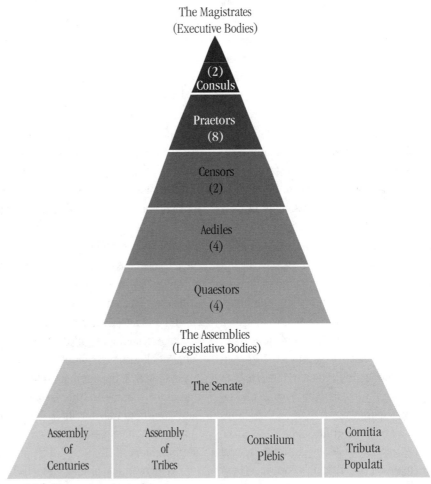

Figure 8-16 *The government of Rome*

The Magistrates
(Executive Bodies)

(2) Consuls
Praetors (8)
Censors (2)
Aediles (4)
Quaestors (4)

The Assemblies
(Legislative Bodies)

The Senate

| Assembly of Centuries | Assembly of Tribes | Consilium Plebis | Comitia Tributa Populati |

republic, a number of men were appointed to administer the decisions of the consuls and the Senate, and to assist the tribunes elected by the Concilium Plebis. These officials included *quaestors, praetors, censors,* and *aediles.*

The quaestors served as assistants to the consuls. They oversaw the financial administration of the republic and investigated cases of murder. Originally, the consuls appointed the four quaestors but, after 447 BCE, the Comitia Tributa Populi won the right to elect them. This change represented another concession that the republican government granted the plebeians.

After 366 BCE, the Comitia Tributa Populi elected eight praetors within the republic. These officials were responsible for the administration of justice, and for relations between Roman citizens and non-Roman citizens. When the consuls were absent from Rome, one of the praetors would take charge of the city. He would substitute for the consuls in the Senate, and would even assume command of the army during times of emergency.

The government created the office of censor in 433 BCE. The Assembly of Centuries elected two censors for a five-year term. The censors assessed all of the property holdings and assigned them to the appropriate tribes and companies. Censors had added power within the republic because they also enforced public morality. They had the authority not only to appoint new senators, but to expel any senators from office if they considered them unworthy.

The Comitia Tributa Populi elected the four aediles to arrange public games and supervise the grain supply. Two of the aediles represented plebeian interests and two represented patrician concerns. These four magistrates operated as a committee.

GOVERNMENT IN THE ROMAN EMPIRE

During the Roman empire, the nature of government changed considerably. The emperor exercised almost total power. Some emperors, like Octavian, did so with the approval and goodwill of the Roman citizens, particularly the goodwill of the Senate, which remained influential throughout most of the imperial period. No emperor ruled quite as successfully as Octavian did. Because of his distinguished reign, all emperors who followed were given the name Augustus in addition to their own. Later emperors, however, abused their power and, because there were no clear laws outlining how a new emperor should be chosen, bloody struggles for succession were common.

THE PROVINCES

For administrative purposes, the Roman empire was divided into provinces, each about the size of a small modern country. Britain, for example, was one province. Gaul or modern France was divided into four provinces, Spain was divided into two, and Portugal was administered as one.

The highest-ranking official in each of the provinces was the governor. For the provinces on the frontier, where the risk of trouble was greatest, the emperor kept direct control and chose the governors from the Senate. For the more settled provinces, the Senate itself assumed control. Being chosen governor was an honour that brought prestige to the senator and his family. Rome paid governors well for their duties, but treated them quite harshly if they were poor administrators.

The governor's primary responsibility was to keep watch over his subjects from a distance. He interfered very little in the province's affairs as long as the people paid taxes and sent recruits to the Roman army. In the outlying provinces, a procurator managed the finances and reported directly to the emperor. In the established provinces, the governor's second-in-command looked after the accounts. Retired army officials often helped the governors to perform their duties.

In general, the Romans decided to treat the conquered nations the way the Romans would treat themselves. They shared the advantages of the empire with their subjects and encouraged the people's allegiance. But they took precautions as well. While they allowed each province to govern itself, they still maintained a small local army in case the people rebelled against Rome. They established excellent communication links between the provinces and the capital, and kept roads in good repair so that the governor could call in legions from Rome or other provinces if necessary. To secure the conquered nation's loyalty, Rome allowed people in the provinces to become army officers and Roman citizens.

Late in the imperial period, the emperor Diocletian changed this system of administration. The empire was facing serious internal and external problems that jeopardized its very survival. Inflation, for example, had spiralled so high that Roman currency was almost worthless. Mediterranean pirates were disrupting the food supply to Italy, and foreign invaders were threatening the frontiers.

Diocletian decided to divide the provinces into smaller units called ***dioceses*** to make them easier to administer and defend. Each diocese was governed by a nominee directly appointed by the governor.

THE TOWNS AND VILLAGES

Town councils and mayors also played an important role in Rome's political organization. Municipal officials took care of the specific concerns of their town and the surrounding countryside. According to the Roman system of local government towns elected their officials every year. They usually voted in four to six administrators, including mayors and magistrates. To hold municipal office, a candidate had to fulfill a minimal property qualification. Councillors and mayors needed to own between 12 and 16 ha of land. Although this requirement did not represent a large property, it usually restricted public office to merchants, shopkeepers, and retired army officers.

The mayors and councillors administered public services such as police and fire protection, water supply, drainage, roads, markets, temples, festivals, and public entertainment.

The highest-ranking official was the mayor. Every town always had two mayors so that one could watch over the actions of the other and protect the interests of the citizens. The two mayors had to agree on any major town project before work could begin.

In addition to elected officials, every town had a council to advise the mayors and monitor their performance. These town councils were composed of former mayors, who became councillors for life after their term in office.

on the Greek system. The Greeks had believed that reason governed the universe, and the Romans incorporated that notion into their law codes.

When two people had a legal dispute, the court requested the advice of a panel of jurists. The panel members were educated patrician men who were interested in the study of law. Over several centuries, these panels refined the system of personal law more and more.

But the Roman judicial system was not without problems. One of the more serious drawbacks to a Roman court was the absence of a public prosecutor. Without a public prosecutor, the court depended on private citizens to provide information about crimes. Rarely did the court bother to investigate the motives of these witnesses—or informers, as they were called. In cases that involved the interests of the emperor, the court asked even fewer questions. Therefore, regardless of an informer's honesty, the petitioner or defendant in a case had to accept the jurists' verdict.

When the emperor Constantine transferred the capital of the empire to Constantinople, the new city became the centre of Roman law. By the time Justinian became emperor in 527 CE, the legal code had grown so much that it included thousands of statutes, decrees, and ordinances, and millions of lines of legal commentary and case records. Justinian decided to have this body of law collected, edited, systematized, and condensed into a manageable form. The result was the Corpus Juris Civilis, or the system of civil law. Roman law later influenced the legal systems of Scotland, France, Quebec, Louisiana, and most countries of South America.

REFLECT AND ANALYZE

1. What steps did the plebeians take to acquire greater political recognition within the republic? How effective were these steps?

2. Assume the role of a Roman consul, tribune, censor, or aedile. Write a series of decrees or directives to deal with problems under your jurisdiction in the latter years of the republic.

3. "The successful administration of the Roman empire depended on a clear hierarchy of officials and checks on the power of any individual or region." Do you agree or disagree with this statement? Support your position.

LAW AND JUSTICE

The Roman laws remained unrecorded until the plebeians insisted on a written code to address the injustices in the system. In 449 BCE, a commission of ten patricians drafted a code of traditional Roman laws. The laws were written on 12 bronze tablets and set up in the Forum for all to see. These laws covered nearly every aspect of Roman life, including wills, property rights, court cases, and even the public behaviour of citizens. The code, called the Law of the Twelve Tables, remained the foundation of Roman civil and criminal law for a thousand years.

The Romans were proud of their legal system, particularly those aspects that dealt with private disputes between individuals. They modelled their system of personal law

THROUGH THEIR EYES

Law of the Twelve Tables

Read the excerpts from the Law of the Twelve Tables. Whom do these laws seem to favour? How would you describe the punishments listed in these excerpts? How could a public record of these laws possibly serve the common people?

Table III

When a debtor has been acknowledged, or judgement about the matter has been pronounced in court, thirty days must be the legitimate time of grace. . . .

Unless they make a settlement, debtors shall be held in bonds for sixty days. During that time they shall be brought before the praetor's court in the meeting place on three successive market days, and the third market day they shall suffer capital punishment or be delivered up for sale abroad, across the Tiber.

Table VIII

If any person has sung or composed against another person a song such as was causing slander or insult to another, he shall be clubbed to death.

If a person has maimed another's limb, let there be retaliation in kind unless he makes agreement for settlement with him.

If he has broken or bruised a freeman's bone with his hand or club, he shall undergo penalty of 300 as [bronze coin] pieces; if a slave's, 150.

Any person who destroys by burning any building or heap of corn deposited alongside a house shall be bound, scourged, and put to death by burning at the stake, provided that he has committed the said misdeed with malice aforethought; but if he shall have committed it by accident, that is, by negligence, it is ordained that he repair the damage, or, if he be too poor to be competent for such punishment, he shall receive a lighter chastisement.

If theft has been done by night, if the owner kill the thief, the thief shall be held lawfully killed.

It is forbidden that a thief be killed by day . . . unless he defend himself with a weapon; even though he has come with a weapon, unless he use his weapon and fight back, you shall not kill him. And even if he resists, first call out.

No person shall practise usury at a rate more than one twelfth [probably 8½%]. . . . A usurer is condemned for a quadruple amount.

. . . a person who has been found guilty of giving false witness shall be hurled down from the Tarpeian Rock. . . .

Table XI

Intermarriage shall not take place between plebeians and patricians.

REFLECT AND ANALYZE

1. How do the laws and punishments contained in the Law of the Twelve Tablets compare to those found in Hammurabi's law code?

2. What are the positive and negative features of the Roman legal system? If you were accused of a crime in ancient Rome, how might you prepare your defence?

3. Write a letter to the emperor, suggesting ways to improve this legal system.

ROME:
Society and Culture

According to legend, Rome was founded by a single individual named Romulus. Romulus was the son of Mars, the god of war, and a beautiful princess, Rhea Silvia. Rhea's uncle, Amulius, had seized the throne and imprisoned the princess so that she could not produce an heir. But mysteriously she bore twins, fathered by Mars. The children were Romulus and Remus. Amulius immediately ordered the boys killed, but his command was disobeyed and the babies were set adrift in a basket on the Tiber River. When the basket ran aground, the boys were discovered by a she-wolf, a sacred animal of Mars. The she-wolf warmed and nursed the twins until a shepherd found them, took them to his home, and raised them.

When they grew up, Romulus and Remus dethroned Amulius, avenged their mother, and decided to found a city where the she-wolf had discovered them. But they quarrelled, and Romulus killed his brother. As sole leader, Romulus gave the new city its name—Rome.

Figure 9-1
Romulus and Remus

The story of Romulus and Remus is one of the central legends of Rome's early history. It was well known by the beginning of the third century BCE, and was retold by Roman historians such as Livy. According to the legend, Romulus founded Rome in 753 BCE, and all Roman dates are reckoned from that year. How does this story of Rome's origins compare with the creation myths and legends of other civilizations?

Other accounts of Rome's origins stress the virtue and dignity of the early Romans, and try to draw parallels between Greek and Roman civilizations. Some sources, for example, suggest that Rome's ancestors were Greek and Trojan heroes. One version claims, for example, that Rome was founded by Aeneas, a hero of the Trojan War. According to this story, Aeneas and his followers conquered the native Latin tribes and intermarried with them. Why would the Romans claim a close association with Greek civilization?

RELIGION

GODS AND GODDESSES
Roman religion was influenced by contact with the Greeks and Etruscans in the Italian peninsula. Like the Greeks, the Romans adopted a pantheon of deities, six gods and six goddesses, who directed the affairs of the world with their superhuman powers. But while these principal Roman gods had close associations with the Greek Olympians, many also shared characteristics with early Latin and Etruscan deities. Jupiter, the supreme god of the Roman pantheon, was probably originally an Etruscan deity. His character and functions,

however, resembled closely those of the Greek god, Zeus. Like Zeus, Jupiter was a sky god and protector of the people. Some deities, such as Mercury, were simply Roman versions of Greek gods (Hermes, in this case). Others, such as Janus, the god of beginnings, were original Latin deities. Roman religion was a synthesis or blending of Latin, Greek, and Etruscan influences.

The names of many Roman gods and goddesses will sound familiar. Several planets in our solar system were named after Roman gods. Other names, such as Vulcan, have become part of our language in another form. Because the Romans believed that Vulcan made thunderbolts under Mount Etna, today we call fiery and explosive mountains volcanoes.

The Roman Pantheon

JUPITER	king of the gods and god of the sky and weather
JUNO	queen of the gods and goddess of women (protector of women during childbirth)
NEPTUNE	god of the sea and god of earthquakes, caused by banging his trident on the ground
MINERVA	goddess of science and crafts (an old Etruscan goddess)
CERES	goddess of agriculture
VESTA	goddess of fire
APOLLO	god of sun and prophecy, adopted directly from the Greeks
DIANA	goddess of the moon, hunting, and fertility
MERCURY	god of communications, business, and trade
VENUS	goddess of love
VULCAN	god of metalworking
MARS	god of war

In addition to the 12 principal gods, the Romans believed in a number of minor deities and in a spirit world. Spirits were everywhere—in fire, water, stones, and trees. Spirits also watched over everyday activities such as planting seeds and baking bread. The success and happiness of a family depended on the goodwill of various household spirits. People regularly made sacrifices and performed rituals to appease these supernatural beings. Each day, for example, the head of the family made offerings of wine and incense to the various household spirits on behalf of the family.

One group of spirits was called the *lares*. These were the spirits of family ancestors who protected the household. Families kept statues of the *lares* in a little shrine called the *lararium*, located in the main living room of their house. Another important group of spirits was the *penates*, who protected the cupboards or storehouse, making certain the family had enough to eat.

RELIGIOUS BELIEFS AND PRACTICES

The Etruscans and the Greeks influenced not only Roman gods, but also Roman religious practices and beliefs. Like Greek religion, Roman religion was based on rituals and traditions, rather than on dogma (a clearly defined or written code of beliefs).

The Romans honoured their gods and sought their goodwill mainly by festivals and rituals such as sacrifices. When an animal was sacrificed, it was important to speak the right words and perform the proper actions at the appropriate moments. The people held religious festivals every month except September and November. The Saturnalia was one of the most popular festivals. It was held each December in honour of Saturn, the god of agriculture and the father of Jupiter. During the festival, masters changed places with their slaves, and people exchanged gifts. In some ways, this religious holiday resembled the celebration of Christmas today.

Roman priests were officials of the state, elected by the people. The chief priest within the hierarchy was called the Pontifex Maximus. He supervised the work of various groups of priests who performed religious duties for the state. Some gods and goddesses had their own priests, called *flamens*. The Flamen Dialis, for example, was the priest of Jupiter, while the Flamen Martialis was the priest of Mars. The Vestal Virgins were priestesses who served the goddess Vesta. Other groups of priests, called augurs and haruspices, were mainly concerned with looking for signs from the gods.

The Romans believed in omens, curses, spells, and a form of astrology.

Figure 9-2
A participant in the Dionysic mysteries

Many of these beliefs, as well as the art of **divination**, probably came from the Etruscans. Divination is the practice of interpreting the will of the gods through signs and omens. For example, priests might search for signs by examining the size, shape, and colour of an animal's internal organs after it has been sacrificed.

DEATH AND THE UNDERWORLD

The Romans did not believe that the after-life necessarily promised happy immortality. Like the Greeks, they believed the spirit of the dead passed to an underworld, called Hades. But first the body had to be ferried across the river Styx, which separated this world from the one beyond. Anyone crossing the river had to pay Charon, the boatman, and therefore relatives placed a coin in the mouth of the departed to pay the fare. The Romans believed that both fearful demons and good spirits inhabited the underworld.

When a Roman died, family members washed the body with warm water, anointed it with sweet-smelling oils, and dressed it in white. They then placed it on a funeral couch so that relatives and friends could pay their last respects. As symbols of mourning, lamps were lit around the funeral couch and a cyprus tree was placed outside the house. To signify loss, the fire in the hearth was put out.

Since poor people could seldom afford a proper funeral, they buried their dead at night in a common grave without ceremony. But for those who could afford the costs, professional undertakers would organize a funeral. After a dinner held by family and friends, the burial began with a procession. Flute players, horn players, torchbearers, and women hired as professional mourners led the way. Next came slaves carrying the funeral bier with the body, followed by members of the mourning family. Some participants carried portraits of family ancestors in the procession.

When someone in a Roman household died, the relatives made a sacrifice to the lares to purify the house. Nine days after burial, a special sacrifice was made to the departed spirit, or *manes*, of the dead person. Then, each year in May, the head of the household carried out a ceremony to persuade the spirits of the dead to leave the house and not haunt it.

CHRISTIANITY

When Christianity began in the first century, the Romans dismissed it as a minor Jewish sect (religious group), centred in Jerusalem, that would have little effect on the rest of the world. Originally, Christianity was based on Judaism, a **monotheistic** religion that taught that one true God governed all aspects of life. God's word was recorded in a sacred book (the *Torah*), and God's laws (the Ten Commandments) had been handed down to the people through the prophet Moses. This belief in a single, all-powerful deity and a written dogma (code of beliefs) was unique in the world at the time.

Around 30 CE, Jesus Christ began teaching that the prophecies in the Torah were being fulfilled—the Kingdom of God had come to earth. The followers of Jesus believed that he was the Son of God and their personal saviour. He preached kindness, compassion for others, and faith in a loving, forgiving God. His teachings, however, brought him into conflict with powerful leaders in the Jewish religion, who could not accept his claim to be the sole agent of God and the forgiver of sins. They believed that only God had such power. Jesus also angered Roman officials because people saw him as the **Messiah**, who had come to free the Jewish people from Roman rule. Jesus was betrayed by one of his own followers, arrested, and crucified for claiming to be "King of the Jews," although there is little evidence that he sought any form of earthly power. Christians—believers in Jesus Christ the Saviour—continued to follow his teachings. By 395 CE, in fact, Christianity had not only spread throughout the Roman empire, but had become the official religion of Rome.

How can we account for the remarkable spread of the Christian faith? Why did the Romans come to view Christianity as a threat to the empire? Originally, Roman officials had not worried about the new religion. Two significant developments, however, increased the power and appeal of Christianity and caught the attention of Rome.

First, Christianity gradually built a strong church organization with a hierarchy of leaders. At the top of the hierarchy, bishops had the most authority. Below them, priests conducted services for the people. This organization, along with a clear body of sacred writings and the strong convictions of devoted followers, attracted many converts. Rome grew suspicious of the potential danger of this new church and its leadership. No other religion at the time had such a powerful and far-reaching organization.

The other important development was the Christian break with Judaism. The Christians separated themselves from the Jewish nation by establishing a non-Jewish or Gentile church. Founded by the apostle

Figure 9-3 *"The Triumphant Christ": a mosaic from an early Christian church*

Paul of Tarsus, this church was open to all who would genuinely accept the faith, whether slave or noble, Jew or non-Jew. The Christians preached equality in the eyes of God, and promised everlasting life after death for the worthy. These ideas comforted many people, especially as the official Roman religion was less personal and did not promise equality or eternal happiness in the afterlife.

The Romans began persecuting Christians as early as the first century CE, even though government policy officially tolerated foreign religions until the second century. In 64 CE, Rome used Christians as scapegoats for a great fire that destroyed much of the city and that many claimed had been started by the emperor Nero.

Roman leaders were most concerned about the Christian message that all people were equal in the eyes of God. This view contradicted traditional Roman values, which accepted the authority of the husband over the family, the parents over their children, the master over the slave and, above all, the emperor over all Roman citizens.

During the second century, the persecution intensified because Christians refused to worship either the emperor or the Roman gods. To the government, this refusal was intolerable because most Christians were citizens and bound to obey Roman laws.

Many Romans blamed the Christians for disasters such as floods and famines. Tolerating the Christians' strange beliefs, they thought, likely angered the Roman gods. They saw Christian rituals such as eating the bread (body) of Christ and drinking the wine (blood) of Christ as forms of cannibalism. Other rituals they associated with black magic.

Unofficial persecutions called **pogroms** were launched against the Christ-

THROUGH THEIR EYES

Christian Persecution by the Emperor Nero

Tacitus, the Roman historian of the first century CE, tells how the emperor Nero tried to blame the Christians for the great fire of Rome in 64 CE. How does this account reflect the writer's own bias? How did Nero's actions against the Christians actually work against his own interests?

But neither human resources, nor imperial munificence, nor appeasement of the gods, eliminated sinister suspicions that the fire had been instigated. To suppress this rumour, Nero fabricated scapegoats— and punished with every refinement the notoriously depraved Christians (as they were popularly called). Their originator, Christ, had been executed in Tiberius' reign by the governor of Judaea, Pontius Pilatus. But in spite of this temporary setback the deadly superstition had broken out afresh, not only in Judaea but even in Rome. All degraded and shameful

practices collect and flourish in the capital.

First, Nero had self-acknowledged Christians arrested. Then, on their information, large numbers of others were condemned—not so much for incendiarism as for their anti-social tendencies. Their deaths were made farcical. Dressed in wild animals' skins, they were torn to pieces by dogs, or crucified, or made into torches to be ignited after dark as substitutes for daylight. Nero provided his Gardens for the spectacle, and exhibited displays in the Circus, at which he mingled with the crowd . . . . Despite their guilt as Christians, and the ruthless punishment it deserved, the victims were pitied. For it was felt that they were being sacrificed to one man's brutality rather than to the national interest.

Tacitus

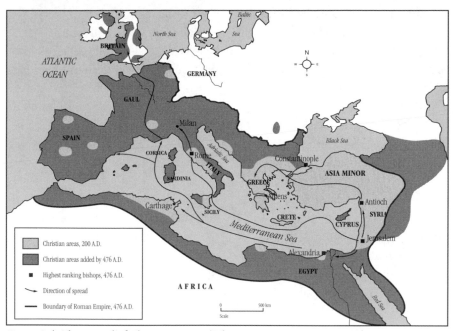

Figure 9-4 *The spread of Christianity to 476 CE*

ians in many parts of the empire during the second and third centuries CE. Because the government did not organize them, these pogroms were not considered official; yet the government also did nothing to stop them. Despite the persecution, more people converted to Christianity and, by the end of the third century CE, about a tenth of the Roman empire's population was Christian. Many who were executed were seen as **martyrs**, people who were willing to die for their beliefs.

Persecution accelerated during the rule of Diocletian at the end of the third century. Diocletian saw himself as a god-like figure, and resented the fact that the Christians did not share this view and would not worship him. With severe economic problems and the constant threat of invasion on the empire's borders, Diocletian blamed the Christians for these misfortunes. He launched several official persecutions, and the last one, launched in 303 CE,

continued a few years after his reign.

The emperor Constantine looked upon the Christians more favourably and even turned to Christianity himself. His conversion was gradual, however, and he continued to worship Roman gods even as he accepted the new religion. In 312 CE, in response to a vision, he ordered his soldiers to wear Christian monograms on their shields into battle to show respect for the Christian God. The following year he issued the Edict of Milan, declaring that Christians were free to practise their religion openly and without persecution. This was a turning point for Christianity, paving the way for greater acceptance and authority in the years ahead. During his reign, Constantine used state funds to construct Christian churches, and he encouraged citizens of the empire to convert by offering them rewards and jobs. Constantine himself was baptized on his deathbed in 337 CE.

His successor, Theodosius, made Christianity the official religion of the empire in 380 CE. Christianity had gained such legitimacy and power that Theodosius even outlawed all other religions. He declared, "We authorize the followers of this law to assume the title of Catholic Christians . . . ." Christianity was now the only accepted religion, and any religious persecution to come would occur in its name.

REFLECT AND ANALYZE

1. How did the Greeks and the Etruscans influence Roman religion?

2. a) Create a chart to compare and contrast the major features of ancient Roman religion and Christianity.
   b) As a Roman citizen who has converted to Christianity, write a letter or journal entry describing what attracted you to the Christian faith and how your conversion has affected your daily life.

3. What is a scapegoat? In what ways were the Christians in Rome used as scapegoats? Give an example of another group of people being used in this way.

4. Defend or dispute this statement: "Persecution by the Romans strengthened Christianity and encouraged its spread."

SOCIAL STRUCTURE

Social standing in ancient Rome depended on two different factors. One factor related to birth: whether you were born a free Roman citizen or a slave. The other factor related to wealth and family influence. During the Roman empire, the emperor was at the top of the social pyramid, whether he acquired his position through heredity or force.

The patricians, or wealthy and influential families, formed the Roman upper class. These freeborn Roman citizens belonged to two separate groups, the senators and the knights. The senators, whose wealth exceeded 1 000 000 sesterces (a Roman coin), numbered about 600 after the reign of Augustus. Their wealth enabled them to buy and sell urban real estate, large country houses, and blocks of flats in the city. They avoided careers in trade or industry, preferring instead to fill high positions in the public service.

Also within the upper class were the knights, whose wealth exceeded 400 000 sesterces. They were the empire's businessmen and, at the time of Augustus, several thousand lived in Rome and in the larger provincial cities. They owned factories, ships, farms, ranches, and vineyards, and competed with one another to gain government contracts to build roads and harbours, work mines, or collect taxes.

The common citizens or plebeians made up the lower class. Some of the poorest people were hardly better off than slaves. Many had originally been small farmers, but had been displaced when the wealthy bought up most of the land and organized it into larger units worked by slaves. Many plebeians then went to the cities in search of jobs, but soon discovered that they had to compete with slave labour there as well. Some were fortunate enough to work independently as shopkeepers or craftspeople, and found places to live in the poorer districts of the cities.

At the base of the social pyramid, the slaves included both freedmen—slaves released by their masters—and current slaves, who could be bought and sold. Romans imported slaves from Britain, Greece, Egypt, and North Africa, and sold them to the most well-to-do families of Rome. Slaves were considered property, not people, and had no rights. Some acted as domestic servants and took care of housework, cooking, and shopping. Others worked on official building projects or trained as gladiators. Some educated slaves were employed to keep accounts or other records, or to teach children. Slaves had to do their master's bidding; any insubordination could lead to punishment or death.

A Roman could grant a slave freedom as a reward for loyal service. Slaves could also buy their freedom if they could save enough money. Some freedmen became quite wealthy later in life. Although many slaves received good treatment from their owners, many others suffered under brutal conditions and took any opportunity to escape.

Between 73 BCE and 71 BCE, thousands of runaway slaves revolted against Rome. The uprising was organized by a group of Roman gladiators led by the slave Spartacus. With early successes, the slave army increased in number to nearly 70 000, and it defeated several Roman forces sent to suppress the revolt.

When Spartacus and his followers tried to cross the Apennines to the Alps, the Roman legions cut them off. Nevertheless, the slaves succeeded in forcing the Roman army to retreat. However, a second Roman assault led to the death of Spartacus and thousands of his soldiers. The Romans nailed 6000 captured slaves to crosses along the Appian Way to serve as a lesson for future rebels.

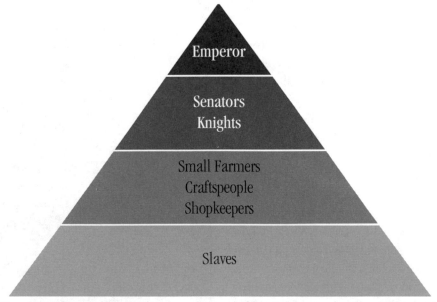

Figure 9-5 *The social pyramid*

REFLECT AND ANALYZE

1. What factors determined social status in ancient Rome? Why do you think these factors were sources of conflict and discontent within Roman society?
2. Create a cartoon that highlights an issue of social concern in ancient Rome.
3. What role did slaves play in Roman society? What problems do you think a dependency on slave labour might cause?

EVERYDAY LIFE

THE FAMILY

The family was the foundation of society in ancient Rome. A family's status and prestige tended to mark an individual's place in society. As property passed from father to son, couples wanted to have at least one male child. Men who had only female children could divorce and remarry at will. The head of the family (usually the father) held absolute authority over all other family members and household slaves. By law, this authority included the right to sell his children into slavery and to abandon unwanted infants.

When a Roman child was born, the father picked up the infant to signify that he recognized the baby as his own legitimate offspring. If the father did not pick up the child, the infant was considered illegitimate, had no rights to inheritance, and could be left to die or be adopted. Eight or nine days after birth, a child received his or her first name, and the parent would hang a *bulla*, or good luck charm, around the baby's neck to ward off evil spirits.

The family assumed responsibility for raising the child during the first six years of life. The father acted as overseer, and usually insisted on strict discipline. The mother, nurses, and slaves looked after the infant's day-to-day needs and upbringing.

Sixteen was an important age for a Roman boy. On that birthday, he exchanged his white, purple-bordered toga, associated with boyhood, for an all-white one, signifying manhood. The bulla given to him when he was a baby was offered up to the gods in thanks for bringing the youth safely to adulthood. His name was officially recorded in the list of citizens, and he was eligible to vote.

At 16, a Roman male might also decide to marry, although boys could marry as young as 14 and girls as young as 12. A couple might marry for love or the couple's parents might arrange the marriage. An engagement provided the occasion for a party to celebrate the signing of a marriage contract. During the festivities, the bride's father presented the groom with a dowry in the form of money or jewellery.

Until the first century CE, wedding ceremonies were common in Rome. After that time, an arrangement somewhat similar to today's common-law marriage became common. Couples living together were

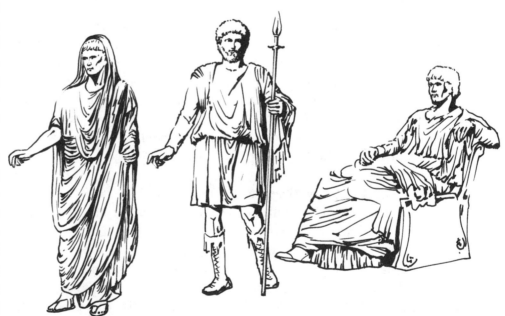

Figure 9-6 (left) *The Roman toga, worn pouched in front and drawn over the head*

Figure 9-7 (centre) *The long-sleeved tunica, worn during the later empire*

Figure 9-8 (right) *The stola, a long tunic that reached to the feet, was worn by Roman women. It sometimes had five pleats and was brightly coloured. A shawl, or palla, which was really a large white blanket, was draped over the shoulders and worn as a hood outdoors. Sandals completed the outfit.*

Figure 9-9 *Some Roman hairstyles*
Hairstyles were important to wealthy women who trained their slaves in the newest and most elaborate fashion. In the days of the Republic hair was evenly parted and drawn back into a chignon, a fashion revived by the Emperor Claudius. The rest of the emperors saw their wives and court ladies with hair piled high, tier-upon-tier. Sometimes hair was dyed, and if it was thin, hair pieces and wigs were available.

considered married, and a formal ceremony was unnecessary. But when a formal wedding did take place, the bride and her family made many preparations. They brought out the busts of family ancestors for display, and decorated the house with flowers. They also prepared the food for the wedding feast or reception, held at the bride's home.

The evening before the wedding, the bride dedicated her toys and her bulla to the family gods who had guarded her childhood. On her wedding day, she wore a white ankle-length tunic made from a single piece of cloth belted at the waist. Her hair was parted in the middle, braided, and tied with ribbons, and an orange veil was placed on her head. The groom wore a white toga.

As the couple stood before the priest, the priest asked the gods if it was a lucky day for a wedding. If there was no sign to the contrary, the ceremony continued. The solemn moment came when the matron of honour took the right hand of the bride and joined it with the right hand of the groom. This act signified the union of the couple. They signed the register in front of several witnesses and prayed for happiness in their married life. The ceremony ended with a sacrifice to the gods.

EDUCATION

Primary education for Roman children, which began at the age of six or seven, was not compulsory. Only the wealthy could afford to send their children to a school, or *ludus*, because the teachers charged high fees. Very rich families often hired private tutors to instruct the children at home. The goal of a primary education was to teach students reading, writing, and counting. Daughters learned to read and write just as sons did, but few girls went on to the secondary level. Instead, they stayed home, where they were taught the skills needed to run a household.

A ludus might be located in a small room next to a shop or a house. The students arrived with a satchel, in which they carried their own books, pens, writing tablets, and ink. In fact, the books were really scrolls of papyrus paper, the pens were made from feathers, and the ink came from soot or dye. The children also wrote on wooden writing tablets covered with wax, using a sharp-pointed stylus of wood or metal to mark the surface.

Most boys left school after the elementary level. For the few who could afford to continue, secondary education began at the age of 10 or 11. At the *grammaticus*, the boys studied Greek and Roman literature, language, and some history, geography, geometry, music, and astronomy. When the students were 13 or 14 years of age, they began a serious study of oratorical and

Figure 9-10 *Scene from a sarcophagus showing the upbringing of a Roman boy*

debating skills, taught by a *rhetor* or expert in the field. (We get our word "rhetoric" from this Latin name.) The Romans considered both skills essential for anyone interested in Roman law or politics. Students spent long hours reading the works of great Roman writers such as Cicero.

WOMEN IN ROME

Roman women played an active and important role in the family, social events, and business ventures. They enjoyed more freedom and independence than their counterparts did in Greek society, although they were still subject to the authority of their fathers and husbands. Roman women attended state functions, the public games, and the theatre. They could own property, work outside the home, and manage their own businesses, but they were never allowed to hold official government positions or vote. Nevertheless, some women exerted considerable influence over political affairs.

One example is Julia Mamaea, the mother of Alexander Severus (221 CE–235 CE), who became emperor at the age of 13. Because of his young age, Julia Mamaea

exercised the real power in his name. It was her goal to restore the prestige and authority of the Senate in order to reduce the power and influence of the military. To accomplish this, she instituted three significant policies. First, she placed the management of the empire in the hands of a small council of senators. Second, she attempted to control the powerful Praetorian Guard by placing them under the command of a distinguished lawyer named Ulpian. Third, she attempted to stave off any frontier disturbances that might lead to military action and any glory for military commanders. Next, she focused on civilian policies. For example, she subsidized teachers and scholars. She also instituted a program excusing landowners who improved their properties from paying taxes and she set up a special guild for manufacturers and merchants who served the interests of the capital. Her efforts succeeded in bringing 12 years of peace and stability to the Roman empire during a very difficult period.

REFLECT AND ANALYZE

1. Why can the family be considered the foundation of Roman society?

2. Compare the type of education offered to students in Roman society with education in our society today. How might you account for the similarities and differences?

3. What is rhetoric? Why would rhetoric have been particularly important for a Roman citizen entering law or politics? Give examples of how rhetoric is used in society today.

4. Stage a conversation between a Greek and a Roman woman to discuss how they view their various rights, privileges, and roles in their societies.

URBAN AND RURAL LIVING

The design of typical homes, and the artifacts found within them, can often tell us a great deal about the daily lives and activities of the inhabitants. Imagine what archaeologists in the future might be able to tell about your lifestyle from your home! In ancient Rome, upper-class urban citizens lived in town houses of various sizes and designs.

A wealthy Roman's town house usually featured a large central atrium or living room, with smaller rooms such as bedrooms, kitchen, storerooms, and lavatories built around it. The two rooms fronting the street were often let out as shops, sometimes run by former household slaves.

Because the Romans did not consider the outward appearance important, houses had few exterior decorations. They also had few windows—a blessing in a noisy city like Rome. Sometimes wealthy city-dwellers cultivated a small garden at the back of the house, away from the main entrance.

The richest citizens built larger and more splendid town houses that looked more like two houses joined together. These homes usually featured a *peristylium*, an elaborate garden that took its name from the colonnade surrounding it. Inside, the walls of the principal rooms were painted in brilliant colours with hunting scenes and still lifes added for decoration. Mosaic floors were patterned from small cubes of coloured stone in a cement base. The Romans furnished their dining room, or *triclinium*, with couches because they followed the Greek practice of reclining while eating.

Some of the more fortunate upper-

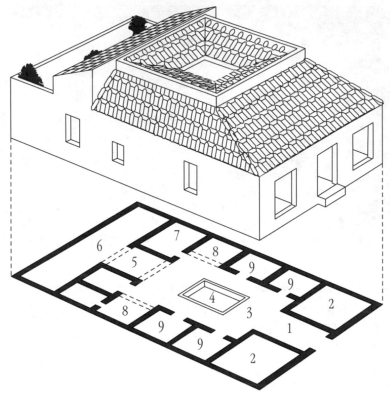

Key
1. *fauces* – entrance passage
2. *tabernae* – shops
3. *atrium* – hall
4. *impluvium* – rainwater basin
6. *hortus* – garden
7. *triclinium* – dining room
8. *alae* – side-rooms
9. *cubiculum* – bedroom

Figure 9-11 *The basic plan and design of a Roman town house*
A town house was constructed with an opening in the centre of the roof, called a compluvium. Similar to a modern sky-light, it let in light, air and rain water. The rain water was collected in an impluvium or pool below

class Romans could afford to own a home in the country. A country villa included a large stone house with many rooms, a walled courtyard, private bath houses, swimming pools, statues, and countless fountains. Sometimes a villa was more than just a home. For example, some villas operated as the centre of a self-contained farming industry.

The stone house had a long covered verandah, offering shade to the rooms op-

ening onto it. The main wing included the dining room, kitchen, storeroom, and guest rooms. The family rooms and the baths were located to the right of the courtyard, and the slaves' quarters to the left.

Inside the house, the Romans plastered and painted the walls, and decorated the floors in important rooms with mosaics. Like the town houses, villas had little furniture. Simple wooden beds with leather webbing served as couches during the day.

Families kept a few chairs for guests or the elderly, and wooden stools for children and slaves. They stored their valuables in boxes or chests. The most prized pieces of furniture were tables made of rare wood, bronze, or silver with inlays of wood, ivory, or tortoiseshell.

The town houses and country villas of the wealthy Romans contained a means of central heating called a *hypocaust*. In this heating system, small stoke-holes were located at the side or in the basement of the main building. When a fire was lit, the hot air and smoke circulated under the floor, then passed up special flues in the walls and provided heat throughout.

In large towns, land prices were often so high that members of the middle and lower classes could not afford town houses. Instead, many lived in overcrowded apartment buildings called *insulae*. In a census taken in 350 CE, it was reported that Rome had 20 times as many insulae as private homes.

These four- to five-storey structures appeared more attractive on the outside than many of the largest private homes. Windows and balconies on the outer walls

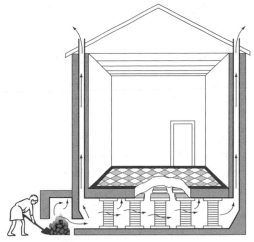

Figure 9-12 *How a hypocaust worked*

THEN AND NOW
The Roman Banquet

What do you find most unusual about a Roman banquet? How does the Roman banquet compare with the Greek symposion? What kind of event do we have today that we could compare to a Roman banquet?

Figure 9-13 *A Roman banquet*

Upper-class Romans enjoyed holding lavish banquets that featured a wide variety of foods imported from all over the empire.

During a banquet, male and female guests reclined on couches in the dining room and selected their food from dishes set out on low tables. They had spoons and knives but no forks, so usually ate with their fingers. Slaves wandered among the couches, offering basins of water and towels to the guests.

A banquet often ran for hours, usually involving at least three heavy courses and many types of entertainment. As they nibbled on delicacies and sipped on wine, the wealthy citizens listened to poetry and music, and applauded jugglers, acrobats, and dancers.

A Roman Banquet Menu

FIRST COURSE
salt fish-balls in wine sauce
boiled eggs
chicken giblets

SECOND COURSE
steamed lobster
roast peacock
roast boar
assorted vegetables

THIRD COURSE
stuffed dates
nut custard
bread and cheese
sweet-wine cakes

wine

created a sense of openness, and each of the small rooms overlooked either the street or an inner courtyard.

But this outward appearance was misleading. The poor construction of the insulae made living conditions rougher and more precarious. Often only the ground floor was built solidly of stone. Workers added upper storeys more hastily by filling a timber framework with rubble, leaving the structure weak and dangerous. Residents had no running water, and therefore no bath or lavatory. For winter heat, they relied on charcoal braziers or stoves, which created a constant threat of fire.

ENTERTAINMENT

Roman forms of public entertainment have fascinated and horrified people for centuries. Some historians suggest that we should not be surprised at their violent games and competitions because the Romans were at war throughout their history. Violence was almost part of their daily life.

Chariot racing and gladiatorial games were two of the most popular forms of entertainment. The Romans held chariot races on an oval track, or circus. The largest and most famous track was in the Circus Maximus, a stadium that seated about 250 000 spectators. During a race, chariots usually made seven laps around the 550 m track. As many as 24 races ran each day, interspersed with acrobatic displays.

Huge crowds gathered at the Circus Maximus before dawn to get good seats. The wealthy sent their slaves or hired people to stand in line for them. Overcrowding in the stadium was common, and

INNOVATIONS
The Roman Baths

What purpose did the baths play in the everyday lives of Roman citizens? What do we have in our contemporary society that might compare with the Roman baths?

The Romans believed in the motto *"mens sana in corpore sano,"* which means "a healthy mind in a healthy body." But because few houses had bathrooms, Roman citizens frequently visited the public baths. The first Roman baths appeared in

Figure 9-14 *The public baths*

the second century BCE as small wash houses for men only. But by the later days of the empire, they became magnificent structures with marble pillars and mosaic-decorated walls. The baths built by the emperor Diocletian could hold 3000 people and were open to men, women, and children.

For a very small fee, a Roman citizen could use the public baths. Most patrons typically began their visit with a hard work-out, either in an open area beside the bath or in an attached gymnasium. Afterwards, they entered first a warm room and then a hot room to sweat the dirt out of their pores. Using a small wooden or metal scraper called a *strigil,* slaves scraped each person's skin clean and rubbed the body down with olive oil. Finally, patrons made their way into a cold room for a plunge into cold water to close the pores.

A visit to the public baths could fill hours. A visitor could make a day of it by participating in athletics or games in the sports hall, sitting with friends and enjoying a drink or a game of dice, or browsing through the library on the premises. The baths were for more than just personal cleanliness—they featured prominently on a Roman's social calendar. To prevent citizens from whiling away too many hours in these pleasant surroundings, later emperors had to restrict the bathhouses' hours.

on more than one occasion the seating collapsed. The worst disaster occurred during the reign of Diocletian, when approximately 13 000 people were reported killed.

Men and women sat together in the stadium on cushioned seats. The emperor sat in a special loggia, or gallery. Seats of honour were reserved for various wealthy or influential citizens: senators and knights, those who supported the races financially, and those who organized the competitions. A jury awarded prizes to the winners.

To start the race, a consul threw a white cloth from a raised platform. At the signal, the chariots burst from their barriers and hurtled into the first lap, the drivers fighting to control the light chariots as they careened along. The reins were bound tightly around the charioteers' bodies to hold them in place as they jostled for position.

A charioteer wanted to be on the inside of the track, close to the partition. To win the race, the driver had to turn so sharply that his chariot would graze the stone turning-post. But too sharp a swerve would overturn the chariot and leave the charioteer dragging along behind the horses. The only way to get free was to cut the reins with a knife.

When the winner crossed the finish line, a storm of applause burst out from the audience and especially from the charioteer's supporting faction, which was identified by their colour—white, green, red, or blue. The Romans idolized the most successful charioteers as heroes.

The popular gladiatorial games took place in amphitheatres such as the famous Colosseum in Rome. Unlike the chariot races at the Circus Maximus, these games were held only on special occasions, but usually on a grander scale. The emperor Trajan once organized a display that lasted 117 days and involved nearly 10 000 gladiators. Women attended these brutal events, but were not allowed to sit in the same sections of the amphitheatre as the men.

Before the gladiators, the games

Figure 9-15 *Roman gladiators in the arena*

THROUGH THEIR EYES

The Gladiatorial Games

The Roman writer and philosopher Seneca comments on the gladiatorial games in 50 CE. How does he feel about the competitions? Why? Do you agree or disagree with this view? Explain.

The other day, I chanced to drop in at the midday games, expecting sport and wit and some relaxation to rest men's eyes from the sight of human blood. Just the opposite was the case . . . it was plain butchery. The men had nothing with which to protect themselves . . . every thrust told. The common people prefer this to matches on level terms or request performances. Of course they do. The blade is not parried by helmet or shield, and what use is skill or defence? All these merely postpone death. In the morning men are thrown to bears or lions, at midday to those who were previously watching them. The crowd cries for the killers to be paired with those who will kill them, and reserves the victor for yet another death. . . .

"But he was a robber." What of it; did he kill anyone? "Yes, he did." Well, just because he committed murder, did he deserve to suffer this? And you, poor man, what have you done to deserve to have to watch it? "Kill him, lash him, brand him! Why is he so frightened of running against cold steel? Why does he die so feebly? Why is he so reluctant to die or to be driven to his death by the lash? They must both inflict wounds on each other's bare chests. Ah, now there's an interval. Let's have some men strangled to fill the time."

opened with a series of acts to stir up the audience's enthusiasm—much like at a concert today. The entertainment then, however, was considerably more violent. After a performance by acrobats, wild beasts might be set loose to tear each other apart. Unarmed men might be led into the arena to be pitted against lions or bears. Just before the main event, hunters might demonstrate their skills or actors might present a short comedy routine to put the spectators in good humour.

When the trumpets sounded, the gladiators marched into the arena, stood before the emperor, and saluted. Many gladiators were prisoners of war, criminals, or slaves. They were equipped with a net, a trident (three-pronged spear), and a dagger, or a small shield and a curved sword. All swore an oath to fight to the death, although a losing gladiator could appeal to the emperor for mercy. Usually the emperor would read the mood of the crowd and then signal either "thumbs up" to save the gladiator, or "thumbs down" for death. Victory brought great prestige to Roman gladiators. Freemen might be awarded large sums of money and slaves might receive their freedom.

REFLECT AND ANALYZE

1. How are Roman house styles similar to modern North American styles? Provide examples.

2. Evaluate life in the insulae. What are the positive and negative aspects of living in this type of housing? What comparisons can you make with life in apartment buildings today?

3. Based on the information in this section, write a detailed account of a day in the life of an ancient Roman citizen of either the upper or lower class.

4. Defend or dispute the following statement: "The nature and purpose of public entertainment in ancient Rome was very different from the nature and purpose of public entertainment in contemporary North America." In a two-column chart, outline the major points in your argument and list specific facts to support each point.

THE ECONOMY

AGRICULTURE

Like the economies of other ancient civilizations, Rome's economy depended on agriculture. During the early years of Roman history, the typical citizen was a peasant farmer tending his own small plot of land, producing enough food to support his family, and selling the surplus to the growing towns. Beginning in the second century BCE, when wealthy townspeople bought many of these smaller land holdings and created larger estates, many peasant farmers became renters or tenants.

Land ownership was a measure of wealth in ancient Rome. At the height of the empire, therefore, the large landowners were generally the wealthiest citizens. As their estates grew, and they looked for ways to reduce their costs and increase their profits, many of them turned to slave labour. Most of the empire's land was still worked by free citizens, however.

Almost all farms grew wheat for bread, the staple item of the Roman diet. Because the expanding urban areas kept up a high demand for grain, the large estates specialized in its production. But as Rome grew to become a metropolis, the demand for grain outstripped the supply. The Romans then had to import much of their wheat from North Africa, Egypt, and Sicily.

In addition to grain, the Romans grew olives and pressed them into olive oil, which they used for cooking and for oil lamps. In the later period of the republic, farmers cultivated grapes for wine. All three of these crops—wheat, olives, and grapes—were grown in the Italian countryside and throughout the empire. Sheep raised in the hilly districts provided both wool and meat, and most lowland farms kept cattle and pigs.

The Romans developed a number of agricultural innovations. One of the most important was an improved plough. The ancient Egyptians had an iron-tipped ploughshare to turn over the soil. When the Romans added an iron coulter, or sharp cutting tool, ahead of the share to cut the soil, they made the task of turning a furrow much easier.

The Romans also invented an efficient hand mill, called a *quern*, for grinding grain. The mill consisted of two stones that would grind together when someone turned a handle on the top stone. The wheat was poured through a funnel in the centre of the upper stone, the handle was turned, and flour came out the bottom. The quern was such an excellent tool for making flour that the Romans built water mills to work on the same principle. The much larger stones of the water mill could grind corn into flour.

INDUSTRY

Workshops were located both on the large estates and in the major towns of the empire. They employed anywhere from a single craftsperson to over a hundred labourers. Many craftspeople, such as potters, drapers, and shoemakers, worked alone in their own small rooms, earning just enough to buy food and clothing for their families. Sometimes a wealthy citizen or entrepreneur hired a few craftspeople, assembled them in a workshop, and produced greater quantities of goods to sell to a larger market. But because there were no machines, workers made everything by hand. Therefore, the workshops—large or small—never became factories like the ones we have today.

Workshops also employed slaves because the entrepreneur could make them work longer and harder than hired employees. However, buying, training, and keeping the slaves cost money as well. In a typical Roman workshop, therefore, hired craftspeople worked alongside slaves.

In the towns, most workshops were originally located around the forum, or marketplace, where farmers from the countryside set up their stalls on market days. Nearby streets were lined with smaller shops selling a wide variety of goods. Some

Figure 9-16 *A Roman shop*

sold food, some sold imported goods, and some sold locally produced metal goods, pottery, or shoes. Later, when public buildings such as the Curia replaced the shops of the Forum, new shopping areas were provided in other parts of the city by both Julius Caesar and the emperor Augustus.

Merchants—the people who actually sold the goods—made more money than either the craftspeople or the small farmers. But few of them achieved great personal wealth because they did not own land.

Roman craftspeople established clubs for those who shared their skill or trade. Each club had its own president, who was elected annually, and its own treasurer, who looked after club funds. Each had its own patron god, and some had a priest to serve that god on behalf of the members. The carpenters' club in Rome even had its own doctor.

To be a member in good standing of such a club, each craftsperson had to pay an annual fee. The fee entitled him to all of the privileges associated with membership, including a monthly dinner meeting. Clubs also paid the funeral costs of departed associates, thus freeing the bereaved family of the burial expenses.

TRADE

Ostia, Rome's chief port, was a busy trading city at the mouth of the Tiber River, about 24 km from Rome. Warehouses lined its docks and wharfs, and a huge force of porters and stevedores worked constantly loading and unloading merchant ships. Since the surrounding countryside could not meet all the needs of this growing city, Rome imported wheat, wine, olives, and other products from the outlying provinces and abroad.

Rome's location at the centre of the Mediterranean region gave it a trading advantage, even though the port at Ostia tended to favour trade with the west rather than the east. The emperors took steps to develop trade between the various provinces and between the empire and other countries. They constructed an extensive network of straight, well-paved, well-drained roads to help knit the sprawling empire together. They built lighthouses to help ensure the safe passage of trading vessels. They even attempted to have the waterways policed to keep pirates in check.

The Romans imported much more than food. They shipped in antiques from Greece, linen from Syria, cotton from Egypt, hunting dogs from Britain, gold and silver from Spain, ivory and wild animals from Africa, and slaves from all parts of the empire. From beyond the empire, they purchased furs from the Baltic countries, silk from China, and pepper from India.

Goods unloaded at Ostia were transferred onto barges and hauled up the Tiber to Rome by teams of oxen or gangs of slaves. On their return trip to Ostia, the barges carried pottery and other products for export to the provinces and countries abroad. But the balance of trade did not favour Rome. That is, Rome imported more than it exported. This dependence on imported goods left the empire vulnerable. When wars disrupted trade routes, for example, Rome suffered. Imports also discouraged new entrepreneurs and technological innovations at home. Eventually, these weaknesses would threaten the survival of the empire.

REFLECT AND ANALYZE

1. What agricultural innovations did the Romans introduce? Why were they important?

2. What benefits did a craftsperson gain by joining a craft club in ancient Rome? Do we have anything similar to these clubs in our society today?

3. a) What weaknesses in the Roman empire's economy could adversely affect its development?
   b) Assume the role of a Roman emperor. Draft a list of reforms and decrees that you would institute to put the empire on a more stable economic footing.

THE ARTS

Modern western culture owes a great deal to Roman traditions. While both the Greeks and the Etruscans influenced Roman art and architecture, the Romans made some important advances of their own. A look around North American cities today reveals evidence of Roman architectural and artistic styles. As well, we use the Roman alphabet and have been influenced by Roman writers and orators.

LITERATURE

Most historians would agree that, unlike classical Greece, Rome did not produce great philosophers. But it did produce a galaxy of prominent writers of Latin prose and verse, as well as several notable historians. The Romans admired no form of intellectual and artistic expression more than literature. The final years of the Roman republic and the early years of the empire set the stage for a burst of literary achievement known as the golden age of Latin literature.

Among the notable and popular writers of this period were Catullus, Cicero, Virgil, and Livy. C. Valerius Catullus (84 BCE–54 BCE) came to Rome from a wealthy family in Verona and quickly became part of the most fashionable circles of the city. His most significant works, which are filled with wit and character analysis, provide us with glimpses into the lives of Rome's upper class. Over 2300 of his verses survive today.

Marcus Tullius Cicero (106 BCE–43 BCE) was a man of varied interests. He was a writer, orator, politician, and statesman.

Cicero first gained a reputation as a brilliant orator in the law courts of Rome. After he entered politics, he was elected consul in 63 BCE and served as governor of Cilicia for a year in 51 BCE.

Cicero's writings were as varied as his interests. He wrote speeches intended to be read as well as heard, treatises on the techniques and training of orators, and books on government, law, friendship, duty, and old age. At least 800 private letters exchanged between Cicero and relatives and friends have also survived.

It was the quality of Cicero's prose that made him a famous writer. Critics admired his skilful use of long sentences and subordinate clauses. They praised his powers of description, his wit, and his use of pathos—all designed to keep the audience spellbound. Cicero was also known for his authoritative grasp of his subject matter. He took great care to collect and present evidence in a convincing manner. Cicero's prose style was so popular that he influ-

enced writers in Latin and other languages for centuries.

Cicero wrote many of his most famous letters to an equestrian named Atticus during the political crisis of 49 BCE, when Julius Caesar was about to seize power in Rome. The letters reveal a great deal about both Cicero and his society. Like other prominent Romans, Cicero had to decide whether to support Caesar or Pompey, Caesar's rival for power.

One of the most famous Roman writers from the early empire was the great poet Publius Vergilius Maro (70 BCE–19 BCE), or Virgil. A prolific writer, Virgil is noted in part for a series of pastoral poems inspired by the years he spent growing up on his father's farm in northern Italy. (Pastoral poetry depicts country life, often in an idyllic fashion.) His most famous work, however, is a patriotic 12-book epic called the *Aeneid*, which he completed shortly before his death.

Commissioned by the emperor

THROUGH THEIR EYES

Cicero's Letter to Atticus about Caesar

The following excerpt is from one of Cicero's letters to Atticus before Julius Caesar crossed the Rubicon River. In the letter, Cicero expresses his view of Caesar and the impending crisis. What does Cicero intend to do? How does he describe his dilemma? What stylistic techniques does he use?

Formiae, c. December 18, 50 BCE
The political situation alarms me deeply, and so far I have found scarcely anybody who is not for giving Caesar what he demands rather than fighting it out. The demand is impudent no doubt, but more moderate than was expected(?). And why should we start

standing up to him now? ... You will ask me what line I shall take in the House. Not the same as in my own mind. There I shall vote for peace at any price, but in the House I shall echo Pompey, and I shall not do it in a spirit of subservience either.

> *Cicero*
> **Letter to Atticus**

When the final confrontation came between Caesar and Pompey, and Caesar led his army across the Rubicon on January 11 in 49 BCE, Cicero followed Pompey east. Later, he returned to Rome and received Caesar's pardon.

Figure 9-17 *Virgil, with the Muses of history and tragedy*

Augustus as part of his program to promote patriotism and reverence, the *Aeneid* tells the story of Aeneas, a Trojan prince who escaped the Greek destruction of his city and founded the kingdom that became Rome. In describing the hardships, setbacks, and final triumph of Aeneas, Virgil underlined the struggle and achievement of Rome, and the great promise of its empire under Augustus. In the following excerpt, Aeneas learns of Rome's future when he visits his father in the underworld.

Now bend your gaze this way, look at
*   that people there!*
They are your Romans. Caesar is there
*   and all Ascanius'*
Posterity, who shall pass beneath the
*   arch of day.*
And here, here is the man, the promised
*   one you know of—*
Caesar Augustus, son of a god, destined
*   to rule*
Where Saturn ruled of old in Latium,
*   and there*
Bring back the age of gold: his empire
*   shall expand*
Past Garamants and Indians to a land
*   beyond the zodiac*
And the sun's yearly path, where Atlas
*   the sky-bearer pivots*
The wheeling heavens, embossed with
*   fiery stars, on his shoulder.*

Even now the Caspian realm, the
*   Crimean country*
Tremble at oracles of the gods predicting
*   his advent,*
And the seven mouths of the Nile are in
*   a lather of fright.*

Virgil, *Aeneid*

Titus Livius (59 BCE–17 CE), or Livy, was a prose writer who devoted his career to a 142-volume history of Rome from its beginnings to Livy's own time. Beside this vast project, the work of other Roman historians appears almost insignificant. Today, only 35 of the volumes (or rolls of original papyrus) survive, each representing about 30 to 50 printed pages in a modern context. Although they make up only part of the manuscript, these volumes provide historians with an invaluable source of information. Livy drew upon many sources and traditions that can no longer be traced. When he died, no comparable historian emerged for almost a century.

THROUGH THEIR EYES

Livy Speaks of Hannibal

In his history, Livy always attempted to promote the cause of Roman patriotism. Even so, he was forced to recognize the dauntless courage of Hannibal of Carthage. What qualities does Livy see in Hannibal, even though Hannibal is the enemy? What evidence do you think Livy has for this portrayal?

He was fearless in exposing himself to danger and perfectly self-possessed in the presence of danger. No amount of exertion could cause him either bodily or mental fatigue; he was equally indifferent to heat and cold; his eating and drinking were measured by the needs of nature, not by appetite; his hours of sleep were not determined by day or night, whatever time was not taken up with active duties was given to sleep and rest, but that rest was not wooed on a soft couch or in silence, men often saw him lying on the ground amongst the sentinels and outposts, wrapped in his military cloak. His dress was in no way superior to that of his comrades; what did make him conspicuous were his arms and horses. He was by far the foremost both of the cavalry and the infantry, the first to enter the fight and the last to leave the field.

History of Rome
Livy

ARCHITECTURE

Immense palaces, stadiums, temples, and victory arches are perhaps the most impressive testimony of Rome's grandeur. We remember Romans for the great monuments they built to show their power and dignity, and for their important architectural innovations. Today, we can still find Roman-style buildings in Europe, Spain, the Middle East, and North America.

Roman temples were intended primarily to house the statue of a particular god or goddess. Typical temples consisted of a central rectangle or *cella*, constructed on a high platform. A marble colonnade surrounded the rectangle and supported a sloping roof. People could only enter the temple by climbing the steps at the front.

From the Greeks, the Romans learned to use rows of stately columns and rectangular forms. But, by the third century CE, the Romans were also using the arch more extensively and had developed the dome. They discovered that curved structures, such as the arch, could support their own weight better than straight ones. On this principle, the Romans were able to construct much larger buildings than the Greeks.

Figure 9-18 *A model of the city of Rome in the second century CE*

THEN AND NOW
The Roman Colosseum

What features of the Colosseum's design are Roman innovations? Provide examples of modern buildings that are similar to the Colosseum. How do they compare?

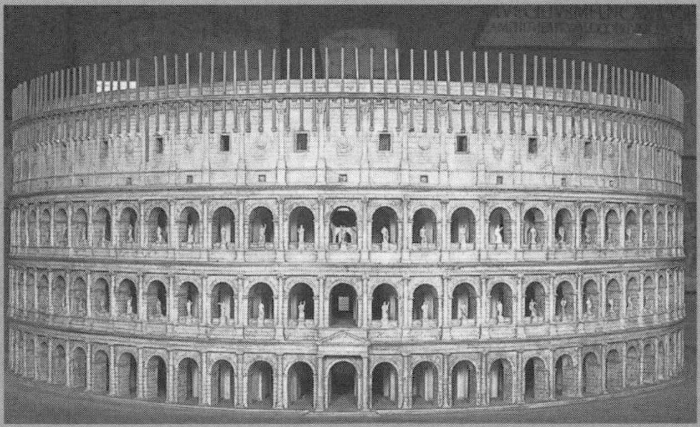

Figure 9-19 *The Colosseum then*

Today, we can see only part of the Colosseum because earthquakes during the thirteenth and fourteenth centuries CE shook much of the outer arcade to the ground. During Roman times, however, the Colosseum was an impressive structure. Wide corridors allowed spectators to enter and exit safely and easily. Inside, six tiers of seats accommodated 45 000 to 50 000 spectators.

Beneath the centre of the arena was an elaborate complex of passages and rooms designed to store properties and cages for animals. Systems of trapdoors and

Figure 9-20 *The Colosseum now*

pulleys transported the animals into the arena from the underground chambers. Over the top of the Colosseum, an enormous awning provided shade for spectators when needed. A service corps drew the giant awning forward using ropes tied to the upper cornices of the building.

The Colosseum presented gladiatorial combats and wild beast hunts. Scents were sprayed into the auditorium to mask the smell of blood and the stench of rubbish.

Another important innovation was concrete. We take concrete for granted today, but it offered the Romans several advantages over traditional stone construction. They could put up buildings more economically because the materials were cheap. As well, most of the work could be done by large numbers of unskilled workers, usually slaves and prisoners of war, rather than by skilled stonemasons. Concrete was also stronger and more adaptable. A well-built concrete vault (a roof made of arches) could enclose a much larger space than any form of stone construction. Concrete vaults were common features in the Roman baths because they resisted dampness and were fire-proof. Roman architects also used these vaults in the great Roman amphitheatres.

Many of the finest public buildings in Rome were constructed by emperors who hoped to leave a personal legacy. The emperor Vespasian, for example, began the construction of perhaps the most distinctive and imposing of all Roman monuments—the famous amphitheatre called the Colosseum. Construction began sometime between 70 CE and 75 CE, and was completed in 80 CE by Vespasian's son, the emperor Titus. Titus introduced the Colosseum to the public with a series of gladiator shows that lasted for 100 days.

PAINTING AND SCULPTURE

The Romans imported thousands of Greek statues to decorate their homes, gardens, and public buildings. It is not surprising, therefore, that Roman sculpture was influenced by Greek and Hellenistic styles. In fact, the Romans often tried to copy the Greek models as closely as possible.

Some Roman sculptors, however, adopted a realistic style that was very different from the idealized forms preferred by the Greeks. The Romans tended to concentrate on the head and face, rather than the whole body, and portrayed their subjects with every wrinkle and wart. These sculptors of the late republican period emphasized the model's maturity and individual character (with an expression of haughty pride or smugness, for example), rather than his or her good looks. During the empire, sculptors turned to creating large works that celebrated Roman victories or demonstrated Rome's influence and power.

Roman painters were not considered important members of Roman society, so although many examples of their work remain, we know little about the artists themselves. Many seemed to favour detailed still-life subjects, which they painted on the stucco walls of rooms to make them look larger. In some Roman villas, paintings of magnificent landscapes or scenes from myths gave the houses a palatial feeling. Portraits were also popular. Pictures of departed family members, for example, were commonly placed in tombs.

Another popular Roman art form was

Figure 9-21 *A Roman bust, possibly of Marcus Brutus*

the **mosaic**, a picture or pattern made from small chips of coloured stone or marble. Those that survive tell us a great deal about the lives and interests of the ancient Romans. They depict everything from gladiators in the arena to people in their daily routines. Christian themes became popular in the later years of the empire.

REFLECT AND ANALYZE

1. What contributions did Catullus, Cicero, Virgil, and Livy make to our understanding of ancient Rome?

2. a) What important innovations did the Romans make in architecture? Why were these innovations significant?
   b) Provide examples of buildings in your community or in a nearby city that have Roman architectural characteristics. Draw sketches or create a photo portfolio of these buildings. Include labels and captions pointing out Roman features.

3. Compare an example of Greek classical sculpture with an example of Roman sculpture. Account for the similarities and differences.

4. Ovid and Horace were two other important Roman writers. Do some research to find out what contributions these writers made to Roman literature and how they influenced later writers.

THE SCIENCES

ENGINEERING— THE ROMAN ROADS

"All roads lead to Rome." When we examine the extensive network of roads that linked the distant parts of the Roman empire, we can easily understand this famous expression. Roman roads were the empire's lifeline, essential to its survival and defence. Troops marched quickly and easily along these roads to parts of the empire where they were needed. Essential supplies travelled along these roads to the frontier, where soldiers guarded the empire's borders. But the roads had great economic importance as well. They were the main transportation routes used by the Roman merchants, who traded with the outlying provinces of the empire.

The Romans demonstrated a particular genius for solving some of the practical problems of engineering. They built their roads so well that some of them are still used today. Others have formed the basis of modern highways.

What was so remarkable about Roman roads? First, they were wide and straight—unlike earlier roads, which were narrow and winding. Turns usually occurred at higher elevations because the surveyors made their sightings from one high point to the next. Second, the roads were durable, largely because of their solid foundation. Workers dug a trench a metre or so deep and filled it with large stones tightly wedged together. They then covered this stone base with a layer of smaller stones, sometimes bound together by cement. The top layer was gravel, small flints, or stone slabs (when available).

Sometimes the Romans built the

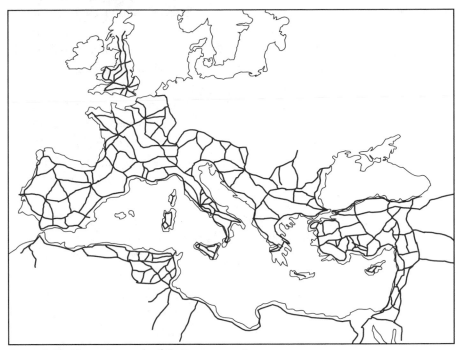

Figure 9-22 *The main roads of the Roman empire*

foundations by piling earth up in a mound and laying stones on top. This embankment, 12 to 15 m wide, was called an *agger*. When the Saxons invaded Roman Britain, they saw these aggers rising above the surrounding fields, often as high as a metre, and called them "high ways." We get our word "highway" from this source.

The workers raised the roads in the centre so that water would drain off quickly into the ditches dug alongside. They also cleared trees around the roads to eliminate hiding places for animals or enemies along the route. The Senate took responsibility for keeping the roads in good repair. A special

board of traffic control maintained the roads.

Approximately every 1.5 km along a Roman road, markers indicated the distance to the nearest fortress. At 18 km intervals, stations provided a place to change horses. At 36 km intervals, inns were constructed to provide overnight accommodation for travellers. The most famous Roman road was the Via Appia, or Appian Way, which stretched over 200 km, linking Rome to Capua. The Via Appia was completed in 312 BCE and was named after its builder, Appius Claudius.

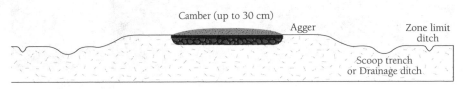

Figure 9-23 *Cross-section of a Roman road*

AQUEDUCTS

The Romans developed aqueducts to transport water. Basically, aqueducts were stone channels built above ground and supported on arches or bridges. They provided vital water supplies to many towns and cities throughout the empire. In Roman Britain, most centres had easy access to water in rivers and wells, so aqueducts were not often needed. But in the long, dry summers of Italy, southern France, and Spain, they were essential. In Rome alone, more than 640 km of these channels brought water into the city.

The aqueducts carried water from a source gradually downhill to where it was needed. At the source, the water was pooled so that workers could control the amount flowing into the channels. The Romans covered the channels to avoid contamination and overflow from rainstorms. Workers had to build some sections high above valley floors. Sometimes they also had to tunnel through hills that were too difficult to bypass.

The Romans constructed wells and reservoirs in their cities to store the water transported by the aqueducts. Poorer citizens fetched their water from these public sources. Wealthy citizens had water piped directly to their homes and paid a tax according to the size of the pipe leading into the house. Some aqueducts are still in use today.

MEDICINE

In the early years of the Roman republic, doctors relied on herbs, amulets, and prayers to ward off disease. Most citizens accepted these methods and showed little interest in medical science. After contact with the Greeks, however, the Romans began to examine new methods of treating illness.

Initially, the Romans did not hold doctors in high regard. As most doctors were Greeks or slaves, the Romans looked upon them with suspicion. The military was the first sector of Roman society to understand the importance of medical science. Julius Caesar valued doctors highly and recognized their work officially by granting them Roman citizenship.

Archaeologists have found a variety of surgical instruments among the ruins of Rome. Doctors administering to soldiers in military hospitals and to gladiators in arenas had to develop surgical techniques. By trying to save the lives of men damaged in violent sports or wars, doctors learned how to mend fractures, remove surgical abscesses, and even amputate limbs. Without anesthetics, these operations must have been very painful.

By dissecting apes, doctors learned more about the human anatomy. Unfortunately, these investigations also led them to assume too many similarities between the anatomy of humans and other primates. Nevertheless, Roman doctors contributed to our knowledge of the structure and functions of the human body.

MATHEMATICS

The Romans did not develop a sophisticated system of mathematics. They had no concept of zero, and used only seven symbols in their counting system: I (one), V (five), X (ten), L (50), C (100), D (500), and M (1000).

To create the numbers from one to ten, the Romans used the first three symbols: I, II, III, IV, V, VI, VII, VIII, IX, X. Note that the number four (IV) was one less than five and nine (IX) was one less than ten.

Mathematical operations such as division and multiplication were very difficult in this numerical system. Even writing a

Figure 9-24 *The aqueduct of the Pont du Gard, built between 63 BCE and 13 BCE, to bring water to Nîmes, France*

date could be a daunting task. For example, 1888 is written MDCCCLXXXVIII while 1995 is MCMXCV. Nevertheless, we still use Roman numerals in special instances today. For example, we use them to distinguish popes and monarchs with identical names (Pope Pius X, Henry VIII, Elizabeth II). Publishers also use lowercase Roman numerals for the introductory pages of books, before the formal chapters begin (see the front of this book for an example). Where else in our society do you see this numerical system?

TIME

The Romans likely got their first calendar from the Greeks. The earliest republican calendar was a lunar one of 354 days with the moon's cycle of 10 months. Priests kept watch for the new moon in order to record the cycles and the changing months. The year originally began in the spring when vegetation started to grow.

According to tradition, Numa Pompilius, who succeeded Romulus as king of Rome, reformed the calendar so that special religious holidays could be named by date and observed by all. The reformed calendar had 12 months and corresponded to the solar year.

But by the time of Julius Caesar, the new year was falling in the middle of winter and the calendar was in a hopeless state of confusion. In 45 BCE, therefore, Caesar imposed a new calendar on Rome. The Julian calendar had a standard year of 365 days, with an extra day added in February every fourth year. It also had 12 months: Januarius, Februarius, Martius, Aprilis, Maius, Junius, Julius, Augustus, September, October, November, December. July was named in honour of Julius Caesar and August after

Augustus. September, October, November, and December were taken from the Latin words for the numbers seven, eight, nine, and ten. Januarius was sacred to Janus, the god of entrances and beginnings. Martius was dedicated to a festival in honour of Mars, the god of war and agriculture. Juno, the wife of Jupiter, gave her name to Junius (June), the month considered most advantageous for marriage.

The Julian calendar remained in use for centuries. But, despite the adjustment every four years, the calendar was still one

day out every 128 years. By the sixteenth century CE, it had drifted nearly two weeks ahead of the seasons. In 1582, therefore, Pope Gregory XIII reformed the calendar. Some eastern European and Greek Christian faiths, however, still follow the Julian calendar to mark their religious days.

The Romans divided the period of actual daylight into 12 hours. Therefore, the duration of an hour varied according to the length of the day. The Romans did not count the night hours.

REFLECT AND ANALYZE

1. What evidence suggests that the Romans focused their energies on practical matters?

2. "In matters of science, the Romans were not very innovative." Do you agree or disagree with this statement? Explain.

3. You are a citizen from an outlying province of the empire visiting Capua. You have decided to extend your holiday and travel the Appian Way to Rome. Create a journal entry describing the nature and quality of the road system, and your general impressions of road travel.

LOOKING BACK

Roman civilization affected the lives of millions of people across Europe and the Mediterranean region for more than eight centuries. Today, we still feel the legacy of that civilization. The Romans adapted many ideas from other Mediterranean peoples, especially the Greeks. They built on Greek achievements in art and architecture, and made their own practical contributions in areas such as road construction and aqueducts. Roman literature, art, and architecture helped to preserve Greek

forms, and ensured that both cultures became part of the heritage of the western world.

The Roman language of Latin gave birth to the romance languages of French, Italian, Spanish, Romanian, and Portuguese. Roman law provided ideas for future legal systems in Europe. Roman government served as a model for later constitutional designs.

When Rome granted official recognition to Christianity, it took a critical step in shaping the future course of western civilization. Under Roman influence, the

Christian church became an institution, taking advantage of the government's support to build its power and prestige during the last century of the empire.

The western and eastern parts of the Roman empire followed quite different paths, as we shall see. To the east, the Byzantine empire maintained some of the glory that had been Rome, creating a sophisticated culture, art, and unique form of Chritianity. But in the west, as small, fierce Germanic tribes fought one another, the achievements of Rome were mostly lost, and life continued to be unsettled for many years. For this reason, the early part of the Medieval period has sometimes been called the **Dark Ages**.

MAKING CONNECTIONS

1. You are a reporter for a contemporary Canadian magazine assigned the task of putting together a 2 – 3 page feature story under the banner headline, "Sparta Revisited." Develop a collection of articles, based upon your observations of life in this unusual Greek polis, that will interest your readers and provide them with a clear understanding of Spartan life and values.

2. Ancient Greek philosophers like Plato and Aristotle called many established ideas of their times into question. What contemporary ideas or issues do you think Plato might have questioned? Prepare a response that he might have delivered to his pupils about the idea or issue you have selected.

3. Rome grew from a collection of mud huts along the Tiber River into one of the greatest empires of all times. What factors were most instrumental in this transformation?

4. One of the most widely studied aspects of Roman history is the decline and fall of the Roman empire. What lessons do you think modern nations can learn from the decline of the Roman empire?

5. The ancient Romans are admired for many different reasons. One reason was their practical nature. In what ways did Roman emphasis on the practical help to unify the Roman empire?

6. Rome borrowed heavily from Greek civilization. Civilizations often borrow from their neighbours. Identify a present-day example where one civilization or culture is strongly influenced by another. Provide evidence to support your example.

DIGGING DEEPER

7. Read the excerpt in the text from Homer's epic poem *The Odyssey*. Find a translation or retelling, and read more of Odysseus' adventures. Choose one of these adventures, and create a scenario to present to the class.

8. Ancient Greek architecture has greatly influenced the architecture of the modern world. Find resources in your library with local pictures of contemporary architecture that illustrate a strong Greek influence. Label the pictures to identify them, noting the particular Greek influence. Create a montage or a bulletin board display.

9. One of the principal ways that Rome influenced the societies that followed it was through its law. Research some of the ways in which Roman law is still central to our legal concepts today, and find a way of presenting your findings to the class.

10. Choose one of the following people, and research his or her life and importance. Present your findings to the class.

Pythagoras	Socrates	Plato
Alcibiades	Hypatia	Alexander the Great
Pericles	Zenobia	Caligula
Constantine the Great	Attila the Hun	St. Augustine

11. "Ancient Minoan civilization gave greater equality to women than any society until our own. "

"It is impossible to imagine the modern world without the legacy of ancient Greece."

"Slavery was the curse of the Roman world."

Choose one of these statements, and collect evidence to support or refute it. Present your findings to the class.

SKILL DEVELOPMENT: DEVELOPING AN ISSUE ANALYSIS ORGANIZER

In order to understand history, it's often necessary to analyze specific issues or questions. Doing this can help us understand what happened in a particular period, and connect it to important issues in our own time.

Process

1. Make sure you have a clear subject that you are analyzing. For example: "Was the system of government instituted in Rome during the period of the republic a satisfactory form of government?"

2. Place the alternatives at the top of the first two columns of the issue analysis organizer. Make a third column for potential compromise positions.

	Yes - The republican system of government was satisfactory	No - The republican system of government was not satisfactory	Ways in which the republic could have been improved

3. Now come up with a common set of **criteria** to write in the blank left-hand column. These criteria are questions you can ask of either alternative, or common areas in which you can compare the two. For example, you could compare the different executive positions and legislative assemblies in the Roman republic. As common answers emerge, you can begin to group your criteria together. For example, you will likely find the same answers with all of the popular assemblies. This might generate a new question about whether the popular assemblies were effective or not. As you consider your material, do new criteria emerge? Do potential solutions suggest themselves?

CRITERIA	Yes - The republican system of government was satisfactory	No - The republican system of government was not satisfactory	Ways in which the republic could have been improved
Criteria Related to Structure executive branch - magistrates legislative branch - senate - assemblies			

4. Use the text or other resources to find information to fill in your categories.

5. Compare the "yes-no" columns. Do you find compromises to fit in the alternative column?

CRITERIA	Yes - The republican system of government was satisfactory	No - The republican system of government was not satisfactory	Ways in which the republic could have been improved
Criteria Related to Structure executive branch - magistrates legislative branch - senate - assemblies	• a large number, so less power concentration • provided stability • an attempt to represent all citizens (Tribes) • an attempt to be democratic (Tribes/Curia)	• not enough public input in selection process • too much the reserve of one class • too many assemblies • too much emphasis on wealth (Centuries) • organization too complex	• elect at-large or use an assembly to select • open to other classes or reduce power • reduce number of assemblies to one or two

Criteria Related to Function executive branch - magistrates	• attempts in place to control or limit their powers • areas of responsibility and powers are clearly defined		
legislative branch - senate		• too much power concentration	• reduce its legislative powers
- assemblies		• too much ceremonial rather than real power	• redistribute some of the senate powers here
Criteria Related to Checks on Power Abuse executive branch - magistrates	• separate areas of responsibility were assigned • consuls shared imperium and veto power • consuls alternated power monthly, daily during war		
legislative branch - senate			
- assemblies		• too little control over the power of the senate	• limit senators term or devise a way to override the legislative position of the senate

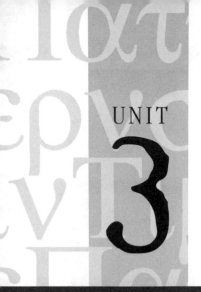

UNIT

3

The Medieval World
400 CE - C. 1500 CE

EUROPE, THE BYZANTINE EMPIRE, AND ISLAMIC CIVILIZATIONS

The disintegration of the Roman empire ushered in a new and different age—the medieval period. In European history, this is also called the Middle Ages. It was a time of turmoil and change during which two new religions gave birth to three great civilizations. Two of these civilizations were Christian. When the western Roman empire collapsed, the eastern empire continued as the ***Byzantine*** civilization. The Byzantines called themselves "Romans" and built a sophisticated and wealthy society founded on Christian and classical traditions. Western Europe, on the other hand, was plunged into chaos and ignorance for centuries. Slowly, an entirely new civilization developed, which blended Christian principles, Germanic culture, and surviving influences from ancient times.

South and east of the Mediterranean lay the Muslim empire based upon a religion called Islam. Born on the Arabian peninsula, Islam spread to the eastern Mediterranean, North Africa, Spain, and central Asia. The Muslim world was larger than either the Byzantine empire or Europe. Its tradition of classical learning, scientific innovations, and vast wealth had a major impact on the other two civilizations that bordered the Mediterranean.

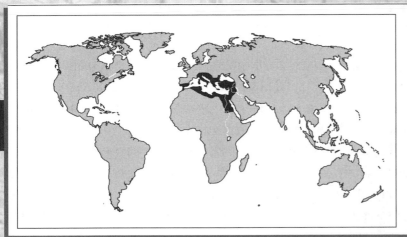

THE BYZANTINE
EMPIRE

MEDIEVAL EUROPE:
The Age of Chivalry

I t is dawn. Squire William Dowdeswell of Gloucester, England, has spent the night in church in prayer. His suit of metal plate armour and his helmet lie on the altar before him. On this morning in 1312, he is to be knighted in a special ceremony. His lord, Sir Henry Wakefield, will publicly recognize the completion of William's training by dubbing him on each shoulder as he kneels before a large assembly.

The son of a noble family, William had always wanted to become a knight. His training began at the age of seven, when his father sent William to the Wakefield home to serve as a page for seven years. During this time the ladies of the household taught him manners and how to act in company.

When he turned 15, William became a squire to Sir Henry. For the next five years he looked after Sir Henry's horse and armour, and served the lords and ladies of the household. He was trained in the use of weapons and accompanied Sir Henry on occasions when he went into battle.

Once knighted, William must follow the **code of chivalry** expected of all knights. Chivalry was a code of behaviour that combined Christian values and the virtues of a noble warrior. Sir William is expected to be brave, generous, and loyal; to protect noblewomen; and to defend the honour of his family.

Figure 10-1
A knight and a lady as depicted in a fifteenth century illuminated French manuscript

Nowadays, we have a romantic view of the Middle Ages, especially of knights in shining armour and their ladies. But during the early medieval period, full of warfare and strife, living conditions were quite primitive and basic necessities hard to come by for the average person. Even in castles, daily life lacked the technological and cultural refinements which Roman citizens had enjoyed. To understand how a completely new civilization in western Europe rose out of the ruins of the Roman empire, we need to look at how geography, the character of the Germanic peoples, and a budding Christian religion all came together.

THE LANDS OF WESTERN EUROPE

A Roman citizen in the dying years of the empire would not have understood what we mean today by the term "western Europe." The Roman world, like that of the Greeks before them, had a Mediterranean focus, extending to Spain, north Africa, and what is now the Middle East. The northern provinces of Gaul (now France) and Britain were the least significant of Rome's holdings.

The geography and climate of Europe are very different from that of the Mediterranean region.

Europe is the smallest continent, and might be thought of as a peninsula attached to the large land mass of Asia. It is divided from Asia by the Ural Mountains, the Caspian Sea, and the Caucasus Mountains to the east. The Mediterranean and Black seas form the southern boundary, while the Atlantic and Arctic oceans lie to the west and north. Although small in area, Europe has a very long coastline that snakes around the northern Scandinavian peninsula, the western Iberian peninsula, and the southern Italian and Baltic peninsulas. Along this coast are many good harbours and navigable rivers leading inland. Off the northwest coast of the mainland, halfway between the Scandinavian and Iberian peninsulas, lie the British Isles.

A vast, fertile plain, suitable for cultivation, covers most of the central area. Unlike in the Mediterranean, crops planted on the European plain do not grow year-round. However, the fertile soil and more plentiful rainfall make it possible to grow a wider variety of crops and to produce more abundant harvests. Europe's numerous rivers are another advantage. Many rivers became important routes for commerce, although trade did not develop for some time. Three key waterways are the Rhine, the Danube, and the Volga.

Several mountain ranges, notably the Alps and the Pyrenees, tended to keep communities separate, helping to foster a diversity of cultures and languages. However, good mountain passes allowed people to cross these barriers fairly easily.

The vegetation of Europe is varied, with scrubland in the south, deciduous woodlands in the central lowlands, and evergreen forests in the north and mountainous areas. The climate is similarly

Figure 10-2 *The fertile valleys of the Rhineland*

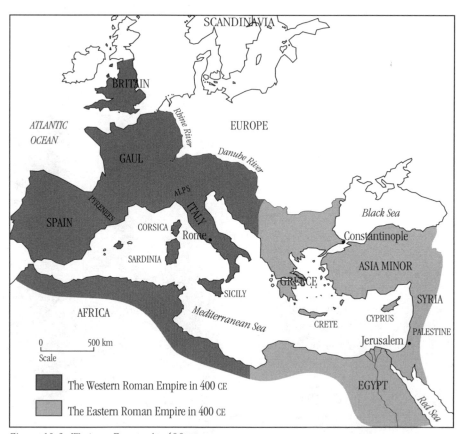

Figure 10-3 *Western Europe in 400 CE*

varied, ranging from mild temperatures year-round in the south to extreme cold in the far north. Valuable resources of the region include timber, furs, and tin.

HISTORICAL OVERVIEW

The period following the end of Roman civilization, during which western Europe took shape, is called the Middle Ages. The adjective **medieval** comes from two Latin words, *medium aevum,* which mean "the middle age." Latin, the language of Rome, did not die when the empire ended. It was destined to become the language of the Christian church and of scholars in the Middle Ages.

The medieval period in Europe can be divided into two phases. The Early Middle Ages, from 476 to about 1050, was a period of perpetual strife among various Germanic peoples. During this unsettled period, once called the Dark Ages, there was little development in trade or social structure. In the Late Middle Ages, 1050 to about 1450, a more stable society developed, and along with it, growth in agriculture and trade.

AFTER THE FALL OF ROME

As we saw in Chapter 8, numerous Germanic tribes had lived on the fringes of the Roman empire for centuries. Nomadic, aggressive, and fiercely independent, many of these groups occupied different parts of the empire by the time it fell in 476. Each group was ruled by its own king. Rome's centralized form of government had collapsed.

A number of tribes succeeded in establishing small independent kingdoms. The Ostrogoths ruled the Italian peninsula and surrounding area for about 30 years before another group, the Lombards, took over the northern part of the peninsula. The Visigoths formed a kingdom in the Iberian peninsula, while the Vandals ruled in North Africa. The Germanic Angles and Saxons from the mainland invaded Britain in the mid-400s, taking over the eastern half of the island from the native Celts.

The chiefs of these tribes gave lands to their warriors, in return for their services in war. These warriors, in turn, ruled over various smaller landowners and the common people who lived and worked on the land. This hierarchical social structure, with the king as overlord, warriors or lords at differing levels below him, and common people at the bottom, is called **feudalism**. Feudalism developed first on the

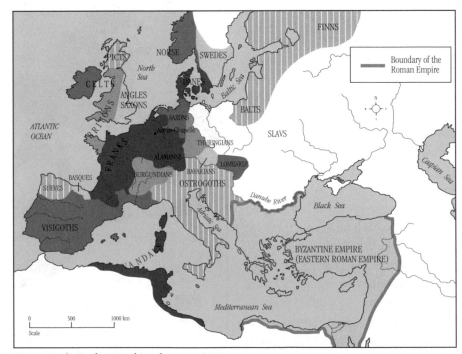

Figure 10-4 *Barbarian kingdoms, c. 500 CE*

continent and later in Britain. In a feudal society, as we shall see in the next chapter, ruler and ruled had clearly defined duties and responsibilities toward each other. This helped to create a sense of order even during unsettled times.

THE KINGDOM OF THE FRANKS

The largest and most powerful kingdom of the Early Middle Ages was established in the former northwest Roman province of Gaul. Clovis (480–511), leader of the Franks, became ruler over territory stretching from the Pyrenees Mountains to central Europe.

Clovis is recognized as the founder of the French monarchy. When he converted to Christianity, he won favour with the church in Rome, becoming the only Roman Catholic king in western Europe. By gaining a foothold in the Frankish kingdom, Christianity was set to play a role in other developing societies of Europe. Having won the acceptance of local chiefs, Clovis ruled over a relatively stable kingdom. Unwisely, he bequeathed his kingdom to his four sons, which led to two centuries of infighting among his descendants, the Merovingians. The Merovingian kings further weakened their power by appointing a royal official, called the "mayor of the palace," to handle the running of the government.

During the eighth century, the Frankish kingdom was threatened by Muslim invaders, originally from north Africa, who had gained a hold in Spain. When the Muslims entered the south of Gaul in 732, they were turned back by forces led by a mayor of the palace named Charles Martel (688–741). An able and ambitious leader, Martel forged ties with Christian leaders, recognizing that the church's increasing influence could help to strengthen his own authority. The church, in turn, needed the protection of the Franks as it sought to spread Christianity throughout northern Europe. With the church's help, Martel's son, Pepin (714–768), was elected king by the Frankish nobles, securing a new line of rulers, the Carolingians. Pepin rewarded the church with lands near Rome, which became the Papal States. As a result of this alliance, the church would be closely involved in political affairs throughout the Middle Ages.

Charlemagne

Pepin was succeeded in 768 by his son Charles (768–814), who set about increasing the size of the kingdom and strengthening its central rule. He waged numerous war campaigns, defeating the Lombards in Italy, the Muslims in Spain, the Saxons in northern Europe, and the Avars in the east. His military achievements were so impressive that he was called "Charles the Great," or Charlemagne.

Figure 10-5 *The coronation of Charlemagne in the fourteenth century illumination* Grandes Chroniques de France

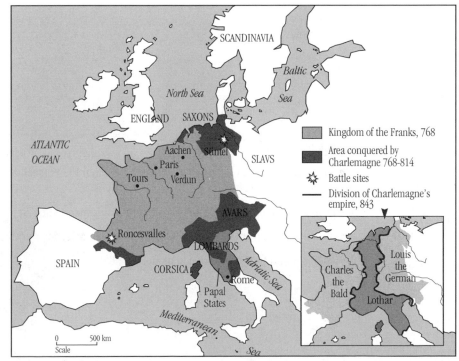

Figure 10-6 *Charlemagne's empire*

MEDIEVAL EUROPE: A DEVELOPMENTAL TIMELINE

EARLY MIDDLE AGES (DARK AGES)
476-c. 1050

POLITICAL DEVELOPMENTS

- small, independent kingdoms spring up in Italy, Gaul, Spain, Germany, Belgium, and Britain (400s)
- Clovis establishes the Frankish kingdom (around 500 ce)
- the pope crowns Charlemagne "Emperor of the Romans" (800)
- the Vikings invade Europe and Britain (800s–1000)
- the Vikings (called Normans) occupy northern France (911)
- Otto becomes ruler of the Holy Roman empire (936)
- the Capetians start the first French royal dynasty (987 onwards)

CULTURAL DEVELOPMENTS

- missionary monks bring Christianity to pagans in northern and eastern Europe (400s–1100)
- St. Benedict establishes the monastic Benedictine Order (500s)
- the epic of *Beowulf* is written by an unknown author in Old English (700s)
- Charlemagne reintroduces education and literacy in western Europe (800s)
- the illuminated *Book of Kells* is created in Ireland (900)
- Romanesque cathedrals are built in France and England (starting about 1000)

TECHNOLOGICAL/ECONOMIC DEVELOPMENTS

- wooden medieval castles are built
- agricultural innovations such as the heavy plough, the horseshoe, and an improved harness contribute to higher crop yields
- farmers develop the three-field system for soil conservation
- the stirrup is invented, making horseback riding easier for warriors (900s)
- horses begin to replace oxen in ploughing (900s)

LATE MIDDLE AGES
1050-c. 1450

- William of Normandy defeats the Anglo-Saxon king Harold in the Battle of Hastings and establishes the Plantegenet monarchy in England (1066)

- the four Crusades are launched against the Muslims in the Holy Lands (1096–1200s)

- John of England signs the Magna Carta (1215)

- Edward I establishes the first formal English parliament, called the Model Parliament (1295)

- Philip IV establishes the Estates General in France (1302)

- the Hundred Years' War ends English control over French territory and marks the decline of feudalism (1337–1453)

- the English War of the Roses ends with a new monarchical dynasty, the Tudors, ascending the throne (1485)

- the Bayeux Tapestry commemorates the Norman Conquest of England (late 1000s)

- works of Roman law and the philosophy of Aristotle are reintroduced to Europe from the Byzantine empire and the Muslim world (late 1000s onward)

- medieval Europe undergoes a cultural renaissance and the first universities are established (1100s)

- the Roman Catholic church establishes the Inquisition to investigate suspected heretics (1100s)

- a common law is established in England, applying to all citizens equally (1100s)

- the code of chivalry becomes a popular theme in literature (1100s–1200s)

- Gothic cathedrals replace Romanesque ones (late 1100s–early 1500s); Chartres Cathedral is completed in 1220

- Thomas Aquinas argues that there is no conflict between reason and belief in Christianity (1200s)

- Dante and Chaucer influence the development of literature written in vernacular languages (1200s and 1300s)

- larger stone castles replace simple wooden castles (1100s onward)

- heavy armour as well as swords, lances, and other weapons are developed for use by knights in warfare

- towns develop and large-scale trade is revived (1100s onward)

- merchant and craft guilds are established to protect and regulate their industries (1100s)

- Roger Bacon employs the scientific method of observation and experimentation (1200s)

- mechanical clocks are invented (1300s)

- trade revives, and annual trade fairs displaying international goods become common

- the windmill and the waterwheel are adopted in Europe to provide power for grain mills (1100s)

On Christmas day in 800, the pope crowned Charlemagne "Emperor of the Romans," the first to rule in western Europe since classical times. This title was intended to demonstrate the rebirth of the old western Roman empire. The church also wanted to show that it was the spiritual leader of the realm, the "crowner of kings," just as Charlemagne was the political leader.

Charlemagne kept a tight rein on his empire from his court at Aachen (in present-day Germany). He attempted to establish uniform laws throughout the kingdom, appointing local judges to see that they were upheld. Local nobles were required to regulate justice within and guarantee defence of their own territories. To keep these same lords under control and suppress any threat of rebellion, Charlemagne sent out royal inspectors every year to check on different parts of the kingdom.

Perhaps Charlemagne's most significant activity was to revive learning and literacy. He invited scholars to his court, and became a student himself at the palace school. With his encouragement, monasteries set up schools and libraries throughout the empire. Art and culture also thrived during his reign.

After Charlemagne's death, civil war broke out as his heirs fought for control of the kingdom. In 843 his three grandsons signed the Treaty of Verdun, dividing the empire among them. The western part included most of France, the eastern part included most of Germany, and the middle part stretched from the North Sea to Italy. However, further conflicts and invasions from outsiders continued to break up Charlemagne's empire.

REFLECT AND ANALYZE

1. Why are the Early Middle Ages sometimes called the "Dark Ages"?

2. What was a "mayor of the palace"? Why was this official more powerful than the Frankish king?

3. The pope crowned Charlemagne "Emperor of the Romans." In your opinion, was Charlemagne a "new" Roman emperor? Give reasons to support your opinion.

4. Why do you think Charlemagne asked the church to set up and run new schools? Give as many reasons as possible.

OTHER EUROPEAN INVASIONS

In the late ninth century, western Europe was once again threatened by peoples from outside its boundaries. The nomadic Magyrs (Hungarians) from Asia drove the Slavs from their lands in northeastern Europe, and soon both Slavs and Magyrs were attacking western Europe. In the southeast, Muslims threatened Italy. But the most serious invasions came from the Germanic Vikings in the north.

The Vikings were pagan warriors and expert sailors from Norway, Sweden, and Denmark. Probably due to overpopulation and inhospitable conditions in their own lands, they sailed out in small, well-designed ships to search for new resources. Along the coasts of Europe and Britain, they burned and looted towns, castles, churches, and monasteries. Their violent attacks made them greatly feared among the peoples they invaded. Vikings from Sweden attacked eastern Europe and Russia, while others settled in Iceland and Greenland. The Danes occupied a section of England. Around 1000, a group of Vikings led by Leif Ericson sailed

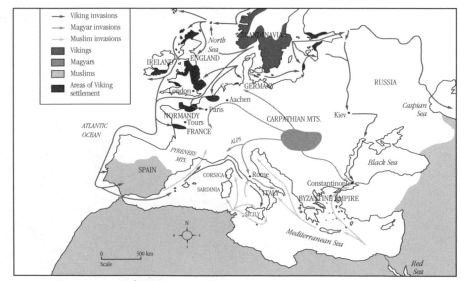

Figure 10-7 *Invasions of Europe, 700–1000 CE*

right across the Atlantic Ocean to North America, where traces of their settlement still remain in Newfoundland.

In 911 the king of the Franks was forced to surrender part of northern France to the Vikings. The region surrendered came to be called Normandy, based on the French word *Norman,* which means "Northmen."

BRITAIN

Despite three centuries of occupying England, the Jutes, Angles, and Saxons still tended to fight one another. But the Viking threat brought them into a union of sorts under the Anglo-Saxon king, Alfred the Great (871–899). Alfred established a code of law, improved local governments, and founded schools. He also built a strong army and navy to protect Britain against further invasions. After he died, however, weak rulers were unable to keep back the Danes. The Danish king Canute defeated the Saxons in 1016, becoming king of England.

One of the most significant events in English history occurred 50 years later. In 1066, William, Duke of Normandy (1066–1087), crossed the English Channel with his army of about 7000 and invaded England. At Hastings, his forces met, and conquered, those of the Saxon king, Harold. Harold himself was killed on the battlefield. The Battle of Hastings is the most famous battle in English history and it set the stage for England's future development.

William, hailed as the Conqueror, became the first Norman king of England. All British monarchs since 1066 can trace their ancestry back to William. He established himself and fellow Normans firmly in control. The large land holdings of the Anglo-Saxons were divided up and given to Norman nobles. William also selected important nobles and church leaders from among the Normans. In return, Norman lords had to swear an oath of loyalty to their king. In this way, William built up a strong, central monarchy, although some rebellions broke out after his death.

FRANCE AND THE HOLY ROMAN EMPIRE

As you recall, Charlemagne's grandsons had divided the Frankish empire into three parts. The western part, which became France, was battered by the Viking invasions and did not have a strong, overall ruler until 987, when the feudal lords elected Hugh Capet, Count of Paris, as king. Hugh Capet (987–996) controlled only the lands around Paris, but over the next three centuries, his descendants gradually brought all of France under their control, including Normandy and other mainland territories controlled by the English. The Capetian kings also made the crown a hereditary title to ward off any rivals.

In the eastern part of the old Frankish empire, Charlemagne's heirs lost power to local nobles called dukes. These dukes chose the Duke of Saxony to be King Otto I (936–973). Seeking to gain control of the central region (Italy), Otto allied himself with important church officials. When the pope appealed to Otto for assistance against powerful Italian nobles, Otto sent forces to defend Rome. In 962, a grateful pope crowned Otto "Holy Roman Emperor," like Charlemagne before him.

Otto brought Germany and most of Italy together into one kingdom, which became known as the Holy Roman Empire. But few German rulers after Otto I were able to successfully control both Germany and Italy. After Otto's death, the Holy Roman emperor lost Italy, regained it again during the reign of Frederick I (1152–1190), only to lose it again in 1268. German rulers spent so much time trying to conquer Italy that other dukes were able to split both territories into hundreds of small states. Not until the nineteenth century did these states finally unite into the countries of Germany and Italy that we know today.

REFLECT AND ANALYZE

1. What caused the Vikings to invade Europe? What advantages did their ships provide for their raids and explorations?

2. a) What measures did William the Conqueror introduce to establish a strong Norman monarchy in England?
   b) Do you think William was wise to implement these measures? Give reasons for your opinion.

3. What are the advantages of making the crown a hereditary title? Are there any disadvantages? What might these disadvantages be, and what actions might arise from them?

4. In a group, draw up a list of the characteristics of a nation. Consider all of the aspects that define a nation, including politics, culture, language, etc. Decide if France, England, and the Holy Roman Empire, as they existed in the year 1000, were nations.

THROUGH THEIR EYES

The Bayeux Tapestry

The Bayeux Tapestry is the most famous wall hanging in western art. After you read this account and look at pictures of the tapestry, can you explain its importance today? What modern art forms would you compare it to? Try drawing your own "tapestry," illustrating another event in history or an event in your life

C *Norman soldiers set fire to a house*

Figure 10-8 A *After the battle victorious Normans pursue the English*

B *Duke William's invasion fleet*

D *Harold is told of the appearance of a comet*

After William's successful defeat of England, his half-brother, Bishop Odo of Bayeux, commissioned the making of a large wall hanging to commemorate the event. Known as the Bayeux Tapestry, the work is actually an embroidery of coloured woollen threads on a white linen background. Bayeux is a small French town near the coast, but evidence shows that the tapestry was designed and embroidered in England. (Anglo-Saxons were known for their skill in illustration and needlework.)

Over 70 m long and half a metre high, the tapestry vividly depicts the story of King Harold of England and Duke William of Normandy, including the invasion and the Battle of Hastings itself. There are about 75 different scenes, with 623 human figures (only six of them women), 190 horses, 55 dogs, 505 other animals, 41 ships, and 49 trees. The story is told through lively gestures and movements, accompanied by short phrases in Latin. The battle scenes show the violence of war, with soldiers hacking each other to pieces and bodies strewn about the battlefield.

Completed just a few decades after the Conquest, the Bayeux Tapestry provides a revealing, contemporary glimpse of one of the historic battles of English history.

THE CRUSADES

As western Europe entered the first millenium, the various kingdoms were still struggling to form distinct political identities. But they were united in at least one respect: allegiance to the Christian faith. The church was the single most influential force affecting the development of medieval Europe. No event demonstrates the power and reach of Christianity better than the wars in which all of Europe was engaged: the **Crusades**.

The Crusades were a series of holy wars waged against the *Saracens*—non-Christian Arabs, Turks, and Moors, most of whom were Muslims. The Saracens called all Europeans "Franks." The term *"crusade"* is derived from the French and Spanish words for "cross." The uniforms of the Christian soldiers were emblazoned with large crosses across the chest.

Since the second century, Christians from Europe had been making the difficult pilgrimage to the "Holy Land," Jerusalem and other sites where Jesus had preached. Muslims and Arabs conquered this area, called Palestine, in the seventh century, but they generally tolerated Christian pilgrims. However, in 1071 a group of hard-line Muslims called the Seljuk Turks took Palestine, closing it off from Christians. They also threatened to invade the Byzantine empire. The Byzantine emperor appealed to the pope in Europe for help.

Although the Roman Catholic and Byzantine churches had split earlier in 1054, Pope Urban II called upon the kingdoms of western Europe to prepare for a crusade, or holy war. Urban II believed that all of Europe had a duty to win back the Holy Land for Christianity. He also hoped to reunite the two churches and to distract European leaders from their constant warring. Christian soldiers, called crusaders, were promised forgiveness of their sins, a share of the spoils of war, and release from debts and punishments.

The First Crusade was launched in 1096 and may have involved as many as 34 000 soldiers. Some were trained knights, but many more were poor peasants unused to warfare. Despite being poorly armed and trained, the Europeans were surprisingly successful, taking Muslim territory along the eastern Mediterranean shore, which they renamed the Christian States. The crusaders captured the Holy Land itself (Palestine and Syria) and the holy city (Jerusalem) in 1099.

The First Crusade was the Christians' only victory. A second crusade was launched in 1147, when part of the Christian States was retaken by the Muslims, but this attempt to regain these states failed. The Third Crusade saw three kings of Europe unite against the great Saracen

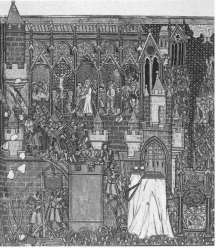

Figure 10-9
Crusaders storming the walls of Jerusalem

leader Saladin after he captured Jerusalem in 1187. This crusade is best known because it involved Richard the Lionheart, the English king who appears in the Robin Hood legend. Richard's forces fought valiantly, but neither he nor Saladin could defeat each other. In 1192 the two sides called a truce, which allowed Christian

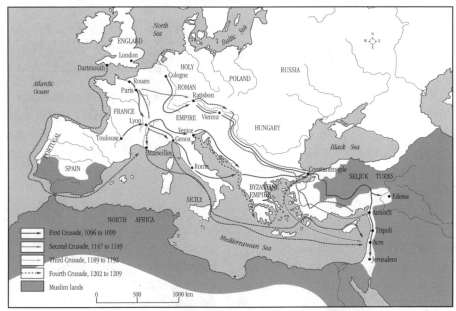

Figure 10-10 *The routes of the four crusades*

pilgrims to visit Jerusalem without persecution. The Fourth Crusade, begun in 1202, did not even reach the Holy Land. Instead, the crusaders, led by the city of Venice, used the occasion to conquer Constantinople, the Byzantine capital and Venice's fierce rival in trade. This attack on Constantinople left the Byzantine empire seriously weakened.

The crusaders, who had sought to subdue the Muslims, were themselves changed by the holy wars. The pope and the Roman Catholic church gained prestige from the successes of the First and Third Crusades.

(However, the church was criticized for corruption in the misguided Fourth Crusade.) Kings became more powerful, since so many lords and knights who might have challenged them were killed in the holy wars. The Crusades had a significant economic impact as well. It opened the eyes of the Europeans to the cultures and the riches of the east, including cotton, spices, sugar, and perfumes. Trade, which was revived between the Byzantine empire and Europe during this period, was greatly stimulated by this contact with the east.

disrupt England's wine trade with Gascony, as well as its thriving wool trade with Flanders.

Fed up with France's interference, the English king Edward III laid claim to the French throne, based on the fact that his mother, Isabella, was the sister of three former French monarchs. In 1337, the English attacked France.

What came to be called the Hundred Years' War was actually a series of conflicts that lasted from 1337 to 1453. In the early years, the English easily defeated the French, due to better strategy and an effective new weapon: the longbow. The English army consisted mostly of archers on foot, while the French relied on heavily armoured knights on horseback. With their longbows, English archers could shoot showers of arrows farther and more quickly than French crossbow archers. Knights, knocked off their horses by arrows, were not effective fighters on foot. Later in the war, cannons, loaded with gunpowder, were used. Gunpowder, a Chinese invention, was probably introduced to Europe during the

REFLECT AND ANALYZE

1. Do you think the European Christians were justified in launching a holy war against the Muslims?

2. "The Fourth Crusade was about economics, not religion." Do you agree or disagree with this statement? Use arguments to defend your position.

3. During the Crusades, Muslims occupied most of the Holy Land. What advantages would this have given them in fighting the wars?

4. For the Europeans, the Crusades were a failure. Did the wars have a positive or negative effect on Europe? Explain your answer.

THE DECLINE OF MEDIEVAL EUROPE

Beginning in the fourteenth century, Europe experienced a wave of natural disasters and prolonged warfare that led to severe social and economic decline. The population had grown rapidly due to improvements in agricultural production. But a series of poor harvests, caused by cooler, wetter weather, resulted in widespread famine between 1314 and 1317 and periodically throughout the century. France and England clashed over territory on the continent in the Hundred

Years' War, which actually dragged on for over 100 years. Overshadowing all of these events, however, was a terrifying epidemic that spread a blanket of death over Europe (see box on opposite page).

The Hundred Years' War

Since the Norman Conquest, England and France had never been the best of friends. England still controlled lands on the continent, which the French wished to reclaim. The two nations also engaged in bitter trade disputes. France, for instance, attempted to

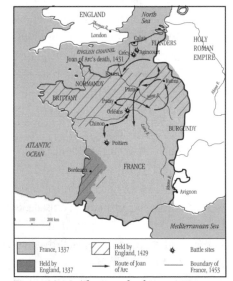

Figure 10-11 *The Hundred Years' War*

Crusades. Early cannons were rather primitive, but they signalled the beginning of a new kind of warfare and the end of the feudal knight.

Despite being outnumbered, the English army were victorious at Crécy, and later captured Calais, a key port in Flanders. At Poitiers, the French seemed at first to have the upper hand against the Black Prince, son of Edward III, but once again the English longbows prevailed. The king of France was captured at Poitiers and, in 1360, signed a treaty turning over one-third of all French territory to the English.

Over the next half-century, the French won back much of their lands through small-scale fighting. The English resumed major campaigns in the early fifteenth century, and appeared close to a final vic-

Figure 10-12 *The Battle of Crécy*

tory. In 1428 they were laying siege to Orléans, when a significant turn of events took place. A 17-year-old peasant girl emerged to save the day for France.

In 1429 Joan of Arc (1412–1431) went to see Charles, the heir to the French

PERSPECTIVES ON THE PAST
The Black Death

Why was the plague called the Black Death? How did it change medieval society? Are there any parallels to the plague in modern society? Do you think an epidemic similar to the Black Death could ever happen again?

The bubonic plague, popularly called the Black Death, first broke out in Asia. Rats harbouring fleas infected with the plague were carried on cargo ships sailing from east to west. The plague first struck Black Sea ports in 1347. From there it spread rapidly along the major trade routes to Italy, France, and England in 1348, and other parts of Europe by 1350.

Figure 10-13
The Triumph of Death *depicting the Black Death*

The poor living in crowded and unsanitary settlements were most affected, although no class of society escaped the plague.

Victims bitten by infected fleas would develop swollen glands and lumps, called buboes, in the armpits or groin. Some buboes were as large as an apple. These were followed by black or red spots that developed into open sores. As the disease spread through the bloodstream, victims would often cough up blood. Once stricken, very few people survived. Death occurred within days, or even hours.

In some communities, one-third to one-half of the population died. There was no defence against the disease, since no one knew what caused it or how to treat it. Panic rose to such a degree that people showing signs of illness were sometimes walled up in their homes to keep the plague from spreading. Other people fled in terror, abandoning shops and farms. The flourishing commerce of the twelfth and thirteenth centuries, which had contributed to the growth of towns, collapsed. Because there were fewer peasants to work the farms, there were frequent food shortages and famines.

With no explanation for such an overwhelming affliction, people believed God was punishing them for their sins. They performed rites of penitence in the hope of stopping the terrible scourge. Yet outbreaks of plague recurred throughout the next century. More than one-third of Europe's population died from the disease, and thousands more were killed in related famines and wars. The psychological trauma of so much disease and death was enormous. Many people thought it signalled the end of the world.

Western Europe did not recover from the demographic, social, and economic ravages of the plague until the early 1500s.

Figure 10-14 *The spread of the plague*

throne. Joan claimed to have received a message from God in the form of a dream, telling her to save France. She asked Charles for command of the army at Orléans, and Charles reluctantly agreed. Dressed in full armour and mounted on a horse, Joan led the French forces to victory over the English at Orléans. The French, weary of the war, took fresh courage from "the Maid of Orléans," who appeared to have God on her side. When Charles was crowned king of France, Joan stood with him.

Joan led other battles, but Orléans was her only victory. In 1430 she was captured by the people of Burgundy, allies of the English. Fearful of Joan's influence, the English tried her for witchcraft and burned her at the stake at Rouen in 1431. Unfortunately for the English, Joan's death made her a martyr in the eyes of the French people. By 1453 the French had recaptured all of their territory, except Calais.

Figure 10-15 *Joan of Arc*

THE END OF FEUDALISM

The Hundred Years' War had important consequences for both France and England. Their victory united the French with a sense of collective pride, which benefited the monarchy. During the rebuilding of France, the king assumed greater powers, eventually leading to complete control over government.

England, weakened internally by the long years of war, now faced a civil war on its own soil. Two noble families, the House of York and the House of Lancaster, fought each other in a 30-year conflict called the War of the Roses. The war was so-named because the Yorks' emblem was a white rose, while that of the Lancasters was a red rose. In 1485, Henry VII of Lancaster defeated the king of York, but took a York noblewoman as his queen. Thus united, the two families formed a strong new dynasty,

1 ▲ Bison from the cave at Lascaux,
Montignac, France (c. 15 000 BCE).

The Granger Collection, New York.

2 Head of a bull from the cave at Lascaux,
Montignac, France (c. 15 000 BCE).

The Granger Collection, New York.

3 The Code of Hammurabi, engraved black basalt stele,
   originally from Babylon (c. 1792-1750 BCE) found at
   Susa, Iran. Detail: Hammurabi standing, God
   Shamash sitting.

Erich Lessing/ART RESOURCE, New York.

4 ▲ The Standard of Ur, enamelled panel (c. 2500 BCE), found at the Royal Cemetery at Urin Mesopotamia. Depicts the war and triumph of a king of the First Dynasty of Ur.

Erich Lessing/ART RESOURCE, New York.

5 The procession road to the Ishtar Gate, Babylon, Mesopotamia, enamelled tile frieze (c. 7th century BCE). Detail: A lion.

Erich Lessing/ART RESOURCE, New York.

6 The Pharaoh as Osiris, with insignia and typical
pose with arms crossed. Relief from one of the
chapels off the inner Hypostyle Hall at the Temple
of Abydos (c. 14th century BCE).

Erich Lessing/ART RESOURCE, New York.

7 Painted and gilded mummy case of the musician-
priestess of Amun, Djed-maat-es-ankh,
(9th century BCE).

Royal Ontario Museum, Toronto, Canada.

Egypt

8   The Banqueting Scene. Copy of a
    wall painting from the Tomb of Two
    Sculptors, Nebamun and Ipuky, from
    the 18th Dynasty (c. 1380 BCE).

*Egyptian Expedition of The Metropolitan
Museum of Art, Rogers Fund, 1930
(30.4.105).*

9 ▲ The Queen's chambers, Palace of Knossos, Crete
Greece (c. 1625 BCE).

Vanni/ART RESOURCE, New York.

10 Bronze sculpture of Apollo, with copper incrustations,
Greece (c. 5th century BCE).

Erich Lessing/ART RESOURCE, New York.

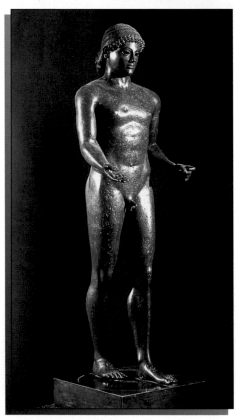

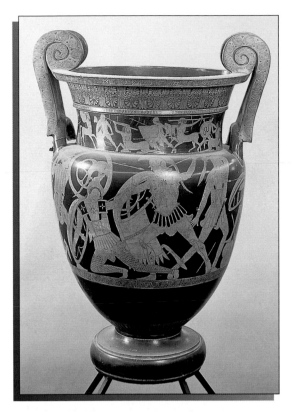

11 Painter of the Niobids, vase showing a battle scene from Gela, Greece (c. 475-450 BCE).

Scala/ART RESOURCE, New York.

12 ▼ Fresco painting of Minoan court ladies, Palace of Knossos, Crete, Greece (c. 1625 BCE).

Michostzovaras/ART RESOURCE, New York.

13 ▲ Fresco from the Villa of Mysteries: A wall
in the "Sala del Grande Dipinto," Pompeii,
Italy (c. 1st century BCE).

The Granger Collection, New York.

14 Fresco from the Villa of Mysteries: Bacchantes
in the "Great Painting," Pompeii, Italy (c. 1st
century BCE).

The Granger Collection, New York.

15 Dioscuros of Samos, Roman mosaic from
Cicero's villa, Pompeii, Italy (c. 1st century
BCE). Detail: Musicians in a street scene.

Erich Lessing/ART RESOURCE, New York.

16 ▼ Mosaic thought to represent Christ, from
a Roman villa at Hinton St. Mary, England
(c. 4th century CE).

The Granger Collection, New York.

17 ▲ An illuminated manuscript from Austria (1448 CE). Detail: The building of cathedrals.

The Granger Collection, New York.

18 The Winchester Bible (c. 10th century CE). Detail: Elijah and the Messengers, from Ahaziah and Elijah in the Fiery Chariot.

Sonia Halliday Photographs.

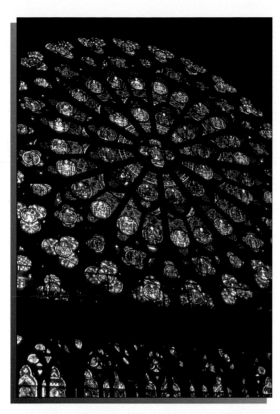

19 Stained glass window from the Cathedral of Nôtre Dame, Paris, France (1163 CE).

Adam Woolfitt/Woodfin Camp & Associates.

20 ▼ Cathedral of Chartres

Philippe Giraud/Sygma/Publiphoto.

21 ◄ El Greco, *The Burial of Count Orgaz*, S. Tome, Toledo, Spain (1586 CE).

Giraudon/ART RESOURCE, New York.

22 ▲ Raphael, *The School of Athens*, fresco from Stanza della Segnatura, the Vatican (1509-1510 CE).

The Granger Collection, New York.

23 Titian, *Bacchus and Ariadne* (1523 CE).

The Granger Collection, New York.

24 ▲ Theodora and her Court, Byzantine mosaic from San Vitale, Ravenna, Italy (c. mid-6th century CE).

The Granger Collection, New York.

25 ▶ The Virgin of Vladimir: Russian icon painted at Constantinople (c. 1131 CE).

The Granger Collection, New York.

26 The Praying Virgin in the Apsis, a fresco from the Monastery Church, Ohrid, Yugoslovia (1295 CE).

Erich Lessing/ART RESOURCE, New York.

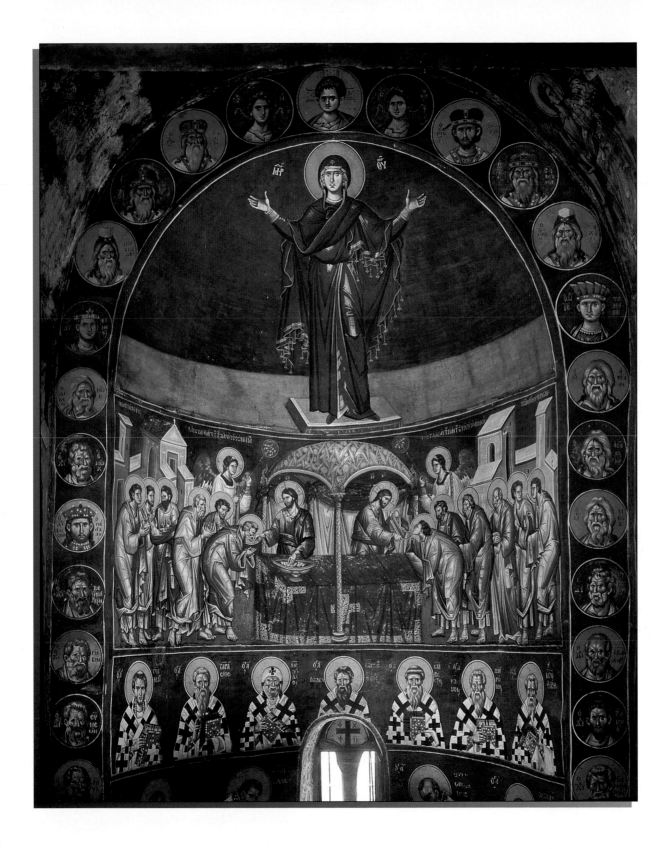

Byzantine

27 The Travellers Abu Zayd and Alharith
Arrive in a Village, an illuminated manuscript (date unknown).

Sonia Halliday Photographs.

28 Meeting of the Sultan Suleyman the
Magnificent's Ministers, an illuminated
manuscript from Suleymanname
(c. 1520-1566 CE).

The Granger Collection, New York.

the Tudors. As in France, the monarchy in England grew stronger, but it shared responsibility for governing the country with an important new body called ***parliament***. You will read about the English parliament later in this chapter.

The stirrings of national pride in both France and England signified a break from the long-established feudal system. With strong, central governments in control, people switched their allegiance from local lords to the monarchy itself. This was the beginning of the development of nations, in which people are bound together by a common government, language, culture, and perhaps most important of all, set of ideas. At the same time, two other potent symbols of the Middle Ages, the fortified castle and the armoured knight on horseback, were being eroded by such military innovations as gunpowder and the longbow. Europe was changing.

REFLECT AND ANALYZE

1. Why was the longbow such an effective weapon against knights on horseback?

2. Joan of Arc was a peasant woman, untrained in the art of warfare. Yet she believed she could save France. In your opinion, did she save France? Give reasons to support your answer.

3. "Nationalism won the Hundred Years' War for France." Do you agree or disagree with this statement? Give reasons for your opinion.

4. What are the characteristics of a nation? How does a nation develop? Do you think the use of force is necessary in developing a nation?

GOVERNMENT

In the Early Middle Ages, hundreds of Germanic territories were ruled by an overlord or king. Warrior nobles swore loyalty to their leader, and received weapons and a share of the spoils of war in return for their military service. Even when some kings began to expand their territory, the real power still lay in the hands of local lords. They jealously guarded their privileges and landholdings, knowing that the king needed them for military support. It took exceptional leadership and administrative abilities, as well as a certain amount of cunning, for kings to gradually centralize their power and form strong royal governments called ***monarchies***.

ENGLAND
The first great monarchical dynasty of England was formed by the Plantagenets, descended from William the Conqueror. The family line included members from both English and French nobility, which enabled Edward III to argue his claim to the French throne in the Hundred Years' War. Figure 10-16 shows a partial genealogical chart for the Plantagenets.

After the Norman Conquest, William I sent out envoys to gather information about the property in his new kingdom. In each village, a group of men were required to swear a solemn oath about the value of local property. Such groups were called juries, from the French word *juré,* meaning, "sworn under oath." During the reign of William's great-grandson, Henry II, juries would become important in the dispensing of local justice.

In 1086, every person, farm animal, and piece of property, no matter how small, was compiled into a huge record called the Domesday Book. The Domesday Book was used to determine the amount of taxes people owed.

Henry I (1100–1135), son of William the Conqueror, replaced hereditary office holders with paid royal officials, believing that they would be more loyal to him if they owed their jobs to the king. Henry I kept accurate tax records and increased royal income by allowing landowners to make money payments instead of providing military service. All revenues were gathered into a central treasury called the exchequer. With control of the exchequer, the king had large sums of money at his disposal, allowing him to finance major projects such as war campaigns.

But the expansion of royal power and wealth under the Plantagenets did not go unopposed by other nobles, called barons. King John (1199–1216), son of Henry II, faced a rebellion of his nobles in 1215. He exacted heavy taxes in order to finance a war with France—an unsuccessful war, in which England lost lands held since the Conquest. He guarded his royal privilege jealously, and quarrelled with the pope over who was to be the next Archbishop of Canterbury. Angered by John's heavy-

How many Plantagenet monarchs are identified in the family tree? What seems to determine the order or line of succession? Where does there appear to have been a break in the natural order of succession? Can you suggest why this might have happened?

THE PLANTAGENETS

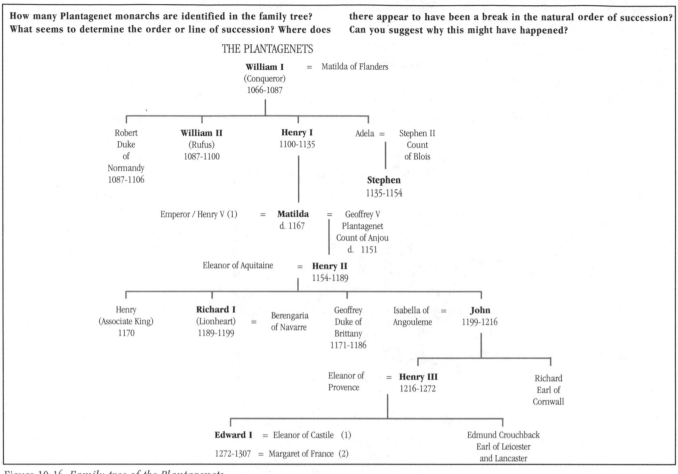

Figure 10-16 *Family tree of the Plantagenets*

THROUGH THEIR EYES

The Domesday Book

Figure 10-17
A page from the Domesday Book

Examine the translation from this entry in the Domesday Book for the village of Fobbing, in the county of Essex. Why did King William want to record such information? How is such a record useful to a government? What similar records of population and property are compiled in Canada today? What are they used for?

Brictmer, a thane of King Edward's, held FOBBING for 5 hides, as one manor. Now Count Eustace holds it in lordship. Always 4 ploughs in lordship; 5 men's ploughs.

Then 8 villagers, now 3, then 8 smallholders, now 22; then 12 slaves, now 6.

Woodland, 700 pigs; pasture, 700 sheep; 1/2 fishery. 31 pigs, 717 sheep.

handed ways, a group of barons drew up a document, called the **Magna Carta** or "Great Charter," which they forced the king to sign in 1215. The Magna Carta listed the rights of nobles and the king's responsibilities and privileges in governing. The king could not set new taxes without first consulting his Great Council, made up of lords and clergy, and he had to obey the law like all his subjects. The charter also recognized some of the rights of common people and of the church. Over time, the rights granted to nobles by the Magna Carta were extended to all citizens.

Parliament

William the Conqueror started the Great Council to advise him in governing. It consisted of high church officials and nobles whom the king trusted. The Magna Carta changed the function of the Great Council from merely advising the king to actively participating in government. No longer could the king act solely on his own authority.

By the thirteenth century, meetings of the Great Council had begun to include lesser knights and representatives from the towns.

THEN AND NOW

The Magna Carta

Read the provisions below from the Magna Carta. What important concepts are included to protect the rights of common people in the thirteenth century? To what extent are these provisions in place today? Does the Magna Carta have any modern parallels? How might it have affected the development of governments in other countries, such as Canada?

Figure 10-18
King John signing the Magna Carta

John, by the Grace of God, king of England, lord of Ireland, duke of Normandy and Aquitaine, count of Anjou; to the archbishops, bishops, abbots, earls, barons, justiciars, foresters, sheriffs, reeves, servants, and all bailiffs and his faithful people greeting.

1. *In the first place we have granted to God and by this our present charter confirmed ... that the English church shall be free, and shall hold its rights entire....*
   We have granted moreover to all free men of our kingdom for us and our heirs forever all the liberties written below, to be held by them and their heirs from us and our heirs....
12. *No scutage [a tax paid instead of military service] or aid [tax] shall be imposed in our kingdom except by the common council of our kingdom....*
14. *And for holding a common council of the kingdom concerning the assessment of an aid ... we shall cause to be summoned the archbishops, bishops, abbots, earls, and greater barons..... [In addition], we shall cause to be summoned by our sheriffs and bailiffs all [our other vassals] ... for a certain day ... and for a certain place.*
    ...
39. *No free man shall be taken, or imprisoned, or dispossessed, or outlawed, or banished, or in any way destroyed, except by the legal judgment of his peers or by the law of the land.*
40. *To no one will we sell, to no one will we deny, or delay, right or justice.*

Meetings of these representative groups came to be known as *Parliament,* from the French word *parler,* meaning "to talk."

In 1295, when Edward I (1272–1307) needed money to pay for wars with France, he summoned a meeting of Parliament to gain support for the new taxes. He invited not only great nobles and bishops, but also two knights from each county and two citizens from each town. As the king declared, "Let that which toucheth all be approved by all." He recognized that consulting a wider group of people could help limit the power of the nobility, as well as increase support for his proposals. The meeting of 1295 was called the Model Parliament, because it represented most citizens. It formed the basis for later parliaments.

When Parliament first met, the great nobles and bishops made the decisions, while the lesser knights and townspeople stood at one end of the room and listened. They expressed their opinions only when asked to do so. Later the two groups met separately. The division finally resulted in two houses of Parliament: the **House of Lords**, made up high nobles and bishops, and the **House of Commons**, made up of lesser knights, clergymen, and townspeople. The beginnings of a representative government brought ordinary citizens into government, helping to strengthen the nation's unity and sense of identity.

FRANCE

Powerful feudal territories in France made it difficult for a monarch to govern them and unite them into one nation. When Hugh Capet was made king in 987, he ruled over a small territory, and the other feudal lords thought he would be easy to control. Instead, he founded a dynasty that continued unbroken for 300 years. Figure 10-19 shows a partial genealogical chart for the Capetians.

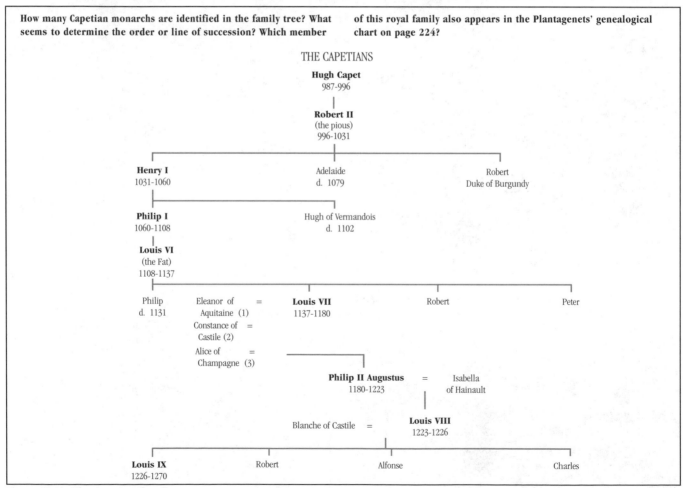

How many Capetian monarchs are identified in the family tree? What seems to determine the order or line of succession? Which member of this royal family also appears in the Plantagenets' genealogical chart on page 224?

Figure 10-19 *The Capetian family tree*

Many French nobles, as well as English ones, controlled larger territories in France than the king himself. Slowly, the Capetians added to their small land holdings through diplomacy, marriage, and war. Philip II (1180–1223), known as Philip Augustus, acquired the vast territories of Normandy, Anjou, and Poitou from the English when he successfully waged war against King John. Later, Philip Augustus gained control of Flanders and also seized lands in southern France. Other monarchs added to the royal holdings so that by 1328, the king ruled most of central and southern France.

Philip Augustus and his successors established an efficient royal bureaucracy, a group of officials who governed through departments. Educated clergy, lesser knights, and townspeople were appointed to administer the various districts. All royal officials were selected for their ability and paid a salary. The king was better able to command the loyalty of such salaried workers than that of nobles, who might feel inclined to challenge his authority.

Philip Augustus and other monarchs also supported the growth of towns, where the revival of industry and trade was forming a new class of prosperous, and therefore

PERSPECTIVES ON THE PAST

Eleanor of Aquitaine

After reading this account, decide whether or not Eleanor of Aquitaine's power was equal to a king's.

Even if she had not married two European monarchs, Eleanor would have been a powerful noblewoman in her own right. As the only living child of the Duke of Aquitaine, she inherited the responsibility of ruling and defending an estate covering one-third of present-day France— larger than the French king's own territory. To secure these lands and vassals, King Louis VII married the 15-year-old Eleanor in 1137.

Figure 10-20
Eleanor of Aquitaine

She courageously joined her husband on the Second Crusade against the Muslim Turks. But when their 15-year marriage failed to produce a son, she showed as strong a determination in fighting to get a divorce from Louis. Within a few months of the divorce, she married Henry II of England. She proved an able partner to Henry, helping to govern their joint lands in France and ruling England during his frequent absences.

When their sons had grown, Henry and Eleanor disagreed over how to divide up their lands among them. Eleanor and her sons attempted to overthrow Henry, but she was captured by her husband while her sons escaped to France. Rather than submit to Henry, Eleanor chose to live in captivity for 15 years. She was released by her favourite son, Richard the Lionheart, when he became king, and she in turn used all her powers to help him. She raised 100 000 silver marks as ransom when he was captured on crusade, and, at age 77, assembled an army to defend English territory in France against Philip Augustus.

Eleanor was a political force to be reckoned with, but she was also a lifelong patron of the arts. Whether in London or in her court at Poitiers, she surrounded herself with poets, musicians, ambitious young academics, and witty courtiers. Reading literature about courtly love and heroic deeds was a favourite pastime. When the great queen died at the advanced age of 82, she was buried in a coffin carved with an image of her lying at rest with a book in her hands.

influential, citizens. All of these developments added to the monarchy's power while weakening that of the feudal lords.

The Estates General

The French equivalent of the English parliament was the **Estates General**. Philip IV assembled this group in 1302 during his clashes with the pope over church taxation. The Estates General was made up of three estates or social classes: clergy, nobles, and townspeople. The Estates General was not as powerful as the English parliament, because it did not have control over taxation or other money matters. The king tended to consult the body whenever it suited his purposes, and it never provided a check on royal powers. Instead, the monarch and his efficient royal bureaucracy increasingly controlled all aspects of government.

THE HOLY ROMAN EMPIRE (GERMANY)

The five great duchies or provinces of medieval Germany were Saxony, Franconia, Lorraine, and in the south Swabia and Bavaria. The dukes of these and other territories exercised such great power that it was difficult for a monarch to unite the area into one lasting kingdom. Otto I, known as Otto the Great, succeeded where others had failed, but the achievement was not a lasting one.

Otto was chosen as king by the other dukes in 936, but he emphasized his supremacy right from the beginning of his reign. During his coronation ceremony, for instance, he used nobles as household officers. He appointed relatives to ducal offices and formed alliances with the clergy. He relied on these relationships for their

loyalty and for their help in governing.

In the Holy Roman Empire, the church in Rome played a central role in politics. The emperor protected the pope, while the church, in turn, supported the emperor against the powerful dukes. But power struggles developed between emperor and pope, as each sought to increase his own authority. The emperors attempted to gain control of northern Italian lands and to appoint high church officials. The popes responded to these challenges by limiting outside interference and sometimes even by **excommunication**—banishing the emperor from the church. Feudal states thrived in Germany long after France and England became centralized monarchies. In Italy, the pope controlled the Papal States and surrounding areas, while city-states such as Venice de-

Figure 10-21 *The Coronation of Otto I*

veloped into great centres of commerce and culture.

REFLECT AND ANALYZE

1. Describe the similarities and differences between the English Parliament and the French Estates General. Which group better represented the interests of common people? Why?

2. The monarchy in France came to be called an "absolute monarchy." What do you think this term means? Do you think it is an apt description? Why or why not?

3. Compare the medieval English parliament with Canada's parliament today. Is parliament an effective form of democratic government? Give reasons for your opinion.

4. Explain why the pope and the Holy Roman emperor were sometimes allies and sometimes enemies.

5. The king of England wants to raise taxes to finance war with France. Organize a session of Parliament in the classroom. The king should be present, as well as nobles, church members, and townspeople. Determine if the king gets his wish.

LAW AND JUSTICE

In the Early Middle Ages, justice was based on unwritten custom. Feudal lords administered justice for lesser lords and peasants living on their lands. What written laws did exist were usually lists of fines to be levied as punishment for specific crimes. Whether based on custom or written, laws were mainly designed to prevent feuds between families.

Custom, for example, recognized the right of an individual to be tried by his peers or equals. And lords themselves were also bound by custom not to act in grossly injust ways, such as taking over a lesser lord's estate without recognizable cause.

Charlemagne was the first monarch to establish a royal court, and William the Conqueror did the same later in England. In both instances, royal justices were sent out to uphold law and order. These royal judges would hear local cases that had not been resolved to everyone's satisfaction. Even if a person had no complaints, he or she could attend the hearings just to listen.

A feudal lord presided over two kinds of courts. The lord's court dealt with matters concerning lesser nobles, called *vassals,* who owed allegiance to the lord, while the manor court handled disputes among peasants living on the manor.

Conflicts between a lord and his vassal, if not settled by war, were decided in court or in trial by combat. If the case was heard in court, the lord summoned his vassals to meet to decide the issue. All free men and women had the right to be tried by their peers, although the court's decision could be overruled by the lord. The accused had the option of admitting guilt and receiving a sentence that was usually a fine. In trial by combat, the accused knight had to fight another knight in personal combat. Women and clergymen could not participate, so a champion was selected to fight for them. Following the principle that "might equals right," the accused was considered innocent if he won, guilty if he lost.

The manor court was presided over by the lord or by his deputy, called a *bailiff.* The court was held in the great hall of the lord's house or manor. Disputes or crimes involving peasants were generally minor. They included such things as allowing a farm animal to wander into a cropfield or stealing a neighbour's firewood. Those found guilty were usually fined.

Ordinary people could also be tried by ordeal, in which the accused person had to undergo a harrowing physical test. In a trial by ordeal, it was believed that guilt or innocence would be decided by God. The accused might be forced to carry a red-hot poker over a certain distance or to plunge his or her hand into a pot of boiling water. The hand was then bandaged for three days, and if after that period the blisters festered, the person was guilty. A popular ordeal was to tie up the arms and legs of the accused and throw him or her into a pond or river. If the person floated, he or she was considered guilty.

Not surprisingly, many people were unhappy with the system of trial by ordeal, and it was banned in the early thirteenth century. To replace it, Henry II of England (1154–1189) introduced wide-ranging legal reforms. He sent royal justices into the countryside to investigate crimes and disputes. Before the justices, groups of local citizens were sworn to report anyone "accused or publicly known as a robber or murderer or thief." These groups were called grand juries.

A smaller jury of 12 men, known as a petit jury, then appeared before the royal justice to explain what it knew about the accused person and the crime. Based on this statement, the judge decided if the accused was guilty or innocent. Later, jury members themselves decided guilt and innocence, while the judge's role was to set a punishment. The jurors, selected from among local people, reached their verdicts based on the facts as they were generally known. Although these early juries heard cases, no witnesses appeared and no evidence was presented. However, with only a few improvements, the practice of trial by jury continues today in many countries.

Henry II also expanded the power of the royal courts, which replaced those of the individual lords and of the church. Any freeman could bring a case before a royal court. Serious crimes such as murder were now tried only in the royal courts by royal judges. The expanded royal courts increased the power of the king, particularly since the fines and fees that were imposed ended up in the royal treasury.

Another important reform to the legal system credited to Henry II was the development of **Common Law**. All of the decisions of the royal courts were written down or recorded, and these decisions became the basis for common law. Common Law refers to all of the accepted legal principles that were applied to everyone throughout England. It was the beginning of the idea of equal justice for all English citizens.

REFLECT AND ANALYZE

1. What different types of courts operated in medieval western Europe ?

2. Prior to the legal reforms of Henry II, why can it be said that the "interests of justice were not always served" in the legal system ?

3. How have the English legal reforms instituted by Henry II influenced our present judicial system ?

The period following the end of Roman civilization, during which western Europe takes shape, is called the Middle Ages. The adjective *medieval* comes from two Latin words, *medium aevum*, which mean "the middle age." Latin, the language of Rome, did not die when the empire ended. It was destined to become the language of the Christian church and of scholars in the Middle Ages.

The medieval period in Europe can be divided into two phases. The Early Middle Ages, from 400 to about 1050, was a period of perpetual strife among various Germanic peoples. During this unsettled period, once called the Dark Ages, there was little development in trade or social structure. In the Late Middle Ages, 1050 to 1350, a more stable society developed, and along with it, growth in agriculture and trade.

MEDIEVAL EUROPE:
Society and Culture

I Urban II, Pope of the Holy Church of Rome, do hereby pronounce the Peace of God
and the Truce of God....

, In accordance with the Peace of God, all warfare is thus banned against women,
children, elderly people not involved in combat, or clergymen. The pillaging of
churches, monasteries, and other holy places is forbidden. Church sacraments will be
withheld from any who violate this pronouncement.

In accordance with the Truce of God, all fighting is prohibited on weekends, that is,
between sunset on any Wednesday and sunrise of the following morning. All fighting is
also prohibited on the countless Holy Days, and during such seasons as Lent, the seven
weeks before Easter, and Advent, the four weeks before Christmas. Any knight found to
be in violation of the truce shall face the threat of excommunication from the Church.

Figure 11-1
*Pope Urban II and
clergy blessing the
church of Cluny*

Pope Urban II (1088–1099) issued this proclamation in the late eleventh century. Why do you
think he felt such a proclamation was necessary?
Would such an order from the pope have been
effective? What might have been the results?

RELIGION

The Middle Ages is sometimes called the "age of
faith." All people in medieval Europe were expected
to live according to the Christian doctrines set
down by the Roman Catholic church. More powerful than kings or nobles, the church reached into
every part of Europe. It could make kings by
supporting their right to rule and officiating at
their coronation. It could also unmake kings by
excommunicating them.

The church had its own government, laws,
courts, and system of taxation. It provided educa-

tion through its schools, monasteries, and convents. It looked after the poor and sick. It encouraged merchants to charge fair prices for their
goods, and forbade **usury**, the practice of charging interest on loaned money. It provided spiritual
comfort during constant wars, famine, sickness,
and other troubles. In many ways, then, the
church's influence on peoples' lives was far greater
than that of their rulers.

In the Early Middle Ages, the church focused
on converting non-Christians. Missionaries travelled
to remote areas, especially in the north where there
were still large numbers of heathens. As early as 432
CE, a monk named St. Patrick reached Ireland's
shores and set up several monasteries there. St.
Augustine landed in Kent, England, in 597, and
became the first Archbishop of Canterbury—the
highest church official in England—in 601. St.
Boniface carried Christian teachings to the peoples
east of the Rhine River in Germany. Other mission-

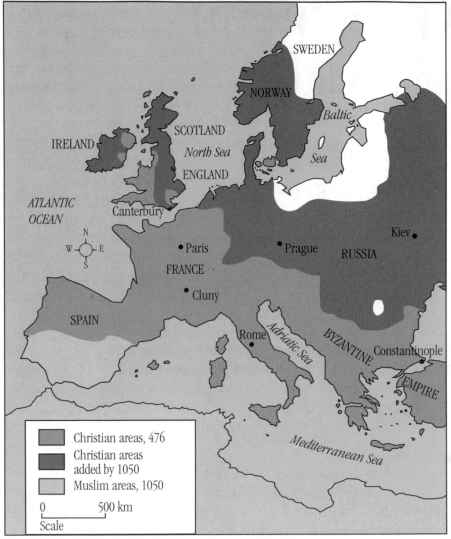

Figure 11-2 *The spread of Christianity in Europe, 476-1050*

the right to inherit the property of these church officials after they died.

CHURCH ORGANIZATION

Most people lived in scattered rural communities during the Early Middle Ages, and hence the church sent priests to serve in local areas called parishes. Usually located in a village, the parish consisted of a small church and a house for the priest, and served the faithful from the village and surrounding countryside.

For most people, the parish priest was their only contact with the church. His life was a busy one, performing daily services of worship and helping the poor and sick. He presided over the important rituals in people's lives, such as baptism, marriage, and the last rites, or blessings, given to a dying person. He was often the village's only teacher. Yet, in the early days, many priests were poorly educated themselves, barely understanding the Latin phrases they recited during Mass, the main religious service. Charlemagne, an early supporter of rural parishes, insisted that priests be able to read and write Latin. Throughout the Middle Ages, education was always a primary function of the church.

Every year the village priest collected a tax, called a ***tithe***, from all church members. The tithe was one-tenth of a person's income. It paid for the priest's services and was also used to fund charities, hospitals, and schools. Using the tithe, the church built up large reserves of money and bought land to build more churches and religious communities called monasteries and convents. Before long, the church owned more land than any noble or monarch.

Neighbouring parishes were grouped together into a larger unit called a *diocese*

aries went further north and east to preach among the Slavs, Magyars, and Vikings. By 1100, almost all of Europe was Christian.

Early political leaders such as Charlemagne recognized that the church could help further their own ambitions. As the seat of learning, the church produced educated clergy who often were the only members in society who could read and write. Kings and nobles used such educated clergy to administer their affairs. With

these positions in government came great influence in politics.

The church itself held vast areas of land and grew very wealthy from the taxes and fees it received for its services. Many nobles, with their own feudal lands, were appointed as high officials within the church. Such church leaders sometimes had to decide between loyalty to the church and loyalty to their feudal lord or king. Monarchs also battled with the church over

or see. A diocese was ruled over by a bishop, usually a well-educated noble. In turn, a group of dioceses was governed by an *archbishop*, a church official of high rank. Some archbishops governed relatively small territories, while others, such as the archbishop of Canterbury, were responsible for an entire kingdom. *Cardinals* were high bishops appointed by the pope to advise him in church doctrine and other important matters. Cardinals also selected a new pope after the current one died.

The *pope* himself was the head of the Roman Catholic church ("pope" comes from the Greek word for father). From Rome the pope wielded enormous power, setting down church teachings, or **doctrines**, to be followed in every part of Christian Europe. His power also extended to the secular, or non-religious, realm, since no king could safely rule without his approval. As ruler of the Papal States in Italy, the pope controlled a large territory that was not subject to any political leader. Thus, even though some leaders tried, the pope could never be "conquered" in the way that secular leaders could be. It is no wonder, then, that kings at various times envied, befriended, or feared the pope.

Any Christian who disobeyed or questioned church teachings faced various punishments, the most serious being **excommunication**. Excommunication was dismissal from the church and its sacraments—rites of penitence for sins and rites of salvation. People who were excommunicated could not marry or be buried on church grounds. They were treated as outcasts and often lost their property and rights. Furthermore, church doctrine taught that unsaved souls would burn forever in hell. No doubt the fear of excom-

munication caused many a Christian's faith to burn brighter.

Although excommunication was usually reserved for major religious offences, the pope sometimes used it as a political tool. Kings who clashed with the pope risked excommunication. For example, Pope Innocent III (1198–1216) excommunicated King John of England when the two disagreed over who was to be the next Archbishop of Canterbury. An excommunicated king was vulnerable to challenges by other lords, because the pope could release royal subjects from their feudal obligations to the king.

CHRISTIAN BELIEFS AND VALUES

Christianity taught that life on earth was less important than eternal life in heaven, free from pain or want. This must have been a very comforting doctrine to many people whose daily lives were harsh and difficult. When disaster struck in the form of war, famine, or plagues, people turned to their faith to get through the difficult times.

Another reassuring aspect of Christianity was the belief that all people were equal in the sight of God. Anyone who was a good Christian, man or woman, noble or commoner, could gain entry into heaven. Women could worship alongside men at church services. Women could also serve God as nuns, although they were not allowed to conduct services or hold positions of authority in the church.

The route to heaven lay in salvation—forgiveness of one's sins—and the **sacraments** of the church administered by a priest. The alternative to salvation was eternal suffering in the fires of hell. The only way to be saved was to be a Christian;

people of other religions were considered lost souls. Thus, in the early days of Christianity, the church's mission was to convert as many people as possible.

Because of this emphasis on salvation within the church, Christianity soon became intolerant of other religions, especially those of Jewish and Muslim peoples. In Roman times, Christians were persecuted for following their religion; in the Middle Ages, Christians fought holy wars against the Muslims. These conflicts were as much about power as religion, since the Muslims felt as strongly about their faith and periodically invaded the Christian world.

Within Christianity itself, the Byzantine and Roman Catholic churches disagreed over church teaching and practices. For instance, Byzantine services were held in Greek, while Roman Catholic services were held in Latin. Pope Gregory I (590–604) established the idea of **purgatory**, a place where the souls of the dead atone for their sins before being admitted into heaven. Purgatory did not exist in Byzantine belief. Over the centuries, the differences built up to such an extent that the two churches separated in 1054.

To ensure Christians adhered to church teachings, the Roman Catholic church set up a special court in the twelfth century to deal with a serious offence called **heresy**. **Heretics** were people who held different beliefs from those of the church or who questioned church doctrine. The special court was called the **Inquisition**. (Inquisition means "inquiry" or "investigation"—church officials investigated the faith of individuals who came before them.) If a heretic called before the Inquisition showed penitence and renounced

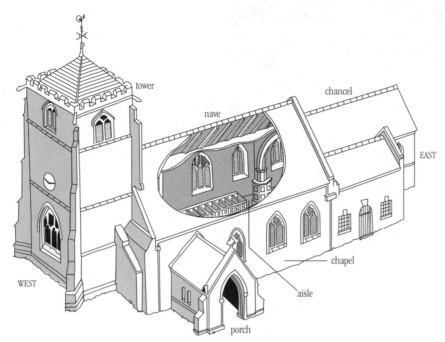

Figure 11-3 An early medieval church. The porch was the entrance and the area where most parish business was conducted. Worshippers stood in the long central area called the **nave**. *The* **chancel** *was the space around the altar for the priest and choir. One or more* **chapels**—*separate rooms along the church's wall*—*were built by wealthy parishioners for private worship. Finally there was the cross-topped tower where bells summoned people to worship.*

his or her earlier statements against the church, the court often set a suitable punishment and released the accused. If a person did not confess right away, he or she was often tortured. For those found guilty of heresy, the punishment was death by burning at the stake. Such harsh punishment was considered justified to prevent the evil ideas of heresy from spreading to other people.

RELIGIOUS ORDERS

The word monk comes from the Greek word *monos,* which means "single." Early Christian monks were religious men who lived alone, without worldly possessions, devoting their lives to God. Eventually monks grouped together in communities called monasteries. Similarly, groups of religious women, called nuns, lived together in convents.

In the sixth century a monk named St. Benedict established a monastery at Monte Cassino in Italy. He drew up a set of rules, called the *Rule* (or *Code) of St. Benedict,* for monks to follow. According to the Benedictine Rule, a monk could own no property, not even a writing tablet or a pen. He had to remain celibate and to swear absolute obedience to the abbot, the head of the monastery. All activities had to be carried out in silence, since idle talk could easily lead to sinful words and thoughts.

Daily life in the monastery revolved around prayer and hard work. At dawn, monks rose to attend the first service. A bell signalled other services throughout the day. Between services, monks were busy with assigned duties, such as labouring in the fields owned by the monastery, copying manuscripts, teaching, or performing household activities. Long periods were also spent reading the Bible and in silent meditation. In winter, one simple meal a day was served; in summer, when monks toiled in the fields, there were two daily meals. Bedtime came soon after sunset, when the light from candles was too faint to continue reading or working.

From the eighth to twelfth centuries, monasteries and convents based on the Benedictine Order were established all over Europe. They especially flourished in the north, possibly due to the energy and devotion of the missionary monks who founded them. Monks made ideal missionaries for the church since their celibacy and discipline enabled them to endure the rigours of travelling to the hinterlands.

Monasteries and convents performed important services in feudal society. They provided charity for the poor and homeless, and tended to the sick. They acted as hostels for Christian pilgrims travelling to holy shrines. They operated schools attended by the children of nobles. Some orders maintained well-run hospitals, while others developed improvements in farming methods.

The religious orders performed another function that was invaluable for posterity: they preserved and copied ancient Greek and Latin texts that doubtless would have been lost during the turbulent Early Middle Ages. Monks and nuns copied these manuscripts as a form of daily industry, often not greatly understanding what they were copying. In any case, the secular

PERSPECTIVES ON THE PAST

Hildegarde of Bingen (1098-1179)

Figure 11-4
Hildegarde of Bingen

What evidence shows that Hildegarde of Bingen believed men and women to be equal? Did male church leaders share her view? Explain your answers.

In our day Hildegarde would probably be called a motivational speaker. She was in great demand as a sage and advisor among royalty and nobility, scholars, church leaders, and even the pope. She was celebrated not only for her religious visions, which she wrote down in a widely read book called *Know the Way*, but also for her medical knowledge and her talent in composing music.

Born into a noble German family, Hildegarde was placed in a Benedictine convent as a child. She received her education there and became a nun at age 14 or 15. Later she rose to the position of abbess, or head, of the convent. In response to a vision, she founded a new convent near Bingen on the Rhine River and began speaking tours to raise money for the settlement.

Today Hildegarde is regarded as an early feminist, and her writings, which often imply an equality between men and women, are studied in universities. Recordings of her musical chants have also become popular.

The abbess used her reputation as a prophet to admonish great men to act justly and religiously; yet the power she and other learned religious women enjoyed would not last. In the centuries after Hildegarde's death, the church took away the rights of holy women to preach, administer sacraments, and hear confessions. Women also lost their access to higher education when exclusively male universities took over as centres of learning from the monastic orders in the twelfth century.

---

nature of classical literature made it unsuitable reading material for most Christians, and these works were mostly ignored for centuries. However, some great Christian scholars, such as St. Augustine of Hippo, studied the classics.

Some monasteries became distinguished centres of learning and art. They housed extensive libraries and produced beautifully scripted and illustrated copies of the Bible. These ***illuminated manuscripts***, as they were called, were one of the great art forms of the Middle Ages (see box on page 236). Monks and nuns had no musical instruments, so they composed simple, sacred chants for the unaccompanied human voice. Sung in Latin and Greek on the way to and during services, these haunting chants created a sense of harmony with God.

Reform within Monasteries

By the 10th century, some monasteries had grown rich and rather corrupt. The monks no longer worked the land themselves but engaged peasants, like any feudal landowner. Disregarding their vows of poverty, they allowed themselves luxuries.

In response to growing calls for reform, a new monastery was established at Cluny, France, in 910. The abbot of Cluny was determined to restore the Benedictine virtues of piety and hard work, and to take orders only from the pope, not from nobles. These reforms were quickly embraced by other monasteries, and hundreds of them joined the Cluniac order. To limit outside interference, all Cluniac houses reported to a single authority, the abbot of Cluny.

In the Late Middle Ages two other important religious orders arose, partly out of concern that the church had become worldly and materialistic. Both of these orders, the Franciscans and the Dominicans, dedicated themselves to poverty, teaching, and service to humanity.

Francis of Assisi, who founded the Franciscan Order in the early thirteenth century, was the indulged son of a well-to-do Italian merchant. In his 20s he experienced a vision, and gave up everything to become a friar. (A friar was a monk who travelled in the towns and countryside, preaching the gospel to the

THROUGH THEIR EYES
Medieval Illuminated Manuscripts

Why do you think medieval manuscripts were made by hand? How would monks and nuns have benefited from their labour in creating these manuscripts?

The word illuminated means "brightened with light." Medieval Christians believed that just as the word of God enlightened the soul, so should the written text of the Bible and other sacred works be lavishly decorated to symbolize that spiritual light. Thousands of these precious manuscripts were made by hand during the Middle Ages.

The Book of Kells, created by Irish monks on the island of Iona, is a famous early illuminated manuscript. Completed around 900, this book of the gospels shows interlacing patterns and fabulous intertwining beasts that reflect the early Celtic and Viking people's love of intricate detail.

Figure 11-5
A page from The Book of Kells

Such designs were also a feature of the fine metalwork, such as belt buckles, of the region. (In Figure 11-5 can you identify an element that looks rather like a belt buckle?)

Medieval manuscripts often took years to complete and were made from expensive materials. The pages were vellum (fine parchment prepared from the skins of sheep or calves), and the lettering was done with gold paint as well as ink. The covers were often embellished with gold and jewels. But the hand lettering and illustrations were the finest decorations of all. Capital letters were given special treatment by being greatly enlarged and imaginatively ornamented. Colour plate 18 shows a capital P, decorated with human figures and animals, from the Winchester Bible in England.

---

poor.) St. Francis extolled the virtues of poverty, humility, and kindness to animals as well as to fellow humans. The Franciscans lived on charity, mostly from a sympathetic and prosperous middle class, and devoted their lives to teaching and helping the poor.

At about the same time, a Spanish priest named St. Dominic founded his order of Dominican friars. St. Dominic and others were disturbed by heresies arising from a new interest in science and a rediscovery of classical philosophy. The Dominicans sought to affirm the supremacy of church teaching through education and reasoning. They established schools in the growing towns of the twelfth and thirteenth centuries and gained fame as scholars and teachers. In fact, a Dominican friar named

St. Thomas Aquinas became the preeminent scholar of his time (see page 257).

CONFLICTS BETWEEN CHURCH AND STATE

In medieval society, church and state (political) affairs were so intertwined that it was often difficult to separate the two. As we have already seen, nobles often held high church positions, while educated clergy were closely involved in running the government. Such a close association greatly benefited both institutions. As kings and the church each grew in strength, however, they sought to take over, or limit, parts of the other's authority.

An epic confrontation took place between the Holy Roman emperor Henry IV

and Pope Gregory VII in the eleventh century. Henry claimed the right to appoint church officials, hoping to surround himself with powerful and sympathetic clergy in his battles against the German dukes. Unfortunately for Henry, Gregory was a zealous reformer who was determined to end this interference in church matters. He banned the practice of lay (non-clerical) appointments of church members in 1076.

Henry refused to obey the ban, whereupon Gregory excommunicated him and called on the German dukes to elect another emperor. To save his throne, Henry was forced to seek the pope's forgiveness. In the winter of 1077, he stood barefoot and rudely clothed in the snow for three days outside the castle where Gregory was staying. Gregory could not refuse to forgive a confessed sinner, but when Henry again disobeyed the ban he was excommunicated a second time. This time Henry led an army against the pope in 1081, forcing Gregory into exile.

The battle over the right to appoint bishops continued until 1122, when the church and the emperor reached a compromise known as the Concordat of Worms. (Worms, pronounced "Vourms," is a town in Germany.). By this agreement, church officials elected bishops and abbots, while the emperor kept the privilege of granting any lands and secular powers that accompanied church offices. Newly appointed clergy would attend two swearing-in ceremonies, one religious and one secular. Neither the king nor the church found this arrangement very satisfactory, so there continued to be struggles, though they were less intense than before.

Although much farther from the pope's reach than Germany, England was also the site of conflicts between church and state. A notorious stand-off occurred between King Henry II and Thomas Becket, Archbishop of Canterbury. As discussed in chapter 10, Henry brought the feudal legal system under royal control, and he wished to do the same with the church courts. Henry appointed Becket, his former chancellor (royal secretary), archbishop in 1162, hoping to find in him an ally. But Becket turned against the king, insisting that the church retain its privilege of trying and sentencing clergy.

Becket's stubbornness led to exile in France for six years. Henry finally pardoned him, and Becket returned to England. Demonstrating that his resolve had not changed, he excommunicated friends of the king who opposed his views. These actions drove Henry into a fit of rage, during which he ranted against Becket and expressed a strong desire to be rid of him. Four knights overheard the king and took him at his word. They made their way to Canterbury, confronted the archbishop, and murdered him as he prayed. This event of 1170 horrified Henry and the Christian world. In penitence, Henry submitted to the pope's decree that the church had jurisdiction over church affairs. Nevertheless, Henry continued to approve church appointments, thereby maintaining considerable control over the church in England.

The fact that the church did not pay government taxes on its vast land holdings riled many a European monarch. Yet the church itself levied a tax on all lay members, clergy, and monasteries, greatly enriching its own coffers. In an attempt to get a share of this wealth, Philip IV of France set a tax on the French clergy in 1294. Pope Boniface VIII ordered the clergy not to pay.

Figure 11-6 *Thomas Becket being slain at Canterbury Cathedral*

Philip then instituted the Estates General in 1302 to show that he had popular support. When this did not work, he sent troops to Rome to seize Boniface. A badly injured Boniface managed to escape, but died a few weeks later.

Philip engineered the election of a French pope, who moved the papacy (papal government) to Avignon in southern France in 1309. There the papacy remained, a pawn of the French monarchy, for almost 70 years despite protests from other European kings. This period was named the Babylonian Captivity, a reference to the 70-year period when the ancient Hebrews were captives in Babylon.

DECLINE OF THE CHURCH

At the end of the twelfth century, the church was at the height of its power. Earlier reforms had abolished corrupt practices such as the selling of church offices, increased the authority of priests, and momentarily subdued royal interference. The success of the early Crusades had increased the church's prestige and popular support. The monasteries were thriving, and large, grand churches called cathedrals were being built everywhere, their height and splendour inspiring religious awe in the humblest of worshippers.

Things changed in the thirteenth and fourteenth centuries. After the disastrous Fourth Crusade, people criticized the pope for not controlling the Venetians in their self-serving attack on Constantinople and the Byzantine church. The ravages of the plague undermined people's belief in a merciful God; nor were their moods cheered to see priests fleeing in fear and a remote pope refusing to venture outside his palace. The Babylon Captivity was a particularly

THROUGH THEIR EYES
Murder in the Cathedral

Some scholars have suggested that Thomas Becket chose martyrdom, since he did not flee Canterbury but almost seemed to invite the knights to kill him. One of the archbishop's attendants, Edward Grim, wrote this eyewitness account of Becket's death.

Based on this account, do you believe that Becket chose to be a martyr? What is your opinion of him and why do you think he acted as he did? Decide whether or not this account is an objective portrayal of his death.

Coming close up to him they [the knights] said: "We declare to you that you have spoken in peril of your head." "Have you then come to slay me?" said he. "I have committed my cause to the great Judge of all mankind; wherefore I am not moved by threats, nor are your swords more ready to strike than is my soul for martyrdom." ...

The archbishop then returned to the place where he had before been seated, consoled his clerks and exhorted them not to fear; and, so it seemed to us who were present, he sat there waiting as unperturbed, although his death alone was sought, as if they had come to invite him to a wedding. Ere long back came the murderers in full armour with swords, axes and hatchets, and other implements suitable for the crime on which their minds were set. Finding the doors barred and unopened at their knocking, they turned aside by a private path through an orchard till they came to a wooden partition, which they cut and hacked and finally broke down. Terrified by the noise and uproar, almost all the clerks and the servants scattered hither and thither like sheep before wolves. Those who remained cried out to the archbishop to flee to the church; but he, mindful of his former promise that he would not through fear of death flee from those who kill the body, rejected flight....

Then they made a rush at him and laid sacrilegious hands upon him, pulling and dragging him roughly and violently, endeavouring to get him outside the walls of the church and there slay him, or bind him and carry him off prisoner, as they afterwards confessed was their intention....

Next he received a second blow on the head, but still he stood firm and immovable. At the third blow he fell on his knees and elbows, offering himself a living sacrifice and saying in a low voice, "For the Name of Jesus and the protection of the Church I am ready to embrace death." But the third knight inflicted a terrible wound as he lay prostrate. By this stroke the sword was dashed against the pavement and the crown of his head, which was large, was separated from the head in such a way that the blood white with the brain and the brain no less red from the blood, dyed the floor of the cathedral with the white of the lily and the red of the rose, the colours of the Virgin and Mother and of the life and death of the martyr and confessor.

---

low point, during which the pope lived in luxury in Avignon and church leaders were open to bribes.

When the French pope died in 1378, reformers elected a new pope in Rome, while the French cardinals chose their own pope. Most of Europe supported the Roman pope, while only France, Scotland, and parts of Spain recognized the French pope.

Yet a third pope was elected in 1409. This disorganized state of affairs, called the Great Schism, did not end until 1417, when a church council met to choose a single pope to lead the church.

DEATH

Before Christianity took root, many Germanic tribes honoured the dead and disposed of their bodies by cremation. Cremation was especially favoured among the Angles, Saxons, and Vikings. Vikings sometimes placed their dead leaders, dressed in armour and surrounded by their weapons and other treasures, on their ships to be burned as a vast funeral pyre. Other peoples, such as the Jutes, followed the Roman practice of burial.

Figure 11-7 *Tombs of the Plantagenet kings, with the tombs of Richard the Lionheart, Eleanor of Aquitaine, and Henry II*

As Christianity spread, cremation was abandoned in favour of burial so that the dead might have bodies to return to on the Day of Judgment. In Christian teaching, Judgment Day was the end of the world, when God would judge all souls, sending the saved to heaven and the damned to hell. All Christians, from the highest noble to the humblest peasant, were given a funeral ceremony in a church. The priest blessed the deceased and commended his or her soul to God in a funeral mass, thus helping to ensure the soul's entry into heaven. The body was also buried in hallowed ground, most often the church cemetery. The church frowned upon the earlier Roman and pagan customs of burying valuables, such as weapons, jewellery, and coins, with the body for use in the afterlife. It was thought that such material things were unworthy and unnecessary for a saved soul in heaven.

Peasants received only a simple funeral. The body was wrapped in a cloth called a shroud and carried to the church on a bier, or stand, draped in black. After the funeral, the body was lowered into the ground in a rude wooden coffin, if the family could afford it, or simply in the shroud itself.

Kings, bishops, and high nobles had much grander burials. Their tombs were given places of honour inside a church, often along the walls or in the crypt, an underground chamber. The body was laid in a heavy stone coffin called a **sarcophagus**, covered by a lid carved with an effigy of the dead person lying peacefully at rest. Sometimes an internal organ such as the heart, a lock of hair, a snippet of clothing, or other personal effect was removed from the body of an important person, such as a saint, and placed in a precious, elaborately decorated container. These **relics**, as they were called, inspired great religious devotion, drawing pilgrims (travelling worshippers) from near and far to worship before them. Most relics were displayed at a church associated with the saint, but some were taken on medieval road tours so that large numbers of worshippers could see them.

REFLECT AND ANALYZE

1. Do you think the Middle Ages can rightly be called the "age of faith"? Explain why you agree or disagree in a short essay, giving reasons and evidence to back up your opinion.

2. Was the medieval church a purely religious institution? Explain what its functions were in medieval society, and whether these were strictly spiritual in nature.

3. Many people of noble birth entered the religious orders. Some monks and friars were the younger sons of nobles, who were not able to inherit the family estate. Noblewomen, too, entered convents to become nuns and abbesses. Describe the features and activities of monasteries and convents that would have attracted people to them.

4. Decide whether you would prefer to have been a king or a pope during the twelfth century. What would have been your powers and privileges? What difficulties would you have faced, and how might you have dealt with them?

SOCIAL STRUCTURE

FEUDALISM

During most of the Middle Ages, life was based on an economic, political, and social organization called *feudalism*. By means of mutual agreements and obligations between well-defined groups or classes of people, feudal society functioned effectively despite the lack of a sophisticated system of law. There were three aspects to feudalism. Economically, it regulated the distribution of land, and therefore of wealth. Politically, it ensured the protection of all people of a territory, the weak as well as the strong. Socially, it provided a hierarchical structure which determined each person's place, rights, and responsibilities in society.

As Figure 11-8 shows, medieval feudal society looked like a stacked pyramid, with the king at the top, peasants (who made up 90 percent of the population) at the bottom, and layers of lords, lesser lords, and knights in-between. Interestingly, the Roman Catholic church, with its pope, archbishops, bishops, and priests, had a very similar structure.

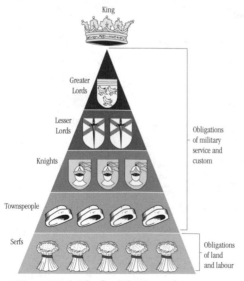

Figure 11-8 *The feudal pyramid*

The feudal system, which reached its height around the eleventh century, grew out of the customs of the early Germanic tribes. Tribal warriors swore an oath of loyalty to their chief and fought for him whenever required. In return, the chief looked after their needs and provided weapons and horses. The barbarian warriors were skilled horsemen, which had been an advantage against the Roman legions who fought on foot. In the eighth century the stirrup was invented, making horseback riding easier and allowing warriors to wear more protective armour and wield heavy weapons. These mounted, armoured warriors were called knights. Knights and the women they married became the nobility. Powerful nobles were called lords and their wives were called ladies.

Charles Martel, leader of the Franks, started the practice of preparing and arming knights to be battle-ready at all times. Trained knights, of course, were invaluable to an ambitious leader trying to expand his kingdom through invasions and wars. But paying knights, as well as providing their equipment and horses, was very expensive. So Charles Martel gave his knights land instead of money, so that the knights could provide for themselves. The parcels of land were called fiefs. They ranged in size from several hectares to hundreds of hectares. Greater lords were given larger fiefs than lesser lords and knights.

Through war, gifts from the king, and marriage to wealthy noblewomen, some lords built up vast territories and became very powerful. These lords divided up their lands among lesser lords who were sworn to serve them. The lesser lords were called vassals. A lesser lord, in turn, granted land to his own vassals. The hierarchy continued down to the lowest knight, who had no vassals and owned just enough land for his family to live on. Lords and vassals were central to feudalism from the tenth to twelfth centuries.

The king was the only member of feudal society who did not have a lord. The highest lords in the kingdom were his vassals and bound to provide military service to him. However, in the Early Middle Ages, a king's power was limited by the very fact that he had to rely on these lords to defend and administer their own territories within the kingdom. Many nobles owned more land and commanded more vassals than the king, making him vulnerable if one or several of these nobles decided to challenge him. Only a few exceptional rulers, such as Charlemagne, were successful in controlling these feudal lords and suppressing rebellion. The formation of monarchies in France and England in the eleventh century made the king's position more secure, since his vassals shifted their loyalty from his person to the crown itself.

Below the lowest knights were commoners, most of whom were farm labourers called peasants. Other commoners were artisans such as blacksmiths and carpenters, and lower clergy such as priests. Originally free men and women, peasants were forced to seek the protection of a lord during the war-torn, dangerous Dark Ages. In return for this protection and a place to live, they performed all the manual labour needed on the lord's estate—planting and harvesting crops, looking after farm animals, and numerous other activities. By the eleventh century, peasants called *serfs* had become legally bound to their lord's estate. They were not slaves because they

PERSPECTIVES ON THE PAST
The Medieval Knight

The medieval knight was a trained warrior, whose only occupation was fighting. Unlike earlier Germanic warriors, who farmed or hunted or fished when they were not fighting, knights were trained from childhood in the art of war. You have already read about a boy's development from page to squire to knight. Only men of noble birth could be knights.

A knight wore a suit of metal armour that covered him from head to toe. This suit was so heavy that he had to be helped onto his horse. All knights rode horses. (In fact, the French word for knight, *chevalier*, means "horseman.") Holding a lance and with a sword by his side, a knight charging on horseback was a formidable foe. On the other hand, if you could knock him off his horse, his unyielding armour made effective hand combat almost impossible.

Since knights were so expensive to train and arm, they were more often captured for ransom money rather than killed. In the thirteenth-century Battle of Lincoln involving 1000 knights, one knight was killed. But 300 were held for ransom!

could not be bought or sold, but neither were they free to leave the estate. They lived their entire lives on a single estate and were considered part of it. If the estate changed hands, the new lord took over the feudal responsibilities toward the serfs.

As fiefs were passed down to succeeding generations, they tended to get divided up into smaller holdings. The network of feudal obligations could become quite complex. A powerful lord might acquire land through marriage or war that made him the vassal of a weaker noble. Vassals might hold several fiefs, each subject to a different lord. Since loyalty was owed to each lord, problems of conflicting obligations could easily arise.

With the birth of towns in the eleventh century came a new class of people who were neither serfs nor nobles. Townspeople included free citizens as well as serfs who had escaped from their estates or who had secured their freedom by paying a fee to discharge their feudal obligations. In the towns, people worked as merchants and skilled craftspeople. As the towns grew in size many people prospered, earning enough money to buy small plots of land and build their own houses. No longer dependent upon a lord for a living, they formed what we now call the middle class. In England, towns were called *boroughs* and their citizens were *burgesses* or *burghers*. The German word for townsperson was also "*burger*," and the French word was "*bourgeois*" (pronounced "bor-ZHWUH"). Among townspeople, social status was based on wealth rather than on a hereditary title and fief.

FEUDAL OBLIGATIONS AND RIGHTS
Lords and Vassals

The mutual exchange of responsibilities between lord and vassal is sometimes referred to as the feudal contract. It was not written down, as our contracts are today, but it was binding all the same.

The bond between lord and vassal was recognized in a formal ceremony, which took place whenever a fief was granted or a son inherited his father's estate. Kneeling and placing his hands between his lord's hands, the vassal pledged his loyalty and service. The lord accepted this oath of homage with a kiss and granted the vassal the rights to the fief, giving him a handful of earth or a wooden stick as a symbol. Technically, the lord still owned the land, but the vassal had the right to use it and pass it on to his heirs.

Besides granting fiefs, a lord had other responsibilities toward his vassals. He provided military protection and a court for settling disputes between vassals. If a vassal died, the lord acted as guardian to the young heir and his family.

A vassal's obligations to his lord were more numerous and specific. The most important was military service, usually 40 days a year. (In later centuries, money payments could be substituted for military service, a relief for vassals who served several lords.) A vassal spent time guarding his lord's castle and serving his lord on special occasions. He helped to dispense justice in the lord's court. He acted as host and provider whenever the lord paid a visit

Figure 11-9
Vassal kneeling to swear loyalty to his lord

to his fief. He had financial obligations, including payment of an annual relief or fee, and ransom money if the lord was captured in battle. The payments, in fact, could be quite burdensome. The vassal contributed a sum when the lord's eldest son was knighted or when his eldest daughter was married. He contributed to war campaigns, castle-building, and any other major activity requiring money. When he died, his heir paid a fee before he could inherit the fief.

Lords and Serfs

A lord had obligations to his serfs, although not nearly as many as the serfs had to their lord. The lord protected his serfs during wars or raids. He provided them with land to build modest homes to live in, and strips of farmland to grow crops. He administered justice through the manor court. Custom dictated that he treat his serfs fairly and that he could not seize their land unless they failed to meet their obligations.

In return for these privileges, the serfs performed hours of back-breaking labour and paid numerous taxes and fees. They had to work three days a week on the lord's land, farming his fields, digging the moat, and repairing castle walls and roads. Extra labour was required in busy seasons such as harvest time. The serfs paid an annual tax for their homes and their strips of field. They paid fees to use the lord's road and bridges, his mill for grinding grain, his oven for baking bread, and his wine press.

They were sometimes allowed to fish in lord's streams, again paying a fee for the privilege. There was a marriage tax and special payments at Christmas and Easter. After the head of the household died, his widow had to pay a death tax, usually the family's best animal, for the right to continue using the land. Serfs paid their taxes in the form of labour, farm produce and animals, and goods such as woven cloth, a piece of furniture, or a pot. Not surprisingly, after all of these payments there was very little left over for the serfs themselves.

REFLECT AND ANALYZE

1. How did feudalism provide order and some stability to Europeans at a time when wars raged constantly and there were few laws protecting people?

2. Feudal society has been described as being shaped like a pyramid. Why is this analogy appropriate? Draw a large diagram, showing where people belonged in the pyramid. For each group, write a one-paragraph description of who the people were, what they did, etc. Use information from this chapter to write your descriptions.

3. a)   Do you think the feudal agreement between lord and vassal, or that between lord and serf, was a fair one? Provide reasons to support your opinion.
   b)   The serfs supplied the most important product in medieval society—its food. Do you think that the serfs realized the power they possessed? Could they have improved their lives if they had asked for more privileges in exchange for farming? Explain your answers.

4. Compare medieval feudal society with the social structure of ancient Rome. How were they similar and different? Explain whether a connection can be drawn between the two systems.

EVERYDAY LIFE

THE FAMILY

As in most rural societies, the family was central to medieval life. The eldest son born to a vassal was his heir, and he and his younger brothers could serve as knights to their lords. Sons born to peasants were welcome additions as heavy labourers, while daughters also worked in the fields as well as in the home.

Babies were born at home with the help of a midwife. A priest baptized the child soon afterwards in case of early death. Infant mortality was very high in an age of poor hygiene and sanitation and scant medical knowledge. A healthy child, especially if it was an heir, was a cause for rejoicing. Nobles celebrated the birth of a child with a feast, while peasants celebrated much more modestly. Sometimes serfs were visited by their lord who came to see their newborn child.

Peasants and nobles alike swaddled their infants, wrapping strips of cloth tightly around the child's arms and legs so that it could not move. This made the child easy to carry around and also kept it quiet by depressing its bodily functions. Swaddled children cried less and slept more. However, swaddling stunted their growth and increased their susceptibility to ailments.

In peasant families, children were put to work at an early age, running errands and doing chores. They received no or very little education and were illiterate throughout their lives. The children of nobles were usually sent, at age six or seven, to the household of their lord or another noble family. A boy destined to become a knight served the lord as a page and, later, as a squire. Boys who had no taste or talent for military life might prepare to enter the priesthood or a monastery. A girl learned the manners of the nobility and other skills she would need as a future lady.

MARRIAGE

Serfs who wished to marry had to obtain their lord's permission and pay a marriage fee, such as several hens. The wedding was performed by the church door in the presence of the priest. (The custom of weddings inside churches did not start until after the Middle Ages had ended.) The priest first asked if there were any barriers to the marriage, meaning a close family relationship between groom and bride. If there were no barriers, the groom pledged his commitment to his bride by giving her a ring. The ring was a symbol of the groom's dower, or gift, that his wife would receive if she were widowed. The dower was a portion of the groom's goods and access to farmlands. Likewise, the bride's family brought a dowry to the marriage. A poor family might give a new robe and tunic as a dowry, while a richer family might give a chest, bedding, and some money.

Some peasants did not bother with a religious ceremony at all, much to the chagrin of the church. These couples would simply acknowledge their commitment to each other wherever was convenient—an open field, a forest, or a tavern. Even when there were no witnesses, as often was the case, the marriage was considered valid since both parties had agreed to it.

Marriage among nobles was a much more formal and strategic affair. Nobles arranged marriages to increase their wealth or social standing. Kings used marriage to strengthen their political authority or to change an enemy or potential enemy into an ally. Child marriages were not uncommon among royalty and higher nobles: for instance, the nine-year-old daughter of Henry II of England and Eleanor of Aquitaine was married to the 12-year-old ruler of Castile in Spain.

Wealthy grooms gave dowers of land and castles, which their brides, if widowed, had use of as long as they lived. Brides usually brought dowries of money. If a bride owned land, her husband ruled it after their marriage. But in cases where a marriage was dissolved, such as Eleanor of Aquitaine's first marriage to Louis VII of France, the woman retained her land rights.

The wedding itself was an occasion of much lavish display and feasting. A priest officiated at the exchange of vows and gifts, the giving of the ring, and the bride's kneeling in acceptance of her husband's authority. In a second, secular ritual, the bride's father also gave her hand to her new husband.

EDUCATION

During the Dark Ages, the learning of classical Greece and Rome was lost. There were no schools, except a few within the church, and most people were illiterate, even the priests. Charlemagne was the first European leader to revive learning on a large scale. He invited scholars from Spain, Italy, and England to his court to advise him on education.

The most influential scholar at Charlemagne's court was an Anglo-Saxon monk named Alcuin, who set up a palace school to educate the emperor's children and the children of other nobles. Alcuin was also responsible for establishing schools and libraries in the monasteries throughout the kingdom.

Under his direction, monks began the practice of copying ancient Greek and Latin manuscripts. In doing so, they developed a new form of writing, with capital and lower-case letters, that was easier to read than Roman capitals. This script is the basis of written Italian, French, English, and other European languages today.

Education for girls and women in noble families focused on practical skills. Young women learned spinning, weaving, embroidery, and medical remedies for illnesses. They learned to supervise the many activities involved in the feeding, clothing, and care of a large household. Some, but not all, learned to read. Noblewomen of ability often educated themselves in literature and poetry, written both in Latin and in their native tongue, and in music. When convents and monasteries were first established, nuns could expect to get as good an education as monks, but starting in the twelfth century the church severely restricted such opportunities.

Universities

The twelfth century saw a flowering of academic enquiry and scholarship in medieval Europe, leading to the birth of universities. Two major factors contributed to this flowering. One was a flow of knowledge into Europe from other cultures that had started in the eleventh century. From the Muslim world came new translations of Aristotle and other Greek philosophers as well as mathematical and scientific knowledge; from the Byzantine empire came works of Roman law. The second factor was the rapid growth of towns, where churches had established free schools for the children of merchants and artisans. More people were able to read than ever before, and wealthy townspeople as well as nobles were able to afford higher education for their sons.

Scholars also came to the towns to meet together. The earliest universities were associations of students and teachers. Like trade guilds, these university associations protected the interests of students and teachers, prescribed courses of learning, and set standards. They also barred women from being admitted to universities.

Universities operated under the authority of the church or the king. The universities of Paris and Bologna were the first to be established. When France and England went to war, English students in Paris returned home and founded the University of Oxford. A group of Oxford students later formed a university at Cambridge.

All universities offered a course of study in the seven liberal arts: grammar, rhetoric, and logic; arithmetic and geometry; astronomy; and music. This curriculum was based on ancient Roman teaching. Universities also developed expertise in other disciplines. Bologna was a centre for the study of law; Paris and Oxford excelled in religious studies and philosophy; and Salerno was known for medicine.

University life was rigorous, with few human comforts. Students rose before dawn for their first lesson of the day, and attended their last review session after supper. They sat for hours on hard benches in unheated rooms, listening to lectures. Before the founding of colleges in the thirteenth century, students had to arrange their own lodging and meals, as well as pay for tuition, texts, and writing supplies.

Students trained for highly respected professions in law, medicine, government administration, teaching, and the church. After completing a basic course of study in three to six years, a student took a final examination to gain the degree of Bachelor of Arts. A master's degree, which qualified a person to teach at a university, could take up to 10 more years of study.

WOMEN IN MEDIEVAL SOCIETY

In a society as preoccupied with war as medieval Europe, women were relegated to a

Figure 11-10 *A medieval university*

secondary position. The church, too, taught that women were inferior to men. According to the Biblical story, Eve was created from Adam, and she was also responsible for the couple's banishment from Eden. Woman, said the church, led man into sin.

Noblewomen lived under the guardianship of men, first as daughters, then as wives. Only widows were mistresses of their own estates. Noblewomen could inherit a fief, but were not allowed to rule it. Still, they played a far more active role in affairs than these outward restrictions suggest.

When her husband was away fighting, as he frequently was, a noblewoman was head of the manor. Out of necessity, she had to know how to supervise the vassals and serfs, conduct business matters, collect taxes, and direct the defence of the castle if necessary. Of course, there were advisors and officials to help her, but she made the final decisions.

Some women raised money to finance wars or to pay ransoms if their husbands or sons were captured in war. A few even endured the hardships of war itself, accompanying their husbands on the Crusades.

At least one high-born woman, Eleanor of Aquitaine, was a formidable power in royal politics. She initiated her divorce from Louis VII of France and persuaded Henry II of England, 12 years her junior, to marry her. She ably ruled England on occasions when Henry, and later her son Richard the Lionheart, were away. She also endured 15 years of imprisonment when she joined her sons in rebellion against Henry.

For women of lower rank, necessity dictated a more equal partnership between the sexes. In addition to their own responsibilities of raising children, preparing food, and weaving cloth, peasant women did virtually the same farm work that their husbands did. They planted, weeded, gathered, and threshed crops; milked cows; and sheared sheep. Widows had the greatest responsibility, being required to work on their lord's land and pay taxes in their husbands' place.

In the towns, too, women worked alongside their husbands in trades and businesses. Many women were employed in their own right as domestic servants, spinners, weavers, and brewers. However, they earned lower wages than men, and most women were barred from becoming members in male-controlled trade guilds.

The Code of Chivalry

When the rough-and-tumble ways of early feudalism gave way to more courtly behaviour in the twelfth century, the image of women also changed. The code of chivalry required knights to act as men of honour as well as valour. They had to fight fairly in war—for instance, not attacking another knight before he was armed—and to treat noble prisoners well. They were to uphold and defend Christianity, and to be generous to the poor and weak. The legends of King Arthur and Sir Lancelot provided a model of knighthood.

Knights were expected to act gallantly toward ladies and to respect, cherish, and protect them. In the code of chivalry, women were seen as chaste, virtuous beings, inspiring goodness and ardent love in knights. This notion of chivalry found greatest expression in literature, poetry, and love songs, which were becoming popular modes of entertainment in courtly households. Troubadours, or wandering poets, travelled from castle to castle, singing songs about courtly love and chivalrous deeds. Songs and long narrative poems called romances celebrated knights and ladies as equals, although this was an idealized vision rather than one based on reality.

Figure 11-11 *Noblewomen in medieval society*

REFLECT AND ANALYZE

1. "The Middle Ages was a time of great ignorance but also a time of great learning." This statement sounds contradictory, but it is true. Explain why.

2. Compare the purpose of higher education in ancient Greece and Rome to the purpose of education in medieval universities.

3. There were two sharply contrasting ideas of women in medieval Europe, put forward by two different groups in society. What were these two ideas, and who created them? In popular culture and movies today, can you think of a similar contrast in the images of women? Do you think such images are accurate?

4. Compare the status of a medieval noblewoman to that of a Roman matron. Which enjoyed better rights and education? Would you prefer to have been a well-born Roman woman or a medieval noblewoman? Explain your opinion.

Figure 11-12 *Warwick Castle, Warwickshire and the river Avon*

URBAN AND RURAL LIVING

Who has not at one time thought how wonderful it would have been to have lived in a castle? Well, the reality of medieval castle life, particularly in the Early Middle Ages, was quite different. For one thing, castles were built more for protection than for comfort. Early castles were simple structures consisting of only two rooms: a lower hall where the lord conducted his affairs, and an upper private chamber. The stone walls were thick and usually damp, and there were no windows. Narrow slits high up in the walls let in some light, but they also let in cold winds, rain, and snow. Fires were lit for warmth, but because there were no chimneys, the air was always filled with heavy, choking smoke.

In the great hall, the king or lord received guests and officials, and provided them with a feast and entertainment. People ate with daggers or their hands and threw their scraps to the dogs. After dinner, they were entertained by wandering minstrels who sang or recited poetry. The table in the great hall also served as a bed for the guests and knights. Servants slept on the floor.

The family retired to their private chamber above the great hall. The lord and lady slept in a large bed, while their children slept in smaller beds. Any personal servants slept on the floor.

In the Late Middle Ages, larger castles were built, with multiple rooms and more comfortable furnishings. These refinements came about when trade increased and the nobility had greater leisure. Castles were viewed more as homes than as strongholds. Especially in France, courtly manners reigned and elegant tapestries warmed the walls. Still, there were discomforts. Castles were crowded places, housing not only the lord's family but also servants, knights, cooks, blacksmiths, brewers, bakers, and other workers. When the castle was under attack, serfs and other people from the countryside took refuge within its walls, adding to the congestion.

ENTERTAINMENT

Noblemen spent much of their leisure time in forests and wild lands, hunting foxes, deer, wild boar, hares, pheasants, grouse, ducks, and herons. Hawking was a favourite sport of both men and women. The lord's falconer trained hawks or falcons to perch on the lord or lady's wrist. The hawk's head was covered by a hood. When a suitable quarry was sighted, the hood was removed and the hawk could fly up into the air for the kill.

To keep themselves in fighting form between battles, knights engaged in dangerous contests called tournaments. Tournaments were also a training ground for young knights. Noblewomen as well as men enjoyed watching these combats, often supporting a particular knight, who fought as her champion. Even peasants were allowed to attend the events.

At early tournaments, a large gathering of knights were divided into two teams which then fought each other. The knights

INNOVATIONS
The Medieval Castle

What features in the structure of a medieval castle were designed specifically as security measures for the occupants? Which features of the design do you think offered the greatest security? Why?

Early medieval castles were built of wood, which in the twelfth century was replaced by stone. Castles were built on hilltops or mounds, or by rivers, to make them more difficult to attack. To prevent an enemy from tunnelling under the walls, many castles were surrounded by a *moat*, a deep ditch filled with water from a nearby river. A *drawbridge* across the moat, which could be raised in the event of an attack, allowed people to enter and exit.

A wall called a *curtain*, with a gatehouse for guards, surrounded the castle. A sentry walk was built along the inside top so that soldiers could keep watch and shoot arrows at the enemy. Inside the curtain were one or more flat, open areas called *baileys*. Peasants and farm animals would take refuge here if the castle came under siege. (During a siege, the enemy would surround the castle for an extended period, hoping its inhabitants would run out of food or water and surrender.)

The entranceway of the gatehouse was protected by a *portcullis*, a strong heavy grating which blocked entry inside. The portcullis was winched up and down by a rope, and its bottom was spiked, making it a deadly weapon if it were suddenly dropped on an enemy.

The main tower or stronghold of the castle was called the *keep*, because this was where the lord and his knights lived or were "kept." The walls of the keep might be as much as 8 m thick. Many keeps were square, but later ones were round to allow a better view of the enemy. The various levels of the keep allowed for halls, dining rooms, private apartments, lavatories, storage rooms, and a chapel.

The tops of the castle walls had upright stones called *merlons*. Defenders hid behind these, and when they were ready they threw rocks or fired arrows through the gaps between the merlons called *crenels*. Inside the keep, soldiers and servants poured boiling water and molten lead on attackers through gaps in the walls at the higher levels.

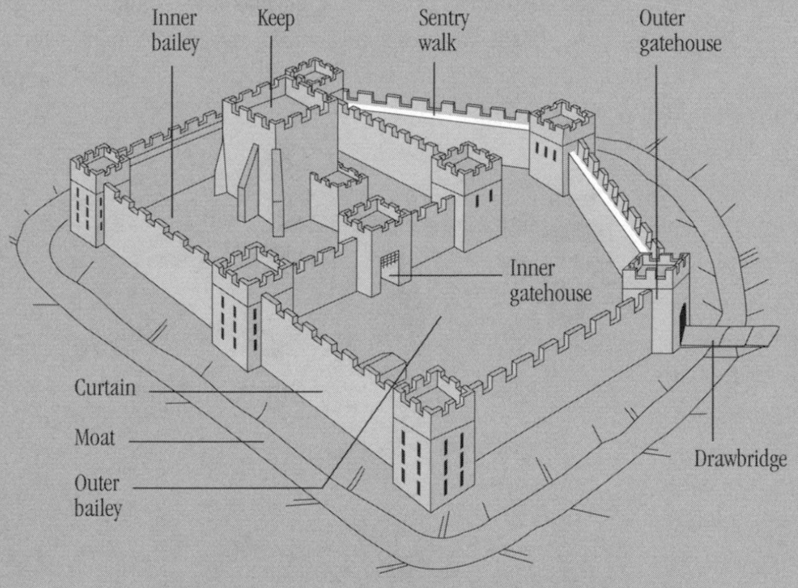

Figure 11-13 *A typical medieval castle*

who were defeated had to pay a ransom or hand over their horses and weapons to the winning team. English kings banned this type of tournament since they feared that such a large assembly of armed knights might result in a rebellion.

Tournaments then became mock battles that were fought between two knights. This type of combat, called ***jousting***, took place on a special field. At each end of the field, each knight was armed with a blunted lance and mounted on horseback. The two

Figure 11-14　*A medieval tournament*

knights then galloped toward each other, with their lances levelled, trying to unhorse their opponent. The pair might engage in as many as three rounds of jousting, followed by three rounds of fighting with battle-axes, swords, or maces. Participants were sometimes killed or maimed in these contests.

Later, jousting gave way to ***tilting***, where the knights charged at each other in narrow lanes, called lists, that were separated by a low fence. Again, the aim was to knock the other knight off his horse with a lance.

Only the king or the wealthiest nobles could afford to sponsor a tournament and entertain the throngs of knights and their followers who attended.

MANOR LIFE

During the fifth century, Germanic farmers moved onto large estates that had been abandoned by the Romans. These and similar estates gradually evolved into rural ***manors***. Large fiefs contained numerous manors, each or several of them administered by a single lord or knight.

Everyday feudal life revolved around the manor. As Figure 11-15 shows, it consisted of the lord's castle or manor house, fields for crops, grazing pastures, a barn and stable, a cluster of cottages where the peasants and other commoners lived, a church, a mill, a blacksmith's shop, and one or two other buildings. A typical manor might be about 400 ha in size.

The manor was a small, self-sufficient rural community. The peasants were expected to produce enough food for the entire community. They grew grain, vegetables and fruits, and kept egg-laying hens, geese, and ducks as well as a few pigs and cows. In the pastures sheep grazed, raised for their wool, which was spun and woven into cloth. Oxen for pulling heavy ploughs were expensive, so peasants shared one or two teams in the early days. A blacksmith made tools and weapons, while grain was ground into flour at the mill. In the days before towns became widespread, only a few items came from outside the manor. These included iron for metal implements and salt for seasoning and preserving food.

The lord employed a bailiff or steward to advise him on agricultural matters and to supervise the serfs. The bailiff also acted as the lord's deputy in the manor court.

The three fields of the manor were divided into narrow strips, a third of which belonged to the lord. The rest was rented to the peasants. Although the lord kept the best land, called the *demesne* (pronounced "di-MAYNE") for himself, the other strips were scattered among the serfs so that good and

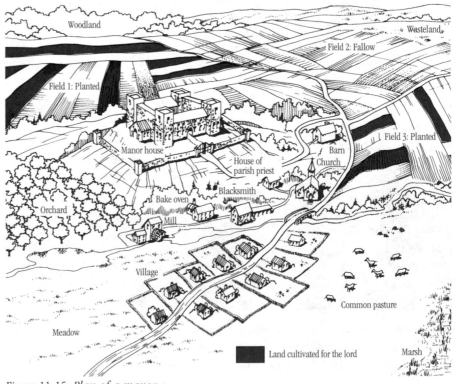

Figure 11-15　*Plan of a manor*

bad land was distributed more or less equally. The forests on the manor's boundary were strictly the lord's preserve. Anyone caught poaching wild game was severely punished.

The life of a peasant was anything but easy. The men and boys rose at sunrise, eating a breakfast of bread washed down with watery ale. Their day might be spent ploughing the fields, tending their small flock of sheep, or working in their vineyard. Heavy work, such as chopping down trees, carting wood, building fences and roads, and mowing land, was usually a joint venture among the men of the village. When not working for his lord, a serf tended to the small garden outside his cottage, where apples and pears, and a few vegetables such as beans, peas, cabbages, turnips, and onions, were grown.

The women worked equally hard at home, sheering sheep, feeding the hens and pigs, spinning wool, and sewing garments. Women also worked in the fields, especially during the planting and harvesting seasons.

The main meal of the day was in the early evening. It might consist of a thick vegetable soup, or pottage, along with ale or cider to drink. Breads and puddings were other staples. Occasionally there might be pork or fish from the stream, but meat was a luxury seldom enjoyed. Late winter was often a time of hunger or famine for peasants.

The family's cottage was small with only one or two rooms. The walls were made of layers of mud and the roof was thatched with straw. The only furniture was a few wooden stools, a small table, and a wooden chest that held all of the family's clothing. Bags of straw covered by rough blankets served as beds. In a two-room cottage, the family occupied one room, while livestock and tools were kept in the

other. Otherwise, humans and animals slept together in one room.

The hard days of work were broken by Sunday and by holy days and festivals when little or no work was done. Everyone celebrated these special days by attending a church service, followed by sports and dancing on the village green. Christmas and Easter holidays lasted a week. On Christmas day, the lord threw a feast which was followed by games of chess, football, bowls, and blind man's buff.

TOWN LIFE

In the eleventh century, a growing population and an increase in trade even before the Crusades led to the rise of towns. Italian ports were the first towns, where merchants gathered to trade with the Byzantine empire, the Muslim world, and points even further east. Artisans such as metalworkers, tanners, carpenters, textile makers, and many others flocked to these centres, knowing they could find customers for their services. Country people came to sell farm produce and to look over the dizzying array of wares, none of which existed in the small market of the manor. Thus a town's growth quickly took on a life of its own.

Goods from Italy's cities were transported by river to other places, so the earliest northern European towns often sprung up around manors situated by major rivers. The lord of the manor offered some measure of protection to a fledgling town, but feudal lords were not happy to see their serfs fleeing to these new settlements. The lords dealt with this by taxing all the inhabitants of a town that was situated on their land.

Eventually, townspeople asked the king to grant them a *charter*, a legal document guaranteeing their rights and giving

Figure 11-16 *Shops in a medieval town*

them some control over their own affairs. Kings, recognizing that townspeople would make valuable allies against feudal lords, readily granted these charters. The charters prevented the lords from seizing the townspeople's property and stipulated that they should charge a flat rent for the land instead of numerous separate fees. Another important provision granted freedom to serfs who spent a year and a day in a town.

Even though most medieval towns had a population of only a few thousand, they were always crowded. A few towns had populations of 10 000, while the cities of Venice, Genoa, and Paris had over 100 000 inhabitants! A typical town was surrounded by thick defensive walls. An open square with a clock tower lay at its centre, with the church, guild halls, and the homes of the wealthiest citizens situated close by. Narrower houses and shops were located on the cramped, winding, unpaved streets that led from the square. The streets were often named after traders or craftspeople who had their shops there.

Closely packed houses, as high as five or six storeys, blocked out daylight along the streets. At the front of a townhouse was a large hall, often two storeys high, and at the back was a storeroom downstairs with private bedrooms upstairs. Most towns had no sewers—people simply flung waste out the window with scarcely a warning cry to anyone below. As a result, the streets were filthy and smelly, even though households were supposed to clean the section of lane in front of their home.

Most town buildings were made of wood, and once a fire started it quickly raged out of control. Thieves and pickpockets roamed the streets. Some towns had night patrols, but assaults could occur at any hour. The greatest dangers in towns, however, were the terrible epidemics of smallpox, typhoid, and plague that were made worse by overcrowding.

Despite the drawbacks, towns thrived. Ordinary people who worked hard could save money and raise their social status— things they could not do when they were serfs on the manor. Life was never dull, for there was always work, street entertainments, and shops to occupy one's attention. Townspeople grew so prominent that they were given a voice in government, along with the king and nobles.

REFLECT AND ANALYZE

1. a) Describe all the features protecting a castle.
    b) If you were a noble with an army of knights who wished to attack a castle, how would you overcome all of the obstacles in your way?

2. How did the medieval pastimes of hunting and holding tournaments reflect that era? Do you think you would have enjoyed these pursuits? Are there any activities nowadays that are similar or that provide a similar release of energy?

3. Why did manors have to be self-sufficient communities?

4. a) Do you think the design of a medieval town was a good one? What would have been the advantages and drawbacks of its layout and the construction of buildings?
    b) What physical changes to cities have more recent urban planners made to make them more pleasant and convenient places to live in?

THE ECONOMY

AGRICULTURE

The light, wooden Roman plough, which was adequate for turning over the light, dry soils of the Mediterranean region, was useless in northern Europe. Here, the soil was dark and dense and frequently soaked by the abundant rainfall. Nor could crops be grown year-round, as they could be further south. During the Early Middle Ages, crop yields were barely sufficient to meet the needs of the population. But by the Late Middle Ages, agricultural production had improved so much that surpluses were being produced. What led to this dramatic improvement?

Several revolutionary inventions and farming techniques were the secret. A heavier plough was invented which dug more deeply and forcefully into the soil. It was mounted on wheels, which made ploughing easier and faster, and also allowed larger fields to be cultivated. Yoked oxen were used to pull the ploughs, but in the tenth century they began to be replaced by horses. The innovations that made this possible were the horseshoe, an improved harness, and the padded horse collar. Unlike the yoke, the horse collar was fastened around the back of the animal's neck, which allowed horses to pull with their full weight. Previously, they would have been strangled by a yoke across their throats. (Oxen had much thicker, fleshier necks that could bear a yoke.) Horses were faster than oxen, so ploughing was speeded up even more.

Crop rotation, using the three-field system (see box on page 251), kept the soil from being depleted of nutrients. A greater variety of crops could be grown, reducing the threat of famine among the peasants if one of the crops failed.

Early Europe was covered by vast forests and some swamps. Starting in the 11th century, the forests were cut down and the swamps drained and filled to make more land available for agriculture. In less than two centuries the face of Europe was transformed. Kilometres of farmland stretched in every direction, and only a few forests remained. This "Great Clearing" has left its mark on Europe today.

Figure 11-17 *An agricultural scene from a fifteenth-century French calendar manuscript*

The lords cleared their lands in order to grow large quantities of food that could be sold to people in the towns. This change benefited many serfs. Their labour was badly needed to clear the woodlands and farm the new fields. Many lords offered serfs their freedom in exchange for these activities, while other serfs were able to save enough to buy their freedom. Newly independent serfs became tenants who paid rent on the land where they lived and worked.

Farming moved from being a subsistence activity to being an industry. In 1300, European farmers were growing four times as much grain as farmers had during the Dark Ages. Some farmers were engaged in new activities such as the growing of grapes for wine and sheep farming. Wool, in fact, became a major export of England and Flanders (modern Belgium).

The population of Europe experienced explosive growth, tripling between 1050 and 1300. Most of these people moved to the towns, stimulating economic activity. Yet despite the great gains made in agriculture, ordinary people remained vulnerable to hunger and famine whenever there was a major crop failure.

INDUSTRY

In the towns, artisans produced goods that were in demand by townspeople and people living on the manors. The surplus wares were sold by merchants and traders along the major trading routes of Europe. Among the many artisans to be found in medieval towns were bakers, butchers, brewers, spinners, weavers, wool dyers, clockmakers, stonemasons, tanners, shoemakers, saddle makers, hatmakers, candlemakers, as well as woodworkers and metalworkers of all kinds.

Craftspeople engaged in a particular trade tended to congregate in the same part of a town. For example, hatmakers and everyone connected with hatmaking would have their shops along the same street. This system worked well, since the suppliers of raw materials, the wholesalers, and the consumers could all meet in the same place. To protect their interests, people working in the same profession began meeting informally in groups. These groups evolved into more formal organizations called ***guilds***.

The earliest guilds were formed by

INNOVATIONS
The Three-Field System of Farming

Why was crop rotation important? How was the three-field system more efficient than the two-field system? What impact would the three-field system have on the amount of work that a peasant did?

The fields of early medieval farms were divided into two parts. One field was planted with crops and the other field was left *fallow*, or unplanted, so that the soil could rest and be fertilized with the droppings of farm animals. The next season, the uncultivated field was planted and the other field remained fallow.

To increase their yields, farmers reduced the amount of fallow land by dividing the fields into three, instead of two, parts. Although a seemingly small change, this system allowed two crops to be grown at different times of the year. In spring, one field was planted with a crop such as oats, barley, peas, or beans and harvested in the fall. The second field was planted in the fall with a crop that could survive the cold winter, such as wheat or rye, and harvested in the late spring. The third field was uncultivated.

The crops were rotated among the three fields in a three-year cycle. In this way, food production was spread out more evenly over the year. The different harvest times also reduced the likelihood of famine.

merchants who wanted to protect their business from outside competition. They controlled the buying and selling of goods, restricted the activities of foreign merchants, agreed on prices and standards of workmanship, and settled disputes among guild members. Each guild had its own town hall and had the power to punish members who disobeyed guild rules. Because they controlled the sale of all goods, the merchant guilds were the most powerful in town and played an active role in local politics.

Artisans also formed guilds to protect and regulate their businesses. Craft guilds insisted that only their members could ply their particular profession in a town. The guilds imposed strict rules regarding working hours, wages, the number of people a shop could employ, and training. To uphold standards, guild officers would examine the goods produced by all workers.

Figure 11-18 *A cabinetmaker and his family from a fifteenth-century illuminated manuscript*

The church preached vigorously against profit-making, so guilds set a "just" price for their goods. A just price included the cost of materials plus a reasonable, but not excessive, profit. Guilds did not allow price competition among the various artisans selling the same goods. Once a price had been set, it could only be changed by the guild.

By the late 1300s, craft guilds began restricting their membership, partly to prevent an oversupply of labour and goods. A person now had to complete a long period of rigorous training before being accepted into a guild. At age eight to ten a boy became an apprentice in a business. An apprentice learned the trade from a master who was a guild member. The apprentice earned no wages but was housed, fed, and clothed by the master. After three to 12 years, the apprentice became a journeyman who earned wages while perfecting his skills. When he had saved enough money, he would pay an entrance fee and submit a "masterpiece" to the guild as proof of his abilities. If his work was acceptable and his character deemed worthy, he was admitted into the guild and could assume the title of master. Only master craftspeople could open their own shops.

Women often worked alongside their husbands in the family business, helping to supervise apprentices and production, keep the books, and sell wares. Although women were mostly barred from guilds, a widow who took over her husband's business was sometimes allowed to join, especially if the shop was thriving and she had demonstrated her business skills. Working women formed their own guilds in such industries as silk-spinning, weaving, and lace-making in which the majority of workers

were women. A young girl, like a boy, could serve as an apprentice in these trades.

Guilds were more than trade associations; they were social and communal groups as well. They looked after sick or needy members. If a member died poor, the guild would arrange his funeral, provide for his family, and help the sons find apprenticeships. Each guild had its own patron saint and feast day, which were celebrated by festivities and grand parades through the streets. Guilds also contributed to the building and repair of churches, and presented outdoor religious theatrical performances called *mystery plays* and *miracle plays*.

TRADE

During the constant warfare of the Early Middle Ages, trade in Europe was virtually non-existent. The roads so prized by the Romans had fallen into disrepair and feudal lords charged heavy tolls to travellers using their roads. Worse still, bands of roving thieves made land travel dangerous. What markets did exist were small and local.

As societies stabilized in the tenth and eleventh centuries, trade began to revive. During the Crusades, Europeans regained control of the Mediterranean from the Muslims, who had dominated it for centuries. The northern Italians were the first to benefit from this new access, sending fleets of ships east and south to buy sugar, spices, silk, and other precious goods. The Byzantine empire was the gateway to the distant lands of China and India. The empire's efforts to control its lucrative trade in silk and spices led to an attack on Constantinople by the Venetians in the Fourth Crusade.

From the Italian seaports, goods were transported to other parts of Europe by river. Rivers were the new "highways" of

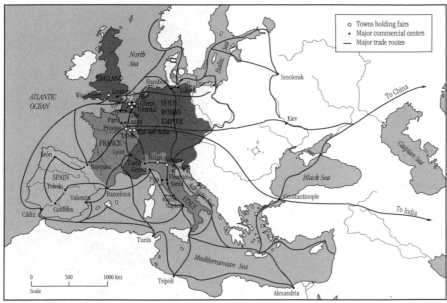

Figure 11-19 *Medieval trade routes in Europe*

ing. The large fair in Troyes, France, brought in traders from both north and south. Italians bought raw wool, Russian furs, and hides, while northern merchants bought luxuries from the eastern Mediterranean, weapons, armour, and horses.

Because people attending a fair often had to travel large distances, trading lasted at least a month. Each day was given over to the selling of a particular commodity— wool one day, for example, and furs the next. Visitors to the fair were entertained by jugglers, tumblers, dancing bears, and travelling musicians, and other performers. The final day was reserved for the exchange of foreign currencies and the settling of accounts.

trade, water transportation being much faster and safer than transportation over land. While Italy traded mostly in goods from afar, northern Europe traded in native products such as wool, furs, and skins. England sent wool across the North Sea to Flanders, where weavers turned it into a fine cloth prized all over Europe. Vikings brought their furs and skins, honey, and a rough woollen cloth to the Flemish trading centres of Antwerp and Bruges.

Local merchants did most of their buying and selling at large trade fairs held in different locations throughout Europe. Nobles were eager to host these fairs since they could earn a handsome profit by renting booths to exhibitors, charging an entrance fee, and imposing a sales tax on all transactions.

Many fairs were held in Flanders and northern France. The Fair of St. Denis, which operated outside the gates of Paris every October, attracted dealers in foreign foods and spices, precious metals and gems, and cloth-

REFLECT AND ANALYZE

1. Explain why it was important for farmers in northern Europe to find better methods of farming. What disadvantages did they face? How did they overcome them?

2. a) What modern organizations are like the trade guilds of medieval times? b) In the Late Middle Ages, the guilds made becoming a member more difficult by increasing the training requirements and requiring examinations. Why did the guilds restrict membership in this way? Do you see any parallels in modern society? Explain.

3. Prosperity and increases in population usually go hand in hand. In an essay, describe how social, economic, and agricultural factors came together to produce growth and economic vitality in Europe from 1000 to 1300.

4. Research and create a presentation on one of the following subjects: a) craft guilds and guild regulations; b) history of the wool trade; c) the silk route between China and Europe (or Marco Polo); d) the trade history of Flanders (cities of Antwerp, Bruges, and Ghent), Venice, or London. Present your work in any form you choose, such as an illustrated history, an annotated map, a "tapestry," etc.

THE ARTS

ARCHITECTURE

The greatest art form of the Middle Ages was the **cathedral**—an immensely tall, grand stone church whose beauty and engineering still awe us today. France was the home of the greatest achievements in cathedral-building. Its **Gothic** style of architecture spread to other northern European countries, most notably England, where builders adapted the style to create their own distinctive version of Gothic architecture. ("Gothic" comes from the name of the Germanic Goths. Later Europeans used the word "Gothic," in the disparaging sense of "barbaric," to refer to medieval architecture.)

Most Christian churches, large and small, were built in the shape of a cross. The shape was adapted from the basilicas of Roman times. The main entrance of the church faced west, while the altar was situated near the church's east end.

All the large cathedrals followed this basic plan. A cathedral was the main church of a diocese, where the bishop's throne, or *cathedra*, was located. Such a church had to a be worthy monument to God's grace and inspire all who worshipped in it. Bishops, nobles, and townspeople alike contributed money to build the tallest, brightest, most beautiful cathedral possible.

The building of a great cathedral could easily take 30 years or much longer. A master builder drew up plans for the church and supervised its construction. He, along with the quarrymen, stonemasons, mortar makers, carpenters, and sculptors, spent their entire lives working on a cathedral that possibly would be completed by their children or grandchildren. Sometimes money would run out during a cathedral's construction. Work would not resume until years or even decades later, when enough money was raised to continue the project.

Around 1000, Norman towns and monasteries began building large stone churches in a style called the **Romanesque**. These churches showed the influence of Roman architecture in their use of round arches and the barrel vault, a round-arched ceiling. Thick walls and large piers (pillars) supported the heavy weight of the barrel vault. Because windows would weaken the walls, only small openings were cut into the walls near the roof. Although they were the highest churches of their time, Romanesque churches were dark inside and solid and heavy in appearance.

Several innovations in engineering (see box on page 255) made possible the building of Gothic cathedrals—much taller, brighter churches, whose walls seemed to dissolve into air and coloured light. The effect was the result of decorative openings that could now be cut along the length of the wall, and slender piers at ground level. The coloured light came from multicoloured stained-glass windows that were new in churches.

One of the most celebrated Gothic cathedrals of all is Chartres Cathedral, not far from Paris. Begun in 1194, after the old church burned down, Chartres was completed in an astonishingly short 26 years. It rises to a height of over 35 m, equal to a 16-storey building. Chartres is not the tallest or grandest of the Gothic cathedrals, but its proportions are considered classic. It is also one of the few churches whose original 13th-century stained-glass windows survive.

Gothic churches were built from the

Figure 11-20
The interior of Chartres Cathedral

1150s to the 1500s. On the outside they were decorated with statues of saints, while inside they housed beautifully illustrated copies of the Bible and other religious manuscripts (see colour plates 17 and 18).

STAINED GLASS

Gothic cathedrals were decorated with huge windows made of many pieces of different-coloured glass. The windows showed scenes of the life of Christ or of saints. This was an important part of religious teaching, since many people were unable to read.

Glass-making was a highly skilled and expensive art. The glass was made from beechwood ash and washed sand mixed and melted together at a high temperature. The result was glass of a greenish colour. Different metal compounds, such as iron and copper oxides, were added to create different colours of glass. Glass-blowers

INNOVATIONS
Cathedrals of Light

After reading this article, explain how Gothic builders were able to construct tall cathedrals that appeared light and bright inside.

Through trial and error (some of their churches collapsed), Gothic architects learned how to build higher cathedrals and to remove as much mass as possible from the walls. But the churches were not held up by a miracle: the weight of the roof and walls had to be shifted to other supporting structures.

Pointed arches, instead of Romanesque round arches, were both more esthetically pleasing and better at directing weight downward to piers and outward to structures on the church's exterior. The vertical lines of the piers caused the eye to look heavenward, to the stained-glass windows and the rib vault ceiling. A rib vault ceiling was made up of a series of pointed arches with the spaces filled in with stone blocks.

Flying buttresses along the church's exterior supported the outward thrust of the ceiling and walls. They were called *flying* buttresses because the sloping parts "flew" over the low aisle on either side of the church before attaching to the thick vertical shaft of the buttress. With these outside supports in place, the inside wall could be reduced to a mere skeleton, with large windows and arcades in the upper part, supported by slender piers. Flying buttresses were themselves esthetically pleasing, adding to the interest of the church's exterior.

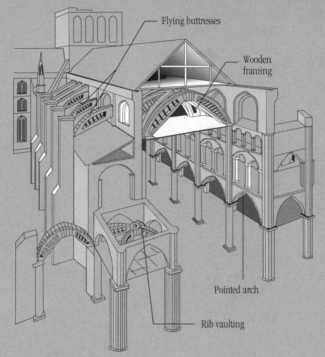

Figure 11-21 *The structure of a Gothic church*

Flying buttresses

Wooden framing

Pointed arch

Rib vaulting

---

then scooped up the molten mixture on the end of a hollow pipe and blew it into a balloon shape. The glass balloon was removed from the pipe and flattened.

When it had cooled and hardened, the glass was laid over a drawn pattern and cut into the shapes and sizes needed for the window. Pieces were joined together by strips of lead to form a picture. The faces of people or the folds of their robes were painted on the glass. Sections of these leaded pictures were held together with iron rods and fitted into the carved stone window frames. Some windows were the height of three storeys.

One of the most intricate and beautiful patterns in stained glass is the rose window, shaped like the flower. Colour plate 19 shows one of the rose windows in Notre Dame Cathedral in Paris, made by two craftsmen around 1270.

LANGUAGE AND LITERATURE

Medieval scholars wrote religious treatises, histories, and other works in Latin, the language of the church. Legal documents such as town charters were also written in Latin. Yet most people, whether commoner and noble, could not read or write the language.

During the twelfth and thirteenth centuries, a new style of literature developed, written in the **vernacular**, the everyday language of the people. The vernacular was used for songs and narrative poems. The languages of France, Spain, Italy, and Portugal were strongly influenced by Latin and today are called Romance languages.

The vernacular languages of Germany, Scandinavia, and England were based on German and are called Germanic languages.

Troubadours and singing minstrels, travelling from court to court, helped to spread the vernacular languages. Their songs and poems focused on love and the heroic deeds of legendary warriors. Poets began to write down these stories, which were popular among the nobility.

The legend of *Beowulf,* written in Old English in the 700s, is one of the earliest and greatest European epic poems. It tells the story of a great Anglo-Saxon hero, Beowulf, who battles an evil monster named Grendel. The French wrote heroic epics called *chansons de geste* (literally, "songs of heroic deeds"). One celebrated work, the *Song of Roland,* describes the heroic death of Roland, a knight in Charlemagne's army, while on a crusade against the Muslim Moors in Spain. Poets in other countries wrote celebrations of their own heroes.

Among townspeople, animal fables were popular. The best known fables were about Reynard the Fox, whose human-like tricks and weaknesses reminded people of their own. These stories are very similar to folk tales found in other cultures around the world.

Toward the end of the Middle Ages, several poets became masters of the narrative poem. The Italian poet Dante Alighieri lived in Florence from 1265 to 1321, and is considered one of the greatest authors in world literature, along with Homer and Shakespeare. His most famous work, the *Divine Comedy,* depicts religious faith as a great journey, progressing from the darkness of doubt to the glorious light of faith. (This is why the work is called a "com-

edy.") In the poem, Dante is guided by the Roman poet Virgil through the circles of hell and purgatory. During his visit to hell, Dante talks with great classical figures such as Homer and Ajax, the Greek warrior. Learning from their wisdom and mistakes, he journeys upwards through purgatory to heaven, where his childhood love, Beatrice, is his guide and inspiration.

Writing in a completely different style and tone was the English poet Geoffrey Chaucer (1340–1400), the son of a London merchant. Whereas Dante wrote about imagined historical and ideal figures, Chaucer wrote about ordinary people, describing their characters in sharp and comical detail. His *Canterbury Tales* tells the stories of 29 travellers on their way to Canterbury Cathedral, a popular destination of pilgrims. The pilgrims—a knight, a miller, a cook, the five-times widowed wife of Bath, a friar, a prioress, and others—represent typical personalities of the period and are wonderfully portrayed.

REFLECT AND ANALYZE

1. Latin was the language of the church. Why do you think secular (non-religious) literature, such as poetry and stories, developed in vernacular languages?

2. a) Compare the design of an earlier medieval church (page 234) with that of a Gothic church (page 255).
   b) What economic benefits might a splendid Gothic cathedral have for a medieval city?

3. Are there any similarities between the decoration of Gothic cathedrals and the decoration of medieval manuscripts? What might have been the importance of such lavish decoration?

4. Choose one of the characters from Chaucer's *Canterbury Tales.* Read a modern translation of his or her tale, and then dramatize and stage it for the class.

THE SCIENCES

PHILOSOPHY

The rediscovery of Aristotle's works in Europe via the Muslim world provoked great debate and soul-searching among Christian scholars. Aristotle indicated that humans should use reason and examine a subject from all sides to arrive at the truth. Medieval Christians, however, were re-

quired to accept church teaching as the one true way of looking at the world. Questioning any part of one's faith would be heresy.

Scholars worked to resolve the differences between faith and reason. They developed a school of thought called *scholasticism,* which used reason and logic to affirm Christian beliefs. One scholar in particular, Thomas Aquinas (1225–1274),

Figure 11-22 *Thomas Aquinas*

emerged as the most important religious philosopher since St. Augustine of Hippo in the fourth century. Born near Naples, Aquinas joined the Dominican Order and studied theology (religion) at the University of Paris. He wrote comprehensive, rigorously reasoned works reconciling the knowledge of the ancients with Christian doctrine.

Aquinas sought to show that there was no conflict between Christian faith and humans' free will and capacity to think for themselves. The ability to reason was a gift from God, and so too was religious faith. If a conflict arose between faith and reason, Aquinas argued that the problem was faulty reasoning and mistaken assumptions rather than a failing of Christianity.

His most famous work, the massive *Summa Theologica,* is a summary of theology and philosophy for students. In it, Aquinas posed more than 600 questions on such fundamental issues as whether God exists. For each question, he looked at a number of popular answers, including the arguments of skeptics, and then gave his own reasoned opinion. Aquinas was not afraid to examine the beliefs of heretics, which led some church officials to condemn his own writings as heretical. But his arguments defending Christianity were so powerful that the church declared

him a saint in 1323. His work has continued to influence Christian thought to the present.

EXPERIMENTAL SCIENCE AND TECHNOLOGY

Starting in the ninth century, scientific advancements from Asia and the Muslim world slowly made their way into western Europe. Europeans learned the Indo-Arabic system of numbers, which had many advantages over clumsy Roman numerals, from Spanish Muslims. Aristotle's observations of the physical world revived a long-absent interest in science among medieval scholars. Unfortunately, any real scientific advancement was hampered by the church's ultimate authority in such matters and by people's acceptance of classical knowledge (such as the astronomer Ptolemy's mistaken belief that the sun revolved around the earth) without making observations of their own.

Roger Bacon (1214–1292), an English Franciscan monk, was one of the few medieval scholars who employed the scientific method of observation and experimentation. He conducted many experiments in optics (the study of light and vision), which much later led to development of eyeglasses. He also predicted the invention of engines and their use in cars, flying machines, and ships. Unfortunately for him, his experiments and uncompromising views resulted in a confrontation with the church. Bacon would only accept facts based on scientific observation and stated that clergymen and others should spend more time observing and conducting experiments. The church, for its part, was suspicious of his strange experiments and condemned his free thinking.

Bacon was imprisoned for 24 years for his activities. Not until two centuries after his death did his methods become accepted practice in Europe. Today, he is recognized as the father of modern experimental science.

Alchemy was a much-favoured science in the Late Middle Ages. Alchemists had two aims: to change rather worthless metals such as lead into precious gold, and to find an "elixir of life" that would make humans immortal. Alchemists were part philosopher, part scientist, and part magician. They mixed and heated up substances in workshops that resembled modern-day laboratories. Although the alchemists did not succeed in either of their goals, they acquired knowledge that would lead to the development of chemistry and the preparation of medical drugs.

Technological inventions in the Middle Ages included the windmill and waterwheel, used to provide power for grain-grinding, grape-pressing, and other activities. One of the most significant inventions in the fourteenth century was the mechanical clock, driven by weights. Mechanical tower clocks, often decorated with working calendars, figures that moved, and chimes, were a source of wonder and pride to the townspeople who kept time by them.

MEDICINE

Although some fine physicians were trained at renowned medical universities such as Salerno and Montpellier, most people lacked access to doctors. They relied on folk medicine, a combination of traditional remedies, superstition, and Christian beliefs. Since many people believed that illnesses were the work of evil spirits, they

Figure 11-23 *Medieval alchemists*

prayed to the saints for cures or made pilgrimages to holy shrines. In extreme cases, surgery was performed to release the evil

Figure 11-24 *Medieval medicine*

spirits. People used astrology in an attempt to explain afflictions such as the Black Death and to predict future plagues based on the positions of the planets.

Natural remedies concocted from herbs, roots, and flower essences were used for minor ailments like headaches and toothaches. Since medical knowledge was poor, most of these remedies had little effect. One remedy for toothache was a mixture of vinegar, oil, and sulphur placed in the mouth of the patient. A presciption for headache called for peony root to be mixed with rose oil. Linen was soaked in the mixture and applied to the sufferer's forehead.

Medieval people believed that good health depended on a balance among four bodily fluids called **humours**: blood, phlegm (mucus), black bile (gall), and yellow bile (also called choler). Illness developed when there was too much or too little of one of these fluids, and the goal of any treatment was to restore balance in the body. The humours were also thought to affect a person's temperament: for instance, too much choler caused bad temper, too much phlegm resulted in sluggishness, and too much black bile led to melancholy or depression. A common treatment for humour-related illnesses was bleeding of the patient. Sometimes this had a beneficial effect, but more often than not it weakened the sufferer and exposed him or her to infection from dirty surgical instruments and fingers.

TIME

The Julian calendar, developed during Julius Caesar's reign (see page 201), was so effective in marking the seasons that its use continued throughout the Middle Ages. By 1400, Christian Europeans had added an important element to the numbering of years. They made a distinction between the years coming before and after Christ's birth. The year in which Christ was born was called the *Anno Domini,* meaning "the year of our Lord." All years after 1 A.D. were marked with the abbreviation A.D., while all years before 1 A.D. were counted backward and carried the designation B.C. ("before Christ"). In recent times, A.D. has been changed to CE (which stands for "Common Era") and B.C. has become BCE ("before the Common Era").

REFLECT AND ANALYZE

1. Did foreign sources influence the development of science and philosophy in Europe? Explain your answer.

2. Christian thinkers such as Thomas Aquinas sought to reconcile religious faith and reason in their work. What kinds of conflicts do you think might have arisen between Christian beliefs and logical reasoning?

3. Based on your understanding of the medieval humours, what do the words *phlegmatic* and *choleric* mean? After writing definitions, check your answers with a dictionary.

4. Can you give a reason why medieval people made a distinction between the years before and after Christ's birth?

5. Based on what you have learned in science classes, can you explain why the alchemists were unable to turn metals such as lead, tin, and silver into gold?

LOOKING BACK

Although the Middle Ages began in chaos and lawlessness, many important political and social institutions were established by the time it ended. In France and England, strong kings united people together politically and culturally into nations. Representative government had its beginnings, allowing ordinary people as well as kings and nobles to participate in the making of laws. As well, a justice system based on common law served all citizens equally. Today, many democratic countries have governments and legal systems that hark back to those medieval institutions.

The university was born during the Middle Ages. Many of its traditions, from the study of the liberal arts to the granting of different levels of degrees, are still with us today. A student's university experience has probably changed less in 800 years than we might think. And although medieval scholars lost much classical learning from the past, they rediscovered some of it through their contact with the Byzantine and Muslim civilizations.

The Roman Catholic church is another important and enduring legacy. The church united Europeans through faith, despite their differences in nationality, culture, and language. It established parishes, monasteries, and schools, which greatly influenced people's lives. It also built the great cathedrals and created the illuminated manuscripts that are considered artistic masterpieces today.

Through their innovations in farming, the people of the Middle Ages made Europe one of the world's most productive agricultural regions. Ordinary people, who once laboured as lowly serfs on feudal manors, were able to better themselves by becoming artisans or merchants in the towns. Medieval women, as well as men, could work in trades to support themselves.

Economic prosperity gave rise to a middle class. This new group could afford to pursue greater educational and economic opportunities than previous generations. Thus the stage was set for a great revival of classical learning and exploration of new ideas in the period known as the Renaissance.

FROM RENAISSANCE TO REFORMATION:
Europe Beyond the Middle Ages

Figure 12-1
Michelangelo's David

Pope Julius II had heard much about the young Florentine sculptor Michelangelo Buonarroti. Several years earlier, in 1504, Michelangelo had caused a sensation when his statue of the Biblical hero David was unveiled in the entrance of Florence's city hall. What Florentines saw was the full-length, standing figure of an ideal male nude, whose pose, grace, and facial features recalled the classical sculptures of ancient Greece. Rather than showing David in triumph, as earlier artists had done, Michelangelo showed him in contemplation before his fight with the giant Goliath. The body was relaxed yet alert, and the figure gazed intently to the left as if mentally preparing to do battle. Florentines were delighted with their new statue and hailed Michelangelo as a genius.

Now Julius wanted Michelangelo to come to Rome to work at the Vatican, the pope's court and residence. Julius asked the young master to paint the huge ceiling of the Sistine Chapel with scenes from the Bible. Despite his initial reluctance, Michelangelo could not refuse such an important request.

It would take him four years to complete the mammoth task. He spent long hours lying on his back on scaffolding 18 m above the floor, working in dim light while paint dripped into his eyes. At night he often slept on the platform so that he could begin again early in the morning. Beneath his brush, 343 larger-than-life human figures, classically inspired and almost sculptural in their beauty, took form.

The *Creation of Adam,* showing a nude Adam reclining with his arm outstretched to receive the spark of life from God, would become the Sistine Chapel's most famous scene. When Michelangelo finally finished the ceiling in 1512, he was recognized as one of the greatest artists Europe had ever seen. That judgment still holds true today.

The works for which Michelangelo (1475–1564) was celebrated were unlike any art seen in medieval times. A medieval pope living two centuries earlier would have been scandalized by the idea of an oversized nude adorning any kind of religious building, let alone one at the Vatican. This difference signifies the radical shift in ideas about humans and their relation to God and the world that marked the end of the medieval age and the beginning of a new one, the ***Renaissance***.

Figure 12-2 *Creation of Adam*

Although the Renaissance overlaps the medieval period, modern scholars generally agree that it started in Italy in the early fifteenth century, later spreading to northern and western Europe. The Renaissance lasted less than 200 years, but the extraordinary ferment of ideas affected every aspect of life. Even the church was not immune to deep questioning: it was permanently altered by a movement called the **Reformation**. This chapter gives you only a glimpse of the developments in society, politics, learning, culture, and religion that transformed Europe and extended its influence far beyond its borders.

HISTORICAL OVERVIEW

The word *renaissance* means "rebirth" or "revival." What was revived, on a greater scale than ever before, were the ideas and ideals of classical Greece and Rome. As we have seen, there were several earlier "renaissances" of learning during the Middle Ages, notably Charlemagne's reign in the ninth century and the founding of universities 300 years later. These earlier revivals mainly affected people of education and privilege, leaving the greater population untouched. A number of circumstances in the fifteenth century came together to create a new Renaissance that would change European society itself. This change did not happen overnight; rather, it built upon the learning and discoveries of earlier times. As well, medieval influences continued well into the Renaissance, particularly in the north.

The difference between the Middle Ages and the Renaissance is most clearly seen in the visual arts. During the medieval period, art was created to glorify God and artists mostly laboured in anonymity. During the Renaissance, artists became known by name and their works celebrated the beauty of the human form and the achievements of great people. Whereas the monks and nuns who created medieval manuscripts lived behind monastery walls, Renaissance artists were worldly and embraced society. This emphasis on human abilities and the secular world was one of the key elements that separated the Renaissance outlook from the medieval one.

Italy was the birthplace of the Renaissance for several reasons. It was the home of ancient Rome, with numerous architectural ruins and other artifacts that continually reminded Italians of their glorious past. The church in Rome had preserved ancient manuscripts, which Renaissance scholars began studying in earnest. As the achievements of antiquity were rediscovered, the Italians came to admire their ancestors and strived to follow their example in thought and art.

Italy differed from its northern neighbours in other ways. Since Roman times, it had been torn in power struggles between the pope, the Holy Roman emperor, and various noble families. Nor had the feudal

FROM RENAISSANCE TO REFORMATION: A DEVELOPMENTAL TIMELINE

	THE RENAISSANCE **c. 1430-1600**	**THE REFORMATION AND** **COUNTER-REFORMATION** **c. 1517-1565**
POLITICAL DEVELOPMENTS	• the Italian city-states of Florence and Venice become leaders of the Renaissance movement (early 1400s) • Cosimo de' Medici becomes governor of Florence, establishing a powerful dynasty (1434) • Lorenzo de' Medici (the Magnificent) becomes governor of Florence (1469) • Machiavelli writes *The Prince*, dedicating it to Lorenzo the Magnificent (1513)	• northern and southern Swiss cantons sign a treaty allowing each district to choose its religion (1531) • Henry VIII establishes the Protestant Church of England (1534) • Mary I (Queen of Scots) (1553–1558) attempts to restore Catholicism in England • Elizabeth I re-establishes Protestantism and brings prosperity and a cultural Renaissance to England (1558–1603)
CULTURAL/RELIGIOUS DEVELOPMENTS	• Giotto paints realistic human figures and architectural settings (c.1290–1337) • Flemish artist Van Eyck paints the highly detailed *The Marriage of Arnolfini* (1434) • Brunelleschi builds the dome of Florence's cathedral (1436) • Michelangelo creates the sculpture of *David* (1504) and paints the ceiling of the Sistine Chapel (1508–1512) • Leonardo da Vinci paints the *Mona Lisa* (1505) • Dutch humanist Erasmus writes *In Praise of Folly* (1509) • Titian is a leading figure of the Venetian school of painting (c 1510–1576) • El Greco paints visionary religious works in Spain (c. 1561–1610) • William Shakespeare writes his great plays and sonnets in Elizabethan England (1589–1613) • the Italian city-states (Venice, Florence, Milan, Genoa, Pisa, Naples) dominate international trade in Europe (1400s) • Gutenberg perfects the printing press in Germany (1453) and publishes the first printed Bible (1455) • the first stock exchange is established in Antwerp, Belgium (1460) • Leonardo's notebooks contain sketches of flying machines and submarines (c. 1470–1519) • Copernicus states that the earth revolves around the sun (1530) • Flemish anatomist Vesalius publishes *Seven Books on the Structure of the Human Body* (1543) • Kepler shows that the planets move in elliptical, not round, orbits (1620)	• persecution of heretics gives rise to witch-hunting among Catholics and, later, Protestants (c. 1480s–1750) • Martin Luther nails *Ninety-Five Theses* on the door of a church in Wittenberg, Germany (1517) • the Catholic church and the German Imperial Diet excommunicate Luther (1521) • Luther translates the Bible into German and founds the first Protestant church • Swiss Protestant Zwingli establishes communion as a symbolic, not literal, representation of the Last Supper (c. 1525) • Calvin presents a doctrine and structural organization for Protestant churches (1536) • the Catholic Society of Jesus (Jesuits) is founded (1540) • the Council of Trent meets to review and strengthen Catholic principles (1545–1563) • by 1600, Europe is fragmented into many different Christian denominations

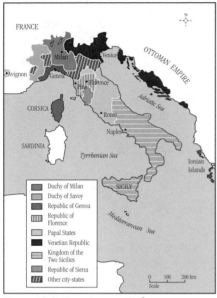

Figure 12-3 *Renaissance Italy*

system of northern Europe really taken hold; instead, political and social life in Italy was centred around powerful, bustling cities with enormous populations of 100 000 people or more. The city-states of Florence, Venice, Milan, Genoa, Pisa, and Naples, as well as the Papal States, had their own governments and ruled the regions surrounding them (see Figure 12-3).

Whereas other European economies were based on agriculture, the Italians earned their living through trade and commerce conducted in urban environments. Port cities like Venice and Genoa were prime locations for trading with distant peoples and gaining an appreciation of their cultures. Italians were cosmopolitan in outlook and open to exploring new ideas in art and learning. As middle-class citizens amassed huge fortunes, they displayed their taste and education by sponsoring artists, writers, and scholars. They also tended to play a larger role in

civic affairs than the townspeople in feudal societies. Thus the Italian cities of the Renaissance in many ways resembled the ancient Greek city-states of Athens and Sparta. There was even a similar rivalry between the cities as each sought to outdo the others in commercial activity and artistic splendour.

During the Middle Ages Gothic countries had dominated politics, religion, and culture, but the tide turned once again to Italy in the 1400s. In a sense, the disasters of the fourteenth century wiped the social slate clean. Famine and plague had reduced populations everywhere, and France and England further exhausted their resources during the Hundred Years' War. The church suffered a century-long crisis, as different factions tried to control the papacy. In fact, people's loss of confidence in the church and other institutions

prompted their movement toward human and individual goals.

FLORENCE AND THE MEDICI FAMILY

The heart of the Italian Renaissance was Florence, situated on the Arno river. Although only the fourth largest city in Italy, it was the wealthiest due to its activities in banking, manufacturing (especially the production of fine woollen cloth), and trade in fine silks, tapestries, and jewellery from the east. The city also nurtured the finest artists, writers, and thinkers, including Botticelli, Michelangelo, da Vinci, Dante, Petrarch, and Machiavelli.

In the fifteenth century the richest family in Florence, the Medicis (pronounced "MED-i-chee"), became governors of the city. The Medicis were aristocrats who acquired their immense fortune through

Figure 12-4 *Procession of the Medici*

banking and trade. They moved in the highest circles and were bankers to the pope himself; yet they were popular with commoners as well. For decades they dominated Florentine life, both as rulers and as influential patrons, or sponsors, of the arts.

Cosimo de' Medici became head of the government in 1434, after winning a power struggle against other leading families. He was popular among the middle and lower classes because he supported their interests. He also worked to establish peace between Florence and its rivals, Venice and Milan. His grandson, nicknamed Lorenzo the Magnificent, was the most famous of the Medicis. Lorenzo was noted for his charm and wit, as well as his cunning and ruthlessness in politics. He escaped an assassination attempt in 1478 and used his influence to have his 14-year-old son made a church cardinal.

Most importantly, Lorenzo was an extremely generous and discerning patron of culture. He used up much of the family fortune buying ancient manuscripts and sponsoring the work of artists, poets, and philosophers. A talented poet himself, he supported the development of a vernacular Italian language. During his rule, Florence gained recognition as Italy's cultural capital, filled with magnificent buildings, paintings, and statues.

VENICE

Venice, "Queen of the Adriatic," was Florence's rival in trade and artistic achievement. Built on 118 small islands on the northern Italian coast, Venice was the main trading port between Europe, the Middle East, and Asia. Its citizens were great merchants, shipbuilders, and travellers, the best-known example being Marco Polo and his family, who travelled to China in the late thirteenth century.

Through their monopoly in trade, the Venetians amassed large fortunes, enabling them to build grand palazzos, or palaces, along the banks of the canals which were the city's streets. The Venetian head of government was the *doge* (duke), elected by a council. The government built the Grand Canal, the city's main waterway, and St. Mark's Square, which was surrounded by the doge's palace, the cathedral, a tall bell tower, and other magnificent structures. Both public and private buildings were filled with paintings by renowned Venetian artists—Giorgione, Titian, Tintoretti, and others—whose work was distinct from that of the Florentines. You will learn more about the different styles of Renaissance painters later in this chapter.

THE RENAISSANCE IN THE REST OF EUROPE

News about the artistic splendours of Italy was brought to other parts of Europe by scholars, traders, and even enemy soldiers who attacked various Italian cities. However, it was the invention of the printing press in the 1450s that made it possible for average people in London or Madrid or Cologne to read classical and Italian works for themselves and to view reproductions of Italian art and architecture.

Renaissance culture was the first to be disseminated to a "mass" audience in Europe. The northern countries of Flanders, Belgium, and Germany produced fine painters who interpreted Italian models according to their own traditions. Writers in England, France, and Spain were influenced by classical mythology and Italian authors. Even as the Renaissance was coming to an end in Italy in the early 1500s, it continued on in other countries for another 100 years.

REFLECT AND ANALYZE

1. List the differences between the Italian Renaissance that started in the fifteenth century and earlier medieval renaissances.

2. Why were business people such as bankers and merchants important to Renaissance artists? Explain whether the artistic achievements of the Renaissance could have occurred without them.

3. Both Michelangelo's *The Creation of Adam* (page 261) and the tenth-century *Book of Kells* (page 236) show human figures from the Bible. What are the differences in style and feeling between the Renaissance work and the medieval one?

4. Compare Michelangelo's statue *David* (page 260) with the *Laocoon* (page 146) created in Hellenistic times. Do you think Michelangelo studied Greek and Roman sculpture? Does the word *renaissance* accurately describe fifteenth-century Florentine art? Explain.

PHILOSOPHY AND LITERATURE

HUMANISM

The focus on human concerns and classicism during the Renaissance was called **humanism**. In the universities, scholars studied the humanities—classical subjects such as grammar, rhetoric, poetry, and history—more carefully and objectively than their medieval predecessors had.

Early humanists first rediscovered many long-forgotten Roman works such as Livy's *History of Rome* and Cicero's speeches and letters. Later they were introduced to Plato and other Greek authors by Byzantine scholars, who fled to Italy when Constantinople fell to the Ottoman Turks in 1453. Unlike medieval scholars who rejected any ideas or beliefs that went against church teaching, the more secular Renaissance thinkers saw no conflict in studying pagan literature and depicting classical deities in art. They admired and copied the ancients, but they also drew a clear distinction between them and their own Christian age.

During the Middle Ages, the harshness of life and the teachings of the church motivated people to prepare themselves for a better life in heaven. The Renaissance humanists, on the other hand, embraced life on earth in all its forms. They discarded the view that society and material values were evil, seeking instead to improve humans and society through enlightened education and action. Thus the Renaissance was a period of optimism, self-confidence, and explosive creativity.

ITALY

Three Florentine writers—the late medieval poet Dante Alighieri, Francesco Petrarch, and Giovanni Boccaccio—paved the way for other authors who followed them. Dante wrote in vernacular Italian as well as Latin, used classical references, and adopted a highly personal voice that foreshadowed Renaissance humanism. Petrarch (1304–1374) is considered the "father of humanism." He was trained in law and religion, but preferred to spend his time searching monasteries and churches for old, classical manuscripts by Cicero, St. Augustine, Virgil, Homer, and other ancient writers. He and other researchers inspired by his example were responsible for reintroducing neglected classics to western Europeans.

In his own writings, Petrarch imitated the style, content, and form of classical literature. He wrote biographies of historical figures, letters in Ciceronian Latin, and epic poems. His love poems, inspired by a married woman named Laura whom he adored from afar, were written in vernacular Italian and consisted of 14 lines in a specific rhyming pattern. This verse form became known as the Petrarchan or Italian *sonnet*. Petrarch celebrated earthly love and action in his sonnets, rejecting the medieval ideal of a contemplative, chaste life.

His friend Giovanni Boccaccio (1313–1375) could not have been more different. Whereas Petrarch preferred to live a quiet life in France, Boccaccio moved to Florence to take advantage of its stimulating urban environment. Although he also wrote love poems, he is most celebrated for an earthy, humorous, often bawdy collection of stories called the *Decameron*.

The book, whose title means "ten days," contains 100 stories set in Florence during the Black Death. Three men and seven women seek refuge from the plague in a country villa and pass the time telling stories about love affairs involving dissatisfied wives and deceived husbands. The work was a Renaissance best-seller, perhaps partly due to the frank sexuality of some of the stories, but also because the tales reflected every segment of society, from noble aristocrat to earthy commoner. Many great writers were influenced by the *Decameron*. Chaucer, living in still-medieval England, fashioned his *Canterbury Tales* in the style of Boccaccio's work.

In the world of politics where expediency is often considered a virtue, Niccolo Machiavelli (1469–1527), took the idea to new heights in his handbook for rulers, *The Prince*. Machiavelli worked in the Florentine government, where he saw first-hand the intrigues, brutal displays of power, assas-

Figure 12-5 *Niccolo Machiavelli*

THROUGH THEIR EYES

The Prince by Niccolo Machiavelli

What do you think of Machiavelli's comments about cruelty and mercifulness in the following excerpt? Do you agree with his views about human nature? Why or why not? The word "Machiavellian" is used to describe a particular kind of politician. What characteristics would such a politician possess?

Whether It Is Better to Be Loved or Feared

I say that every Prince should desire to be accounted merciful and not cruel. Nevertheless, he should be on his guard against the abuse of this quality of mercy. Cesare Borgia was reputed cruel and yet his cruelty restored Romagna, gave it solidity, and reduced it to order and obedience; so that if we look at things in a true light, it will be seen that he was in fact far more merciful than the people of Florence, who, to avoid the reputation of cruelty, suffered Pistoja to be torn to pieces by factions....

And here arises the question whether it is better to be loved rather than feared, or feared rather than loved. It might perhaps be answered that both are best; but since love and fear can hardly exist together, if we must choose between them, it is far safer to be feared than loved. For of men it may in general be affirmed that they are thankless, fickle, false, studious to avoid danger, greedy of gain, devoted to you while you are able to confer benefits upon them, ... but in the hour of need they forsake you. The Prince, therefore, who has built wholly on their professions leaving himself bare of other preparation is undone. For those friendships which we buy with a price, and do not gain by greatness and nobility of character, though they be fairly earned are not made good, but fail us when we have occasion to use them.

---

sination attempts, and wars that were a part of political life. As an envoy to France, he observed how a strong monarch benefited the French and wished for a similar stability in Florence. The Medicis, despite their dominance, were always fighting off rivals; and they were driven from the city for several years when France invaded Italy in the 1490s. Italian life would be disrupted for half a century by repeated invasions by France and Spain.

Machiavelli himself lost favour with the Medicis, was imprisoned and tortured, and spent a long period in exile. During that time he wrote *The Prince* (1513) and dedicated it to Lorenzo the Magnificent, hoping that it would win him back his job. Machiavelli believed that only an absolute ruler could achieve stability and keep enemies firmly in control. His book therefore recommended a course of action necessary for a ruler to gain absolute power, citing numerous examples from classical history and contemporary European politics.

The Prince shocked—and continues to shock—many people by suggesting that a ruler should not hesitate to use violence and deception when necessary to achieve the goal of stability. In fact, Machiavelli took the troubles of the world to heart and wished to write about them in the cold light of reality rather than with naive idealism. His observations showed that he well understood the difference between appearance and reality. For example, he cautioned that it was better for a ruler to be feared rather than loved, and to be miserly rather than generous to keep the government's finances from ruin.

NORTHERN AND WESTERN EUROPE

The Renaissance reached the countries north of the Alps in the late fifteenth century. Here, where religious devotion and Gothic traditions were strong, humanism took a somewhat different form than in Italy. Scholars in Germany and the Low Countries (Holland and Flanders) looked to the classics and the writings of the early Christians for moral lessons and spiritual guidance. Northerners tended to be more sober and less concerned with grand display than the Italians. While they embraced the humanist belief in people's ability to learn and achieve, they also maintained a sense of humility before God.

The Dutch priest and scholar Desiderius Erasmus (1466–1536) was the greatest humanist of the Northern Renaissance. He travelled constantly through the Low Countries, France, Germany, England, and Italy throughout his career, earning an international reputation for scholarship and reform. As an educator, he wrote about the classics and the Bible, believing that the study of both would improve people's understanding and moral character. As a reformer, he produced scathing satires such as *In Praise of Folly* (1509), in which he ridiculed stupidity and corruption among members of society and the clergy. He was particularly critical of the church's emphasis on outward trappings and superficial rituals. A devout Christian, he believed that piety should come from within, not simply from a priest administering sacraments or from superstitious practices such as the worship of saints. His belief was shared by other religious reformers in the north who would lead the movement for change in the church.

In the 1500s, the universities of Oxford and Cambridge became known for their classical scholarship and new translations of the Bible. Erasmus often worked in England and became friends with Thomas More (1478–1535), a respected humanist scholar and official in the court of King Henry VIII. More did much to fuel the English Renaissance by encouraging the study of Italian literature and by spreading humanist ideas through his writings. His most influential work was *Utopia,* in which he criticized such evils as poverty, war, unearned wealth, and religious perse-cution and painted a picture of the ideal society based on justice, tolerance, kindness, and hard work. More placed this model society on an imaginary island, reflecting his interest in the voyages of European explorers to unfamiliar lands. His opposition to Henry VIII's divorce from his first wife, Catherine of Aragon, resulted in his execution by the king's order in 1535.

The greatest writer in English literature, William Shakespeare (1564–1616), was a product of the late English Renaissance. Shakespeare, of course, is best known as a playwright whose tragedies, comedies, and historical dramas are masterpieces. He wrote his plays mainly in verse, but also used prose to convey the speech patterns of ordinary, working-class characters. He greatly enriched the vocabulary and the expressive possibilities of the English language. Besides plays, he wrote 154 sonnets which focus on friendship and the constancy and fickleness of love. These sonnets include such famous lines as "Shall I compare thee to a summer's day?" and "My mistress' eyes are nothing like the sun." Shakespeare used an English sonnet form adapted from Petrarch's greatly admired Italian sonnets.

In France, the Renaissance was embodied by two writers, François Rabelais and Michel de Montaigne. Rabelais (1483–1553) was a Franciscan monk who abandoned religion to study first medicine and then the classics. A master of earthy humour and exaggeration, he created fantastic stories about a giant with an enormous appetite, Pantagruel, and his father Gargantua. These stories were actually satires attacking religious and educational institutions which Rabelais felt were in need of reform. His targets included stuffy scholars and narrow-minded monks. The frank bawdiness and irreverence of his works caused them to be censored by his Franciscan superiors and by the Sorbonne, a university in Paris.

Montaigne (1533–1592) created a new literary form, the personal essay. He lived during a period of bloody religious wars in France, which convinced him that moderation in both faith and reason was the best approach in life. Too much of one or the other, he felt, bred intolerance and fanaticism that could easily lead to violence. In his *Essays* of the late sixteenth century, he tried to show how good-will, tolerance, and self-knowledge could help people live together in harmony. His portrait of the skeptical, modest, and honourable man was a model for many people caught in the turmoil of civil war.

Miguel de Cervantes (1547–1616) was the most gifted writer of the Spanish Renaissance. In his long comic novel *Don Quixote,* he satirized the image of the chivalrous soldier-poet, idealized in Spanish heroic literature, painting, and sculpture. Cervantes tried to show that this medieval model had become antiquated in modern Spanish society. Don Quixote fancies himself a knight and sets out to be a champion of honour and right. Unfortunately, his old-fashioned ideals are impractical and cause more problems than they solve. He saves people who do not want to be saved and fights danger where there is none. For instance, he tilts with windmills, believing them to be dangerous giants.

REFLECT AND ANALYZE

1. Draw a map showing how the influence of Italian Renaissance literature spread to other parts of Europe. Include the names of major writers and the dates of their important literary works. Also indicate whether a specific work was a model for a later work. Do extra research if necessary.

2. Have two teams of students debate Machiavelli's opinion that "The ends justify the means." The rest of the class should decide which team presents the most convincing arguments.

3. Compare Machiavelli's view of society with that of Thomas More. How are humanist ideas reflected in both their perspectives?

4. Thomas More painted the picture of the ideal society in *Utopia*. Write a short essay describing what changes you would make to modern society to make it ideal.

scale paintings did not exist; only in the Late Middle Ages did they begin to appear in the form of altarpieces and wall frescos.

A revolutionary figure in European art was a Florentine named Giotto di Bondone (c. 1266–1337). He electrified his contemporaries by painting startlingly lifelike, rounded figures in settings that looked three-dimensional. He did this by using different shades of light and dark paint to create an illusion of depth. It is not known how Giotto developed this technique, but it was the first time since ancient Roman days that a European artist had painted in such a realistic manner. His focus on human emotion and gesture in religious scenes was another radical departure from the blank facial expressions of medieval

PAINTING, SCULPTURE, AND ARCHITECTURE

The achievements we most readily associate with the Renaissance are painting, sculpture, and architecture. Renaissance artists did not simply copy ancient classical models; rather, they developed numerous innovations in style, technique, and subject matter that represented a revolutionary break with the past. No other age in European history has produced so many great painters, sculptors, and architects.

PAINTING

In the medieval period, pictorial art existed mostly as vivid illustrations in manuscripts and on tapestries. Medieval artists stressed the divine and symbolic qualities of human beings rather than their individual and physical characteristics. Figures were brightly coloured, two-dimensional, and often set against a plain, flat background. Large-

Figure 12-6 *A scene from Giotto's* Life of Christ

figures. In this respect, Giotto was a forerunner of the Renaissance humanists. Other artists immediately began imitating his style, setting the stage for even more realism in painting.

Another very important innovation was the development of **perspective**, a mathematical technique for rendering three-dimensional objects on a two-dimensional surface. Renaissance architects probably discovered perspective during their studies of the proportions of Roman buildings. A picture drawn in perspective shows objects close to the viewer as large and objects farther away as smaller, thus creating a sense of three-dimensional space (see Figure 12-7). Artists mastered the principles of perspective, enabling them to plan the correct size and placement of objects even in very large, complex paintings.

Renaissance painters incorporated classical imagery, such as mythological gods and famous figures of antiquity, in their work. Sandro Botticelli (1444–1510) painted one of the first female nudes of the Renaissance in his *Birth of Venus,* which shows the Roman goddess coming toward the shore on a seashell. As humanism took hold, artists also began painting scenes of nature, as the ancients did, and portraits of real people. In their efforts to achieve realistic light and shadow, they experimented with different paints. The quick-drying tempera paints of medieval times were eventually replaced by oil-based paints, which could be blended together to create many new colours and which dried slowly, allowing artists to build up layers of subtle shading and depth.

Two Italian Renaissance artists stand out above the rest: Leonardo da Vinci and Michelangelo. Both were geniuses and true

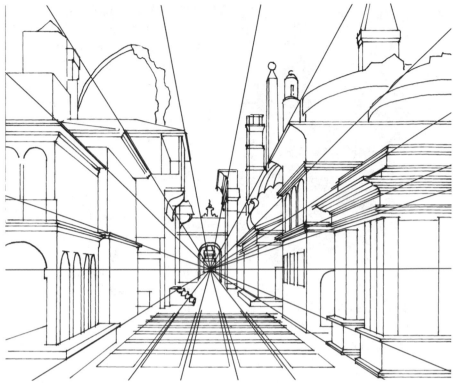

Figure 12-7 *A sketch demonstrating perspective*

"Renaissance men"—individuals whose energy, curiosity, and talent allowed them to excel in many fields. Leonardo's famous *Mona Lisa* and *Virgin of the Rocks* show his masterful use of gradual shading to reveal human qualities and the texture of human skin. With their serene expressions, Leonardo's figures often have an air of mystery about them. Michelangelo was a well-rounded artist, brilliant in painting, architecture, and especially sculpture (see following section).

In Rome, Raphael Santi (1483–1520) made his name as a great painter of the Madonna and infant Jesus and of portraits. At age 19 he studied anatomy, drawing, and perspective with Leonardo da Vinci in Florence. The pope, who hired only the best artists, invited Raphael to decorate the papal apartments in the Vatican at the

same time that Michelangelo was working in the Sistine Chapel. Using the bright colours favoured by artists in his native Umbria, Raphael painted four frescoes on the walls of the library. Four fields of study were depicted: philosophy, theology, the arts, and law. The most famous scene is the *School of Athens* (colour plate 22), which shows the great philosophers of antiquity, including Socrates, Plato, and Aristotle, assembled together and discussing their ideas in a grand basilica. In typical Renaissance fashion, Raphael includes the faces of actual people—Michelangelo, Leonardo, and himself among others—in the group.

The great artists of Venice developed a style of painting all their own. Whereas the Florentines emphasized mathematical form, drawn outlines, and anatomical accuracy in their work, the Venetians were

Figure 12-8 *Detail of Leonardo (right) in Raphael's* School of Athens

masters of vibrant colour and movement. They used fluid brush strokes without hard-edged lines, and focused on the emotional and intimate aspects of human nature rather than its grandeur. Titian ("TI-shun"), who lived in Venice from about 1488 to 1576, was an artist equal to his Florentine contemporaries. He was remarkably prolific, producing an average of one picture a month during his long life. While he earned great wealth painting the portraits of popes and kings, his reputation stems from his paintings of mythological and allegorical subjects. In his *Bacchus and Ariadne* (colour plate 23), the Greek god of wine and revelry springs upon a startled Ariadne after she has been abandoned by the hero Perseus. The emotional drama of the moment is captured with dynamic gestures and glowing colours.

In northern Europe, artists focused less on classical subjects and more on scenes of everyday life. Flemish artists, in particular, were renowned for their realism and attention to detail. In fact, one Italian critic called Jan van Eyck ("Yan van IK")

(1390–1441) the leading artist of the day. Van Eyck painted exquisitely detailed works such as *The Marriage of Arnolfini,* which shows every fold in the bride's dress and daylight reflecting off the chandelier. He even included a small convex mirror in the background, in which an image of himself painting the picture is barely visible. Renaissance artists enjoyed putting such witty visual effects in their work. Another Flemish painter, Pieter Brueghel ("BROI-gul") (c. 1525–1569), found inspiration in the modest lives of peasants. His scenes of these people working and celebrating, such as *Peasant Wedding,* influenced generations of northern artists who followed him.

The work of German artist Albrecht Dürer (1471–1528) reveals a psychological depth unusual even in the humanist environment of his age. In his *Self-Portrait* he gazes out intently toward, but not quite directly at, the viewer. With a northerner's love for detail, Dürer delineated even the fine hairs of his fur collar. Drawing upon

the German tradition of woodwork and metalwork, he also created some of the finest, most intricate woodcuts and copper etchings in art. These works were reproduced in black and white on paper and sold in large numbers. In an etching called *Melancholia,* a quietly brooding winged figure portrays the introspection and sombre mood that characterizes a melancholy disposition.

El Greco, "the Greek" (1541–1614), was born on the island of Crete, studied painting in Italy, and settled in Toledo, Spain. His mystical vision was evident in most of his work, even his portraits and landscapes. Despite constant battles with patrons, some of whom felt uneasy with his depictions of heavenly saints and angels, El Greco remained true to himself and became even more experimental as he grew older. *The Burial of the Count of Orgaz* (colour plate 21) presents a contrast between the earthbound, darkly dressed human figures below and the bright, heavenly

Figure 12-9 The Peasant Wedding *by Brueghel*

PERSPECTIVES ON THE PAST

Leonardo da Vinci (1452–1519)

In what different ways does Leonardo da Vinci embody the "spirit of the Renaissance"?

Who has not gazed upon the mysterious smiling face of the *Mona Lisa* at one time or another? Probably the most famous image in western art, the *Mona Lisa*, completed about 1505, is one of only 15 surviving paintings by Leonardo. A wealthy Florentine merchant commissioned the artist to paint a portrait of his wife, Lisa de la Giaconda.

Leonardo took four years to complete the *Mona Lisa* and decided not to part with it after all. It is easy to see why. With her serene, direct gaze at the viewer and her still pose, the figure has a timeless, universal quality. Leonardo gives us few clues about the woman's actual character: she is warm and welcoming, yet deeply mysterious at the same time. This is the genius of the *Mona Lisa*. She is placed not in an interior or urban setting, as might be expected, but in a romantic landscape which scholars have tried for centuries to identify.

Leonardo became famous in his own time for his monumental *The Last Supper*, a Milan wall fresco showing Jesus' last meal with his disciples. Unfortunately, the paint Leonardo used was unstable and it began to deteriorate soon after he completed the work. Many of his

Figure 12-10
The Mona Lisa

other paintings have suffered a similar decay.

Besides being a painter, Leonardo was a natural scientist, an engineer, and an inventor. He observed the world around him with insatiable curiosity, filling more than 5000 pages with sketches and notes. His superbly rendered drawings of human anatomy were studied by medical students, while his drawings of plants, birds, animals, and insects were valued by the scientific community.

As an inventor, he was centuries ahead of his time. He invented a thread-cutting machine and an improved water wheel. In his notebooks are fascinating if sometimes impractical designs for catapults, portable bridges, a canal system for the city of Milan, a machine gun, mechanical diggers, and even a submarine. Fascinated by flight, he made drawings and models of human flying machines, some resembling helicopters.

Figure 12-11
Leonardo's sketch for a bicycle

saints above. El Greco's style and vision are so original that his work is instantly recognizable.

SCULPTURE AND ARCHITECTURE

During the Renaissance, sculptors and architects revived classical ideals of beauty and proportion in the human form and in buildings. Sculptors carefully studied human anatomy and made lifelike statues that accurately showed muscles and joints. Nudes, not seen since ancient times, came back into vogue. The Gothic style of architecture, which reached such a glorious pinnacle in northern Europe, had only limited success in Italy. With the onset of the Renaissance, Italian architects turned their attention to constructing symmetrical buildings, with domes, columns, and friezes, in the manner of ancient architecture.

Two Florentines, Lorenzo Ghiberti and Donatello, were notable sculptors of the early Renaissance. They, along with Filippo Brunelleschi, best known as an architect,

Figure 12-12
Bronze door panel by Ghiberti

were celebrities adored by the public. Ghiberti (1378–1455) won a competition over Brunelleschi to design the massive bronze doors of Florence's Baptistery of San Giovanni. The door panels, which depict stories from the Bible, are decorated with realistic human figures and show an expert use of perspective. The figures closest to the viewer are cast in high relief, those in the background in low relief. The sculpting of two pairs of doors took Ghiberti 48 years to complete. One set of doors is aptly named the "Gates of Paradise."

Donatello (1386–1466) created the earliest free-standing statues of the Renaissance. He travelled throughout Italy, accepting only the commissions that he wanted. His bronze statue of *David,* created for the Medici family, startled people with the sensual, almost living quality of the youthful, nude figure. *David* was a model for later classically inspired statues. Donatello is also famous for a large statue of a Venetian general on horseback, entitled *Gattamelata.*

After his defeat in the Baptistery com-petition, Brunelleschi (1378–1455) turned away from sculpture and set out to become Florence's undisputed master in architecture. Trained in mathematics, he is credited with rediscovering the long-lost principles of perspective during his studies of late Roman, Romanesque, and Byzantine buildings. In 1436 he achieved what was thought to be an impossible task: creating a dome, larger than any in Europe, to cover the vast interior space of Florence's cathedral. Considered by his fellow Florentines as the greatest engineering feat of all time, Brunelleschi's octagonal dome consisted of a strong inner shell and a high, light outer shell that reinforced one another. The cathedral's red dome is still the most recognizable landmark in Florence.

Michelangelo (1475–1564) stands among the anonymous Greek and Roman sculptors as one of the greatest sculptors in art. Although also a great painter, a poet, and later in life, an architect, he considered sculpture to be the most powerful artistic medium of all. The act of taking a huge marble block and discovering the human form within it was, to him, a deeply spiritual process. He said, "Each act, each limb, each bone [is] given life, and lo, man's body is raised breathing, alive, in wax or clay or stone." Besides *David,* his greatest sculptures are the *Pietà,* showing a grieving Mary cradling the dead Christ on her knees, and the heroic, horned figure of *Moses* which decorates the tomb of Pope Julius II.

Still vigorous at age 70, Michelangelo added architecture to his accomplishments. He agreed to complete the dome of St. Peter's Cathedral in the Vatican, which had been designed by an earlier architect in the style of the ancient Roman Pantheon. Borrowing elements of Brunelleschi's dome in Florence, Michelangelo created a smal-

Figure 12-13 *Florence's domed cathedral*

ler, elegantly ribbed circular dome for St. Peter's. He also designed one of Rome's main piazzas, or plazas, a magnificent open space surrounded by stately buildings and classical statues.

Andrea Palladio (1508–1580) started as a humble stonemason, but rose to become the leading architect of the Neo-Classical style. His designs most closely resembled ancient architecture, with classical columns, pediments (the triangular structures resting on top of columns), and rounded arches. He built churches, palaces, and theatres, but he was most famous for the splendid country villas commissioned by noble landowners. The square-shaped Villa Rotunda best illustrates his ideas of classical proportion. It has four porticos (porches), one on each side, that all lead into a central room covered by a dome modelled after the Pantheon. Centuries later, Palladio's designs would be an inspiration for British and American architects.

REFLECT AND ANALYZE

1. In a short essay, discuss either: a) the specific characteristics associated with Renaissance art, sculpture, and architecture; or b) the stylistic and technical developments that made Renaissance painting possible.

2. Research the work of one of the following non-Italian artists: Jan van Eyck, Pieter Brueghel (the Elder), Albrecht Dürer, Hans Holbein the Younger, or El Greco. Choose a painting by the artist that you like. In a report, describe the picture and explain why you like it. Make sure you include a picture of the painting.

3. Develop a collage or bulletin board display that shows the richness of Renaissance art, sculpture, and architecture. Include captions with your pictures or illustrations.

4. Choose and compare a painting by Titian with a painting by Michelangelo or Raphael. Describe the two paintings and the features that make them Renaissance works. Also describe any differences in style and mood that you notice between the two artists.

Figure 12-14 *Villa Rotunda designed by Palladio*

RENAISSANCE SOCIETY, ECONOMY, AND SCIENCE

SOCIETY AND EVERYDAY LIFE

Social changes that had begun in the Late Middle Ages—an influx of people to towns and cities and the growth of a financially based middle class—continued during the Renaissance. Education, training, and books were more available than ever before, especially for those who could afford it. Families began to change. On the medieval manor, large, extended families had been necessary for working the land. In the towns of the Renaissance, where living space was often limited, the nuclear family emerged. (A nuclear family consists only of parents and their children.)

The wealth of towns and cities provided more opportunities for both men and women to work. Young women from the country often became domestic servants in the households of nobles and wealthy business people. Generations of artists and artisans benefited from the heightened appreciation and sponsorship of the arts. Guilds had virtually closed their membership in the late medieval period, but people in newer or more isolated settlements managed to practise trades free of such restrictions.

RENAISSANCE WOMEN

Although most women's lives changed little, the freer intellectual and cultural atmosphere of the Renaissance did benefit women of the upper and middle classes.

Urban schools admitted both boys and girls. Women continued to be barred from pursuing higher education, but some received private tutoring in classical studies in their homes. And for the first time, some queens became the sole rulers of nations, free from the control of a husband or male relative. These queens were Mary I, who ruled England and Scotland from 1553 to 1558, and her half-sister Elizabeth I, patron of William Shakespeare, who ruled from 1558 to 1603. Another queen, Isabella of Spain, was as strong and influential a monarch as her husband, King Ferdinand.

BUSINESS AND TRADE

Humanism, with its emphasis on life on earth rather than the rewards of heaven, led

to the church relaxing its long-standing ban on moneylending and charging interest on borrowed money. It had become apparent that both of these practices were needed to provide the money, or capital, to finance large-scale ventures in manufacturing and trade. This was the start of the economic system known as ***capitalism***, in which wealth created by the charging of interest and by profits from business was in turn used to finance more commercial activities. The result was an astonishing boost to international commerce. The number of European banks increased greatly, many owned and managed by Italians. Banks loaned money to their clients and helped to exchange money from one currency to another, making trade between countries

PERSPECTIVES ON THE PAST
Isabella d'Este (1474–1539)

In what ways did Isabella d'Este represent the ideals of the Renaissance?

One of the smaller but brilliant courts of northern Italy was to be found in the city of Mantua. At the height of the Renaissance it was ruled by Isabella d'Este, an educated, cultured, and witty noblewoman who also possessed uncommon political skill.

Born into the ruling family of Ferrara, a wealthy city-state in the Po river valley, Isabella studied not only the arts befitting a noblewoman—singing, dancing, playing the lute, and embroidery—but also classical literature in Latin and Greek. Her education in the humanities allowed her to converse easily and knowledgeably with scholars and artists, while her interests and accomplishments made her the quintessential Renaissance woman.

When she married Francesco Gonzaga, who later became ruler of Mantua, Isabella dedicated herself to making the city a cultural centre. She set the artistic

fashions and standards of the day. Songs and poems were written in her honour, and printed books were submitted to her for approval. She commissioned paintings from well-known artists, and knew Michelangelo and Leonardo da Vinci. An enthusiastic collector, she acquired so many vases, statues, gems, coins, medals, and clocks that they had to be stored in a separate set of rooms called the "Grotto" (cave). When distinguished guests visited Mantua, Isabella always delighted in showing off her collection.

After her husband was captured by the Venetians in 1494, Isabella ruled Mantua during his absence. Her diplomatic and negotiating skills kept rival princes from taking control of the city. Eventually she secured her husband's release. When he died in 1519, Isabella acted as regent for her son. (A regent governs in place of a ruler who is too young or too ill to rule.) For years, she maintained Mantua's place in the delicate balance among the ruling powers of Italy.

much easier. Businesses also changed: many families formed partnerships with other families to pool their resources for investment.

Venice was one of the main trading and manufacturing centres during the Renaissance. Its location made regular trade possible between Asia, Africa, the Middle East, and Europe. The Rialto, or business district, lay along a stretch of the Grand Canal, attracting traders from near and distant lands. Well-built Venetian galleys transported foreign and domestic goods along waterways to other European ports, such as London, Amsterdam, and Antwerp. Venetian workmanship in the production of fine cloth, glass, and leather goods was also highly valued throughout Europe.

Venice's supremacy began to wane in the sixteenth century, when other European nations, tired of Italy's monopoly in trade, sent out explorers to discover new trade routes to Asia. However, the city remained a vibrant cultural centre even after the Renaissance ended. Trade in the east shifted to the Muslim Ottoman empire, which had replaced the medieval Byzantine empire. Trade in western Europe became dominated by Portugal and Spain, which acquired untold wealth through their discoveries of the Americas as well as their alternative routes to Asia.

The financial capital of northern Europe was the Belgian city of Antwerp, which was under Spanish control in the sixteenth century. Antwerp was the home of the world's first stock exchange, founded in 1460, as well as a lucrative diamond trade. Lyon in France and Amsterdam in Holland were also important northern centres of finance. These cities had their share of well-to-do banking and merchant families, just as the Italian cities did. Across the North Sea, England lagged behind its continental neighbours in exploration and trade until the seventeenth century.

THE DEVELOPMENT OF PRINTING

The advent of the printing press and paper was a genuine revolution. Before they were invented, books were copied laboriously by hand on expensive parchment made from the skin of a sheep or a goat. A simple book with few illustrations might be completed in half a year, while elaborately decorated manuscripts took many years to complete. Several thousand manuscripts existed in all of Europe before the printing press. Virtually all of them suffered from errors and omissions.

The Arabs learned about making paper from the Chinese, and in the 1300s the Europeans acquired this knowledge from the Arabs. Paper was made from rags (especially linen rags) and wood pulp. The growth of Europe's population after the Black Death and a flourishing textile industry resulted in a ready and inexpensive supply of rags for paper-making. Without a cheap source of paper, printing on a large scale might not have been possible.

In Germany and other northern countries, designs were carved on wooden blocks, which were inked and pressed on cloth or paper. By the fifteenth century German engravers had developed movable type, which consisted of small blocks of wood, each engraved with an individual letter. The letters were combined to form words and sentences on a page. When the page had been inked and printed, the letters were taken apart and reassembled into a new page.

The Chinese had earlier invented movable type around 1040, but it is not known whether the Europeans learned the technique from the Chinese or invented it for themselves. In any case, Johann Gutenberg (1400–1468) of Mainz, Germany, is cred-

Figure 12-15 *Modern Venice*

THEN AND NOW
Print Communication

What technological differences can you identify between a Renaissance printing press and a modern press? What other forms of communication now exist? Do you think these newer forms will ever replace printed books? Magazines? Newspapers? Give reasons for your opinion.

Figure 12-16a
A fifteenth-century printing press as depicted in the engraving
The Printing of Books *by Jan van der Straet*

Figure 12-16b
A modern printing press

---

ited with perfecting the printing press around 1453. He used metallic movable type, which did not wear out as quickly as wooden blocks.

Gutenberg published the first printed edition of the Bible in 1455, ushering in the era of printed books. Since most of its pages are 42 lines long, the Gutenberg Bible is sometimes called the 42-line Bible. About 40 copies of this three-volume work survive and are valued among the most precious books in existence.

With the rise of numerous printing shops, inexpensive books could be printed by the thousands and made available to the general public. The wealth of knowledge and learning exploded; moreover, such knowledge could be passed down from one generation to the next. Scholars edited important religious works, while independent printer-publishers produced books on astrology, engineering, botany, and almost any topic of interest. By 1500, at least six million books had been printed in Europe. Gutenberg's printing press was so practical that it remained almost unchanged for five centuries.

SCIENCE

The thirst for learning that greatly advanced the humanities and arts during the Renaissance affected science to a much lesser degree. Leonardo da Vinci made numerous observations about botany, zoology, and human anatomy in his notebooks, yet he was reluctant to make his discoveries known to a wider audience. Most of his notebooks, in fact, were not published until the nineteenth century.

Since classical knowledge was so highly revered, many scientists believed there was little else of value left to be discovered. Others were reluctant to expose themselves to the criticism that new discoveries and theories would inevitably draw from the church and the scientific community. Nevertheless, a few inquisitive and brave individuals made some startling discoveries that contradicted accepted teaching.

The ancient Greek astronomer Ptolemy had taught that the sun, moon, and planets revolved around the earth. The church and European scholars accepted this theory because their general observations seemed to confirm it and because it satisfied their feeling that the earth was the centre of the universe. This view was challenged in the sixteenth century by a Polish astronomer named Nicolaus Copernicus (1473–1543). His book *Concerning the Revolutions of the Celestial Spheres* stated that the sun, not the earth, was the centre of the universe. The earth, Copernicus argued, was just one of the planets that revolved around the sun.

Such a direct contradiction of fundamental beliefs was bitterly opposed by the church and conventional scholars. Copernicus was prevented from publishing his book for 13 years. It was finally published in 1543, the year of his death. Several decades later, the Danish astronomer Tycho Brahe (1546–1601) carefully observed the night sky for years and came to the conclusion that Copernicus was indeed correct. Brahe's assistant, the brilliant German astronomer and mathematician Johannes Kepler (1571–1630), formulated three laws concerning planetary movement around the sun. His calculations showed that the planets moved in elliptical or oval orbits, not in perfect circles, as Ptolemy and Copernicus had believed.

Copernicus, Brahe, and Kepler are considered founders of modern astronomy. They were the first among a growing number of scientists who preferred to observe and experiment for themselves rather than rely on classical or religious authority. The independent spirit and exploratory attitudes encouraged by the Renaissance would ultimately lead to spectacular scientific discoveries in the seventeenth century.

In the fields of anatomy and medicine, Andreas Vesalius (1514–1564) of Flanders was a pioneer. Like Leonardo da Vinci, Vesalius spent hours dissecting corpses in order to study the human body. In 1543 he published *Seven Books on the Structure of the Human Body,* the first detailed and accurate study of human anatomy. His meticulous drawings corrected errors that had existed in medical texts since ancient times.

REFLECT AND ANALYZE

1. Define the word *capitalism.* Explain how you think a capitalist economy would have affected family, social, and religious life during the Renaissance.

2. How important was the printing press to the development of the Renaissance? Write a short essay on this topic, providing evidence to support your statements.

3. "The Renaissance was the age of the individual." Discuss whether or not you think this statement is true, in terms of the development of literature, the arts, and science.

4. Can you give any reasons for the church's opposition to highly independent thinking and experimentation in the sixteenth century?

5. Name one or two inventions of the last 50 years that you feel have had a significant impact on people's lives just as the printing press had in the fifteenth century. Explain the good and bad consequences of these inventions.

THE REFORMATION

"The Word of God cannot be received and cherished by any works whatever, but only by faith. Hence it is clear that, as the soul needs only the Word for its life and righteousness, so it is justified by faith alone and not by any works.…Wherefore it ought to be the first concern of every Christian to lay aside all trust in works, and more and more to strengthen faith alone."

The words above were written by Martin Luther in his work, *A Treatise on Christian Liberty* (1520). These and other statements by Luther signified a fundamental rethinking of the church's role in religious life that would split the single Roman Catholic church apart. Such challenges to the church's authority were not new, but a complex interplay of social, cultural, and political forces in the sixteenth century would radically change Christianity and with it the course of western history. The reforming movement is known as the **Reformation**, and the bold, independent ideas that circulated among religious thinkers were certainly born of the Renaissance atmosphere of inquiry. Before looking at this period, let us first examine earlier challenges to Roman Catholicism, some of which set the stage for the events during the Reformation.

EARLIER CHALLENGES TO ROMAN CATHOLICISM

In the eleventh century, Christians in southern France calling themselves the Albigensians broke away from the Roman Catholic church and established a separate church with its own bishops and priests. The Albigensians viewed human existence and materialism as evil and aspired to live a completely spiritual life free from the worldly influence of the Roman church and its priests. Pope Innocent III declared the Albigensians to be heretics and launched a holy war against them in 1208. The result was a bloody conflict in which 20 000 people, both Albigensian and Catholic, died in one town alone. As the crusaders stormed town after town, many Albigensians chose to die as heretics rather than swear loyalty to the Catholic church.

The corruption and worldliness exhibited by the church during the Babylonian Captivity and the Great Schism laid it open to harsh criticism in the fourteenth century. John Wycliffe (1320–1384), a doctor of theology at Oxford University, argued that the sacraments, clergy, and even the pope were not necessary for salvation. A person could achieve grace simply by reading the Bible and following God's word. To make the Bible accessible to ordinary people, Wycliffe translated it from Latin into English. His ideas were well-received in his own country and other parts of Europe, but Pope Gregory XI branded him a heretic.

The Bohemian philosopher and reformer Jan Hus (1369–1415) also criticized

Figure 12-17 *A woodcut by Lucas Cranach depicting Martin Luther (left) and Jan Hus serving bread and wine at communion*

church corruption and translated Wycliffe's writings into Czech. For his activities, Hus was excommunicated and burned at the stake. As the Italian Renaissance gained momentum, Girolamo Savonarola (1452–1498) of Florence attacked church and secular leaders for luxury and vice. Although his views were influential for a time, eventually he, too, was burned at the stake for heresy.

The church's tactic of generally suppressing dissenting voices rather than ad-

dressing concerns did nothing to improve its image. Once a uniter of Europe, the church was also increasingly besieged by feelings of nationalism among northerners and by a general resentment of papal authority and taxes.

CAUSES OF THE REFORMATION

In the same way that humanists looked to the ancients for inspiration and guidance, religious reformers desired the church to return to the simpler, more genuine values of early Christianity. People's grievances against the church were many. To pay for such ambitious and expensive projects as the building of St. Peter's Cathedral in Rome, for example, church leaders exploited money-making activities to the fullest. Pope Leo X (1513–1521) generated an annual income of more than a million dollars from the sale of over 2000 church offices. Many appointments went to rich nobles who lacked clerical training and who were more interested in the income they received from a diocese than in serving the community.

The sale of letters of indulgence was another heavily criticized practice. Indulgences, in effect, were pardons granted to sinners in exchange for certain acts of repentance or good works. It was believed that if a person undertook such atonement while still living, he or she would lessen the punishment required in purgatory to enter heaven. Originally, indulgences were granted to crusaders, pilgrims, and people who said certain prayers or did good deeds. Eventually, the church accepted money payments in place of acts of service. In the 16th century, the practice had degenerated to the point that indulgences could even be bought for dead souls in purgatory.

Resentment toward the papacy was especially strong in northern Europe. Here, people did not feel the pull of Roman tradition as the Italians did. English and French monarchs had long been displeased to see revenue flow from their lands to the church while it was exempt from government taxation. Ordinary people, too, resented their church payments being spent on extravagant construction projects far away in Italy rather than used for more deserving purposes at home.

Germany, which did not have a strong, central monarchy to defend local interests against the papacy, displayed the greatest anti-Rome sentiment. The Germans, like the Dutch and Flemish, also possessed a natural spirituality that made them impatient with external observances that disrupted the working day and seemed to have little to do with genuine piety. Differences in belief about how the church should be run and what sacraments it should administer were ultimately the source of irreparable rifts among various groups. Even reformers who wanted to change the church from within, such as Erasmus, dared to suggest that the sacraments and priests were not necessary for salvation.

Not surprisingly, perhaps, it was a northerner—a German—who brought long-simmering grievances and doctrinal differences to a head and crystallized them into action. That individual was Martin Luther.

MARTIN LUTHER

The story of Martin Luther (1483–1546) is a long and fascinating one, and needs to be told in some detail for an understanding of Protestantism. He was born into a German peasant family, which eventually prospered in copper mining. As a young man, he was sent to university to prepare for a more prestigious career in law. However, on a July day in 1505, he decided to give everything up to become a monk. What prompted this sudden decision? During a thunderstorm he was nearly struck by lightning, an experience which he interpreted to be a sign from God. Within a few years he was ordained and had accepted a post as professor of theology at the University of Wittenberg.

Scholars have commented a great deal

Figure 12-18 *Martin Luther*

on Luther's gnawing self-doubt and feelings of guilt. For years he was preoccupied with a sense of his own unworthiness to be saved, despite such cleansing rituals as prayer, confessions, and fasting. In despair, he looked to the Bible for guidance and eventually found it in the phrase, "The just shall live by faith." Luther later wrote: "This passage of [St.] Paul became to me a gate of heaven." He realized that humans, as imperfect and sinful beings, could not be saved on their own merit or by good works. Salvation was the result of God's mercy and grace, and therefore an individual's only hope of being saved was to have faith. Everything else, including most of the sacraments and the clergy, was unnecessary.

Despite his penchant for self-questioning, once Luther formulated his convictions, he stuck to them with resolute determination. Accordingly, he did not hesitate to act at the first appropriate opportunity. In 1517, a Dominican friar named Johann Tetzel came to Wittenberg to sell indulgences to finance the building of St. Peter's at the Vatican. Tetzel claimed that every time money entered the box, a soul was released from purgatory into heaven. Outraged by such claims, Luther produced *Ninety-five Theses* (statements) attacking the sale of indulgences and other matters of doctrine. He nailed this list to the door of the university church on October 31, 1517, offering to debate about church reform with other scholars.

The matter might have started and ended in Wittenberg, had it not been for the power of the printing press. Luther's theses were translated from Latin into German, printed, and circulated all over Germany. His views were widely supported, particularly by German nobles who saw an opportunity to free their states from Rome's political and economic control.

The glare of public attention compelled Luther to work out and explain his ideas more fully. In treatises and sermons, he questioned the authority of the pope and church councils and argued that only two sacraments—baptism and the Lord's Supper (the taking of holy bread and wine)—were necessary, having been performed by Jesus and the apostles. He also stated that the priesthood included all believers, not just those ordained by the church, and that priests should be allowed to marry. Pope Leo X could not ignore such heresies and issued an order of excommunication in 1520, giving Luther 60 days to recant, or take back, his statements. On the final day Luther threw the order into a bonfire before a cheering crowd of students and citizens.

With this gesture, he became a hero among German peasants, townspeople, and princes.

A second order of excommunication was issued, which required the approval of the government. Luther was summoned before the Imperial Diet, the parliamentary assembly of the Holy Roman Empire, in 1521. It took courage for him to attend because of the very real possibility of being arrested and tried for heresy. Yet he appeared before the assembly and solemnly declared that to recant would go against his conscience. The Diet declared him a heretic, denied him protection of any kind, and forbade the distribution of his works.

Luckily for Luther, one of the princes in the assembly, Frederick III of Saxony, gave him refuge at his fortified castle in

THROUGH THEIR EYES

Ninety-five Theses, by Martin Luther

What do you think of Martin Luther's statements? Explain the reasons why his words had such a great influence on people in the sixteenth century.

10. *Those priests act ignorantly and wickedly who, in the case of the dying, reserve canonical penalties for purgatory.*

27. *They preach only human doctrines who say that as soon as the money clinks into the money chest, the soul flies out of purgatory.*

28. *It is certain that when money clinks into the money chest, greed and avarice can be increased; but when the church intercedes, the result is in the hands of God alone.*

31. *The man who actually buys indulgences is as rare as he who is really penitent; indeed, he is exceedingly rare.*

32. *Those who believe that they can be certain of their salvation because they have indulgence letters will be eternally damned, together with their teachers.*

36. *Any truly repentant Christian has a right to full remission of penalty and guilt, even without indulgence letters.*

44. *Because love grows by works of love, man thereby becomes better. Man does not, however, become better by means of indulgences but is merely freed from penalties.*

45. *Christians are to be taught that he who sees a needy man and passes him by, yet gives his money for indulgences, does not buy papal indulgences but God's wrath.*

50. *Christians are to be taught that if the pope knew the exactions of the indulgence preachers, he would rather that the basilica of St. Peter were burned to ashes than built up with skin, flesh, and bones of his sheep.*

Wartburg. During his year there, Luther began to translate the Bible into German. With such a Bible available, people would not need the services of a priest to interpret the scriptures for them. On his return to Wittenberg, he set about establishing a new church according to his already declared principles. Services were to be conducted in German, not Latin, with more participation from the congregation. Church structure was simplified and clergy were allowed to marry. There were only two sacraments, with no formal rituals of penance such as fasting. Luther himself wrote several hymns to be sung at services.

His decisive break with the Roman Catholic church lost him the support of Erasmus and other humanists who believed in reconciliatory reform. However, the Lutheran church was embraced by the German nobility for political reasons and by an urban middle class interested in reading the Bible for themselves. By the time Luther died in 1546, northern Germany and most of Scandinavia was Lutheran, while the southern German states remained Catholic. This was just the beginning of religious, as well as political, divisions throughout Europe.

The name **Protestant** arose out of the formal protests made by German princes when, in 1529, the Imperial Diet declared that they did not have the right to set the religion of their subjects. Since that time, any Christian church that is not Eastern Orthodox or Roman Catholic has been called Protestant.

Other Protestant Reformers

Once given life, the Reformation movement grew irresistibly. A Swiss priest named Ulrich Zwingli (1484–1531) took Protestantism even further than Luther did.

Zwingli persuaded worshippers in Zurich to remove all images and decorations from their churches and to adopt a service focusing on sermons rather than rituals. He established the practice of communion as a symbolic representation of the Last Supper instead of asserting, as the Catholic and Lutheran rituals did, that Christ's body and blood were physically present in the bread and wine. Zwingli's ideas were adopted throughout northern Switzerland, but war broke out in the southern states during which Zwingli himself was killed. To settle the conflict, Swiss leaders signed an agreement in 1531 that allowed each district, called a canton, to choose its own religion.

Next to Luther, the most influential Protestant was a humanist named John Calvin (1509–1564). Born in France, Calvin fled to Geneva, Switzerland, as a young law student when his own government began persecuting suspected heretics. He would remain in Geneva for the rest of his life. Calvin's great contribution was to organize the ideas of earlier reformers into a clear doctrine that could be followed by Protestants anywhere. In addition, he specified a four-tiered church structure consisting of pastors, doctors, laypeople called elders, and deacons at the top level.

Calvin introduced the influential concept of **predestination**, which stated that a person's salvation was determined before birth and that nothing could change it. Such a doctrine was not without its problems, as it flew in the face of the idea that salvation could be attained through faith. Calvin's solution was to declare that everyone should live by the highest moral standards, because there was no way of knowing for sure who the elect (the saved individuals) were.

Figure 12-19 *John Calvin*

Calvinists, accordingly, were required to follow strict rules governing every aspect of life. They had to observe the rules given in the Bible, refrain from work or pleasure on the Sabbath, and pursue the virtues of thrift and hard work. Immodest attire and frivolous activities such as dancing and games were outlawed. The Calvinists did not always get their way: although they attempted to replace taverns serving ale with sober coffeehouses filled with Bibles, public protest resulted in the taverns being reopened.

THE SPREAD OF PROTESTANTISM

In one short century, the religious map of Europe was fundamentally changed. In the 1400s, it had been a single, vast expanse united under Catholicism; at the end of the 1500s, it had become a patchwork quilt of distinct religious identities. Now, religion as well as politics divided people and pitted

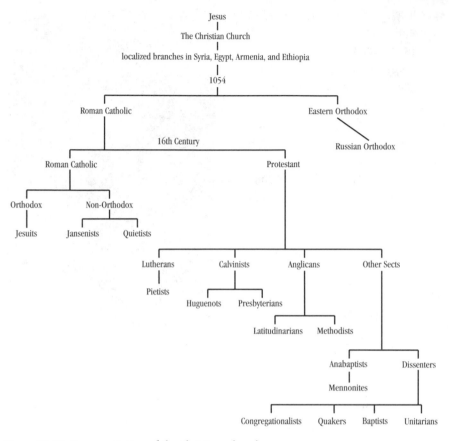

Figure 12-20 *Fragmentation of the Christian church*

violence of any kind. They also preached religious tolerance, in sharp contrast to the uncompromising views of many Protestant groups. One group of Anabaptists fled to Pennsylvania in the New World to escape persecution. Descendants of those settlers became Mennonites, some of whom settled in Kitchener, Ontario. The Amish and the Quakers also trace much of their ancestry to the Anabaptists.

Other branches of Protestantism gained a much wider following. Calvinism was the most popular Protestant church of all, with followers in Holland, Germany, France, and England. French Calvinists were called Huguenots, while English Calvinists were called Puritans. Scotsman John Knox (c. 1514–1572), who studied in Geneva, based his Presbyterian church of Scotland on Calvinist principles.

The Protestant Church of England followed quite a different path of development than the others, being more a product of politics than of religious conviction.

them against one another. Groups of Catholics and Protestants could be equally intolerant, persecuting religious minorities within their own territories and engaging in wars with each other. Some ideological conflicts would last for years, even centuries. A few, such as those that later began in Ireland, have never been resolved.

Specific aspects of Protestant thought formed the basis of some relatively small sects. For example, the Anabaptists adapted the austere principles of Zwingli to create their own religion. Conscientious duty, moral discipline, and a simple life free of materialism were central to the Anabaptists. However, whereas Zwingli advocated the use of force, the Anabaptists opposed

Figure 12-21 *The battle between Huegenots and Catholics in Paris on St. Bartholomew's Day, 24 August 1572*

Henry VIII (1491–1547) desperately wanted a son to become his heir. After 18 years of marriage, he and his wife, Catherine of Aragon, had only one surviving child, a daughter named Mary Tudor. Henry asked Pope Clement VII to grant him an ***annulment***, an official statement declaring the marriage invalid. Henry would then be free to marry another woman. The situation was further complicated by the fact that he was already in love with Catherine's lady-in-waiting, the teen-aged Anne Boleyn.

Although popes had annulled marriages before, Clement did not want to offend Catherine's nephew, the powerful Holy Roman emperor Charles V. He therefore refused Henry's request. The enraged king, supported by advisors who had Protestant leanings, broke with Rome. He appointed Thomas Cranmer as Archbishop of Canterbury, who granted him an annulment. After his marriage to Anne Boleyn, Henry passed the Act of Supremacy through Parliament in 1534, making him "the only supreme head on Earth of the [new] Church of England." Unfortunately for Anne Boleyn, she too produced no male heir, only a daughter named Elizabeth. Henry had her tried for adultery and beheaded. He would marry four more women, only one of whom bore him a son, Edward.

Henry closed down all the Catholic monasteries and convents in England and confiscated their lands, which were sold to nobles, wealthy farmers, and merchants. The Church of England, or Anglican church as it was also known, maintained traditional Catholic practices, although Henry did allow the use of an English Bible and the marriage of clergy.

After Henry's death, religious turmoil erupted in England. The 10-year-old Edward VI was dominated by Calvinist Protestants who wanted more changes to the Anglican church. Thomas Cranmer initiated the *Book of Common Prayer*, outlining the official rituals and prayers for the Anglican service. Some Protestant elements were added, but the service still remained basically Catholic.

When Edward died in 1553, his half-sister Mary Tudor became Queen Mary I. A devout Catholic, Mary attempted to restore Catholicism in England. Her execution of hundreds of Protestants earned her the nickname of "Bloody Mary." Her younger half-sister, Elizabeth, was Protestant and far more popular than she. Fearing that Elizabeth was involved in a plot against her, Mary placed her sister under house arrest for nearly a year. This made the princess even more popular with the people.

When Mary died in 1558, Elizabeth became queen. During her 45-year reign, she would bring much-needed order,

Figure 12-22 *Queen Elizabeth I*

stability, and prosperity to England. In 1570, she passed a new Act of Supremacy, again making the monarch the head of the firmly Protestant Church of England, now the offical religion of the land.

REFLECT AND ANALYZE

1. Explain how political cultural, and economic factors contributed to the drive for religious reform.

2. Why did people in northern countries object to the sale of indulgences, particularly for such projects as the building of St. Peter's basilica in Rome?

3. Do you think Martin Luther's break with the Catholic church was inevitable? What factors prevented his ideas from being accepted by the Catholic church?

4. "The English Reformation was a political instead of a religious development." Do you agree with this statement? Explain why or why not, providing evidence to support your opinion.

THE CATHOLIC REFORMATION AND COUNTER-REVOLUTION

For centuries, the Catholic church had been largely deaf to calls for reform and to suggestions from its best thinkers. Now, with people leaving the church in droves, it was imperative that its leaders seriously reexamine its purpose and principles. Two separate but related movements developed. During the *Catholic Reformation* that started in the 1520s, the church implemented various reforms and engaged in a long period of self-reflection that culminated in a renewed set of Catholic principles. At the same time, the church became more militant, launching a *Counter-Reformation* to deal forcefully with the rising tide of Protestantism.

Most Catholic reforms were aimed at returning the church to some of its earlier, less worldly values. However, its leaders were reluctant to revise the hierarchical structure and emphasis on priestly sacraments which had been their privilege for so long. As in earlier times, the religious orders provided the best and most genuine models of change. Several new orders were established, the most influential being the Society of Jesus. A Spanish nobleman and soldier named Ignatius Loyola (1491–1556) started the order after he was permanently crippled in a war against the French. During his convalescence, he read about the lives of St. Dominic and St. Francis, and resolved to become a holy man like them. The pope officially sanctioned the Jesuit Order, as the society was more commonly known, in 1540.

The Jesuits did much to restore the prestige and power of the Catholic church. Loyola organized the order like an army. Its members were called "Soldiers of Christ," and Loyola was their first "general." Also like military men, the Jesuits swore complete obedience to the pope, underwent a period of rigorous training, and carried out their extensive "missions" with great discipline and conviction.

One of their most important missions was to gain new converts to the Catholic church. To that end, the Jesuits travelled extensively in the New World and Asia, attracting thousands of people to Catholicism. In Germany and Eastern Europe, they brought back many Protestants into the Catholic fold. Known as outstanding, dedicated teachers, the Jesuits also set up hundreds of schools and universities throughout the world.

Pope Paul III, who was elected in 1534, called together a council of high church officials to review Catholic practices. The Council of Trent met in three separate sessions between 1545 and 1563. Taking a conservative position, the council reaffirmed most aspects of Catholicism, including the importance of all of the sacraments and the role of priests as mediators between God and churchgoers. Priests and monks were to undergo better training, to strictly observe celibacy, and to be above reproach in their conduct and teaching. Bishops no longer could live outside of their dioceses. Finally, the council set limits on the sale of indulgences, and banned the sale of church offices altogether.

To combat Protestantism, Catholic leaders issued an index of banned books, which included not only those by Protestants but also many by Renaissance humanists. The church had become wary of the free flow of new ideas, even when they did not specifically concern religion. The Inquisition was revived to deal with heretics and was most active in Spain, Portugal, and Italy. The Spanish Inquisition was especially powerful and especially feared, since centuries of fighting the Muslims had heightened the religious zeal of Spanish Catholics.

Figure 12-23 *The Spanish inquisition*

As religious persecution grew, witch-hunting became popular among both Protestants and Catholics. Many people believed that the devil was to blame for the religious turmoil and that witchcraft was on the rise. Witches who were agents of the devil and possessed magical powers, and therefore had to be rooted out and burned at the stake. Most of those accused of witchcraft were women, although a few men faced similar attacks. Society's outcasts—the poor, the isolated, the mentally unstable—were the main victims of persecution. Between 1450 and 1750, tens of thousands of women and men were killed as witches. Most accusations of witchcraft were based on fear, ignorance, spite, or hatred of women. The witch-hunting craze was strongest in Germany, Switzerland, and France, areas of the greatest religious conflict.

flourished since worldly success was considered a sign of God's favour. The idea of making a profit or lending money at interest was no longer frowned upon.

Yet, the emphasis on the dignity of work had its downside as well. The new system allowed workers to be exploited mercilessly. Women and children were often forced to labour for long hours for low pay.

The Protestant Reformation strengthened the family unit as Protestant preachers spoke about husbands and wives as "helpmates" in the family. The importance of family love was emphasized. Marriage choices were less frequently based on economics and more often made for personal reasons. The wife increasingly played an important role in the moral education of children as the family was considered the best place to teach Christian ideals.

The role of women was also affected by the Protestant Reformation. Whereas the Catholic church provided an environment in which women could devote themselves to religious life, Protestantism did not afford the same opportunity. Yet, by encouraging all followers to read the Bible for themselves, Protestantism encouraged education for women.

REFLECT AND ANALYZE

1. Describe the measures the Catholic church took to combat the spread of Protestantism. How effective were these various measures, in your opinion? Explain your answer.

2. In groups of five students each, imagine that you are the Council of Trent. Formulate five recommendations for reforming the Catholic church and for keeping people from leaving it. Present your ideas to the rest of the class, who should vote on whether or not to accept each recommendation.

3. What made the Jesuits effective missionaries for the Catholic church?

4. Why did witch-hunting become a popular fad? Do you think people accused of witchcraft were being made scapegoats for other troubles? Explain.

THE EFFECTS OF THE PROTESTANT REFORMATION

The Protestant Reformation had profound effects upon European life. Most notably, it altered the religious composition of Europe. It affected attitudes and practices in work and the business community. It helped to reshape public attitudes towards human relationships and the family unit.

Both Calvin and Luther glorified the dignity of work and the "Protestant ethic" of hard work, little extravagance, and careful savings became admirable human qualities. Since Protestantism encouraged individual competition, in the marketplace it was also encouraged. In fact, competition

REFLECT AND ANALYZE

1. Draw up a list of the main differences between Roman Catholic and Calvinist beliefs and practices in the sixteenth century. Explain whether you think these two churches could have overcome their differences and been united into one.

2. Make a visit to one Catholic and one Protestant church in your city or town. Take a look at how the churches are built and decorated. If you like, attend part or all of a service. What differences, if any, do you notice between the two churches?

LOOKING BACK

The Renaissance represents a pivotal point in western history. On one hand, it provides a bridge to the distant past through its revival of classical learning and artistic ideals. On the other hand, it is connected to our own modern age through its emphasis on humanism and belief in individuality.

Like the period during which ancient Greece flourished, the Renaissance was a "golden age" for the arts. Its achievements in painting, sculpture, and architecture became the new "classics" for generations of later artists. The works of William Shakespeare set a standard for literature. When we hear a person described as a "Renaissance man" or "Renaissance woman," we know that he or she has exceptional and diverse talents.

The explosion in new ideas led people to question many things, including church doctrine. The printing press helped to spread ideas for reform quickly and to a large audience, making it much more difficult for the church to fight change than in the past. Today, we still recognize the power of the printed word to communicate information rapidly and inexpensively.

Whereas the Renaissance was a cultural revolution, the Reformation was a religious one. Religion once united Europe; now it divided Europe, sometimes even more strongly than politics. As Protestantism grew, the gap between it and Catholicism became larger. Modern Christian churches are the direct result of developments in both Protestant and Catholic reform.

In addition to the Renaissance and the Reformation, there is a third significant event of this era: the exploration of areas previously unknown to the Europeans. It is worth noting that European domination left a permanent mark on peoples around the world. By exploiting the diverse resources of the Americas and suppressing aboriginal peoples, European countries such as Spain, Portugal, and England grew rich and powerful. By 1700, there were few regions of the world that had not been touched by Europeans.

THE BYZANTINE EMPIRE:
Land at the Crossroads

"Owhat a splendid city, how stately, how fair, how many monasteries therein, how many palaces raised by sheer labour in its broadways and streets, how many works of art, marvellous to behold; it would be weariness to tell of the abundance of all good things; of gold and of silver, garments of manifold fashion, and such sacred relics. Ships are at all times putting in at this port, so that there is nothing that men want that is not brought hither."

The Frenchman Fulk of Chartres is speaking of his impressions of the city of Constantinople in the eleventh century. Like other Europeans, he is dazzled by the busy streets, magnificent buildings, art treasures, and bewildering array of exotic and precious goods to be found in this glittering capital of the Byzantine empire. Whereas the people of western Europe have only recently revived trade with distant lands and started to live in towns, Constantinople has for centuries been a bustling centre of commerce between Mediterranean countries and Asia. With as many as one million people of diverse ethnic backgrounds—Greek, Roman, Turkish, Arab, Jewish, Persian, Northern European, Slavic, and others—roaming its streets, Constantinople is the richest and most cosmopolitan city in the western world.

Figure 13-1
Mosaic showing Constantine holding a replica of his city

The people of the flourishing empire that lay on the border between Europe and Asia did not call themselves Byzantines. The word ***Byzantine*** comes from Byzantium, the name of the small Greek trading town which the emperor Constantine made his "New Rome" in 330 CE. Modern historians use "Byzantine" and "Byzantium" to distinguish this Christian civilization from the earlier, pagan Roman civilization. In fact, the Byzantines considered themselves and their empire to be Roman. As they watched the western part of the old empire fall under the control of the barbarians, the Byzantines strengthened the eastern empire and firmly maintained classical traditions.

THE LAND BETWEEN EAST AND WEST

CONSTANTINOPLE

Constantine called his city New Rome, but it was eventually renamed in his honour. (Constantinople means the "City of Constantine.") The great Roman emperor could not have chosen a

Figure 13-2 *Location of Constantinople*

more advantageous site for his new capital.

The city lay at one of the great junctions of the world, linking east and west, north and south. Situated on a small peninsula that was the easternmost point of the European land mass, Constantinople was directly across a narrow strait from Asia Minor. The strait, called the Bosporus, was 27 km long and less than a kilometre wide—the narrowest water crossing between Asia and Europe. Constantinople was the largest city on the most important land route between the two continents. At the same time, the Bosporus, controlled by the empire's naval fleet, was the only sea passageway for ships travelling between the Mediterranean and Aegean Seas in the south and the Black Sea in the north. Truly, then, Constantinople was the hub of trade from all four directions of the compass.

Shaped like a triangle (see Figure 13-3), with two sides surrounded by water, the city was well positioned to defend itself from attacks by sea or land. An 8-km inlet along the northern shore provided a sheltered harbour, which was further protected by a chain extending across the mouth of the inlet. This inlet was the Golden Horn,

Figure 13-3 *City plan of Constantinople*

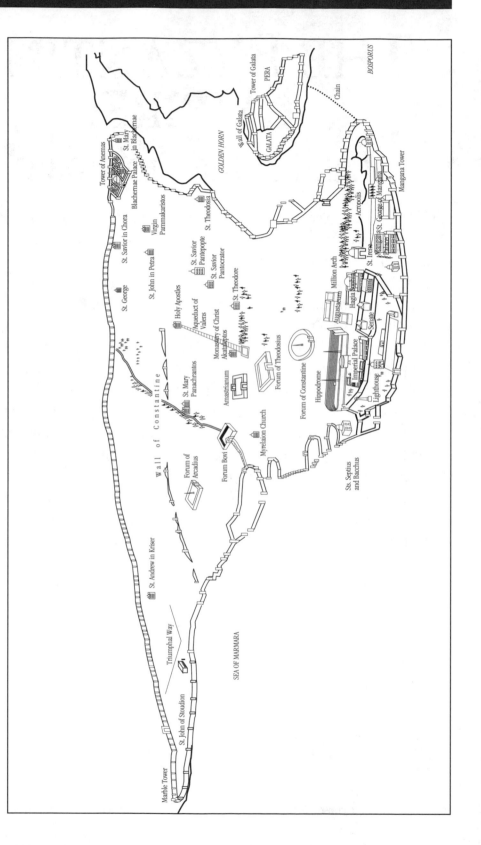

named for its shape and the international riches deposited on its docks. The Sea of Marmara lapping Constantinople's southern shore was constantly patrolled by imperial navy ships. The third, landward side of the city was protected by a thick wall, while walls also extended right around the coastal areas. Constantinople's formidable defences enabled it to withstand numerous raids over the centuries by Muslims from the east and south, and barbarian tribes from the north.

In the fifth century, the wall of Constantine was replaced by a new triple wall further west to make room for the growing populace. The wall was punctuated with numerous watchtowers and fortified gates. At the wall's southwest end was the Golden Gate, the grand, arched entrance to the city used for welcoming newly crowned emperors and victorious generals.

Figure 13-4
Constantine

Constantine liked to point out that his city was built on several hills and was divided into 14 districts, just as Rome was. However, with an area of twenty square kilometres, the Byzantine city was about four times the size of Rome. The main street was called the *Mese* (Middle Road) and ran from the western wall to the imperial district near the waterfront. Along this grand boulevard were several huge forums or squares, enclosed by colonnades and containing tall, ornamental columns and royal statues. All important imperial processions took place along the *Mese*. It was also home to Constantinople's finest, costliest shops. The street ended at the downtown centre where the most important buildings lay: the Hippodrome, a huge entertainment arena; the domed Church of Hagia Sophia ("HI-ya So-FEE-ah"); the Senate; and the Imperial Palace.

GEOGRAPHY AND CLIMATE

Although the size of the Byzantine empire grew and shrank during its thousand years of existence, its influence was mostly contained within certain physical boundaries. To the north, the River Danube and the Black Sea formed a frontier which the empire never crossed, although the Byzantine language and culture would play a significant role in Russia's development. To the west, the mountains along the eastern shore of the Adriatic were another natural barrier. To the east and southeast, mountains again separated the empire from the plains of Persia and Arabia.

Constantinople enjoyed a temperate climate, never too hot or too cold. Fertile valleys west of the city and along the coast of Asia Minor yielded grains for making bread, abundant fresh vegetables, and grapes for wine. The Bosporus and Sea of Marmara teemed with fish. Fresh water was always in plentiful supply, due to a system of aqueducts that led into Constantinople as well as numerous cisterns inside the city for holding rainwater. Being self-sufficient in food and water was a great advantage whenever enemies tried to lay siege to the capital. Only additional grain had to be imported from Egypt to accommodate the enormous population.

In the north, the cold, mountainous lands of the Balkans were covered with forests that provided wood and furs. Copper, lead, silver, and small quantities of iron and gold were mined in Asia Minor. A deep blue stone called lapis lazuli, highly prized as an ornamental gem, came from Nicomedia, an important fortress and stopping point on the road leading west to the Byzantine capital.

Unlike western Europe, the Byzantine empire maintained an excellent system of roads, some built on earlier Roman highways, throughout Asia Minor and other regions. While these land routes were important for commercial and military purposes, the sea routes were Constantinople's most essential link with all of the other civilizations of the world.

HISTORICAL OVERVIEW

The Byzantine civilization began in 330, when Constantinople became the capital of the Roman empire, and ended in 1453 when the city fell to the Ottoman Turks. The Byzantines combined Roman practices with Christianity and eastern influences to create a distinctive culture of their own.

The period can be roughly divided into three parts: the Early Period, from 330 to about 680; the Middle Period, from 680 to the 1050s; and the Late Period, from the 1050s to 1453. Many historians consider Byzantium's "golden age" to be the reign of Justinian in the sixth century, when the empire grew to its largest size and when many distinctive aspects of Byzantine civilization emerged. Although the Byzantines enjoyed influence and wealth for centuries afterward, their civilization never quite reached the same heights again.

THE EARLY BYZANTINE PERIOD

As you read in Chapter 8, the Roman empire was divided into western and eastern parts in the third century. However, Constantine the Great (c. 285–337) defeated three other co-rulers in 323 and reunited the empire. After becoming sole emperor, he decided to make a fresh start in a new capital. Rome, thick with political enemies plotting conspiracies and assassinations, had become too dangerous a place to live. Constantinople was better situated than Rome in terms of trade and defence, enjoyed a better climate, and was far more spacious than the old capital.

Wishing to make Constantinople even more magnificent than Rome, Constantine constructed many buildings and squares on classical models. He imported numerous Roman statues and commissioned other art works, especially huge, carved columns, to decorate public spaces. In one vital respect, however, Constantinople was not like ancient Rome, because it was a Christian city. Constantine built the Hagia Sophia (the Church of Holy Wisdom) in 537 and many other churches, which became filled with relics of the saints. During the medieval period, only Rome rivalled Constantinople as the centre of Christianity.

The Roman empire was again divided into two parts in the fourth century. Whereas the western empire disintegrated under the barbarian onslaught, the eastern empire remained intact due to its location further east, better defences, and most important of all, the skill of its emperors in negotiating with the Germanic tribes. For example, the Byzantines, like the Romans before them, did not force non-Byzantines to adopt their ways. They also engaged German warriors as soldiers in the imperial army, granting them land, money, and other privileges.

It is perhaps no wonder, then, that the eastern empire escaped the fate of its west-

Figure 13-5 *A carved ivory casket showing the triumphal emperor's entry into Constantinople*

ern counterpart and did not lose its classical heritage and traditions. The early Byzantine emperors and government officials were Roman in every way, speaking, writing, and worshipping in Latin. But the empire's eastern orientation dictated that, by the seventh century, the primary language would be Greek. Constantinople itself was on Greek soil, and later emperors, some of them ethnically neither Roman nor Greek, were nevertheless Greek in upbringing and outlook. Despite this fundamental change, the Byzantines always called themselves Romans.

THE RULE OF JUSTINIAN

It was during the reign of the greatest emperor, Justinian (527–565), that the Byzantine civilization matured and took on its own character. Both Justinian and his wife Theodora were people of humble origin, but their ambition and ability enabled them to rise to the top of Byzantine society.

Justinian was born to a family of peasants from Macedonia in the Balkans. Earlier, his illiterate uncle Justin had gone to Constantinople to join the army. Justin rose through the ranks and fought off rivals to become emperor in 518. He gave his nephew a thorough education; and Justinian, in turn, acted as the emperor's most important advisor. When Justin died in 527, Justinian assumed the throne at the age of 45. He brought to his position an impressive military background as well as considerable knowledge in law, music, religion, and architecture.

As emperor, Justinian selected advisors and officials based on ability rather than on wealth or social position. Many of his advisors, therefore, came from common families. Justinian never forgot his own

Figure 13-6 *Mosaic of Justinian and his court from the Church of San Vitale, Ravenna, Italy*

modest background. The sixth-century historian Procopius said that he was "the most accessible person in the world. For even men of low estate and altogether obscure had complete freedom not only to come before him but to converse with him."

A disciplined and energetic man, Justinian set about fulfilling his greatest

dream: restoring the Roman empire to its former glory by reconquering the western lands lost to the barbarians. His first step was to reorganize and strengthen the military forces. He appointed Belisarius as general in charge of the reforms.

The cavalry and the militia were most in need of change. The cavalry consisted of units of mounted soldiers who were hired

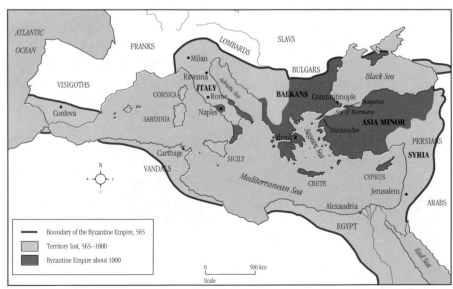

Figure 13-7 *The Byzantine empire, 565–1000*

THE BYZANTINE EMPIRE:

EARLY BYZANTINE PERIOD
330 TO C. 680

POLITICAL DEVELOPMENTS

- Constantine moves the capital of the Roman empire from Rome to Byzantium (330)
- the old Roman empire is permanently split into western and eastern parts (395)
- the western Roman empire collapses (476)
- Justinian becomes emperor (527) and reconquers North Africa, Italy, and southern Spain, restoring the former Roman empire for a short period (533–565)
- Justinian slaughters 30 000 rioters in the Hippodrome during the Nika revolt (532)
- Justinian establishes a legal code based on Roman law (529–533)
- western barbarians and Persians invade the Byzantine empire (568–early 600s)
- Heraclius becomes emperor (610), reorganizes the empire into themes, and gives land to peasant soldiers
- Muslim Arabs conquer North Africa, Egypt, Palestine, Syria, and parts of Asia Minor (660–680)
- the Arabs attack Constantinople but do not capture it (673–678)

CULTURAL DEVELOPMENTS

- Constantine models New Rome (Constantinople) on ancient Rome (330) and builds the first Church of Hagia Sophia (330s)
- icons become popular in the Byzantine empire (330s onward)
- St. Basil writes a code for monastic life (370s)
- Theodosius makes Christianity the empire's official religion (380)
- an early university is founded in Constantinople (425)
- after the Nika revolt, Justinian rebuilds the Hagia Sophia (532–537) and other buildings in Constantinople
- Justinian's reign is a golden age of learning and culture during which Greek replaces Latin as the language of everyday life and the church (527–565)
- the mosaics of Ravenna, Italy, are created during Justinian's reign
- the historian Procopius documents Justinian's life and military campaigns (500s)

TECHNOLOGICAL/ ECONOMIC DEVELOPMENTS

- Constantine introduces the bezant, a gold coin which becomes the most stable unit of exchange in the Mediterranean world
- Chinese silkworms are smuggled into the Byzantine empire (c. 550)
- during Justinian's reign, Constantinople becomes the trading capital of the civilized world
- Callimachus invents Greek fire, which is used for the first time during the Arab siege of Constantinople (670s)

MIDDLE BYZANTINE PERIOD
680-1050s

- Leo III defeats Muslims during a second attack on Constantinople (717) and continues Heraclius's reorganization of the provinces (717–740)
- 10–year-old Constantine VI gains the throne, with his mother Irene acting as regent (780–797)
- Irene rules as the first Byzantine empress (797–802)
- a Macedonian dynasty of emperors reigns over Byzantium (802–1056)
- Basil II becomes emperor (963) and wages war against the Bulgarians for 20 years
- Basil II, "Slayer of the Bulgars," blinds nearly 14 000 Bulgarian soldiers captured in battle (1014)

- the iconoclastic emperor Leo III orders all religious icons destroyed (726)
- Pope Leo III defies the Byzantines by crowning Charlemagne "Emperor of the Romans" (800)
- Byzantine missionaries convert Slavic peoples to Christianity (800s)
- two Greek monks, Cyril and Methodius, create the Cyrillic alphabet so that the Bible can be translated into Slavic languages (800s)
- human figures in wall mosaics become highly stylized and are set against plain backgrounds
- icons are restored in Eastern Orthodox worship (843)
- the heroic epic *Digenes Akrites* is written (1000s)
- officials of the Eastern Orthodox church and the Roman Catholic church excommunicate each other (1054)

- Constantinople becomes extremely wealthy through international trade during the Macedonian dynasty (802–1056)

LATE BYZANTINE PERIOD
1050s-1453

- the Byzantine empire starts a long, slow decline when the emperors abandon Heraclius's military reforms and increasingly rely on foreign armies for defence (1060s onward)
- the Normans seize Byzantine lands in southern Italy, while the Seljuk Turks seize lands in Asia Minor, Syria, and Palestine (1071)
- Alexius I drives back the Normans with Venetian help and asks Pope Urban II for western assistance against the Seljuk Turks
- Pope Urban II proclaims a holy crusade against the Muslims (1096)
- the Venetians attack and plunder Constantinople during the Fourth Crusade (1204)
- the Venetians occupy Constantinople and Byzantine territory (1204–1261)
- Michael Palaeologus rises to power in Nicaea, drives the Italians out of Constantinople, and re-establishes the Eastern Orthodox church (1260s)
- invasions by the Ottoman Turks reduce Byzantine territory to just the area surrounding the capital (1300s to mid-1400s)
- Constantinople falls to Sultan Mehmed II, is renamed Istanbul, and becomes the capital of the Ottoman empire (1453)

- John Scylitzes writes the *Chronicle of Basil I* (1200s)
- Anna Comnena writes a history of her father, Alexius I (early 1100s)
- the Black Death kills two-thirds of Constantinople's population (1347)
- Emperor John VI Cantacuzenus abdicates the throne and writes his memoirs (1350s)
- wall frescoes depicting realistic human figures replace mosaics as the main form of decoration in churches

---

- the government abandons protection of small farmers, resulting in greater concentration of land among large landowners (1060s)
- in exchange for military protection, the Byzantines are forced to grant trading privileges to Italian city-states (1070s onward)
- the Byzantines lose their control over the northern Mediterranean to the Italians (1070s onward)

and paid by noble landowners. Because of this, the units felt more loyalty to their employers than they did to the emperor. The cavalry commanders also acted independently and rarely cooperated with one another. The militia formed the bulk of the army. It was composed of foot soldiers who were called into active service only when needed. At other times, they returned to their homes to live and work. As a result, the militia was not always in fighting form and felt little loyalty to either their commanders or the state.

Belisarius first focused his attention on the cavalry, improving the soldiers' training, providing better weapons and armour, and building bonds of loyalty. The cavalry was made into the premier fighting force, whose example and leadership other soldiers would willingly follow. To win the loyalty of the militia, the government offered parcels of land to peasants in exchange for military service. These farmers were also promised protection from exploitation by wealthy and powerful landowners in the provinces. These measures went a

long way in establishing trust and dedication among the militia.

With his revitalized army, Belisarius stormed into North Africa in 533, defeating the Vandals. From there the general moved onto Italy, capturing Rome from the Ostrogoths in 536. Over the next 20 years, Belisarius and a later general, Narses, reconquered the entire Italian peninsula as well as southeastern Spain. With most of the Mediterranean basin in his hands, Justinian was close to fulfilling his dream.

Because so much of the army was en-

PERSPECTIVES ON THE PAST

Empress Theodora

Why would some Byzantines have considered Theodora an unusual or unsuitable choice for an empress? What is there in Theodora's words that convinces Justinian not to flee? Theodora is an excellent example of a wife who exerts a significant influence over the policies of a public figure. Can you think of any contemporary women who play a similar role in politics?

Theodora, Justinian's empress, was the daughter of a bear-keeper for the Hippodrome. Growing up to be beautiful, graceful, and intelligent, Theodora worked as an actress and dancer (both lowly professions) throughout Syria and Egypt. In Constantinople, she caught Justinian's fancy, and the couple married in 525. Before they could do so, Justinian had to ask his uncle, Emperor Justin, to change a law forbidding marriage between a high government official and an actress.

Two years later, Justinian himself was crowned emperor. Theodora demonstrated keen political insight and became her husband's most trusted advisor. Her strength of character and personal courage showed early on the occasion of the *Nika* rebellion of 532. As protesters moved in on

Figure 13-8
Detail of Empress Theodora from a Ravenna mosaic

the palace, Justinian's advisors urged him to flee. Empress Theodora, however, disagreed. She told Justinian: "My opinion is that the present time, above all others, is inopportune for flight, even though it brings safety. For while it is impossible for a man who has seen the light not also to die, for one who has been an emperor it is unendurable to be a fugitive. May I never be separated from this purple, and may I not live that day on which those who meet me shall not address me as mistress. If now, it is your wish to save yourself, O Emperor, there is no difficulty. For we have much money, and there is the sea; here the boats. However, consider whether it will not come about after you have been saved that you would gladly exchange that safety for death. As for myself, I approve a certain ancient saying that royalty is a good burial-shroud."

Heeding his wife's words, Justinian crushed the rebels and continued to rule for many years. Theodora herself was ruthless in dealing with enemies and those she disliked, but she was generous toward the poor. She built public hospitals and a home for destitute women in Constantinople.

gaged in the Mediterranean, the eastern and northern parts of the empire were left short of military resources. Rather than risk war on these fronts, Justinian agreed to pay an annual tribute to the barbarian tribes in the north and to the Persian emperor in the east. This solution lasted for as long as Justinian lived; but after his death in 565, conflict broke out throughout the empire and along the borders.

In the end, Justinian's restored Roman empire was short-lived. But he is remembered for much more than his military ambitions. Urged by the resolute Theodora (see box, page 294), he ruthlessly put down a rebellion in 532 by citizens protesting against tax increases imposed to pay for the imperial campaigns of expansion. The leaders of the uprising wanted to overthrow Justinian and replace him with a new emperor. Their rallying cry was "*Nika!* (Let us conquer!)" As people rioted in the streets and started a fire that raged for five days, the rebellion threatened to turn into a revolution. When 30 000 protesters poured into the Hippodrome for a mass rally, the emperor ordered Belisarius to surround the arena and execute everyone in it.

The incident left half of the city destroyed, including the Hagia Sophia and parts of the Imperial Palace. Justinian immediately undertook a huge building program, employing the best architect in the empire to construct a larger, more magnificent Hagia Sophia. Under the emperor's watchful eye, the most glorious buildings in Constantinople were erected. Justinian also commissioned the creation of many beautiful **mosaics** (pictures made out of small tiles of coloured stone or glass).

During his reign, Justinian solidified the emperor's role as the supreme political and religious authority. His most enduring legacy was to collect and synthesize Roman legal knowledge into a coherent code of law. These topics are discussed later in this chapter and the next.

INVASIONS AND THE RULE OF HERACLIUS

After Justinian's death, the empire suffered a wave of invasions for almost two centuries. In 568 the Lombards of Germany invaded northern Italy, and in the early 600s, the Visigoths took back southeastern Spain. The Avars, Slavs, and Bulgars invaded the Balkan peninsula in the north, while Persians and Arab Muslims attacked the eastern regions.

Beset on all sides, the Byzantines had neither the military forces nor the finances to resist these advances. After years of costly conquests, the imperial treasury was bare. In addition, fighting among political rivals for the throne weakened the government for decades.

In 610, Heraclius (575–641), the son of the Byzantine governor of north Africa, gained control of the throne. He strengthened the empire by transforming it into a military state. The old provinces were reorganized into smaller divisions called *themes,* each governed by a general called a *strategos*. The *strategos* was both a military and a civilian leader. He was directly responsible to the emperor, but also had the authority to take military action if his theme was threatened. Heraclius continued the policy of granting land to local inhabitants in exchange for military service. The emperor hoped that such soldier-farmers would ensure the security of distant provinces.

By such measures, Heraclius made

Figure 13-9 *Byzantine soldiers*

peace with the Avars. He then turned his attention to the Persians, who had taken over eastern sections of the empire. In four campaigns between 622 and 628, Heraclius broke Persian power in Asia Minor and Armenia, and regained Syria, Palestine, and Egypt. Although his conquests would prove only temporary, his governmental reforms would last for five centuries.

Heraclius's successors faced a new challenge: resisting the wave of Arabs who swept in from the Middle Eastern desert. The Arabs, who had converted to the new religion of Islam, were seeking to bring the light of the Prophet Muhammad to others. During the Dark Ages, the Byzantines had largely escaped the havoc created by the barbarian invasions in western Europe. Now it was their turn to shield Europe from the onslaught of Muslims from the southeast. The Arabs overran the empire's richest provinces in North Africa, Egypt, Palestine, Syria, and parts of Asia Minor. In 655, an Arab fleet inflicted heavy losses on the Byzantine navy in the eastern Mediterranean. Between 673 and 678, Arab ships laid siege to Constantinople itself, cutting the Byzantine capital off from its vital sea routes. To repel the Muslims, the Byzantines developed a powerful new naval weapon called Greek fire, a kind of flamethrower (see page 321).

REFLECT AND ANALYZE

1. Why was it important for the Byzantine emperors to reform the army? Were these reforms effective?

2. Compare the Byzantine empire and medieval France in the year 500. Which society presented better opportunities for ordinary individuals to improve their lot in life? What evidence can you give to back up your opinion? Which society would you have preferrred to live in? Why?

3. a) Why do historians consider the reign of Justinian and Theodora the golden age of the Byzantine empire?
   b) Suggest reasons why Justinian's military conquests did not last long after his death.

4. What are the advantages and disadvantages of a military government versus a civilian government?

5. Compare and contrast the military successes of Heraclius with those of Justinian.

THE MIDDLE BYZANTINE PERIOD

The Middle Period of Byzantium is characterized by several general trends: 1) the constant and troublesome threat of Muslim invasions; 2) the strengthening of Eastern Orthodox Christianity and serious friction with the Roman church; and 3) the spread of Byzantine ideas beyond the empire's borders. During this period, the empire also achieved its greatest prosperity, while some of its rulers committed acts of horrible brutality.

In 717, Constantinople was again besieged by the Muslims. The emperor Leo III (717–740), a general from Asia Minor, suc-cessfully turned back the Muslims and continued the military reorganization of the provinces begun by Heraclius. Leo also supported a religious movement called **Iconoclasm** which sought to abolish the worship of religious images or icons (see pages 316-317). The debate about icons divided not only the Byzantines among themselves, but the Roman and Byzantine churches as well.

In 780, a 10-year-old boy, Constantine VI (780–797), inherited the throne, with his mother Irene, the widow of Emperor Leo IV, acting as regent. The empress was exceptionally ruthless and determined to hold onto power. When Constantine came of age, he had the army seize control and his mother exiled. Unfortunately, he was a weak and ineffective ruler. The banished empress, meanwhile, launched a successful plot to imprison and blind her son so that he would be unable to govern. After his death, Irene became the first woman to rule the empire, from 797 to 802. The strong-willed empress even called herself *basileus* (emperor) rather than *basilissa* (empress).

Irene's reign was controversial. In a bid for popularity, she reduced taxes, which brought about a financial crisis. She also took unpopular positions on religious issues. Pope Leo III in Rome, seeing that no male occupied the emperor's throne, took the opportunity to challenge Byzantine authority by crowning the Frankish king Charlemagne "Emperor of the Romans" in 800. This was a double act of defiance, since the Byzantines considered the emperor to be the religious as well as the political leader of the Romans. Thus, the religious rivalry between Rome and Constantinople escalated.

In 802, Irene was overthrown and exiled to an isolated Greek island. For the rest of her days, she was kept under close guard to prevent her from hatching any more plots.

From the late ninth century to the mid-eleventh century, Byzantium became the commercial centre of the civilized world under a dynasty of Macedonian emperors. A number of these emperors came to power by murdering their predecessors. As the empire acquired untold wealth, its leaders were able to pour money into reinforcing the army and navy. In this way, they were able to stem the tide of Muslim and European invasions for quite a long period.

Constantinople's population grew more diverse, as merchants of all nationalities conducted business in the city. Foreigners took Byzantine ideas home with them. Western Europe, for instance, was beginning to rediscover lost classical works through its contact with Arab Muslims and the Byzantines. But Byzantine religion and culture would have the greatest effect on the newly developing Slavic countries in the north, especially Russia. Constantinople sent missionaries to Kiev to convert the Slavs, and two Greek monks created the Cyrillic alphabet, adapted from Greek, so that the Bible could be translated into Slavic languages. A later Russian city, Moscow, billed itself as the "Third Rome"—the legitimate heir to ancient Rome and Constantinople.

Basil II (963–1025) was the most notorious emperor of the late Middle Period. After defeating an invasion by Egyptian Muslims, he waged a 20-year campaign against the Bulgarians in the northeast. In a battle in 1014, he took 14 000 Bulgarians prisoner. Instead of killing or ransoming them, he inflicted a far crueller punishment. The prisoners were blinded, with only one eye of every 100th man spared so that he could lead his countrymen home. When the Bulgarian king saw his army of maimed soldiers groping sightlessly toward home, witnesses said that he fell senseless in horror and died two days later. This atrocious act earned Basil the title of "Slayer of the Bulgars." The emperor also tried to

THROUGH THEIR EYES

Basil the Magnificent

What work of art produced in medieval western Europe is similar to the illustrated *Chronicle of Basil I?* This pictorial account was created centuries after Basil's death. Do you think the story is accurate? What changes might have occurred in the intervening centuries?

Like a number other Byzantine rulers, Basil I (867–886) rose from humble roots in a peasant family to become emperor. As the founder of a Macedonian line of emperors, he was celebrated in stories. One of the best known is the *Chronicle of Basil I*, by a Byzantine official of the eleventh century named John Scylitzes. Scylitzes' chronicle was illustrated during the 1300s by hundreds of miniatures painted by Sicilian monks.

Figure 13-10a *Basil sits on his throne, dispensing justice.*

Figure 13-10b
One of Basi's admirals tortures Arab sailors who invaded the empire. One sailor is being hanged, the second skinned alive, the third used for target practice, and the fourth lowered into boiling tar.

limit the growing power of the nobility in favour of the soldier-farmers who were so vital to the empire's security.

We close the Middle Period in the 1050s. In 1054, the Eastern Orthodox and Roman Catholic churches excommunicated each other due to their longstanding rivalries and disagreements (see page 307). Two years later, the Macedonian dynasty came to an end.

REFLECT AND ANALYZE

1. In what ways were foreigners: a) beneficial, and b) destructive to the Byzantine empire during the Middle Period?

2. Why did the Byzantines not take lightly Pope Leo III's action of crowning Charlemagne "Emperor of the Romans" in 800? What was the significance of this gesture?

3. Both the Eastern Orthodox church and the Roman Catholic church claimed to have authority over the other. Based on what you have learned about Medieval Europe and the Byzantine civilization, explain why each church had a legitimate claim.

4. How did commercial success and wealth help to keep the empire strong?

THE LATE BYZANTINE PERIOD

In the late centuries of the empire, pressures from within and without led to a steady decline. Inside the empire, the stable social structure began fraying when power shifted from small farmers to wealthy nobles. High taxes forced many a small farmer to sell his land to a powerful aristocrat. These aristocrats were allowed to make money payments instead of performing military service, meaning that the empire was losing its reserve supply of soldiers. Outside the empire, western Europeans gazed with envious eyes at the Byzantines' fabulous wealth and made plans to seize some of it for themselves.

The most dangerous European was Robert Guiscard, leader of the Normans in a region of France. In 1071 Guiscard invaded Byzantine lands in southern Italy, and threatened to march on to Constantinople to seize the imperial crown itself. The Byzantines had neglected to maintain the troops necessary to deal with this aggression and appealed to the Italian city-state of Venice for help. Emperor Alexius I (1081–1118) and the Venetians drove back the Normans, but the Venetians demanded extensive trading privileges as payment for their services. Later Byzantine emperors came to rely more and more on Italian ships for defence and granted similar privileges to Genoa and Pisa. As a result, the Byzantines lost their monopoly on trade and the lucrative marine tolls they used to charge.

Also in 1071, a group of Persian Muslims called the Seljuk Turks took over much of Asia Minor, Syria, and Palestine. The Seljuk Turks had earlier established a sizeable empire in Persia and were now attempting to expand their territory. Alexius stopped their advance into Asia Minor, but feared that the Turkish setback was only temporary. He therefore took an unprecedented step: he asked Pope Urban II in Rome for assistance against the

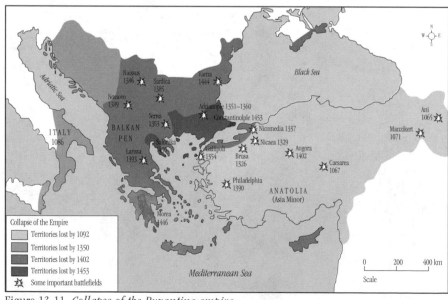

Figure 13-11 *Collapse of the Byzantine empire*

Seljuk Turks. What Alexius wanted was a united defence of Christianity by the western and eastern parts of Europe. Thus, as you read in Chapter 10, the First Crusade was launched in 1096.

The crusades actually created new problems for the Byzantines. The pope did not ask Alexius to lead the First Crusade, as the Byzantines expected, but instead sent European leaders directly to the Holy Land. Eastern Orthodox Christians and western Roman Catholics were suspicious of each other. The Byzantines also soon realized that the Europeans' goal was not the defence of Christianity as a whole, but rather the reconquest of the Holy Land for European pilgrims.

The self-serving agenda of at least some Europeans was made clear in the Fourth Crusade of the early thirteenth century. Venetian merchants, who had long coveted the Byzantines' trading routes and markets, recognized an opportunity to seize control of Constantinople. They offered to transport the crusaders to the Holy Land by ship, in exchange for the crusaders' help in attacking the Byzantine capital. Constantinople, which had resisted every attack since its founding in 330, was sacked and its treasures stolen during three days of destruction in April, 1204. Pope Innocent III publicly condemned this brutal raid by the Venetian expedition, which was to have lasting consequences for both Byzantines and western Europeans.

For half a century, the Venetians occupied Constantinople. The city's Greek population greatly resisted this occupation. Many Byzantine nobles, military leaders, and church officials fled to areas of the empire free from western control and established rival kingdoms. The most important

of these was located at Nicaea in Asia Minor. From here, a Greek noble named Michael Palaeologus launched an attack in 1259 against the Italian coalition that controlled the Byzantine territory. He succeeded in conquering Constantinople in 1261.

The Eastern Orthodox church was restored, and so was the Byzantine empire, although it was a mere shadow of its former self. Michael Palaeologus became Emperor Michael VIII (1258–1282), establishing a dynasty that would survive up to end of the empire.

In the fourteenth century, Constantinople was devastated by the Black Death, just as Asia and Europe were. The plague swept through the city in 1347, killing almost two-thirds of its inhabitants. The huge drop in population further weakened the empire.

A new Muslim power also arose in Asia Minor in the early 1300s: the Ottoman Turks. They steadily chipped away at the Byzantine empire, taking parts of Asia Minor and the Peloponnese. They were intent on capturing Constantinople, but did not succeed the first time they tried in 1402. With aid from the west, the Byzantines managed to hold them off for a number of years; but the Ottoman Turks could not be resisted forever. In March of 1453, the Ottoman sultan (ruler) Mehmed II set out from Adrianople with a force of 100 000 men to launch an all-out assault on the Byzantine capital. For seven weeks, Turkish ships constantly blasted cannonballs at the city's walls and attempted to cross into the well-protected Golden Horn. The greatly outnumbered and weary Byzantines received scant help from the west, since they refused to accept the pope as the head of the

church. When the Turks finally penetrated the city walls on May 29, the last Byzantine emperor, Constantine XI Palaeologus, chose to die fighting rather than surrender. Sultan Mehmed II entered the city a few hours later, enslaving or killing many of its inhabitants. The Byzantine empire was no more.

Constantinople (eventually renamed Istanbul) became the capital of the Muslim Ottoman empire. The Church of Hagia Sophia was converted into a mosque (an Islamic house of worship). But although the Byzantine civilization was over, its traditions and the Eastern Orthodox church lived on in the new nations of northeastern Europe, especially Russia. Byzantine influences formed the basis of Russia's own great empire several centuries later.

Figure 13-12 *The fall of Constantinople to the Turks*

GOVERNMENT

Just as the Roman emperor Diocletian had considered himself a god, the Byzantine emperor, in a Christian era, believed that he was Christ's representative on earth. There was no separation of political and religious authority in Byzantium, as there was in the west. Within his own domain, the emperor was far more powerful than any western European king.

During the coronation ceremony, the emperor was instated as the head of the church as well as of the government. He was crowned by the **patriarch**, the highest official in the Eastern Orthodox church, and swore a solemn oath to defend the faith.

To the Byzantines, human society was a reflection of divine society. People believed that the emperor brought order and harmony to his earthly subjects in the same way that God ruled heaven. Accordingly, the actions of the emperor were invested with symbolic and sacred meaning. He was also bound to follow highly formal and elaborate Byzantine rituals that developed under Persian influence.

Justinian built up the emperor's status as Christ's appointed representative and ruler of a universal empire on earth. Perhaps as a result of the *Nika* revolt early in his reign, he took steps to ensure that he had complete control over religious as well as secular matters in the empire. He appointed all key government and church officials, including the patriarch. He set rules concerning business, trade, and taxation. The Senate, whose role had already waned during the late Roman empire, seems to have all but disappeared in the Byzantine era.

As in Roman times, there was no established system for determining a successor to the throne. The unspoken assumption was that the emperor was chosen by God, and that God's ways were unknowable. In practical terms, this meant that any person who succeeded in gaining the throne—whether by fair means or foul—was considered a legitimate ruler. A murderous plot was just as likely to yield a new emperor as a hereditary claim.

As a result, all rulers, especially weak ones, faced danger from those wishing to replace them. Numerous emperors were killed, maimed, or tortured, some by close relatives. One popular tactic was take the emperor prisoner and blind him to make him unfit to rule. Of the 88 emperors who reigned during the Byzantine period, 29 suffered a horrible and untimely death!

Figure 13-13 *Emperor Justin II presented this jewelled cross to the Vatican in the 500s. The central medallion contains a splinter believed to have come from Christ's Cross in Jerusalem*

PERSPECTIVES ON THE PAST
Unlucky Emperors

What aspects of imperial succession encouraged violence as a means of gaining the throne? What measures might the government have taken to discourage such violence?

Below is a list of the 29 Byzantine emperors whose reigns were cut short by violence. Also included are the dates when disaster struck.

Emperor	Date	Event
Basilicus	477	Starved in prison
Zeno	491	Buried alive
Maurice	602	Beheaded
Phocas	610	Dismembered
Heracleonas	641	Mutilated
Constantine III	641	Poisoned
Constans II	668	Bludgeoned in his bath
Leontius	705	Beheaded
Tiberius III	705	Beheaded
Justinian II	711	Beheaded

Emperor	Date	Event
Philippucus	713	Blinded
Constantine VI	797	Blinded
Leo V	820	Stabbed, beheaded
Michael III	867	Stabbed
Constantine VII	959	Poisoned
Romanus II	963	Poisoned
Nicephorus II	969	Stabbed, beheaded
John I	976	Poisoned
Romanus III	1034	Poisoned, drowned
Michael V	1042	Blinded
Romanus IV	1071	Poisoned, blinded
Alexius II	1183	Strangled, beheaded
Andronicus I	1185	Mutilated and tortured
Isaac II	1193	Blinded
Alexius IV	1204	Strangled
Alexius V	1204	Blinded, maimed
John IV	1261	Blinded
Andronicus IV	1374	Blinded
John VII	1374	Blinded

With bloody intrigue being common in Byzantine politics, how was the empire able to last for over 1000 years? How did the government maintain stability? To begin with, most Byzantine emperors were not weak. A strong emperor faced fewer challenges to his authority and could deal effectively with any challenges that did occur. Secondly, the emperor exercised absolute power. He could pass any laws he wished, without the need to answer to a senate or a parliament. And thirdly, a well-organized, central service kept the country running, even when a weak emperor ruled or when there was a struggle for the crown.

Whereas western European monarchs faced constant challenges from powerful feudal lords, early Byzantine emperors allied themselves with the peasant class, engaging them as soldiers and giving them land so that they could support themselves. Hundreds of ordinary people throughout the provinces owed loyalty and military service to the emperor, which helped to keep aristocratic power under control. In later years, nobles grew more powerful as small farmers sold their land to pay for heavy taxes imposed by the emperor. These farmers then had to work for noble landowners, thus losing their independence. A kind of feudalism developed between greater and lesser lords, although it was never as strong as in western Europe.

Heraclius's reforms, in which civilian provinces were divided up into military themes, kept the government in firm control of the empire when hostile forces threatened all sides. Each theme was governed by a *strategos,* or general. Since the *strategi* were appointed by the emperor, they were usually loyal to him.

Early Byzantine towns were run by a municipal council. All local landowners who met a property qualification, as well as their heirs, were required to serve on the council. It was responsible for repairing public buildings, roads, and aqueducts; keeping the streets clean; regulating the market; running postal services; recruiting soldiers; and other activities. Unfortunately, these duties became so heavy that many people tried to evade municipal service, with the result that the councils were extinct by the mid-500s. The church took over many of these responsibilities, including dispensing justice and overseeing the market. In some cities, the bishop acted as the government administrator—another example of the marriage of politics and religion in Byzantine life.

REFLECT AND ANALYZE

1. As a Byzantine emperor, you face many political enemies. What steps would you take to prevent them from attempting to take over the throne?

2. Describe the ways in which the Byzantine emperor was more powerful than a western European king.

3. Do you think Byzantine emperors were any more or less violent than monarchs in western Europe? Explain your opinion.

4. Would there have been conflicts between church and state in Byzantine society, as there were in western European countries? Explain.

LAW AND JUSTICE

In 528, just a year after he became emperor, Justinian appointed a 10-person commission to systematically gather and organize all of Roman law and legal opinion into a practical code for daily use. Eight centuries of Roman legislation had produced an enormous, unwieldly body of knowledge. Justinian wanted this knowledge to be updated and condensed into a more manageable form.

The task facing the commission, made up of lawyers and scholars, was enormous. The researchers first had to collect and review all existing and previous laws, as well as case records, judgements, and legal commentary. They eliminated items they considered no longer necessary, and then catalogued and summarized the remaining information. After six years of painstaking work, the commission produced the *Corpus Juris Civilis (Body of Civil Law),* popularly known as **Justinian's Code**.

There were three parts to this monumental work. The *Code* itself, published in Latin in 529, was a list of 4652 statutory laws passed by Roman emperors from Hadrian to Justinian. The *Digest,* published in 533, consisted of 50 volumes that summarized legal opinions. Also published in 533 were the *Institutes,* four volumes that together formed a text for the study of law. After Justinian's death, another book was added to the Code. Called the *Novellae,* it documented, in Greek, 175 of Justinian's own legal decisions.

Some of Justinian's laws were more liberal than earlier Roman ones. For example, he made it easier to free slaves and sell land. Widows were guaranteed the right to inherit property, and children were protected from their father's absolute authority over their lives. On the other hand, acts considered to be crimes were severely punished. Heresy was a serious offence—those who strayed from Orthodox Christian beliefs were barred from holding government office and denied their inheritance.

Figure 13-14 *Justinian's wife Theodora had a powerful influence over the emperor's political thinking*

Seducing a young, unmarried woman was a crime carrying the death penalty. If a seducer's victim had willingly submitted, she too was executed.

The importance of Justinian's Code is inestimable. It became the chief source of Roman law for western Europeans, who had lost this knowledge during the Dark Ages. Western scholars visiting Constantinople in the twelfth century eagerly studied and copied the code. Its principles and practices shaped the legal systems of the Roman Catholic church and medieval European countries. Much later, the code formed the basis of legal systems in the Americas and other countries around the world, as well as modern international law.

Just one of many important concepts contained in Justinian's Code was a rule regarding evidence: "The person who accuses someone must prove that the charge is true. This is not the obligation of the person denying the charge." This rule developed into the modern legal principle that an accused person is innocent until proven guilty.

In the eighth century, the code was revised and expanded into a new set of laws called the *Ekologa*. Notable changes in this document included a reduction in the number of crimes carrying the death penalty. Two hundred years later, yet another revision and expansion of the code was undertaken. The resulting code, called the *Basilica,* had the aim of simplifying the laws and making them easier to understand.

REFLECT AND ANALYZE

1. "Justinian's Code was the Byzantine civilization's legacy to the world." Explain whether or not this statement is valid.

2. Do you think a code of Canadian laws and legal history, similar to Justinian's Code, would be a valuable undertaking? Give reasons for your opinion. What kinds of people would benefit from such a code?

3. Can you explain why laws and legal judgements made so long ago and in a very different society are still valuable to us today?

THE BYZANTINE EMPIRE:
Society and Culture

The year is 726. Emperor Leo III has ordered workers to dismantle the great mosaic of Christ which adorns the Chalke gate at the Imperial Palace. A few days earlier, the emperor issued an edict declaring that all religious images, or icons, are to be removed from buildings and destroyed. Leo is one of a small number of Byzantines who believe that the adoration of images of Jesus, the Virgin Mary, and the saints smacks of pagan idolatry, or the worship of idols. Since the Bible forbids idolatry, Leo has decided to ban all icons.

Most Byzantines violently disagree with their emperor's views. In the following months and years, there are protests and riots in support of icons. Monks, in particular, argue vigorously in favour of Christian images, and are greatly persecuted.

In western Europe, the Roman Catholic pope and priests also defend icons. They denounce the attackers of religious images—including the Byzantine emperor himself—as heretics. For more than a century the controversy rages, deepening the divide between the churches of Constantinople and Rome.

Figure 14-1
*Mosaic of Christ from
the Hagia Sophia*

The people who believed that icons were evil were called **Iconoclasts**, or "image breakers." Like all groups with strong ideologies, they had a greater impact than their relatively small numbers would suggest. With powerful supporters on their side—the emperor, military leaders, and government officials—the Iconoclasts succeeded in having religious images banned for the better part of a century, despite bitter opposition from most members of the clergy. To gain an understanding of this debate, let us look at how Byzantine Christianity developed, shaped by earlier traditions and influences from both west and east.

RELIGION

You may recall that the emperor Constantine experienced a religious revelation in 312. On his way to fight Maxentius, a ruler of the western empire, Constantine had either a dream or a vision of the Christian cross, on which appeared these words: "In this sign, conquer." And conquer is exactly what Constantine did, believing that he was protected and blessed by the cross.

As a result, he became the first Christian emperor of the Roman empire and established Constantinople as its first Christian capital. Because of his revelation, Constantine felt that he and the empire were special in the eyes of God. The Byzantines, too, believed that their emperor had divine authority concerning religious matters. Nor could other faiths be tolerated, since Christianity had revealed itself to Constantine as the one true religion. Thus, non-Christians began to be persecuted during his reign.

The next ruler, Theodosius, made Christianity compulsory in the empire in 380. Political as well as religious reasons prompted him to take this action. Christianity, he hoped, would unite the disparate peoples of the empire and inspire them to fight the barbarians pressing in from the west. Christian beliefs, as we saw earlier, were also easily adapted to the cult of the emperor that had existed in earlier times. Church leaders willingly allied themselves with the emperor, eager to have their religion officially recognized and made more powerful. In the sixth century, Justinian established the emperor as the actual head of the church as well as the state.

From the beginning, it was clear that the church in Constantinople and the church in Rome were set on different paths. The leader of Christianity was the pope, the "father" of the church, who presided in Rome. But easterners preserved the notion of the universal Roman empire, of which the emperor was the spiritual as well as the secular head. Westerners, on the other hand, felt no such allegiance to the Byzantine emperor. When Justinian became emperor, he openly disputed Rome's supremacy, claiming that the church in Constantinople was "the head of all other churches." This early rivalry was never resolved and was later compounded by differences in doctrine and practice. Inevitably, the two churches would separate, although

the formal break did not occur until the eleventh century. Even after that date, there were periodic attempts at reconciliation.

Although other religions were outlawed in the empire, Byzantine Christians in fact incorporated old Roman and foreign elements into their practices. For example, since the date of Jesus's birthday was not known, the Christians chose to observe it on December 25, the time of an earlier pagan festival celebrating the winter solstice.

The merging of church and state meant that Christianity was even more integrated into the daily life of the Byzantines than it was in western Europe. Christian crosses, relics, and icons existed everywhere in Constantinople, decorating not only churches but public monuments such as the Imperial Palace and the great column of Constantine. The Byzantine capital was like an enormous *reliquary* (a container for precious relics), which befitted its claim as the centre of Christianity.

CHURCH ORGANIZATION AND PRACTICES

As in the west, Byzantine priests performed services in parishes and individual churches. Above the priests were the bishops who administered the *dioceses,* geographical divisions larger than parishes but smaller than provinces, which Diocletian had created at the end of the third century. Higher bishops called metropolitans (*archbishops* in the west) were responsible for large areas covering a number of dioceses. The most important metropolitan was the bishop of Rome, soon to be called the pope. Other key metropolitans of the eastern empire presided over the important Christian cities of Alexandria, Antioch, Heraclea, and Caesarea. The highest official in the

Byzantine church was the bishop of Constantinople, called the patriarch, whom the emperor appointed to administer church affairs on his behalf. In church hierarchy, the patriarch was second only to the pope.

Unlike Roman clergy, Byzantine priests were allowed to marry. Most higher church officials, however, came from monasteries and therefore were celibate.

Over time, the practices of eastern and western churches grew to be quite different. Throughout western Europe, services were conducted in Latin, the language of ancient Rome. The Byzantines gradually replaced Latin with Greek, which was the everyday language not just of the empire but also of classical Greece. Because of this, the Byzantines did not feel they were abandoning their classical heritage. They also remained closer to early Christian practices than the western Europeans, rejecting such Roman Catholic concepts such as purgatory, introduced by Pope Gregory I in the sixth century.

Figure 14-2 *Greek Orthodox priest*

DEBATES OVER DOCTRINE

In the early days of the church, important officials would meet together in councils to discuss questions concerning Christian doctrine or heresies that had arisen. The first council gathered at Nicaea (in Asia Minor) in 325 to deal with the issue of whether Christ the Son occupied a lower place than God the Father. (The council affirmed that the two were equal.) Another important debate took place in 451, when the Fourth Council met to discuss a challenge to the church doctrine that Christ had two natures, one divine and one human.

Church councils were often called by the emperor who, as spiritual leader of the church, took an active interest in such debates. Ordinary Byzantines, too, discussed these matters with great enthusiasm in their homes and shops. Visitors to Constantinople were amazed by the popularity of esoteric church matters as topics of casual conversation. Let us not forget, however, that the Byzantines viewed Christianity as an integral part of everyday life, much like eating and working. Sometimes their animated discussions would turn into heated arguments leading to fights or riots.

Iconoclasm

The most serious debate, which nearly tore the empire apart and caused a great rift with the church in Rome, concerned the role of icons in religious worship. An *icon* was an image of a religious figure, especially Jesus, the Virgin Mary, or an apostle (one of Jesus' followers). Since the time of Constantine, such images had been important to worshippers, especially those who could not read or understand Latin. By gazing at and praying to a beloved figure such as the Virgin Mary, ordinary Christians could feel close to God.

THROUGH THEIR EYES

The Virgin Mary

What qualities made the Virgin Mary more popular than any other saint? Think of a classmate who is popular. What are the qualities that make him or her popular, and are they similar to those of the Virgin Mary?

Most Eastern Orthodox and Roman Catholic Christians considered the Virgin Mary or Madonna to be their favourite religious figure. Artists depicted her as a warm, compassionate figure who was more approachable than the supremely saintly Jesus. People felt that their prayers to the Mother of God were more likely to be heard and answered.

Certain towns and cities, including Constantinople, felt that the Virgin was their patron saint, or special protector. "You would not find any public place or imperial dwelling, no reputable inn or private house of those in authority where there was not a church or an oratory of the Mother of God," said one Byzantine.

Figure 14-3
An icon of the Virgin Mary

In the northwest part of Constantinople, near the city wall, was a church that housed the most precious relic in the city: the Virgin's robe. It was brought to Constantinople from Palestine during the reign of Leo I (457-474). The people of Constantinople believed that the robe protected their city in times of danger. For example, when the Russians were laying siege to the city in 860, the Virgin's robe was carried around the walls and battlements. Lo and behold, the Russians departed soon afterward.

The patriarch Photius described the event in this way: "Truly is this most holy garment the robe of God's Mother! ... For immediately as the Virgin's robe went round the walls, the barbarians gave up the siege and broke camp, while we were delivered from impending capture and were granted unexpected salvation." It is no wonder, then, that so many shrines and churches were dedicated to the Holy Virgin.

Iconoclasm, the belief that worshipping icons was a superstitious practice akin to worshipping idols—which the Bible expressly forbids—arose in the eighth century. Here is an instance of eastern influences making their way into the Byzantine church. Both the Jewish and Muslim religions flatly prohibited religious imagery. Byzantines living in the eastern regions of the empire were influenced by their close contact with these religions. One such Byzantine was Emperor Leo III, who was born in Syria.

As you read at the beginning of this chapter, Leo ordered all religious images destroyed in 726. He had strong support from people in Asia Minor, the army (mostly recruited from the eastern provinces), and government officials who wished to limit the power of the church. Defending the use of icons were people in the western provinces, the clergy who regarded Iconoclasm as heresy, and Roman Catholics in western Europe. Feelings ran so high that riots broke out when icons were destroyed.

The Iconoclasts did have some good arguments in their case against icons. Many people did, in fact, venerate holy images for superstitious reasons. They believed that praying to icons and *relics* (holy objects) could bring about great miracles, such as the cure of a terrible illness, the restoration of a blind person's sight, or the recovery of a lost ship. If the icon of a particular saint did not bring the desired result, people would abandon it and direct their prayers to the icon of a different saint. The Iconoclasts argued that people devoted too much attention to icons and not enough to the genuine rites of the church. In addition, the Iconoclasts felt that any human depiction of Christ was

improper because it denied his divine nature.

Pope Gregory III called a council of Italian bishops in 731 to examine the matter. The council threatened the Iconoclasts with excommunication and defended the role of icons as intermediaries between humble worshippers and the unseen spiritual world. The Byzantine emperor ignored these arguments. The controversy raged on for many more years, as emperors in favour of or against icons came to the throne. The matter finally came to a close in 843, when icons were restored once and for all.

THE SPLIT BETWEEN THE EASTERN AND WESTERN CHURCHES

The Iconoclastic controversy widened the already existing breach between the Byzantine and Roman churches. When the patriarch of Constantinople refused to recognize the pope as the head of Christianity, the pope broke his ties with the Byzantine emperor and turned to the Frankish kings for protection. As you have already read, Pope Leo III thumbed his nose at the Byzantines by proclaiming Charlemagne as "Emperor of the Romans" in 800. The Byzantines regarded this action as an insult.

In the following years, the Byzantine church engaged in more conflicts and rivalries with Rome. Latin-speaking and Greek-speaking missionaries clashed with each other as they each sought to convert the Slavs of northeastern Europe to Christianity. The pope and the patriarch disagreed over who had religious authority in southern Italy, which was then under Byzantine control.

In a last-ditch attempt to resolve their many differences, the pope sent a delega-

tion to Constantinople in 1054. The patriarch and his officials met their visitors with accusations and insults. The meeting dissolved in anger, with church leaders on each side excommunicating the other. The Christian church was now divided in two. In the west, the pope headed the Roman Catholic church. In the east, the patriarch headed the Eastern Orthodox church.

Today, many differences between the two churches can be traced back to the eleventh century and earlier. The Eastern Orthodox church does not accept the belief in the infallibility of the pope. Whereas Roman Catholic priests must take a vow of celibacy, Eastern Orthodox priests are allowed to marry, although a candidate for the office of bishop cannot be married. Services in the Eastern Orthodox Church are conducted in the language of the people, whereas Roman Catholic services prior to 1964 were conducted only in Latin. Because Eastern Orthodox Christianity allows the use of different languages, different versions of Orthodox churches have developed, such as Greek, Russian, and Serbian.

MONASTERIES

The tradition of holy men living alone originated in Egypt, where the desert and rocky terrain were particularly appropriate for solitary life. Other monks chose to live in quiet, self-sufficient communities. Such communities or monasteries appeared in the eastern empire in the fourth century. They thrived throughout the Byzantine period and after.

In 357 a young Greek named Basil decided to follow the example of his devout mother and sister, and enter religious life. He travelled to Syria, Palestine, and Egypt to

Figure 14-4 *A mosaic of St. Basil*

Figure 14-5 *A Byzantine monk in a cell*

he set down rules for the organization of monasteries. He did not establish a holy order, as St. Benedict did in Italy, but his list of rules became the model for Eastern Orthodox monastic life.

Eastern monasteries and convents were slightly different from those in western Europe. Whereas western monasteries came to stress service to humanity, many Byzantine monasteries continued in the tradition of isolated communities where much time was spent in solitary prayer. Their focus on seclusion meant that eastern monasteries did not attempt to become major centres of learning and culture, as western ones did. Monks and nuns, however, did create fine illuminated manuscripts, mosaics, and murals (wall paintings). They also composed solemn chants for their services.

Most people entered monasteries to lead a chaste, holy life, but a few had other reasons. Anyone with ambitions for

observe monks. He preferred the communal life of monasteries to the solitary life of hermits, and returned home to become bishop of Caesarea around 370. As bishop,

high office had to be a monk, since bishops were mostly recruited from monasteries. Monks were also exempt from serving

THEN AND NOW
Byzantine Monasteries

Why do you think the monasteries of Mount Athos have changed little since Byzantine times? What might be the appeal of monastic life for people of today?

Mount Athos is an isolated highland on a narrow Greek peninsula in the Aegean. Here, 20 monasteries and 200 hermitages that were established under Byzantine emperors still exist today, with scarcely any change. They continue to operate under the jurisdiction of the patriarch of Constantinople.

Hermits began coming to Athos in the ninth century. Several tiny hermit's huts are still perched in isolated alcoves on top of rocky mountains. Since there are no easy pathways, these huts are difficult to reach, and

must have been even more difficult to build.

In the monasteries of Athos, the monks wear heavy black habits and hood-like hats that date from Byzantine times. The monastery walls are covered with splendid murals of saints painted in the Byzantine style. The monks strictly observe three vows set forth by St. Basil: poverty, chastity, and absolute obedience to the abbot. Their poverty is demonstrated by their lack of possessions, frugal meals, and stark cells. To ensure chastity, most monasteries forbid women within their walls. A daily routine of fasting, meditating, and praying develops piety and obedience. Each monk is also assigned a specific job, such as tending the vineyard, making works of art, or repairing buildings.

in the army, which would have attracted those trying to avoid their obligations of military service.

Throughout most of Byzantine history, the monasteries did not have to pay state taxes. With their huge tracts of land, many monasteries became powerful and rich. In the tenth century, the devout emperor Nicephorus II complained that monks thought only of acquiring land and livestock, not about the virtues of poverty.

Yet, as monasteries evolved, many assumed an important social role. Believing that all Christians were responsible for the well-being of others, monks and nuns provided a variety of essential services to Byzantine citizens. They provided relief to the poor, constructed hospitals, and operated schools for needy children. Their example inspired the general population as well. Wealthy Byzantines, including members of the imperial household, formed organizations to care for the poor, the aged, and the blind. The emperor and the government likewise took pride in building public works and supporting good causes.

Byzantine monks and nuns believed that they could convert more people to Christianity if church services and the Bible were presented to non-Christians in their own language. Two Greek monks, Cyril and Methodius, travelled to eastern Europe in the ninth century to convert the Slavs. Their ability to speak Slavic languages gained them many converts to Orthodox Christianity. Since the Slavs had no written language, the monks created a new alphabet, based on Greek letters, so that the Bible could be written down for Slavs to read. The Cyrillic alphabet, as it was called, is the written script that Russians, Ukrainians, Bulgarians, and Serbs use today.

REFLECT AND ANALYZE

1. a)   Explain how the Byzantine church incorporated beliefs and ideas from pagan Rome into its practices.
    b)   Why did the Byzantines feel that their church could claim to have authority over the church of Rome?

2.   Set up a debate in class. One group of debaters is made up of Iconoclasts, the other group consists of defenders of icons. Each group should present compelling arguments supporting their position. The rest of the class, as the church council, decides which position becomes church doctrine.

3.   Today, we still use the word "iconoclast" with a modified meaning. Write a modern definition for this word, based on your knowledge of Byzantine history. Then check your definition with a dictionary.

4.   Divide the class into groups. Put the groups in pairs, with one group representing the Roman pope and the other group representing the Byzantine patriarch. Imagine that you are at the 1054 meeting when the two churches separated. Instead of separating, try to work out compromises that each church head can live with. Is this possible?

5.   Compare the features of Eastern Orthodox monasteries and Roman Catholic monasteries. How were they similar, and how were they different? Do you think the monasteries might have been able to find a way to reconcile the two churches? Explain your answer.

SOCIAL STRUCTURE

Although Byzantine society was hierarchical in nature, few barriers existed to prevent a person from moving from one social class to another. We have already seen how individuals of low birth were able to become emperors or empresses.

The emperor and his family, while in power, held the highest position in society. They were surrounded by a court of advisors and subordinates who attended to their every need.

Next in stature to the imperial family were various levels of government officials. Civil servants were highly educated and well-trained for their duties. They administered both civilian and military affairs of the empire. Many individuals in the government vied with one another for power and prestige, seeking the favour of the emperor. Sometimes they were involved in intrigues to depose one emperor and enthrone another.

Ranking below civil servants were church leaders, wealthy landowners called *decurions,* and merchants. Many in this group rose quickly to positions of promi-

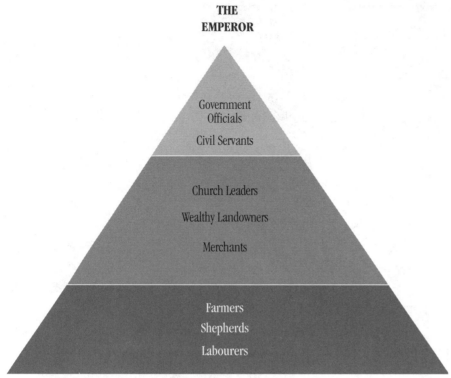

THE
EMPEROR

Government
Officials

Civil Servants

Church Leaders

Wealthy Landowners

Merchants

Farmers

Shepherds

Labourers

Figure 14-6 *The Byzantine social pyramid*

EVERYDAY LIFE

THE FAMILY AND MARRIAGE

Most Byzantines, urban and rural, considered their families to be the centre of their social life. Marriage, accordingly, was a sacred institution in the eyes of both the church and the state. A bride brought to her marriage a dowry in the form of a certain amount of money or property agreed to by the two families. Her groom was required by imperial law to provide her with property equal to the value of the dowry.

Traditional village weddings in modern Greece observe some customs dating back to Byzantine times. Such village marriages were once arranged by the parents, although this is rare nowadays. Since the church forbids weddings during Lent (the 40 days of penitence and fasting before Easter), many weddings take place directly after Easter. On the day itself, the groom, following an ancient custom, leads a band of musicians to the bride's home. During the ceremony, the couple wear crowns made of paper and flowers, joined by a

nence. Church officials, in particular, were held in great esteem because of the church's importance in daily life. The patriarch and the metropolitans of important jurisdictions had the highest status of all, virtually equal to governors. Decurions were fairly numerous and were required to sit on the town councils that acted as local governments. They and the merchants were essential to the economic well-being of the empire.

Farmers, shepherds, and labourers occupied the bottom of the social pyramid. They were by far the most populous group, and most of them lived in rural areas and villages. Their lot improved when Heraclius introduced his military reforms in the early seventh century. Large numbers of them were recruited into the militia and given land by the government and protection against wealthy landowners. Heraclius

and other astute emperors always respected this group, since it formed the greater part of army and was vital for the empire's defence.

REFLECT AND ANALYZE

1. a) Were people in Byzantine society more socially mobile than people in feudal Europe? Explain your answer.
    b) Taking either western Europe or Byzantine society, consider what factors hindered, and what factors helped, people to overcome any socioeconomic obstacles they faced.

2. Compare the social pyramid of the Byzantine civilization with the feudal pyramid of western Europe. Describe any similarities or differences between parallel groups.

3. Compare the lot of the independent small farmer in the Byzantine civilization with the manorial serf in feudal Europe. Which individual, in your opinion, was better off? Why?

ribbon signifying the bonds of marriage. The priest leads the couple and their bridal party three times around the altar, while well-wishers cheer, sing songs, and throw rice.

Another significant event in the life of a newly married couple was the birth of their first child. It was celebrated by a gathering and the most important ceremony, the baptism.

EDUCATION

Byzantines considered good education a virtue and a must for everyone wishing to better himself or herself. Primary-level instruction was widely available in the cities and in some villages. At about age seven, boys (and sometimes girls) would be sent to an elementary teacher who would teach them the basics: reading, writing, basic points of grammar, and how to count numbers. Wealthy families occasionally hired distinguished tutors to teach their children at home. These tutors were particularly important for girls, since they were not often sent out to a teacher.

A girl's formal education usually ended after the elementary level. Boys, on the other hand, had the option of pursuing secondary and higher education. A well-rounded secondary education consisted of literature (Greek and Roman), arithmetic, geometry, astronomy, and musical theory.

Higher education was available only in the large cities. In Byzantium's early days, boys of about 15 years of age would seek out a higher-level instructor to teach them. If a student wanted to pursue a subject such as law or medicine, he would travel to the city which had the best teachers in that subject. The quest for higher learning was synonymous with travel.

In 425, an early form of university was established in Constantinople with government support. Among the subjects taught there and at various other academies were medicine, law, philosophy, arithmetic, geometry, astronomy, grammar, and music. The great works of classical Greek writers, such as Homer, Sophocles, and Plato, were also widely studied. Near the end of the empire, when Byzantine scholars were fleeing from Constantinople to the cities of western Europe, they brought these literary works along with them. In this way, western Europeans were reintroduced to the works of Greek antiquity which had been lost to them for a thousand years.

The church established religious schools throughout the empire to train priests and scholars. The leading centre of religious studies was the patriarchal academy located in Constantinople. Interestingly, Byzantine monasteries never became involved in the mass education of children as western European monasteries were. St. Basil deemed monasteries unsuitable places for the teaching of "secular" children, and therefore such an activity was discouraged throughout the Byzantine period.

WOMEN IN THE BYZANTINE EMPIRE

Byzantine custom dictated that women live partly in seclusion. Women had separate quarters in their homes and in church. In the home, they were primarily engaged in household tasks. On the occasions that they appeared in public, they often veiled their faces. This custom was due to a general prejudice toward women in Byzantine society, a belief that the sight of a woman's exposed face might cause a man to forget

Figure 14-7 *Empress Theodora (centre) and her court attendants*

himself and behave immorally. This harsh assessment of womanhood found parallels in Persian and, later, Islamic societies where women were also required to cover their faces.

Yet, in the eyes of the law, Byzantine women had quite a favourable status. As mentioned in Chapter 13, married women were guaranteed rights of inheritance. In certain circumstances, such as on being widowed, a woman could control her husband's property as well as her own. She also enjoyed equal authority with her husband concerning her children's upbringing.

Although education opportunities for women were limited, resourceful individuals from well-to-do families could manage to acquire a good education, if they chose. A few women even entered such professions as medicine.

Some women ran their own businesses or managed large estates, and thus needed a shrewd grasp of economics. The strong wife of an emperor could wield considerable influence in politics. A number of women ruled the empire as **regents**, or temporary rulers, for their young sons not yet come of age. One or two female regents, such as the empress Irene, later ruled in their own right, although for only brief periods.

The influential Empress Theodora, wife of Justinian, championed the rights of married and widowed women. She was responsible for gaining the right for a wife to own land equal in value to her dowry. She also succeeded in improving the condi-tions for widows who, due to her efforts, were allowed to raise their children without governmental interference. They also gained the right to control their late hus-band's property.

Divorce, although not forbidden, was difficult to obtain, and remarriage was considered socially unacceptable. Repeated marriages brought severe penalties from the church.

REFLECT AND ANALYZE

1. Compare educational opportunities and standards between western Europe and Byzantium: a) around 500, and b) around 1450. Take into consideration other events that might have had an impact on education in these periods.

2. Which group do you think enjoyed more freedom and personal opportunities in their society: Byzantine women or medieval European women? Consider women of all classes.

3. Why did Byzantine women veil their faces in public?

URBAN AND RURAL LIVING

A TRAVELLER'S DIARY OF CONSTANTINOPLE

Imagine, if you will, that the fictitious Leon of Rome is visiting the great Byzantine capital for the first time in the seventh century. What sights will he see? What con-versations will he overhear? What will his impressions be of the Byzantine people?

June 5, 628

This is my first day in Constantinople, and I cannot help but notice some simi-larities between the city and my lovely Rome. My Byzantine host, Philippucus, tells me that Constantinople is built on seven hills, although I count only six. I suppose that's close enough. I have also heard there are 14 districts, just like in Rome. But one major difference is the magnificent harbour. On this hilltop, I can look out to the sea glittering with such a variety and number of ships as I have never seen before. It's a wonder that they do not crash into one another.

Walking along the grand Mese, *the city's main street, I've heard quite a variety of languages. I can understand a fair bit of Greek and have picked out some German and French, but the other languages are unfamiliar to me. Philippucus says he can identify Jewish, Arab, and Persian words, even though he does not understand them. There is such a great diversity of people compared to Rome!*

June 6

Continued my explorations today. What a breathtaking city this is, like a bigger, showier version of Rome. No wonder Con-stantine called it "New Rome." The for-ums along the Mese are enormous—such long arcades and such tall decorated columns! Such grand arched entrance-ways and public baths! All these public monuments look Roman in appearance, but are built on a scale that dwarfs my beloved city.

There is even an arena here similar to the Circus Maximus back home, but it seems twice the size. The Hippodrome has 40 000 seats and is shaped like an oval. The Byzantines come here and sit under silk awnings to watch races, public pa-geants, and circuses, or to cheer and welcome home their victorious generals.

My host took me to a chariot race in the Hippodrome this afternoon, which seems to be a favourite entertainment among the Byzantines. There are two factions of charioteers, the Blues and the Greens, and each has its share of eager supporters. The aristocrats support the Blues, while the working-class people support the Greens. There was such a yelling of insults and angry gesturing between groups of fans that I feared a riot would break out. After the races, when we were walking home, Philip-pucus told me the story of how a riot broke out in the days of Justinian that nearly toppled the emperor. To think that 30 000 people were slaughtered in the Hippodrome! Such a thing could never happen in my beloved Rome.

Figure 14-8 *A map of medieval Constantinople*

The dome of the Hagia Sophia looks beautiful in the moonlight. Inside, the golden mosaics on its walls dazzled my eyes like the sun.

June 7

The narrow side streets that lead off the Mese and the other broad avenues are a bewildering maze. Philippucus says there are about 3000 streets! No wonder I got hopelessly lost. But my ramblings gave me an idea of how ordinary Byzantines live.

The streets are crammed with tenement houses for the poor and covered markets where every imaginable kind of ware (and many more I have never imagined) are for sale. It is impossible to walk quickly—there are so many peddlers and porters and stray dogs getting in one's way. Refuse lies everywhere, and the stench is overwhelming on this warm day. I've seen numerous rats scurrying about. Disease, they say, spreads easily in these overcrowded streets. I imagine it must take a heavy toll on the poor.

Middle-class people, like my host's family, live in modest yet comfortable wooden houses rather than tenements. The rich live in townhouses made of stone or brick. Many of these houses are constructed in the old Roman style, with two storeys built around a central courtyard. From what I can tell, the homes are richly decorated and filled with luxurious furnishings. I am a little surprised to see everyone—rich, middle class, and poor—living side by side. A great stone mansion belonging to a government official and his family might be located right next to a shabby, crowded tenement apartment housing dozens of inhabitants.

Despite the wide gulf between rich and poor, the citizens of Constantinople demonstrate a genuine and active concern for the less fortunate. I have seen church and government hospitals which provide free medical care to the poor. Philippucus's wife says that wealthy people also have set up charitable organizations to care for the poor, the aged, and the blind. Free bread is distributed daily to the hungry, and the monasteries provide shelter to travellers and the homeless.

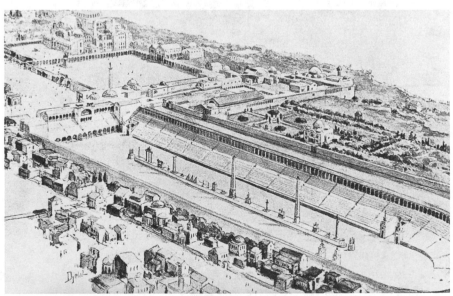

Figure 14-9 *The Hippodrome*

Figure 14-10 *Byzantine society*

Alas, this is my last day with my wonderful hosts. But I shall carry the memories of their hospitality and their jewel-like city with me always.

REFLECT AND ANALYZE

1. Does Leon of Rome's diary give you a detailed picture of life in Constantinople? Explain. What features of the diary do you like? Which do you find useful? Based on Leon's description, would you want to visit Constantinople in 628?

2. What do you think of the Byzantines' favourite entertainment (chariot races)? What are the appealing aspects of this sport? What are the unappealing aspects? Which modern sports inspire a similar intense competitiveness among their fans?

3. Do you think it was a good or bad thing that citizens of different classes lived next to one another in Constantinople? Explain any advantages or drawbacks.

4. How did the people of Constantinople demonstrate their civic concern? How does their attitude compare with modern attitudes toward the disadvantaged today?

THE ECONOMY

AGRICULTURE

During the Byzantine period, most farms were small and independent. Farming was mainly a family venture, with the occupants focused on growing enough food to feed their own families. Some farms raised cattle, ducks, and geese as well as crops, or grew cash crops for sale in the local market. The women and children of the family helped in the fields, while still fulfilling other responsibilities associated with running the household.

The empire was able to grow a variety of vegetables and fruits adequate to the population's needs. However, Byzantium was not able to grow sufficient quantities of grain. Additional supplies of grain had to be imported from Egypt. After the Muslims conquered Egypt, most of the additional grain came from Asia Minor.

The small farmer, despite his independence, was always vulnerable to exploitation or takeover by big landowners. Heraclius's seventh-century measures were well received by small farmers, since they were given some protection from the more powerful landowners. In return, the farmers had to pay heavy taxes to the imperial government and serve in the army when called upon.

In the twelfth century, the government removed its protection of small farmers. It was felt, wrongly perhaps, that the fighting power provided by the farmers was no longer essential for the empire's defence. The powerful, landed aristocrats began to take advantage of peasants who were unable to pay their taxes. The landowners bought up the farmers' lands, making the farmers themselves into hired hands on

Figure 14-11 *Byzantine farming*

what had once been their own land. Thus many farmers were reduced to serf-like individuals labouring to support a large landowning class who spent most of their time in luxurious urban townhouses.

INDUSTRY

Byzantine industry was heavily regulated by the emperor as well as by the merchants and craftspeople themselves. The imperial government set wages and prices, determined the hours of business, stipulated working conditions, and specified weights and measures. Merchants and artisans engaged in a particular trade or industry organized guilds to protect their interests and provide mutual aid to one another. These guilds were more limited in scope than those in western Europe, since the Byzantine government had so much control over the terms and conditions of working.

Guilds set rules to uphold the reputation and standards of their trade. Any member who broke guild rules faced possible expulsion from the guild. Any merchant of a trade guild who tried to cheat purchasers was severely punished. The son of a guild member was required to follow his father's occupation and become a member of the same guild.

For centuries Constantinople was the wealthiest commercial centre of the Mediterranean basin. Although a great trading city, it was also known for the quality of certain goods produced by its inhabitants. Cloth, enamelware, and jewellery were manufactured in Constantinople and traded to both Asia and Europe. The Byzantines learned the secret of making silk when silkworms were smuggled out of China and brought to Constantinople around 550. Apart from the Chinese, the Byzantines were almost the only people who manufactured silk, which became an extremely lucrative industry for the empire. Rich, embroidered fabrics and garments were produced primarily for the emperor, his court, and the church. So valuable was the Byzantines' monopoly on silk production outside of Asia, that the government maintained an iron control over the industry to prevent its secrets from reaching western countries.

TRADE

Constantinople's prime location for both land and sea routes was its greatest asset in trade. The city became a centre of trade between Europe, Asia, and the Middle East. Ships brought in spices, tapestries, leather goods, metalwork, and grain, while other ships transported them to new locations. Imperial officials closely monitored the movement of all trade goods. Trade created a great deal of revenue for the Byzantine government, since it collected taxes on all goods flowing in and out of the city.

Geography was only one of three overall factors contributing to the empire's supremacy in trade. The second factor was the attitude of the Byzantine people toward commerce. In ancient Rome, trade had not been a highly regarded activity, and people of noble birth had shunned business activities. The opposite was true in Constantinople, where the nobility invested and participated in all kinds of commercial ventures.

The third factor in the empire's trading success was a strong monetary system. At a time when a money economy was nonexistent in western Europe, the Byzantine currency, the gold *bezant,* was the world's most stable and widely used unit of exchange. The bezant made trade possible between Europe, the Mediterranean, the Middle East, and even Asia. Introduced by Constantine, the bezant would maintain its stability for 700 years.

Constantinople's trading monopoly began to decline in the eleventh century, when the Italian port cities of Venice, Genoa, Pisa, and others stepped up their trading activities and became formidable competitors. At the same time, the Byzantine empire was finding it more difficult to

Figure 14-12 *Byzantine bezants*

keep Muslim invaders at bay. The government's failure to maintain its military forces meant that the empire increasingly called on western nations to come to its aid.

The fact that the Byzantines needed to ask their fiercest rivals in trade—the Italians—for military aid was surely a sign of decline!

REFLECT AND ANALYZE

1. How was the Byzantine government able to acquire immense riches from the industry and trade of the empire?

2. a) Describe the important factors that contributed to Constantinople's success as a centre of trade.
   b) Describe the factors or weaknesses that led to its decline as a trading centre.

3. As Constantinople's star was falling in terms of commerce, Venice's star was rising. In a chart, record the respective rise and decline of the two cities. Include significant political, social, and economic events and their dates, and note the impact that each city had on the other. When you have finished your comparative chart, see if you notice any patterns.

THE ARTS

VISUAL ART

Most Byzantine art was devoted to religious subjects, created by anonymous monks. Anonymity allowed a work of art to glorify God rather than focusing attention on the artist or artists who created the work.

Icons

The distinctive qualities of Byzantine art are well illustrated in its icons, which became important for everyday worship early in the empire. Icons were created in many media—mosaics, small paintings on wooden panels, and frescoes—for display in churches, shrines, and homes. Their main purpose was to inspire religious devotion, especially among illiterate churchgoers. Icons therefore emphasized the sacred, symbolic aspects of Biblical figures over their human, physical qualities. Most depictions were two-dimensional, with static poses and serene facial expressions revealing little human emotion. You can see an example of an icon of the Virgin Mary on page 317.

Artists creating icons were required to follow certain conventions. Each holy figure was to be rendered with distinguishing features, such as a particular hairstyle, beard, or colour of clothing. Christ was usually shown wearing blue and gold robes before the Crucifixion (His death on the cross), and purple and gold robes after the Resurrection (His rising from the dead on the third day after the Crucifixion). The Holy Virgin was typically clothed in blue and purple. The apostle St. Peter was al-

Figure 14-13
A mosaic of John the Baptist (detail)

ways depicted as an elderly man with white hair and beard, while St. John the Baptist was a young man with a straggly brown beard. St. Paul was always bald. The Greek saint Demetrios could be recognized by the suit of mail that he wore.

Since the church dictated these conventions, the depiction of holy subjects did not change greatly over the course of Byzantine history. Nevertheless, different periods are recognizable by their differences in style. In the Early Byzantine Period, when classical influences were still strong, human figures were quite expressive and lifelike and often set in landscapes. During the Iconoclastic controversy of the Middle Period, human figures were replaced by purely symbolic items such as crosses and by abstract designs of foliage. When icons were restored in the ninth century, the naturalism of the early era was completely abandoned. Instead, the importance of icons was reaffirmed by flat, highly stylized representations which minimized human individuality. Landscapes were replaced by dazzling gold backgrounds that drew the eye immediately to these precious images. In the Late Period, expensive mosaics were mostly replaced by fresco paintings which, once again, depicted weightier, more realistic human figures. The three-dimensional appearance of these figures anticipated the rebirth of classicism in the Renaissance.

The hierarchy of holy subjects was reflected in their placement in churches. Jesus, the "Lord of the Universe," looked down upon worshippers from the highest position, the main dome of the church. Below him, in order of importance, were the angels, scenes of Christ's life, the apostles, Biblical prophets, and at the lowest level, the saints. The Mother of God generally occupied a place of honour in an arched ceiling behind the altar. By looking at the precisely placed images in any Byzantine church, the devout could easily "read" the story of Christianity.

Mosaics

Byzantine art attained its most glorious expression in mosaics. A ***mosaic*** is a picture or design made out of small pieces of coloured stone, clay, or glass called *tesserae*. The tesserae are held together with cement. Whereas many pictures created with pigment on walls, parchment, wood, or canvas have long since perished, numerous ancient mosaics still exist due to the durability of their materials.

In Roman times, floor mosaics were common. These were replaced by wall mosaics in the Christian era, since the floor was not a fitting place for holy subjects. The floor was reserved for scenes of everyday life.

Early Christians did not allow depictions of people or animals, and created mosaics in simple geometric patterns. These restrictions were lifted in the fifth century, allowing Jesus and the saints to be portrayed in mosaics in the upper walls of a church. Imperial palaces were decorated with formal portraits of emperors as well as with animal figures (see Figure 14-15).

Mosaic artists were skilled at using tiles of various colours to create subtle

Figure 14-14 *A late thirteenth-century Byzantine fresco showing the Virgin Mary, from the Church of St. Clement in Ohrid, Yugoslavia*

Figure 14-15 *An animal mosaic from Constantinople*

close range, they blend into an intricate and natural-seeming image when viewed from the proper distance.

ARCHITECTURE

Few examples of Byzantine secular architecture survive. Archeological excavations and artistic depictions in ivory or mosaics (see Figure 14-17) show that imperial palaces and other civic buildings were mostly based on Roman models.

The most distinctive form of Byzantine architecture was the Eastern Orthodox church. Early Byzantine churches, like those in western Europe, were based on the basilica of Roman times. However, architects gradually modified this oblong plan into a more compact and centralized shape to accommodate the Greek custom of performing mass in the central part of the nave. The square shape of the Greek cross was the model for many Byzantine churches.

effects of shadows or drapery folds. The folds of a red robe might be rendered in dark blue to create a distinct contrast. Although such colours appear to clash at

THROUGH THEIR EYES
The Mosaics of Ravenna

Why are the churches of Ravenna valuable sources for early Byzantine art?

Almost all early Byzantine art created in Constantinople was destroyed during the Iconoclastic period that lasted from 726 to 843. However, glorious mosaics dating from the Early Period are preserved in such sites as Ravenna in Italy, which became part of Justinian's empire in the sixth century.

The Church of San Vitale houses the most celebrated mosaics of the early era. Imperial portraits showing Justinian and Theodora, surrounded by royal attendants and church officials, decorate facing walls (see colour plate 24). It was customary for the Byzantine emperor, as mediator between God and the people, to

be portrayed as a holy figure in churches (although, naturally, he occupied a lower level than the saints).

Other mosaics, like that of St. Mark, show realistic landscapes and animals typical of early Byzantine art. These features would disappear in later church decoration

Figure 14-16
*St. Mark and
the lion at San Vitale
in Ravenna*

Figure 14-17 *A mosaic of a palace from the church of San Apollinaire, in Ravenna*

LANGUAGE AND LITERATURE

By the middle of the seventh century, Greek was the universal language of the Byzantine empire, binding together the diverse peoples living within its boundaries. All educated Byzantines spoke and read "Atticized" Greek, derived from the language of classical literature. This "pure" form of Greek differed somewhat from the vernacular spoken by the masses which, naturally, had undergone changes over the centuries. The Greek language also influenced the development of languages in northeastern Europe. As you read earlier, it became the basis of the Cyrillic alphabet used by the Russians and other peoples.

Until the reign of Justinian, students were taught both Latin and Greek classical literature. However, when Greek became the main language, the Byzantines focused almost solely on the Greek authors, especially Homer. After the Bible, the *Iliad* and the *Odyssey* were the most familiar and most widely quoted works in the empire. The Byzantines were proud of their classical heritage and emphasis on learning, which they felt made them superior to the unschooled barbarians of the west.

Byzantine religious literature focused upon salvation of the soul and obedience to God's will. Christ and the Virgin Mary were praised in poems and hymns. Romanus the Melode, a sixth-century clergyman, and St. John of Damascus, who lived in the eighth century, wrote some of the finest hymns of the Byzantine church. The nun Casia, who turned down the chance to become empress in order to devote her life to God, also wrote religious poems. Other popular religious writings were the lives of the saints, which read like novels and told of dramatic events, travel, adventure, and miracles. These

The idea of a central dome crowning the church probably came from the domed buildings of Rome and Persia, as well as the domes adorning the tombs of early Christian martyrs in the Holy Land. Byzantine architects solved the difficult problem of placing a circular dome on top of a square building in two basic ways (see below). In later periods, churches again became oblong and included multiple smaller domes. However, no other church matched the early architectural achievement of the Hagia Sophia in Constantinople (see box next page).

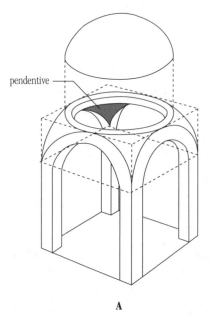

A

A pendentive is a curved, triangular vault over a pillar forming one corner of a square building.

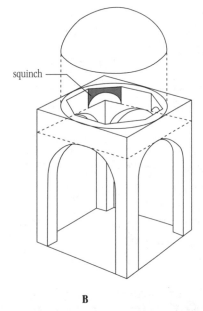

B

A squinch is a section of vaulting that with other squinches makes up an octagonal shape, easily accommodating a round dome.

Figure 14-18 *The two ways of placing a dome over a square*

INNOVATIONS

The Hagia Sophia

Based on what you have learned, can you explain why Constantinople's Hagia Sophia needed to be the most splendid church in the Byzantine empire?

Figure 14-19a *Exterior of the Hagia Sophia*

One of the world's great architectural landmarks, the Hagia Sophia, or Church of Holy Wisdom, was designed and built by Anthemius of Tralles and Isodorus of Miletus. Justinian commissioned these two architects, considered the best of their day, to construct a new building when Constantine's church was destroyed during the *Nika* revolt. Between 532 and 537, nearly 10 000 labourers were employed in the church's construction. Justinian himself visited the site daily to view the building's progress.

The dome, which dominated Constantinople's skyline, was the largest ever constructed in Europe. Its enormous weight was supported on four great half-domes situated more than 18 m above the floor. These arches were in turn supported on massive piers built out of limestone blocks, with the cracks between the blocks reinforced with molten lead. The dome was constructed of light bricks made especially in Rhodes. Each brick was stamped with the words, "God founded this work and God will come to its aid."

The Hagia Sophia was the first church to use this design, which has inspired architects ever since. The dome collapsed several times during the frequent earthquakes that rocked the region, and was rebuilt each time.

The church's vast interior, 30.5 m wide and nearly 55 m high, was as impressive as its exterior. Forty arched windows around the dome's circumference allowed sunlight to pour in, creating the impression that the dome was floating on air. The mosaics decorating the walls created such a wealth of colour that one Byzantine historian exclaimed, "One would think we had come upon a meadow full of flowers in bloom. Who would not admire the purple tint of some and the green of others, the glowing red and the glittering white, and those to which nature, like a painter, has marked with the strongest contrasts of colour?"

When the Ottoman Turks captured Constantinople in 1453, the church became a mosque and its gleaming mosaics were whitewashed. The Turks also erected four slender Mulim towers, called minarets, outside each corner. In 1922, the government of Turkey removed the whitewash from the mosaics and turned the Hagia Sophia into a museum.

Figure 14-19b *Interior of the Hagia Sophia*

Α	Β	Γ	Δ	Ε	Ζ	Η	Θ	Ι	Κ	Λ	Μ	Ν	Ξ	Ο	Π	Ρ	Σ	Τ	Υ	Φ	Χ	Ψ
a	b	g	d	e	z	ē	th	i	k	l	m	n	x	o	p	r, r̥h	s	t	u	ph	kh	ps

А	Б	В	Г	Д	Е	Ж	З	И	Й	К	Л	М	Н	О	П	Р	С	Т	У	Ф	Х	Ш	Щ	Ы	Э	Ю	Я	Ц
a	b	v	g	d	e	zh	z	i	í	k	l	m	n	o	p	r	s	t	u	f	kh	sh	shch	y	e	yu	ya	ts

Figure 14-20 *The Greek and Cyrillic alphabets*

works were intended to teach moral lessons.

Byzantine writers of secular literature, not surprisingly, were often highly influenced by the classical past. However, work of distinction and originality was produced in some fields. For example, a short, pithy form of poetry was popular. Such poems, written in Atticized Greek, resemble epigrams in their focus on a single idea and use of witty language.

Another admired literary form was the romantic or heroic epic, usually written in the vernacular. The best-known epic, *Digenes Akrites,* was written in the 11th century and has been compared to the medieval French romance, the *Song of Roland.* The hero, whose last name Akrites means "borderer" in Greek, is caught between two worlds. Born of a Muslim father and a Christian mother, Digenes displays the bold individuality and fearlessness of those who live on the frontier. Besides battling wild beasts and roving bandits, he also kidnaps and woos the lovely Eudoxia, a wealthy nobleman's daughter, who becomes his bride. Like western Europeans, Byzantines admired the chivalric ideal represented by such literary heroes as Digenes.

Byzantines also excelled as chroniclers of history. Procopius, an advisor to the general Belisarius, wrote a detailed account of Justinian's military campaigns. He also produced a *Secret History,* severely criticizing Justinian and portraying Theodora as a scheming monster. Anna Comnena, regarded by scholars as the first important female historian of Europe, wrote an analytical account of the reign of her father, Alexius I (1081–1118). Comnena portrayed the Venetian crusaders as greedy barbarians. John VI Cantacuzenus, who abdicated as emperor in 1354, wrote his memoirs, which provide a revealing glimpse into the turbulent history of the Balkans in the later years of the empire.

REFLECT AND ANALYZE

1. Why were icons important to Eastern Orthodox Christianity? Can you explain why so many Byzantines argued against icons being removed from churches during the Iconoclastic controversy?

2. a) Can you give a reason why the mosaic became a popular art form in the Byzantine civilization but not in western Europe?
   b) What art form in Gothic churches might Byzantine mosaics be compared to? Explain whether the two art forms served similar functions.

3. Why do you think few examples of Byzantine secular architecture exist today?

4. The interiors of a central-plan Byzantine church and a French Gothic church both create a sense of religious majesty in very different ways. Describe the main architectural and decorative elements that contribute to this effect in each church.

5. Using small squares of coloured paper, create a mosaic that might be found in a Byzantine church or palace.

6. Can you explain the Byzantines' interest in recording contemporary events for posterity?

THE SCIENCES

One of the most important legacies of the Byzantine empire was the preservation of classical Roman and Greek knowledge, including the work of mathematicians and scientists such as Pythagoras, Ptolemy, Euclid, and Archimedes. The writings of the second-century Greek physician Galen were also preserved and later formed the basis of Byzantine and medieval European medicine. Through the Byzantines, ancient learning was disseminated first to the Arabs and, much later, to the people of western Europe.

GREEK FIRE

Callimachus, a Syrian engineer, invented the highly effective and much feared weapon of the Byzantines known as *Greek fire*. This highly combustible substance would ignite on contact when catapulted through tubes, in the manner of a flamethrower, or when packed in clay pots and tossed, like hand grenades. Water could not douse the flames, making Greek fire especially useful for naval battles.

It was first used during a siege of Constantinople by Muslim attackers in the seventh century. The flaming liquid caused considerable damage and death when launched at enemy ships. Its use in land battles was prohibited by the fact that even a slight jolt on a bumpy road caused the liquid to explode.

The formula for Greek fire was a state secret and never written down. Modern scholars speculate that its main ingredients were petroleum, saltpetre, sulphur, and quicklime. Time and again, Constantinople was saved from defeat by its strong defences and use of Greek fire.

TIME

Like the medieval Europeans, the Byzantines used the Julian calendar and the term *Anno Domini* to distinguish between the years coming before and after Christ's birth. When Pope Gregory XIII slightly reformed the Julian calendar in 1582, western Europeans adopted the new version, which was called the ***Gregorian calendar***. Byzantine and eastern Europeans took longer to switch over to the new calendar, and continued to use the Julian calendar to mark their religious days. Today, Orthodox Christians celebrate Christmas on January 6, which is December 25 in the Julian calendar.

REFLECT AND ANALYZE

1. Education in the Byzantine empire was freely available to most people. Despite having such an educated population, explain why the Byzantines did not make noteworthy advances in mathematics and science.

2. Do you think the Byzantines' reliance on their "super weapon," Greek fire, contributed to their later neglect of the militia (foot soldiers)? Explain your opinion carefully, considering as many factors as possible.

3. Give reasons why, despite Constantinople's strong defences, efficient navy, and use of Greek fire, hostile enemies from both east and west repeatedly tried to capture it throughout the Byzantine period.

4. "The Byzantine legacy of preserving the heritage of the Greek and Roman world was more important than the empire's original contributions to science." Do you agree or disagree with this statement? Explain your answer.

LOOKING BACK

For most of its 1123-year history, the Byzantine empire stood in sharp contrast to the feuding, and feudal, kingdoms of western Europe. Byzantium was, in fact, a continuation of the Roman empire—Christianized, but maintaining a strong, central government, classical institutions, and people's powerful identification with their emperor that had characterized the pagan empire.

At the same time, when the capital was moved from Rome to Constantinople, the empire was exposed to powerful and lasting influences from the Middle East that would further sharpen the differences in ideas, beliefs, and customs between the Byzantines and western Europeans. For almost 1000 years, the empire traded mostly with the countries of the eastern Mediterranean, North Africa, and Asia. In such matters as Iconoclasm, we can also see a definite eastern influence. In certain respects, then, the Byzantine civilization was as much eastern as it was western. Its heavy influence on the development of eastern European countries—Russia, the Ukraine, and others—meant that those countries, too, would draw distinctions between themselves and the rest of Europe. Today, differences in religion, culture, and political organization between western and eastern Europe are still very much in evidence.

The most potent symbol of the divide between east and west was Christianity. The church took divergent paths in Byzantium and western Europe from the very beginning. The history of its development reflects the power struggle not only between Rome and Constantinople but also between two medieval world views. The eastern view mostly looked backward, safeguarding the traditions and knowledge of two illustrious ancient civilizations. The western view looked forward, forging new social and political institutions out of chaos and struggle.

Let us remember, however, that the Byzantines' preservation of the past made possible yet another future era in Europe. The literature of ancient Greece and the laws of ancient Rome, which Byzantine scholars brought to western Europe, were two pillars on which Renaissance learning and humanism rested.

At its height, Constantinople was the richest, and probably the most powerful, city in Europe and the Middle East. Belonging neither to the Roman Catholic west nor to the Muslim east, it was greatly coveted by both sides for economic and religious reasons. Taking this into account, it is remarkable that the Byzantine empire lasted as long as it did.

CHAPTER
15

THE ISLAMIC CIVILIZATIONS:
The Land of Muhammad

"**G**o forth into battle, as followers of Islam, against the Persians. It is our common goal to carry the word of Muhammad to other peoples. It is our duty to struggle against evil and the enemies of God. Muhammad showed us the way by defending his followers and leading them into battle for eight years. The ***Qur'an*** [the holy book of Islam] tells us that we have a religious duty to struggle for the faith, even by armed force. These wars we fight against infidels and unbelievers must be viewed as a *jihad* [holy war]. There is no more noble calling for a true believer. Those who are killed in battle shall receive immediate entry into paradise."

Such words might have been spoken by Umar, the second *khalif*, or successor, to the great Prophet Muhammad, the Arab founder of the religion of ***Islam***. Only a few years after the prophet's death, Arabs would carry his message to distant lands. Today, about one-fifth of the world's population are ***Muslims*** (followers of Islam), and it is the fastest growing religion in the world.

Figure 15-1
The Prophet Muhammad

THE LANDS AND PEOPLES OF THE MIDDLE EAST

Europeans invented the term "Middle East" to describe the region between the Near East (a term sometimes used for the area of ancient Egypt, Asia Minor, Syria, Palestine, and Mesopotamia) and the Far East (Asia). While the name is Eurocentric, it has been universally adopted for convenience, including by the peoples of this region themselves.

GEOGRAPHY
The boundaries of the Middle East reflect in large part the history of Muslim conquests and assimilation. The heart of the region is the Arabian penin-

sula, the largest in the world and the birthplace of Islam. Egypt lies to the west, while Iraq (Mesopotamia) and Iran (Persia) lie to the north and northwest. When Muslim peoples conquered first Palestine and Syria (sometimes called the Holy Land), then parts of Turkey (Asia Minor), and finally the rest of the Byzantine empire, these areas also became part of the Middle East. Farther flung lands that do not belong to this region yet were deeply influenced by Islam include parts of eastern Europe, central Asia, and the territory occupied by modern Pakistan and northern India.

Although outsiders tend to think of the Middle East as virtually all desert, its geography is more diverse than that. It is true that in this vast region,

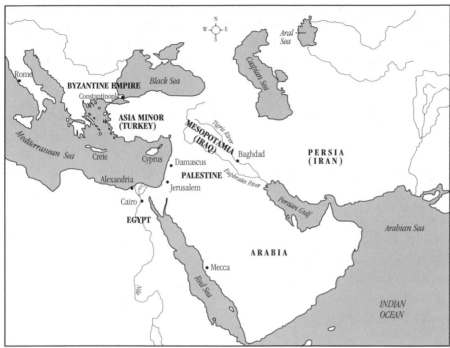

Figure 15-2 *Historic lands of the Middle East*

there are only two large river systems: the Nile in Egypt and the Tigris and Euphrates in Iraq (the home of ancient Mesopotamia). These flat, wide river basins provided water for irrigating field crops, giving rise to the world's earliest civilizations and their huge populations.

Other fertile areas were to be found in the mountain ranges along the coasts of the Mediterranean and southwestern Arabia and in the high plateaus of central Turkey (Asia Minor) and Iran. Here, where seasonal rains fed the mountain streams, crops could also be grown although not as abundantly as in the river basins.

Semi-arid steppes or grassy plains covered much of Iraq and Iran and sections of Arabia. Because rainfall fell irregularly, the steppes were inhabited by sparse populations of nomadic peoples, who used the land to graze their livestock.

Finally, there were the deserts—

expanses of sand or pebbles where almost no rain fell. Apart from the alluvial plains flooded by the Nile, Egypt was essentially a vast desert. The Arabian peninsula was also mostly covered by desert, which extended north into Palestine, Syria, and western Iraq. The deserts were largely uninhabited, except in spots of fertile land that lay over underground water sources. These fertile spots, called **oases**, served as stopping points for caravans, long lines of people and camels travelling across inhospitable terrain. A few oases, such as Damascus in Syria, were large and fertile enough to support an urban population.

Temperature, climate, vegetation, and crops varied throughout the Middle East. The fertile plains of Egypt were major sources of wheat and cotton. Other southern fertile regions were hot and humid, ideal for growing date palms and, later, coffee. Olives and cotton were cultivated in the Mediterranean climate of Turkey's coastlands, while various grain crops were planted on the more temperate inland plateau. The deserts were searingly hot during the day, and dryly cool at night. In the north, the mountains were covered with snow caps year-round.

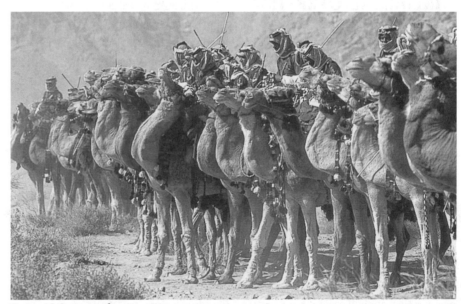

Figure 15-3 *A camel caravan*

ETHNIC GROUPS

While the word "Arab" has been used as a synonym for "Middle Eastern" and sometimes for "Muslim," only a small proportion of people in this ethnically diverse region are, in fact, Arab. The original Arabs came from the Arabian peninsula and differed from the Egyptians, the Jews, and the Syrians (whose ethnic background was closer to that of the Greeks). The Iraqis were mainly of ancient Mesopotamian and Persian origin, while the Iranians were Persian. The Turks, who originally came from central and northeast Asia, moved west into Asia Minor and south into northern Iraq.

REFLECT AND ANALYZE

1. In your view, is the name "Middle East" an appropriate description for the area that encompasses the Arabian peninsula and surrounding lands? Give reasons for your opinion.

2. Explain how physical geography and the availability of water would affect land use and the size of the human population in several of the following: a) a wide, flat plain near the Nile; b) a desert oasis covering an area of three hectares; c) a vast grass-covered steppe with not much rainfall; d) a narrow valley and stream between rugged mountains; e) a sandy desert bare of any vegetation.

3. Can you explain why people crossing the desert travelled in caravan groups rather than alone?

HISTORICAL OVERVIEW

Before the seventh century, the desert peninsula of Arabia was unimportant in world history. Surrounded on three sides by water, it was largely untouched by the great ancient civilizations of Egypt, Mesopotamia, Israel, and Persia that flourished not far from its borders. Most of its inhabitants were nomads called Bedouins, who moved from place to place with their herds of camels, sheep, and goats. These "people of the tent" were tough, independent, and strongly attached to their own tribe or clan. Tribal wars were a fact of life, and the Bedouins celebrated their victories and their heroes in poetry recited at night around campfires.

Other Arabs led a more settled existence, living permanently in oasis towns that sprung up along Arabia's western coast to accommodate trade between Asia, Africa, and Europe. One such town was Mecca, situated halfway along the caravan route connecting Yemen, in the southern tip of Arabia, to Syria and Egypt north of the peninsula. Exotic and precious goods from China, India, Persia, and east Africa arrived by ship in Yemen and were transported north, bound for the great Byzantine empire. A long and exhausting war between the Byzantines and the Persians in the seventh century had disrupted the land roads between them, forcing the traffic of goods to be rerouted south to Arabia.

Mecca's importance was heightened by another factor: the presence of the peninsula's holiest temple, the Ka'ba. The Ka'ba was a tall, windowless building that housed images of about 360 Arab gods and spirits, including their creator and lord, Allah. The Ka'ba also contained a huge black stone (probably a meteorite) believed to have been sent to earth by Nabie Ibrahim (the prophet Abraham). Once a year, Arab tribes would make a pilgrimage to Mecca to worship in the temple and to attend an annual fair. Local merchants profited greatly from the selling of goods to visiting pilgrims.

MUHAMMAD AND THE BIRTH OF ISLAM

Islam is a *monotheistic* religion; that is, its followers believe in one all-powerful God. The rise of Islam in the seventh century was made possible by two earlier monotheistic religions: Christianity and its predecessor, Judaism (the Jewish religion). Muslims believe in the same God, whom they call *Allah*, as Christians and Jews. However, Muslims consider Muhammad to be the last, and the most authoritative, of all the prophets.

Muhammad was born to a family of poor merchants in Mecca around 570. Having lost both parents when he was young, he was raised by his grandfather and his uncle. As a young man, he led trading caravans for a rich widow named Khadijah. During the long, tedious journeys through the desert north to Syria or south to Yemen, he had plenty of time to ponder the meaning of life and God. In the north he would have encountered many Christians and Jews from Syria, Palestine, and Egypt.

Figure 15-4 *Muhammad and the angel Gabriel. Since Islam forbids idolotry, the Prophet's face is veiled.*

At age 25, Muhammad married Khadijah, 15 years his senior. With his newly gained financial security, Muhammad was able to spend more time in solitary prayer and meditation in the desert. In his musings, he was influenced not only by Christian and Jewish teachings, but also by the *hanifs,* religious Arabs who rejected the pagan gods and worshipped a single God of their own.

According to Islamic tradition, Muhammad experienced a vision during a night in the month of Ramadan in 610. While sleeping in a cave on Mount Hira, near Mecca, the angel Gabriel appeared, telling him to recite the words of God. When he told Khadijah about his vision, she was convinced that God had chosen him to be a prophet, or divine messenger. She and other close relatives and friends were Muhammad's first followers.

He began preaching among the people of Mecca the new religion of *Islam,* a word which means "submission to Allah," the one true God. Those who submit to Allah are called Muslims. Followers of Islam would receive their rightful reward in heaven, but worshippers of pagan idols would suffer eternal damnation in hell. Since he could not read or write, Muhammad recited the divine messages he received. After his death, his recitations were written down, forming the holy book of Islam, the Qur'an.

Muhammad believed that he had been chosen by God to restore the religion of Abraham, which had been distorted by the Jews and Christians. In Islamic teaching, Jesus is viewed as a prophet, not as an incarnation of God. Muslims flatly reject the Christian concept of the Trinity (God the Father, Son, and Holy Spirit) which, in their view, denies the unity of God. Muhammad is seen as the final, and truest, prophet, but not a god himself. The words of the Qur'an are considered to be the actual words of God, not a paraphrase or an interpretation by Muhammad. Islam, then, differs significantly from Judaism and Christianity. You will learn about the teachings and duties of Islam in the next chapter.

Not surprisingly, Muhammad's message that all idols should be destroyed and that people should worship only Allah was not well received by many Meccans. Merchants and innkeepers feared the loss of prestige of their city's idol temple as well as the loss of business generated by visiting pilgrims. People also opposed Muhammad's teaching that duty to Allah was more important than duty to one's family or tribe. Faced with persecution, Muhammad

and his followers decided to leave Mecca secretly in 622.

The Hijrah to Medina

Muhammad's destination was Yagrib, another commercial town about 400 km north of Mecca. Muslim converts in Yagrib had earlier invited him to preach and act as a judge among them. Muslims call Muhammad's journey from Mecca to Yagrib the *hijrah* (departure) and designate the year 622 as the first year of the Muslim calendar. Yagrib was later renamed Medina, "the city of the Prophet."

The *hijrah* was a turning point for Islam. In Medina, the new religion acquired political and social authority, with Muhammad as ruler and lawgiver as well as prophet. His mission also changed. He

Figure 15-5 *The Mosque of the Prophet is visible in this photograph of Medina*

THE ISLAMIC CIVILIZATIONS:

	MUHAMMAD AND THE BIRTH OF ISLAM 610-661	**THE FIRST KHALIFS 632- 530 BCE**	**THE UMAYYAD DYNASTY 661-750**
POLITICAL DEVELOPMENTS	• the angel Gabriel speaks to Muhammad in a cave on Mount Hira (610) • Muhammad recites the messages of Allah (God) in Mecca (610 onward) • Muhammad and his followers leave Mecca to avoid persecution (the hijrah) in 622; this date is the first year of the Muslim calendar • Muhammad becomes leader and lawgiver of the first Muslim community in Medina (622) • Muhammad captures Mecca in the first jihad and turns the Ka'ba into Islam's holiest site (630) • Muhammad dies, having converted most Arab tribes to Islam (632)	• Abu Bakr is elected as the first khalif (successor) to Muhammad (632) • Abu Bakr sends out Muslim Bedouins to attack the Byzantine and Persian empires (634) • Umar becomes the second khalif and conquers Syria, Palestine, Persia, and Egypt before being assassinated (634–644) • after Umar's death, Muslims are divided over how their leader should be chosen, leading to the eventual Sunni-Shi'a split (644 onward) • Uthman, an Umayyad, is elected khalif (644) • Ali, the Prophet's cousin and son-in-law, becomes khalif, leading the first Muslim civil war with Mu'awiya, Uthman's relative (656)	• after Ali's assassination, Mu'awiya becomes the first Umayyad khalif and moves the khalifate from Medina to Damascus, Syria (661) • Mu'awiya changes the khalifate from an elected to a hereditary office • the leader of the Shi'as, Husayn the son of Ali, is killed, leading to a permanent rift between Shi'as and Sunnis (680) • the Umayyad khalifs greatly expand Islamic territory, conquering North Africa, Spain, much of central Asia, and western Pakistan • the Umayyads appoint only Arabs as provincial governors and impose a heavy tax on non-Arabs • non-Muslim subjects and non-Arab converts to Islam oppose Umayyad rule and Arab domination
CULTURAL/RELIGIOUS DEVELOPMENTS	• Bedouin tribes compose heroic desert odes called *qasidas* (500s to 600s) • Muhammad establishes the five pillars (essential duties) of Islam	• the Sunnis believe that khalifs should be chosen by Muslim leaders • the Shi'as reject the rightly guided khalifs and their successors, feeling that khalifs should be descendants of the Prophet's cousin and son-in-law Ali • Muhammad's divine recitations are compiled into the Qur'an (650) • the earliest stories of the Arabian Nights emerge in Persia	• Arabic is made the universal language of the Islamic empire • the death of Husayn is a defining event in Shi'a Islam (680 onward) • the Dome of the Rock, the earliest Muslim mosque, is built in Jerusalem (691) • Muslims absorb Byzantine influences • Umayyad poets compose desert qasidas in urban environments • Sufi mysticism develops and appeals to ordinary Muslims (700s onward)
TECHNOLOGICAL/ ECONOMIC DEVELOPMENTS			• the alchemist Jabir performs experiments and keeps careful scientific records (c. late 700s)

THE ABBASID KHALIFATE 750–1258

- the Abbasid family and Persian Shi'a rebels capture Damascus and defeat the Umayyads (750)
- Abu al-Abbas becomes the first Abbasid khalif (750)
- all the Umayyads are killed except Abd al-Rahman, who establishes an independent khalifate in Spain (756)
- the Abbasids move the capital of the Islamic empire from Syria to Baghdad, Persia (762)
- the Abbasids appoint non-Arabs (Persians and Turks) to high positions in government and the army
- the Abbasids establish peaceful relations with non-Muslim nations in order to engage in trade
- Turkish slave soldiers take control of the khalifate (860s)
- various provinces assert their independence, leading to fragmentation of the Islamic empire

---

- Abbasid rulers become major patrons of the arts, resulting in a golden age of Islam (763–809)
- the historical chronicle becomes an important form of non-fiction
- the Moors in Spain construct the Great Mosque of Cordoba (785)
- the Abbasids adopt Persian imperial and cultural customs
- the House of Wisdom is founded in Baghdad (early 800s)
- Muslim women veil their faces and are segregated from men in harems

---

- Baghdad becomes the most important trading city of the medieval world (c. 780)
- numerous hospitals are opened in Baghdad and Muslims become renowned medical authorities
- Muslim mathematicians adopt Hindu-Arabic numerals and create algebra and trigonometry

INVASIONS OF ISLAMIC LANDS C. 800–1258

- the Shi'a Fatimids establish an independent khalifate in Cairo, Egypt (969–1171)
- the Seljuk Turks invade Persia from the east and take Baghdad (1055), establishing themselves as sultans
- the Seljuk Turks take Syria, Palestine, and most of Asia Minor from the Byzantines (1070s–1080s)
- European Christians of western Europe launch the Crusades and capture Jerusalem (1099)
- Saladin recaptures Jerusalem for the Muslims (1187)
- the Mongols blaze a trail of mass murder and terror through central Asia, Persia, and Mesopotamia (1218–1260)
- the Mongol chief Hulagu seizes Baghdad and deposes the Abbasid khalif (1258)

- during the Fatimid reign, Cairo is a centre of Egyptian and Arab culture
- the Fatimids found the mosque university of al-Azhar in Cairo (970)
- the Seljuk Turks make Persian the second language of the Muslim world
- the Moorish philosopher Ibn Rushd (Averroes) writes about Aristotle and applies logic to the study of religion (late 1100s)
- the world's first full-time astronomical observatory is built (1259)
- the Tunisian historian Ibn Khaldun writes the Muqaddima (1300s)

- al-Hasan studies optics (c. 900)
- al-Razi writes an important book about children's diseases (early 900s)
- Ibn Sina (Avicenna) compiles a Canon of Medicine (c. 1030s) that becomes the standard medical reference in the Muslim world and Europe until the seventeenth century

ISLAM AROUND THE YEAR 1500

- the Mamluks rule Egypt, Syria, and Palestine
- the Ottoman Turks capture Constantinople (1453) and establish a large empire encompassing Asia Minor, the Balkans, Greece, and parts of Persia
- Spanish Christians defeat the Moors and expel them from Spain (1492)
- the Shi'a Safavids take control of Persia from the Mongolian Il-Khans (c. 1500)
- the Ottoman Turks defeat the Mamluks of Egypt, establishing their dominance over the Muslim world (1517)
- Babur establishes the Mughul dynasty in northern India (1520s)

- in the Ottoman period, Turkish becomes a third important language of Islam
- Ottoman artists begin to paint portraits and scenes of historical events

---

- Muslim astronomers discover that the earth is round and measure its circumference
- the Mamluks' monopoly of Middle Eastern trade causes the Portuguese and Spanish to search for alternative ocean routes (late 1400s onward)

Figure 15-6 *A mosque in Cairo, Egypt*

believed that God sent him a message to fight infidels or unbelievers. His use of armed force, not just persuasion, to bring people to Islam was the origin of the belief in *jihad,* holy war, as a religious duty. Muslims who fought for Islam were assured of a place in paradise. Thus the stage was set for a wave of Arab conquests following Muhammad's death.

In 630 he and 10 000 Muslim soldiers marched to Mecca and captured it. Muhammad ordered all of the idols of the Ka'ba to be destroyed, except for the holy black stone, which he dedicated to Allah. Mercy was shown to all Meccans who accepted Islam. The pagan shrine was transformed into the holiest shrine of Islam, the place to which all Muslims must make a pilgrimage at least once in their lives.

During the last two years of Muhammad's life, most of the tribes of Arabia accepted the Islamic faith. Although some people adopted it in name only, many others were greatly attracted to the message of one God, the equality of all believers, and the promise of paradise. Muhammad's words, later compiled into the Qur'an, also contained a clear code of conduct, which people found useful for organizing their lives.

After a short illness, the great Prophet died in 632 and was buried in the Mosque of the Prophet in Medina.

REFLECT AND ANALYZE

1. What made Mecca an important town on the Arabian peninsula in the years before Islam? How might it have changed after becoming the centre of Islam?

2. Explain how Muhammad was influenced by Christianity and Judaism in proclaiming the new religion of Islam.

3. a) How was Muhammad different from a Christian or a Jewish prophet?
    b) After his flight to Medina, how did his views and activities change?

4. Explain the origin of the Muslim belief in *jihad*, or holy war. In many Muslim countries, members of the army are highly respected. Why?

THE FIRST KHALIFS

Muhammad had left no clear instructions as to who should be the next leader of the Muslim community. A group of influential disciples chose Abu Bakr, a close friend of Muhammad and one of his earliest converts, as *khalif,* or successor, of the Prophet. He and the next three Khalifs were called the "rightly guided Khalifs" because they had personally known Muhammad and heard his teachings.

Abu Bakr faced fiercely independent Bedouin tribes who rebelled against Islam after Muhammad's death. There were also Muslims who opposed his leadership. How could he control these rebels? Abu Bakr's plan was to unite all Arabs by spreading Islam among the infidels. Soldiers would be sent out in a grand campaign of Islamic conquest. The fact that Arabs also needed more arable land, which was scarce on the peninsula, provided another incentive for invasion. The khalif's plan would succeed brilliantly, providing a model for his successors to follow. Nevertheless, conflict among Arabs was always in danger of breaking out.

With Abu Bakr's consent, Bedouin tribes attacked the Byzantine and Persian empires along Arabia's northern border. Both empires had been weakened during a 26-year war against each other. Abu Bakr died in 634, just as the *jihad* had begun.

Umar, the new khalif, was another close associate of Muhammad. Within a few years, he conquered the Byzantine provinces of Syria and Palestine, and then turned his attention to the Persians. During a four-day battle in 637, the Arabs killed 30 000 Persian soldiers as well as their king. The Persian empire quickly fell to the Muslims. Umar also captured Egypt before his assassination by a Persian slave in 644.

Division among Arab Muslims

After Umar's death, controversy developed over how the khalif was to be chosen. The majority of Muslims, who eventually became known as the *Sunnis,* felt that khalifs should be elected by a committee of Muslim leaders, as earlier khalifs had been. A small group of Muslims, however, believed that Muhammad had designated his cousin and son-in-law Ali as his successor.

All khalifs, therefore, should be descendants of the Prophet through his closest male relative, Ali. This group of Muslims came to be called the *Shi'as.*

As well as clashing over the question of leadership, Sunnis and Shi'as disagreed fundamentally as to the proper interpretations of the Qur'an and Muhammad's own actions (*sunna* in Arabic). It is probable that tribal rivalries and personal ambition also played a role, since the *khalifate* (office of khalif) carried significant political power. For instance, Ali's chief competitors were members of the influential family of Umayya, distantly related to Muhammad, but who had opposed his early preaching in

Mecca. The family converted to Islam at a late stage, perhaps when it realized it could no longer avoid doing so.

Muslim leaders elected an Umayya named Uthman as the third khalif, instead of Ali. When Uthman was murdered by warriors who opposed his leadership, the Shi'as chose Ali as leader. Uthman's kinsman, Mu'awiya, who was governor of Syria, refused to recognize Ali and garnered Sunni support for his claim to the khalifate.

Ali tried to avoid armed conflict, which the Qur'an forbids between Muslims. Some people viewed his refusal to fight as a sign of weakness, which led to a loss of support for the Shi'a movement. Ali's

PERSPECTIVES ON THE PAST

Arab Warriors

In the mid-600s, the Muslim battle cry of "Allah is most great!" was heard far and wide. Arabs conquered a large part of the Byzantine empire and shattered the Persian empire. More conquests were still to come. Why were Muslim warriors so successful?

First, a belief in holy war created a sense of unity and purpose. Before going into battle, Muslim warriors were guided in prayer by their military commander.

Second, Bedouins, who made up a large part of the early armies, were already skilled in fighting. For generations, they had engaged in tribal warfare. They were also nomads, accustomed to moving about from place to place. This gave them an advantage over, for example, Byzantine soldiers, who were mostly farmers and only called into action when necessary.

A third factor was the Arab style of fighting. Rather

Figure 15-7 *Arab warriors*

than launching all-out offensives with huge numbers of soldiers, Muslim commanders preferred surprise attacks with small groups. Lightly armed with lances and swords, and carrying few supplies, Arab warriors were highly mobile yet aggressive, easily overcoming the slower and heavily armoured enemy soldiers.

The last, and perhaps most far-reaching, factor was the Muslims' treatment of conquered peoples. The Arabs established military settlements in newly captured territory to keep it under control. At the same time, they acted leniently toward their former enemies. Although the goal was to convert all people to Islam, Christians and Jews were allowed to practise their faith in peace, as long as they paid a tribute or tax to their Muslim rulers. This tolerant attitude, along with Islam's simple, powerful message, attracted many people to the religion.

attempt to negotiate with Mu'awiya failed, and for the first time Muslims were divided by civil war. Ali himself was assassinated by a disenchanted follower.

With his rival dead, Mu'awiya became the undisputed khalif in 661. He moved the khalifate from Medina, where there were many Muslims loyal to Ali, to the Syrian capital of Damascus. A new era in Islamic leadership was beginning.

REFLECT AND ANALYZE

1. What prompted the first khalif, Abu Bakr, to undertake a *jihad* soon after Muhammad's death? Why did Arab tribes eagerly join in this Islamic expansion?

2. Explain whether there was a difference between religious and political leadership in early Muslim communities. Compare such a community with the organization of a feudal village in medieval Europe.

3. Explain the origin of the split between the Sunni and Shi'a branches of Islam. What part did family rivalries play?

4. Are there any parallels to the Sunni/Shi'a schism that you have learned about in history? If so, describe the similarities and differences between the two situations.

5. Why do you think the majority of Muslims favoured the election of khalifs rather than succession based on family blood?

THE UMAYYAD DYNASTY

The Arab tradition of strong loyalty to one's clan resurfaced with Mu'awiya. He made the khalifate a hereditary office, replacing the more egalitarian principle of election. He also set up a council of Arab *shaykhs* (sheiks) or chiefs to assist him in governing and to ensure that political power remained in Arab hands.

The Umayyad dynasty dominated Islam from 661 to 750. Their control of the khalifate was bitterly opposed by Shi'as, who increasingly used Persia as their home base. When Mu'awiya's son Yazid became khalif in 680, a group of Shi'as elected their own successor, Husayn, the son of Ali (the Prophet's cousin). In Persia, Yazid's troops confronted and killed the dissenters, including Husayn. This event united and mobilized all Shi'as, angered by the slaying of one of the Prophet's family. Martyrdom and sacrifice became a theme of the Shi'a cause. Sunnis and Shi'as were permanently divided in a second, violent civil war that only ended when another Umayyad khalif negotiated peace in 692.

Under the Umayyads, the borders of Islam were greatly expanded. Muslims advanced west beyond Egypt, conquering all of North Africa and Spain. They continued north into France, but were stopped by the Frankish king Charles Martel. Resuming their assault on the Byzantine empire, they laid siege to Constantinople but did not manage to capture it. Further east, they advanced into the area occupied by modern Afghanistan and western Pakistan. Remarkably, these conquests were accomplished with relatively little bloodshed.

The Umayyads maintained control of their steadily expanding Islamic empire by appointing Arab governors in all of the provinces. The Arab rulers, who did not pay taxes themselves, grew extremely wealthy from the high taxes they imposed on non-Arabs. Educated non-Arabs, such as Jews, Byzantine Greeks, and Persians, were employed in local government, but the Arabs dictated that all state business was to be conducted in Arabic.

The Umayyad ruling elite faced increasing dissent in the later years of their reign. As increasing numbers of non-Arabs converted to Islam, they resented the privileges enjoyed by Arab Muslims, namely higher salaries and lower taxes. The new Muslims could quote the Qur'an in support of their grievances. Had not the Prophet stated that all followers of Islam were equal in the sight of God?

Figure 15-8 *An Umayyad Khalif*

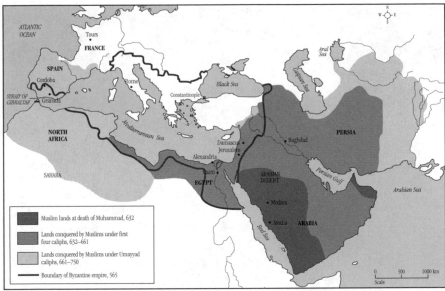

Figure 15-9 *Islamic conquests up to 750*

The Shi'as also renewed their fight for a new leader chosen from among certain branches of the Prophet's family. They hoped to find an *imam* (leader) in the Abbasid family, who were descendants of Muhammad's uncle Abbas. The Arab Shi'as were supported by large numbers of Persians and Turks, who had converted to Shi'a Islam. The Turks wanted to break free of the Arab empire and form their own state.

With so many forces of opposition within the Arab empire, a revolution was brewing.

REFLECT AND ANALYZE

1. Do you think historians are right to describe the Umayyad line of khalifs as a "dynasty"? In what ways did these khalifs resemble imperial rulers?

2. Describe the event that was a critical moment in the history of the Shi'a Muslims and the consequences of this event.

3. How did the Umayyads maintain control of their greatly enlarged Arab empire?

4. How did non-Arabs benefit under Umayyad rule? What disadvantages did they face?

5. "There are parallels between the ancient Roman empire and the Umayyad Arab empire." Discuss whether or not you agree with this statement, taking into consideration a variety of aspects.

THE ABBASID KHALIFATE

Although the Abbasids were Sunni, not Shi'a, Muslims, they found support among the Shi'as because of their close blood ties to Muhammad the Prophet. The head of the clan was Abu al-Abbas. He turned to a charismatic Persian named Abu Muslim to lead rebel fighters to Damascus, which they captured in triumph in 750. Al-Abbas was hailed as khalif, the rightful heir of the Prophet. He invited the defeated Umayyads to a banquet, during which he had them massacred. Only one Umayyad, Abd al-Rahman, escaped alive, fleeing to Spain where, in 756, he set up an independent khalifate in Cordoba (see box on page 334).

Unfortunately for the Shi'as, Khalif al-Abbas cut his ties with them as soon as he was in power. The Abbasid khalifate would be a Sunni one. The family established their capital in Baghdad in 762, then a market village in Persia. Whereas the Umayyad capital, Damascus, had belonged to the Greco-Roman world, Baghdad was heir to the sophisticated and cultured Persian empire which had flourished before the advent of Islam. The move of the khalifate from Syria to Persia resulted in an eastern influence on the religion.

The Arabs themselves learned much from their exposure to the knowledge and culture of the peoples they conquered. From the Byzantines, for example, Arabs acquired knowledge of the ancient Greeks and Romans, whom they grew to admire. Classical texts of literature, philosophy, and medicine were translated into Arabic and widely studied by Muslim scholars. Several centuries later, western Europeans would be reintroduced to their ancient Roman heritage through their contact with the Muslims.

The Abbasid khalifate lasted from

PERSPECTIVES ON THE PAST
Muslim Spain

When Muslim warriors stormed across north Africa and crossed the Strait of Gibraltar, they captured Spain with surprising ease from the Visigoths who ruled it. Between 711 and 718, the Muslims gained all of the Iberian peninsula except for the northern mountains which were considered not worth capturing.

Spain's great distance from the Umayyad capital in Damascus, Syria, meant that Muslim rule was fairly tentative during the early years of occupation. A journey between Damascus and Seville in southern Spain could take four months, if travel was not disrupted by local uprisings in North Africa. The situation in Spain stabilized when the last of the Umayyads, Abd al-Rahman, arrived in 756 after escaping from the Abbasid massacre of his family.

Figure 15-10 *The arches in the Grand Mosque of Cordoba, Spain*

Al-Rahman established his government in Cordoba, a town in southern Spain. This branch of Umayyad rule would last until 976, more than twice as long as the earlier Umayyad dynasty in Damascus. The Muslims in Spain (referred to as *Moors*) named their kingdom al-Andulus, which gave rise to the modern name of Andalusia.

Far from the Abbasid centre of power in Baghdad, Spain developed into a prosperous and culturally sophisticated Islamic kingdom. Its wealth came from trade with North Africa, the Byzantine empire, and the eastern Mediterranean. Arabs, Berbers (a people of North Africa), Christians, and Jews all made distinctive contributions to Moorish society and culture.

Khalif al-Rahman began construction on the Great Mosque of Cordoba which, in 785, had a capacity of 5500 worshippers. Succeeding khalifs finished and made additions to the building. This magnificent example of Moorish architecture incorporates different artistic and architectural influences. The classical columns and capitals are Byzantine in origin, as are the horseshoe arches and the use of contrasting colours of stone. The ornamental, abstract carvings on the stone blocks are a typically Arab feature.

In the thirteenth century, the Christian kingdoms in the north conquered (reconquered in their view) most of Spain, leaving only the southern province of Granada in Muslim hands. When two Christian kingdoms, Castile and Aragon, were united by the royal marriage of Ferdinand and Isabella, the fate of the Muslims was sealed. Isabella was a devout Catholic who was determined to punish Christian heretics and to expel the Muslims and Jews from Spain. In 1492, the deed was done and al-Andalus was no more. However, it left its mark on the architecture, literature, and some of the social customs of southern Spain.

750 to 1258. In its first 100 years, the Arab Islamic empire attained its zenith. Many achievements were made in the arts and sciences, and the Muslim rulers lived in immense luxury like the ancient kings of Persia. Commerce and trade formed the basis of this vast wealth, which the Abbasids and their subjects pursued assiduously rather than engaging in further Islamic conquests. The Abbasids developed mainly peaceful relations with non-Muslim nations—*jihad* was used to defend the established boundaries of Islam rather than to expand them.

Muslim ships voyaged to India and China, bringing back spices, silk, and other precious goods. The ships also patrolled the waters of the Mediterranean to protect the Muslims' lucrative trade with the Byzantine empire and Africa. Baghdad became the marketplace of the world, so wealthy that even its buildings gleamed with gold and precious stones. Talented artists and distinguished scholars flocked to the Islamic capital. At its height in the ninth century,

Figure 15-11 *Baghdad, on the banks of the Tigris, was a major centre on the main trade route between Asia, and Europe and Africa*

Baghdad surpassed the great Byzantine city of Constantinople in size, prosperity, and cultural achievements.

The Abbasid khalifs made important changes to Islamic society and politics. They eliminated discrimination against non-Arab Muslims, stressing equality and unity through Islam and use of the Arabic language. Arab Muslims lost their dominance, as non-Arab Muslims assumed high positions in government and the military. The khalifs appointed a *wazir* (vizier), or chief minister, to manage the running of government. The wazir was almost invariably an educated Persian. In the army, Arab tribesmen were increasingly replaced by Persian mercenaries (soldiers for hire) and Turkish slave-soldiers.

Influenced by Persian imperial tradition, the Abbasids exalted their role as head of the Islamic empire, adopting flowery titles such as "Prince of the Faithful" and "He who is made victorious by God."

Individuals admitted before the khalif were required to bow down and kiss his feet or the floor.

Harun al-Rashid

Perhaps the most famous Abbasid khalif was Harun al-Rashid (786–809), whose reign is considered Islam's golden age. Well-educated and literate, Harun encouraged artists and rewarded them lavishly. He could well afford to be generous, since his wealth was enormous. One story tells how Harun, delighted by some beautiful verses, ordered his treasurer to pay the poet the vast sum of 10 000 dirhams. The overwhelmed poet bowed low and said, "O Prince of the Faithful, your words of praise are better than my verse." Even more delighted, the khalif gave the poet another 100 000 dirhams.

A great traveller, Harun visited outlying areas of the empire, thus gaining the respect and affection of the local inhabi-

tants. In 796, he made a pilgrimage to Mecca, walking the 400 km of the journey to gain greater merit. He showed diplomatic skill in dealing with other nations, yet did not hesitate to employ his well-trained army on appropriate occasions, such as when a new Byzantine emperor refused to pay the customary tribute to the Muslims. Later generations of Muslims would view Harun as the ideal Islamic ruler.

Fragmentation of the Empire

During the first century of their reign, the Abbasid khalifs maintained a strong central government from Baghdad. However, in the ninth century their power began to deteriorate, although they continued to exist, often in name only, for another 400 years.

Like the Roman emperors of former times, the khalifs found it difficult to govern such a far-flung empire. They increasingly relied on the provincial governors to raise taxes and administrate local affairs. Some governors took the opportunity to form their own territorial dynasties and armies, paying mere lip service to the distant khalif. Ironically, it was during Harun al-Rashid's reign, the high point of the Arab empire, that a governor (of a province in North Africa) first became virtually independent of Baghdad.

Harun's successors encountered difficulties with the army which, as mentioned earlier, was mostly made up of non-Arabs. Early recruits were mainly Persian mercenaries from the eastern province of Khurasan. The Khurasanians were Muslim and loyal to the khalif. When Khurasan became autonomous in the mid-800s, the khalifs turned to Turkish slave soldiers, who were renowned if brutal fighters, to fill army ranks. The Turks at that time were mostly heathen, did not speak Arabic, and felt no particular loyalty to the empire.

They also proved to be an unwise choice. Turkish generals soon took control of the government, casually murdering khalifs whenever it suited them and appointing new khalifs in their place. The Turks stopped short of eliminating the khalifate altogether, since in it rested the spiritual leadership of Islam. But with the khalifs mere puppets in the hands of the military, even more provinces, such as Egypt, broke away. The empire fragmented to such an extent that the khalifs only effectively maintained authority in Baghdad and the surrounding area.

REFLECT AND ANALYZE

1. "The Abbasids restored the principle of equality of all Muslims, which the Umayyads had disregarded." Discuss whether or not this statement is true, drawing arguments from history.

2. Draw a map of the Mediterranean region, placing ships in the areas controlled by the Arabs, and different ships in the areas controlled by the Byzantines. Which fleet dominated? Why? Explain why the two empires fought for control of the Mediterranean.

3. Name the factors that made the early years of the Abbasid khalifate the "golden age" of Islam.

4. Describe the events that led to the fragmentation of the Muslim empire and the Abbasid khalifs' loss of power.

INVASIONS OF ISLAMIC LANDS

The Islamic empire had fallen into disarray and was vulnerable to seizures of power and invasions. A group of Shi'a Muslims, claiming descent from the Prophet's daughter Fatima, established their own khalifate in Cairo, Egypt, in 969. The Fatimids, as they called themselves, regarded the Abbasid khalifs as illegitimate holders of the office. The Fatimids acquired control of all of Egypt, Syria, and much of North Africa and Arabia, but were unable to advance further.

During the Fatimids' reign, which lasted until 1171, Cairo became the centre of a vibrant Egyptian and Arab culture and literature. The Fatimids also founded one of the world's earliest universities, the mosque-university of al-Azhar, in 970. Unfortunately, the Fatimids lost Syria to the Byzantines in the tenth century. Syria and Palestine would pass between Christian and Muslim powers for several centuries to come.

Meanwhile, a tribe of nomadic Turks swept into Persia from the northeast, conquering Baghdad in 1055. These Turks, newly converted to Sunni Islam, were led by the Seljuk family. They allowed the Abbasid khalifs to retain their position as religious leaders, but assumed all political and military power. For the first time, religious and political authority were divided in an Islamic state.

The Turkish rulers, who called themselves *sultans,* ended the long-standing Arab leadership of Islam. Obsessed with empire-building, the Seljuk Turks revived *jihad* in their quest for new lands. They regained Syria and Palestine from the Byzantines, and invaded Asia Minor, a territory new to Islam.

Overwhelmed by the Seljuk Turks, the Byzantine emperor appealed to western Europe for help. When enthusiastic Christian soldiers marched into the Holy Land, the fragmented Islamic world was unable to resist them. However, the Seljuk Turks managed to keep their territory in Asia Minor, much to the chagrin of the Byzantines. The Muslims generally viewed the Crusades as a minor inconvenience, since the Christians' victories were short-lived, with the single exception of Spain.

Islam itself changed under the influence of the Seljuk Turks. They gradually adopted Persian customs and language. Instead of learning to speak Arabic, they made Persian the language of their empire. In a flowering of culture, Persian poets and artists set new standards of excellence in Islamic literature and art.

The Mongols

In the eleventh century, the Seljuk Turks had successfully taken control of the Muslim world; in the thirteenth century, another threat appeared from the east. The Mongols were a heathen nomadic people of eastern Asia, skilled in horsemanship and brutal tactics of war. United under their leader Chingghis Khan, they blazed a path of mass destruction and terror through central Asia, moving steadily westward. Their mode of

PERSPECTIVES ON THE PAST
Saladin

In your opinion, who won the standoff between the Muslims and the Christians in the Holy Land: Saladin or Richard the Lionheart?

Salah ad-Din, known to the Europeans as Saladin, was the most famous Muslim war hero of the Crusades. He became sultan of Egypt in 1171 when, as general of the army, he overthrew the last Fatimid khalif. Egypt thus came under Sunni rule after two centuries under the Shi'a Fatimids.

Saladin spent the first 12 years of his reign consolidating his hold in Egypt, Syria, Palestine, and northern Mesopotamia. He then launched a sustained military campaign against the Christian crusaders then occupying parts of the Holy Land. Within a few years, he had conquered numerous cities held by the Christians. His most important victory came in 1187 when Muslim forces captured the holy city of Jerusalem. After 88 years of occupation in the Middle East,

Figure 15-12 *Saladin*

the European Christians were left with only one stronghold, the well-fortified city of Tyre.

Saladin's impressive victories caused the Europeans to launch a counterattack in a third crusade. For two years, the crusaders, under Richard the Lionheart, laid siege to the Palestinian city of Acre. Richard's forces finally defeated the Muslim army at Arsuf in 1191, but they were not able to retake Jerusalem. Peace was negotiated between the two sides in 1192 when Saladin agreed to allow Christian pilgrims to visit Jerusalem without being harmed.

During their long standoff, Saladin and Richard came to respect each other's military skill and persistence. When Richard fell ill with a high fever, the sultan sent his personal physician and supplies of fresh fruit to the enemy camp. After the peace treaty was signed in 1192, Richard vowed to return to conquer Jerusalem. Saladin replied that if he were to lose the city, he would rather lose it to Richard than to any other man.

operation was to terrify people into surrendering without a fight. The entire population of a settlement would then be rounded up and slaughtered, regardless of age or sex. The city or town itself was stripped of its valuables and burned to the ground.

In 1258 Chingghis Khan's grandson, the Mongol chief Hulagu, descended upon Baghdad. After battering down its walls, the Mongols assembled all of the inhabitants and shot or slashed them to death. Historians estimate that perhaps 8000 people were killed. The superstitious Mongols

sewed up the khalif in a sack and had him trampled to death by horses, so that his blood would not be on their hands. Baghdad's buildings, which housed centuries of accummulated knowledge and art treasures, were utterly destroyed. Thus ended, in a flash, the Abbasid khalifate and, with it, the Arab leadership of Islam.

This was another critical moment in Islamic history. The Mongol rulers plunged the eastern Muslim world into a dark age. Virtually nothing remained of its sophisticated urban culture. Agriculture also

slumped due to neglect of the all-important irrigation networks. With the population, economy, and agriculture devastated, those who survived were often reduced to begging on the streets or living at barely a subsistence level. Central Asia, Persia, and Mesopotamia would not fully recover from this disaster for centuries.

Later generations of Mongol rulers were less brutal than their ancestors. They converted to Islam and were gradually integrated into Persian-Turkish life.

REFLECT AND ANALYZE

1. What important changes did the Seljuk Turks make to Islam?

2. In Islamic history, groups of foreign invaders almost always adopted the Muslim religion rather than impose their own faiths. What reasons can you give to explain this phenomenon?

3. Describe how the coming of the Mongols resulted in a dark age in Islamic history.

ISLAM AROUND THE YEAR 1500

Although the Muslim world was dealt a severe blow by the Mongols, it survived, regained strength and was, by 1500, many times larger than the Christian world. Christianity had reclaimed almost all of Spain by 1492, but apart from that, Islam's influence was greater than ever before. Through gradual assimilation, as well as conquest, the Muslim religion extended well into the African subcontinent, northern central Asia, India, and even southeast Asia. Despite the various independent states, khalifates, and empires that existed, Islam itself and the Arabic language of the Qur'an were universal elements throughout the Muslim world.

The Turks in particular strengthened Islam, enabling it to repel the Christian crusaders and embark on more conquests. Turkish leadership resulted in Turkish joining Arabic and Persian as an important language of Islam.

There were four major centres of power in the post-Mongol period. Egypt, Syria, and Palestine were ruled by the Mamluks, a group of elite Turkish slave soldiers. When Baghdad fell under Mongol rule, the Mamluk capital of Cairo became the main repository of Islamic learning and culture for two and a half centuries. The Mamluks stopped the Mongols' westward rampage in 1260 and expelled the last Christian crusaders from Palestine in 1293.

Persia was initially ruled by the Mongol conquerors, calling themselves the Il-Khans, who were soon followed by a series of Mongol and Turkish dynasties. In the

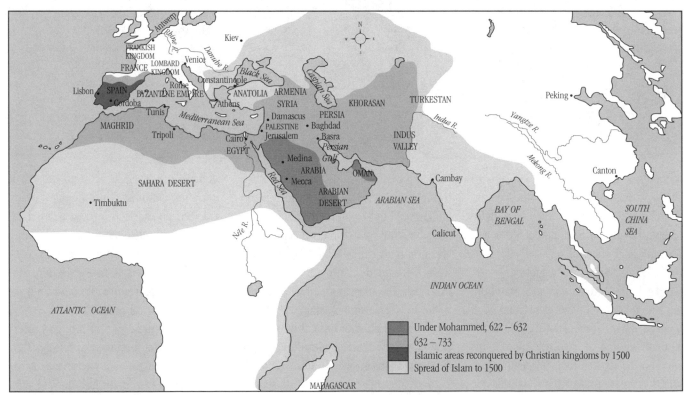

Figure 15-13 *Islamic expansion to 1500*

fifteenth and sixteenth centuries, a Shi'a group called the Safavids came to power. Strongly religious and anti-materialistic, the Safavids made Persia into a Shi'a state—the one exception among nations dominated by Sunni Islam. The Safavids are the ancestors of the fundamentalist government that rules Iran today.

Islam penetrated the northwestern border of India as early as the eighth century, but it was the Turks who established northern India (present-day Pakistan) as a strong Muslim state. A powerful dynasty, the Mughuls, was founded in the 1520s by Babur, who traced his lineage back to Chingghis Khan and the notorious Turkish ruler Timur-i Lang (Tamerlane). Islam developed in a unique way in India, influenced by Hinduism and Indian cultural traditions. Mughul rule was a far cry from the egalitarianism of the original Arab Muslims. The Mughuls were a royal dynasty, presiding over a splendid, stately court in Delhi.

The fourth and greatest of all Islamic centres was the Ottoman empire in Asia Minor and eastern Europe. The Ottoman Turks became a formidable power in the fourteenth century, about 100 years after the fall of the Seljuk Turks. The Byzantine emperor John VI Cantacuzenus, like the earlier Abbasid khalifs, recruited Turks in his army only to soon regret his decision. The Ottoman Turks rapidly occupied the remaining Byzantine portions of Asia Minor, Greece, and the Balkan lands north of Constantinople. The city was the only remaining stronghold of the Byzantine empire, in its final death throes after a long, slow decline. Barraged by a determined Turkish attack, Constantinople fell in 1453.

The Ottoman Turks saw themselves as heirs of both Islamic tradition and classically rooted Byzantine tradition. They soon overthrew the Mamluks in Egypt and exerted strong, if not complete, control over Persia. Thus, by the end of the sixteenth century, the Ottoman empire encompassed virtually all of the Middle East and portions of eastern Europe. Its reign would last in varying forms until the end of World War I.

Figure 15-14 *A sixteenth-century Ottoman manuscript showing the coronation of a sultan*

REFLECT AND ANALYZE

1. "The Muslims expanded the borders of Islam at the expense of Christianity." Decide whether or not this statement is true by charting, on a map, the wave of Islamic conquests from 661 to 1500. Sum up your findings in a short presentation.

2. Draw a map illustrating the territory controlled by each of the four main centres of Islam in 1500.

3. Choose one of the following topics regarding Mughul rule in India to research, and report your findings in a presentation format of your choice: a) history of the Mughul dynasty; b) social structure; c) architecture; d) mathematics, science, and technology.

GOVERNMENT

THE ARABS

The early political organization of the Arabs was tribal. All of the families of a tribe or clan appointed a chief, or *shaykh*, as their leader. The shaykh was expected to lead the men of the tribe in battle, protect the tribe's interests, and respect tribal customs. In return, the members of the clan obeyed his orders. A council of elders advised the shaykh in important matters.

People's loyalty to their tribe was extremely strong, and most often exhibited in battles against rival tribes. Since all of the shaykhs felt equal to one another, they preferrred to fight rather than submit to another's dominance. Despite the constant warring, relatively little blood was shed and few prisoners were taken. Clashes were seen more as a defence of the tribe's honour rather than a means of taking over another group.

The independent, egalitarian spirit of the Arabs, the intense competition between tribes, and the desert landscape worked against the formation of political unity. A unity of sorts was achieved by the end of the Prophet Muhammad's lifetime, but it was the result of religion, not politics. Under the banner of Islam, Arab tribes mostly continued to maintain their independence and manage their own affairs. In Medina, Muhammad established the model for all future Muslim communities, one that was both a religious and a political entity.

After Muhammad's death, the khalif assumed the role of political and religious leader of the Muslims. At that time, when his political power was still in the early stages of development, the khalif was a sort of grand shaykh over all of the shaykhs of Arabia. He attempted to keep them from breaking away from Islam and sent them to wage holy war against the infidels.

True political power and the makings of government emerged when the Umayyads took control of the khalifate. You may recall that the first Umayyad khalif, Mu'awiya, assembled a council of shayks to advise him. The Umayyads also made Arabic the official language of the empire, and adopted the existing government structures of the Byzantine and Persian peoples. While Arab governors ruled the provinces, the actual work of government was carried out by local people trained in administration.

During the age of the Abbasid khalifs, government underwent significant changes. The Abbasids reduced the power of Arab governors, who were potential rivals, by appointing non-Arab Muslims in the highest governmental positions. The khalif Mehedi created the position of *wazir,* or chief minister, to head the governmental bureaucracy, reserving a largely symbolic and ceremonial role for himself. Whereas earlier Arab khalifs had ruled as tribal shayhks, the Abbasid khalifs governed in the manner of divinely appointed Persian kings. They maintained their mystique by making isolated public appearances and engaging in elaborate court rituals at which only a few, specially chosen officials were present.

THE TURKS

When the Seljuk Turks conquered Persia, they instituted a separation of politics and religion in Islam. They adopted the title of **sultan**, an Arabic word for "government" or "governor." In Turkish usage, the word came to mean the head of the government and the army. The sultan was usually an army general; hence, Turkish government had a military flavour. The Seljuk Turks allowed the khalif to continue to exist, but confined his role to that of head of the faith and imam, leader in prayer.

The rise of the Seljuks, and later the Ottomans, resulted in Turks replacing Arabs as the ruling class of Islam. Turks dominated government, even in places where the majority of the population consisted of Persians, Arabs, Egyptians, or other nationalities.

The sultans, as men of the sword, were often illiterate and relied on their *wazirs* to manage governmental affairs. Unfamiliar with Arabic, the Seljuk Turks adopted Persian as the language of government as well as of everyday life. The form of Persian used, however, was written in the Arabic script and borrowed many Arabic words.

The khalifate, which had been relegated to a secondary position since the late Abbasids, disappeared altogether after the Ottoman Turks came to power. The Ottoman sultans incorporated the duties of the khalif into their role as supreme leader of their empire.

The Safavids of Persia, being Shi'as and the enemy of Sunnis, formed their own government institutions. The most important official was the *shah,* the head of the Persian state.

REFLECT AND ANALYZE

1. Describe the social and cultural customs of the Arab tribes. Can you explain why the early Muslims had no organized government? What influence, if any, did Arab customs have on Muhammad's organization of Islam?

2. Use an organizer to chart the history of Islam from its beginning to the year 1500, focusing on the significant developments brought about by: a) Arab, and b) Turkish control of Islamic leadership and government.

3. Explain whether or not you think the disappearance of the khalifate during the Ottoman empire was inevitable.

LAW

In the medieval Muslim world, religious law governed all personal and social behaviour. Muslims were ever mindful of Judgement Day and wished to act according to God's desires. The Qur'an, the **sunna** (the practices of Muhammad), and the **hadiths** (authorized records of Muhammad's sayings and actions) formed the basis of Islamic law.

The Qur'an discussed many matters with legal and political implications, such as organization of the Muslim state; crime; marriage and divorce; the status of women, children, and slaves; and inheritance rights. Suitable punishments for various violations were also mentioned. The *sunna* provided a model for Muslims to follow. For example, the Qur'an might tell people to pray, but only Muhammad's actions showed them how to do so. The *hadiths,* which were not written down until at least a century after the Prophet's death, were accounts of what he had said or done given by eyewitnesses and reliable sources. Sunnis and Shi'as each have their own versions of the *hadiths*.

While Muhammad was alive, he acted as judge and lawgiver for the Muslim community. After his death, the rightly guided khalifs performed the same role. As the Islamic empire grew in size and complexity, however, the khalifs spent most of their time in governing the state. To decide issues of law, they appointed *qadis,* or religious judges.

A *qadi* was often assisted by a judicial official called a *mufti,* who provided expert advice on technical points of law. A *shahid* was a witness who testified that a certain action had occurred, such as the signing of a contract. Lawyers have never existed in the Islamic legal system. The *qadi* decided cases based upon evidence presented by the involved parties and witnesses, and upon advice from a *mufti.* Since commerce was such a vital part of the Muslim economy, special officials called *muhtasibs* enforced Islamic law in the marketplace.

In the ninth century, the Abbasid khalifs recognized that a more formal code of law was needed that could apply to all Muslims equally, no matter where they lived or what their nationality was. Muslim religious scholars called the *ulema* compiled this code of law, the **shari'a**, which in Arabic means "the straight path." The *shari'a* consisted of two parts. The first part dealt with doctrine and morality—the ideals that should govern the actions of every pious Muslim and that will make possible his or her entry into heaven. The second part presented rules about religious practices, civil law, and criminal law. Since the *shari'a* represented God's law, any Muslim who violated it was committing a sin as well as a crime.

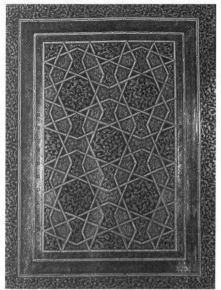

Figure 15-15 *The decorative cover of a copy of the Qur'an*

No formal government existed in Muhammad's day, and hence the Qur'an was silent on the role and powers of government. The holy book also did not address public law (the regulations all citizens of a state are required to follow). To cover these areas, Muslims created a second, secular body of law known as the **kanun**.

REFLECT AND ANALYZE

1. How did Islamic law differ from law in Christian Europe and the Byzantine empire?

2. Why did a formal code of law not emerge in Islamic society until the ninth century?

3. Was there a separation of religious and secular law in Muslim society? Explain.

THE ISLAMIC CIVILIZATIONS:
Society and Culture

Figure 16-1
*The Royal Mosque
in Isfaban, Iran*

"There is no God but Allah, and Muhammad is his servant and Prophet."
Muslim Declaration of Faith

In the name of Allah, the Compassionate, the Merciful:
Praise be to Allah, Lord of the Creation,
The Compassionate, the Merciful,
King of Judgement Day!
You alone we worship, and to You alone
we pray for help.
Guide us to the straight path,
The path of those whom You have favoured,
Not of those who have incurred Your wrath,
Nor of those who have gone astray.

*The Qur'an
Sura 1, The Opening*

RELIGION

For Muslims in the Middle Ages, Islam was not just a faith but a complete way of life. They were guided in their behaviour by the Qur'an and the Prophet's own life, and lived under the laws of the *shari'a*. The complete integration of society and religion is one of the hallmarks of Islam and is evident in many Muslim societies today.

THE TEACHINGS OF ISLAM
As in Judaism and Christianity, the fundamental teaching of Islam is that there is one God, all-knowing and all-powerful, who is the Creator. All other principles and duties of Islam derive from this essential fact. It is people's duty to submit to Allah and to follow the teachings of His Prophet Muhammad. Those who fulfill their religious duties will gain eternal happiness in paradise, while unbelievers and the negligent will be eternally punished in hell. When the world ends, the dead will be resurrected and God will make His final judgement.

Islam is a more concrete religion than either Judaism or Christianity. The Qur'an provides detailed instructions to guide Muslims in every aspect of life, not just religion. Various chapters deal with, for example, the number of wives a man may have, divorce, and the rights of women, children, and slaves.

Islamic law strictly forbids idolatry, or the worship of images. This includes images of Muhammad and other religious figures, whose faces are often veiled in Islamic art. Copies of the Qur'an are devoid of any figural illustrations. Mosques are decorated with geometric and abstract designs, as well as verses of the Qur'an written in Arabic calligraphy (an art form in itself).

There are five essential duties that every Muslim must carry out. These are known as the **pillars of Islam**.

First Pillar: Declaration of Faith

New converts to Islam must declare their faith, aloud and in front of witnesses, with the words, "I witness that there is no God but Allah, and that Muhammad is his servant and Prophet." In Arabic, this statement is called the *shahada*. Muslims recite these same words every time they pray, in a constant reaffirmation of their belief.

Second Pillar: Prayer

The second pillar of Islam is called *salat*, or worship. Five times a day, all Muslims turn toward Mecca and pray. The times of prayer are dawn, noon, mid-afternoon, sunset, and evening, and Muslims can worship in any place considered clean and appropriate. Travellers often carry small,

PERSPECTIVES ON THE PAST
The Qur'an

Can you explain why the Qur'an is essential reading for every Muslim? Why is it often read aloud?

For 23 years Muhammad received divine messages, which he recited to his followers. These recitations were memorized or written down on pieces of bone, parchment, clay, and other convenient writing surfaces. After Muhammad died, Khalif Uthman appointed a man named Said Ibn T'abit to compile an authoritative version of the Qur'an, with the help of Muslims who could recite the words by heart. When the book was completed in 650, all other written versions were destroyed.

Thus there is only one text of the Qur'an. This makes it markedly different from the New Testament of the Bible, which contains four different versions of Jesus' life, told by four different disciples.

Muslims regard the Qur'an as the direct word of God, and therefore the original text in Arabic has never been altered. Again, this is different from the eyewitness accounts of the New Testament. Many Muslims do not approve of translations of the Qur'an, since these are written by fallible human beings in another language. Devout Muslims try to learn Arabic, even if it is not their native language, so that they can read the Qur'an in its original form.

Written in rhymed prose, half in prose, the book contains revelations, prophecies, and stories. It also sets forth the duties and rules which every Muslim must follow, such as abstaining from alcohol, pork, and gambling. **Suras** (chapters) such as "The Spider," "The Cow," and "The Elephant" illustrate aspects of the religion of Abraham.

Because of its sacred nature, the Qur'an is always stored in a higher place than any other book. Muslims wash before touching it and refrain from talking or eating while it is read aloud. Men and women also cover their heads while reading the book to show their respect for the word of Allah. Reciting passages from the Qur'an, as Muhammad might have recited them, is an important part of Islamic worship.

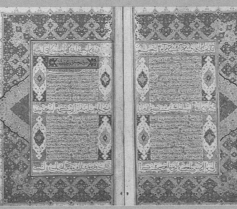

Figure 16-2
Pages from a Qur'an written by a Persian scribe in 1773

Figure 16-3 *The flag of Saudi showing the Muslim declaration of faith in Arabic*

clean mats with them, so that they can pray anywhere.

In Islamic countries, a caller, or *muezzin*, summons people to prayer from the top of a minaret of a mosque. A minaret is a slender tower outside a **mosque**, an Islamic house of worship. When Muslims hear the voice of the muezzin, they stop whatever they are doing to pray. Nowadays, the call to prayer is often prerecorded and broadcast from loudspeakers.

Before praying, Muslims must do a ritual cleansing. Cleanliness is an important part of Islamic worship. The Qur'an explains how one must wash one's hands, arms, face, and feet before praying. Every mosque has a fountain for this purpose. People must also take off their shoes before entering the mosque, so that dirt is not carried into a holy place.

Salat begins with worshippers standing and facing Mecca. (In a mosque, a niche called a *mihrab* indicates the proper direction.) Worshippers follow a set routine of standing, bowing, and kneeling, while reciting the opening prayer (reprinted at the beginning of this chapter) and other passages from the Qur'an in Arabic. To physically show their submission to God, Muslims kneel and bow with their forehead and hands touching the ground.

People who are ill are excused from praying. The Qur'an also permits prayers to be shortened or even joined together on such occasions as when one is travelling or in a non-Muslim location.

During the week, Muslims can pray at home, a mosque (where men and women worship in separate sections), a school, or a place of work. On Fridays men always go to a mosque for midday prayer. This ceremony, while outwardly similar to a Sunday church service for Christians, does not involve priests or sacraments. It is simply a communal prayer, guided by an *imam*, or prayer leader. After the prayer, there is a sermon.

Third Pillar: Alms-giving

Zakat, giving alms to help people in need, is the third pillar of the faith. Through alms-giving, Muslims acknowledge that all riches flow from God and make atonement for their sins and selfishness. In earlier times, alms-giving was also a means of redistributing wealth within the community, in accordance with the belief that all Muslims were equal in the sight of God.

Traditionally, alms were collected in the form of a money payment or a portion of one's possessions, such as animals or grain. Eventually, a charity tax—equal to 2.5 percent of a person's income—was levied on all Muslims. This levy still exists in modern Islamic countries. The state collects the tax as aid for the poor and to pay for schools and some other public services.

Besides paying this tax, Muslims are expected to engage in charitable acts of their own and to act justly toward one another. For example, Muhammad exhorted the merchants and businesspeople of Mecca to charge fair prices for their work instead of inflating their rates.

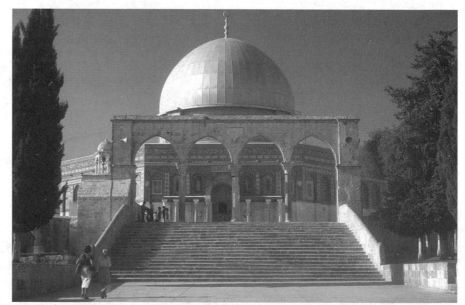

Figure 16-4 *The Dome of the Rock, in eastern Jerusalem, Islam's oldest monument. Completed in 691, the shrine covers a rock from which Muhammad is thought to have ascended miraculously to heaven. In Jewish tradition, the rock is the place where Abraham attempted to sacrifice his son.*

Fourth Pillar: Fasting

During Ramadan, the ninth month of the Islamic year, all Muslims over the age of 12 are required to fast from sunrise to sunset. Pregnant women, the aged, and the sick are excused from fasting, but are expected to make up the fast when and if they are able.

Ramadan is a sacred month for Muslims for two reasons. It was during Ramadan that the word of God was first revealed to Muhammad. Several years later, the Muslims' first victorious battle against the Meccans also occurred during this month.

For the 29 or 30 days of the month, Muslims abstain from all food and drink (including water) during the daylight hours. Smoking and sexual relations are also forbidden. The activity of fasting (*sawm* in Arabic) expresses self-discipline, moderation in one's desires, and submission to the will of God.

While the body fasts, the soul is nourished by a recitation of one-thirtieth of the Qur'an each night. When the new moon appears, signalling the end of Ramadan, Muslims celebrate their breaking of the fast with the joyous, three-day festival of Id al-Fitr. During this celebration, people say prayers of thanksgiving, visit their families and friends, exchange presents, and take children to carnivals.

Fifth Pillar: Pilgrimage to Mecca

The fifth pillar of Islam is a pilgrimage, or *hajj*, to the Ka'ba in Mecca (in present-day Saudi Arabia) at least once in a person's lifetime. Every year, over two million Muslims from around the world congregate in the holy city. The *hajj* is the most difficult duty to carry out, and hence Muslims are required to undertake it only if they have the means. People who are unable to go may entrust this duty to others.

The pilgrimage takes place during four days in the month of Dhu'l-Hijja. Markers 9.5 km outside of Mecca indicate that pilgrims are entering upon the *hajj*. At that point, Muslims must wash and put on simple white robes to show their equality with all other believers. Within the boundaries of the holy city, they walk barefoot and neither shave nor cut their hair or nails.

When they reach the Ka'ba, pilgrims must walk around the sacred black stone seven times in an counter-clockwise direction. The pilgrims then visit several holy sites around Mecca, where they perform prayers or certain rituals. Their pilgrimage ends with the Festival of Sacrifice, in which they make an offering of a sheep or goat to the poor before enjoying a feast themselves. (Because so many pilgrims visit Mecca nowadays, just part of an animal, slaughtered by a butcher, is a sufficient sacrifice.)

Before leaving Mecca, Muslims circle the Ka'ba another seven times. Successful pilgrims call themselves *hajjis,* and usually also pay a visit to Islam's second holiest site, Medina, to see the Prophet's tomb.

In the Middle Ages, the *hajj* brought together people from different regions and contributed to an exchange of ideas and culture. Merchants would often combine their pilgrimage with a business trip, while scholars took the opportunity to meet colleagues, attend courses, and buy books. People could read a wealth of travel literature describing journeys and encounters with fellow Muslims in distant lands. The *hajj* fostered a powerful feeling of solidarity and oneness among Muslims. Today, this pilgrimage is the largest annual religious gathering in the world.

Figure 16-5 *Muslim pilgrims worshipping at the Ka'ba in Mecca. Only Muslims are allowed into this holiest of Islamic shrines.*

Jihad

Jihad, holy struggle or holy war, is often considered to be an unofficial sixth pillar of Islam. There are two main aspects of *jihad*. The greater *jihad* is the internal struggle of the soul to be worthy of God and to live according to His principles. The lesser *jihad* is the external struggle, namely, the use of force to fight for one's beliefs.

Since Muhammad's time, *jihad* has been interpreted in military terms. While it was sometimes viewed as a defensive measure, more often it was a rallying call to bring the entire world to Islam by conquest. Muslims believe that those who are killed "in the path of God" are martyrs and are rewarded with immediate entry into paradise.

According to the *shari'a*, it is permissible to wage war against infidels (unbe-

THEN AND NOW
Journeying to Mecca

In earlier times, what difficulties might Muslims have experienced in undertaking the *hajj* from distant places? What problems might exist today concerning the vast numbers of pilgrims visiting Mecca?

The custom of making the pilgrimage to Mecca has existed since Muhammad's lifetime, but the modes of transportation have changed greatly since then.

In the Middle Ages, pilgrims made the long and arduous journey by caravan (i.e., in groups), carrying adequate supplies of food, water, and medicine with them. Some pilgrims rode camels and some rode horses; but many ordinary Muslims simply walked. Even those who could afford transportation often undertook part of the journey on foot to show their piety. For

example, Harun al-Rashid, the Abbasid khalif, walked the 400 km of his *hajj* from Baghdad to Mecca.

Today, many pilgrims cover even greater distances in a much shorter time, but their journey is still often tiring and uncomfortable. During the *hajj*, ships, planes, trains, and buses are crammed with thousands of pilgrims, as is Mecca itself. Less affluent Muslims from the countryside might arrange a ride on a truck bringing goods into the city. In villages along the Nile, Egyptian Muslims decorate the outside walls of their homes with paintings of the vehicles they took on their pilgrimage.

Pilgrims are housed in a tent village in Mina, 5 km outside of Mecca, where they are organized into blocks according to nationality. Poorer pilgrims live in the streets and under bridges.

---

lievers), lapsed Muslims, rebels, and bandits. Muslim law also discusses how war should be conducted and what should be done with prisoners and seized property.

RELIGIOUS ORGANIZATION

Historically, Islam had no priests or organized hierarchy. The role of an imam in a mosque was to lead worshippers in prayer, not to administer sacraments or to mediate between God and ordinary people. Special training and ordination were not required for imams or even for the head of the faith, the khalif.

Eventually, a class of Muslim scholars developed, who had expert knowledge of the Qur'an and the sayings (*hadith*) and actions (*sunna*) of the Prophet. This group, called the *ulema,* became the interpreters of religious law. They created the *shari'a* and added many provisions to it over the centuries. Members of the ulema

ranged from the local official of a village or mosque to the highest dignitary, the *qadi* or religious judge. The ulema were recognizable by the turbans and distinctive robes that they wore.

Rulers and ordinary people alike respected the authority of the ulema. The khalif or sultan usually consulted them in matters concerning holy law and sometimes in aspects of secular law as well. Often, the ruler would ask the scholars to provide religious justification for actions he wished to take, such as the launching of a *jihad*. Ordinary people called upon their local jurist to mediate disputes or to officiate at weddings. In such cases, the religious scholar combined the functions of a clergyman and a judge.

SHI'AS VS. SUNNIS

In the previous chapter you read how the split between Sunni and Shi'a Muslims

occurred a few decades after Muhammad's death. We will describe here only a few differences between the two sects.

The Sunni majority felt that the leaders and scholars of the Muslim community were qualified to elect the khalif and to interpret the Qur'an and the *sunna*. The Shi'a minority, on the other hand, firmly adhered to a hereditary principle of leadership. They believed that descendants of Muhammad's cousin Ali were the only legitimate leaders of Islam. (Later Shi'as also recognized descendants of Muhammad's uncle Abbas and daughter Fatima.) By virtue of their kinship with the Prophet, these successors had special insight into the faith; accordingly, only they and their appointees were qualified to interpret the Qur'an and religious law—not the Muslim community as a whole.

The Shi'as did not recognize the rule of the rightly guided khalifs and their successors. Instead, they elected their own leaders whom they called imams. The Shi'as also followed their own versions of religious doctrine, law, sunna, and hadiths. While the differences between Sunni and Shi'a beliefs were relatively minor, the Sunnis saw the Shi'as as heretics. The Shi'as, in turn, felt persecuted as a minority and greatly wronged when Ali's son, Husayn, was slain by the Umayyads in 680. The anniversary of this event, called Ashura, is one of the most important dates in the Shi'a calendar.

Most Shi'as belong to the group called the 12-Imam Shi'as. Historically, this group was moderate in its beliefs and focused on contemplative, scholarly activities. The last imam, Muhammad al-Mahdi, disappeared under mysterious circumstances in the ninth century, and the 12-Imam Shi'as believe that he will return on Judgement Day. Other, smaller Shi'a groups have been much more radical and military in their outlook.

SUFI MYSTICS

The Sufis, who emerged in the eighth century, were individuals who sought a mystical union with God through meditation, prayer, chants, and trances. Like Christian and Buddhist monks, they adopted an ascetic lifestyle and came to be organized into brotherhoods. They did much to popularize Islam and make it meaningful for ordinary people who had no interest in the complex legal matters that preoccupied religious scholars.

The name Sufi likely came from the Arabic word for wool, *suf.* The early Sufis wore rough woollen robes as a symbol of their piety and poverty. Later called *fakirs* in Arabic and *dervishes* in Persian and Turk-ish, Sufi monks believed that one's inner experience of God was more important than the religious laws and customs which governed most people's lives. By repeatedly chanting such phrases as "There is no God but God (*la ilaha illa llah*)," the monks would transport themselves into a state of religious ecstasy. Poetry and music would move them to perform whirling dances as an expression of their love for God.

Orthodox Muslim worship did not permit music or poetry, so the Sufis were regarded with disapproval by both Sunni and Shi'a scholars. Common people, however, were greatly drawn to the monks, who provided a priestly function and role model missing in Islam. The Sufis encouraged the worship of saints and holy places—a practice which religious scholars considered idolatrous but which helped illiterate Muslims feel closer to God. In fact, many Sufi practices and sayings subtly criticized conventional religion and politics.

Wandering Sufi monks helped to spread Islam among country and tribal peoples, including the Seljuk Turks and Byzantine Christians after they came under Ottoman rule. Despite their distaste for religious dogma, some mystics became influential philosophers and theologians, whose teachings are still evident today. Other Sufis became poets whose verses about love and other popular subjects entertained the masses.

DEATH

The Muslims regarded death as a release from the troubles of this world. When speaking of the deceased, people would say "*Allah Karim* (From Allah we came and to Him we shall return)." This was a reference to the Day of Judgement when all souls will be judged and given entry into either the garden of paradise or the fires of hell.

The Qur'an describes paradise as a lovely garden on a cool mountaintop with flowers, trees eternally bearing fruit, cold springs, and golden pavilions. Here, the blessed enjoy all the pleasures of the senses from which they abstained while living. Attended by voluptuous virgins called houris, they can eat and drink to their hearts' content while reclining on sumptuous couches. To Muslims living in the arid deserts and infertile steppes, the concept of the garden of paradise held boundless appeal. It was often used as a motif in carpets, manuscripts, and other forms of art.

By contrast, hell is a flame-filled pit where condemned souls suffer forever. They drink water from a salty well that increases their thirst, and their only food is a strong-smelling plant that causes hunger.

Figure 16-6 *The Taj Mahal. When his wife died in 1631, Emperor Shah Jahan started building a memorial for her. The Taj Mahal was constructed by 20 000 workers in 22 years.*

Burial

After a ritual washing, the body of the deceased person was wrapped in at least three white sheets. At the funeral ceremony, only a few prayers were said before the body was laid on its right side, with the face turned toward Mecca, in a grave at least 2 m deep. Muslims have a saying that the grave should be deep enough so that the dead person can sit up to answer questions during the Last Judgement without his or her head appearing above ground. The graves are not marked with a headstone.

Muhammad did not want Muslims to build tombs to commemorate the dead; yet, tombs were built throughout the Islamic world. The Taj Mahal, in the northern Indian town of Agra, has been called the most beautiful building in the world. It is actually a tomb built by the Mughul emperor Shah Jahan in the seventeenth century in memory of his beloved dead wife Mumtaz Mahal. A rectangular pool in front of the Taj Mahal shows a shimmering reflection of this serenely beautiful monument.

REFLECT AND ANALYZE

1. Islam has been called a "religion of law." Explain whether or not this is an accurate description.

2. How is the Qur'an different from the New Testament of the Bible? Explain the role that the Qur'an plays in the lives of Muslims.

3. Which of the five pillars of faith do you think had the greatest impact on the non-Islamic medieval world? In what way? Was it likely a positive or negative impact? Explain your answer.

4. How did the activities of the Sufis deviate from orthodox Islam? Can you explain the great popularity of Sufism among ordinary Muslims?

5. It was once customary for young Muslims to learn the entire Qur'an—all 6000 verses of it—by heart. Why would this have been considered valuable?

SOCIAL STRUCTURE

In early Islamic history, people under Muslim rule were classified into four main groups, each with legally defined rights and obligations. The first group consisted of Muslim freemen (and freewomen) who were the Arab ruling elite. They held all of the high government positions and paid few, if any, taxes. In effect, they were a relatively small, aristocratic class who drew their income from taxes paid by their non-Muslim subjects. The Arabs who enjoyed the highest status were members of the Quraysh, the tribe of the Prophet.

The second group was made up of freedmen or clients. These were former Arab and non-Arab slaves who had gained or been given their freedom, and who were employed by their former masters. The status of freedmen was influenced by Roman law and Arab tribal custom. In Roman tradition, a freedman became a client, or dependant, of his former master; in Arab custom, he became an adoptive member of the tribe. While freedmen did not enjoy the full rights of Arab freemen, as Muslims they occupied a higher social position than non-Muslims. Capable freedmen were often given positions of considerable responsibility, including the governorship of some provinces.

Non-Muslim subjects comprised the third social group. These "people of the pact," as they were called, were bound in an unwritten contract with their Muslim overlords. According to this contract, non-Muslims had to acknowledge the supremacy of Islam and their Muslim rulers and pay a special tax. In return, they were protected by the state and allowed to practise their professions and religions. (Only Jews, Christians, and Persian Zoroastrians were given freedom of religion—worshippers of multiple pagan gods were forced to renounce their beliefs.) Educated non-Muslims formed a large part of the civil service, but were prohibited from bearing arms.

Because they paid higher taxes, non-Muslims were often discouraged from converting to Islam by their Arab rulers. Nevertheless, many non-Muslims did convert and found that they still occupied a lower social status than their Arab counterparts. This inequality contradicted the teaching of Islam, and as non-Arab Muslims grew in number, the Umayyad khalifs found them increasingly restive. When the Abbasids came to power in the eighth

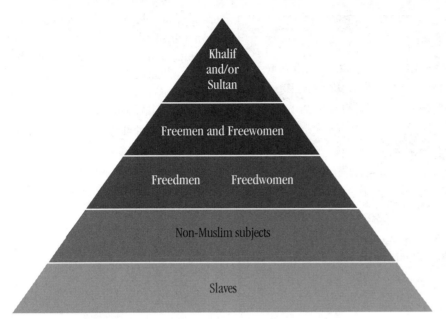

Figure 16-7 *The Muslim social structure*

century, they abolished the inequalities between Arab and non-Arab Muslims.

The fourth social group consisted of slaves, who were mainly heathens captured in battle and people born into slave families. The position of slaves was a complex one. They outwardly occupied the lowest social category; yet some female slaves were educated and trained in the arts, while many Turkish male slaves were recruited into the army where they reached high positions and eventually took control of the Abbasid khalifate.

Before Islam, slaves were entirely at the mercy of their masters. Islamic law assumed that humans were born into a free state, and therefore put limits on slavery. Muslims could not enslave other Muslims. Only infidels (excluding Jews and Christians) from outside the Muslim world could be captured or bought as slaves. Owners were forbidden to overwork their slaves and were required to provide them with food, medical attention, and assistance when

old. Slaves who converted to Islam were still bound to their masters, but they could more easily acquire their freedom than heathens.

In the early years, most slaves were recruited from North Africa, Egypt, and Ethiopia. As the Islamic empire expanded, Slavic peoples from eastern Europe (the name Slavic comes from "slave"), Turks from central Asia, and black peoples from sub-Saharan Africa formed the majority of the slave population.

Unlike ancient Egypt, Greece, and Rome, Arab society was not primarily slave-based. Slaves were mainly used for domestic service and in the army. Many female slaves were concubines (female companions to the male head of the household) in the **harems** of wealthy Muslim homes. (A harem, which lived in its own quarters, consisted of all the women in the household—wives, concubines, female relatives—as well as the servants who attended to them.) Female slaves often provided

entertainment as dancers, singers, or musicians. Male slaves of African origin were employed in homes, shops, mosques, and mines, while Turkish male slaves filled the ranks of the army.

Classification by Profession

Medieval Muslim society, like so many others, might also be classified according to profession. In this case, a pyramid structure is not entirely appropriate, since certain groups existed side-by-side, rather than above or below, each other.

Men of the sword and men of the pen enjoyed the highest prestige. The Turks established military regimes in which the sultan was both commander of the army and political ruler. There were two groups of literary and learned men: a secular class called the scribes, which ran the government, and the religious scholars called the ulema. Unlike in medieval Europe, where the clergy was heavily involved in politics and government, the Muslim ulema viewed politics as sordid and unsuitable as a vocation. Such aloofness gave them immense moral authority in Muslim society.

Merchants, traders, and manufacturers formed a powerful and wealthy class below the military and scholarly elites. Trade was the lifeblood of the Muslim economy, since agriculture was confined to the few areas that could be adequately watered. Below the businesspeople were individuals engaged in professions, such as physicians, scientists, astronomers, engineers, teachers, and architects. Next came the artisans who produced numerous goods needed in the local economy. Finally, there were the slaves, and illiterate peasants and nomads who lived in the countryside, far from the urban centres of power.

REFLECT AND ANALYZE

1. Compare the social structure of early Muslim civilization with that of ancient Greece or Rome. How were slaves used in the two different societies? Are there parallels between the social classes in the two societies? Explain.

2. Describe Islam's position on slavery. How were former slaves and slaves able to gain positions of power and responsibility in the Muslim world?

3. Muhammad was a merchant. Based on what you have read so far, make predictions about how business was viewed by Muslims. Check whether your predictions were correct when you read about these topics later in this chapter.

EVERYDAY LIFE

THE FAMILY AND MARRIAGE

As in other areas of life, Islam had rules and laws concerning marriage and children. The Qur'an taught that husband and wife were spiritual equals, but that each had different roles and responsibilities. The man was the provider, protector, and head of the family, while the woman took care of the children and the home.

In pre-Islamic Arabia, **polygamy** (marrying more than one wife) was permitted. The Qur'an limited polygamy, stating that a man could have no more than four wives and that all of them had to be treated equally. Thus, only wealthy individuals could afford to have more than one wife. Islam also granted women the right to inherit property and to dispose of it as they wished.

Polygamy was practised for several reasons. It kept the birth rate high, helping to restock the male population depleted by civil conflicts and wars of conquest. It was also a way to protect and provide for women, such as widows, who might have had no other means of support. In Arab culture, it was a chivalrous and generous act for a man to marry as many women as he could provide for. Finally, it was considered a great indignity if a woman remained single or married below her social status. Eligible bridegrooms often received more than one offer of marriage from families competing with one another to provide the most attractive dowry.

Muhammad himself married several women, and all historical sources indicate that he was fond of them, treated them well, and respected their abilities. In his day, women enjoyed relatively high freedom, especially when compared to the restrictions of later Muslim society.

A Muslim male married for the first time at about age 20, while his bride was usually between 12 and 20. Marriages were arranged, with the bride's parents negotiating an appropriate dowry with the bridegroom's family. The groom also had to provide a bridal gift. The Qur'an stated that a woman should give her consent to her marriage and not be forced against her will; in practice, she usually had little say in the selection of her husband. Marriage between cousins was preferred because it strengthened tribal ties and kept property within the family.

The marriage ceremony itself was very simple. Each partner declared their commitment to each other in front of two Muslim witnesses. Music and feasting were also part of the marriage celebrations.

As soon as a baby was born, the head of the family whispered the Muslim declaration of faith in its ear, bringing the child into Islam. No other baptism was needed. In some Islamic societies, a naming ceremony called *aqiqah* took place seven days after birth. The child's hair was cut and the weight of the hair in gold or silver was given as alms. In the case of a boy, two animals (sheep or goats) were sacrificed; in the case of a girl, one animal was sacrificed. The meat was given to the poor.

A Muslim household included all of the wives of the male head of the family, their children, and other family members such as a widowed mother. In this patriarchal society, sons were preferred over daughters. However, the Qur'an forbade female infanticide, which had been the custom of some Arab tribes during times of hardship.

The Qur'an allowed divorce, although it was frowned upon and was only to be used after due consideration. To divorce, a man had to say the words "I dismiss thee" three times, give his wife back her dowry and the bridal gift he had made to her at the wedding, and allow her to live in his home for another three months. Thereafter, the woman was once again the responsibility of her family. Women could not initiate divorce, but they could raise the matter with their husbands.

EDUCATION

Although Muhammad was illiterate, he had a deep respect for education and knowledge which became essential parts of Islamic culture. Religious education was the most important, but Muslims also valued poetry, mathematics, and science.

At age six or seven, boys went to a school associated with a mosque. Students learned to read and write using the Qur'an, copying great chunks of the text and learning it by heart. They also studied grammar, arithmetic, and the lives of the prophets. The schools exercised strict discipline and harsh punishment for misbehaviour.

Boys from wealthy families were sometimes taught by private tutors. Besides studying the Qur'an, these boys learned to appreciate poetry. Their fathers also instructed them in how to be gentlemen and leaders in the Muslim community.

Girls were taught at home by their mothers or by educated slave women. While some girls learned how to read and write, their education mainly focused on the running of a household, in preparation for their future marriage. Like the boys, they learned to recite passages of the Qur'an by heart.

When the Muslims conquered Byzantine and Persian territories, they acquired the knowledge of these earlier civilizations. Muslims especially admired Greek philosophy and science, and Roman law, and translated many of these works into Arabic. Later, Muslim scholars passed on these same works to western Europeans.

In the early ninth century, the Abbasid khalif al-Ma'mun established the House of Wisdom in Baghdad, a higher institution which became famous throughout the Muslim world. The House of Wisdom included several schools, a vast library, astronomical observatories, and impressive facilities for translating classical and Persian texts into Arabic.

Other academies of higher learning, called *madrasas,* were established in great numbers by the Seljuk Turks in the eleventh century. A *madrasa* was a religious college usually associated with a prominent urban mosque. Here, young men could undertake advanced studies of the Qur'an, Islamic law, and theology. Large *madrasas* had libraries containing books on non-religious subjects such as philosophy, mathematics, medicine, astronomy, and music. The libraries were open to students pursuing these other fields.

Madrasas and other advanced academies were much like the university colleges of western Europe. Eventually, institutions that might be called universities were established, offering studies in philosophy, science, mathematics, and astronomy.

WOMEN IN MUSLIM SOCIETY

The status of women changed significantly over the course of Islamic history, despite the fact that Allah's word was unvarying. The cultural traditions of Arabia, the Byzantine empire, and Persia shaped how women were viewed and how the Qur'an was interpreted regarding female dress and behaviour.

Pre-Islamic Arab tribal culture was practical in nature. Although women were subordinate to men, they were actively engaged in the social, political, and religious life of their clan. They provided counsel in

Figure 16-8 *Modern Iranian women wearing the shador, a black robe covering the entire body*

matters concerning the tribe, composed poetry, and sometimes acted as religious leaders. Free women in the towns wore veils to distinguish themselves from slaves, but otherwise women were not veiled.

The widow Khadija, who became Muhammad's first wife, prospered in her own trading business. She was not a typical Arab woman, but she demonstrates that at least some women had considerable responsibility and power in seventh-century Arabia.

Muhammad stressed that loyalty to Islam was more important than loyalty to one's family. Hence he welcomed women who became Muslims even when their husbands or fathers did not. Some women made the *hijrah* from Mecca to Medina alone. Others accompanied their men in the wars of conquest, tending to the wounded and supervising prisoners.

Initially, Islam improved the lot of women. Whereas previously women had no inheritance rights, the Qur'an specified that females were to inherit half as much property as males, which took into account the man's need to provide for his family. Married women were entitled to a share of their husband's property even if the couple divorced. Muhammad also stated that men should be kind to their wives and treat them equally.

Women, said the Qur'an, should be modestly dressed and chaste in appearance so as not to tempt men. The holy book did not, however, specify veiling of the entire female body or segregation of the sexes. These practices were Persian and possibly Byzantine in origin, only becoming part of Islam when Muslim khalifs established themselves first in Damascus and later in Baghdad.

The Abbasid khalifs were greatly impressed by the splendour and elaborate ceremony of the Persian empire they conquered. They abandoned Muhammad's concept of equality and democratic rule in favour of Persian imperial tradition, where the king maintained a majestic distance between himself and even his most trusted advisors. The Abbasids also adopted the Persian institution of the harem, which separated women from men and mostly confined women to their domestic quarters. The veil, which had been the mark of a Persian noblewoman and had shielded her from the eyes of common men, now became the required attire for Muslim women.

The khalifs encoded these restrictions in the *shari'a,* and subsequent generations of religious scholars viewed such practices as having always been a part of Islam rather than as later adaptations. In fact, later authorities were even more conserva-tive in their interpretation of religious law, and mandated veiling from head to toe for women appearing in public. Peasant women and female slaves not living in harems did not wear veils, but they too suffered from the narrowing of women's options.

After the first century of Islam, women no longer played a role in public life. Five hundred years later, they ceased to have any contact with men who were not husbands, male relatives, or servants. While they retained their property and inheritance rights, they could only carry out legal matters through a male relative acting on their behalf.

Nevertheless, women went about the task of raising their children and running the household. They exerted influence on their husbands quietly and behind the scenes, and had their own clan networks and sources of information. Some female slaves gained fame as entertainers in the harems of their owners.

In modern times, some Muslim countries, such as Saudi Arabia, Oman, Yemen, and Iran, still require heavy veiling for women and separation of the sexes. Other countries (including Egypt, Morocco, Tunisia, Iraq, and Pakistan) are more moderate, while a few are almost completely secular (Turkey and Indonesia). Feminists working for the rights of Muslim women base their arguments on the Qur'an itself and on early Arab Islamic culture.

REFLECT AND ANALYZE

1. How was polygamy viewed in Muslim society? What were its advantages? Do you see any disadvantages to this custom?

2. Can you explain why the study of Islamic law was so important in Muslim society? What profession would most men studying at the *madrasas* have entered?

3. Explain how Islam initially improved the status of women in the seventh century.

4. Did Byzantine and Persian influences have a positive or negative influence on the role of women in Muslim society? Explain your answer.

URBAN AND RURAL LIVING

TOWNS AND CITIES

Although some Muslims lived in rural or desert areas, Islamic civilization was primarily urban in nature. In the arid Middle East, only well-watered towns and cities could support sizeable populations. Muhammad had lived in Mecca and Medina, two important trading towns on the Arabian peninsula. Damascus, Baghdad, and Cairo, occupied by different dynasties of khalifs, became centres of commerce, culture, and learning.

The layout of a Middle Eastern city

was determined not only by geography but also by the water source. Mesopotamian and Egyptian cities were located along the flat and even flood plains of the major rivers. In Persia, long underground channels called *qanats* carried water to urban settlements and fields. Other cities relied on aqueducts, cisterns, or canals.

Most cities were protected within a wall and divided into two general districts. The public district housed businesses, government buildings, and religious institutions. The palace of the khalif or sultan, the main mosque, and other important buildings were surrounded by walls. Mosques with their domes and tall, slender minarets dominated the skyline, while hospitals and *madrasas* were located nearby.

The heart of the district was the large marketplace, called a *suq* in Arabic and a *bazaar* in Persian and Turkish. The bazaar was covered with a roof to protect shoppers from the blazing sun. Shops selling the same kind of goods were grouped along the same street. Located near the bazaar were warehouses and large inns, called *caravanserais,* where out-of-town merchants stayed and conducted business. The multitude of goods, both local and imported, to be found in a Muslim bazaar would have astonished most Europeans, who did not resume large-scale trading until the eleventh century.

The other main district, residential in nature, was a tangle of narrow, winding streets where houses were closely packed together. Many of these streets were also covered. The houses, constructed out of mud bricks or stone, had plain, white-plastered exteriors to reflect sunlight and only a few, small windows looking out onto the street. The windows were covered with wooden screens to keep out noise and light, and to maintain the privacy of the women living in the house.

HOMES

For most Muslims, their home (*dar* in Arabic) was an oasis of comfort and tranquillity. Domestic life was enjoyed in strict privacy, with only family friends and business associates invited into the home. Men and women ate meals and entertained guests separately.

A typical upper- or middle-class house consisted of one or two storeys oriented around a central courtyard. Wealthy homes

Figure 16-9 *A turkish painting of Ankara, an important Muslim commercial city in Turkey*

had decorative stonework and columns around the courtyard, with a porch overlooking it on the upper floor. There were taps with running water in some of the rooms. Poor families lived in small mud huts surrounding a common courtyard or in multi-storeyed apartment buildings.

The courtyard was the focal point of the home, where the family could sit and contemplate nature or entertain their guests. The courtyards of the rich had fountains and well-tended fruit trees and flowers. In more modest homes, a pleasing effect could be obtained with a few small bushes or flowerpots. These family gardens were common throughout the Muslim world, a reflection of the Middle Easterner's love of greenery to brighten a desert environment. All gardens, large and small, were a reminder of the garden of paradise.

Muslim homes contained almost no furniture, but lots of textile furnishings and art objects. Solid furniture consisted of one or two small chests, decorated with inlays of different coloured woods or bone, and perhaps a low table. Wood was expensive due to the lack of forests in the Middle East. Textiles, on the other hand, were inexpensive and readily available. The main piece of furniture was the divan, a low sofa extending around three sides of a room. It was piled high with cushions for people to lean against. Meals were eaten while reclining on a divan.

Other textiles in the home included beautifully decorated carpets, rugs, and wall hangings. People slept on low mattresses that were rolled up and put away during the day. Clothes and blankets were piled up in a corner of a room or stored in a cupboard or chest. Small niches along the walls held books or displayed art objects. Domestic items that were both functional and decorative included trays, oil lamps, pottery, and glassware.

Food

During meals, family members would sit on the floor in a circle and eat from large trays of bread, meats, and fruits. People used their fingers or spoons and knives for certain foods.

Muslims, like Jews, were forbidden to eat pork, which spoils quickly in hot climates. Animals that were used for meat (mainly goats and sheep) had to be killed in a special way. An animal was blessed before its throat was cut with a very sharp knife and its blood drained out. During the slaughter, people recited the words *"B'ism Allah* (In the name of God)" and prayers of thanksgiving. Only then was the meat considered *halal* (pure and cleansed) and suitable for eating.

THE COUNTRY

Land was the principal source of wealth in the Muslim world. The state held most land, including that gained by conquest. In the early years, the government granted large areas of newly acquired territory to Arab tribesmen who had fought for Islam. The new landowners collected high taxes from the local non-Muslim inhabitants, submitting part of the revenue to the state and keeping the rest as income.

As Muslim civilization developed, it became mainly urban, not rural. By the Abbasid period, most landowners were government officials who lived in the cities and who often only visited their holdings to collect taxes. The land was farmed by local farmers and peasants. Slaves were not used in agricultural production.

Although landholders tried frequently to establish hereditary rights to their land, they were usually foiled by the government which wished to maintain central control. This, coupled with the scarcity of arable land, prevented Muslim landowners from becoming a powerfully independent group, like the landowning nobles of Europe.

ENTERTAINMENT

For nomads living on the steppes and borders of the desert, composing and reciting poetry was the main form of recreation. In pre-Islamic Arabia, women as well as men were noted for their oral compositions.

In sophisticated, urban Muslim society, the telling of stories was also a favourite pastime, as the popular collection of folk tales *Arabian Nights* attests. In Persia, aristocratic men were often entertained in the luxurious and sensual environment of the harem, where skilled slave women danced, sang, played music, and recited poetry and stories.

The martial Turkish sultans were fond of game-hunting on a grand scale, in which hundreds of military men took part. The hunt provided soldiers with exercise and training in the use of weapons. Other physical activities included racing on horses and camels, gymnastics, and archery. Also popular were the spectator sports of horse-racing, wrestling, and cock-fighting.

Like the ancient Romans, Muslims had public bath houses which people used at least once a week. Bathing, which took several hours, was an occasion to relax, talk, and listen to professional storytellers. Bathrooms had taps with running cold and hot water. After a person had bathed, an attendant would rub down his or her body with oils. The bather could use a steam room to open the skin's pores and a cold room to splash on cold water to close the pores up again.

The town bazaar was a main meeting place where people could see friends, exchange news, conduct business, and be entertained. Musicians, snake charmers, storytellers, and other entertainerss could always be found in the bazaar.

Coffee-houses were also popular gathering places. The practice of drinking coffee (*qahwa*) first arose around the fourteenth century in Ethiopia, where coffee plants grew wild and were later cultivated. Merchants and pilgrims spread the habit first to the Arabian peninsula and then to the rest of the Muslim world. Tea had been introduced earlier by the Mongols from the east, but coffee was by far the more popular beverage. Since the Qur'an banned alcohol, coffee-houses and teahouses were the Islamic equivalents of European ale taverns.

eggplant, artichokes, and spinach, were enhanced in Middle Eastern cooking by spices grown in the region or imported from India and Southeast Asia.

Crops were also grown for the trade market. Olives, used for oil, were the main crop in North Africa and parts of Asia Minor. Sugar, refined from sugar cane, was grown in Egypt and exported to Europe, while coffee was mostly consumed within the Muslim world. Two important non-dietary crops were cotton and flax.

Techniques of cultivation did not change significantly from those used in ancient times. The light, wheel-less wooden plough remained adequate for turning the loose soils of the Mediterranean region and the annually flooded river plains. Middle Eastern farmers continued to use the irrigation systems of ancient peoples, with a few adjustments and improvements.

Unlike in Europe, where scholarly monks experimented with new agricultural methods, educated Muslims did not concern themselves with farming. As the centuries progressed, lack of innovation and soil erosion caused by grazing animals and wars led to a significant decline in crop yields. Once fertile areas reverted to grassland or became desert. The social and economic disruption caused by the Mongol invasion of 1258 also had disastrous results for Middle Eastern agriculture.

The rearing and care of livestock was handled not by farmers but by nomadic peoples living on the steppes and the boundaries of the desert. Always in search of new grazing land for their herds, the nomads often attacked farmers who cultivated areas of steppe land. Indifferent to government authority and venturing into the cities only to trade, nomadic tribes

---

REFLECT AND ANALYZE

1. Compare a medieval Muslim suq or bazaar with a modern urban shopping mall. Consider the following factors: location, appearance, arrangement of shops, purpose, and nearby amenities.

2. Did the layout of a *suk* make it easy or difficult to buy goods and conduct trade and business? Explain.

3. How does a Muslim *dar* (house) compare with a Roman villa in structure, comfort, furnishings, and types of people living in the household? How does a *dar* compare with an early medieval European castle?

4. Compare and contrast life in a medieval Muslim town with life in a medieval town in western Europe.

THE ECONOMY

AGRICULTURE AND LIVESTOCK

Although naturally fertile land was confined to the river valleys and the few areas that received adequate rainfall, Middle Easterners increased the amount of land available for cultivation by building irrigation systems in areas of steppe land.

The crops grown in the Middle East were surprisingly diverse. Since antiquity, cereals such as barley and millet had been grown on the banks of the Nile. In the medieval period, Egypt was a major producer of wheat. Rice was introduced to the Middle East from India sometime after the seventh century.

Dates, figs, and grapes were grown along the Mediterranean and Arabian coasts. Peaches, apricots, and citrus fruits were introduced from Asia. Peas, beans, lentils, and chickpeas were important dietary staples and widely cultivated. These legumes, along with such vegetables as

Figure 16-10 *A Bedouin herder tending his animals*

sometimes posed a threat to the ruling establishment. Both the Seljuk Turks and the Mongols were nomads who overthrew the existing regimes.

The nomads' sheep and goats provided meat, wool, and hides. Goat's milk was made into yogurt and cheese. Camels, the "ships of the desert," were used for transportation and as pack animals. They were ideally suited to desert conditions, since they could travel over 300 km a day and did not need to drink water for 17 days. Horses were rare in pre-Islamic Arabia, but later generations of Arabs built up sizeable herds by importing animals from central Asia. The Arabs became expert horse breeders, producing the swift Arabian horses well suited to racing. Owning a fine herd or stable of horses became a mark of prestige.

INDUSTRY

Both farming and the raising of livestock provided the raw materials for the main Middle Eastern industry, textiles. The region lacked the sources of energy, such as wood for fuel and flowing rivers to power water mills, necessary for other kinds of industry. Textile-making, by contrast, relied on human labour.

Wool, cotton, and flax were woven into cloth by artisans working at home or in small shops. Most cloth was used locally to make clothes and home furnishings, but some textiles were traded internationally. Middle Eastern carpets, produced primarily in Persia and Turkey but also in Egypt, North Africa, and Spain, were renowned for their quality and intricate geometric or floral designs. Egyptian linen and cotton were ideal for making the lightweight yet durable robes worn in the summer. People of the Middle East favoured bright colours and vibrant patterns as an antidote to the monotony of the physical landscape.

The manufacture of silk and brocade were government-controlled monopolies. The Byzantines had earlier discovered the secret of silk-making and established a highly lucrative trade that continued after their empire fell to the Turks. Brocade was a heavy silk fabric covered with an intricate raised design. It was very expensive and was worn only by Persian Muslim rulers and by

Figure 16-11 *A jeweller, apothecary, butcher, and baker in a bazaar, from a thirteenth-century Turkish illuminated manuscript*

individuals to whom brocade robes were given as a special honour.

Artisans in tool-making, leather working, perfume-making, and many other industries belonged to guilds and occupied their own quarters in the bazaar. Many guilds were associated with the Sufi brotherhoods. Polluting trades such as tanning, brick-making, and animal slaughtering took place on the outskirts of town. Craftspeople produced most of the artistic wares for the local population, including ceramics, glassware, and embroidered wall hangings. Calligraphers and illustrators were employed in making manuscripts and books by hand. (Because of the intricacy of the Arabic and Persian script, printing was slow to take hold in the Muslim world.)

Parchment and papyrus from Egypt were early writing materials. The textile industry produced a plentiful supply of rags that were used to make paper from the mid-eighth century onwards. The Arabs learned paper-making from the Chinese and in turn passed it on to the Europeans.

Besides controlling important industries such as silk-making and sugar refining, Mamluks of Egypt tried to fix prices for valuable goods such as spices. Their tactics backfired when the Portuguese, frustrated by heavy regulations and high prices imposed by the Muslims, sought an alternative trade route around Africa in the fifteenth century.

TRADE

"Allah has permitted trading and forbidden usury," says the Qur'an. Trade was the most important economic activity in the Muslim world, and second only to land ownership in generating wealth. The high social status enjoyed by traders and merchants was due not only to their wealth but also to the fact that the Prophet himself had been a trader.

In the ninth century, the Abbasid khalifs established peaceful relations with their non-Muslim neighbours to facilitate trade. Baghdad became the most important trading city in the world. Its links to markets in three continents brought immense riches to its rulers and citizens. Muslims in other locations also prospered.

Camel caravans with as many as 4000 animals travelled over land routes to China, bringing back silk and fine paper. Spices, tea, precious gems, and tropical hardwoods came from India. Gold and slaves were imported from Africa.

Land travel was slow, expensive, and made dangerous by highway robbers. Only easily transportable, non-perishable, luxury items yielded high enough profits to justify the risks and the cost. Along the Middle Eastern trading routes, caravanserais were located at regular intervals and in the towns and cities. A caravanserais was a two-storey building surrounding a huge courtyard that could accommodate the merchants' camels. Cargo was stored on the ground floor, while guest rooms were located on the second floor.

Transportation by water was much faster and safer than land travel. Muslim ships controlled the waters of the Mediterranean for centuries, with only some competition from the Byzantines. In the fifteenth century, the Italian city-states came to dominate the Mediterranean. Both Muslims and Italians later lost ground to the Spanish and Portuguese when the new Atlantic route around Africa to Asia resulted in the decline of the traditional land and Mediterranean routes.

Several key ingredients contributed to the Muslims' spectacular success in large-scale trade and commerce. Since the Qur'an approved of commerce, there was no shame attached to it, as there was in early Christianity. (Jesus, after all, had expelled money-

Figure 16-12 *Engraving of a Caravanserais at Guzel Hisar*

lenders from a holy temple.) From Spain in the west to the Indian border in the east, the entire Muslim world was bound together by a common religious and political system. Arabic was understood across this vast region, as were Persian and Turkish in later centuries. Although the Qur'an banned usury, religious authorities interpreted the law in such a way as to make investment and banking possible. Last but not least, the annual pilgrimage to Mecca brought together Muslims from all areas, forging a sense of common identity and cooperation rather than competition. As a comparison, trade in medieval Europe was hindered for centuries by fighting between different national groups and by the multiplicity of languages and customs.

REFLECT AND ANALYZE

1. Explain how social instability would have a negative effect on:
   a) agriculture, and b) business and trade.

2. What reasons would nomadic tribes such as the Seljuk Turks and the Mongols have had for attacking agricultural and urban settlements and overthrowing the government?

3. Why is it not surprising that trade was the mainstay of the medieval Middle Eastern economy?

4. List the factors that contributed to the success of Muslims as international traders. Would the type of physical geography found in the Middle East have been a factor in the Muslims' success? Explain.

5. In what ways do you think that trade in the medieval Muslim world was similar to and different from modern international trade?

THE ARTS

ISLAMIC ARCHITECTURE

The mosque was the most distinctive form of architecture in the Muslim world. The word *mosque* is derived from an Arabic word meaning "place of prostration." In other words, the mosque was a place where worshippers knelt and bowed before God. The design of mosques varied from region to region, but there were several basic architectural elements: a high, wide, vaulted interior, the *mihrab* or niche indicating the direction of Mecca, and the *minbar* or pulpit (always located to the right of the *mihrab*). All mosques had one or more minarets or slender towers, which were as recognizable a feature as the crosses on Christian churches.

The interior of a mosque was simple, austere, and devoid of furniture. Worshippers knelt in tight rows on a carpet in the central space. To prevent any possibility of idolatrous worship, paintings and especially sculptures of Muhammad or other Muslim leaders were completely forbidden in religious buildings. As a result, decoration consisted of abstract designs and inscriptions of the Qur'an rendered in swirling, decorative calligraphy on the walls and ceiling. For Muslims, looking upon the words of the Qur'an, whether reproduced in a book or on a wall, was an act of worship.

In Arab regions, a mosque's exterior was generally plain and unadorned. Farther east, in Persia and India, intricate, colourful designs decorated mosques both inside and out.

Early Arab mosques used rows of columns and curved arches borrowed from classical Greek and Roman architecture. Christian churches in Egypt and Syria also provided architectural models and were even converted into mosques when the majority of the local inhabitants adopted Islam. Arab mosques had a single minaret, either attached to the mosque or freestanding. Early minarets were rectangular, but the cylinder would eventually become the preferred shape throughout the Muslim world.

Sometimes Arab architectural elements were carried far afield, such as when the last remaining Umayyad established independent rule in Spain in the eighth century. The horseshoe arches, numerous columns, and alternation of red and white stones in the Great Mosque of Cordoba are Syrian influences.

During the Abbasid period, mosques began featuring domed roofs, an element borrowed from Persian and Byzantine architecture. Persian mosques were also characterized by their large courtyards, enclosed on all four sides by rows of arched vaults, and by the double minarets that flanked the entranceway.

Turkish mosques were based on Byzantine church models. The Ottoman Turks

Figure 16-13 *The Badshahi Mosque in Lahore, Pakistan*

celebrated the triumph of Islam over Christianity by turning the great Church of Hagia Sophia in Constantinople—which had been the headquarters of Orthodox Christianity—into a mosque. Like Byzantine churches, Turkish mosques often incorporated smaller domes and half-domes around the great central dome. The imposing massiveness of the mosque was counterbalanced by dainty, pointed minarets which resembled arrows ready to fly up to heaven. Four, or even six, minarets were arranged symmetrically around the mosque.

DECORATIVE ART AND PAINTING

One of the most characteristic motifs of Islamic art was the **arabesque**, a curving, often interlacing design pattern that was sometimes abstract and sometimes embellished with plant stems, leaves, flowers, stars, and similar elements. The arabesque (which literally means "in the Arabian fashion") could be found on book covers and pages, walls, ceilings, tiles, pottery, carpets, swords, and almost any other surface that could be decorated.

Arabesques are a good example of the highly ornamental nature of Islamic art. Similar patterns used geometrics, florals, scrolls, "starbursts," and even the flowing lines of Arabic or Persian script. Such designs could be found everywhere in the Muslim world, spread by Arab conquerors and travelling artists.

The popularity of these intricate, highly stylized designs was largely due to the ban on depicting human and animal figures in religious art. This aversion to figures often spilled over into secular art. Nevertheless, human figures were depicted quite frequently in Islamic painting.

Small illustrations in books and manuscripts, called *miniatures*, were the predominant examples of Islamic painting. In these works, human figures were just one element in a design that also incorporated calligraphy, decorative borders, and background patterns. Because the Arabs had no tradition of painting, Muslim artists drew upon existing local models. For instance, Syrian manuscripts showed humans wearing Byzantine-style draped robes, while

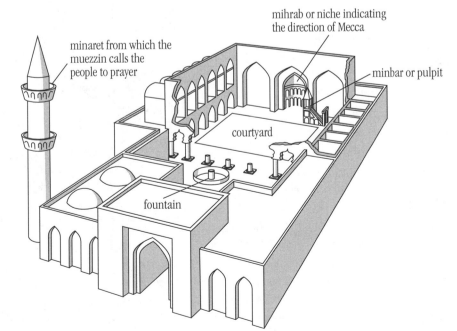

minaret from which the muezzin calls the people to prayer

mihrab or niche indicating the direction of Mecca

minbar or pulpit

courtyard

fountain

Figure 16-14 *A cut-away plan of a mosque*

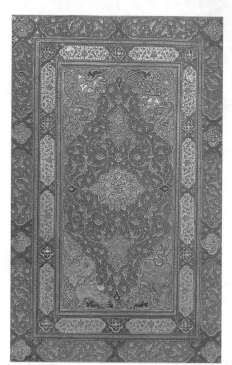

Figure 16-15 *An arabesque pattern on a cover of the Qur'an*

Figure 16-16 *A painting of Mehmed II from a sixteenth-century geneological manuscript*

Persian manuscripts showed male figures wearing Persian clothes and turbans. Later, during the Mongol period, painted human figures looked distinctly Asian.

Larger paintings did not develop until the Ottoman period in the fifteenth century. Turkish paintings depicted historical events and genuine people in a more realistic and weightier style. Figure 16-16 shows a manuscript portrait of Mehmed the Conqueror, the Turkish sultan who defeated the Byzantine empire. In the painting, Mehmed's face appears regal yet real, engaging the viewer's attention despite the busy patterns covering his clothes and the background.

LANGUAGE

The Arabic script was developed so that the word of God, the Qur'an, could be written down. All the characters of the alphabet were consonants, while vowel signs (small marks above or below the characters) were used to ensure proper pronunciation. (See box on page 361.) Arabic was written from right to left. The graceful lines of the Arabic characters and the importance of the Qur'an's text contributed to the development of a highly ornate Arabic script. Some forms of Arabic calligraphy were so highly embellished that they were illegible. In such cases, legibility took a back seat to the script's decorative possibilities.

Arabic was the primary language used in Arabia, Syria, Palestine, Egypt, and North Africa. When Persian became the second language of Islam, it was mainly used in Persia and central Asia. Islamic Persian took a different form than Persian before the Muslim wars of conquest. Islamic Persian derived many words from Arabic and was written in Arabic script. However, it was a different language, in the same way that English differs from French despite the incorporation of many French words in the language after the Norman Conquest.

Turkish became the third language of Islam during the Ottoman empire. It was the primary language in Asia Minor and was used more intermittently in central Asia, Egypt, Syria, and Palestine.

LITERATURE
Poetry

Even before Islam, poetry had been a celebrated cultural tradition among the Bedouin tribes. Although Muhammad had disapproved of poetry because of its pagan roots, it was revived and enjoyed renewed prestige in the Umayyad period and succeeding eras. Muslims of all ethnic and linguistic backgrounds—Arab, Persian, and Turkish—viewed literature as the highest form of artistic achievement, far

Figure 16-17 *This bird-shaped calligraphy says "In the name of Allah, the most compassionate, the most merciful."*

PERSPECTIVES ON THE PAST

The Arabic Alphabet

What aspects in the development and appearance of the Arabic script make it ideal for calligraphy?

The Arabic script is based on the earliest known alphabet, the North Semitic, which originated in Palestine and Syria around 1700 BCE. The Arabic alphabet consists of 28 characters, all consonants, and six vowel signs (three of which are also consonant characters). A character can have four different forms, depending on how it is used.

Form	Name	Form	Name	Form	Name	Form	Name
ا	alif	د	dāl	ض	dād	ك	kāf
ب	bā	ذ	dhāl	ط	tā	ل	lām
ت	tā	ر	rā	ظ	zā	م	mīm
ث	thā	ز	zāy	ع	ʿayn	ن	nun
ج	jīm	س	sīn	غ	ghayn	ه	hā
ح	hā	ش	shīn	ف	fā	و	wāw
خ	khā	ص	sād	ق	qāf	ى	yā

above the mundane arts of painting and music.

To Muslims, the Qur'an was not only the word of God, but also the greatest work of literature in Arabic. But there were many other distinguished literary forms. One of the earliest and most copied was the *qasida,* a heroic desert ode perfected by Arab tribes in the sixth century. The expressive imagery and high literary quality of *qasidas* impressed the later Umayyad poets, who composed their own versions even though they had long left behind a desert lifestyle.

A *qasida* began with the poet sitting in a deserted campground, reminiscing about lost love and past adventures with his tribe. The poet then related the earlier events that had occurred—stirring battles, thundering rides across the desert, and a great love affair that ended unhappily because the woman belonged to a hostile tribe. The *qasida* was elegiac in tone, a lament for happier days that have passed, yet it ended on an upbeat with the poet boasting about his tribe or himself. Umayyad poets turned this boast into lavish praise for their patron.

Love poetry, called *ghazal,* was another widely practised literary form. Urban *ghazals* were light-hearted and sophisticated, while *ghazals* from the desert were anguished expressions of unrequited or tragic love. The melancholy tone of tribal verse was likely the result of the conditions of nomadic life—a life in which one might discover one's true love in another tribe, only to have to pack up and leave the next day. Love poetry written in Moorish Spain influenced the development of courtly love poetry in medieval France.

The most famous literary love story was that of Majnun and Layla, two young people whose romance was typically ill-fated. Majnun's perpetual search for his lost love Layla inspired Arabic, Persian, and Turkish poets to retell the story in their own ways. The twelfth-century Persian romantic poet Nizami focused on the human lovers, while the great sixteenth-century Ottoman Sufi poet Fuzuli likened Majnun's longing for Layla to the desire of human beings to be one with God.

The Abbasid khalifs and the Turkish sultans during the Seljuk and Ottoman periods were great patrons of poets. Unfortunately, this patronage resulted in much

THROUGH THEIR EYES

The Mystical Poetry of Rumi

Can you explain the popularity of Sufi poets among ordinary Muslim people?

Sufi mystics were devoted practitioners of poetry, music, and whirling dancing—all activities frowned upon by orthodox religious authorities. Sufi poets mainly wrote about love, using the language of conventional romantic love to express devotion to and longing for God. Sufis called God "the Beloved" and themselves "lovers."

Jalal al-Din Rumi, founder of the Whirling Dervish Order, was one of the greatest and most accessible Sufi poets. Born in Afghanistan in the 13th century, he fled the horrors of the Mongol invasion and found a home among the Seljuk Turks. His poetry is simple, direct, and powerful. Below are two of his quatrains.

O how the Beloved fits inside my heart—
Like a thousand souls in one body,
A thousand harvests in one sheaf of wheat,
A thousand whirling heavens in the eye of a needle.

Wait till you look within yourself and see what is
*   there.*
O seeker,
One leaf in that Garden is worth more than all of
*   Paradise!*

fawning verse being produced by individuals eager to gain favour and financial reward. Generally, poetry of lasting significance was written not by court poets but by outsiders—the anonymous nomadic Bedouins and the wandering Sufi monks who brought Islam to the Turks.

Prose

As is usually the case with literature, prose developed later than poetry in the Muslim world. Storytelling was a popular activity, and Islamic stories in prose first appeared in the eighth century. The ninth-century Abbasid writer al-Jahiz wrote highly acclaimed, wittily entertaining animal tales and anecdotes about urban life.

In a much more fantastical vein is the *Thousand and One Nights* or *Arabian Nights,* which for westerners is the quintessential Arabic literary work. The stories come from a variety of sources, the earliest possibly originating in India and brought to Persia in the sixth century. Other stories were added over the centuries from Baghdad and Cairo.

The different stories are linked together by the central figure of Shahrazad, the grand wazir's daughter, who tells the stories but is not involved in any of them. In Europe, Boccaccio copied this literary structure in his *Decameron.* The world depicted in *Arabian Nights,* with flying carpets, genies and demons, mythical beasts, and caves full of treasure, is not highly typical of Muslim literature.

Historical chronicles and biographies were the main forms of non-fictional prose. History and chronology had been important in Islam since its beginning. Muhammad was the last of God's prophets, superseding those who had come before him. His followers recorded his life, his actions, and his sayings. The Qur'an itself reminded people about historical Biblical figures and events. Muslim rulers, especially the khalifs, were conscious of their place in history and anxious to leave a record of their actions.

At first chronicles recorded yearly events, but later they focused on the lives and actions of the rulers. The fourteenth-century Tunisian historian Ibn Khaldun produced a seven-volume history of the Muslim world, describing events, leaders, battles, and other topics of interest. However, it is not the history itself but its introduction, called the *Muqaddima,* that is famous for its philosophy of history. Ibn Khaldun stated that scholars should look at the causes of events in order to understand them.

Other important genres of non-fiction were religious dictionaries, aimed at helping people read the Qur'an in its native Arabic, and political science texts that provided advice to rulers and civil servants.

THROUGH THEIR EYES
The Revenge of the Sultan

In the Prologue of *Arabian Nights* Shahrazad is introduced. She is the older daughter of the grand wazir (chief minister) of the sultan Shahrayar, who rules a mythical kingdom in India and Indochina. Below is a summary of the background story of Shahrazad and Shahrayar.

After reading this Prologue, decide if it is an effective beginning to *Arabian Nights* and give reasons for your opinion.

The sultan Shahrayar loved his wife dearly, but when he discovered her committing adultery, he flew into a terrible rage and order that she be executed. Convinced that all women were faithless and worthless, Shahrayar vowed to take a new wife each night and have her killed the next morning. The grand wazir had the grievous duty of finding a new woman for the sultan every night and having her executed at daybreak.

As all of the young women in the kingdom were dying in this way, their fathers and mothers clamoured in grief, cursing the sultan and praying to the Creator for deliverance.

The wazir himself had two daughters, the older named Shahrazad and the younger Dinarzad. Shahrazad was intelligent, knowledgeable, wise, and cultured. She had studied books of literature, philosophy, history, and medicine, and knew poetry by heart. She conceived of a plan to end the executions and asked her father to present her to the sultan as his next bride.

Horrified, the wazir tried to change her mind, but Shahrazad stood firm. With a heavy heart, the wazir went to the sultan. Shahrayar was astonished that his chief minister would offer his own daughter, but the wazir explained that it was Shahrazad's wish.

Figure 16-18
Shahrazad telling the sultan a story

Pleased that the sultan agreed to have her as his wife, Shahrazad spoke with her younger sister Dinarzad. She said that she would send for Dinarzad to spend the evening with the sultan and herself. Before daybreak Dinarzad was to ask Shahrazad to tell a story.

All went according to Shahrazad's plan. That evening, in tears, she asked the sultan if he would allow Dinarzad to come and sleep in their chamber so that the two sisters could say goodbye to each other in the morning. The sultan agreed. When all three were together, Dinarzad said, "Sister, if you are not sleepy, tell us one of your lovely stories to while away the night; for I do not know what will happen to you tomorrow." The sultan gave his permission, and Shahrazad began her story...

* * *

Just as she got to the most interesting part, dawn came and she immediately fell silent. In suspense, the sultan resolved to let her live one more day so that he could hear the end of the story. However, she would still die the following morning.

So it happened that each night Shahrazad finished a tale and started a new one, always leaving it unfinished by morning. She had enough tales to last a thousand and one nights, during which time she bore the sultan three sons. He became so convinced of her wisdom and wifely devotion that he spared her life, and the two of them ruled together happily and justly.

REFLECT AND ANALYZE

1. What factors influenced the type of visual art mostly practised by medieval Muslim artists?

2. Describe the main features that characterize Arab, Persian, and Turkish mosques. Research and include pictures of each kind of mosque in your report.

3. a) Can you explain why the desert tribal odes called *qasidas* were greatly popular among urban citizens?
    b) Following the basic pattern of a *qasida*, compose your own heroic or romantic ode such as "Ode of the Classroom" or "Ode of the Workout Gym."

4. Umar Khayyam (Omar Khayyam) was a Muslim version of a "Renaissance man," who gained fame as a mathematician, astronomer, and poet. Research one of the following topics: a) his life, b) his poetry collectively called the *Ruba'iyat*, c) his contribution to mathematics and astronomy.

THE SCIENCES

From the eighth to tenth centuries, scholars and scribes in the Muslim world translated works of Greek philosophy, mathematics, science, and astronomy into Arabic. (Many translators were local Jews and Christians who had extensive knowledge of Greek.) Medical sources from India and Asia were also translated into Arabic. Muslims built upon the knowledge of earlier civilizations by adding their own significant contributions to the fields of mathematics, medicine, and science. They rigorously applied scientific methods of observation and experimentation, correcting errors in earlier texts whenever they found them. Western Europe was greatly influenced by Arab learning.

PHILOSOPHY

The work of the twelfth-century Moorish philosopher Ibn Rushd (known to Europeans as Averroës) had a significant impact on medieval Christian philosophers, notably Thomas Aquinas. Ibn Rushd, who lived in Cordoba, studied the writings of Aristotle and advocated the use of logic and reason in the study of all knowledge. His books on Aristotle were translated by Latin scholars in Spain and made their way into the rest of Europe. His unorthodox religious views led to Muslims burning many of his writings.

MATHEMATICS

Muslim mathematicians adopted the written symbols for numbers used by Hindus in India, including the concept of zero (*sifr* or cipher). Indians had discovered that only ten figures or numerals could be used to express even the largest quantities. The zero indicated the absence of quantity. Two hundred and fifty years before the zero was used in Europe, the Arabs were employing the *sifr* as a placeholder in arithmetical calculations "to keep the rows." The Indo-Arabic system of numerals eventually replaced cumbersome Roman numerals, and is the system we use today.

The Muslims studied and wrote scholarly treatises on Greek geometry. They also created new branches of mathematics, algebra and trigonometry. (Algebra comes from the Arabic word *al-jabr*.) In the fifteenth century, the Persian mathematician al-Khwarizmi produced *The Key to Arithmetic*, a comprehensive and easy-to-use textbook for merchants, financial clerks, astronomers, surveyors, and anyone else who used numbers extensively. This work became a standard text throughout the Muslim world and attracted attention in Europe. Perhaps its most valuable contribution was the author's discussion of decimal fractions.

MEDICINE

Muslim medical practitioners did much to advance medical knowledge and the general practice of medicine. They believed that diseases had natural causes and observed their patients' symptoms in order to reach a diagnosis. They successfully performed surgery and developed many medical instruments, including the syringe. Their knowledge of eye diseases and optics was renowned.

During the Abbasid period, numerous hospitals were opened in Baghdad and elsewhere, some of them free to the poor. (The wealthy, however, paid high fees for medical treatment.) There were separate wards for men and women as well as for different types of illnesses. Physicians practising in hospitals and privately had to receive

Figure 16-19 *A page from an Arabic translation of a Greek medical text. The illustration shows medicine being made from honey.*

formal training and pass an examination.

Muslim medical texts were justly famous for their comprehensive knowledge of diseases, treatments, and herbal remedies. Zakiriya al-Razi (865–925), the head physician at Baghdad's chief hospital, developed many new treatments for ailments and wrote nearly 200 medical books. He emphasized the importance of careful observation of patients and was the first to write about children's diseases. His descriptions of the symptoms of smallpox and measles helped later physicians to diagnose and treat these illnesses. His largest textbook was a compilation of all medical knowledge known at the time, including Greek, Syrian, Hindu, and Persian practices as well as Muslim remedies.

The Muslim medical authority best known to Europeans was Hakim Ibn Sina, (called Avicenna in Europe). Ibn Sina spent most of his active life in the courts of eleventh-century Persia. His vast *Canon of Medicine,* which listed over 4000 prescriptions, was translated into Latin in the thirteenth century. For the next 400 years, the book was the most widely used medical text in Europe.

One serious drawback for physicians was that they did not perform autopsies or dissections of humans after death. Muslims believed that a person's body had to be whole in order for him or her to be received in heaven.

CHEMISTRY AND OPTICS

The Muslims were deeply interested in the physical world and, unlike the ancient Greeks, routinely carried out observations and experiments. Muslim scientists believed that base metals such as tin, iron, and lead could be changed into gold and silver. Their experiments and observations in search of this transforming process became the medieval science of **alchemy**, the forerunner of modern chemistry.

The noted Muslim alchemist Jabir, who may have lived before 800 although most work attributed to him appeared later, explored the chemical processes of oxidation, crystallization, and filtration. He kept careful records of the equipment he used, the steps he took in his experiments, and the results. Such practices would later become standard in the study of science.

The Muslims' contribution to optics, the study of light and vision, was outstanding. Al Hasan, who lived during the ninth and tenth centuries, is sometimes called "the father of optics." He wrote about the principles of convex and concave mirrors and the refraction of light. Whereas ancient scientists had believed that the eye emitted rays toward the objects it sees, al-Hasan's work led him to conclude that it was light travelling from an object to the eye that allowed the object to be seen.

ASTRONOMY

Arab astronomers were not content to just simply study the work of the Greek astronomer Ptolemy, but made detailed studies of the moon, planets, and stars of their own. They used the compass to measure the distances between heavenly bodies and the astrolabe to measure their heights. The astronomers charted the movements of heavenly bodies, creating star maps and astronomical tables that for centuries were used not only in the Muslim world but in Europe and Asia as well.

The world's first full-time astronomical observatory was built in central Asia in 1259 and employed about 20 astronomers, including one from China. At this observatory, astronomers made and recorded ob-

Figure 16-20 *Muslim astronomers*

servations for a continuous period of 20 years. They measured the earth's circumference, with fair accuracy, 600 years before the Europeans admitted that the world was round.

The Muslims gave many stars the names they still have today. They also described solar eclipses and showed conclusively that the moon causes the ocean tides on earth.

TIME

The Muslim calendar dates from 16 July 622, when Muhammad made his *hijrah* or journey from Mecca to Medina. Because the Muslim calendar is lunar, a year has either 364 or 365 days. Every 32.5 years in the Gregorian calendar is equivalent to 33 years in the Muslim calendar.

Lunar months are slightly shorter than Gregorian months, about 29 days and 12 hours long. This means that the first day of a Muslim month falls about 13 days earlier in each successive Gregorian year. Thus the month-long fast of Ramadan does not occur in the same season every year. The names and lengths of the Muslim months are shown below.

Name of Month	Number of Days
Muharram	29 or 30
Safar	29 or 30
Rabi I	29 or 30
Rabi II	29 or 30
Jumada I	29 or 30
Jumada II	29 or 30
Rajab	29 or 30
Sha'ban	29 or 30
Ramadan	29 or 30
Shawwal	29 or 30
Dhu'l-Qa'dah	29 or 30
Dhu'l-Hijjah	29 or 30

REFLECT AND ANALYZE

1. Do you think European science and philosophy could have existed without the Arabs? Explain your answer as fully as possible.

2. List the different ways in which Muslim mathematical and scientific knowledge could have spread to Europeans.

3. Considering how much medieval Europeans learned from the Muslims, can you provide reasons why the scientific contributions of Muslims are not generally known to westerners?

LOOKING BACK

The birth of Islam in the seventh century changed the face of the world. The religion transformed the social and political organization of the Arabs and motivated them to build one of the largest and most durable civilizations the world has ever seen. Whereas Europe's transformation by Christianity was not attributable to any single ethnic group, the Islamization of the Middle East was almost entirely due to the Arabs. Yet even while Arabs and their language spread throughout the Middle East and central Asia, they were themselves changed by the cultures they encountered—Persian, Byzantine, and Indian in the east.

The great wealth and cultural sophistication of the medieval Muslim world stood in stark contrast to the poverty and backwardness of medieval Europe. The international trade between the Middle East, Asia, Africa, and the Byzantine empire was in full force while Europe was still living in the Dark Ages. Muslim thinkers were making significant advances in mathematics and science at a time when most Europeans were illiterate. By the end of the Middle Ages, however, the Europeans were

poised to enter a period of great cultural vitality and to extend their influence around the world through voyages of exploration. The Muslim world, while still impressive, had by this time passed the peak of its achievements.

The legacy of earlier developments live on in Islamic practice and custom today. The pilgrimage to Mecca still brings Muslims from around the world together and strengthens their faith. Iran, Saudi Arabia, and several other modern Islamic countries strictly abide by the laws of the *shar'ia*, the religious code of Islam. In some societies, Muslim teenaged girls and women are required to always cover their heads (a modern form of veiling) and not to show their arms or legs. It should be noted that men also often dressed modestly, in accordance with the rules of the Qur'an.

While some Islamic countries today denounce western influences, historically, the Arabs willingly learned from foreign cultures. They freely adopted useful ideas and valuable knowledge, whether the source was Byzantine, Persian, Indian, or Chinese. The Muslims provided a valuable service to future generations by preserving the learning of ancient civilizations, not only that of classical Greece but also Mesopotamia and Egypt. When Europeans finally emerged from centuries of ignorance during the Middle Ages, a significant part of their learning and rediscovery of the past came from Muslim sources.

The medieval Muslims also consistently practised religious tolerance toward the Christians and Jews in their realm, making no attempt to convert them. European Christians were not nearly so tolerant of Muslims and Jews. However, it is interesting to observe that whenever Christians and Muslims mingled or clashed with each other, such as during the Crusades, the Muslim side usually prevailed in the long run.

MAKING CONNECTIONS

1. How is Islam related to and different from Christianity and Judaism? Create one or more large maps showing the spread of Christianity through Europe and the Byzantine empire, and the spread of Islam through the Middle East up to the year 1500. You may wish to use overlays to show how Islam took over Christian areas. Why do you think both of these religions became such a dominant force in the life of medieval people?

2. a) Compare the depiction of Christ in medieval European manuscripts and Byzantine mosaics with the depiction of Muhammad in Islamic manuscripts. Are there any similarities?

   b) Compare and contrast an illuminated page from a medieval European manuscript with a comparable page from an Islamic manuscript. Note how the design of each page uses calligraphy, illustration, decorative borders, and any other features. Based on your findings, do you think there might have been any cross-cultural influences between the two civilizations?

3. Assume the role of *either* a lord *or* a serf living on a medieval manor in western Europe. Write a report explaining the advantages and disadvantages of the manorial system as you see it.

4. Read one of the tales in the *Arabian Nights* and write a brief summary of the tale. Create an additional tale that might be included in this collection.

5. Read the first chapters of Chaucer's *Canterbury Tales* and Boccacio's *The Decameron*. What similarities do you notice between the two works? Why were these two books so popular in their day?

6. Muslims examine the sayings and behaviour of Muhammad as closely as the Qur'an itself. Explain in a few paragraphs what you think Muhammad might have meant by the following statement: "The ink of the scholar is holier than the blood of the martyr."

7. Do the following activity with a partner. Read or dramatize your diary entries in class.

   a) One partner takes the role of an English medieval knight participating in the siege of Acre during the Third Crusade. Write a diary entry describing some of your military experiences, what you have seen or experienced in the Holy Land, your feelings for your leader Richard the Lionheart, and how well you are upholding the code of chivalry.

   b) The other partner writes a diary entry for a Muslim Turkish soldier defending Acre in the same siege. Describe your feelings for your leader Saladin, tactics against the Christians, your impressions of the Christians, and any religious ceremonies that occur during the day.

DIGGING DEEPER

8. The dome was used in Byzantine, Islamic, and Renaissance Italian architecture. Research three domed buildings, one from each civilization. Describe what each building was used for, and compare the buildings, especially their domes. Discuss how use of the dome might have spread from one civilization to another.

9. Islam is an important religious and political force in many parts of the world today. Research one or more of the following topics.

    a) In which modern nations is Islam a major influence? Draw a world map showing predominantly Islamic countries or regions. In which regions is there armed conflict between Muslims and non-Muslims?

    b) Describe the role of Islam and Islamic customs in modern Saudi Arabia in a report. Use photos to illustrate different aspects covered in your report.

    c) Describe events leading up to and after the Ayatollah Khomeini's Islamic revolution in Iran.

10. a) There are many different Protestant denominations today. Research the history and beliefs of one of the following:

Calvinists	Presbyterians
Puritans	Methodists
Quakers	Baptists
United Church	

    b) Research how the Russian Orthodox church developed out of the Eastern (Greek) Orthodox church. Describe any differences.

11. a) Women played an important, if often hidden, role in medieval European, Byzantine, and Muslim society. Research the status of women in more depth in one of these civilizations, and create a written or oral presentation.

    b) Alternatively, write a profile on or dramatize the life of one of the following historical women or an individual of your own choosing.

Rabi'a al-Adawiyya (Sufi mystic)	Byzantine Empress Irene
Lucrezia Borgia	Marguerite of Navarre
Queen Isabella of Spain	Lady Margaret Beaufort
Mary Queen of Scots	Elizabeth I

12. Religious holidays were important in the medieval period. Research and report on one Christian and one Muslim holy day or festival. Describe the purpose of each celebration, when it is observed, its length, and its customs. Do you see any parallels between the two festivals?

SKILL DEVELOPMENT: RESEARCHING A TOPIC

Before writing a report on a topic, you first need to research it. Finding and recording your research involves three separate steps:

1. Identifying and locating sources of information.

2. Crediting the source material.

3. Recording the data.

Process

Step 1: Identifying and Locating Sources of Information

In this stage, you identify and locate the resources you need for your research assignment. The type of resources can vary considerably. Clarify each of the following issues before proceeding with your research.

1. How many different resources do you think you need to examine?

2. What types of resources do you need to examine? Specifically,
   - do you need only **secondary** (researched) resources?
   - do you need **primary** (historical) sources?
   - can you use **newspapers** and **magazines** as well as books?
   - can you use **videos**, **sound recordings**, **CD-ROM**s, and other forms of information?

3. Identify the places in your school, neighbourhood, and city where you can find the resources you need. Consider whether you might contact government, social, or cultural organizations in your community for information.

4. Who, or what, can assist you in locating the research resources you need?

Step 2: Crediting the Source Material

Each source you use must be clearly identified so that you can keep track of where you have obtained data. You also need this information in order to compile a complete bibliography for your final report.

For each source from which you draw information, record the following:

- the author(s) of the publication. Record the full name of each author credited and note whether he or she is a writer, editor, or translator.
- the complete name of the publication. Include a volume number or a subhead, if there is one.
- the name of the publisher(s) and the place of publication (e.g., Toronto, Ottawa, New York, London, England).
- the date of publication. This is usually designated with a copyright (©) sign. If there is more than one date, record the original publication date as well as the date of the latest edition or revision.
- for a periodical, the volume or series number (if there is one), the issue date, and the pages on which the article appears.
- the page numbers from which you have recorded any data.

Step 3: Recording the Data

There are many ways to record the information that you have found. The important thing is to develop an organized or systematic plan. Here are some tips:

- Keep all of your research notes together in a research folder.
- Start with a fresh page for each new resource that you consult. Put the credit information at the top of the page. Record page numbers where you find information down the margin. This will make it easier to go back to the source later, if necessary.
- If you prefer, use large index cards rather than pages to record your data.
- When you locate a fact, concept, or idea you wish to record, write it in point form in your own words.
- If you wish to quote a primary or secondary source, use quotation marks before and after the statement. Record the entire passage word for word. If you wish to leave out a phrase or section, make sure you use an ellipsis (three dots) to indicate the gap. (If in doubt, do not leave out any words at all.)

Indicate the writer or speaker of the quoted passage, and record the page number on which the quotation appears in the source.

- Make a note of any maps, illustrations, photos, audio clips, etc., that you would like to use in your final presentation. Consult your teacher or a librarian about whether you will need to obtain permission to use the material.

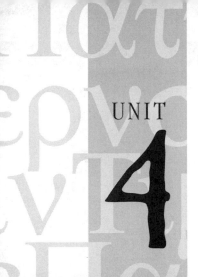

Early Asian Civilization
4500 BCE - 1185 CE

CHINA AND JAPAN

Two important civilizations associated with ancient East Asia are those of China and Japan. China originated as a river valley civilization, and gradually grew to include an enormous geographical area. Japan was an island civilization whose early history was very much influenced by the sea and its island location.

During this period China developed a very advanced civilization and enjoyed a remarkable degree of cultural continuity. Although there were periods of significant upheaval, Chinese traditions survived these upheavals. The Chinese introduced many important innovations to the rest of the world. Japan came under the influence of China for a time and adopted many of its institutions and cultural traditions. Japan then underwent a process of assimilating these outside influences with indigenous traditions to develop a purely Japanese way of life.

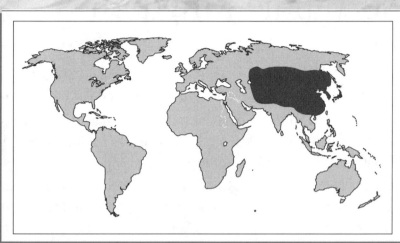

THE CHINESE EMPIRE

THE JAPANESE EMPIRE

CHINA:
The Middle Kingdom

The most influential philosopher of ancient China was Confucius (Kong Fuzi), who was revered as a great teacher and philosopher. Confucius aspired to political office, and travelled to the different courts of his day in the attempt to find a position. He was unsuccessful in this, but his experiences led him to articulate a philosophy that influenced life in China for most of its history.

Confucius himself did not write down his teachings. His followers compiled them in a book called the *Analects*, which consists of a series of questions and answers. In the following excerpt from the *Analects*, Confucius is questioned about the role of government.

Zigong inquired about governing. The Master said, "Make food supplies sufficient, provide an adequate army, and give the people reason to have faith."

Zigong asked, "If one had no choice but to dispense with one of these three, which should it be?"

"Eliminate the army."

Zigong continued, "If one had no choice but to get rid of one of the two remaining, which should it be?"

"Dispense with food," the Master said. "Since ancient times, death has always occurred, but people without faith cannot stand."

Figure 17-1
Confucius

THE LAND OF ANCIENT CHINA

Unaware of the great civilizations in other parts of the world, the ancient Chinese thought of their country as the "Middle Kingdom," or the centre of the world. Isolated during their early history, the Chinese developed a unique civilization and a strong sense of cultural identity.

Geographic factors lay at the heart of this isolation. China was well protected by natural barriers. The south and west borders of the country consisted of the forbidding Himalaya Mountains to the south and the burning Taklimakan Desert to the west. On the east, the Pacific Ocean acted as a barrier to contact with others. Only from the steppes, or grassy plains, of the north was China easily accessible.

Within China, civilization developed in the fertile river valleys of the Huang He and the Chang Jiang.

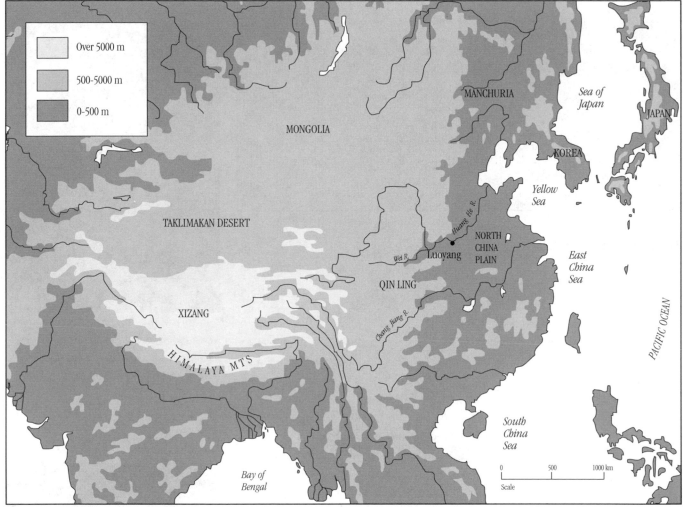

Figure 17-2 *China*

The Huang He in the north winds for 4300 km through the North China Plain. It was the first river to play an important role in the history of ancient China. It is sometimes called "the great sorrow" because of its tendency to flood its banks frequently, destroying villages and fields. It floods frequently because it carries a large amount of yellow-coloured silt. This silt is a fine yellow soil, called *loess*, that blows onto the North China Plain from central Asia. As it builds up in the Huang He, the river floods depositing more of this silt on the countryside. In some areas of the North China Plain the *loess* is over 75 m in depth.

North China was very attractive to people from the northern steppes, where the drier and colder climate prevented the successful practice of agriculture. The earliest Chinese civilization was centered on the Huang He in the north of China.

In later times, the Chang Jiang River Valley became a more important settlement region because it was easier to navigate along the great length (5150 km) of this river. Travel between the two great settlement areas was slow and difficult because they are separated by the Qin Ling mountains.

The climate in northern China contrasts with that in the south. Northern winters are cold due to winter winds sweeping down from the Asian continent. Summers are hot and rainfall is irregular. The Qin Ling mountains block the warm humid monsoon winds from the southeast that provide south China with a moist warm tropical climate year round.

REFLECT AND ANALYZE

1. Why might the ancient Chinese believe that their country was the centre of civilization in the world?

2. Which geographic features facilitated and hindered communication within China?

3. How large is China? Using an atlas, find out the size of China in terms of its area and its population. Compare China to other countries in the world. In terms of both size and population, where does it rank?

Figure 17-3 *The Huang He River and the North China Plain. The foreground shows terraced fields irrigated by the river, whose level changes according to flood seasons*

HISTORICAL OVERVIEW

Around 3000 BCE, farming communities began to develop along the Huang He River and its tributaries. As these communities took shape, they initiated a civilization that would be the longest continuous civilization in the world.

From the beginning of their recorded history, the Chinese were ruled by a series of dynasties in which the reigns of specific ruling families were used to name the historical time periods.

THE SHANG DYNASTY
1700 BCE-1027 BCE

The first historical dynasty began about 1700 BCE, when a Shang king established his rule in the valley of the Huang He by defeating other rulers. He began the Shang Dynasty that lasted until 1027 BCE. During their 600 years of control, Shang rulers used the horse-drawn war chariot to extend their influence over most of the Huang He Valley and beyond.

The Shang did not control this enormous area on their own. They relied on princes and nobles who were loyal to them to rule the various territories not under their direct control. In 1300 BCE the Shang established a capital at Anyang, where they built homes and temples for the ruling family, chief priests, nobles, and court advisors.

The Shang were particularly noted for their skill in working bronze, using techniques that have never been surpassed. As a valuable commodity, the use of bronze was reserved for weapons and for elaborately decorated ceremonial vessels. Wood and stone tools were used for everyday activities.

The Shang also had a system of pictographs and ideographs that later evolved into writing. This early writing was discovered on oracle bones that were used to predict the future. A question would be inscribed on animal bones or tortoise shells, that were then heated until cracks appeared. The interpretation of these cracks provided the answer to the question.

The Shang dynasty was an agricultural society. The Shang developed a calendar based on the positions of the moon so they could schedule the planting and harvesting of crops. The Shang had developed a fairly sophisticated economy. As well as manufacturing bronze, they also manufactured silk. The economy had developed sufficiently to require money, and cowrie shells were used for this purpose.

Figure 17-4 *A bird-shaped bronze wine vessel from the Shang dynasty*

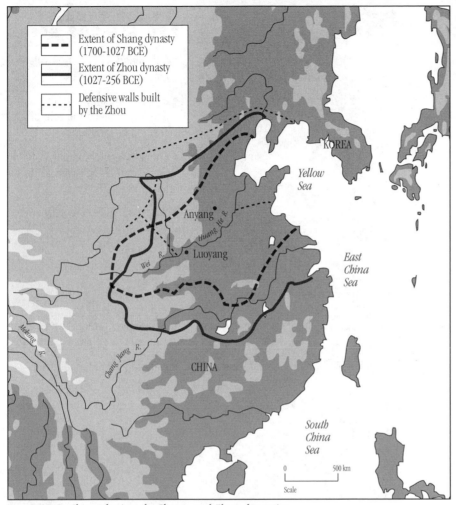

Figure 17-5 *China during the Shang and Zhou dynasties*

THE ZHOU DYNASTY
1027 BCE-256 BCE

The Shang dynasty was overthrown in 1027 BCE by the Zhou who invaded from the valley of the Wei River, a western tributary of the Huang He. Their rule over China, nearly 800 years, was the longest of any single dynasty in Chinese history.

The Zhou themselves had developed neither writing nor bronze technology, but they readily adopted the traditions of the Shang. The Zhou dynasty is often referred to as the Classical Period of Chinese history because of the developments that took place in these years.

The Zhou established a feudal state by granting large tracts of land to families who agreed to rule on behalf of the Zhou in return for paying the Zhou an annual tribute in jade or grain. The Zhou enlarged the extent of their territory far beyond that of the Shang, moving into central China and the Chang Jiang basin.

The Zhou were the first to build walls in an attempt to defend China from the nomadic peoples of the steppes. In addition to this, they improved their techniques of warfare by inventing the cross-bow and replacing chariots with cavalry.

Under the Zhou, many important cultural and economic developments took place. The Shang system of writing was refined and the first books were written. Agricultural productivity increased enormously as the use of iron became common in farming, the ox-drawn plough was introduced, and large-scale irrigation projects were built. Rainfall in the north of China was uncertain, and the use of irrigation was essential to ensure good harvests. Trade expanded, aided by the building of canals to link the far flung dynasty and by the introduction of copper coins as currency.

However, it was difficult for the Zhou to maintain central control. Each feudal territory was actually a small city-state, and although its ruler owed obedience to the Zhou king in theory, in fact the ruler was essentially independent. As time went by, these rulers gained more power and built walled towns that dominated the surrounding countryside. From these bases, the nobles fought with each other to increase the size of their territories.

An alliance of rebel states and nomadic tribes from the steppes invaded the Wei Valley in 770 BCE. The Zhou fled east and set up a smaller capital at Luoyang. Gradually, the Zhou kings, dependent on the nobles for funding and military forces, lost all their power and were reduced to a ceremonial role.

By 481 BCE the wars among the rival rulers had become so numerous that an interval known as the Period of the Warring States ensued. It was during these years that Confucianism, Daoism, and Legalism were

A TIMELINE OF ANCIENT CHINA

	THE SHANG DYNASTY 1700 BCE-1027 BCE	THE ZHOU DYNASTY 1027 BCE-256 BCE	THE QIN DYNASTY 256 BCE-202 BCE
POLITICAL DEVELOPMENTS	• the Shang overcome a number of smaller states and establish a capital at Anyang • horse-drawn chariots are used in warfare	• the Zhou establish a feudal system and expand China's territory • the cross-bow is invented and cavalry begins to replace chariots • the first walls are built to defend China against the nomads of the steppes • the first law code is written • the capital is moved to Luoyang (770 BCE) • the period of the Warring States pits aristocrat against aristocrat as central control breaks down	• Shi Huangdi is the first ruler to call himself "emperor" • officials appointed in the capital begin to replace the role of aristocrats in government • Chinese territory expands to include the Chang Jiang River Valley and north Vietnam • the Great Wall is constructed
CULTURAL DEVELOPMENTS	• oracle bones, used to predict the future, contain an early form of writing • kings are buried with their servants and possessions	• the Chinese writing system evolves • Confucianism, Daoism and Legalism develop during the Warring States period	• Shi Huangdi orders the burning of all history and philosophy books • calligraphy is standardized
TECHNOLOGICAL/ECONOMIC DEVELOPMENTS	• the art of silk-making is well known • bronze weapons and ceremonial vessels are made with a technology that has never been surpassed • wood and stone tools are used in everyday pursuits • cowrie shells are used as money • lunar calendar is developed	• iron replaces bronze in weapons • iron farming tools and the ox-drawn plough are introduced • large-scale irrigation projects are built; canals are dug • copper coinage is introduced	• the tax system, coinage, weights, and measures are standardized • roads are built

THE HAN DYNASTY 202 BCE-220 CE	THE PERIOD OF CHAOS 220 CE-589 CE	THE SUI DYNASTY 589 CE-618 CE	THE TANG DYNASTY 618 CE-907 CE
• Confucianism becomes official government doctrine • schools and a system of examinations are set up to provide competent people for the bureaucracy • Chinese territory expands to include Manchuria, Korea, and part of central Asia • the use of cavalry is expanded and a more efficient cross-bow is developed	• China fragments into a number of kingdoms competing with each other to found a new dynasty	• China is re-united with a strong central government • the Great Wall is re-built • the Grand Canal is begun to link the Huang He and the Chang Jiang • extensive public works are undertaken • emperors engage in many wars to restore lost territory	• a centralized bureaucracy, based on merit, is established to govern the empire • more schools are established to train students for the government examinations • the landholding system is revised to make it fairer for the peasants • the Empress Wu breaks tradition by ruling in her own name
• scholars recover many of the writings lost during the Qin dynasty and an enormous amount of new literature is written	• Buddhism spreads to China from India • Daoism becomes a popular religion	• peace and order encourage literary and artistic expression, especially Buddhist	• a "golden age" for culture • the great age of sculpture in China • literary criticism begins and many encyclopedic works of literature are written • an era of cultural tolerance; many visitors are welcomed to China
• the shoulder collar is invented to increase the efficiency of draft animals • paper is invented • pottery glazes pave the way for the invention of porcelain • overland trade expands with the opening of the Silk Road • more canals are built • the water-powered mill is invented	• daily life at the local level continues much as usual • the stirrup is invented	• the economy improves as a result of the public works projects, but the peasant conscripts who build them are overburdened	• great population growth in the Chang Jiang River Valley • Changan becomes a city with a population of almost two million • porcelain is invented late in the Tang dynasty • gunpowder and the wheelbarrow are invented

developed. All three schools of thought sought the means to achieve a peaceful and orderly society. Confucius believed that human nature was essentially good, and that the family was the core of society. Family members had well-defined roles, according to Confucius. Those in authority, such as parents, should be kindly and loving. In return, those in an inferior position, such as children, owed obedience to their superiors. Confucius believed that the state was similar to the family. Rulers were obligated to set an example by ruling wisely, and the people were obligated to be obedient in return. Legalism was quite different. According to Legalists, people were selfish by nature, and would not voluntarily follow the good example set by those in authority. People had to be forced to obey through fear of punishment. Daoism was a philosophy that sought to harmonize the relationship between humans and the natural world.

The Zhou were eventually conquered by the Qin, the westernmost of the Warring States in 256 BCE. By 221 BCE, the Qin had defeated all the other Warring States and founded a new dynasty.

Figure 17-6 *Tourists viewing the Great Wall of China today*

REFLECT AND ANALYZE

1. What key developments occurred during the Shang and the Zhou dynasties in the evolution of civilization in China? Which one of these developments made the most significant contribution? Provide evidence to support your position.

2. What evidence is there to suggest that a centralized state was desirable in early China? Suggest three or four reasons, and explain each one.

3. If you were a territorial ruler owing loyalty to the Zhou, how would you justify ignoring your obligations in the pursuit of greater wealth and power for your territory?

THE QIN DYNASTY
256 BCE-202 BCE

The Qin dynasty lasted only a short time, but its political contributions to China were enormous. The Qin prince who defeated the Zhou and the other Warring States called himself Shi Huangdi or "first emperor." He reunited and expanded China and began a new kind of political system.

Shi Huangdi expanded China's territory to include the entire Chang Jiang River Valley, most of south China and north

Vietnam. He also connected the series of shorter walls that had been built by the Zhou into the Great Wall to improve China's defenses against the roaming nomads of the steppes. The wall was 2200 km long, 7.5 m high and 4.5 m thick. A dirt mound was made first and then large stones were cut and put into place on the mound. Fortified towers and a roadway were built along the top of the wall. About 300 000 labourers from all across China were conscripted to build the Great Wall. Work con-

tinued at all times, regardless of weather. Herded together in huge primitive camps with very little food, many thousands of workers died.

In addition, Shi Huangdi made important changes in the way China was governed. Because the feudal system of government had been ineffective, Shi Huangdi set up a system designed to neutralize the power of the territorial rulers. He divided the land into provinces that were administered by governors he appointed and who were responsible only to him. In addition, Shi Huangdi required the former rulers to move to the capital of Changan, where their actions could be closely scrutinized. Shi Huangdi ignored hereditary territorial rights in order to impose centralized control.

Shi Huandi introduced other measures to unify the empire. He established a common currency, a standard system of weights and measures, a single law code, and a single tax system for the entire country. He built more roads and canals to improve communications, and standardized the writing system, which had developed many different forms over the years.

Shi Huangdi also conducted a book-burning campaign. He wanted to establish a new empire, and thought that many of the philosophies and literature of the Shang and Zhou dynasties would undermine this new empire. He ordered that all books be burned. Failure to comply would result in forced labour on the Great Wall. Anyone who criticized Shi Huangdi or his policies was killed, along with their families.

Shi Huangdi's successor was unable to control the empire. Shi Huangdi had ruled too harshly and had offended too many people. Widespread revolts broke out, and rival generals fought one another in a bid for power. One of these generals, Gaozu, was successful and founded a new dynasty in 202 BCE.

THE HAN DYNASTY 202 BCE-220 CE

Gaozu was the first emperor of the Han dynasty. The Han dynasty paralleled the Roman Empire in power, prestige, and historical importance.

The Han maintained and expanded the centralized government system developed by the Qin. They kept the practice of appointing governors to administer the provinces of the empire, and continued to reduce the power of the old nobility. In order to provide the loyal and capable administrators needed to govern the empire, the Han set up schools and started a system of examinations that candidates had to pass in order to be eligible for a government position. China's government

Figure 17-7 *Chinese rulers were buried with terracotta figurines to serve them in their afterlife. These warriors in battle array were found in Shi Huangdi's tomb*

became one based on merit, not birth.

Wudi, the sixth Han emperor, expanded China's borders to the south. As well, through a combination of conquests and alliances, he extended the Chinese empire into Manchuria, Korea, and far into central Asia.

Wudi imposed government control over the economy by building canals to improve communication and trade. Great camel caravans were organized to travel west in search of horses and markets for China's silk, resulting in the Silk Road, a trade route to western Asia. Under the Han, a trickle of overseas trade also began.

Han scholars worked diligently to restore China's literary heritage after the book burning of the Qin. Many books had survived, hidden away, but much had to be carefully pieced together again from fragments and memory. There was a great increase in literary activity under the Han.

Many different kinds of books were written, from dictionaries to encyclopedias to stories and poetry.

The Han era was rich in technological inventions. A shoulder collar increased the weight that draught animals could pull. The water-powered mill was invented, as well as the rudder and the magnetic compass for ships. Advances in pottery glazing techniques paved the way for the later invention of porcelain. Perhaps the most important development during these years was the invention of paper.

The later Han emperors were less capable, and the people grew discontented with increasing taxes, natural disasters, such as famine, flood, and drought, and the threat of external invasion. Court plots and rebellion broke out. The Han emperors became little more than puppets in the hands of their generals and the last emperor was forced to surrender his throne in 220 CE.

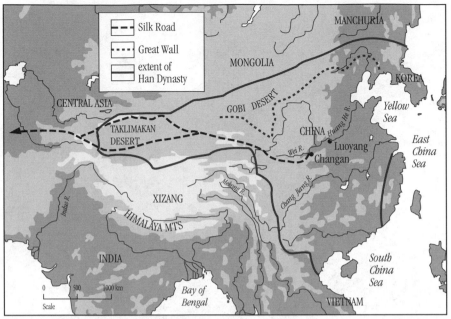

Figure 17-8 *The extent of the Han dynasty*

THE PERIOD OF CHAOS
220 CE-589 CE

With the end of the Han dynasty, China entered a period of almost four hundred years of political turmoil. No single leader was able to hold the empire together. China was fragmented into a number of kingdoms, each competing with the others for power. At the level of ordinary life, things went on much as usual, since the conflict was confined to the ruling classes. Buddhism spread to China from India during these years. Perhaps the uncertainties of the times enhanced the appeal of a religion that was designed to overcome human suffering. This period of disunity was not ended until the Sui dynasty was founded.

THE SUI DYNASTY
589 CE-618 CE

After years of war, an official of one of the kingdoms of China formed an army in 589 and successfully founded the Sui dynasty. This was a short-lived dynasty, lasting only thirty years, but it was one of great accomplishment.

Above all, the Sui were successful in re-uniting and revitalizing China. They instituted an extensive program of public works, constructed large granaries to store grain for distribution during times of famine, fortified the Great Wall, restored the territory of the empire, and undertook the construction of the Grand Canal. The Grand Canal was built to link the Huang He with the Chang Jiang and the coast by connecting a series of older and shorter canals. Internal communication within China was becoming increasingly important as the Chang Jiang region became a major food-producing area.

All of this was achieved at a great human cost, however. Hundreds of thousands of people were forced to work on the public works programs in the cruelest of conditions, or were drafted into the army. The Sui, short of money, ordered that taxes be paid ten years in advance. Before long, rebellions broke out, the second emperor was assassinated in 618, and a new dynasty was founded.

THE TANG DYNASTY
618 CE-907 CE

The Tang dynasty lasted almost 300 years, and was one of the most powerful and creative dynasties in the history of China. It expanded the empire, reformed government and education, and produced a golden age of art and literature. It was also a time of technological achievement.

REFLECT AND ANALYZE

1. What positive contributions did Shi Huangdi make to the development of China? Why did he want to erase the traditions of the past?

2. What contributions did the Han make to the development of China?

3. As a Chinese scholar, write a letter to a friend explaining your thoughts and feelings about Shi Huangdi's book-burning policy.

4. Using an organizer, compare the importance to the world of the Roman empire and the Han dynasty. What categories of comparison should you use? What research will you need to conduct? What conclusions will you make about the significance of these two empires?

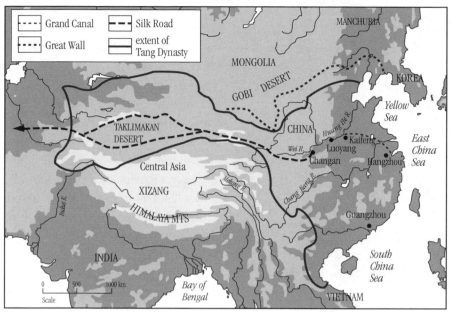

Figure 17-9 *The extent of the Tang dynasty*

The Tang expanded the borders of the empire to include much more central Asian territory. The Tang ruled a vast empire that stretched from southern Siberia west to the Caspian Sea and south into southeast Asia. Around the borders of the empire were vassal states that paid tribute to the Tang.

The Tang reintroduced strong central government. One of the most important reforms made by the Tang was a redistribution of land. China's government depended heavily on the tax revenues from farmers, and over the years, the number of farmers who owned their own land and paid taxes had decreased substantially. Many farmers had been forced into tenancy. Under the land redistribution policy, each male was to receive 5.5 ha of land and the number of days of public labour he owed to the government was fixed.

The Tang entrenched the concept of a bureaucracy based on merit not birth. Schools and the examination system were expanded enormously and were opened to all classes of society, although in most cases only the wealthy were able to take advantage of this.

An unusual event occurred during the Tang dynasty. Empress Wu began to rule on her husband's behalf when he had a stroke in 660. After his death in 683, she continued to rule, deposing her own sons. In 690 she proclaimed herself emperor, the only woman who took this title in all of Chinese history. She was not deposed until 705, when she was over eighty and ill. Many women exerted a great deal of influence on the government of China, but unlike the Empress Wu, they usually exercised their power behind the scenes.

The Tang dynasty enjoyed a period of cultural flowering. Some of China's greatest artists and poets lived during this time. It was a great era for sculpture and painting, a great deal of which was Buddhist in inspiration. Literature flourished, as did calligraphy, astronomy, and music. In the field of technology, the making of paper was refined, and porcelain was invented. Gunpowder and the wheelbarrow were also invented during the Tang dynasty.

The world of the Tang was a tolerant one. Trade brought the Chinese into contact with other parts of Asia. Chinese cities had special areas reserved for foreigners, who found a warm welcome. Interregional, overland, and overseas trade flourished under the Tang. Tea was introduced to China at this time.

All parts of the economy were prosperous. A profound change in agriculture had its beginnings under the Tang. The government encouraged farming in the lands south of the Chang Jiang. Rice production

Figure 17-10 *Taizong, the second emperor of the Tang dynasty*

increased, and population growth in the south began to outpace that in the north, since rice was more nutritious than the grains grown in the north.

During the latter years of the dynasty, the Tang system began to break down. Enemy attacks, high taxes, and dishonest government officials took their toll. China split into many small states. It was not until 960 that a general from one of the states was able to unify China once again and found another dynasty.

role, but it became more ceremonial and ritualized.

An important theory of government, called the **Mandate of Heaven**, evolved from Confucian philosophy. The Mandate of Heaven originated in the myth that China's first ruler was the son of the sky god and an earthly mother. His children, the emperors following the first ruler, were therefore the Sons of Heaven, who obtained the right to rule from the highest spiritual power in the universe. They kept this authority to rule only so long as they ruled worthily, with benevolence and concern for the people's welfare.

If a dynasty failed to govern well, the dynasty's Mandate of Heaven would be lost, and it would then pass to a new dynasty. The Chinese people thought of their history as a series of cycles, in which dynasties rose and for a period governed well. Inevitably, the dynasty would decline and a new cycle would begin.

The political role of the emperors varied considerably with each individual emperor. Many were actively involved in the decision-making and government of the empire, while others were not. Some emperors were more inclined to pursue their private interests, such as painting, and leave the running of the empire to the bureaucracy.

REFLECT AND ANALYZE

1. Why was the Sui such a short-lived dynasty?

2. Explain the reasons for the wealth and power of China under the Tang dynasty.

3. As a Chinese peasant, explain the benefits of the government's land reform policy from your point of view and from the government's point of view.

4. Find information on one of the famous Tang poets or painters. Provide a short biography for the person you select, some examples of his or her work, and explain why he or she was so highly regarded.

5. Imagine that you are a visitor from the West living in the Tang capital, Changan. Write a letter home describing your impressions of China and the Chinese.

GOVERNMENT

The focus of government in China was always on a strong centralized state. One reason for this was the need for massive public works projects. To feed the large population, the Chinese needed to practise intensive agriculture. Huge water control projects were necessary to irrigate crops and to manage the Huang He River. Only a centralized system could provide the necessary resources and technology to undertake such large-scale efforts. A strong centralized government was also needed for defence. The nomadic groups from the steppes to the north were a constant threat to Chinese stability. The Chinese built the Great Wall and maintained a large army ready to protect China at all times.

THE EMPEROR

China's rulers were more than just political leaders. They also fulfilled a spiritual and ceremonial role. In Shang and Zhou times, it was believed that the king held special powers that allowed him to communicate with the spirits of nature and his royal ancestors on behalf of all of the people. After the Qin ended the feudal system and introduced a new kind of centralized rule, the emperor continued this spiritual

THE CIVIL SERVICE

The Shang and Zhou dynasties were feudal kingdoms. The ruler lived in the capital and controlled as much territory as possible directly. In an era of poor communication, however, the king was forced to delegate power to nobles to govern in his name. One of the means used to expand the size of the kingdom during the Shang

THROUGH THEIR EYES
The Role of the Emperor

This account of the emperor's duties, according to
Confucian theory, was written during the Han dynasty.
How does the author define the emperor's roles?

*He makes the sacrifice (to Heaven) in the
   suburb with utmost respect;
He serves his forefathers in the
   ancestral shrines;
He elevates and illuminates both filial and
   fraternal piety;
He displays what is unique in filial conduct.
By these means he honors the Heavenly base.*

*He holds the ritual plow and tills in person;
He gathers the mulberry and tends the silk
   worms himself;*

*He breaks the grassland and propagates cereals;
He opens ground and clears it away—for
   adequate clothing and food.
By these means he honors the Earthly base.*

*He founds a Round Academy and village
   centers of learning;
He cultivates filial and fraternal piety, respect
   and deference;
He enlightens through instruction and conversation;
He inspires by ceremony and music.
By these means he honors the Human base.*

and Zhou periods was to send nobles out to establish new states loyal to the king. Most of the nobles were eventually able to exercise power in their territories quite independently of the king.

When the Qin came to power, they wished to curb the power of the nobles in favour of the central government. To do this, they began to replace the hereditary nobles with appointed officials responsible only to the central government. Later dynasties refined this practice, leading to the concept of a civil service based on merit rather than birth, often called a **meritocracy**. In this system, government officials gained their rank only because they were responsible and capable people, and not as a result of hereditary right. It was not until the later years of the Tang dynasty that the meritocracy was fully put into place. It took a long time to remove

all the hereditary noble families from their positions of authority. Succeeding dynasties continued to promote the concept of a meritocracy.

The Chinese needed a way to select those capable enough to be civil servants. The Han rulers introduced civil service examinations to do this. Candidates were tested on their knowledge of literature and Confucianism. They were also expected to be knowledgeable about more practical matters such as mathematics and engineering, but the real prestige came from being Confucian scholars. Over time, the more practical subjects became less and less important. Those who were successful in the examinations were appointed to government posts in the capital or in the provinces.

Initially only members of the upper class were allowed to take the examina-

tions. Under the Tang, the examinations were opened up to the general population. Since many years of schooling were needed to prepare for the examinations, relatively few families could afford the expense, but it was possible for less wealthy families or for villages to band together to give their sons the opportunity for an education leading to government office.

Over the years, the bureaucracy became very complex. Specific governing departments such as agriculture, crime and justice, public works, finance, and the military were created. Each department had a chief minister and numerous minor officials, much like the modern civil service that is found in our own country. The civil service had 18 grades, or ranks in all.

Figure 17-11 *These would-be bureaucrats are awaiting the results of the civil service examinations*

REFLECT AND ANALYZE

1. What was "the Mandate of Heaven"? Was it the same as the European concept of the divine right of kings? Explain your answer.

2. Explain the differences between rule based on birth and rule based on merit.

3. As a Chinese bureaucrat, trained in Confucian traditions, explain how you would react to the news of famine in one of the provinces.

4. How important is education as a qualification for election to government or a job with the civil service in Canada? Compare the role of education in our system and in the Chinese system, pointing out any similarities or differences.

LAW AND JUSTICE

Confucian values knit China so closely together that in many ways Confucianism played the same role that legal codes or religious doctrines played in other early civilizations. Confucianism defined the ideal way to behave. As a result, many aspects of behaviour were family, not state, matters in China.

While government and society in China were based on Confucian principles, the early legal system was based on a rival philosophy known as Legalism, which developed at the same time as Confucianism.

Legalism was an authoritarian philosophy that taught unquestioning obedience to authority. Among its chief advocates was the philosopher Han Feizi who felt that the only way to achieve a stable society was to give the ruler absolute power. Legalists believed that human nature meant that people were too easily swayed by greed, self-interest or fear to ever behave voluntarily in the interests of the common good. Legalists compared the people of a state to children. Just as children were too immature to make wise decisions and needed the guidance of their parents, Legalists believed that only a strong ruler could protect the interests of society as a whole. To do so, the ruler must reward obedience to the laws and punish disobedience severely.

During their rule, the Qin developed a code of laws for the entire empire based on Legalist principles. The laws were strict and violations were punished harshly. The Han, having adopted Confucianism, moderated the legal code to some extent. The Tang published a law code in 653 and revised it in 737. Although later dynasties made a variety of changes, the Tang code remained the basic law code of China.

The law was divided into various categories, such as administrative regulations, families and marriages, treasures, thefts and violence, and trial and imprisonment. In addition to the law code, government departments and provincial governments issued many rules and regulations. Families and local communities were expected to resolve minor legal disputes on their own, guided by Confucian principles.

There were five standard punishments for breaking the law, and each punishment had different levels of severity. When the

PERSPECTIVES ON THE PAST

The role of the examination system

There were both benefits and drawbacks to China's examination system. Considering both short-term and long-term effects, do you think that the examination system contributed positively or negatively to China on the whole?

Everyone in China who went to school to study for the examination system learned the same curriculum. The examinations system produced a nation that was intellectually unified. Government officials helped to unify the nation even more. As they spread out from the capital to the far corners of the empire, they took with them the same vision of the empire. They also took with them knowledge of new developments in medicine or agriculture or other new technologies. When officials reported to the capital, they passed on new developments occurring in their provinces. As a result, information was spread quickly throughout the entire empire.

At the same time, however, the emphasis on the literary, historical, and scholarly traditions of China meant that government officials looked to the past to provide answers to current questions. Over the years, practical subjects, such as mathematics and science, lost their role in the curriculum, which came more and more to emphasize Confucianism. The bureaucracy also became increasingly rigid and hierarchical, so concerned with the preservation of Confucian ideals that it seemed unable to cope with change.

---

death penalty was called for, death could be by strangulation or decapitation. Three different distances were prescribed when the penalty was exile. Penal servitude could last for three different time periods. There were five levels of beatings with a heavy stick, and five levels of beatings with a light stick.

Chinese law included the principle of collective responsibility. The whole family was held responsible for the crime of any one member, and anyone who failed to report a crime was considered as guilty as the offender.

The law was not equally applied. One of the benefits of holding public office in China was that exemptions from punishment were part of the rewards of public office. The higher the rank in the bureaucracy, the fewer the legal penalties that could be applied.

REFLECT AND ANALYZE

1. In what ways was Legalism a totalitarian philosophy?

2. Why did the Han make Confucianism rather than Legalism their official doctrine?

3. Was it a coincidence that Legalism developed during the Warring States period?

4. Which of the lesser punishments under Chinese law would you prefer to undergo—exile, prison or beatings? Explain the reasons for your answer.

CHINA:
Society and Culture

Figure 18-1
*The symbol for yin
and yang*

F*rom the beginning there were two forces in the world, the Yin and the
Yang. These forces were opposites as light is to darkness, active is to
passive, heat is to cold, dryness is to moisture. Yin and Yang had to be in
balance if all was to run smoothly.*

*The Yang, the lighter part, went skyward to form the heavens; the Yin, the
heavier part, went downward to form the earth. With this division, Yang and Yin,
the male and female principle came to be. Yang produced fire, hence the sun. Yin
produced water, and hence the moon. Their active and passive forces mingled,
producing the stars, the seasons, and all the products of earth including rivers,
rain, dust and all creatures.*

Ancient Chinese beliefs

The concept of yin and yang was one of the earliest Chinese beliefs about the world
they lived in. Later, two great philosophies and one religion contributed to the rich
cultural past of China. They were Confucianism, Daoism, and Buddhism.

RELIGION

From the earliest days, the Chinese believed that
the universe was an interdependent whole. They
believed that all parts of the universe, whether
animate or inanimate, were governed by a force or
energy called *qi*. The Chinese worshipped the spirits of nature, especially the spirits of earth and sky
that could affect their crops.

The Chinese viewed nature as dual, symbol-
ized by yin and yang. Yin and yang represented
opposites—yin represented water, dark, cold, femi-
nine, and yielding while yang represented sun,
heat, masculine, and dominance—yet these forces
were not in opposition to each other. Both contained elements of the other within it and were
interdependent, part of a harmonious whole.

The Chinese also believed that all phenomena
were made from various combinations of five basic
elements—water, wood, fire, earth, and metal. All
phenomena were thought to be in a constant state
of change that was cyclical in nature.

It was important that humans not disturb the
harmony of nature. *Qi* was thought to flow through

the surface of the earth, and it was important to position buildings and tombs correctly in order not to disturb *qi*. Experts in *fengshui* (wind and water) would be consulted about the correct positioning of buildings.

The Chinese also revered and consulted the spirits of departed ancestors, believing that they could communicate with the gods as well as influence the lives of the living. The ancestors could either help or harm. To please ancestral spirits, the living made offerings of food, flowers, fruit, vegetables or animals which were burned in the belief that the smoke and aroma would drift into the spirit world to sustain the ancestors.

At first, the practice of ancestor worship was restricted to important families. It was thought that the gods would respond more favourably to the prominent than the lowly. Gradually, however, all families consulted their ancestors for mediation with the gods or for advice on important decisions.

RELIGIOUS BELIEFS AND PRACTICES

In addition to their beliefs about the interdependence of the universe and the role of ancestors, the Chinese had three major belief systems. Only one, Buddhism, was properly speaking a religion. Chinese belief systems were not dogmatic. The three belief systems existed side by side and borrowed freely from each other.

CONFUCIANISM

Confucius or Kong Fuzi is thought to have lived during the Warring States period. As a result, he was exposed to constant warfare, and disapproved of the social disorder this caused.

Confucius spent a number of years travelling throughout northern China as a teacher. Later generations of scholars came to revere him, and his teachings eventually became an important basis for Chinese society and government.

Confucius viewed the Zhou era as a model of security and order, and studied the classic texts of ancient China looking for the values that had made this peace and order possible. He concluded that the family was the primary model of social harmony. If the family defined the status, duties, and obligations of each individual clearly, the result would be a harmonious family. The same model could be applied to society at large.

Confucius identified five virtues and five relationships as the basis of an orderly society. The five virtues were benevolence, righteousness, propriety, wisdom, and trustworthiness. These virtues were to be taught to people by the family and the state.

The five relationships were father and son; ruler and subject; older brother and younger brother; husband and wife; friend and friend. The father was the master of the household, and the son must honour and respect his father. In return, the father must be benevolent and loving towards the son. Older brothers were superior to younger brothers, husbands were superior to wives and so on. These relationships were mutually beneficial. While inferiors must show deference and respect, those in superior positions were expected to be benevolent to their inferiors.

The relationship between ruler and subject echoed these family relationships. Rulers were expected to govern with the welfare and interests of their subjects in mind, in return for their subjects' obedience and loyalty.

The Confucian view of society was ordered and hierarchical. There were many rules and regulations about how people ought to behave in various circumstances. The family and society were built on positions of superiority and inferiority.

The significance of Confucian theory was its moral content. Confucius believed that good government was primarily a matter of ethics. He did not question the right of rulers to rule, but he did insist that their first duty was to set a proper example of ethical conduct. The people's contentment was the measure of political success.

DAOISM

Daoism developed chiefly from the teachings of Laozi who may have lived between 604 and 517 BCE or may have been a legendary figure, created by Daoists to make their philosophy appear to be older than Confucianism. In about 300 BCE, Daoist teachings began to appear in writing.

Daoism was an important way of thought in China for many years. Unlike Confucius, Daoists were not interested in the rational ordering of society. Instead, Daoism sought to harmonize the world of humans with the world of nature. According to Daoists, human society should emulate the balance and harmony of the natural world. To do this, people needed to follow the "Dao," or the "Way," by understanding the interactions and cycles of nature so that individuals could live in harmony with it.

Daoists disapproved of anything that interfered with the relationship between individuals and nature. In their eyes, the

Figure 18-2 *A Daoist vision of paradise, painted in the mid-eighteenth century. What aspects of Daoist thought are evident in the painting?*

struggle for wealth, power, and status were human inventions that led inevitably to war, instability, death, and disorder. The rules and regulations of government were similar, because they imposed restrictions on individuals, interfering with their efforts to live in harmony with nature.

Daoism was popular with the common people, since it was a form of protest against the demands of government. It was popular with the educated elite as a relief from the rigidity of Confucian society.

BUDDHISM

Buddhism spread to China from India during the late Han dynasty and became popular during the turbulent times of the Period of Chaos. The influence of Buddhism peaked under the Tang dynasty in the eighth century. Buddhism brought to China a belief in the need to live properly in order to achieve nirvana, or the ending of all desires. Buddhism stressed that life was painful, and that this pain was caused because people were full of desire. To avoid this pain, one should free oneself from earthly desires through meditation and an ascetic lifestyle.

The most popular version of Buddhism in China was called Mahayana Buddhism. The emphasis in Mahayana Buddhism was on salvation through the efforts of another, rather than self-salvation. Buddhism in China eventually developed a huge number of semi-deities who would assist in this salvation, as well as a new type of deity known as a *Bodhisattva*. *Bodhisattvas* had already achieved nirvana on their own account, but were willing to stay in the world to help others achieve it.

Over time, Buddhist monasteries came to provide services as inns, public baths, and banks, becoming very wealthy. Buddhism contributed enormously to the artistic heritage of China but did very little to change Chinese society fundamentally in any respect. By the ninth century Buddhism was in decline as Confucianism became state doctrine.

DEATH

Early Chinese rulers were buried in tombs with their weapons, pottery, tools, ornaments, and even their household servants. In one early imperial grave, twenty-four women, seventeen men, horses, chariots, and dogs were buried with the emperor to keep him company in the next world. In

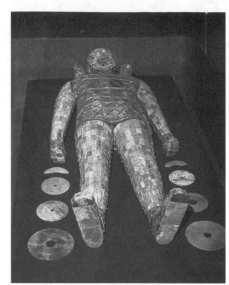

Figure 18-3 *The Chinese associated jade with eternity. The rare substance was difficult to obtain, and so hard that it could only be worked using an abrasive sand. An imperial burial of the Han dynasty revealed two figures covered entirely in jade. Two thousand separate squares of jade had been sewn together with gold wires to preserve the bodies*

later days, pottery figurines were buried with the body, rather than actual people or animals. Historians have learned a great deal about the earlier years of Chinese history from these grave figurines. In many cases, no other artifacts have survived the passage of time.

SOCIAL STRUCTURE

The social structure of China went through a process of evolution, but by the time of the Han dynasty the basic pattern was in place. This pattern existed until the twentieth century.

During the Shang and Zhou dynasties, Chinese society was feudal. The kings and nobles were the upper layer of society. The nobles owed an annual tribute of grain or jade to the king. By the time of the Zhou, there were several categories of nobles. Those associated with the ruling family had more wealth, power and prestige. They dressed in elaborate clothing and were the only ones allowed to learn to read and write or study astronomy. Most of the commoners were farmers who worked the land of the upper class. They owed taxes, labour, and military service to their landowner, in return for leadership and protection. A few of the commoners were artisans.

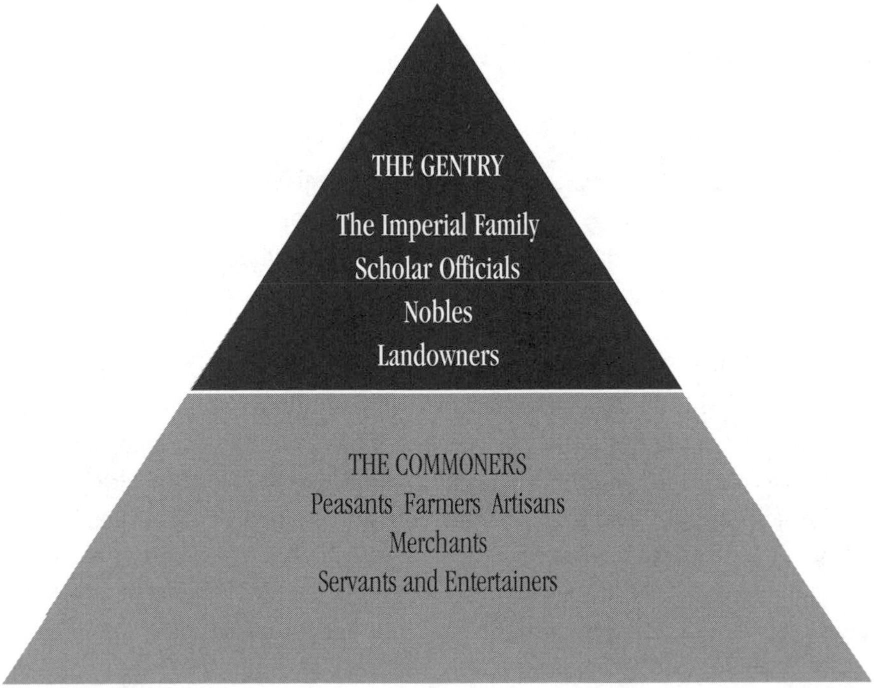

The Qin introduced a major change in the social structure when they began to centralize the government. They appointed people loyal to the emperor to rule as many provincial territories as possible, instead of using the hereditary rulers. The Han carried this practice even further, and opened the way to a whole new group in society—scholar officials, who gradually displaced the hereditary nobles. The displaced aristocracy retained their lands and wealth and a great deal of power, but by the time of the Tang dynasty, scholar officials were in charge of the government.

Peasant farmers continued to make up the majority of the Chinese population. They owed taxes to the government, labour for public works projects such as the Great Wall and irrigation systems, as well as military service in time of war. Peasants were heavily taxed, providing most of the revenue for the central government. Most of the upper class did not pay taxes.

Circumstances varied greatly among the peasantry. Many owned their own land and some became wealthy. Others were tenant farmers, working the land of the large landowners. Most of the peasants were extremely poor. Villages were collectively

THE GENTRY

The Imperial Family
Scholar Officials
Nobles
Landowners

THE COMMONERS

Peasants Farmers Artisans
Merchants
Servants and Entertainers

Figure 18-4 *The Social Pyramid from the Han dynasty on*

responsible for submitting their taxes and arranging for the public labour the inhabitants owed. It was possible for some peasants to acquire a leadership role in this, enhancing their own economic status in the process. During the Tang dynasty, peasant families could also aspire to improve their social status by sending a clever son through the examination system. If the son became a government official, the family entered the upper class.

The rest of the commoners were artisans, merchants, servants, and entertainers. Artisans were respected members of society, but merchants were not. Confucian scholars believed that merchants contributed little to society. They did not grow food or make useful products; they worked for profit. As a result, their social rank was low. In spite of this, many merchants acquired great wealth and power which they used to enter the upper ranks of society, by becoming landowners or sending their children to school to be trained as bureaucrats. Entertainers and servants formed the lowest class of people in ancient China.

labour. Striking an older cousin was worth a hundred strokes of the rod. A father who seriously harmed a son while administering punishment was liable to a less severe punishment than if he had harmed a stranger.

The head of the family was the eldest male, usually the grandfather. He chose his children's wives and husbands and decided what work his sons would do. His eldest son would assume this leadership role upon the father's death. The head of the household also conducted the ceremonies honouring the family's ancestors.

Male heirs to carry on the family line were considered so important that a man could take a concubine to provide him with sons if necessary. Large families were desired, since it was through family, rather than individual, effort that families maintained their wealth and prestige.

In spite of the rigid rules of conduct they were required to learn, young children were allowed a great deal of freedom in their early years. About the age of seven, children began school or helped their parents with whatever work they did.

Many families could not achieve the family ideal, especially those in the lower classes. Natural disasters, wars or other problems could quickly reduce a family's wealth and status.

REFLECT AND ANALYZE

1. How did the structure of the gentry class change in ancient China? Explain the significance of this change.

2. In what ways were the conditions for peasant farmers in ancient China similar to those of peasant farmers in other ancient civilizations?

3. Social mobility is the opportunity to improve your social standing. What avenues of social mobility were open to commoners in early China? What avenues of social mobility are available to Canadians? Explain whether or not there are any similarities or differences.

4. Create a dialogue between a Confucian scholar and a merchant on the value of the merchant's contribution to society.

EVERYDAY LIFE

THE FAMILY

The family, the embodiment of Confucian ideals, formed the core of Chinese society. The ideal family was an extended family, consisting of three generations—grandparents, married sons, and grandchildren. Each family member had roles based on the family hierarchy. The youngest members were required to be obedient to their parents, and even more obedient to their grandparents. Complex traditions outlined the nature of the duties and obligations that were owed to anyone in a superior position. For example, if a son went walking with his father, he had to walk behind the father. If, during this walk, they met a senior person, the son had to put his feet together and clasp his hands.

These obligations were so important that they were embodied in the law code during the Tang dynasty. Anyone who assaulted a parent or grandparent was beheaded. Assaulting an older brother or sister brought two and a half years of forced

WOMEN IN ANCIENT CHINA

Women in China occupied a subservient position, according to Confucian principles. They were expected to defer to men. However, women acquired status as they aged, since younger women in the family owed obedience to the older women. Sometimes a strong-willed grandmother became the head of the family. On marriage, women joined the husband's household, and became members of that family.

Marriage was an alliance of families, used to establish ties of kinship that could enhance the family's social and economic position. Among the poor, marriage could be an old age security measure, making certain that there would be someone able to support the older generation in their old age.

The women of the upper class led secluded lives. When they went out, upper class women were carried in a curtained chair to hide them from view. Nevertheless, women were responsible for running the household, which in wealthy families could be quite a responsibility, because the households were so large. In spite of these family responsibilities, upper class women also had a great deal of leisure, with many servants to do the actual work.

Women usually received no formal education, although upper class families frequently educated their daughters. Some of China's most famous poets were women. Few professions apart from nursing or domestic service were open to women, but the wives of merchants and artisans often helped to assist their husbands by keeping the accounts or running the store. China's silk was manufactured primarily by women. The wives of farmers were extremely busy and played a major role in looking after the farm, running their households, and raising their children.

EDUCATION

Scholarship was a revered Confucian tradition. All members of the upper class were expected to be familiar with the Confucian classics and a great deal of literature. A number of emperors were famous for their skills in writing or painting. Education became even more important when the government began to rely on trained scholars to administer the empire.

Prior to the Han dynasty, education was carried out primarily by private tutors. During the Han dynasty, schools were opened to help prepare students for a future role in the Chinese bureaucracy at the local, provincial, and national levels. Schools were also provided by monasteries, and by groups of families who banded together. Tutoring remained an avenue to an education among the wealthy.

Students studied the Confucian classics, literature, law, calligraphy, engineering, and mathematics, but the greatest emphasis was placed on the classics and literature, which had to be memorized. In addition, students had to master specific forms of composition, including poetry. It took about six years of study to prepare for the lowest level of examination.

Examinations were held at the local, provincial, and national levels. A student had to pass the local examination in order to study for the next level. Earning a degree entitled the holder to certain privileges, such as exemption from public labour and corporal punishment.

The government examinations were rigorously supervised. They lasted for about five days. Each morning, students were locked in small rooms, after verifying their identity with someone who knew them

THROUGH THEIR EYES
A Girl's Upbringing

What does the poem have to say about the status of women in Chinese society?

How sad it is to be a woman!
Nothing on earth is held so cheap.

. . .

No one is glad when a girl is born:
By *her* the family sets no store.
When she grows up, she hides in her room
Afraid to look a man in the face.
No one cries when she leaves her home—
Sudden as clouds when the rain stops.

She bows her head and composes her face,
Her teeth are pressed on her red lips:
She bows and kneels countless times.
She must humble herself even to the servants.
His love is distant as the stars in Heaven,
Yet the sunflower bends toward the sun.
Their hearts more sundered than water and fire—
A hundred evils are heaped upon her.
Her face will follow the years' changes:
Her lord will find new pleasures. . . .

Fu Xuan

Figure 18-5 *A scholarly gathering in the eighth century. Two men study a scroll, while another composes a poem*

personally. The examination papers were given a number, and were re-copied by scribes so that the markers would have no means of identifying the students. These security measures were taken to prevent any form of cheating. However, many students smuggled in "cheat sheets." Key passages and model essays were hidden in clothing and food. Undergarments with the entire text of the classics in tiny writing have been found. The punishments for cheating were very severe.

REFLECT AND ANALYZE

1. Would you have liked to be a woman in ancient Chinese society? Why or why not?

2. Do some research on important women scholars or poets in the Han and Tang dynasties. Select one or two, and explain her contributions. Include samples of her work.

3. Compare the early Chinese curriculum with the curriculum in your school. Give three reasons how and why your life would be different if you were being educated in early China.

4. What rules and regulations does your family have regarding the way you treat your parents, grandparents and siblings, and are treated by them in return? How rigid are these rules and regulations? What happens to you if you break one of them?

URBAN AND RURAL LIVING

During the Shang and Zhou dynasties the kings and nobles lived in fortified hilltop cities along with local artisans. In later dynasties, cities became much larger and more sophisticated. They were always laid out on a strict grid pattern, with the streets running north and south and east and west. The palace (or government buildings) were at the north end of the city, because to face south was a sign of superiority. Markets were located in the eastern and the western parts of the city. Each city grid was surrounded by walls and had its own local government. Under the Tang, Changan was the largest city in the world, measuring around 10 km by 8 km. Including its suburbs, Changan's population was well over one million. It boasted zoos, floating restaurants and fairgrounds, as well as the extensive buildings of the imperial palace.

The peasants lived in rural villages, surrounded by their agricultural lands. Larger market towns were located within walking distance from a number of villages. In turn, these towns and villages were clustered around the large cities.

HOMES

The homes of the Shang and Zhou nobility were constructed of wooden frames with walls of packed earth and roofs of thatch. During later dynasties, the outer walls were more apt to be built of fired brick and the roofs made of tile. The homes of the well-to-do were distinguished by walled gardens and open-air courtyards. At least two courtyards were needed—one for receiving guests and another reserved for family use.

Figure 18-6 *Detail of a painting called "Going up the River at the Spring Festival" showing a scene of urban life. Although this dates from the Song dynasty (960-1279), it is likely that Changan under the Tang dynasty looked a great deal like this*

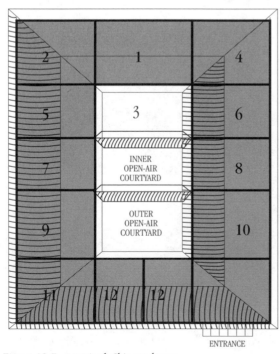

KEY

1. Quarters of the head of the family
2. The Family Hall
3. Garden
4. Ancestral Shrine
5. Eldest son and family
6. Second son and family
7. Storeroom
8. Library and Study
9. Guestroom
10. Guestroom
11. Kitchen
12. Servant's Quarters

Figure 18-7 *A typical Chinese house*

The homes of the very wealthy contained innumerable courtyards devoted to specific uses, such as viewing the moon or listening to crickets. The interiors of wealthy homes were sumptuous, decorated with sculpture, painting and carpets.

Prosperous peasants built themselves comfortable homes not unlike those of the wealthy. Other peasants were desperately poor, and lived in very humble homes of wattle and daub construction.

FOOD

The most common foods in ancient China were millet and rice. Millet, a grain, was used as a porridge or ground up and made into bread and wine in the north. Rice was grown in the south. Oranges, lemons, soybeans, peanuts, sesame seeds, and melons were also common in ancient China. Soybeans were the most important source of protein, and were used in numerous inventive ways, such as in sauces or as tofu.

The ancient Chinese were fond of spices. In 1972 the tomb of a Han dynasty noblewoman, dating from about 165 BCE, revealed hordes of ginger, cinnamon, and other spices, along with grain, meat, fish, and fruit. Ginger was such a popular spice that it was grown in pots on board ships so that it could be eaten fresh.

The ancient Chinese invented chopsticks, the world's second most common eating utensil, likely during the third century BCE. Short of fuel, the Chinese learned to use heat as effectively as possible. Pots often contained two or three sections so that more than one dish could be cooked at the same time, and the Chinese also invented the wok, which is an extremely heat-effective pan.

REFLECT AND ANALYZE

1. What distinguishing characteristics made Chinese cities different from the cities of other civilizations?

2. How did Chinese homes differ from homes in our society?

3. What were the dietary staples of ancient China?

4. Analyze the painting in Figure 18-6. Select three different scenes, and describe what you think is happening in these scenes. How could you verify your interpretation?

THE ECONOMY IN ANCIENT CHINA

AGRICULTURE

Irrigated agriculture was the mainstay of the Chinese economy. The north produced grains and the south produced rice. New crops, improved irrigation methods and innovations in farming practices were constantly being invented to increase food production that in turn allowed the population to increase.

The farmers of the Shang dynasty used stone tools, and raised cattle, sheep, goats, chickens, and mulberries for the silk industry. The food supply was supplemented by fishing and hunting. By the ninth century BCE, the use of iron was common in agricultural tools. The ox-drawn plough and scythes came into use during the Han dynasty. One of the most important agricultural tools the Chinese developed was the seed drill. It allowed farmers to plant their crops in rows, making sowing, weeding, and irrigation much easier.

Landowners and government officials undertook large-scale water control programs, particularly in the north which lacked reliable rainfall. A high degree of engineering technology was employed in these constructions. Around 250 BCE, near Chengdu, the capital of Sichuan, for example, a river was diverted into two channels. One channel fed an extensive irrigation system. The amount of water flowing through both channels could be controlled. During droughts, the channel feeding the irrigation system was fully opened and the other one was closed. In times of flood, both channels were opened fully to allow the water to flow freely, to continue to irrigate crops but not flood the river banks.

To extend the amount of arable land terraces were cut in the hillsides. Farmers were strictly regulated as to the amount of land they could devote to the cultivation of mulberries for silk production because this decreased food production.

INDUSTRY

During the early dynasties of China, most artisans lived in the larger towns or cities and worked for local nobles. Some made pottery and others fashioned bronze. Still

Figure 18-8 *This Shang bronze elephant was made using the piece-mould method. Inner and outer clay or stone moulds were made, and the molten bronze poured between them. When cool, the moulds were removed and the bronze was polished*

others drilled or cut and polished jade. Silk-making was also an important craft.

Over time, the small-scale production of the early artisans developed into large-scale production with a great deal of specialization and technological innovation.

The Chinese maintained their early skill at bronze-making. In later dynasties, Shang and Zhou bronzes became "collectibles" for the wealthy. Eventually, expert advice was needed to distinguish true antiques from modern reproductions.

The Chinese had made fine pottery from the earliest times, and their expertise in this area led to the development of porcelain. By late Tang times the Chinese had learned to add feldspar to the clay and to fire it at a very high temperature. The result was porcelain, demanded world-wide for its hardness and translucent beauty.

Lacquerware was another important craft. Lacquer is a natural varnish obtained from a sumac-like tree. The Chinese used it to paint images on buildings, preserve and decorate wooden articles, leather shoes, and silk hats. On occasion, gold dust or red pigment were added to the lacquer to create visual display. Pliable and easily worked until hardened by submersion in water, lacquer would resist even the corrosion of acids.

Iron and salt were key industries. By 806, China was producing 12 247 t of iron a year. This level of production was not achieved in the West until the eighteenth century. Salt was an essential commodity in the preservation of food. Under the Han, the Chinese were the first to undertake deep bore-hole drilling in their quest for salt. A hole was drilled in the earth from which brine and natural gas were drawn off and passed to a processing room. The brine was put into a tank, and the natural gas was used to heat the brine and crystallize the salt.

TRADE

Trade with other cultures remained relatively limited until the Han dynasty. The ancient Chinese were self-sufficient and remote from other culturally developed areas. Confucian values also may have played a role—merchants occupied one of the lowest levels in Chinese society.

By the Han dynasty, however, an overland trade route to India and the Mediterranean region had been opened. This was the famous Silk Road, a 6400 km route through central Asia. The Silk Road was an arduous route, so that caravans changed hands several times along the route. The most important trade products from China

INNOVATIONS
Silk-making

Why did the Chinese want to keep the silk-making process a secret?

Figure 18-9 *This painting shows women spinning and pounding the newly spun silk fabric to tighten the weave. Silk was usually manufactured by women*

Silk, one of the world's oldest textiles, was the most desired fabric for clothing in ancient times. The Chinese had discovered the process of silk-making by the Shang dynasty.

Silk threads are produced by silkworms that feed on mulberry leaves and then envelop themselves in cocoons. Each cocoon is made of a single continuous silk filament.

The silkworm chrysalis inside the cocoon was killed by steaming, damping with salt or drying in sunlight. The silk filament of the cocoon was then made into thread and spun into cloth. Dipped into brilliant dyes, the cloth exhibited vibrant colours with a rich, lustrous look.

Silk-making was a closely guarded Chinese monopoly. The death penalty was handed out to anyone who attempted to betray the secret of the production of silk. Finally in 552, silkworms were smuggled out of China in bamboo tubes, along with the secrets of the technology, to the Byzantine Emperor Justinian in Constantinople.

were the much desired silk, hence the road's name, and spices. From the west came gold, horses, furs, muslin, glass, and metals. The Silk Road was in operation from the first century BCE until the seventh century CE.

China also began a maritime trade during the Tang dynasty. Arab traders began using Guangzhou as a trading port, acting as intermediaries in the trading activities of China and Europe. Guangzhou came to contain a large Islamic community. Much of the knowledge the Arabs gained about China was subsequently passed on to Europe. These trading links increased enormously in the next several centuries. Both Chinese and foreign traders would eventually ship goods to and from China, South Asia, West Asia, and Africa.

One of the earliest units of exchange in China was the cowrie shell. A string of five or ten cowrie shells was a basic monetary unit in Shang times. About 600 BCE under the Zhou, copper coinage began to appear. The Qin standardized the currency. Bales of silk and silver, measured by weight, were also used as currency. These mediums of exchange were

Figure 18-10 *These terra cotta funerary figurines show a loaded camel and caravaneer from the Tang dynasty*

all difficult to ship. By late Tang times, a form of paper money appeared. The government issued "flying cash" in 811; "flying cash" were money drafts redeemable in the capital.

THE ARTS

PAINTING

A great deal of early Chinese painting has not survived to modern times. There were a number of different schools of painting in China, and painting styles and techniques varied over the years. The subject matter of Chinese painting included portraits, scenes of daily life or of nature, and religious themes. Paintings provide us with an invaluable glimpse into the traditions and values of traditional Chinese society.

Painting and calligraphy were very closely related, since both used the same kind of brush. Great emphasis was placed on skillful use of the brush. Painters practised for years to develop the muscular control needed to produce swift, delicate brush strokes that conveyed energy, move-

REFLECT AND ANALYZE

1. What was the basis of China's economy?

2. In what areas did the Chinese demonstrate their technological inventiveness?

3. Select one example of China's advanced technology. Do some research to find out when it was developed, how it worked, and what improvements resulted from this technology. Prepare an illustrated report.

4. What factors limited trade in early China?

5. Write a journal account of a trip along the Silk Road. Include descriptions of the geographical areas through which you passed, the people you met along the way, and your adventures. Illustrate your journal.

Figure 18-11 *This is a painting from the mid-sixteenth century of an emperor fording a river. What characteristics of Chinese painting can be seen in the painting?*

ment, and life to the subject of the painting. The quality of "life" was the most important aspect of any painting. The composition of a painting also required the artist to balance the different elements of the painting. Particular attention was devoted to achieving three-dimensional space. Vivid colour, important during the Tang period and in Buddhist art, became much more subdued in later dynasties as painters attempted to match the hues of nature.

Chinese landscape paintings stressed the harmony between nature and the human spirit. Generally, human figures are small in order to suggest that human life is only part of a greater whole. Poems were often added to landscape paintings as part of the overall design.

WRITING

The symbols which the Shang scratched on oracle bones are the earliest known form of Chinese writing. The Chinese system, like that of the Egyptians, was pictographic, with pictures representing objects. However, some of the symbols were ideographic, combining several symbols to represent an idea. For example, a woman under a roof means "peace." A woman beside a child means "good" or "to like." A third category of symbols were phonetic, indicating the pictographic symbol was being used to represent a word that was pronounced the same way but had a different meaning.

The symbols in Chinese writing are called characters. During Shang times, 5000 characters were in use, but only 1500 of these have been deciphered. The Chinese later added many thousand additional characters and gradually altered the style of writing—the characters became more stylized, so that the "picture" element became much less obvious.

Calligraphy, or fine writing, became an art form in itself, giving an aesthetic value to writing. Different scripts were used to reflect the calligrapher's mood or subject. The strength, balance, and flow of the strokes were thought to convey the calligrapher's moral character. Expertise at calligraphy was so highly regarded that it became a basis for promotion in the civil service during the Tang dynasty.

The first writing was done on bamboo, bronze, pottery, wood, jade or silk, until the invention of paper sometime around the second century. With the invention of printing around the eighth century, the number of books proliferated, and Chinese culture was spread throughout the empire more rapidly than ever before. All Chinese speakers could read Chinese writing, even though they might not be able to communicate verbally with each other, since many of the Chinese dialects differed from each other so much.

LITERATURE

The body of Chinese literature began during the period of the Zhou dynasty, when ruling families and nobles began to write down the deeds of family members and compose essays and poems. One of the first Chinese books, written sometime before 600 BCE, was the *Book of Changes*, containing ancient beliefs about the nature of the universe. The *Book of Songs*, a collection of poems about war, farming, and everyday life, was written about the same time.

The Han period was noted for a vast outpouring of literature. Scholars attempted to recreate all the books that had been burned by the Qin emperor. Many of these recreations were likely very flawed, since much depended on memory and the scattered fragments of books that still existed. Having reclaimed their literary past, the Han went on to add prolifically to this literary heritage. One of the literary achievements of the Han period was the writing of history. The historian Sima Qian wrote a monumental work of 130 chapters, covering all of Chinese history to that time. His writing was distinguished by being based on fact rather than myth and supposition, as had been the case with earlier histories.

The Tang left behind an extremely varied body of literature, some devoted to the classics, some devoted to Buddhism, as well as a great deal of secular literature reflecting personal relationships, nostalgia for the past, or a reverence for nature. The Tang dynasty was famous for its poets and its love stories. Over 48 900 poems survive from this period,

written by 2200 poets, and an academy for poets was established. A famous Tang love story tells of an examination candidate, Zhang, who fell in love with a distant cousin, Yingying. He wrote her numerous poems, trying to win her affections. He finally did so, but then had to go to the capital to write the examinations. Yingying accused him of unfaithfulness for this. Meanwhile, Zhang had second thoughts about Yingying, coming to the conclusion that beautiful women cause too much trouble. Eventually both Zhang and Yingying married the partners that their families selected for them.

Figure 18-12 *Paper was made from tree bark, hemp, old rags and fishing nets, which were beaten into a pulp. The pulp was rolled into thin sheets, strengthened with starch and coated with gelatin. Colour was frequently added. In the back of the shop, the paper sheets were hung on racks so that customers could make their selection*

REFLECT AND ANALYZE

1. How did the Chinese system of writing evolve over the centuries?

2. What characteristics make Chinese landscape painting distinctive? Find several examples of landscape painting to illustrate your answer.

3. What kinds of literature did the early Chinese write?

4. There are many Chinese dialects. Find out the names of these dialects, and where they are spoken. How important is it that all Chinese people, regardless of the dialect they speak, can read Chinese writing? Explain your answer.

THE SCIENCES

TECHNOLOGY

By the end of the Han dynasty Chinese technology far surpassed that of any other civilization. Four Chinese inventions made an especially great contribution to the rest of the world: the compass, gunpowder, paper, and printing.

Magnetic compasses with dial pointers had been invented by Han times. Used initially to locate buildings that conformed to *fengshui*, the military and miners soon recognized the value of the compass in

finding directions underground. The use of the magnetic compass was not applied to navigation until the later Song dynasty. Its use allowed sailors to sail out of the sight of land without getting lost.

The properties of potassium nitrite were known to the Chinese very early, and by the seventh century they had learned how to combine potassium nitrate with the proper proportions of charcoal and sulphur to make an explosive. Until the eleventh century gun powder was only used in fire crackers in public festivals—not for warfare.

Printing was likely an off-shoot of the practice of ink rubbings. The Han began the practice of carving important books in stone to preserve them for the future. Soon, Chinese students began to make rubbings of these carvings by brushing ink on a piece of paper held over the engravings.

In the block printing process, wood was cut into page-sized blocks and softened with paste. The material to be printed was written on a two-page sheet of very thin paper. The paper was spread over the wood and rubbed so that the ink would stick to the paste on the wood. A woodcutter then carved around the written characters so

Figure 18-13 *The Diamond Sutra, a Buddhist text, was produced in 868 and is the earliest existing book printed by the block-printing method. It consists of one rolled page 4.5 m long*

that they stood out from the surface of the wood. The printer brushed ink on the block and pressed blank sheets of paper on it to make the print. Later, the Chinese invented moveable type.

The ancient Chinese also excelled in manufacturing practical items. They developed the breast-strap harness for animals that made it possible to transport heavier loads, and invented the stirrup that gained enormous importance in warfare. They also invented wheelbarrows, the water mill, and bellows. They built machines to record earthquakes and were the first to devise suspension bridges.

MEDICINE

The oldest Chinese texts on medicine preserved today were compiled about 200 or 300 BCE. These texts identify the major organs of the body by size, weight, and col-our, and contain a rudimentary notion of the circulation of the blood. By Han times, the circulation of the blood was well known.

A great deal of China's medical knowledge came from the Daoist search for the elixir of life. One strand of Daoism became preoccupied with the search for immortality during the Period of Chaos. Daoist experiments with many different substances lead to a wide variety of useful drugs from both plant and metal sources. They learned for example, that although mercury in large amounts would kill people, its use in very small quantities could kill bacteria. By Tang times, Chinese dentists were filling holes in teeth with silver-tin amalgams. The Daoist preoccupation with the need for the parts of the body to be in harmony, to conform to the principles of yin and yang, led to acupuncture as a method of treatment.

By the tenth century, the Chinese had discovered a form of inoculation for smallpox. Doctors took swabs from smallpox pustules, dissolved them in water and kept them at body temperature for a few weeks. The substance produced in this way was then placed on cotton balls in the nose of a healthy person. The person would get a mild dose of smallpox and thereby develop an immunity to a severe case.

Medical texts on treatment and drugs were among those carved in stone by the Han. With the growth of cities, public health increasingly became a matter of concern, since epidemics could spread so rapidly in crowded conditions. Though the Tang established a college of medicine, most doctors were trained outside such institutes. Medicine was a respectable profession because it served people, and it was passed down from generation to generation. Chinese medicine recognized a number of

THEN AND NOW
Acupuncture

What is this ancient Chinese medical treatment? Why has it become popular in the West in recent years?

Acupuncture is the treatment of illness or pain by the insertion of needles into the patient's body at points that are believed to be connected to whatever internal organ is causing the illness. Acupuncture needles are used to stimulate *qi*, the life energy, and to increase yin or yang; whichever is required, to restore balance in the affected organ. There are over 365 acupuncture points.

No one is certain how old the practice is. During the Tang dynasty there was a professor of acupuncture on staff at the Imperial College of Medicine. He had ten assistant teachers and twenty craftsmen to manufacture the needles required for acupuncture. There are also two textbooks on the art of acupuncture. One is the *Class of Acupuncture*, written by Huangfu Mi sometime between 256 and 282. The other is the *Nei Ching*. Some claim that this book was written around 2600 BCE. It is more likely that the book was compiled over several generations, taking its final form sometime around the first century BCE.

Acupuncture is becoming increasingly popular in the West as an alternative form of medical practice. It has been used successfully in the treatment of such ailments as sciatica, lumbago, sprains, asthma, migraine, ulcers, strokes, drug addiction, angina, and neuralgia.

speciality areas, such as dentistry, obstetrics, rheumatism, and ophthalmology.

As well as drug therapy and acupuncture, a great deal of medical practice consisted of the use of charms and talismans. It was thought that demons could invade the body to cause illness, and the charms were designed to chase them out.

ASTRONOMY AND TIME

From the earliest days of Chinese society, astronomy was an important preoccupation. The emperor's role required him to mediate between the people and the forces of nature. He was responsible for maintaining the water control system and for warning people when a famine or some other natural disaster was imminent. He was also expected to predict eclipses and other unusual astronomical events. As a result, the Chinese studied astronomy very closely. The first observatory was built around 1000 BCE, and meticulous records were kept of the events in the night sky. Before 1500 CE, Chinese astronomers were able to predict the periodic arrival of at least 40 comets, among them Halley's comet.

The emperor published a calendar every year specifying the days on which the important agricultural events for that year should take place. The earliest Chinese calendar may date from 2397 BCE. The Chinese calendar was lunar, consisting of twelve months of alternately 29 and 30 days. The lunar year thus totaled 354 days. In order to keep in step with the solar calendar of 365 days, an additional month was periodically inserted.

Although China adopted the Gregorian calendar in 1912, the ancient system is still used in many Chinese communities.

In the Chinese calendar, twelve animal names have become associated with successive years. The animal names in order of occurrence are: rat, ox, tiger, hare, dragon, snake, horse, sheep, monkey, fowl, dog, and pig. The cycle of years was used for astrological purposes much the same way as the twelve signs of the zodiac are used in the West to describe personality characteristics and tell fortunes.

REFLECT AND ANALYZE

1. What are the major technological accomplishments associated with ancient China? Why were they so important?

2. Why were the Chinese preoccupied with astronomy and calendars?

3. Select another ancient civilization and, using an organizer, compare the extent of medical knowledge in that civilization with the extent of Chinese medical knowledge.

LOOKING BACK

The various dynasties of ancient China developed a unique civilization. Some dynastic leaders were better than others, but by the end of the Tang dynasty China had become the richest and most powerful empire in the world.

The successes of the later dynasties of China were due in no small measure to the centralized political authority and the bureaucracy based on merit developed by the earlier dynasties.

The uniqueness that defined ancient China went beyond government. It was evident in the economic strength of the country, based on a foundation of agriculture, industry, and trade, and it was demonstrated also by the advanced state of the arts and technology.

LOOKING BEYOND

THE SONG DYNASTY
960 CE-1279 CE

Following the wars that dominated the years after the downfall of the Tang dynasty, the Song dynasty was founded and ruled China for almost three hundred years. The Song Dynasty was another cultural "golden age" for China. The Song restored peace, reintroduced central government, expanded the civil service examinations, repaired public works, and extended China's trade with the rest of the world.

Militarily, the Song were less strong than their predecessors, and the Jurchen Mongols captured the Song capital of Kaifeng in 1126, carrying off the Song emperor to captivity. The Song dynasty continued, however. A younger son of the emperor moved the dynasty south to Hangzhou and the Southern Song dynasty continued for another 150 years, carrying on the "golden age" traditions.

Eventually the Southern Song succumbed to the Mongol armies of Khubilai Khan. Khubilai, a grandson of Chiggis Khan, had established the Yuan dynasty in 1271 in north China, and by 1279 south China also came under his control.

YUAN DYNASTY
1271 CE-1368 CE

The Mongols, a group from central Asia, were fearless horsemen who attacked their enemies by surprise and who fought under even the worst of conditions. Under their leader, Chiggis Khan, the Mongols had built an empire that stretched from the eastern coast of China across Asia to eastern Europe. By 1300 the Mongols had assembled the largest empire in history.

In some ways, China benefited from the Mongol conquest. Khubilai rebuilt Chinese cities, repaired canals, and extended the Grand Canal. Under Khubilai, China's trade with other nations, such as India, Japan, and the East Indies was greatly increased. Chinese traders travelled more than ever before, and Arab and European merchants came to China. China became one of the most important states in the Mongol Empire.

In other ways, however, the rule of the Mongols was very difficult for China. The Mongols had caused an enormous loss of life and destruction in their campaigns to defeat the Song. Large areas of the countryside were depopulated, and the economy was in ruins. Furthermore, the Mongols discriminated against the Chinese, reserving all the higher government offices for themselves. In addition, the Chinese were punished much more severely for any infractions, while the crimes of the Mongol inhabitants were ignored. In their determination to rebuild public works the Mongols behaved quite ruthlessly towards the general populace. Over time, the Mongol emperors became less able than Khubilai, and social and political institutions and public works began to decline and fall into disrepair. During the

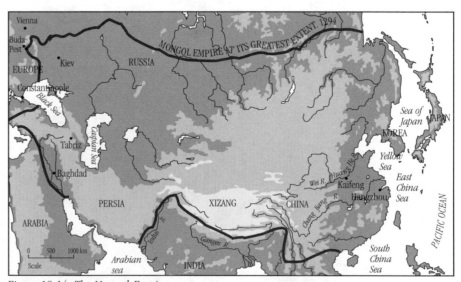

Figure 18-14 *The Mongol Empire*

fourteenth century, revolts against Mongol rule broke out all across China.

THE MING DYNASTY 1368 CE-1644 CE

By 1368 the Ming dynasty had forced the Mongols out of China. The Ming set up a new Imperial Court at Beijing. Inheriting China in a state of much-needed repair, the Ming set about the task of rebuilding. After the years of alien rule, the Ming were determined to restore traditional Chinese culture.

The Ming re-established the central government and the system of civil service examinations, removing all vestiges of Mongol traditions and laws. Under the Ming, the examinations came to emphasize Confucian teachings more than ever. The Ming emperors were more autocratic than the emperors of earlier dynasties, and the Ming court was divided by warring factions much of the time.

The Ming restored the economy of China. In addition, during the early years of Ming rule, contact with outsiders continued. Admiral Zheng He led government-sponsored maritime expeditions to many parts of South and Southeast Asia and to Africa. These expeditions were only partly trading expeditions. The Ming insisted that other countries recognize China's primacy by paying tribute before they allowed trade to occur.

The expeditions suddenly ceased in 1433. No one really knows why but it is probable that the Ming government found them too expensive to continue. In addition, in their desire to restore Chinese traditions after the years of rule by the Mongols, the Ming turned inward. Chinese ships were forbidden to sail to other countries and Chinese citizens were forbidden to leave the country.

Some foreign traders were still allowed to enter China and settle in selected seaports. By the end of the Ming dynasty, China was coming into direct and increasing contact with Europeans. The era of European overseas expansion had reached the shores of China.

JAPAN:
The Land of the Rising Sun

*T*he Asian lands laying farthest to the east were associated very early in their history with the rising sun, and eventually this became the basis of the country's name. Japan's name came from the Chinese *Jih-pen, meaning sun-rise islands, and was pronounced in the Chinese language as* Nippon. *The Japanese pronounced these same characters* Nihon.

Jih-pen *was corrupted by Westerners into "Japan." The Japanese used* Nihon *and* Nippon *interchangeably for years. Shortly before the Second World War, the Japanese government officially endorsed* Nippon, *even though it was the Chinese rather than the Japanese pronunciation. Today,* Nippon *is still officially the correct pronunciation, but many Japanese continue to use* Nihon *when they speak of their country.*

The evolution of the name for Japan is indicative of much of its historical development. Peopled by migrants from the Asian mainland, Japan was influenced by many mainland cultural traditions. However, isolated by geography, Japan developed many indigenous traditions as well. The outstanding achievement of the Japanese was their ability to adapt outside influences to indigenous traditions to create a unique civilization.

THE LAND OF ANCIENT JAPAN

Japan is an **archipelago**, a chain of islands off the northeast coast of Asia. The four main islands are Hokkaido, Honshu, Shikoku, and Kyushu. Stretching over 2000 km along the coast of East Asia, these islands are the tops of volcanic mountains that rise from the ocean floor. The river valleys and coastal plains of Japan are separated from each other by rugged mountains. Japan, as part of the Pacific Ring of Fire, is subject to frequent earthquake and volcanic activity.

The climate of Japan is affected by two ocean currents, the warm Japan Current and the cold Oyashio Current. As a result, southern Japan is warm, with hot humid summers and mild winters. In northern Japan, summers are cool and heavy snow falls in the winter. Rain falls on all of the islands year round, but the south experiences a rainy season in June and July. As well as being subject to earthquakes and volcanoes, Japan lies in the path of fierce typhoons.

The soil of the river valleys and coastal plains is fertile, but because the land is so mountainous, only about twenty percent of Japan is suitable for farming. In order to maximize agricultural production, the Japanese learned early to practise intensive agriculture and to terrace the hills.

Figure 19-1
Mount Fuji, Japan's highest peak

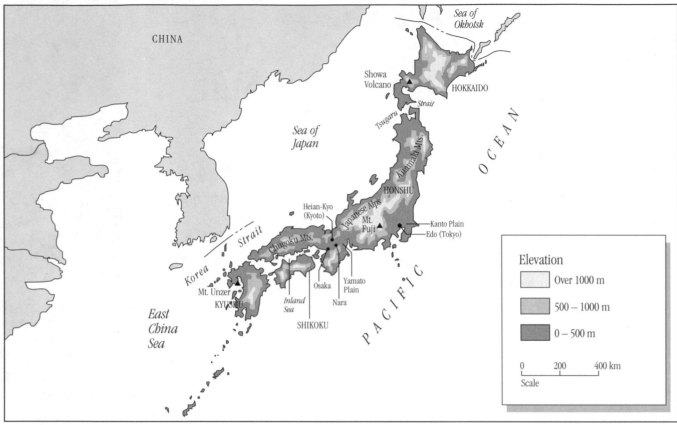

Figure 19-2 *The archipelago of Japan*

Figure 19-3 *Japanese farmers at work in their terraced fields*

The sea was very important to the development of early Japan. The Inland Sea served as a highway to link the fertile areas and the islands together. The sea also provided a rich source of food for the Japanese, who fished the coastal waters. However, the sea acted as a barrier as well. Korea is about 160 km to the west, and China lies some 800 km away. The Sea of Japan was hazardous to cross in early times. The Asian mainland was close enough to allow cultural contact, but too far away to make conquest feasible. The Sea of Japan allowed the Japanese to be selective about their contact with the Asian mainland.

HISTORICAL OVERVIEW

THE JOMON PERIOD
4500 BCE-250 BCE

Until the end of the last Ice Age (around 10 000 BCE), the islands of Japan were linked to the mainland by land bridges. During this period, Japan experienced waves of migration from the Asian mainland. The early arrivals were joined by later migrants who made their way to Japan after the land links were severed. Very little is known about early Japanese history, and it was not until about 5000 BCE that a distinctive culture began to appear. This culture was called Jomon, which means "rope pattern." It is a reference to the rope-like decoration which the people of this culture frequently used on their pottery. Clay statuettes depicting human figures have also been identified with the Joman culture.

The people of the Jomon culture were sedentary, living in small communities of sunken pit houses with steeply pitched roofs. They were hunters, fishers, and gatherers. Nuts and shellfish were part of their diet. Archaeological evidence indicates that their tools were made of deer horn and fish bones.

One of the mysteries of ancient Japan relates to the Ainu, a group of people who predate the Jomon. The Ainu were fairer skinned and had more body hair than other peoples in the neighbouring areas of Asia. Their culture and language were also different. The origin of the Ainu has been the subject of controversy. At one time, it was suggested that they must be a Caucasian group that had somehow made its way to Japan. It is now believed that the Ainu were Asiatic in origin. Throughout Japanese history, the Ainu were continually forced to retreat northward, finally settling

Figure 19-4 *The rope pattern on Jomon pottery was made by wrapping rope around the wet clay, leaving imprints of the rope on the surface*

on the island of Hokkaido. Today, there are a few Ainu descendants living along the Hokkaido coast where they continue to hunt and fish in much the same fashion as their ancestors.

THE YAYOI PERIOD
250 BCE-250 CE

Around 250 BCE a new culture displaced the Jomon. The people of the Yayoi culture were farmers with a knowledge of wet rice cultivation, likely passed on from southern China through Korea. This period is also associated with the use of bronze, iron, glass, and mirrors, all of which came from China too.

JAPAN: A DEVELOPMENTAL TIMELINE

	THE JOMON PERIOD 4500 BCE-250 BCE	THE YAYOI PERIOD 250 BCE-250 CE	THE KOFUN PERIOD 250 CE-710 CE
POLITICAL DEVELOPMENTS	• the Jomon culture emerges and spreads throughout Japan • the Ainu culture is also present in Japan • a period of early clan or tribal organization	• farming villages appear • Yayoi culture spreads east to the Kanto Plain from the Yamato Plain • small states begin to appear, ruled by hereditary clan chieftains	• an aristocratic society, led by warriors with iron weapons • the Yamato establish themselves as the most powerful clan in Japan from 100-300 CE • the mythology of the imperial line is established • the Taika Reforms (646 CE) and Taiho Code (702 CE) are instituted
CULTURAL DEVELOPMENTS	• known for their richly imaginative pottery styles and clay figurines	• bronze, iron, glass, mirrors, and textiles are introduced from the Asian mainland	• the practice of building tomb mounds begins • Chinese influence in Japan expands; Chinese writing is introduced • Buddhism enters Japan in 552 CE and is established at court • the earliest Japanese written records appear
TECHNOLOGICAL/ECONOMIC DEVELOPMENTS	• sedentary hunters and fishers, using tools made of deer horn and fish bone • live in sunken pit houses	• wet rice cultivation is introduced to Japan from Korea, leading to increased agricultural production • wheel-made pottery appears	• iron is used for agricultural tools • houses are thatched structures, raised off the ground • trade accompanies the cultural exchange with the Asian mainland

THE NARA PERIOD
710 CE-794 CE

- the first permanent capital is built at Nara
- Chinese influence in Japan reaches its peak
- government and law based on the Chinese models are implemented

- many Chinese cultural traditions are adopted
- first Japanese anthologies are compiled; Japanese history-writing begins
- Buddhism expands throughout society; Buddhist art is created

- large-scale architectural works and irrigation systems are undertaken
- bronze-casting technology improves
- paper making begins
- roads and bridges are built to improve internal communication; volume of internal trade increases

THE HEIAN PERIOD
794 CE-1185 CE

- the Imperial Court is established at the new capital, Heian-kyo
- the Fujiwara clan rises to power at the Imperial Court
- the central government begins to lose power
- a new class, the samurai, develops
- the Heian period ends with the establishment of the first shogunate

- Japanese fascination with China declines
- the Imperial Court is the centre of cultural life
- the "Golden Age" of ancient Japan, as a distinctively Japanese culture emerges
- *kana* is developed, leading to a proliferation of Japanese literature; *The Tale of Genji* is written
- Japanese traditions in painting and sculpture develop

- art of sword-making reaches new heights; swords become a major export
- construction techniques are refined to withstand earthquakes and typhoons
- trade and contact with the Asian mainland decrease significantly after 894

Throughout the Yayoi period, the number of farming villages steadily increased. Typical villages were small, averaging about ten houses. The pottery excavated from this period indicates a wide variety in style. By the end of the first century BCE, the Yayoi had spread their farming villages to the plains of western Kyushu and western Honshu.

Sometime during the second century CE, small neighbouring farming villages began to organize into small states. Rivalry between these states became common and warfare often broke out. According to a legend that archaeologists and historians have not been able to prove, Himiko, a queen of one of these small states, ended the wars and created a unified state called Yamatai. The source of this legend was the *Wei Zhi*, a Chinese chronicle dating from the third century CE, which was written for the Chinese court based on reports by Chinese visitors to Korea and Japan.

became the first emperor, Jimmu, in 660 BCE. The establishment of the date 660 BCE was a result of the adoption of the Chinese calendar around this time. According to archaeological records, the Yamato rise to power occurred sometime between the second and fourth centuries CE, many years after Jimmu's supposed rule. Nevertheless, 660 BCE became the official date for the establishment of the Japanese imperial line, and all subsequent emperors have come

REFLECT AND ANALYZE

1. How did the culture of the Yayoi period differ from that of the Jomon period?

2. According to legend, what attempt at political unification was made during this period?

3. How can you find out about the history of an area if written records are scarce or misleading? Explain the reasons for your answer.

THE KOFUN PERIOD
250 CE–710 CE

The word *kofun* means tomb mound. Beginning in the Yamato region around 250 it became common for political leaders to be buried beneath a large earthen mound. For this reason, the period is known as the Kofun period or the period of the Tomb Builders.

The Tomb Builders were a warrior people, organized on the basis of clans. They fought fiercely on horseback, carrying the long, straight sword associated with northern Asia. Two other important symbols are attached to their rule—a huge comma-shaped jewel, and a round bronze mirror representing the sun. The sword, the curved jewel, and the bronze mirror are symbols still used by the Japanese royal family today.

The Kofun period is important for two reasons. First, Japan emerged from a collection of small independent states into a unified state controlled by a powerful clan. Second, cultural influence from the Asian continent began to be felt more strongly in Japan.

The Yamato clan rose to prominence during this period. After subduing a number of other clans, the Yamato established a state on the Yamato Plain of Honshu. To legitimize their authority, the Yamato claimed that they were direct descendants of the sun goddess, Amaterasu. Legend states that Japan was created when two deities, male and female, stirred up the sea and created the islands of Japan. The children of these deities became the gods, and the eldest, Amaterasu, became goddess of the sun. Her great-great-grandson supposedly

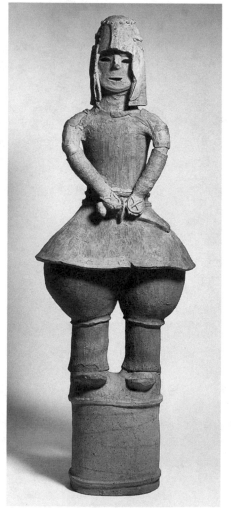

Figure 19-5 Haniwa *were earthenware figures buried with Kofun rulers in their tombs. This is a* haniwa *of a Kofun warrior*

from the Yamato line, making it the longest-ruling imperial line in the world.

In 552, Chinese Buddhist missionaries came to Japan by way of Korea. Their arrival set Japan on a new path. Buddhism became the vehicle for spreading Chinese culture in Japan. Prince Shotoku (574-622), a member of the Yamato ruling family, became fascinated by Chinese civilization. He learned to read and write Chinese, and studied Chinese literature. Under his leadership the pace of borrowing from China increased. Shotoku sent three embassadors to China to study its government, history, philosophy, arts, and sciences from 607 to 614. The Japanese returned with dazzling reports of Chinese achievements, and Japan began to borrow many Chinese ideas.

In 646 a set of reforms called the Taika Reforms was issued. These reforms were designed to model the Japanese system far more closely on Chinese institutions. The reforms called for the establishment of a strong centralized government under the authority of the emperor. Court ranks were to be reorganized and the authority of the central government was to be extended to the provinces. All officials would be appointed and controlled by the emperor. All land was declared the property of the state, and was to be redistributed following a census. The reforms were intended to reduce the power of the leading clans by centralizing power at the Imperial Court. In addition, the Chinese systems of taxation and law were to be adopted. These reforms were implemented gradually over the next half century with mixed success. The reforms were made law in the Taiho Code of 702.

Figure 19-6 *This seventh-century silk painting shows Prince Shotoku between one of his brothers and his son*

THROUGH THEIR EYES

The Writings of Prince Shotoku

Prince Shotoku was influenced in his thinking by the Chinese philosopher Confucius. What is it about Chinese philosophy that Prince Shotoku admires, according to this excerpt from his writings?

Harmony should be valued and quarrels should be avoided. Everyone has his biases, and few men are far sighted. Therefore some disobey their lords and fathers and keep up feuds with their neighbours. But when the superiors are in harmony with each other and inferiors are friendly, then affairs are discussed quietly and the right view of matters prevails. Then there is nothing that cannot be accomplished!

Do no fail to obey the commands of your Sovereign. He is like Heaven, which is above the Earth, and the vassal is like the Earth, which bears up Heaven. When Heaven and Earth are properly in place, the four seasons follow their course and all is well in Nature. But if the Earth attempts to take the place of Heaven, Heaven would simply fall in ruin.

The Ministers and officials of the state should make proper behaviour their first principle, for if the superiors do not behave properly, the inferiors are disorderly; if the inferiors behave improperly, offenses will naturally result...

To subordinate private interests to the public good—that is the path of a vassal. Now if a man is influenced by private motives, he will be resentful, and if he is influenced by resentment he will fail to act as harmoniously with others. If he fails to act harmoniously with others, the public interest will suffer. Resentment interferes with order and is subversive to law...

THE NARA PERIOD 710 CE-794 CE

In 710, the emperor decided to build Japan's first permanent capital, following the example of the Chinese. In the past, the location of the capital was moved each time an emperor died because death was regarded as a form of pollution. Moving the capital with each new emperor avoided the possibility of natural disasters as a result of this pollution. The site chosen for the new capital city was Nara. The city was modelled on the Tang capital of Changan.

The Nara period was the time when Chinese influence in Japan reached its peak. The government organized expeditions to China to learn more about its culture. Hundreds of men participated in these trips. The result was an enormous infusion of Chinese culture into Japan.

Japanese libraries were filled with collections of Chinese literature and learning. The court adopted Chinese styles in art and literature and the nobles studied Confucian and Daoist philosophies. Palaces and Buddhist temples reflected Chinese styles of architecture. Even Japanese clothing showed the impact of Chinese culture. The Japanese wrote the first book on Japanese history at this time, as well as a number of literary works.

The emperors of the Nara period were not without their problems, however. The era was marked by periods of pestilence and poor harvests. Emperor Shomu (724-749) believed that Buddhism offered the best solution to improving the social and economic conditions in Japan. He ordered each province to build a major Buddhist temple and convent. The temple-building program was not so much a belief in the power of Buddhism as an attempt to unite the people and create a sense of community in the face of difficulties. As a result, a legacy of the Nara period is the many magnificent temples, such as the Todaiji, that dot Japan's landscape.

Toward the end of the Nara period, Buddhist influence threatened the security of the royal lineage. In 764, the Empress Shotoku fell under the influence of an ambitious Buddhist monk, Dokyo, and made him minister of state. Court officials became afraid that Skotoku might one day make the monk emperor to satisfy Dokyo's ever-growing personal ambitions. However, Shotoku died before anything like this could happen, and Dokyo was exiled.

Figure 19-7 *The Todaiji temple, the world's largest wooden building, was built in 745. Building a temple was a major undertaking. Transporting the huge timbers needed for the columns and beams was extremely difficult in the mountainous terrain. Thousands of artisans had to be trained to work on the interior decorations*

The incident was enough to make the new emperor wary of the motives of Buddhist monks. He decided to create a new capital that would be free of Buddhist influence. In 794 he selected Heian-kyo, "the capital of peace and tranquillity," as the site for the new capital. About 40 km from Nara, Heian-kyo was eventually renamed Kyoto. It remained the imperial capital of Japan for over a thousand years.

REFLECT AND ANALYZE

1. How did this period get its name?

2. In what ways did China influence the development of Japan during the Nara period?

3. Based on the story of the Empress Shotoku and the monk Dokyo, write a letter to a friend who is away from the Imperial Court, describing the problem with court life that it illustrates.

THE HEIAN PERIOD
794 CE-1185 CE

The Heian period was the "Golden Age" of ancient Japan. It was an era when a specifically Japanese art and culture began to flourish. As the Tang dynasty declined in China during the ninth century, the Japanese fascination with China decreased. The last successful Japanese expedition to China was in 838, when the Tang dynasty was breaking up. All official contact ended in 894, although trade and travel continued on a reduced scale.

During the Heian period, a Japanese culture of great refinement, distinct from that of China, emerged. Countless Japanese literary works were produced using *kano*, a phonetic alphabet devised to express the Japanese language. Painting and sculpture took on a distinctly Japanese style. A cult of beauty in nature and art emerged. Life at the Imperial Court was devoted to the pursuit of the aesthetic, down to the most minor details of clothing, makeup, and deportment. Members of the Imperial Court became so remote from the concerns of everyday life that they came to be called "the dwellers among the clouds."

However, court life also increased rivalries among the noble families, as they vied with each other for imperial favour. Noble families fought for ranks and privileges, accumulating as many as possible. One of the most influential of these families was the Fujiwara clan, which had become very powerful by the early ninth century. The Fujiwara had gained so much political power that the emperor actually held power in name only. The influence of the Fujiwara did not decline until the twelfth century.

Another trend that developed during these years was the growth of powerful provincial lords. Junior members of noble families in the capital managed family estates in the countryside on behalf of senior family members. Over time, the provincial families increased their lands and wealth and power by fighting and intriguing against each other. Gradually, the powerful provincial lords became independent of the central government. They often refused to pay taxes, claiming the same tax-exemption privileges granted to vari-

Figure 19-8 *The Heian cult of beauty in nature and art*

ous religious organizations and court nobles. Peasants became increasingly willing to turn their lands over to these tax-exempt provincial lords. In return they were guaranteed a lower tax and protection from the unrest in the countryside.

As the central government increasingly weakened, and as disorder in the provinces escalated, the provincial lords began training family members and their followers in the martial arts. They became warriors pledged to defend their lord. Over time, these warriors developed into a new class known as the **samurai**.

REFLECT AND ANALYZE

1. Why was the move of the capital from Nara to Heian-kyo considered so significant?

2. Why is this period called "the Golden Age" of ancient Japan?

3. Research one aspect of life at the Heian court that demonstrates how and why members of the Imperial Court became known as "the dwellers among the clouds."

4. As a member of the Japanese nobility, write a journal entry in which you express your feelings about the development of a specifically Japanese culture.

5. What caused the collapse of the Heian period?

GOVERNMENT

During the earliest periods in ancient Japan, the Japanese were organized into clans, each of which had a clan god. The clans were headed by hereditary chiefs who acted as both military and religious leaders. Over a period of time many of these clans banded together to form small states or countries. There is a reference in the *Han Shu*, a first-century Chinese history, describing ancient Japan as being divided into over 100 small countries. Most of the recognized states at that time were located in northern Kyushu.

By about the fourth century, the Yamato clan emerged as the strongest clan in Japan. Their claim to descent from the sun goddess Amaterasu was very important.

By claiming divine descent, Japanese emperors legitimized their authority and gained the respect and support of the people. Emperors were always regarded as the ultimate source of authority in Japan, even when they played no more than a ceremonial role.

During the Nara period, the Japanese attempted to implement China's pattern of centralized government, as outlined in the Taika Reforms and the Taiho Code. The emperor held supreme authority and he appointed the officials who operated the eight ministries of government that were set up. A bureaucracy to administer the government ministries was also set up. The country was divided into provinces, each run by a governor appointed by the central government. Each province was further divided into districts, villages, and hamlets. Postal stations were established along public roads to link the countryside with the capital. Taxes went directly to the central government rather than to local leaders.

However, the Chinese model of government was never a success in Japan. Noble families retained too much power and privilege for a truly centralized imperial bureaucracy to work. The Japanese tradition of hereditary rank was too strong for them to accept the concept of a civil service based on merit. Consequently, it was hereditary nobles rather than scholars who obtained the newly created official positions in the central government. At the provincial level, existing provincial leaders were given the official posts. In time, the new positions became hereditary, and any vestige of centralized control was lost.

By the ninth century, the attempt to impose Chinese political traditions was abandoned. In theory the emperor remained the supreme authority but in practice he became a figurehead whose chief duties were religious and ceremonial. The government was run by the powerful Fujiwara family.

Toward the end of the Heian period, the Fujiwara influence finally waned. Two other clans, the Minamoto and the Taira, rose to prominence and became bitter rivals for power. Their rivalry resulted in a civil war, the Gempei War (1180-1185). Minamoto no Yoritomo was the eventual victor. Taking the title **shogun**, which meant military dictator, he established a military government at Kamakura at the mouth of Tokyo Bay. The attempt at a centralized government based on the Chinese model had failed, and Japan would be ruled by shoguns for more than six hundred years.

PERSPECTIVES ON THE PAST

The Role of the Fujiwara Clan

What allowed the Fujiwara clan to maintain its position of supremacy at the Heian court for more than three hundred years?

The Fujiwara clan, not the emperor, were the true rulers of Japan from 806 to 1160. Having begun their rise to dominance in the mid-seventh century, by the ninth century the Fujiwara were more powerful than any other clan.

Part of the Fujiwara success can be explained in terms of their wealth. They owned large estates—their revenue was said to have been greater than that of the emperor. They used their wealth to maintain the imperial household in style, thereby gaining influence with the emperor.

The Fujiwara also took bold measures to protect their position of power. When the emperor died in 858, he was succeeded by his seven-year-old son, who also happened to be the grandson of the head of the Fujiwara family, Yoshifusa. Yoshifusa moved quickly to have the boy declared emperor and to assume the role of Regent. In the past, Regants had come from the imperial family. The Fujiwara never gave up their role as Regents, even when adult emperors came to the throne.

To reinforce their role as Regents, whenever possible, the Fujiwara made sure that the emperors married Fujiwara women. They also married the women of the family to other noble families who could add to their power and wealth. The Fujiwara further ensured their position by monopolizing government positions.

The real secret of their success, however, was that they did not challenge the supremacy of the imperial line. They always ruled in the name of the emperor, and never tried to assume imperial power directly. They were content to exercise their power behind the scenes.

Figure 19-9 *This panel from a thirteenth-century scroll painting shows an attack on the Imperial palace that took place during the fighting between the Taira and the Minamoto*

REFLECT AND ANALYZE

1. Why did none of the leading clans ever attempt to become emperor?

2. Why did the attempt to institute the Chinese system of government fail in Japan?

3. What changes might follow the institution of a military government? Imagine that you are a visitor to Japan at this time and outline the possible advantages and disadvantages of military rule, supporting your answer with reasons.

LAW AND JUSTICE

Law in Japanese society, prior to the institution of Chinese law in the Nara period, was extremely harsh. Punishments for breaking the rules of the community were most severe. Guilt was determined by practices such as seeing if the culprit could be burned by placing a hand in boiling water. Conviction of a criminal offence led to slavery, usually shared by the entire family, not just the criminal.

In his writings, Prince Shotoku had offered government officials some advice regarding the administration of justice. He stressed the importance of impartiality in dealing with legal complaints, and warned that judges should have no opportunity to make personal gain while resolving legal disputes; otherwise, the poor would have little faith in the law and little reason for behaving as they should. Shotoku also advised officials to reward good and punish evil.

The Taiho Code, adopted in 702, has not survived, so the only things known about it are from later commentaries. It duplicated the Chinese criminal and civil legal codes. There were four categories of law: a penal code, a civil and administra-tive code, as well as two other codes of regulations. The Taiho Code continued to be the basis of the legal system for centuries, in theory at least.

Laws were issued as declarations or edicts. The most important were those issued by the Imperial Court. These were implemented or acted upon by all of the provincial or district administrators throughout the land. They in turn issued their own edicts in order to implement imperial policies or to regulate the conduct of the peasants living in their districts.

Provincial and district administrators also established the punishments for violations of the law.

Following the Chinese model, the laws were very strict. Death, exile, and floggings were frequent punishments. Communal punishments were also used. If a peasant was declared guilty of violating an edict, for example, punishment was meted out not only to him but also to the entire village. The entire community was held responsible for the individual's actions.

With the influence of Buddhism, Japanese courts became reluctant to apply the death penalty and granted amnesty to prisoners on many occasions. By the ninth century, the central government had lost almost all of its ability to enforce the law. The law code was revised in 927 in an attempt to reassert central control that failed. By the end of the Heian period, control of the law had passed to the provincial magnates, who administered a sort of customary law that blended traditional Japanese laws with the Chinese-inspired law codes.

REFLECT AND ANALYZE

1. What advice did Prince Shotoku offer to those who were responsible for administering justice in ancient Japan?

2. Was the advice offered by Prince Shotoku good advice in your opinion? Explain, giving reasons for your answer.

3. What might happen in a country that lacks a law code common to all the inhabitants?

JAPAN:
Society and Culture

Suddenly there came a messenger
Who told me she was dead—
Was gone like a yellow leaf of autumn.
Dead as the day dies with the setting sun,
Lost as the bright moon is lost behind the cloud,
Alas, she is no more, whose soul
Was bent to mine like bending seaweed!
      When the word was brought to me
I knew not what to do nor what to say;
But restless at the mere news,
And hoping to heal my grief
Even a thousandth part,
I journeyed to Karu and searched the market place
Where my wife was wont to go!
      There I stood and listened,
But no voice of her I heard,
Though the birds sang in the Unebi Mountain;
None passed by who even looked like my wife.
I could only call her name and wave my sleeve.

Kakinomoto Hitomaro
A Court poet. 8th Century CE

Figure 20-1
*Caligraphy is an art
form still practised in
Japan today*

Kakinomoto Hitomaro was one of Japan's most famous poets, best known for writing long poems. Poetry-writing was an essential social skill among the nobility of Japan, whether one was a warrior or courtier. Poetry was regarded as the highest expression of the human heart, and was supposed to reflect important moral values, the poignancy of interpersonal relationships, or the artful expression of a fleeting emotion. Court poetry readings and contests were among the most significant occasions at the Imperial Court during Heian times.

RELIGION

SHINTO

The religion that came in later times to be known as Shinto, to distinguish it from Buddhism, began in Japan in prehistoric times. Shinto was an ***animistic*** religion, involving nature worship along with an element of ancestor worship. The word itself means, "the way of the gods." At the heart of the religion was the belief in a variety of *kami* (spirits or souls). The Japanese believed that all natural objects, such as mountains, waterfalls, and trees contained *kami*, and that the *kami* controlled the forces of nature. The Japanese were in awe of nature, which could be bountiful and beautiful, but could also erupt into natural disasters. These disasters were attributed to bad behaviour on the part of either humans or the gods.

In addition to the *kami*, each clan had a god thought of as the clan ancestor. It was the responsibility of the clan leader to maintain the cult of the clan god.

The practices associated with Shinto were relatively simple. Shinto did not contain an organized philosophy or moral code, and it had no sacred texts. Shinto was more a religion of festivals and rituals, particularly those associated with agriculture.

The emperor was the chief priest. Because he was considered a descendant of the goddess Amaterasu, the chief deity over the other clan gods, the emperor was expected to inform the gods of the nation's problems and seek their guidance. He was also responsible for conducting numerous religious festivals related to agriculture, such as festivals for rice-planting or for tasting the new fruit crops.

One important concept associated with Shinto was that of purity. Events such as childbirth, illness, death, or murder were considered impure or polluting. Cleansing rituals and abstention were required to remove the impurities.

By the eighth century, the Japanese countryside was dotted with three thousand officially recognized shrines to a variety of *kami*. Most were dedicated to Inari, the god of rice. The shrines were located in places of great natural beauty, and were indicated by a *torii*, or gateway, composed of two upright posts and a crossbar.

Private worship involved ritual purification as a first step. Purification could be achieved by washing the mouth with water, by sprinkling salt, or by waving a sacred branch. Worship consisted of reciting prayers, bowing, and making an offering of food, drink, or a wand containing a piece of cloth or paper inscribed with religious messages. Worshippers might ask for a good

Figure 20-2 *A modern-day Shinto ceremony in Kyoto*

harvest at a shrine to Inari, or for help in finding a husband at a shrine to the *kami* Konsei. The protection of a *kami* was also sought before battles, journeys, childbirth, or any new ventures.

Festivals were held at the various shrines on days of importance. These were happy occasions, attended by all. The priests would perform a variety of rituals and dances. The approaches to the shrines were filled with food and amusement booths, to increase the day's pleasures.

BUDDHISM

Buddhism came to Japan from India by way of China and Korea. It officially arrived in 552 when a group of Chinese Buddhist missionaries accompanied a Korean delegation on a visit to Japan. One of the more important families in the Yamato court warmly welcomed the arrival of Buddhism in Japan. The Soga clan, important state administrators, saw the Buddhist emphasis on peace as a way to ensure their own power.

Prince Shotoku (574-622), a member of the Yamato clan, became a devout Buddhist, maintaining a Korean tutor and studying Buddhist writings. Shotoku also pursued an extensive program of temple construction. By 624 Japan had 46 Buddhist temples, served by 816 monks and 569 nuns. Between 646 and 710, an additional 486 Buddhist temples were built in Japan.

Buddhism gradually moved from the Imperial Court to the general population. To many, Buddhism was not a threat to the Shinto religion since it could be viewed as a set of cultural values rather than as a religion. For example, Buddhist ideas about family and ancestors were easily absorbed because they reinforced Japanese tradi-

Figure 20-3 *Golden Japanese Buddha at the Todaiji temple*

tions. Shinto gods were regarded as local manifestations of Buddhist deities. A gradual process of assimilation took place and by the late Heian period Shinto and Buddhist ideas had blended together. Nevertheless, Shinto remained more popular with the peasants than did Buddhism.

The emperor had to be careful about embracing Buddhism too closely. It was the Shinto religion that recognized the emperor as a descendant of a Shinto god. If Japan turned exclusively to Buddhism, the emperor would lose his claim to divine descent and therefore his power. In 740, when the emperor wished to erect a statue of Buddha, a Buddhist monk was sent to the shrine of the sun goddess to see if this would offend her. After seven days and nights of praying, Amaterasu indicated that Shinto and Buddhism were simply different forms of the same religion. The emperor went ahead and constructed his Buddha.

Over time, the Buddhist monasteries and temples became very wealthy and powerful, and acquired vast holdings of land. This brought them into conflict with other powerful landowners. Buddhist influ-ence at court became so great at the end of the Nara period that the capital was moved to Heian-kyo, to free it from this influence. Nevertheless, Buddhism remained an important force in Japanese life.

DEATH

The development of the tomb mounds associated with the early Kofun period was unique to that period of Japanese history. The early tombs had a small room containing a coffin and personal objects such as beads, bracelets, mirrors, necklaces, swords, and agricultural implements. Gradually, the burial tomb mounds became larger. The largest of these tombs was built for the Emperor Nintoku in 399. It measured 486 m long by 305 m wide and 34 m high. About 20 000 terracotta figures, or *haniwa*, were placed in the mound, which was surrounded by a double moat.

The costs involved in erecting these tomb mounds became so prohibitive that even the wealthiest found it difficult to maintain the practice. Until the fifth cen-tury, the tombs had been constructed on flat plains. By the sixth century, they were being constructed by tunnelling into hillsides. The tunnelled tombs were rarely more than 3 m long, with a low corridor opening out into a vault-shaped rectangular chamber with a stone floor. The chamber was only wide enough for the bodies to be stretched out. Dividers separated the area if there were two or more bodies.

Later, with the growing influence of Buddhism, cremation became common as a burial practice. The first cremation to be conducted is thought to have been that of the Buddhist monk Dosho in 700. Cremation spread through the upper classes after it was adopted by the imperial household. Following Buddhist tradition, the ashes were placed in one or more containers and buried in a small mound with a stone marker, a small pagoda, a wooden tablet, or some other indicator. Once cremation was accepted by the nobility, it became widespread through all ranks of Japanese society.

REFLECT AND ANALYZE

1. Why can Shinto be described as an animistic religion?

2. How did burial practices change over time?

3. What evidence is there that the ancient Japanese were tolerant in their religious views? Why were they tolerant?

4. Imagine that you are a peasant child of ten and that a Shinto festival is taking place tomorrow. Write a journal entry anticipating what the day will be like.

SOCIAL STRUCTURE

Deference to rank was a tradition dating from the earliest days of Japanese society. The earliest social system was based on clans, which were ruled by hereditary chiefs. The hereditary chiefs were ranked in importance according to the status of their clan. Below the level of the chiefs, the rest of the people were organized according to occupational groups known as *be*, such as agricultural workers, fishers, or weavers. Those of a lesser station always showed their inferior position by squatting or kneeling when addressing a superior, or by stepping to the side when passing on the road.

During the Kofun period the Chinese system of court ranks was adopted, and these had replaced the older clan ranks by the mid-eighth century. The emperor was at the top of the social pyramid. Below the emperor were eight ranks of nobility, each with two or more subdivisions. The distinction of rank was marked at court by the colour of the head-dress worn by the noble. The highest rank of court nobles wore shades of violet. Other ranks wore other colours and shades to distinguish their position. Lesser nobles, who were not allowed to enter the court of the emperor, wore a different style of head-dress.

Distinctions among the nobility became even more pronounced during the Heian period. At this time, many nobles began to live in the capital on a permanent basis. Such nobles were distinguished from the provincial nobles, who were of lesser rank. The provincial nobles also had many subdivisions of rank. The nobles at the Imperial Court became known as "the dwellers among the clouds" because of their exalted status.

Deference to rank was so important that it permeated language usage as well as other social customs. Different terminology was required when addressing someone of superior rank. The terminology depended on a detailed calculation of the difference in rank involved. Similarly, there was a very complicated formula to be used in terms of the proper way to bow or kneel, in order to show the correct degree of deference.

The gap on the social scale between the lesser nobles and the rest of society, composed of peasants, artisans, and traders, was even greater than that between the upper and lower nobility.

Most of the population of Japan were peasants. During the Heian period, the estimated population of Japan was five million. Of these, ninety percent were peas-

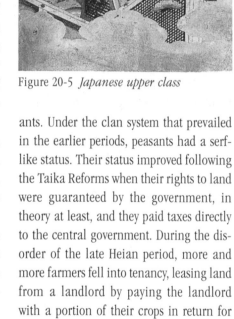

Figure 20-5 *Japanese upper class*

ants. Under the clan system that prevailed in the earlier periods, peasants had a serf-like status. Their status improved following the Taika Reforms when their rights to land were guaranteed by the government, in theory at least, and they paid taxes directly to the central government. During the disorder of the late Heian period, more and more farmers fell into tenancy, leasing land from a landlord by paying the landlord with a portion of their crops in return for the landlord's protection.

There were subgroups within the ranks of the peasants. Those who worked their own land ranked higher than those who were tenants. A third group of peasants were like slaves and did the lowest jobs of all. Many of these people were in this position because they had broken the law or had got into debt.

Artisans and merchants were not held in high regard in ancient Japan and belonged to the same class as peasants. The low status assigned to these groups was due to the fact that Japan was primarily an

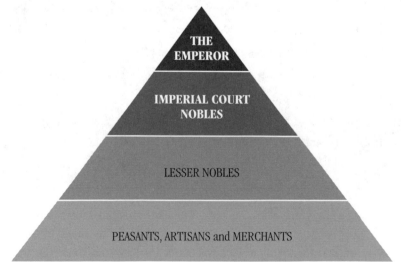

THE
EMPEROR

IMPERIAL COURT
NOBLES

LESSER NOBLES

PEASANTS, ARTISANS and MERCHANTS

Figure 20-4 *The social pyramid of Japan after the mid-eighth century*

agricultural nation. This was reinforced by Confucian ideas imported from China. Confucius had felt that the contributions of artisans and merchants to the common good of society were less valuable than those of farmers.

REFLECT AND ANALYZE

1. What means were used to distinguish the different ranks of Japanese society?

2. Why were the ancient Japanese so concerned with rank?

3. How do Canadians show deference to rank?

4. Rank is still important in Japan today. Research the language usage that determines how a variety of people address one another today in Japan. Present your research findings by drawing a series of cartoons with dialogue.

EVERYDAY LIFE

FAMILY

The family unit was highly valued within ancient Japanese society. Members of the nobility were taught that loyalty to other family members was valued above all else. Each family member was expected to assist other family members in whatever way was required. This might involve going to war against family enemies or contributing money to relatives in distress. Peasants felt the same close attachment to the family unit as well. All of the members of a peasant family needed to work together to raise the food needed to survive. Peasant wives and young children worked in the fields alongside their husbands and fathers.

Families in ancient Japan inherited their positions within society. That is, a family inherited the right to be farmers, weavers, potters, or nobles. If there were no sons to carry on the family line, the family could adopt a son through the marriage of one of its daughters. In this case, the adopted man transferred his loyalty to his adopted family.

The organization of a family was typically an extended family unit. That is, a family might include a married couple and their children, the husband's elderly parents, his eldest son's children, and his unmarried younger brothers and sisters. Younger sons left the family home after marriage to establish their own junior branches of the family. The head of the family was always the eldest male, who had great authority over the lives of family members.

Children were adored. They were seldom beaten and were given a great deal of freedom. They were, however, expected to obey their parents at all times. Children came of age at thirteen. Their marriages were always arranged by the head of the family. Marriage was regarded as a contract between families, so that women of all classes, but especially the noble class, were married to those who could add to the power and wealth of the family.

During the earlier periods of ancient Japan women sometimes held high positions. In the Yayoi period, for example, the legendary Himiko, a woman, was credited with beginning a process of political unification. During the Nara period, almost half the imperial rulers were women until the Empress Shotoku so upset the Imperial Court by her intrigues with the monk Dokyo that no other woman was allowed to rule again until the seventeenth century.

The Taiho law code reduced the status of women with its adoption of Confucian and Chinese ideas, and social conventions became much more strict. By Heian times, for example, noblewomen were not allowed to be seen by men other than family members. However, Japanese women retained a significant degree of legal and economic protection. They could inherit and manage estates, and could participate in politics. The physical abuse of women was prohibited and women were even permitted some sexual freedom, like taking a lover, as long as they were discreet. Above all, women had enormous cultural influence, determining what was considered fashionable or tasteful. Lower-class women were freer from the social conventions than noblewomen because of their lower status in society.

EDUCATION

The attempt during the Nara period to establish schools to train bureaucrats on the Chinese model failed because the Japanese never accepted the concept of a bureaucracy based on merit. However, a university to educate the sons of the court nobility was built in Nara.

Education was primarily a family affair. Formal education usually began at the age of six or seven, and was reserved for nobles, officials, and monks. Generally, all male students learned to read and write in Chinese. Female students learned to read and write in Japanese. The curriculum was strongly oriented to Confucianism, and students spent a great deal of time memorizing poems and court rules about manners.

Peasant children frequently received no formal education at all. Commoners were allowed to attend schools operated by Buddhist temples, and wealthier peasant families might provide an education for their sons or daughters. Usually, however, children were taught only the essentials of reading and writing. Since occupations were hereditary, education reflected the requirements of the occupation in question. Boys were taught the skills they would need to become farmers or they studied the same trade as their fathers. Girls were taught the details of managing an effective household by their mothers.

ings reputedly were of great magnificence. Since the Japanese built in wood, rather than in stone, very few buildings remain from earlier time periods.

Like the palaces, the homes of nobles and officials came to be built on a grand scale. The design featured a main central room surrounded by many smaller rooms. One of the interesting features of these homes was the way in which the rooms were divided. Movable bamboo screens, sliding paper screens, or even cloth drapes were hung as dividers. Screens were beautifully decorated with painted landscapes or poems. The organization of rooms could easily be altered as needs changed. Screens, for example, could be removed to make one large area.

The home had little furniture, which consisted mainly of mats and cushions, possibly a bamboo chest, and some low tables. The common practice was to sit or kneel at the low tables for meals. Raised

REFLECT AND ANALYZE

1. How was a typical family organized in ancient Japan ?

2. How were women treated in ancient Japan both within the family unit and within society in general ?

3. What would be the advantages and disadvantages of hereditary occupations? Make a list of the advantages and disadvantages from the point of view of a noble child and a peasant child. Support your answer with reasons.

URBAN AND RURAL LIVING

During the earlier periods of Japanese history, houses were primitive for nobles as well as for commoners. In Jomon times, pits were dug into the earth and then roofed. At some point, houses began to be built on the surface with tree poles and bark walls, lashed together with ropes. Floors were made of packed earth, with a fire pit for cooking and heat. The roof was made of thatch. Beds were made of straw. All houses were constructed this way—rank in society was demonstrated by the size of the house, rather than by its refinement.

Peasant homes did not improve upon this basic structure very much over the years. A rare luxury, towards the end of the Heian period, might have been the addition of wooden floor-boards or raised sleeping platforms.

However, sharp contrasts between the homes in the peasant villages that dotted the countryside and those in the well-planned capital cities of ancient Japan did become evident in later time periods. Both Nara and Heian-kyo copied the Chinese model of cities and were constructed using a grid pattern. Heian-kyo was larger and more luxurious than Nara. It measured 5.6 km by 4.8 km. Streets divided the city into 1200 city blocks. Canals bordered with a profusion of flowering trees ran beside the main streets. Almost all of the early cities have been destroyed, but the palace build-

Figure 20-6 *Phoenix Hall, the only surviving buiding of Fujiwara palace*

wooden platforms, about 50 cm above the ground, were used as beds. These were covered with mats and cushions and surrounded by screens.

By Heian times, architects were developing building techniques to decrease the amount of damage that the frequent earthquakes and typhoons could cause.

CLOTHING

During the Kofun period, few fabrics were available to anyone, whether noble or peasant. People dressed in fabrics made of cotton, hemp, or mulberry bark, woven and dyed using ancient techniques from the earliest days of Japanese history. Social rank was designated by the style of garment. The upper classes wore loose tunics and straw sandals of white, to distinguish their rank. The lower classes used coarser fabrics and were required to wear black. Everyone wore *geta*, platform shoes to keep out the mud. Hairstyles, however, were elaborate. Men parted their hair in the centre, and tied it in bunches at their ears. Unmarried women allowed their hair to flow free, but married women added a topknot.

During the Nara period, the Japanese nobility adopted Chinese styles of dress, and finer textiles like silk became available. By Heian times, clothing was very luxurious and elaborate. The emperor's court robes were woven with raised motifs of imperial symbols, to be worn over a scarlet kimono and pleated over-apron, along with a jewelled girdle, two pairs of trousers, silk stockings, and black lacquered shoes.

Nobles and court officials dressed in fine silk clothing according to court etiquette. Men wore box-like hats painted with glossy colours, short-sleeved silk jackets, and loose silk trousers. Women wore silk trousers and brightly coloured silk robes. Many different brightly coloured silk robes might be worn at the same time, with the sleeves of each robe being a little shorter than the previous one. This ensured that all of the robes could be seen.

Women shaved their eyebrows and then painted them in again using upward-rising strokes. They dyed their teeth black, since white teeth were considered ugly. The choice of a kimono was of great importance — the wearer might lose social status at court if her kimono was not pleasing enough. Men were just as vain. They powdered their faces white, and cultivated a perfectly groomed chin beard.

Peasants in the Heian period wore cotton clothing. Men wrapped long cloths around their waist and drew the excess cloth up between their legs. On cooler days they wore long-sleeved jackets. Women wore long-skirted, long-sleeved kimonos. Sometimes the men wore short kimonos. Both men and women wore broad-brimmed, round, slightly pointed hats for protection from the sun. Heavy shawls were worn in colder winter weather. To distinguish their rank in society, peasants in the later periods were required to wear yellow.

FOOD

Food and diet reflected the geographic conditions of the country, with small amounts of arable land and the close presence of the sea. The diet was generally very simple, based on rice as the staple food. Very little meat was eaten, partly due to the lack of land available for grazing animals and

Figure 20-7 *Heian clothing*

partly as a result of Buddhist influences. Soya bean soup cooked with parsley, celery, or lotus leaves and flavoured with spices, was common fare. Rice, vegetables, pickles, and tea usually rounded out the meal.

Nobles could afford a more elaborate diet and often included fish such as trout, salmon, carp, bream, or bonito. Fish was usually cut into thin slices and eaten raw after being dipped in soya sauce. Other times it was added to green salads and tossed with a vinegar dressing. Prawns and lobsters were popular as well.

The popular drink of the ancient Japanese was *sake*, or rice wine. This was a strong wine made from partly cooked rice that had gone mouldy. As with all spirits made with cereals, the mould was essential to convert the starch in the grain into sugar which was then fermented by adding yeast.

rice land was divided into units. Each male over the age of six received three units and each female above the age of six received two. The census register was updated and adjusted every five or six years.

The central government also fostered the development of the technology to establish irrigation systems that would increase yields from the rice fields. Irrigation systems were extremely difficult to build in a country as mountainous as Japan. The government also encouraged the terracing of hillsides and the use of iron farming tools to increase agricultural productivity.

With the decline of the central government's power during the later stages of the Heian period, the regular redistribution of land fell into disuse. Farmers' plots became smaller and smaller as they were divided up among their children. A great many farmers were forced into tenancy as a result.

The rice crops were also easily destroyed by insects, typhoons, floods, or other natural disasters. Serious famines resulted. To guard against this, the Japan-

REFLECT AND ANALYZE

1. Why is it that we know so little about the daily living conditions of the peasant population of ancient Japan?

2. What aspects of the homes of the Japanese nobility were somewhat unique?

3. Elegance, grace, and beauty were all important qualities of the ancient Japanese. How were these qualities reflected in their homes and their dress?

4. What aspects of the housing, clothing, and food in ancient Japan appeal to you the most? What appeals to you the least? Give reasons for your answer.

THE ECONOMY

AGRICULTURE

Farming was the basis of the economy in ancient Japan and rice was the main crop. The Japanese had very little arable land from which to feed its population. As a result, all classes of society ate relatively simple meals.

During the Nara period the central government actively promoted the development of rice as a staple crop. It wanted to increase the amount of land being put to agricultural use. One of its first measures was a redistribution of land suitable for growing rice. Based on a census, the arable

Figure 20-8 *Contemporary workers in the rice field*

ese also raised small crops of vegetables, soya beans, and fruit. Such crops were often planted on the borders of the rice fields since advantage had to be taken of even the smallest amounts of arable land.

INDUSTRY

Although farming was the basis of the economy of ancient Japan, the Japanese took advantage of other resources available to them. Fishing was a major activity. They fished for sole, mackerel, sardines, bream, mullet, and trout and they harvested seaweed and sea salt.

The abundant forests of the islands were exploited for the building of temples, monasteries, palaces, and homes. Wood was a very important resource, since the Japanese did not build with stone. Wood was also used for much of the sculpture of early Japan, as well as for making paper. The ancient Japanese became experts at producing fine textured paper that was used both as writing paper and for the construction of the large screens used to divide rooms.

A great variety of crafts flourished in Japan. Artisans used coloured lacquers to create fine inlaid boxes of gold, silver, or mother-of-pearl. Japanese metalworkers crafted excellent bronze sculpture as well as iron items for household use and fishing gear. Sword-making began to develop toward the end of the Heian period with the rise of the samurai. By the end of the tenth century Japanese swords were of such excellent quality that they were in great demand in China.

TRADE

During the earlier periods of Japanese history, Japan functioned primarily as a self-reliant economic unit based on agri-culture. Trade formed a very small part of the economy. In addition, following Confucian precepts, trade was not a highly regarded occupation. There was some internal trade among the various islands of Japan, as well as trade with the mainland of Asia.

Trade within Japan was hampered by the lack of roads and bridges. Those that did exist were poorly built and maintained. During the Nara and Heian periods, communication routes were improved and internal trade expanded a great deal as a result. Travel remained difficult in spite of this. Short journeys took many hours, as ox-drawn vehicles rumbled over bumpy roads at a rate of less than 3 km per hour. The disorders in the late Heian period added a new obstacle to trade— armed bandits increasingly roamed the countryside, raiding travellers.

Currency came into existence in 708, when the central government issued copper cash. In spite of this, the great bulk of trade still occurred on the basis of barter, and peasants still paid their taxes in kind or in labour. In the tenth century, as the central government weakened, it ceased to produce currency.

The main foreign exchanges during the ancient period were those that took place during the Kofun, Nara, and early Heian periods with China and Korea. What began initially as a cultural exchange extended into the realm of economics. The Japanese exported fine woods, products of the sea, and some weapons. Their main imports from China were silks, porcelains, and books. In this trade, one of the main units of exchange was rice.

REFLECT AND ANALYZE

1. What were the most important economic activities of ancient Japan?

2. How did the early Japanese attempt to make agriculture more productive, and what obstacles did they face?

3. Trade is the most important component of the economy of modern Japan. Why was trade not as important to ancient Japan?

THE ARTS

WRITING

Writing came to Japan from China. The spoken Japanese language was very different from the Chinese language, but in spite of this, the Japanese adopted China's writing system. Chinese characters were given Japanese pronunciations. The Japanese had difficulty reproducing Japanese names and words that did not exist in Chinese. A number of complex writing conventions were adopted to resolve the problem.

During the ninth century, simpler ways of writing Japanese were devised. One of these systems was called *kana*. *Kana* was a phonetic alphabet developed to reproduce the Japanese spoken language. Although it made writing simpler, Japanese men continued to write in Chinese, considering *kana* less refined than the Chinese writing system. The *kana* system was primarily used by women to record their spoken language.

Like the Chinese system of writing, written characters were formed with brush and ink, with each character or letter drawn separately from other letters. Calligraphy was considered an art, and was often regarded as more important than the content of the writing itself. Poor penmanship could cost a court official his job.

LITERATURE

The literature of the Nara and Heian periods has served as a valued source of information on Japanese society. Japanese literature began in the Nara period with the collation of an anthology of myths, stories, and poems in 712. This first book was followed by many others, especially an-

thologies of poetry. The first Japanese history was also written during the Nara period.

Some of the best works of Japanese literature were produced during Heian times. Noblewomen were especially influential in developing a distinctly Japanese literature, because they wrote in *kana*, and could express themselves freely. The literary works of Japanese men tended to be stilted and lifeless because they continued to write in Chinese, in spite of the fact that it did not fit the Japanese language well.

The world's first novel was produced by a Heian woman at the Imperial Court about 1022. Lady Murasaki, a lady-in-waiting to the empress, wrote *The Tale of Genji*, a very long novel that runs some 630 000 words in a slightly incomplete English

translation. The novel describes the many adventures of a legendary prince, Genzi, the young son of a Japanese emperor. The plot is intricate and well-developed, and the many characters are all portrayed with an understanding of human psychology.

Another important woman writer of the Heian period was Sei Shonagon, who was also a lady-in-waiting at the emperor's court. She wrote a book called *The Pillow Book* because she is said to have kept her writing materials by her pillow so that she could jot down notes at any time of the day or night. She recorded the things she saw, did, or heard while in service at the court. She did not organize her writings in any particular way, but simply developed a collection of anecdotes, reflections, and observations. This style of writing has been

INNOVATIONS
An Excerpt From *The Tale of Genji*

What can we learn about life in the Heian period from *The Tale of Genji?*

Though it seemed a shame to put so lovely a child into man's dress, he was now twelve years old and the time for his Initiation was come. The Emperor directed the preparations with tireless zeal and insisted upon a magnificence beyond what was prescribed. . . . The ceremony took place in the eastern wing of the Emperor's own apartments, and the Throne was placed facing towards the east, with the seats of the Initiate-to-be and his Sponsor (the Minister of the Left) in front.

Genji arrived at the hour of the Monkey [3 P.M.]. He

Figure 20-9 *A twelfth-century painting of a scene from* The Tale of Genji

man's dress went down into the courtyard and performed the Dance of Homage, which he did with such grace that tears stood in every eye....It had been feared that his delicate features would show to less advantage when he had put aside his childish dress; but on the contrary he looked handsomer than ever.

looked very handsome with his long childish locks, and the Sponsor, whose duty it had just been to bind them with the purple filet, was sorry to think that all this would soon be changed and even the Clerk of the Treasury seemed loath to sever those lovely tresses with the ritual knife....

Duly crowned, Genji went to his chamber and changing into

THEN AND NOW

The Japanese Garden—Art Through Nature

During the Heian period, gardening became an art in Japan. It developed as a natural extension of the Japanese emphasis on nature and on the importance of delicacy and grace. Nobles created the first gardens. They began by developing detailed landscaping plans that incorporated many elements— artfully located areas of flowers, shrubs and trees, flowing streams of mountain water, and artificial but natural-looking lakes, perhaps filled with gold and silver fish. Some gardens included the construction of

Figure 20-10 *The* Rikugi-en *garden in Kanazawa today. The stone lantern in the foreground is named* Kotoji-dourou

islands, bridges, pavilions, and elaborate fountains. As an art form, gardening of this sort took a great deal of patience and was very expensive.

The Japanese interest in this art form has continued to the present day. It has also been extended to the popular art form of creating miniature gardens through the art of *bonsai*. This involves dwarfing trees by careful cutting and pruning. The end result allows trees to be grown in bowls as perfect replicas of full-sized trees. Grace and elegance remain the ultimate goals of the gardener.

copied in Japanese literature many times since. The public popularity of her writing comes from the excellent descriptions she provided of life in the period, her great sense of humour, and her defence of women.

MUSIC AND DRAMA

The Imperial Court was livened by a varied fare of musical and dance performances. *Bugaku* were formal court dances. More than a hundred of these dances have survived, and are performed today. Masks were frequently worn in the court dances.

Puppetry was just beginning to come into fashion by the eighth century. Puppets performed while a tale was told to the audience. Later, musical accompaniment was added to the performance. The popularity of such performances led to later developments in Japanese theatre.

REFLECT AND ANALYZE

1. What is *kana?* Why did it develop?

2. Why were most of the significant literary contributions of Japan written by women?

3. Why are the writings of Lady Murasaki Shikibu and Sei Shonagon such historically important works?

4. Try an experiment. English writers of today attempting to write in the English of Shakespeare might encounter something of the same problem as Japanese writers using the Chinese language. Neither is a natural form of expression for the writers involved. Write a journal entry in Elizabethan English about a topic to do with daily life, in as natural a way as you can.

THE SCIENCES

MEDICINE

The Shinto religion had an abhorrence of disease, physical mutilation, the sight of blood, and death. As a religion, Shinto was oriented toward life, and anything other than good health was considered repulsive or polluted. The word for wound is *kega*, which means defilement. Not surprisingly, in view of this, medicine was held in low regard in ancient Japan.

However, this does not mean that medicine was not practised. In the early days, individuals from the highest ranks of the nobility were selected for medical training. The first treatment was to wash the body of the afflicted, to purify it. The sick frequented hot springs as ideal places to purify themselves and relieve their ills. Other treatments included massage, incantations, and exorcisms.

The Buddhist monks who arrived in Japan from Korea brought with them knowledge of Chinese medicine. Some Japanese regarded the Chinese approach to medicine as too philosophical, but many came to view the Buddhist priests as having mysterious powers that allowed them to control sickness. Eventually, many of the practices of Chinese medicine, such as acupuncture and herbal medicine, were adopted by the Japanese. The Japanese insistence on personal hygiene made the Japanese less susceptible to many diseases.

TIME

During his period as regent to the empress of Japan, Prince Shotoku adopted the Chinese-style calendar for Japan. The calendar examined time in terms of sixty-year cycles. The fifty-eighth year of each cycle was considered to bring with it some significant change. The year 601 was the fifty-eighth year of one of these cycles, and a year of great change in Japan during the lifetime of Prince Shotoku.

The sixty-year cycles were also charted. The fifty-eighth year of every twenty-first cycle of sixty years was thought to record events of even greater importance. That is, once every 1260 years an event of monumental importance would take place. It was on this basis that the year 660 BCE was determined to be the beginning of the Yamato line in ancient Japan.

possible invasion from the Asian mainland. It was extremely hazardous to sail to Japan in early days. Thus, Japan was allowed the opportunity to develop a distinct culture of its own. However, a second role of the Sea of Japan was to provide a conduit to the civilizations of the mainland, most notably those of Korea and China. Cultural, social, and economic interchange between these two ancient civilizations and Japan was a key aspect of the development of ancient East Asia.

In shaping their own culture, the ancient Japanese borrowed selectively from their interaction with the Chinese and the Koreans. They adapted many elements of Buddhist, Korean, and Chinese cultural teachings to enhance their own traditions. By the Heian period Japan had become a very sophisticated society with a distinctive national outlook. A new social order was beginning to emerge in Japan in the late twelfth century. This outlook would dominate national development over the next six centuries.

LOOKING BEYOND

By the end of the Heian period the social order of Japan was changing dramatically as the attempt at instituting a strong central government on the Chinese model collapsed. A feudal-like system grew up in its place, as provincial landowners armed themselves against the increasing disorders that accompanied the decline of central government in Heian-kyo. Provincial landlords became warrior-landlords with bodies of armed retainers to protect them. The armed retainers became known as samurai—"one who

REFLECT AND ANALYZE

1. What views were held by the followers of the Shinto religion regarding medicine?

2. What changes did the coming of the Buddhists and the influence of China have upon the practice of medicine in ancient Japan?

3. How does the use of the Chinese view of time help us to understand the disagreement over the date when the Yamato line is thought to have begun?

4. In what ways would the Japanese insistence on cleanliness have made the Japanese more advanced than Europeans in medical practices during the same time period?

LOOKING BACK

Unlike China, the civilization of ancient Japan is identified with the sea rather than with a river valley. The Inland Sea and the coastal waters of the islands were a vital communication link for the various fertile areas and islands of Japan. The Sea of Japan, on the other hand, played a dual role. One role was to serve as a natural barrier against

serves." A samurai vowed to protect his lord and all of the peasants working the lord's land. The warrior-landlords sought alliances with other warrior-landlords to increase their power. Eventually, a hierarchy of provincial lords came into existence, all of them striving to improve their position in relation to the others.

THE KAMAKURA SHOGUNATE (1185 CE–1333 CE)

The waning of the Fujiwara influence in the twelfth century spelled the end of Heian Japan and led to the establishment of the shogunate government. Following the Minamoto victory in the Gempe War, the first shogun, Yoritomo, established the Kamakura shogunate, which ruled Japan from 1185–1333.

In theory the title of shogun granted Yoritomo only military powers. In practice it gave him almost absolute power over Japan. He controlled taxes, issued laws, and commanded the samurai who had pledged to serve him. The emperor remained officially at the head of the state, and continued to live in Kyoto. But as had happened under the Fujiwara, the emperor performed only religious and ceremonial duties. The shogun was the actual ruler of Japan.

Yoritomo placed the most loyal of his samurai as governors or other officials in the provinces. Society was organized along feudal lines, with the shogun at the top. The strongest samurai were below the shogun in the new order. They carved out large estates for themselves, and gave some of their land to lesser samurai in return for military service and a pledge of personal loyalty. In this way, the stronger samurai built up personal armies. The peasants, artisans, and merchants remained far

Figure 20-11 *Yoritomo established a code of honour among his samurai. Known as bushido, it was intended to create a strong and dedicated warrior class capable of defeating any enemy*

below the samurai in the social scale.

The defence of Japan was the greatest challenge faced by the Kamakura shoguns. In 1274, Khubilai Khan, the Mongol leader from China, attempted to increase his empire by invading the island of Kyushu. Fifteen thousand Mongol troops armed with crossbows attacked the samurai forces armed with inferior bows and swords. It was an unequal match. But nature intervened and a storm sank many of the Mongol ships. The remainder were driven back toward Korea.

The Mongols followed this by sending an embassador to Japan. This time Japan made its rejection quite clear by cutting off the ambassador's head. Japan prepared for another invasion by building a defensive wall along the shores where the Mongols had previously landed. The second Mongol invasion, in 1281, was much larger than the first. The Mongol troops from Korea numbered some 50 000 and there were 100 000 troops from China.

The wall slowed the invasion, but the battle was engaged for fifty days without a decisive victory. Nature again played a significant role in the outcome. A typhoon destroyed most of the Mongol fleet and drowned nearly half of the Mongol force.

Figure 20-12 *This lithograph was published in France in the nineteenth century. It shows a samurai preparing for battle*

The typhoon was named the *kamikazi*, or divine wind. The Japanese believed that the gods had intervened to protect their homeland. Many years later, during the Second World War, the legend of the *kamikaze* was revived. The suicide pilots sent against the enemy warships became known as *kamikaze*.

The Kamakura had successfully defended Japan but at great cost. The war preparations against the Mongols had been very expensive, and the Kamakura had no way to reimburse those who had borne the cost. In addition, there was no booty to be won. The heavy financial burden of the defence destroyed the Kamakura shogunate by 1333, when a new shogun, Ashikaga Takauji, seized power.

THE ASHIKAGA SHOGUNATE (1333 CE-1467 CE)

The period of the Ashikaga shogunate was one of continual unrest. It was never able to develop a strong central government in Japan or to provide law and order. The Ashikaga never managed to get the support of the emperors. Even though the emperors played no real role in government, their support was necessary for any government to flourish. As a result, the leaders of powerful local clans intrigued constantly against the Ashikaga to increase their power and wealth. The most successful of these came to be known as *daimyo*. They were constantly at war with one another, trying to enlarge their holdings. Samurai became loyal to a particular *daimyo* rather than to the shogun. Although the Ashikaga period saw many advances in industry, mining, and public works, it deteriorated into a long period of civil strife. Eventually the Ashikaga lost the struggle against the *daimyo*, whose wealth and military power was too great to be overcome.

FROM CIVIL WAR TO REUNIFICATION (1467 CE-1603 CE)

The Ashikaga shogunate was destroyed by the Onin War (1467-1477), in which two warlords fought each other vigorously. The capital lay in ruins after this war, which was followed by a general civil war where powerful *daimyo* fought one another to extend their influence by absorbing the lands of those they were able to defeat.

By 1550 twelve *daimyo* were in control of Japan. They maintained control through the use of large armies of foot soldiers, a new development, who fought in mass formation like the Mongols. The age of the samurai as the main fighting force had come to an end.

The reunification of Japan was accomplished in 1603, thanks to the efforts of three military leaders. Oda Nobunaga defeated the Ashikaga forces in 1573, and centralized power until he was assassinated by rivals in 1582. Toyotomi Hideyoshi took over following this, and unified Japan by 1590. Afer he died in 1598, Tokugawa Ieyasu seized control in 1603, after a power struggle with rivals, and founded the Tokugawa shogunate, which lasted until 1867.

MAKING CONNECTIONS

1. The year 1997 is the Year of the Ox on the Chinese calendar. Conduct research to find out the Chinese name for the year of your birth. In addition, find out what personality traits or characteristics are associated with people born in the year of your birth. How well do you think these traits or characteristics describe you?

2. The ancient Japanese prized simplicity. Investigate modern Japanese culture to determine the extent to which this love of simplicity has been maintained in modern art forms.

3. Select ten examples of Chinese technological achievement. Using an organizer, explain the workings and the beneficial effects of each technology you select. Find out when the West acquired the same technologies. Note whether they were borrowed from the Chinese or developed independently.

4. Prepare a report on the extent to which acupuncture is used in contemporary medicine in Canada.

5. Create an illustrated timeline for either China or Japan. Include two or three of the most important achievements of each historical time period on the timeline, as well as an explanation of why you selected those achievements as the most important ones.

6. Examine the Heian period of Japanese history in depth. Select two or three developments that demonstrate the synthesis of Chinese culture with indigenous Japanese traditions that took place during these years.

DIGGING DEEPER

7. Ancient China experienced several "golden ages." Research the accomplishments in art for one of these "golden ages" and prepare an illustrated report.

8. By the thirteenth century, China was the richest and most powerful country in the world. What foundations for this wealth and power were laid by the early dynasties of China. Select three or four of the most important, explain why you selected them and how they contributed to China's future wealth and power.

9. After completing some additional research, develop a comparison organizer on the political institutions of early China and early Japan to demonstrate their similarities and differences. Select one specific historical time period for each country.

10. Using an atlas, find out the size of China's or Japan's area, its population, and

the pattern of its population distribution today. Compare these statistics to a particular time period in the history of whichever country you select. What conclusions can you draw from this comparison of the past with the present?

11. Why were both China and Japan open to trade with others at some times, while at other times they preferred to remain isolated?

12. Create a discussion between Confucius, Laozi, and Han Feizi in which you explain their viewpoints on human nature and the proper role of government. Which viewpoints do you agree with and why?

13. Prepare a report on the samurai code of *Bushido*. Explain the most important beliefs, and the reasons for these beliefs. Do you agree or disagree with the beliefs of *Bushido?* Give reasons for your answer.

SKILL DEVELOPMENT: DEVELOPING A WRITTEN REPORT

Understanding of the lessons of history depends to a large extent on the reports that historians write to explain their findings and the conclusions they have reached based on the evidence they have accumulated.

Process

A written report contains three separate sections:
- Introduction
- Body
- Conclusion

1. The **introduction** is the opening paragraph of the report. It should:
   - State the topic or purpose of your report.
   - Indicate the questions or issues that you will examine in each paragraph of your report.
   - State your thesis, or the position your are taking, on the topic.

2. The **body** of the report should develop at least three to five main arguments in support of your thesis statement. Each argument should consist of a paragraph that:
   - States the topic and the argument you will be making in the paragraph.
   - Includes sufficient facts to develop your argument.
   - Links the paragraph to the main thesis of your report.

3. The **conclusion**, or final paragraph, of the report should:
   - Sum up your main arguments.
   - Convince the reader that your thesis is valid.

HELPFUL HINTS IN WRITING A REPORT

Step 1. Develop an outline.
Before you begin to write a draft of the report, develop an outline to make sure that you are on the right track and have all the information you need.

a) Record the purpose of the report.

b) Write down the thesis that you intend to develop in your report.

c) Identify the supporting topics you will use as the focus of each paragraph in the body of your report.

d) State the arguments that you will make in each of the supporting paragraphs of the body of the report.

e) Identify the relevant facts you will include in each of the supporting paragraphs.

f) Develop the summary sentences you will use in your conclusion based on each of the paragraphs in the body of your report.

g) Develop a concluding sentence that links back to your thesis statement.

Step 2. Write the rough draft.
Use the outline to develop a rough draft of your report. Check it over carefully. Have someone else check your report and make suggestions on how it can be improved.

Step 3. Write the final draft.
Use the revisions of the rough draft as a guideline for writing your final report. Check it carefully before printing and be certain that all of the changes that you wanted to make have been included.

Applying the Skill.
Select one of the following topics. Formulate a thesis statement and prepare a written report following the steps outlined in the process above.

1. The role of a strong central government in China.

2. The adaptive skill of the Japanese.

UNIT 5

Central and South America
600 BCE-1572 CE

THE MAYA AND THE INCA

Around 2500 BCE, the cultures of Central and South America ceased to be hunter-gatherers and began to cultivate corn, beans, and squash. With the agricultural revolution came the development of cultures that reached an extremely high standard of social and technological achievement. Two of the most fascinating ancient civilizations to develop in Central and South America were the Maya and the Inca.

The Maya in Central America built large cities with complex buildings and produced magnificent art. They developed a system of mathematics that included the concept of zero, a 365-day calendar, and a writing system. The Inca in South America built irrigation systems, bridges, and roads. They built walls made of huge stones that are so tightly aligned that a knife will not fit between the stones. The Inca also crafted objects of the highest quality from silver and gold.

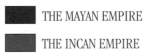

THE MAYAN EMPIRE

THE INCAN EMPIRE

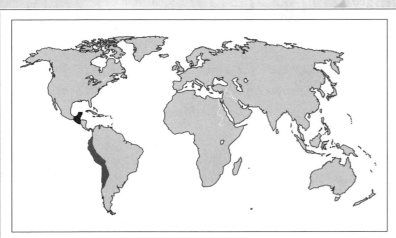

435

THE MAYA:
The Land of the Temple Pyramids

Figure 21-1
The Temple of the Jaguars in the ancient city of Tikal, an important Mayan site, as it appears today

*W*orking *our way through the thick woods, we came upon a square stone column, about fourteen feet [4 m] high and three feet [1 m] on each side, sculptured in very bold relief, and on all four of the sides, from the base to the top....*

We followed our guide who, sometimes missing his way, with a constant and vigorous use of his machete, conducted us through the thick forest, among half buried fragments, to fourteen monuments of the same character and appearance....

We [came] to the base of the pyramidal structure and ascended by regular stone steps, in some places forced apart by bushes and saplings, and in others thrown down by the growth of large trees, while some remained entire. In parts, they were ornamented with sculptured figures and rows of death's heads. Climbing over the ruined top, we reached a terrace overgrown with trees, and, crossing it, descended by stone steps into an area so covered with trees that at first we could not make out its form, but which, on clearing the way with the machete, we ascertained to be a square, and with steps on all the sides almost as perfect as those of the Roman amphitheatre....We ascended these steps and reached a broad terrace a hundred feet [30 m] high, overlooking the river....We sat down on the very edge of the wall, and strove in vain to penetrate the mystery by which we were surrounded. Who were the people that built this city? ....architecture, sculpture, and painting, all the arts which embellish life, had flourished in this overgrown forest; orators, warriors, and statesmen, beauty, ambition, and glory, had lived and passed away, and none knew that such things had been, or could tell of their past existence.

John L. Stephens was an American envoy to the Central American Federation in the 1830s. Fascinated by accounts of mysterious lost cities in the jungle, he searched for and explored nearly fifty Mayan cities, publishing accounts of his discoveries in 1841 and 1843. The city he described above was Copan. Shrouded in jungle foliage, no one knew about the civilization of the Maya prior to the nineteenth century. Only in recent years have some of the mysteries of Mayan civilization been solved. A great deal of archaeological investigation still needs to be done before a fuller understanding of one of the most sophisticated of the early civilizations of the Americas can be obtained.

THE LAND OF THE MAYA

The heart of Mayan civilization was the highlands of Guatemala. From here the Maya spread throughout much of Central America and Southern Mexico. At the civilization's height, Mayan territory measured approximately 324 000 km² and included the modern-day countries of Guatemala, Honduras, and Belize, the western part of El Salvador, and a number of states in Mexico. The Mayan territory was geographically very diverse and can be divided into three regions: the Southern lands, the Central territory, and the Northern province.

The Southern lands included the mountainous highlands of Chiapas, Guatemala, and Honduras, and the Pacific coastal plain of Guatemala and El Salvador. This is a hospitable region, with fertile soils, a moderate climate, abundant wildlife, and natural resources, such as wood for fuel and stone for building. Although Mayan centres developed in the valleys and on the tablelands of the Southern lands, they did not experience the same cultural growth as the other areas. The Southern lands were valued because the golden-green feathers of the quetzal, used by the Maya in ceremonial dress, came from this area, as did jade and obsidian.

The Central territory was located in Tabasco, the Peten district of northern Guatemala, western Honduras and Belize. This is a lowland region threaded by lazy rivers and covered by dense rain forests of mahogany, cedar, rubber, ceiba, breadnut, and other trees. The climate is very humid, with a high annual rainfall and average temperatures of 24°C in January and 30°C in May. The heavy rain leaches nutrients from the soil so that land cleared for farming is exhausted within two or three years. Even though the region is one of the least hospitable in the western hemisphere, this was the region where the Maya attained their greatest cultural achievements, building astonishing cities like Palenque, Tikal, and Copan.

The Northern province took in the Mexican states of Campeche, Quintana Roo, and Yucatan. This is the driest of the three regions, almost totally lacking rivers, and the vegetation consists of scrub thickets and brushwood. A few natural limestone wells, or *cenotes,* and small inland lakes are the main sources of fresh water. There are few natural resources and the chalky limestone soil supports only meagre crops. Monthly temperatures average 22°C in January and 27°C in July. In spite of these obstacles, Mayan culture flowered in the Northern province and Chichen Itza was an important Mayan centre.

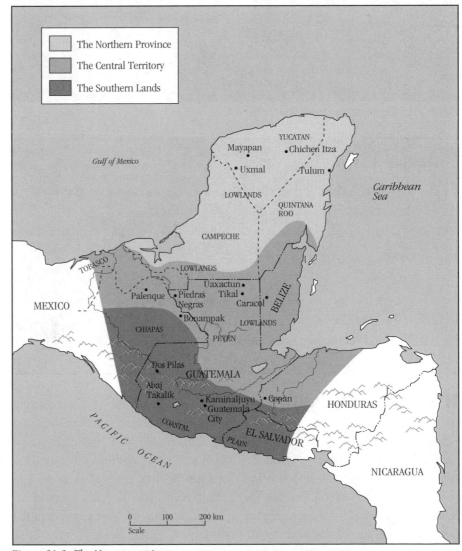

Figure 21-2 *The Mayan empire*

Figure 21-3 *The rain forest of Belize*

REFLECT AND ANALYZE

1. What are the most significant geographical characteristics of the three regions associated with the Mayan world?

2. Why is it surprising that the Central region was the area of highest cultural achievement?

3. Using an atlas, find out how many people, today, live in the three regions of the Maya. Which area has the greatest population? What is the land use in each area? Compare today's patterns of population and land use with Mayan patterns.

HISTORIAL OVERVIEW

Between 300 and 900 CE the Maya developed the most advanced civilization yet seen in the Americas. We have very little written source material on Mayan culture, because the Spanish conquerors of the sixteenth century destroyed almost all the historical records. Non-European and non-Christian civiliza-tions were viewed with the most profound distrust by the Roman Catholic Church and the Spanish government. Only three Mayan manuscripts, or **codices,** survived des-truction by the Spanish, all in a poor and fragmentary state. The major source of in-formation about the Maya comes from the findings of archaeologists. Discoveries of Mayan art, temples, palaces, sculpture, paint-ing, and pottery, and the inscriptions on stelae have helped to solve some of the mysteries associated with the Maya.

PRE-CLASSIC PERIOD 600 BCE-300 CE

Mayan cities first began to appear in the highlands of Guatemala during the Pre-clas-sic period, evolving from the agricultural villages of earlier times. Each Mayan city and its surrounding area formed an independent city-state. The first buildings of any size began to be constructed about 100 BCE. Over the next three hundred years, some of the Mayan city-states grew into large cities like Kaminaljuyu and Abaj Takalik, containing stone temple-pyramids, palaces, terraces, houses, and plazas. The pyramids, used for religious ceremonies, were located in the centre of the city surrounded by large open plazas. Temples were built on the tops of the pyramids. The remains of burials, which in-cluded many offerings, have been found beneath the pyramids and plaza floors.

As the communities grew in size, the population of each city-state began to be strictly regulated according to social class. At the pinnacle were the rulers and the priests, who dominated a large population of peasants living on the outskirts of the city-state. Slaves made up the remainder of the population and performed much of the physical labour.

Each city-state depended upon an economy that was based on agriculture and trade. Corn was the staple food, but farmers also raised many kinds of fruit and vegeta-bles and cultivated cotton and cocoa. Trade in commodities such as salt, cloth, animal skins, and jewellery was conducted between the various Mayan centres and with other peoples in central America.

PERSPECTIVES ON THE PAST
The Olmec

The Maya were not the only civilization to develop in Central America, nor were they the first. The Olmec, a pre-Mayan civilization, first appeared in 1200 BCE and reached their height about 800 BCE. What indications are there that the Olmec may have been the ancestors of the Maya?

The Olmecs lived in the lowland area of Tabasco and Veracruz along the southern shores of the Gulf of Mexico. Archaeological evidence has shown that the Olmec lived in farming villages on the outskirts of religious centres, which were built on hills of mounded earth, topped by temples. They worshipped a jaguar god and had developed a hieroglyphic form of writing, a counting system that included zero, and a calendar.

Figure 21-4
Olmec basalt head from La Venta

The most important Olmec archaeological discovery was made in the 1930s at La Venta, a site that likely flourished from 1500-400 BCE. Four gigantic basalt sculptures of human heads were discovered at La Venta. The largest is nearly 3 m in height. The presence of such colossal monuments suggests a government powerful enough to organize a large and skilled labour force.

The Olmec temple-pyramids also required the same kind of labour force. The Olmec lacked metal tools, draft animals, and the wheel. The necessary stone for these buildings would have had to be brought from quarries at least 100 km away. The only ways to transport the stone would have been to drag it on log rollers through the jungle, and float it down rivers where possible.

Sometime before 300 CE, possibly due to volcanic activity, or to incursions into the area by newcomers from Mexico, the Maya seem to have shifted away from the Guatemalan highlands, and moved into the Central territory and the Northern province, thus beginning a new phase in their history.

REFLECT AND ANALYZE

1. What were the common characteristics of Mayan centres as they began to emerge in the Pre-classic period?

2. Why does it seem likely the Maya were influenced by Olmec culture?

3. Do some research on the methods the Maya used to build their temple-pyramids. Using diagrams, explain how it was done.

4. As a Spanish priest accompanying the soldiers in the conquest of the Maya, explain why you believe that the records of Mayan civilization should be destroyed. As a Mayan noble, explain the importance of these records.

THE CLASSIC PERIOD
300 CE - 925 CE

The shift away from the highlands of the Southern lands was accompanied by tremendous growth in both culture and population. In a relatively short time, about 80 Mayan centres were constructed in the Central lowland region, and dozens more were built in the Northern region. This was the beginning of the Classic period.

The Classic period of Mayan history was the "golden age" of Mayan civilization. Civilization flourished first in the Peten area of Guatemala and adjacent areas of Belize in cities such as Tikal, Dos Pilas, Caracol, Uaxactun, Copan, Piedras Negras, and Palenque. Later, Mayan civilization flourished in the semi-arid scrub lands of northern Yucatan at Uxmal,

THE MAYAN WORLD: A DEVELOPMENTAL TIMELINE

	THE PRE-CLASSIC PERIOD **600 BCE-300 CE**	**THE CLASSIC PERIOD** **300 CE-925 CE**
POLITICAL DEVELOPMENTS	• the Olmec exert a strong influence on the development of the early Maya • some political centralization occurs • some social stratification occurs among the population	• the number of Mayan sites expands to over 80 • a hereditary nobility and priesthood are in charge • Tikal, Copan, and Palenque become important Mayan centres • a period of decline sets in, characterized by an absence of new building or sculpture • major Mayan centres are abandoned
CULTURAL DEVELOPMENTS	• clay figurines begin to portray Mayan ethnic features • stone temples and pyramids are constructed • early development of ideographic writing takes place • carved stelae are constructed • elaborate burials are part of the culture	• carved stelae time records appear at 20, 10, and 5 year intervals • flowering of art, architecture, sculpture, painting, and learning • many pyramids are built • the frescoes are painted at Bonampak • written records or codices are developed • two numerical systems emerge • the *Tzolkin* and *Haab* Calendars are perfected
TECHNOLOGICAL/ECONOMIC DEVELOPMENTS	• game is pursued and agriculture includes maize, beans, and pumpkins, as well as cotton and cocoa • trade in pottery and others items occurs	• many roads are built for trade and communication • the corbel or false arch is developed • slash-and-burn agriculture is supplemented by intensive cultivation • specialized occupational groups appear in the city-states and craft guilds develop • extensive trade routes throughout Mesoamerica are developed

THE POST-CLASSIC PERIOD
925 CE-1250 CE

- new political influences are introduced into the area by the Toltec
- a series of political alliances are formed
- Chichen Itza achieves its splendour and is then destroyed
- Tulum flourishes along the eastern coast of the Yucatan peninsula

THE PERIOD OF DECLINE
1250 CE-1546 CE

- increasing Mexican influence among the Maya
- Mayapan dominates the Yucatan
- there are internal revolts in Yucatan and Guatemala
- Cortez reaches Cozumel in 1519
- the Spanish complete their conquest of the Maya in 1546

- some Mayan cultural continuity is maintained in the Yucatan peninsula
- a Mayan-Toltec style of architecture is adopted
- Maya begin to worship Kukulcan, a Toltec god

- declining standards in art and architecture
- new sculptural motifs reflect new cultural influences

- populous cities based on agriculture continue
- trade continues to thrive

- the economy begins to falter from the impact of regional wars
- population declines as a result of contact with European diseases

THROUGH THEIR EYES

The Stelae of Tikal and Uaxactun

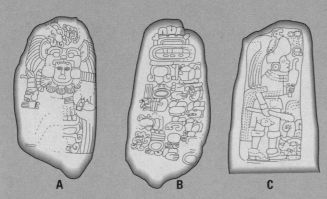

Figure 21-5
A *Stela 4 from Tikal, front view*
B *Stela 4 from Tikal, back view*
C *Stela 5 from Uaxactun*

The gylphs on these two stelae, both from the Peten region of Guatemala, provide some insight into the early history of Tikal, one of the most important Mayan centres of the Classic period. What kind of information is recorded? What details from these stelae would historians find especially interesting? How do you think Smoking-Frog was able to acquire power over Curl Snout?

Both stelae tell of a great military victory by Tikal over the city of Uaxactun on 16 January 378 CE. The victorious ruler, the first king of the city of Tikal, was Jaguar Paw. His brother, Smoking-Frog, was the war chief who planned the battle and oversaw the victory.

According to the glyphs carved on Stela 4 at Tikal, Curl Snout succeeded his father Jaguar Paw on 13 September 379 CE and began a reign that lasted for 47 years. The stelae in both Tikal and Uaxactun confirm that Smoking-Frog married into the Uaxactun ruling family and ruled Uaxactun for 18 to 26 years after the conquest by Tikal.

There is also a strong suggestion that Smoking-Frog was the overall ruler of Tikal as well as Uaxactun during this period. Curl Snout seems to have acted as Smoking-Frog's representative in Tikal. On Stela 4 at Tikal there is a reference to Curl Snout as the *yahau* or "noble of" Smoking-Frog. Other stelae provide additional evidence of this relationship. Stela 31 refers to the accession of Curl Snout in Tikal as taking place "in the land of Smoking-Frog."

The conquest of Uaxactun by Tikal was recorded in both cities on monuments erected to commemorate the event one hundred years after it occurred.

Chichen Itza, and Tulum, among others.

The Classic period is often divided into three time intervals. The first interval occurred between 300 to 625 CE. During this period, the amount of building taking place in Mayan cities increased. The Maya continually replaced earlier temple-pyramids with larger and grander ones. Another sign of the vigour of the period is the number of stelae that were erected. Stelae were free-standing stone monuments covered with carvings and hieroglyphic inscriptions that tell the story of important events. The number of carved stelae increased, and stelae construction took place more frequently, often at intervals of 20 years. Ceramics also became a popular art form during the Classic period. In addition to functional vessels for domestic and ritual use, thousands of ceramic figurines have been recovered from grave sites. These figurines depict musicians, ballplayers, women weaving cloth, and other such scenes from daily life.

Tikal, the largest Mayan city, was the most important centre of the early Classic period. Its population has been estimated at between 50 000 and 100 000, and it covered some 130 km². Tikal contained about 3000 major structures. There were six temple-pyramids in Tikal, one of which was a very lofty 69 m in height. Tikal has been more thoroughly excavated than any other Mayan city. The oldest Mayan inscriptions have been found at Tikal, dating from about 292 CE.

The second interval of the Classic period occurred between 625 and 800 CE. It was marked by a new elegance in art. Palenque became a city of refinement, noted for the grace of its stucco art, and Piedras Negras was noted for its fine statuary. Mayan centres like Dos Pilas stepped up the pace of stelae construction and the interval between the construction of stelae dropped to 5 years.

Figure 21-6 *A view of Tikal today, showing Temple 2 and the North Acropolis*

Mayan city-states were always on alert for possible attack by their enemies. They did not maintain standing armies but recruited peasants during times of crisis. War was usually seasonal, beginning in the dry season of October and ending before planting in May.

Mayan scouts were deployed in advance of a planned battle to determine the location and strength of the enemy. Based upon the scouts' reports, the Maya would then launch a sneak attack. Uttering wild cries, the warriors marched into battle with helmets and large shields. Their officers were resplendent in feathered head-dresses and flashing jewellery. Early in the battle, the main weapons used were the lance and the club. Hand-to-hand combat then followed using daggers and tridents (a wea-pon made from carving three sharp blades from a large seashell).

Many aspects of Mayan warfare were unusual compared to modern wars. Fighting ended at nightfall when the warriors retired for supper. The main goal of a Mayan raiding party was to capture enemy leaders and their warriors. Capturing the enemy leader signalled the end of a battle or raid. The captured leader and his officers were marched to the victor's city and offered for sacrifice. Ordinary warriors became slaves.

The third interval of the Classic period lasted from 800 to 925 CE. It was characterized initially by a rapid decline in artistic and intellectual activity. No new building occurred and some buildings were left half finished. By the end of the period the cities

Figure 21-7 *A copy of the stucco decoration at Palenque showing the king sitting on a two-headed jaguar throne. This copy is not entirely true to life because the original has been almost completely destroyed*

had been abandoned to the jungle, which gradually overtook them. A few Mayans remained in the area but their culture was of a much lower order. People ventured into the city-states only on rare occasions for ceremonies that were pale imitations of earlier ones. It is estimated that in the Central territory alone, a population of 3 million declined to 450 000. The reason for this rapid decline is one of history's great mysteries. Numerous hypotheses have been suggested.

One explanation is that the peasants revolted. Exploited and downtrodden by the ruling class, the peasants may have revolted against their rulers as a protest against the great social and economic gap between the Mayan nobility and commoners. They stopped producing food for the nobility so that the Mayan centres had to be abandoned.

Another explanation is that drought may have led to crop failure, malnutrition, disease, and widespread death. There is some evidence to support this claim. Skeletons unearthed from this period are smaller and show a high incidence of scurvy and rickets, diseases both associated with malnutrition.

It may have been that over-population was a significant factor in the decline of Classic Mayan civilization. As the populations of the various centres increased, it became more and more difficult to grow enough food to sustain the growing numbers. The Mayan may have had to disperse in an attempt to increase the food supply.

It is also possible that invaders from the north were responsible for Mayan decline. There is evidence in the 800s of increasing Mexican influence on the Mayan culture. Even though this outside influ-

Figure 21-8   *A Mayan battle scene from the Temple of Frescoes at Bonampak*

ence may not have been the sole cause of the collapse of Classic Mayan civilization, it might have hastened it.

New archaeological discoveries are bringing these traditional hypotheses into question. These discoveries suggest that there was a third class in Mayan society— a middle class. Middle-class tombs have recently been discovered in Caracol, a major Mayan city in Belize. This means that Mayan society may have been more complex than originally believed. If there was a middle class, then wealth would have been distributed more equitably in Mayan society and peasants would not have had the same cause for rebellion.

Additional finds from the Caracol expedition, as well as findings from excavations at Dos Pilas suggest the Maya

were much more warlike than previously thought. It is possible that warfare between Mayan city-states could have been a major cause of their decline. There is evidence that some time in the eighth century attitudes about war changed. War was no longer ritualistic, with the capture of enemy leaders as the primary focus. Instead, war became a campaign of conquest against neighbouring centres, involving attacks on enemy cities and the burning of their temples. It became a means of expansion and empire-building. In 562 CE, Tikal was conquered by Caracol and in 761 CE one of the cities that was controlled by Dos Pilas rose in rebellion. Eventually Dos Pilas was defeated and the city was abandoned. Similar examples of inter-city warfare throughout the Mayan territory might explain the general abandonment of other centres as well. Whatever the true reason the Mayan centres fell silent.

THE POST-CLASSIC PERIOD
925 CE - 1250 CE

Mayan culture continued in the Yucatan Peninsula after the collapse of the Classic period elsewhere. A cultural and artistic flowering occurred here during the Post-classic period. Among the important centres to develop during this period were Chichen Itza, and Uxmal.

Chichen Itza, located in north-central Yucatan, was one of the largest centres of continuing Maya culture in the Post-classic period. It covered an area of at least 500 ha, and became the most important Mayan centre in the Yucatan between 987 and 1194. In 987, a wave of Toltec people came to Chichen Itza from their desert empire north of Mexico City bringing with them their god Kukulcan, the Feathered Serpent. This Toltec god came to be worshipped at Chichen Itza by both the Maya and the invading Toltec. The architecture and monuments of Chichen Itza show the strong cultural in-fluence the Toltec had upon the Maya.

During this period the ruling families of several city- states in the Yucatan Peninsula formed a series of shifting alliances with each other. One such alliance was formed around 1000 between Chichen Itza, Uxmal, and Mayapan. In 1194, Mayapan betrayed the other partners in the alliance by capturing members of their nobility and holding them prisoner. Chichen Itza was deserted sometime between 1224 and 1244 and the peninsula came under Mayapan control.

THE PERIOD OF DECLINE
1250 CE - 1500 CE

The Period of Decline was a very confused period, about which very little is known. Most accounts come from the Spanish. Mayapan seems to have dominated the Yucatan until about 1441. Its control was marked by an effective central government, but one that was often harsh and abusive even toward its most friendly allies. Eventually Mayapan was attacked and destroyed. Thereafter, the Yucatan was divided into sixteen warring kingdoms which resulted in much social upheaval.

During the years 1250 to 1500, the Mexica were invading the Yucatan in in-

Figure 21-9 *Detail from a doorway at Uxmal, showing the influence of the Toltec culture on the Maya*

creasing numbers, causing additional up-heaval. Contact with this new cultural group appears to have changed many aspects of the blended Toltec/Mayan culture. It is thought, for example, that the Mexica introduced new attitudes about war, and that, as a result of their influence, the number of human sacrifices increased.

In addition to the internal disorders of the Yucatan Peninsula, there were also revolts in Guatemala. These revolts weakened the Mayan city-states in Guatemala just when they faced the challenge of the Spanish. The mighty walled fortress of Tulum, perched atop the craggy cliffs of the Quintana Roo coast of Mexico, was the last outpost of Mayan civilization. Settled late in the Post-classic period, when Mayan civilization was in decline, Tulum was still occupied when the Spaniards first arrived to reconnoitre and trade in 1518.

conquest by the introduction of European diseases like smallpox, measles, and influenza, to which the Maya had no immunity. It is estimated that some Mayan groups lost as much as 75 to 90 percent of their population to European diseases.

In addition, though the Spanish were in theory required to treat the Maya humanely, they in fact behaved with great cruelty. Spanish priests who accompanied the military were shocked by the vicious deeds of the soldiers, although, in their religious zeal the priests themselves often tortured people to enforce their conversion to Christianity. The Maya were forced into service to their foreign masters as slaves. All elements of Spanish rule made a concerted effort to eradicate Mayan culture, and to impose on the Maya European cultural and religious values.

When the Spanish Conquest was complete, the Maya did not disappear with the collapse of their civilization. Today, more than 3 million Mayans live in northern Yucatan, highland Guatemala, Belize, Honduras, and El Salvador and follow a lifestyle quite similar to that of their ancestors. They cultivate corn as their staple crop and live together in extended families in village compounds surrounded by stone walls. Many continue to revere their ancient gods.

REFLECT AND ANALYZE

1. Which centre was the most vital centre of Mayan culture during the Post-classic period and the Period of Decline? Explain the reasons for your choice.

2. What factors contributed to the Mayan decline after the Classic period?

3. Conduct further research to discover how the Toltec influenced Mayan architecture in the Post-classic period. Use illustrations to report your findings.

4. Write an obituary notice for the Mayan civilization, highlighting the strengths and weaknesses of their civilization.

THE SPANISH CONQUEST

In 1519 the Spanish conquistador Hernando Cortez reached the island of Cozumel, off the Yucatan coast, and the Spanish conquest of the region began. The Spanish swiftly defeated the Honduran and Guatemalan regions and were in control there by 1524. Rivalries amongst these kingdoms prevented them from putting forth any united defence against the Spanish. The Spanish shrewdly played them off one against the other.

The conquest of the Yucatan Peninsula was the most difficult for the Spanish. Although Spanish horses and weapons were very difficult for the Maya to overcome, the Spanish did face hardships which slowed their victories. They were unfamiliar with the territory, and they faced a thriving population skilled in warfare. The Maya used guerrilla and siege tactics, so that it took the Spanish until 1546 to complete the downfall of the Mayan civilization in the Yucatan.

The Spanish were aided in their

REFLECT AND ANALYZE

1. Why were the Spanish able to defeat the Maya?

2. How are contemporary Maya a valuable link in filling in many of the missing pieces in the history of Mayan civilization?

3. Do further research on the treatment of the Maya by the Spanish. Explain their actions in the context of the time in which they lived, and explain the difference in attitudes in today's society.

29 Silk landscape painting *The Emperor Guang Wu Fording a River* (16th Century CE).

National Gallery of Canada, Ottawa.

30 Detail from Chinese Taoist Fresco, *Lord of the Southern Dipper* (c. 604-531 BCE).

The Granger Collection, New York.

31 Bronze bird-shaped wine vessel (13th-11th century BCE) from the Shang dynasty.

The Granger Collection, New York.

32 Golden Japanese Buddha, Todaiji Temple (8th century CE).

Dallas & John Heaton/First Light.

Japan

33 ▲ Scroll painting (c. 12th century CE),
depicting a scene from Lady Murasaki's
The Tale of Genji.

The Granger Collection, New York.

34 Phoenix Hall (c. 11th century CE). It is the
only building that remains of Fujiwara
Palace.

Tomomi Saito/Dunq/ Photo Researchers, Inc.

35 Stucco figure of Mayan king, Palace,
Palenque (c. 7th-8th century CE).

D. Donne Bryant/DDB Stock Photos.

36 ▼ Elevated view of Tikal today showing
the ruins of the North Acropolis (right)
and Temple 2 (left), which date from the
late Classic period (c. 6th-10th century CE).

Simeone Huber/Tony Stone Images.

37 Olmecs, a pre-Mayan civilization, sculpted this gigantic basalt human head (1500-400 BCE). It is one of four heads discovered at La Venta.

D. Donne Bryant/DDB Stock Photos.

38 ▼ A fine example of a Mayan corbel arch, Governor's Palace in Uxmal, Yucatan (c. 6th-10th century CE).

D. Donne Bryant/DDB Stock Photos.

39 A French engraving of Atahuallpa (16th century CE).

The Granger Collection, New York.

40 ▲ Machu Picchu, the mysterious lost
city of the Inca, as it appears today.
The peak of Huayna Picchu can be
seen in the background.

Robert Fried/DDB Stock Photos.

41 Gold disks with human faces (date
unknown). They represent the Sun god
which was the Inca's most important
deity.

The Granger Collection, New York.

GOVERNMENT

THE HALACH UINIC

The Mayan ruler of a city-state, called a *halach uinic*, was considered so important that a cloth was always held up before his face to prevent anyone from speaking to him directly. He was the supreme authority and not only was in charge of the civil government, but also played a religious role. The Mayan system of government can be called a **theocracy**, since both religious and political control came under the authority of one person. The *halach uinic's* emblem of civil authority was a rounded sceptre with a carved head at either end. A ceremonial rod was the emblem of his religious authority.

Throughout Mayan history many rulers held the title *halach uinic*. At the time of the Spanish Conquest in the sixteenth century there were about twenty such rulers in the Yucatan Peninsula alone. The hereditary position was usually passed from father to son but, if the line died out, the Council of State selected a new ruler. If a minor assumed the role, the uncles on his father's side formed a regency and ruled in his name until he came of age.

The Council of State was made up of the regional chiefs of the neighbouring towns that surrounded a principal city-state. It also included the more important nobles and priests of the city-state itself. These officials were appointed to their positions by the *halach uinic*. In many instances they were his relatives. Their purpose was primarily to advise *the halach uinic* whose word was ultimately supreme.

SATELLITE CITY-STATES OR COLONIES

The independent Mayan city-states were linked by a common language and trade. Some of the larger centres came to control or dominate smaller local centres, treating them much like colonies. Frequently, large city-states purposely established satellite city-states or colonies in order to expand their territory and power. Eventually some city-states came to serve as the administrative centre for an entire geographic region. Archaeologists believe that two such periods of expansion took place, during the fifth and seventh centuries of the Classic period.

The smaller villages or towns controlled by a larger ceremonial centre were

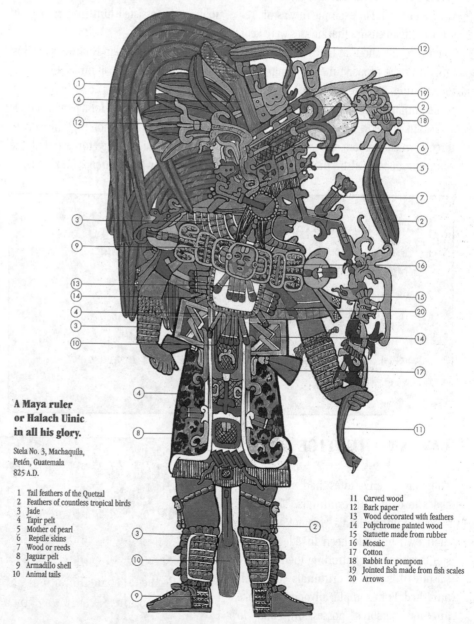

A Maya ruler or Halach Uinic in all his glory.

Stela No. 3, Machaquila, Petén, Guatemala 825 A.D.

1   Tail feathers of the Quetzal
2   Feathers of countless tropical birds
3   Jade
4   Tapir pelt
5   Mother of pearl
6   Reptile skins
7   Wood or reeds
8   Jaguar pelt
9   Armadillo shell
10 Animal tails
11 Carved wood
12 Bark paper
13 Wood decorated with feathers
14 Polychrome painted wood
15 Statuette made from rubber
16 Mosaic
17 Cotton
18 Rabbit fur pompom
19 Jointed fish made from fish scales
20 Arrows

Figure 21-10 *A Mayan ruler, a halach uinic, in ceremonial dress*

treated like conquered territories and were forced to pay tribute. They were administered by a local hereditary chief, called a *batab*, who was appointed by the *halach uinic* from among the ranks of nobles.

The *batab* dispensed justice, collected the tribute owing to the *halach uinic*, and oversaw all the administrative affairs of his village or town. For example, it was his responsibility to ensure that houses were kept in good repair and that fields were cut and burned at the proper time in preparation for planting. He also sentenced criminals and commanded his own soldiers.

Ranked below the *batab* were two or three town councillors, the *ah cuch cabob* who were appointed by the *halach uinic* from among the nobility. Each was in charge of a subdivision of the town and each was empowered to act as an intermediary between the townspeople and the *batab*. The councillors had a vote in local affairs and without their agreement nothing could be done. In addition, the *batab* had two or three appointed deputies, also nobles, who assisted him in carrying out his duties.

There were two kinds of war captains. The *batab* held his position as a war captain through heredity. The second official, the *nacom*, was elected for a period of three years from among the nobility. The *nacom* formulated the strategy for war but the *batab* actually led the troops into battle.

back to the owner or replaced. Sometimes a thief had to work as a temporary slave for the victim until the debt was paid off. On occasion, the cheek and forehead of the guilty person were slashed, leaving a permanent sign of disgrace.

The most serious offences were crimes against a member of your own family or clan. Murder was the most serious offence of all and it was considered to be a crime against the entire clan. The penalty for murder was death, carried out by having the criminal pierced with arrows while tied between two posts, arms in the air.

Some crimes were dealt with by the *batab*, but each Mayan city-state had a building designated as a court. A council of judges assembled there to deal with the criminal cases brought before them. The judges sat on mats on the floor with their backs to the wall to debate the cases. From time to time, runners were sent to a local temple to obtain a sacred decision from the local god. This usually came in the form of an oracle written out on an obsidian block. Sentences were carried out immediately. A guilty verdict against an accused person could result in instant torture or execution right on the central podium of the court.

REFLECT AND ANALYZE

1. What evidence is there to indicate that Mayan government was highly centralized?

2. Write a job description for a *batab*.

3. If you were a Mayan commoner, which government official would you probably approach with a problem? How likely is it that you would obtain a favourable result? Explain, giving reasons for your answers.

LAW AND JUSTICE

The Mayan city-states had strict legal codes to deal with criminals. The Maya believed that criminals were not acting on their own but had been invaded by evil spirits who were controlling their actions. Despite this belief, criminals were still punished. For example, anyone who broke another person's possession, had to replace it. Stolen goods had to be given

REFLECT AND ANALYZE

1. How did the Maya determine the guilt or innocence of an individual accused of a crime?

2. "The administration of justice was humane among the Maya." Do you agree or disagree? Give reasons for your answer.

3. Create a debate that might have occurred in a Mayan court, based on a crime of your own choice.

THE MAYA:
Society and Culture

*I*n *Mayan cosmology the earth was conceived as a flat, four-sided surface lying between thirteen heavens and nine underworlds, which were arranged in layers. At the geographical centre of the earth grew a huge ceiba tree, with smaller trees located at its four outlying corners. Each direction corresponded to a particular colour: white to the north, yellow to the south, red to the east, and black to the west. Specific deities were associated with these directions and colours, and a bird of the appropriate colour supposedly nested in the tree at each corner of the earth. Apparently the Maya envisioned the world as resting on the back of a gigantic crocodile floating in a lily pond...and they believed that the earth had been created several times in the past, only to be destroyed again by calamities.*

The Maya saw time, space, physical reality, and the supernatural as parts of an interdependent whole, in which gods and humans interacted constantly in many different ways. They also believed that human history was cyclical and that events that have occurred once will occur again. The cycles last more than five thousand years and end with a disaster of some sort. According to the Mayan calendar, the present cycle will end in catastrophe on 23 December 2012.

Figure 22-1
The Maya believed the ceiba tree to be the tree of life

RELIGION

GODS AND GODDESSES

The Maya were **polytheistic**, but historians are not certain how many gods and goddesses there were, although one Spanish source lists more than 150. Among the principal gods and goddesses was Hunab Ku, the supreme Mayan god, who seems to have been remote and impersonal. Very little is known about this god. Itzamna, or Lizard House, may have been the son of Hunab Ku. He was the supreme being of the earth and the sky, and the inventor of both the calendar and writing. Ixchel, his consort, was the mother of all of the other gods. She was the goddess of the moon, of healing, and of pregnancy. Chac, the rain or storm god, was the one with whom farmers had the closest relationship, since he had the power to bring abundant harvest and life, or bad weather, famine, and death.

Besides these principal gods and goddesses, the Mayan pantheon held a great many others. There were gods and goddesses associated with the

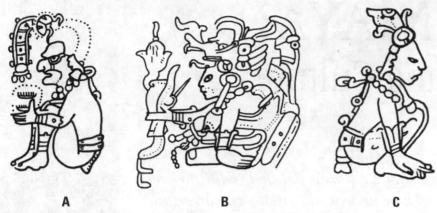

Figure 22-2 *Depictions of* A) *Itzamna,* B) *Moon Goddess,* C) *God of Corn*

sky and the underworld. Other deities controlled day-to-day activities. There were gods associated with death, war, wind, corn, medicine, and even a god of the North Star, who watched over travellers. Mayan gods were unpredictable, and could either help or hinder humans.

RELIGIOUS BELIEFS AND PRACTICES

Since the gods were capricious, only specially trained people could hope to interpret the will of the gods or find ways to please them. Mayan priests were held in high regard and were part of the ruling elite. Some Spanish sources refer to the highest ranking priests as *Ah Kin,* whose functions included divination, prophecy, medicine, and ceremonial practices. They also acted as teachers and instructed candidates for the priesthood in astronomy, mathematics, hieroglyphics, calendrics, and rituals.

The offices of Mayan priests were hereditary, and they were succeeded by the priests' eldest sons or close male relatives. The second sons of nobles could also enter the priesthood if they were so inclined.

Mayan gods were demanding, and it was essential that the priests carry out the correct ceremonies, rituals, and sacrifices at the proper times. Festivals were held at various times throughout the year in honour of the different gods. The most important festivals were those held to honour the gods associated with the harvest. On such important occasions, everyone came to the city-state. They fasted and performed purification rituals, then offered prayers, chants, and dances in honour of the god. Animals such as jaguars, dogs, turtles, and turkeys were sacrificed. Afterwards, there was much feasting.

At times, during natural disasters, human sacrifices were offered to appease the angry gods. It was believed that human blood was essential to sustain the gods. Sacrificial victims were selected from amongst orphans, slaves, captured enemy warriors, or criminals. Children were sometimes stolen from nearby towns or purchased for a handful of beads and offered for sacrifice.

The sacrificial victim was led up the steps of the pyramid, stretched over an altar stone, and, while the arms and legs were restrained, the heart was cut out with an obsidian blade. The corpse was disposed of and idols of the gods were anointed with the blood of the victim. The sacrificial victims were honoured in Mayan society and could look forward to great rewards in their afterlife.

At Chichen Itza there is a great circular well more than 30 m across called the Sacred Cenote. The green, scum-covered surface of the water lies some 20 m below its rim. During Mayan times, the Sacred Cenote was devoted to Chac, the rain god. Precious stones and other objects were thrown into the well as sacrifices to Chac in times of drought. Jade, gold, wooden, and copper artefacts, and balls of copal incense have been recovered from the bottom of the well by archaeologists. The remains of humans, including children, have also been found. Likely they were sacrificed to appease Chac and ensure a good harvest.

Figure 22-3 *The Sacred Cenote at Chichen Itza, where offerings were made to Chac, the rain god*

DEATH

The Maya believed that the sky, or heaven, was arranged in thirteen layers above the earth. Each layer had its own god, dominated by Itzamna, the supreme being of earth and sky. The other realm, the underworld, or hell, was arranged in nine layers below the earth. This was a place of dread and terror where evil gods like the Jaguar God of the Night presided.

Death was feared, even though the Maya believed that worthy individuals who had earned the favour of the gods through proper behaviour would eventually make it to one of the thirteen heavens. When death appeared imminent, a priest was called in to hear the death-bed confession and to drive away any lurking evil spirits.

The traditional view was that elaborate burial customs were reserved for members of the upper class. They were buried in small, stone-lined vaults constructed below the plaza or under the pyramids and temples in the city. Fine pottery, furniture, artwork, jewellery, and ceramic figurines were buried along with the body. Commoners were buried with their tools, food, and drink, beneath the floors of their houses, which were then abandoned.

Recent excavations at Caracol, Belize, have caused historians to question the traditional view of burial customs. The graves of commoners containing jade, pottery, and ritual vessels have been found. The Caracol discoveries also revealed four members of a royal family sharing a tomb. Previously, scholars had believed that the elite received individual tombs.

This practice is called **primogeniture**.

The *ahkinob,* or priests, were particularly powerful members of the upper class. The priests had their own hierarchy. At the top was the *Ah Kin* or high priest. Below the high priest were assistant priests, and, at the lowest level, the local priests in charge of religion in the villages.

As well as playing an important role in the ceremonies of the city-state, the priests were also important in the activities of daily life. They studied the heavens at the day and hour of a child's birth, much like astrologers do today. They celebrated marriages and burials, and ran schools to educate young males of the nobility so that the history of the Maya would be perpetuated.

The *ah chembal uinicob* were the commoners. It is now thought likely that some sort of ranking system existed within the broad category of commoners. Artists, artisans, traders, and minor officials, with their specialized occupations, seem to have occupied a somewhat middle position. It may even have been that a separate middle class existed among the Maya. However, the vast majority of the commoners were farmers, who were also required to help build the city-states. They lived outside the city-state in villages close to their fields.

The *ppentacob,* or slaves, were at the bottom of the Mayan social pyramid. Some of the *ppentacob* were born into slavery, some became slaves as a punishment for crimes, and others were captured as prisoners during wars. Orphans became slaves too. Most slaves seem to have been criminals since the Maya had no jails.

Slaves did everything from the simple task of grinding corn to the heaviest and most dangerous work related to construction. Slaves were also used to carry trade

---

REFLECT AND ANALYZE

1. Why were priests able to exert such a powerful influence in both Mayan religion and society in general?

2. What role did sacrifice play in the religious rituals of the Maya?

3. Write a journal entry explaining the feelings that a captured warrior, a criminal, or a child might have had on learning that he or she had been selected for sacrifice.

SOCIAL STRUCTURE

The halach uinic was the highest ranking individual within each city-state, the most important government and religious figure in Mayan society. The term *halach uinic* means "true man" in the Mayan language.

The *almehenob* were the nobles, the members of the powerful ruling elite. They represented a very small percentage of the total population but they controlled the government, warfare, and commerce. Their administrative positions were hereditary. As an indicator of the power and influence of the nobility, their homes fronted on the central plaza of the city-state, in view of the great temple-pyramid.

Kinship relationships were patrilineal, traced through the male family line. In each generation one member of the family, usually the eldest male, was recognized as its head and inherited all its possessions.

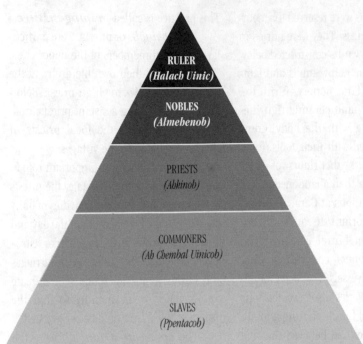

Figure 22-4 *The Mayan social pyramid*

Figure 22-5 *A recent painting done in the style of the Bonampak frescoes, showing the Mayan hierarchy*

goods over the long distances between the highlands and the coast, and to paddle the canoes that transported goods to various destinations along the coast.

REFLECT AND ANALYZE

1. Although there were no theoretical limits to the power of the halach uinic, what practical ones might have existed? Give reasons for your answer.

2. As a Mayan noble, justify the privileges you enjoy over commoners to a visitor in your city who has remarked on the monopoly of power and the prestige enjoyed by the nobility.

3. Which social group would you have preferred to be a member of if you were a Mayan? Explain the reasons for your answer.

EVERYDAY LIFE

THE FAMILY

Depending on their gender, newborn babies were presented to Mayan society by their grandfathers or grandmothers in a traditional ceremony. Nine objects associated with the role of a male or female were offered to the baby by a godparent to signify acceptance of the baby's role in Mayan society. Naming was particularly important and a priest was required to select an appropriate naming-day. A Mayan child was given four names. The first was a private name given at the naming ceremony. Children were known publicly by a nickname. Children also received two more names derived from their parents.

The Maya considered a flattened forehead and crossed eyes to be signs of physical beauty. To achieve this, a wooden frame was strapped to the heads of infants to elongate their skulls, and a ball of resin was dangled above their eyes to cause them to cross. In addition, the ear lobes, nose, and lips were pierced in readiness for personal adornments in later life.

Mayan girls usually married at the age of fourteen and boys at the age of eighteen. Most marriages were arranged by the groom's parents, often with the assistance of a matchmaker. It was important to consider ancestry and favourable astrological signs in the choosing of partners.

The bride's family paid a dowry to the

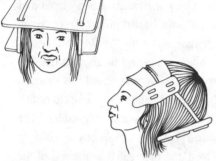

Figure 22-6 *Examples of the wooden frames used to elongate the skulls of Mayan infants*

EDUCATION

All children were trained from early childhood to obey the adult members of the family. Farmers' sons had little opportunity beyond learning how to farm. Formal education was a luxury reserved for the sons of the upper class who were taught reading, writing, and mathematics. Girls of both noble and common backgrounds were trained in the home, learning the skills appropriate to their social class. The daughters of nobles would be able to rely upon household slaves to perform many of the tasks that the daughters of commoners performed on a daily basis.

REFLECT AND ANALYZE

1. Why do you suppose that grooms had to work for the bride's family for the first few years after marriage? Explain your answer.

2. What customs or traditions associated with Mayan family life do you consider to be the most unusual? Why? Do we have any similar traditions in our society? If so, what are they, and why are they practised?

3. The status of women within Mayan society appears to have been inferior to that of men. Do you agree or disagree? Explain the reasons for your answer.

---

groom's family to seal the agreement. After the priest selected a favourable wedding date according to astrological signs, the wedding was held in the bride's home, followed by an exchange of gifts and a feast. Newly married couples lived with the bride's family, to whom the groom owed work, for a maximum of seven years. Only then could the married couple establish their own household.

The Maya lived in extended family units in village compounds. The extended families were combined into larger groups called lineages whose members claimed descent from a common ancestor. Lineages formed even larger units called clans whose members claimed descent from an even more distant ancestor. There were strict taboos against the marriage of two people with the same paternal name, since all people with this name were originally members of the same family.

URBAN AND RURAL LIVING

The city-states were ceremonial centres where the Maya met for political, religious, and social events, or to receive instructions from their leaders in times of emergency. As a result, the most important structures in a city-state were those that served the interests of the government leaders and the priests.

Almost all of the Mayan city-states shared common characteristics. At the heart of each was a central plaza where citizens could meet. It was fronted by one or more temple-pyramids for worship and the palaces that served as the official residences for the *halach uinic*, the high priests, and other leading nobles. All other buildings were constructed in blocks back from the central plaza.

The residences of upper-class citizens were usually divided into two by the construction of an interior partition. This partition, often stuccoed and decorated with paintings, separated the public and private parts of the house. The front of the house served as an entrance hall, a living room, and a reception hall for guests. The rear section was for family use. The furniture consisted of benches, low tables, mats, and wooden beds covered with rush mats.

Slaves maintained the house and prepared meals. The urban upper class ate well. Although their diet was similar to that of the lower classes, the variety and quality of food was much better. They could afford more meat and a wider variety of vegetables to supplement their diet. Among the more popular meat dishes were turkey, venison, and *tzome* a type of

Figure 22-7 *Members of the upper classes dressed elaborately. They wore head-dresses made with a wicker or wooden framework fashioned to represent an animal or god. They also wore many collars, necklaces, wristlets, anklets, and knee bands made of feathers, jade, shells, jaguar teeth, gold, or copper, in addition to nose ornaments, earrings, and lip plugs of jade, stone, or obsidian*

hairless, barkless dog raised for meat.

The village homes of the peasants were little more than huts, usually built to last for one generation. In the lowlands, huts were made of wood or **wattle and daub** over a stone foundation. Roofs were constructed of thatched palm. In the highlands, there was some variation since stone was more plentiful. In these areas the walls were sometimes constructed of rubble and stucco was applied to the surface. Grasses were more often used for the roof than palm.

The huts offered very little privacy since the only door was a blanket draped across the entrance. The interior was small and divided into two sections by a wall or screen. One section served as the bedroom and the other section functioned as the kitchen with a hearth in the centre of the floor. Smoke from the fire was supposed to escape through the roof but often drifted through the building. Furnishings in the huts were sparse, with a few wooden tables to hold storage pots, cooking utensils, and tools, and a few wooden stools for seating.

Village women rose well before sunrise to prepare the morning meal, which might consist of little more than *posol,* a drink made from crushed corn boiled in water, and leftover *tortillas*. With breakfast completed, the men set out for the *milpas*, or fields, to clear, plant, weed, irrigate, or harvest, depending on the season.

The women spent the morning in the time-consuming task of preparing corn for making *tortillas*. The corn was dried and shelled and placed in a cooking pot with enough water and lime to soften the kernels. After boiling, the mixture was set aside to stand overnight. The following morning it was washed free of hulls and ground by hand. Once ground, it was ready for use. A daily supply of *tortillas* was prepared and kept hot in a heated gourd. The average adult male ate twenty *tortillas* at a meal.

There were three meals each day, but only the late afternoon meal was substantial. It might include a stew of meat or fish with added herbs and vegetables. The *tortillas* were used like spoons to scoop up the food and then eaten at the end of the meal. Seasonal fruits were served for dessert. A third light meal was served later in the evening before the family retired for the day.

REFLECT AND ANALYZE

1. What architectural characteristics were common among all of the Mayan city-states?

2. What were the visible signs that identified the wealthy nobles of a typical Mayan city-state?

3. Sketch and label the steps involved in preparing corn for use as food.

THE ECONOMY

AGRICULTURE

Farmers paid tribute to the nobility in both goods and services. They gave up a portion of each crop or paid in commodities like salt, cloth, honey, fruit, and domestic animals. In addition, they performed physical labour as builders, constructing or repairing city buildings.

Maize or corn was the most important crop. In fact, the Maya depended so heavily upon the production of maize that they considered it to be a god. New cornfields, or *milpas,* were created from the dense jungle by slash-and-burn techniques. Farmers felled trees in a chosen area and then burned the brush and as many of the trees as possible to produce a corn field. The *milpa* was never cleared entirely because some large

THEN AND NOW

Chewing Gum

How was chewing gum first discovered? Why was chewing gum considered important by the Maya? What role did chewing gum play in unlocking the key to the Maya's past?

Chewing gum was first discovered by the Maya of southern Mexico. They found that *chicle,* a thick, milky liquid that oozed out of cuts in the wild sapodilla, an evergreen tree, hardened into a tasty gum. Chewing gum gained added significance among the Maya when it became an important part of Mayan mythology. One of their great cultural heroes, Kukulcan, the Feathered Serpent, who later became a god, was a gum chewer.

Under Spanish rule, knowledge of the gum was lost to the outside world for centuries. Only the forest dwellers of Mexico continued to use it.

About 1870, chewing gum was discovered independently in the United States by Thomas Adams. A few years later, William Wrigley also discovered it. Both decided to produce chewing gum as a product, which became extremely popular, and continues to be so to the present day.

The modern demand for chewing gum had an important side effect. Mayans increasingly ventured into the forests for the *chicle* which was in such high demand. It was on these treks that many of the surviving ruins of the great Mayan cities were discovered.

---

tree stumps always remained. The burning process fertilized the field by releasing nitrogen and potassium into the soil. Such fields were only productive for a few seasons. Farmers had either to look for new areas to clear or to leave the fields fallow until they had regained some nutrients.

Each step in the agricultural process was closely regulated by the priests, who calculated the auspicious dates for the various agricultural activities. Mayan farmers had no ploughs, draft animals, or farm implements except for a simple dibbing stick, which was a stick with a point hardened by fire.

Squash was frequently planted between the rows of corn since its broad leaves offered the young corn shoots protection from the sun. Many other crops such as beans, sweet potatoes, pumpkins, chili peppers, avocados, tomatoes, and groves of fruit trees were planted as well. Breadfruit trees were planted as a reserve source of food in case the corn crop failed. Cacao and cotton were grown as cash crops and used for trading.

Domestic animals like cows, pigs, goats, chickens, and sheep were unknown. The only animals raised were turkeys, guinea pigs, ducks, and edible dogs. Bees were raised for honey, particularly in the Yucatan Peninsula. Any surplus farm produce was sold by the Mayan farmers at the city markets.

Many Mayan experts have suggested that the yield of slash-and-burn agriculture would not have been sufficient to support the large Mayan population. An increasing body of evidence shows that the Maya also practised intensive agriculture. In the lowlands, the Mayans increased the amount of arable land by building raised fields and drainage ditches from land that had

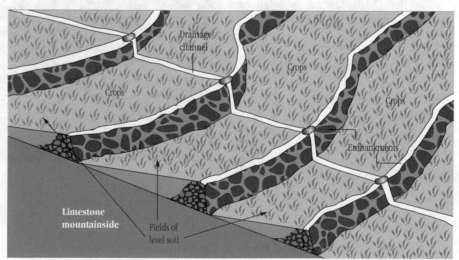

Figure 22-8 *Irrigation canals used to water terraced hillside fields*

formerly been swamp. They also terraced hillsides for agricultural use, and built irrigation canals to water the terraced fields. Aerial photography and radar surveys show widespread canal systems and the grids of raised fields stretching out between drainage channels.

The Maya hunted deer and wild boar using dogs and clubs. Birds were hunted using blow-pipes and pellets of baked clay. Fish were caught using a variety of techniques. An interesting one involved building a dam across a stream and placing a narcotic drug in the water above the dam. The stupefied fish were then scooped from the water by hand as they floated to the surface.

INDUSTRY

The Maya produced pottery and jewellery for household use and for trade. Artisans fashioned the jewellery from jade, copper, gold, and silver, although copper was scarce and gold was used chiefly for religious artefacts. Woven baskets and hampers were also important domestic products as well as trade goods.

By the Classic period, specialized occupational groups had appeared in the Mayan city-states. Members of these groups formed guilds to protect and promote their interests. There is some archaeological evidence to suggest that occupational guilds formed residential groups as well. This development may have led to the rise of a middle class in most of the city-states, although this has not been proven.

TRADE

The Mayan economy depended to a great extent on trade. The Maya obtained a wide range of goods through trade which lead to the evolution of another specialized occupational group as extensive trade routes were developed throughout meso-America.

There were different kinds of trade routes. Some were localized within one geographic zone, such as a highland valley. Others were long-distance trade routes connecting different environmental zones. There were three important long-distance routes. The southern route linked central Mexico to Central America, running along the Pacific coastal plain. The central route ran through the Peten area of Guatemala, and the northern route followed the Yucatan coast. These major trade routes were connected by a number of secondary routes.

Trade had a major impact on the development of the Maya. The north-south trade routes helped to tie the Mayan area together. As well, because of their position between Mexico and the remainder of Central America, and their wealth of jadeite, obsidian, salt, and quetzal feathers, the Maya were able to develop a role of intermediary in the transfer of goods between the two areas. Trade allowed some Mayan centres like Tikal to acquire a great deal of power, prestige, and wealth because its geographical location allowed it to control important trade routes. Finally, trade allowed the Maya to acquire luxuries from peoples of more remote cultures, such as copper bells from central Mexico, gold dishes from Panama, and pearls from Venezuela.

Trade was usually conducted through bartering where goods were traded for goods. Sometimes cocoa beans were accepted as currency. The beans were scarce and spoiled quickly—both excellent qualities for currency—making them difficult to hoard. For localized trade, goods were transported to their destinations on the backs of slaves. In the long-distance coastal trade, canoes large enough to hold forty people were used to transport goods.

REFLECT AND ANALYZE

1. How have recent archaeological discoveries changed thinking about Mayan agricultural practices?

2. Explain why trade was so important to the economic, political, and cultural development of the Maya.

3. Do some research on the Mayan trade routes, and then write a series of journal entries as a trader on one of these routes. Recount the details of your trip, and illustrate your journal.

THE ARTS

PAINTING

The Maya used vegetables and minerals to produce colours for their paints, and they painted both the inside and outside of their buildings. Among the most common depictions in their paintings were those of nobles engaged in the rituals of their office. In some instances rulers were portrayed in their magnificent head-dresses and elaborate jewels, holding the symbols of their authority. On other occasions the rulers were depicted seated on thrones, being carried on litters by attendants, or receiving slaves or tribute. Few good examples of Mayan painting have resisted the harshness of the elements over the centuries.

The best examples of Mayan painting were discovered at Bonampak, Mexico, in 1946, where three rooms of murals have survived. Their historical importance is significant since these murals depict vivid scenes of everyday Mayan life rather than the rituals usually depicted in other ancient Mayan murals.

In the first room of the Temple of the Frescoes are the figures of richly costumed priests, nobles, musicians, and strangely masked impersonators. In the second room, opposing armies are locked in furious battle, and prisoners of war are being judged by chieftains. The third room is adorned with magnificent paintings of dancers in exotic costumes, an orchestra, and scenes of human sacrifice.

POTTERY

Domestic pottery consisted of the pots, tumblers, earthen bowls, and plates needed daily in the home. Since these were clay items used for cooking and preserving food, it is assumed that they were produced by Mayan women. Ritual pots and tumblers, as well as figurines of the gods, are thought to have been made by Mayan men.

Potters used local clay and produced their works by hand since they had no potter's wheel. A variety of design and ornamentation was used, with each piece differing from the next. Pottery not intended for domestic use was fashioned to glorify the gods. Most of this pottery was located in temples and seldom viewed by the general population. It was intended only for the eyes of the gods and the priests.

Styles changed from time period to time period, and were also influenced by styles from other cultures. The late Classic period showed great richness and variety in style with carved, engraved, or painted decorations in blue, purple, yellow, and flesh colours. The motifs include geometric symbols, glyphs, animals, vegetables, and human figures. During the Post-classic period, ceramics were pre-

Figure 22-10 *Vessel from the Classic period, with hieroglyphic captions and a depiction of a noble lord and lady preparing to dance*

dominately orange with black geometric motifs. Flowers and human and animal heads were also often represented in decoration. Tripod (three-legged) vessels became increasingly common.

Figure 22-9 *Musical scene from the Bonampak frescoes*

WRITING

The Mayan system of writing used hieroglyphic symbols rather than words. However, instead of representing objects graphically, as in the case of pictographic writing, the Mayan glyphs are **ideographic**, representing symbols or sounds. Since certain glyphs represent sound values, many linguists believe that the Maya were on the road to developing alphabetic and phonetic writing.

The glyphs were square with rounded corners. Some were simple while others were quite complex. The symbol for water was a jade bead, because both water and jade are green in colour and both are highly valued.

Forty years ago, no one was able to decipher the Mayan glyphs, but today linguists understand the meaning of more than 800 of them, including the symbols for numbers, colours, gods, and ruling dynasties. This has increased our awareness of

Figure 22-11 *Carved stucco hieroglyphs from the Temple of Inscriptions at Palenque*

the Maya considerably, particularly in the areas of history, astronomy, religion, and rituals. Many hundreds of glyphs still remain a mystery.

The glyphs were inscribed on stone stelae, altars, steps, panels, the walls of public buildings, and pottery. Each glyph represented a complete word, and they were arranged in double vertical columns to be read from top to bottom and from left to right. Painted glyphs were also inscribed in books or codices. These are sometimes more difficult to read because they are smaller in size and the blank spaces between words were decorated, making it more difficult to distinguish the words.

Mayan codices were made from a coated bark paper. The inner bark of the wild fig tree was soaked in water, peeled, beaten, mixed with natural gum, and cut into strips 4 cm long. The strips were then coated with lime and allowed to dry. To construct the book, the strips were joined together to a length of approximately 6 m. The pages were then folded like an accordion and a wooden cover was fixed to the front.

Only three codices survive. The Dresden Codex deals with Mayan astronomy and religion and dates from the Classic period. It was taken from Central America to Europe during the sixteenth century as a gift to Charles I, the Emperor of Germany. It is the smallest of the three surviving codices but probably the finest. There are thirty pages in total and the full size of the codex when unfolded is 3 m by 51 cm.

The Madrid Codex was found in Madrid between 1860 and 1870. It is believed that Hernando Cortez took it to the royal court of Spain from Central America. The codex describes ceremonies held by the

Figure 22-12 *A page from the Dresden Codex*

Maya. The Paris Codex was unearthed in Paris in 1860, lying in a basket of rather worthless documents in the National library. Unfortunately, it is incomplete and in poor condition.

ARCHITECTURE

The imposing cities of the Maya were more than mere centres for rituals. Mayan buildings were very large, well-designed, and elaborately decorated. Important buildings were elevated on pyramids or platforms, and both the exteriors and interiors were painted. Nevertheless, the interiors were left plain. Palaces, for example, consisted of a maze of many tiny rooms divided by partitions.

Every city contained a ball court, in which a game called *pok-a-tok*, not unlike basketball, was played. Most of the cities contained sweat baths, artificial reservoirs. underground cisterns, storage places, and burial vaults. Drainage systems carried off excess water, and aqueducts have been found at some sites. Most cities also had buildings that served as observatories. The Maya also built many roads and causeways, as well as irrigation systems. The labour involved in building was enormous. Tons of stone had to be quarried and hauled to the city on rollers, often over very long distances. Wood, stone, and fired clay bricks were also common building materials.

Although the chief expression of Mayan architectural genius is found in the stone buildings of the cities which reached their peak during the Classic period, the Mayans never discovered how to build a

INNOVATIONS
El Castillo: Chichen Itza

What details of construction make El Castillo at Chichen Itza so innovative? Were El Castillo and similar temple-pyramids in other Mayan city-states as innovative as the pyramids of ancient Egypt? Why or why not?

One of the most visited of all of the Mayan ruins are those of El Castillo, a Post-classic temple-pyramid at Chichen Itza. El Castillo is a large four-stairway pyramid with a temple on top, dedicated to Kukulcan. It dominates the northern part of Chichen Itza. El Castillo's sloping sides measure 24 m in height. The balustraded stairways on each side of the pyramid contain 91 exterior steps, for a total of 364 steps. When the additional step to the upper platform of the pyramid is calculated, the total becomes 365, the total number of days in the Mayan year.

El Castillo was built for astronomical purposes. This becomes evident each year on the spring and autumn equinoxes. At about 3 p.m. on those days, sunlight projects on the wall of the balustrade of the northwest side forming a wavy motion. As the sun drops lower, seven isosceles triangles of light and shadow are formed from top to bottom, in the shape of a huge serpent more than 34 m long. The triangles join at the head of the serpent, constructed at the foot of the balustrade. This phenomenon lasts only 10 minutes but thousands of visitors are attracted to the site to witness the event on every occasion.

Figure 22-13 *El Castillo at Chichen Itza*

Figure 22-14 *A corbel arch from the Governor's Palace at Uxmal*

arches or corbels. Corbel arches were shaped like an inverted "V". They were constructed with a series of overlapping blocks, each projecting farther inward until the intervening space between the two walls was bridged by a single capstone. The only support came from the overlap with the block below, counterbalanced by the weight of the stone that held it in place.

Initially, Mayan builders used large stones extending through the entire width of the building's walls to carry the weight. Later, the walls were constructed using smaller stones set in concrete and faced with masonry, an innovation that increased the structural stability of the buildings and allowed for greater freedom in design. Both styles required thick walls and flat roofs made of wooden beams. As a result, the corbel arches lacked the strength to cover large areas. Sites could not exceed 3 m in width, which is why the interiors of Mayan palaces were a maze of tiny, narrow rooms.

true arch. This created problems when it came to constructing the roofs for their great palaces. The Maya constructed false

THE SCIENCES

MATHEMATICS

The Mayan achievements in science, particularly astronomy and engineering, would not have been possible if the Maya had not been skilled mathematicians.

They used two systems to record numbers. One system used stylized pictures of the heads of gods with the numerals remaining constant in their value regardless of their position in a codex or on a stela.

The second system, which was more commonly used, was similar in many respects to our decimal system. However, it was based on units of twenty rather than units of ten. While we use distinct symbols for the numerals zero to nine, the Mayans employed bar-and-dot notations in which the bar had a value of five and the dot had a value of one. A third symbol, a shell, was used to represent zero. The use of the concept of zero was a notable intellectual accomplishment. Some historians believe it to have been the earliest known instance of its use by any civilization anywhere.

Combinations of the bar and dot symbols represented the numbers one to nineteen. Beyond that point, the position of the numerals indicated the value, just as in the decimal system the positions to the left of the decimal point increase by powers of ten. In the Mayan system the values increased by powers of twenty as you moved from bottom to top.

ASTRONOMY AND THE CALENDAR

The Maya were fascinated with time and thought of it as a supernatural force under the control of the gods. They believed that periods of time (days, months, and years) were burdens that different gods carried on

REFLECT AND ANALYZE

1. Why are the frescoes found at Bonampak of such great historical importance?

2. Why would it be assumed that domestic pottery was made by women, and ritual pottery was made by men?

3. How important is it for our understanding of Mayan society that the rest of the Mayan hieroglyphics be deciphered?

4. Some archaeologists and historians consider the Mayan corbel arch to be a major architectural innovation. Others consider it to be a sign of the limitations of Mayan architecture. Debate the issue in your class.

5. Study the Mayan paintings in chapters 21 and 22, taking note of the stylistic details of the paintings. Paint one of your own, in the style of the Mayan paintings, showing a scene from daily life.

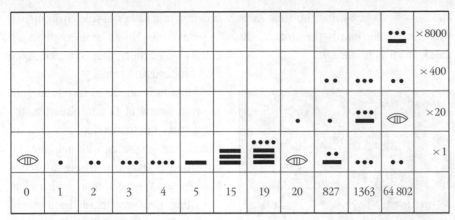

Figure 22-15 *The Mayan number system*

their backs for their allotted span of time, before passing the burden on to the next god. For example, the god of October would pass the burden on to the god of November at midnight on October 31. Some gods were kindly but others were not, so periods of good and bad times were the responsibility of whatever god was carrying the burden of time during those particular intervals. The priests were responsible for determining when beneficial or harmful deities would be ruling time.

The Mayan priest-astronomers studied the sky intently from the tops of their temple-pyramids, plotting the movements of the sun, the moon, and Venus without the use of any optical devices. They undertook intensive studies of lunar eclipses and their observations and records were so exact that they could predict eclipses. Their margin of error was extraordinarily small. The Maya calculated the length of the year at 365.2420 days. The current figure is 365.2422 days.

All of this was accomplished employing primitive techniques of astronomy. The Maya used a *gnomon*, a kind of sight made with a vertical rod, to determine the solstices. The rod produced the shortest shadow on the ground at midday on June 21 and the longest at midday on December 21. They took readings of the sky at sunrise from a fixed point throughout the year, noting the specific angle variations in the movement of the sun. Mayan astronomers calculated these angle variations by using buildings which were aligned to provide observation points, or by using two crossed sticks placed in front of them. All of their measurements were based on sightings, calculations of triangulation, and the movement of shadows.

All data was recorded, providing a database from which the Mayan astronomers developed their calendric system. The Maya used three different calendars—the *Tzolkin*, a 260-day sacred year; the *Haab*, a 365-day solar year; and the Long Count.

The sacred *Tzolkin* calendar contained twenty months of 13 days each. This calendar was reserved for divination and the planning of religious feasts and ceremonies.

The *Haab* solar calendar of 365 days was the agricultural calendar. It was divided into eighteen months, each containing 20 days which made up a *tun* of 360 days. The remaining 5 days were tacked on as an additional five-day month known as the *uayeb*, a period which the Mayans considered to be unlucky and which they devoted to religious ceremonies for the new year.

Each day had two names, one in the *Tzolkin* calendar and one in the *Haab* calendar. Cycles also existed. Seventy-three *Tzolkin* years equalled fifty-two *Haab* years. This 52-year period was called a Calendar Round, an interval comparable to our century. The Maya paid close attention to these time period relationships and calendar cycles. They were considered to have special significance, particularly when it came to building pyramids.

The outstanding achievement of Mayan calendrics was the Long Count, the most accurate of all the calendars developed in the ancient world. Composed of recurring cycles of nine interrelated periods, it allowed the Maya to keep track of enormous time spans. The basic unit was the day or *kin*, the smallest unit of time recorded by the Mayans. Beginning with the *kin*, the sequence was as follows:

		Days
20 *kins* (days)	= 1 *uinal*	20
18 *uinals*	= 1 *tun*	360
20 *tun*	= 1 *katun*	7 200
20 *katun*	= 1 *baktun*	144 000
20 *baktun*	= 1 *piktun*	2 880 000
20 *piktun*	= 1 *kalabtun*	57 600 000
20 *kalabtun*	= 1 *kinchiltun*	1 152 000 000
20 *kinchiltun*	= 1 *alautun*	23 040 000 000

A Mayan date in the Long Count was recorded relative to the total number of days that had passed since the beginning of the Mayan calendar, whose base date has been determined as 3114 BCE on our calendar. A date was usually composed of five numbers. The first recorded the *baktuns*, or the number of times that 144 000 days had passed. The second recorded the *katuns* (7 200 days), the third the *tuns* (360 days), the fourth the *uinals* (20 days), and the fifth the *kins*.

occurred in a rather hostile environment. In spite of this, Mayan centres exhibited a cultural continuity that spanned more than two thousand years.

From their origins as corn farmers in the rain forests of Central America, the Maya went on to develop a society of magnificent city-states, with monumental architecture and astonishing artworks. Nowhere was their skill more evident than in writing, mathematics, and astronomy. Their economy flourished on the basis of agriculture and an extensive trading network. Their accomplishments mark them as one of the most ingenious of the early civilizations.

REFLECT AND ANALYZE

1. Why were the Maya able to make such great advances in the field of astronomy?

2. Use the Mayan Long Count to calculate and record the date 1519 CE and the number system to represent the number 1294. Are there any disadvantages to using the Mayan system?

3. The Mayan priests kept their calendrical and astronomical knowledge a closely guarded secret. Explain why they would feel this was necessary.

LOOKING BACK

The Maya developed a remarkably sophisticated civilization in Central America stretching from the jungles of Guatemala, Belize, Honduras, and El Salvador to the lowlands of the Yucatan Peninsula in Mexico. Most of their greatest achievements

THE INCA:
People of the Andes

Ｈigh on the jungle slopes of the Andes sits the citadel of Machu Picchu, a stunning example of Inca engineering. The fortified city is located on a saddle of land between mountain peaks, about 650 m above the Amazon-bound Urubamba River. The only access to the city was a narrow road winding along the top of the mountains. Machu Picchu remained concealed from the eyes of the world for over four centuries until the American explorer/archaeologist Hiram Bingham discovered it in 1911 along with an 11-year-old local boy who acted as his guide.

Today, Machu Picchu, with over 40 ha of buildings, is the most completely preserved Inca city left, and one of the most important tourist attractions of the Inca world. Tourists reach the citadel first by a train that zig-zags up the mountain and then by a bus which manoeuvres the final hairpin turns before reaching the summit. The only level place in Manchu Picchu is the plaza in the centre of the city. A Sun temple stands on the highest point in the city. Scores of granite shrines, fountains, lodgings and steep stairways joining the different levels of the city make Manchu Picchu the most spectacular remnant of the Inca empire ever found intact.

Figure 23-1
Mystery surrounds the Inca city of Machu Picchu

The mystery associated with Manchu Picchu is that no official records of this city have ever been found. No one knows when it was built, or why it was deserted some time after the Spanish Conquest. It was never attacked. Hiram Bingham thought he had discovered Vilcabamba, the last stronghold of the Inca to succumb to the Spanish invaders. Further explorations proved this supposition to be incorrect. Many other suggestions have been put forth—perhaps it was the birthplace of the Inca empire or a military outpost. Possibly it was an imperial retreat. It is likely that we will never know with certainty.

THE LAND OF THE INCAS

The Inca, a nation of highlanders, developed an empire that extended throughout the Andean area, including contemporary Peru, Ecuador, Bolivia, north-west Argentina, and the greater part of Chile. The Inca empire consisted of three distinct geographical regions: the coastal desert, the highlands, and the eastern slopes of the Andes.

The coastal desert was a strip of land bordering the Pacific Ocean for almost the entire length of the empire. The cold Humbolt current of the Pacific kept this desert cool for many months of the year, but vegetation was sparse and the meagre animal life was limited to lizards, foxes, and owls.

Human settlers clustered around the oases formed by the many rivers descending from the Andes Mountains to the Pacific Ocean. The settlers developed irrigation systems to supply their fields with water, which allowed them to grow cotton, gourds, lima beans, squash, chili peppers, guava, avocado, and maize.

The highland area consisted of the parallel chains of the Andes Mountains stretching from Columbia to Chile. The warmer temperate valleys of the highlands supported small agricultural populations who grew maize, chili peppers, and squash. Potatoes, oca, and a grain called *quinoa* could be grown on the higher elevations. Herds of alpaca, llama, and vicuna were raised, as a source of wool and meat, on the *puna*, or tablelands, between the ranges. The *viscasha*—a large edible rodent—as well as deer and puma also flourished in the highlands.

The highland area was well supplied with water in most areas, containing many lakes and rivers. At 3810 m above sea level

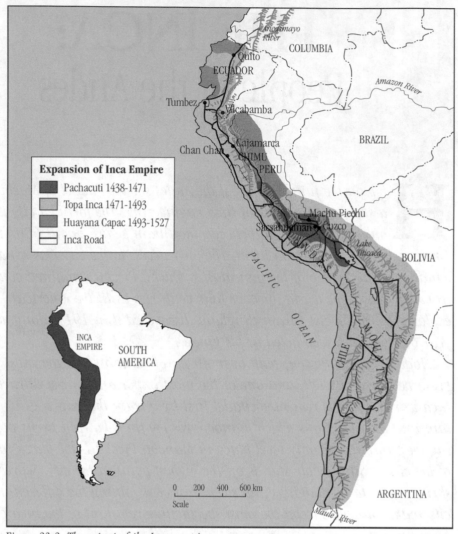

Figure 23-2 *The extent of the Inca empire*

and 8300 km² in area, Lake Titicaca is the largest lake in South America and the highest major body of water in the world.

The third geographic zone, the eastern

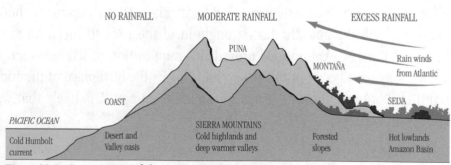

Figure 23-3 *Cross-section of the Andean area*

slopes of the Andes, consisted of forested slopes called *montana*, and a hot tropical rain forest area called *selva*. The *montana* was a transitional zone between the highlands and the rain forest. It abounded with deer, bears, and jaguar. Cacao, manioc, and tobacco could be grown on the *montana*.

The *selva* was a hot, swampy, insect-infested lowland, crossed by slow-flowing rivers that drain into the Amazon Basin. The Inca did not consider this tropical forest area a particularly hospitable region. Generally, the *selva* was important only for the production of a variety of vegetables and fruits.

The early Inca leaders devoted their energies to living at peace with their neighbours while consolidating their position in the valley. Under the guidance of these leaders, the Inca began to develop an economy based on agriculture. Inca pottery became more sophisticated, and weaving became an important craft. A school for boys was opened. The sixth Inca ruler was said to have created a standing army.

Once established in the Cuzco Valley, the Inca began to conquer neighbouring territory. Their conquests began as little more than disorganized looting expeditions, but by the time of the eighth ruler, Viracocha, the Inca had become a small but powerful state.

The Inca state was threatened on three sides. To the south were the Colla and Lupaca. To the west and north-west were the Quechua and the Chanca. The Inca most feared the Chanca. In an attempt to reduce the threat of invasion, the Inca formed an alliance with the Quechua, who acted as a buffer between the Inca and the Chanca. As a result of this alliance, Pachacuti, Viracocha's son, was able to defeat the Chanca when the Chanca invaded the Cuzco area.

REFLECT AND ANALYZE

1. Which region of the Inca territory would be best suited for settlement? Why?

2. Which region of the Inca territory would likely provide the greatest security from outside invasion? Why?

3. Using an atlas, find out how high and how steep the Andes Mountains are. Prepare a report on the effects on people of living at high altitudes.

HISTORICAL OVERVIEW

ORIGINS (1000 CE – 1200 CE)

Between 1000 and 1200, the Andean region was dotted with many isolated communities, each with its own culture and lifestyle. The Inca were merely one of these groups, living in the highland region near Lake Titicaca. Warfare between the various highland groups was common. Chimu, in northern Peru, was the only really powerful state in the area, and its capital of Chan Chan was the only urban centre of any consequence.

According to one version of Inca origin myths, four brothers and four sisters emerged from a cave about 29 km from Cuzco, followed by the people they ruled. The eight brothers and sisters were the children of the Sun god. After wandering for a number of years in search of a suitable site for settlement, only one brother, Manco Capac, was left alive. Manco Capac had a golden rod which he plunged into

the ground at intervals. In one place, this rod embedded itself deeply in the soil, indicating fertility, and the Inca decided to stay in this place. The place was Cuzco and the date was sometime around 1200.

THE PERIOD OF CONSOLIDATION (1200 CE – 1438 CE)

At first, the arrival of the Inca was resisted, but they overcame the opposition and established themselves in the Cuzco Valley.

REFLECT AND ANALYZE

1. Who was the legendary founder of the Inca, and what did he contribute to their early development?

2. How did the Inca become a powerful, though small, state? Of all the measures taken by the early Inca rulers, select one or two that you feel were the most important in allowing them to become powerful. Give reasons for your answer.

3. As a Chimu visitor to Viracocha's court, write a letter to your political leader assessing the role the Inca might play in the future.

THE INCA: A DEVELOPMENTAL TIMELINE

	ORIGINS 1000 CE-1200 CE	THE PERIOD OF CONSOLIDATION 1200 CE-1438 CE
POLITICAL DEVELOPMENTS	• Manco Capac, the legendary leader of the Inca, leads the Inca to the Cuzco Valley	• Inca rulers initially strive for peace with their neighbours • small scale conquests begin as looting expeditions • a standing army is formed • Viracocha forms the Inca into a small but powerful state
CULTURAL DEVELOPMENTS	• The Inca are less culturally advanced than other cultures on the coast	• folklore and poem stories gain popularity • music becomes important at the Inca court • the Inca develop skills in pottery-making and weaving • the first school is established
TECHNOLOGICAL/ECONOMIC DEVELOPMENTS	• The Inca begin to switch from a hunting to an agricultural economy	• agriculture becomes the mainstay of the Inca economy • the Inca use the quipu to keep records • mining begins

THE INCA EMPIRE
1438 CE-1532 CE

- Pachacuti extends Inca territory beyond the Cuzco Valley (1438–1471)

- Cajamarca, the most powerful province in the highlands, is added to the empire

- Pachacuti makes war a profession and military service compulsory

- a centralized system of administration is set up

- Topa Inca extends the empire from Ecuador in the north to Chile in the south (1471–1493)

- Huayana Capac extends the empire north of Quito, setting the imperial boundary at the Ancasmayo River (1493–1527)

- Pachacuti rebuilds the imperial capital at Cuzco, as well as the magnificent fortress of Sacsahuaman

- artisans, particularly weavers, goldsmiths, and silversmiths, gain prominence and expertise

---

- maize and corn develop as the most important agricultural crops

- terracing and irrigation are used to increase the amount of arable land available

- a network of roads is developed to link the regions of the empire

- the technology of building suspension bridges is developed

- a postal service is introduced to improve imperial communication

- extensive land and sea trading routes are developed

THE SPANISH CONQUEST
1532 CE-1572 CE

- Pizarro leads his first expedition into Peru (1524)

- Huayana Capac dies of smallpox (1527)

- civil war breaks out over control of the Inca empire and Atahuallpa emerges as victor (1532)

- Atahuallpa allows the Spanish to enter Cajamarca (1532)

- Atahuallpa is executed and the Spanish install puppet emperors (1533)

- an attempted Inca uprising against the Spanish fails (1536), and the leader flees to the mountains, setting up a rebel Inca state

- the Spanish execute Topa Amaru and bring to an end the existence of an organized Inca state (1572)

- Spanish looting of Inca artefacts begins immediately after Atahuallpa's capture

- European diseases ravage the Inca population

- Inca culture begins to break down

- the Inca are used as forced labour by the Spanish

- road and irrigation systems decline

- Inca lands are seized for Spanish settlers

THE INCA EMPIRE
(1438 CE – 1532 CE)

Pachacuti (1438–1471) was the first Inca ruler to gain and hold territory well beyond the home valley of Cuzco. After defeating the Chanca, he campaigned west and south to add more territory to the Inca empire. Pachacuti then stayed in Cuzco to organize the new territory the Inca had acquired. Meanwhile, his brother extended the Inca conquests to the north, making the Inca supreme in the highlands area.

As well as being a good soldier, Pachacuti was a superb planner, builder, and administrator. Under his leadership, the Inca empire took shape.

Pachacuti made war a profession for the Inca. Military service became compulsory for men between the ages of 25 and 50 in all parts of the empire. Whenever an army was needed, each province sent a contingent of soldiers under a local general. Armies as large as 250 000 were raised for particular campaigns.

Pachacuti established a system of organization and training for the army. Soldiers were organized in groups of tens, hundreds, and thousands. Ten warriors formed a unit under a leader called a *chungacamayoc* who made sure that his men were trained and provided with the necessary clothing, arms, and supplies.

Subsequent groups consisted of 50 and 100, each led by an officer of increasingly higher rank. Such groupings continued up into the thousands. The higher officers were professional career soldiers whose ranks were distinguished by their rich colourful uniforms and plumed helmets. At the top of the military pyramid was the commander-in-chief, who was always an experienced military man and usually an uncle or brother of the ruling emperor.

In addition, Pachacuti developed transport and supply routes for troops in the field. The march to battle was carefully planned. Stops were spaced about every 20 km, where supply bases were located. If a prolonged siege was expected, hill forts were sometimes constructed.

Inca soldiers wore body armour of wickerwood padded with quilted cotton and a wooden helmet decorated with the symbols of their home province. They carried a small round shield of llama skin for added protection. The main weapons were spears with bronze blades and clubs with spiked bronze heads. Slings capable of hurling stones with great force were also carried.

Pachacuti also introduced effective military strategies. Shock troops were held back from battle as a reserve, and then deployed when the startling effect of their arrival might ensure victory.

Victory was sometimes achieved without resorting to battle. Smaller groups often considered it useless to resist the Inca. Frequently, envoys were sent ahead of the army to meet with the enemy and convince them not to fight. The advantages of living in the Inca empire were explained, and the enemy was promised

THROUGH THEIR EYES
The Sayings of Pachacuti

Garcilaso de la Vega, an Inca writer, recorded some of the sayings of Pachacuti, providing us with some idea of the type of ruler he must have been. What suggests that Pachacuti was a successful ruler? What did Pachacuti think was the proper function of government?

Impatience is the sign of a mean low heart that is underbred and full of bad habits.

Judges who allow a plaintiff to visit them in secret must be considered as

thieves and punished with death.

Governors must never forget that he who is unable to run his own house and family, is still less competent to be entrusted with public matters.

He who pretends to be counting the stars, when he doesn't know how to count the knots of a quipu, *deserves to be jeered at.*

Figure 23-4 *Pachacuti, as drawn by Gauman Poma, the sixteenth century chronicler*

that they would not be harmed if they submitted without resistance.

Army life was not all that unattractive for an Inca conscript. It provided commoners with an opportunity to travel. For many, it also offered the opportunity to gain rewards and advancement in return for distinguished service.

Festivities and celebrations were an important part of Inca warfare. Triumphal returns to Cuzco celebrated victory. Enemy captives participated in the triumphal return and only the most dangerous were sacrificed or executed. The triumphs lasted several days and featured displays of booty as well as the prisoners of war. The soldiers were awarded clothing, or gold or silver-plated pendants. High-ranking officers received more luxurious gifts and were sometimes granted promotions or special privileges.

One of Pachacuti's most important contributions to the growth of the Inca empire was how rapidly he imposed effective administration upon the territories and people that he conquered. Shortly after the conquest, engineers and government officials were sent in to complete a census of the new territory. Tallies were made of the population, the amount of arable land, the type of crops grown, and the locations of resources such as tin, gold, or silver deposits. They were very thorough, even preparing clay models of the major settlements and resources.

A labour force was dispatched at once to build roads to the new territory, to build towns or government storehouses and any other public works, such as canals, terraces, and irrigation systems, that might be needed. To facilitate communication within the empire, posts for runners were constructed at 2 to 3 km intervals along the major roads that led from the new territory to the capital at Cuzco. By using a series of runners, news could travel very quickly. The runners could cover some 225 km per day.

Conquered leaders were presented with gifts and granted privileges. Even though the emperor selected from among the Inca aristocracy to appoint a new governor for the conquered province, local officials kept their positions provided they carried out the demands of the emperor and upheld Inca customs and laws. They became "honorary" Inca. The population was allowed to continue to worship local deities and idols so long as they accepted the supremacy of the Inca Sun god.

At times, the sons of local leaders were taken back to Cuzco as hostages to guarantee loyalty. They were educated and prepared for administrative posts throughout the empire. Important local idols might also be removed to Cuzco as further insurance against any possible rebellion.

In extremely rebellious areas *mitimaes,* or troublesome citizens, were removed and resettled in a loyal territory with a similar climate, economy, and altitude. Alternatively, loyal Inca might be moved to the rebellious areas to set a good example for the local inhabitants, teaching them Inca customs and language.

Pachacuti was also responsible for rebuilding Cuzco along imperial lines, making it a capital fit for a great empire. He also built the great fortress of Sacsahuaman to the north of the city.

Pachacuti's heir, Topa Inca (1471–1493), has sometimes been called the "Alexander of the Andean World," because he forged an empire nearly as large as that of Caesar's Rome, stretching from Ecuador over 4000 km south into Peru.

Chimu was the only real obstacle the Inca faced in the northern coastal area. Chimu was well defended except from the north, so Topa launched a campaign as far north as Quito, and then turned south to approach the Chimu unexpectedly from the north. Chimu was defeated and the entire north and central coasts now belonged to the Inca. Subsequently, after another campaign in 1471, Topa subdued the south coast, establishing the southern boundary of the empire at the Maule River.

The last piece of the empire was added under Huayana Capac (1493–1527) who acquired territory north of Quito, setting the northern limit of the Inca empire at the Ancasmayo River. Huayana Capac integrated Ecuador into the Inca empire and built many new towns. It was Huayana Capac who learned that strange bearded men had been seen on the coast. Following his death, two of Huayana Capac's sons, Huascar and Atahuallpa, waged a civil war for the leadership of the empire. When Atahuallpa emerged the victor in 1532 and was preparing for his coronation, the Spanish Conquest of the region was well under way.

THE SPANISH CONQUEST (1532 CE - 1572 CE)

The Inca empire was invaded by the Spanish, led by Francisco Pizarro. Pizarro was stirred by the possibility of making a fortune in the "new world." A soldier of fortune, he travelled with Balboa across the Isthmus of Panama to view the Pacific Ocean. It was here that he first heard stories of the riches of the Inca empire.

Longing for adventure (and wealth), Pizarro managed to get financial backing for an expedition to Peru in 1524. The expedition was plagued by storms and food shortages and had to be abandoned, but not before Pizarro had met some villagers wearing golden ornaments who told him of a great city said to be about a 10-day journey across the mountains. Pizarro decided to lead a second expedition into the heart of the Inca empire, and set out again to do so in 1526. This expedition was unsuccessful in the end as well, but the Spanish presence along the shores of Peru was now becoming known by the Inca.

Huayana Capac was in Quito when word was brought to him in 1527 of the strangers probing the coast. Though the Inca had yet to see the Spanish, the Spanish presence was felt that same year when a smallpox epidemic broke out and Huayana

Capac and his eldest son died. This devastated the royal family and created a crisis between Huascar, Huyana Capac's second son, and Atahuallpa, his half-brother, over who would rule the empire.

The end result was civil war, in which the advantage rested with Atahuallpa. In 1532 the forces of Atahuallpa were victorious. Huascar was captured and imprisoned and Atahuallpa's generals set about consolidating the victory. The empire was in complete disarray as a result of the civil war. Many areas were depopulated and destroyed. Meanwhile, Pizarro and his men had set out on a third expedition to Peru. Landing at Tumbez, they met no opposition. No one opposed their march inland either. The fortresses were empty and the mountain passes were undefended.

Just as Atahuallpa was waiting at Cajamarca for word from his generals that it was safe for him to make his triumphal return to Cuzco, word of the Spanish invaders was received. Atahuallpa sent an envoy to the Spanish, welcoming them in peace to Cajamarca. Pizarro had only 62 cavalrymen and 106 foot soldiers with him. Once in Cajamarca, Pizarro had an initial meeting with Atahuallpa, and invited him to dinner.

Instead of dinner, however, Pizarro

planned to ambush and capture Atahuallpa and the other Inca leaders. It was easy for Pizarro to attempt to do this because the emperor's army of perhaps 50 000 soldiers remained encamped outside the city.

At sundown, Atahuallpa arrived for dinner on a golden litter, preceded by hundreds of chanting sweepers. The emperor was also attended by his finely dressed nobles and an army of servants.

When the signal was given, the Spanish, on horseback, charged the Inca, their swords swinging. In the panic that followed, the emperor's golden litter capsized and he fell to the ground and was seized. More than 6000 Inca were massacred without the loss of a single Spanish life. With Atahuallpa and all the leaders captured or killed, the Inca army fled in panic.

Atahuallpa was held captive and an enormous ransom was demanded for his release. While Atahuallpa was in prison, Huascar was negotiating with the Spanish for his own release. Secretly, Atahuallpa ordered Huascar's execution. The Spanish used this incident to justify putting Atahuallpa on trial. He was convicted and executed by strangulation in 1533. The execution of Atahuallpa signaled the eventual end of the Inca world. Because of the very highly structured nature of the Inca political system, it became paralyzed when there was no Sapa Inca in control.

Pizarro attempted to control the Inca empire by appointing puppet emperors following the death of Atahuallpa. The puppet emperors were ineffective in carrying on the normal administration of the empire, so it began to break up almost at once. One of the puppet emperors, Manco Inca, failed in an attempted uprising against the Spanish in 1536 and fled to the mountains to found

Figure 23-5 *The first meeting between Atahuallpa and Pizarro, from a sixteenth century Spanish drawing*

Figure 23-6 *Contemporary Peruvian drawing of the arrest of Atahuallpa*

a new Inca state. He eventually made his way to Vilcabamba, which became the capital of a rebel Inca state.

Spanish rule over the Inca grew more demanding. Looting began immediately, and eventually millions of dollars worth of gold and silver Inca artefacts were melted down for bullion. The Spanish also seized Inca lands to make room for Spanish settlers, and made increasing demands for the payment of tribute. Roads and irrigation projects fell into disrepair. The working classes were forced to provide labour for the Spanish. Whenever the Inca attempted to revolt against this oppression, as they did again in 1565, the Spanish put down the rebellions with great violence. Probably more decisive than any other factor in the downward fall of the Inca empire was the spread of European diseases. It has been estimated that more than 90 percent of the Inca population died within the first few years of the arrival of the Spanish.

The Spanish regarded the continued existence of any organized Inca state as a threat to their authority. In 1572 the Spanish moved against the Inca stronghold of Vilcabamba, capturing the new emperor, Topa Amaru, and his family, and taking them back to Cuzco for public execution. After this, the Spanish were in complete control of the former Inca empire.

REFLECT AND ANALYZE

1. What attracted Pizarro and the Spanish to the land of the Inca?

2. Describe Pizarro and his men from the point of view of a member of the Inca empire.

3. As a member of Pizarro's forces at Cajamarca, write a letter home, just before the ambush, in which you assess the chances for the success of the ambush.

4. "The Inca should have been able to prevent the downfall of their empire." Explain why you agree or disagree with this statement.

GOVERNMENT

THE SAPA INCA AND THE COYA

The leader of the Inca was called the Sapa Inca which meant Supreme Inca. He was also "son of the Sun" and "benefactor of the poor." These terms express the role of the Sapa Inca. He was the supreme head of government, religion and the army. He had absolute power. This power, however, was to be exercised benevolently, on behalf of his people.

Visitors demonstrated their respect for the Sapa Inca by removing their shoes in his presence and bowing as a token of homage. In 1438 Pachacuti began wearing a fringe of red tassels on his forehead as a sign of royal power.

The Coya was the sister-wife of the Sapa Inca. When a Sapa Inca took the throne he married his eldest sister, who became his queen, even though she was not his only wife. It was expected that their first son would become the next Inca ruler. The Coya was an important person among the Inca nobility even though she possessed no official power. The word *coya* meant "star." The citizens of the empire looked upon her as their mother and referred to her as "she who cares for the unfortunate."

Members of the civil service that ran the empire were Inca of the blood royal. They came first from the family of the current emperor and his wives, but, in addition, there were literally thousands of distant cousins who claimed descent from previous Sapa Incas. This gave them the right to participate in the higher levels of state administration. As the empire increased in size, it became necessary to create a class of "honorary" Inca, to help fill the lower government positions.

The Inca concept of government could almost be called a welfare state. Although the Sapa Inca's power was absolute and the government was monopolized by Inca of the blood royal, the state was held responsible for the welfare of the inhabitants.

Figure 23-7 A coya, attended by her hairdresser

Artisans, for example, were not paid wages. Their living was provided for them by the state in return for their skill at their craft. Similarly, when people became too old to do much work anymore, the state provided for all their needs.

THROUGH THEIR EYES
The Government of the Inca Emperors

Why did the Inca people venerate their rulers? Based on the following excerpt, which was written by Cieza de Leon, one of the Spanish conquerers, do you think that this veneration was justified?

So great was the veneration that the people felt for their princes throughout this vast region that every district was as well governed and regulated as if the lord was actually present to chastise those who acted contrary to his rules. This fear arose from the known valour of the lords and their strict justice. It was felt to be certain that those who did evil would receive punishment without fail and that neither prayers nor bribes would avert it. At the same time the Inca emperors always did good to those under their sway, and wouldn't allow them to be ill-treated, nor that too much tribute should be exacted from them. Many who dwelt in a sterile country where they and their ancestors had lived with difficulty, found that through the orders of the emperor their lands were made fertile and abundant, the things being supplied which before were wanting. In other districts, where there was a scarcity of clothing, owing to the people having no flocks, orders were given that cloth should be abundantly provided. In short....as these lords knew how to enforce service and the payment of tribute, so they provided for the maintenance of the people, and took care that they should want for nothing.

THE INCA HIERARCHY

The Council of Prefects, located in the capital of Cuzco, was composed of four high-ranking Inca or Prefects. Each member of the Council was responsible for one province of the empire. The members of the Council also acted as advisors to the Sapa Inca. They were the highest-ranking officials under the Sapa Inca.

Each of the four provinces in the empire was governed by a *cucuricuc*, or governor, who lived in the provincial capital. The provincial governors were of the blood royal and each reported directly to one of the four members of the Council of Prefects, supplying formal reports on the progress of their province at regular intervals. They had judicial and administrative responsibilities, but their actual powers were quite limited. Their main responsibilities were to ensure that the laws were carried out and that their province was well administered. They travelled about their province constantly and their arrival in a community was cause for celebration. They were welcomed with song and music. They would listen to any citizen's charge of abuse or mistreatment by any government official. They had a hierarchy of lesser officials to carry out the day-to-day tasks of government and to report back on the state of the districts for which they were responsible.

REFLECT AND ANALYZE

1. How did the Inca select the members of their civil service? What strengths and weaknesses can you see in this system?

2. How effective was the administration of the Inca empire? Support your answer with evidence.

3. Explain why you would or would not like to be an inhabitant of the Inca empire.

LAW AND JUSTICE

Many of the laws that were adopted by the Inca came from customs that existed long before the formation of the Inca empire. Justice was administered by judges and officials who wore the large gold ear ornaments that signalled their association with the ruling family. In return for administering justice, judges received their homes, clothing, and food from the royal stores. They received no remuneration from anyone else nor did they ever work for anyone other than the emperor. If a judge was ever caught accepting a bribe he was put to death.

The law was administered at varying levels of authority, depending on the severity of the crime. The more serious the offence, the higher the level of government that dealt with it. At the very top of the system was the Supreme Court. Although not a supreme court in the formal sense as we understand it in Canada, this high court was part of the structure of the central government. It contained 12 judges who heard legal appeals submitted from other courts and its decisions were final. There was no appeal beyond Supreme Court decisions, except for intervention by the Sapa Inca himself.

When a citizen was accused of a crime, he or she, along with any witnesses of the event, were summoned to appear before a judge. The witnesses seated themselves on the ground, forming a circle around the accused. When the witnesses were called upon, they presented their testimony. After the accused had heard the strength or weakness of the case presented, he or she was asked to enter a plea of innocent or guilty to the charges. If the accused pleaded guilty, the sentence was delivered immediately. If the accused pleaded not guilty, and the witnesses had not convinced the court, the case was adjourned for further inquiries.

A citizen with a "criminal record" could be tortured to gain a confession, but if neither the evidence provided by witnesses nor the torture could make an accused confess, he or she had to be acquitted. There was, though, an understanding that if the accused was convicted of any crime in the future, he or she would receive the death penalty.

Some of the punishments for those who violated the law were quite severe. The punishment for robbery, violence, destroying bridges, moving boundary stones, or perjury was a severe flogging for a first-time offender. A second-time offender received the death penalty. The punishment for manslaughter was exile to the hot and humid cacao plantations on the coast. The penalty for killing a disobedient subordinate was the *hiwaya*, which involved dropping a heavy stone on the accused's back from a height of approximately 1 m. The penalty for death using witchcraft was being beaten to death, after which the body was left to be eaten by condors. Treason carried a punishment of a slow agonizing death, following which the culprit's bones were made into musical instruments. For rape, the penalty for the first offence was the *hiwaya* and for the second it was death.

Justice was not equal among the Inca. Inca of the blood royal were publicly reprimanded for their misdeeds, on the grounds that this punishment was more severe than death was to a lower-class citizen!

REFLECT AND ANALYZE

1. What measures were taken in order to help guarantee the integrity of the legal system?

2. What were the rights of the accused?

3. Do some research to compare the laws and punishments of the Inca with the laws and punishments in force in Europe at the same time. Were they more or less severe? Explain the reasons for your answer.

THE INCA:
Society and Culture

Y ou are king of Cuzco,
I am king of Colla, We will drink
We will eat
We will speak
Of what no-one else has spoken.
I am rich in silver
I am rich in gold
Viracocha, symbol of the universe,
I adore,
The sun I adore.

Pachacuti's chronicle.

The Inca had no written language so they used other methods to pass their culture and traditions down through the ages, such as composing story poems of important events. The poem above describes an attempt to form an alliance between the Inca and the ruler of Colla. The ruler from Colla was attending the marriage of Viracocha Inca, and used the occasion to seek the support of the Inca, probably against his rivals in Lupaca. How did he try to make the alliance attractive to Viracocha?

Figure 24-1
A Sapa Inca seated on his throne

RELIGION

GODS AND GODDESSES
The Inca religion was polytheistic and included a large array of major and minor gods. Viracocha was the Supreme Being, who created both heaven and earth. The other chief divinities, the Sun, the Moon, and Thunder, were his servants. The Inca believed that they were the descendants of the Sun, known as Inti, and that the Inca emperor represented the Sun god on earth.

Lesser gods were considered more approachable than either Viracocha or Inti. The lesser gods included Illapa, the Storm god, who was the most revered god after Viracocha and Inti. Pacha-mama, or Mother Earth, was associated with agriculture and was worshipped by farmers seeking protection for their crops. Mama-cocha was the Mother of the Lakes and Sea, worshipped by fishers. The moon and the stars were also important. Mother Moon, the sister-bride of the Sun, was represented on earth by the Coya. The stars, as the children of the Sun and Moon, were worshipped as protectors of many earthly things, such as seeds and the llama herds.

In addition, the Inca also considered a number of places and objects as being associated with the supernatural. These sacred places and objects were called *huacas* and included springs, rocks, caves, and tombs. The mummified bodies of the emperors were also sacred.

RELIGIOUS BELIEFS AND PRACTICES

The Inca insisted that the Sun god be revered by all citizens in the empire, although, apart from this rule, they tolerated the local gods of the areas they had conquered. The government promoted Inti by building temples to the Sun throughout the empire. The Sun god was depicted as a huge golden disc with rays radiating from a human face.

The main Inca temple to the Sun god was the Coricancha in Cuzco, which was used as a model for other temples throughout the provinces. It consisted of a large number of buildings within an enclosure. The masonry of the temple was covered by

Figure 24-3 *Llamas were commonly used in Incan religious practices*

a frieze of thin gold plate. Golden images of the Sun god, the Creator, and the Storm god graced the interior. The Coricancha employed over four thousand priests, and attracted pilgrims from all over the empire.

Temples and shrines were cared for by a hierarchy of priests. The high priest in Cuzco, a close relative of the ruling Sapa Inca, was in charge of all priests. His power at times rivalled that of the Sapa Inca. Ten lesser priests were in charge of religion in

different sections of the empire. Below them were the ordinary priests. The religious establishment had its own lands which were used to support the religious hierarchy.

Religion was an important part of Inca life. Since sin would make the gods angry and bring unhappiness, people were required to confess their sins and to purify themselves following any wrongdoing. Prayers to the gods could be made individually, and traditional prayers were offered during festivals. Purification and fasting were required before festivals and ceremonies, or before making important decisions.

Acllahuasi, or convents for the Sun brides, were attached to the various royal palaces of the emperor. Specially selected young girls were taught religion and domestic duties by *mamacunas,* or teaching nuns. At the age of 13, the girls were taken to Cuzco for the Festival of the Sun. At that time, the Sapa Inca selected some to be his wives, and others to be the wives of members of the Inca family. The rest would serve in shrines or become *mamacunas* themselves.

Divination, or the practice of fore-

Figure 24-2 *Two Inca gold disks with sun faces*

THEN AND NOW
Sacrifices

What kinds of sacrifices did the Inca make? Why do you suppose that animals of different colours were used? Why do you think that the Inca today continue to celebrate important festivals and make sacrifices, centuries after the Spanish imposed Christianity?

Most important Inca festivals, such as the Festival of the Sun, Inti Raymi, involved sacrifices. Although there is evidence that human sacrifices were used at important times, such as inaugurating the reign of a new emperor, or when an emperor was ill, most of the sacrificial victims were llamas or guinea pigs. The blood of a sacrificial animal was offered to the god by smearing it over an idol to the god. White llamas were sacrificed to the Sun god, brown

Figure 24-4 *A contemporary Festival of the Sun in Cuzco, Peru*

llamas were sacrificed to Viracocha, and varicoloured ones were sacrificed to the Storm god.

The Sun god was so important that sacrifices to the Sun were made daily in the main square of Cuzco. A fire was lit as the Sun appeared in the morning. Specially prepared food was thrown into the fire for the Sun to eat, and a llama was sacrificed and burned.

Today, the descendants of the Inca maintain many of the festivals of their ancestors. They continue to hold *Inti Raymi*. Musicians play traditional instruments and people perform traditional dances recounting Inca history. In another echo of the past, the Aymara on Lake Titicaca's Island of the Sun sacrifice a llama to Mother Earth each fall to ask for good crops.

---

telling the future, was also a part of Inca religion. One example was the *calpa* ceremony, performed to determine the chances of success for a military campaign. A priest sacrificed a llama and removed a lung from the animal. The priest would then blow into a vein and observe the colour markings on the surface of the lung in order to assess the outcome of the campaign. The entrails of a llama might also be consulted to help choose a suitable heir to the Sapa Inca.

Fire was often used as a means of communicating with the gods. A fire was built in a metal pot, and dishes of food and drink were set out around the fire. The diviner invited the spirits to speak by chanting. Voices emerging from the fire were then interpreted by the diviner.

DEATH

The Inca believed in life after death. As a result, a variety of rituals were performed. Relatives demonstrated their grief by wearing black, cutting their hair, or smudging their faces with black paint. Relatives also prepared the body for burial, since the soul of the departed might wish to remain in contact with the family. The body was first dried in the sun, then wrapped in layers of cloth, and finally covered by woven mats tied tightly around the body.

The deceased was buried in a sitting position, either in a sand grave on the coast, or in a cave or stone house in the highlands. If the departed were virtuous, the Inca believed that they would go to live with the Sun in the upper world. If they were not

worthy people, they would suffer cold and darkness in the interior of the earth. The deceased were buried with pottery, baskets, jewellery, food, and the tools of their trade. The funeral rites lasted for five to eight days and the family mourned for a year.

The burial of an emperor was particularly elaborate. The body was mummified in such a way that it maintained a very life-like appearance. Many songs and narratives were composed about the emperor's reign. These were recounted throughout the empire for the year following his death. When the year of mourning was over, the mummy was placed in the palace the emperor had inhabited in life, along with all his treasure. Each year, during the Festival of the Dead, the imperial mummies were brought out for public display. Placed on a special carrying chair, they were paraded in elaborate dress around the square in Cuzco. A pure white llama was sacrificed in their honour, and learned men chanted the history associated with their reigns. In death, the Sapa Incas became idols that were worshipped and consulted as oracles.

SOCIAL STRUCTURE

The best way to understand the Inca social pyramid is to examine it from bottom to top. The head of an Inca household was called a *puric*. He held his own section of farmland and was also required to work the lands of the state and the church as a labour tax. In addition, the *puric* was required to provide *mit'a*, or service to the state in the army, on public works projects, or in the mines.

Inca households were grouped together in a larger unit of 10 called an *ayllu*, each headed by a non-hereditary headman. An *ayllu* was both a kinship and an economic grouping, since it was the *ayllu* that was granted land by the state. All *ayllu* in the empire belonged to either a lower-class group, the *Hanan*, or an upper-class group, the *Hurin*. Although upper-class *ayllu* had some precedence over the lower-class *ayllu*, there does not seem to have been any serious social or political disadvantage attached to the *Hanan*.

Inca society beyond the *ayllu* was based upon larger and larger groupings of *purics*. There were groupings of 50, 100, 500, 1000, 5000, and 10 000 *purics*. Each unit of 100 or more was headed by a government official called a *curaca*.

A *curaca* was a government official whose rank became hereditary after he was appointed to his post by the Sapa Inca. *Curacas* were "honourary" Inca, originally chosen from among the rulers of the groups conquered by the Inca.

The *curaca* distributed land and ensured that all work was completed, especially the required amount of labour tax and participation in the *mit'a*. In addition, the *curaca* looked after the welfare of the citizens under his care, resolving local disputes and handling ordinary crimes. He also made certain that his citizens were properly housed, fed, clothed, and doc-

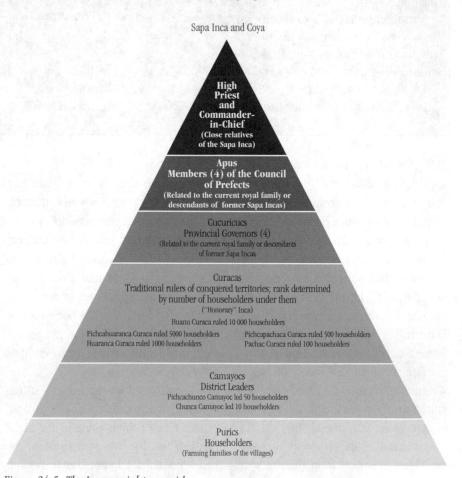

Figure 24-5 *The Inca social pyramid*

tored, and provided with the seeds and tools needed for farming.

The most privileged members of the social pyramid were those at the top, with family ties to the ruling household or that of previous Sapa Incas. This level included the High Priest, the Commander-in-Chief, the four *Apus,* and the four provincial governors.

Figure 24-6 *A silver figurine of a member of the Inca aristocracy. The stretched earlobes were caused by the ear spools that men of the Inca elite wore to show their status.*

EVERYDAY LIFE

THE FAMILY

Daily life in Inca society was regulated by the government to a very great extent. Inca women were expected to marry between the ages of 14 and 18 years, and men generally married between the ages of 25 and 30 years. Marriage was an economic necessity and required the consent of both the bride's and the groom's parents. The couple was also required to get a "licence" to marry from a government official.

Prior to their wedding, the couple went to confession and asked the priest to bless their union. The wedding itself consisted of exchanges of gifts between bride and groom, and much feasting and dancing.

A house was built for the newly married couple, which was furnished by relatives. For the first year of their marriage the couple paid no labour tax. When their first child was born they were given more land, which made the birth of a child an even more welcome event.

Men between 25 and 50 years could expect to be conscripted into the *mit'a* which included service in the army, or labour on public works projects or in the mines. *Mit'a* is a Quechua word meaning "a turn" as in "taking turns." An adult male was expected to take his turn in service to the state, which would involve

Figure 24-7 *A contemporary Peruvian woman weaves cloth*

about five years in total. This was not an onerous requirement since the demands of Andean farm work required only about 60 days per year.

Women between 25 and 30 years had their responsibilities as well. Their primary duty was to support their husbands and care for their families. When husbands were away on *mit'a* service, wives took over all of the daily chores. In addition, government inspectors visited their homes to see that they kept their houses neat, prepared food hygienically, supplied the family with clothing, and reared the children properly. As well as weaving for their families, women were required to weave one garment per year for the government with wool supplied by the emperor.

Citizens between the ages of 50 and 60 years were considered to be semi-retired. Men were no longer expected to perform *mit'a* service or to cultivate land, although they did help out at harvest time. Men in this age group could become servants, record keepers, clerks, storekeepers, statisticians, librarians, historians, official poets, and auditors.

Those over age 60 were expected to do light work if they were able. Men twisted rope for bridge building, collected firewood, looked after poultry and small livestock, or acted as watchmen. They paid no taxes and were provided with food and clothing by the state.

EDUCATION

Children from infancy to age five were called "playing children," and had no responsibilities. After that, however, the state had certain expectations of the children. Children between the ages of 5 and 9 were expected to help their parents by performing small tasks about the house, such as minding babies, feeding animals, or weeding.

There were different expectations for those between the ages of 9 and 25. Most males of the lower class served as *llama michecs*, or shepherds, for the state-owned llama herds until the age of 20. From 20–25 years, they might function as *llama michecs* over the younger shepherds, act as post runners in the communications network of the empire, or serve as pages to officers of rank within the army. These roles were in part intended to give young men an opportunity to see the world and gain some practical experience.

Males of the upper class, the sons of the Inca, and the *curacas,* were the only ones who received a formal education. It was thought that a formal education for the lower classes might provoke rebellion. The best formal education was received in Cuzco at the *Yachahuasi,* or House of Teaching. Boys frequently had to travel long distances to attend the *Yachahuasi,* and were away for four years, the length of the educational system.

Each year of formal education was devoted to a separate subject. During the first year, students studied Quechua, the Inca language, which was generally used throughout the empire. The second year was devoted to religion. The making of *quipus*, the Inca record-keeping device, was the focus of year three, and the fourth year was spent learning Inca history. The teaching was done by wise men called *amautas*. Discipline was strict at the *Yachahuasi* and students could have the soles of their feet beaten up to ten times for misbehaviour.

Lower-class girls between 9 and 12 years were expected to gather flowers and herbs such as coca and quinine for making dyes and medicines. Upper-class girls of this age had no official duties. From 12–18 years, however, after adulthood had been attained, women of all classes worked at home, keeping house and making textiles. Lower-class women might enter into domestic service in an upper-class home. After marriage, women of all classes were expected to look after their families, run their homes, and assist their husbands in whatever way possible, depending upon his status in life. No professions were open to women.

REFLECT AND ANALYZE

1. Although the state regulated a great deal in the lives of its citizens, what did the citizens receive in return?

2. What role were the young men who attended the *Yachahuasi* intended to fulfill? In your opinion, were they given a sound education for this purpose? Give reasons for your answer.

3. As an Inca bride or groom, make a journal entry on the night before your wedding, explaining your hopes for your future life.

URBAN AND RURAL LIVING

The imperial city of Cuzco was built roughly in the shape of a puma, an Inca deity. The four great highways from the provinces met at the central plaza of the city, where citizens gathered for festivals. To the south stood the Temple of the Sun. The top of the Temple of the Sun was banded in pure gold. The paved channel of the Huatanay River carried water into the city and waste away.

To the north of the city was the fortress of Sacsahuaman, which formed the head of the puma. One of the most amazing creations of early American civilization, Sacsahuaman was built by Pachacuti to help protect the capital from invasion. The project required the labour of 20 000 men sent in from the provinces — 4000 to quarry and cut the stone, 6000 to haul it, and the rest to shape the stone and build the walls and towers. The structure was over 600 m long and 20 m high. Some of the stones for the walls were over 8 m in height and width. Many of the walls were assembled with such great care that a knife blade cannot be forced in their joints.

Archaeologists are astonished at the ability of Inca engineers to complete this construction with such precision, using only stone tools. The Spaniards believed that the Inca were incapable of such an accomplishment, and credited it to the black work of the devil, or to the work of giants. Some have claimed that the Inca must have known how to turn wood into stone, while others have expressed the view that the Inca had a herb for softening and shaping rocks. Today, there are even suggestions that Sacsahuaman was built by extra-terrestrials.

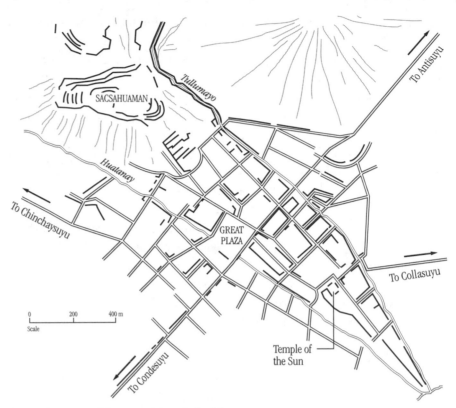

Figure 24-8 *Map of the imperial capital of Cuzco*

Figure 24-9 *A section of the wall of the Sacsahuaman fortress*

Inca cities were almost exclusively government centres, and they all followed the same basic pattern as Cuzco. Each had a temple in honour of the Sun god, a palace for the Sapa Inca, and one for the town governor. There were storehouses to house the taxes of food and clothing from citizens, and an artisans' quarter where crafters produced works for the Inca. Most of the buildings were single-storey, built of stone and thatch. Only the elite lived within the city.

The palaces of the Sapa Incas were large complexes whose main gates were guarded by soldiers day and night. The only access to any of the spacious apartments was through one of the courtyards onto which they opened. The courtyards were filled with gardens. The lavishly decorated living quarters of the Sapa Inca and the Coya were located in the centre of the palace compound. Those of the royal servants were close by.

Commoners lived in satellite towns beyond the city, close to the farmland. Two to eight houses formed a compound developed around a central courtyard used for eating and entertainment. Extended families shared the houses in a compound. As families grew larger, the number of houses within compounds increased. Large villages and cities were actually a series of compounds grouped together.

The homes were rectangular and the general colour scheme was buff and gold. The walls were made of adobe (sun-dried bricks) or sometimes of stone, and the roofs were made of straw thatch. Each house contained a single room that housed a single family.

Furniture was sparse. Along with a few wooden stools, piles of blankets or mats served as furniture for both sitting and sleeping. Niches in the walls served as shelves and cupboards, and a few stone pegs served as hooks. Residents slept together at one end of the house. The stove was at the end of the house farthest away from the sleeping quarters.

Corn and potatoes were the staples of the Inca diet. *Chuno*, dehydrated potato, was made by squeezing the moisture out through repeated freezing and thawing. A traditional drink was *chicha*, made from boiled and fermented cornmeal. The evening meal was the main meal of the day and generally consisted of a stew of potatoes, maize, beans, and other vegetables flavoured with a hot spicy seasoning. On special occasions, the meat from guinea pigs was also eaten.

CLOTHING

The basic clothing style for men was a simple tunic reaching to just above the knees, covered by a big loose cloak. They wore leather sandals or grass shoes. Women dressed in ankle-length gowns, often with a broad waistband and a cape. On their heads they pinned a folded piece of cloth which hung down their backs.

Clothing worn in the highlands was made of wool, but in the warmer coastal regions garments were made of cotton. The fleece of vicunas and alpacas was used to produce wool. Most wool was produced from the fleece of the alpaca but the very finest cloth came from the fleece of the vicuna. Colour obtained from vegetable and mineral dyes was added to the fleece before the fibres were spun.

Clothing demonstrated the artistry of Inca women in weaving. It was decorated with stripes and geometric patterns woven into the fabric using a variety of coloured threads. The finest cloth and the most elegant decorations were reserved for the elite. Their clothing contained elaborate designs made with gold threads and other ornaments. Such clothing was usually only worn on ceremonial and festive occasions.

Figure 24-10a *Men's dress among the Inca*

Figure 24-10b *Women's dress among the Inca*

REFLECT AND ANALYZE

1. What characteristics were common to most Inca cities?

2. What is so astonishing about Inca engineering?

3. Assume the role of an Inca farmer or his wife and write a brief account of a day in your life in your village compound.

THE ECONOMY

AGRICULTURE

All the land in the Inca empire belonged to the state. It was divided into three parts. One part went to the Sapa Inca or the state. A second part went to the Sun god or the religious establishment. A third part went to the common people. The portions allotted were not equal. Inca society was essentially benevolent. In spite of the monopoly of power by the Inca, their primary concern was the welfare of the people. As a result, the portion of land given to the common people was determined first, and it was made large enough to support an acceptable standard of living. After that, the other two parts of the land were distributed to the state and the religious establishment.

The Inca economy depended upon agriculture. The two principal crops were maize and the potato. Maize, the more important crop, was the only food which the Inca considered worthy of being offered to the gods. In every house a shrine was dedicated to "mother maize," containing the best cobs wrapped in the family's finest cloth. Maize was best-suited to the warmer regions of the lower slopes of the Andean highlands and to the lowlands. It required steady watering and fertilizing.

The potato is considered by many to be the most precious gift that Peru has given to the modern world. Through trial and error, a bitter and hard skinned tuber was transformed into the potato, the staple crop of the highlands. Potatoes could be grown at altitudes as high as 5000 m, as long as there was normal rainfall. Potatoes are very hard on the soil, so after a few years the land has to be allowed to lie fallow to allow it to regenerate.

The farm implements of the Inca were quite primitive. The two most important tools were a foot plough and a hoe. The foot plough, a 1.8 m-long pole with a curved handle, a fire-hardened or bronze tip, and a foot rest, was used to break the ground, dig holes, and harvest potatoes. The farmer drove the point into the ground and levered a clod of soil by heaving back and forth on the curved handle. The hoe had a short shaft and a wide, chisel-shaped bronze blade. It was used for general cultivation, breaking up clods of earth, and weeding.

On the high plateaux of the empire, where the climate made agriculture too difficult, the Inca raised the llama and the alpaca. The llama was the only animal large enough to be used as a pack animal. The pasture lands were also divided among the commoners, the state, and the church. Commoners used the wool and meat to barter for other goods they needed. The church used its animals mainly for sacrifice while the emperor's animals were used as pack animals, for food, and for wool.

The Inca had to overcome many agricultural problems in order to obtain an adequate yield from their fields. Fertilizing the maize fields in the highlands meant transporting guano (bird droppings), sardines, and small fish heads from the coast, since the only fertilizer available locally was llama dung.

Maintaining an adequate water supply

for the fields was another problem. Water had to be carried over long distances and across difficult terrain. The Inca became experts at irrigation. Where the land was flat, they dug ditches to transport water. Where the land was hilly, they built stone aqueducts. On gently contoured slopes, they built stone channels about 60 cm in width. On very steep gradients, they constructed a series of steps to allow the water to cascade downward like a small waterfall. In or near towns, hollow masonry blocks were buried end-to-end to transport water.

The Inca also sought every opportunity to increase the amount of arable land. Agricultural terraces were constructed on the sides of valleys. Even the steepest mountainsides were terraced, giving the appearance from below of gigantic staircases climbing to the sky. Agricultural terraces varied in size. On steep slopes they were narrow, but lower down they were quite large. Stones had to be hauled up the slope from the valley floor to build retaining walls, as did fertile soil to fill the terraces. Small stone stairways were built to provide access to each terrace, as well as drainage channels to drain excess water away.

INDUSTRY

Artisans lived in towns throughout the empire, creating objects of great skill and beauty for the elite. Exempt from the usual labour tax, artisans worked full-time at their craft. In return, they and their families were provided with all they needed, including the tools and the materials of their craft. The position of artisan was hereditary. Among the Inca, the most noted achievements were made by goldsmiths, silversmiths, lapidaries, weavers, and embroiderers.

Bronze was the hardest metal used by the Inca. Metalworkers mixed copper and tin in a fire pot filled with burning charcoal. Holes in the sides of the pot allowed air to enter and the temperature to increase. The process was slow and only small amounts of bronze were melted at a time. When the molten bronze was ready, it was poured into a mould or formed into a single sheet to be hammered, depending on the article being made. The Inca made many practical things from bronze, such as needles, earrings, bells, cloak pins, and bronze points for digging sticks.

Gold and silver were used almost exclusively for luxury goods and ceremonial objects. Both minerals were mined in several regions of the empire, and, like the land, they were owned by the state. Gold and silver were important because gold was the symbolic colour of the Sun and the Sapa Inca, and silver was the colour of the Moon and the Coya.

Gold and silver objects were usually worked by hammering the metal into thin sheets using stone hammers. When the sheets of metal became brittle, they were

Figure 24-11 *Agricultural terraces constructed by the Inca, still used today*

Figure 24-12 *Inca goldsmiths were known for the luxury items and ceremonial objects that they fashioned, such as this gold funerary mask*

heated almost to the melting point again. The metal was then formed into the desired shape by cutting it or hammering it over a wooden form to suggest volume. At times, the back of the sheet of metal was hammered to produce a relief on the front. Jewels of many kinds were frequently inlaid in the gold and silver.

Weaving was another important craft. Cotton was grown in the hot coastal lands in six natural colours. Wool was obtained from the highlands. The wool of the vicuna was used for the finest clothing while that of the alpaca provided most of the standard wool. The coarse fleece of the llama was used mainly for cords and woven bags. The finest cloths were woven for the elite of Inca society by professional weavers. Fine garments and the woven *wincha* or headband denoted social and official rank.

TRADE

Trade was conducted by both sea and land. The Inca took advantage of the Pacific Ocean, which provided a natural link for their coastal villages. In addition, they were tireless road builders, constructing numerous roads to link the four quarters of the empire.

Along the Pacific coast great balsawood log rafts, powered by sails or rowers, and steered by a centreboard pushed between the logs, transported trade goods such as pottery, gold and silver, fine cloth, and army supplies. The vessels plied their way south down the coast from village to village, and drifted back northward on the current.

The land links consisted of two main roads which ran north to south, as well as hundreds of smaller roads that crossed them in an east-west pattern, linking the various villages and towns. The roads built in the highlands were paved with stone. The Inca constructed the longest road in the world, extending from Quito to Chile. This great road, joining the far outposts of the empire, was a remarkable achievement. Parts of the road cut through solid rock, and other parts clung to the face of high cliffs. The Incas rivaled and possibly even surpassed the Romans as road-builders.

The roads were important for more than transportation and trade. They made possible the development of an effective postal system. Relays of runners carried messages along the road networks, exchanging at intervals of approximately 2 km. The runners could cover 225 km a day, so that messages could be quickly transported throughout the empire. This communication system was supplemented by a system of beacon fires, which made signals using smoke.

All land journeys were made on foot since the Inca had not discovered the wheel. Rest-houses were built along the routes so travellers could camp, cook, and feed their llamas. Trains of llamas carrying bundles of trade goods or tax grain were the main traffic on the roads.

REFLECT AND ANALYZE

1. The Inca built some of the best roads ever constructed. Why do you think they never invented any wheeled vehicle or cart?

2. What problems did the Inca have to overcome in order to maintain a high level of agricultural productivity?

3. The Inca demonstrated a great deal of ingenuity in making their economy work to its maximum. Do you agree or disagree with this statement? Explain, giving reasons for your answer.

THE ARTS

LITERATURE

It was the duty of the Sapa Inca and other government officials to preserve the history of the Inca people. Because they had no writing, the Inca developed a rich oral tradition. Folklore, poem stories, and narratives were passed down from generation to generation by being sung or recited frequently on important public occasions. Unfortunately, at the time of the Spanish Conquest, only fragments of Inca literature were recorded, and the rich treasury of Inca literature has mostly been lost. It consisted of accounts praising the deeds of the Sapa Incas, myths of creation and other myths, as well as purely secular works about love, nature, and the environment.

Drama was also very popular among the Inca. Many of the plays concerned the heroic exploits, wars, or the greatness of past Inca rulers. However, other plays were comedic, dramatic, or religious. Comedies dealt with themes relating to property and family situations, much like present day situation comedies. Sometimes the plays were accompanied by the music of flutes and drums. Plays were performed for the emperor and the nobility on special feast days. If the performance was good, the performers could expect to be rewarded with gifts and jewels from an appreciative audience.

MUSIC

Music was also important at the Inca court. The main musical instruments were flutes and drums. The most widely used flute was the *quena*, an instrument made from a section of cane open at both ends, with a notch at the edge into which air was blown. The number of finger stops on the instrument varied up to a maximum of eight. A larger type of bone flute was used for playing war tunes. Panpipes were also quite popular. These were made from several sections of cane of different lengths, all tied together, to produce different notes.

Drums were important in war and the triumphal marches in Cuzco after significant victories. They were also used in religious ceremonies. Many of the musical instruments were decorated with gold and silver and set with precious stones. For festivals, smaller drums and tambourines, accompanied by small bells made of copper, bronze, and silver were more commonly used.

ART

The artistic talents of the Inca were demonstrated in a variety of ways. Without a potter's wheel, all pottery was moulded by hand. Pottery was usually fired in open pits, producing a pinky-red or orange colour. The surfaces were then decorated with paints made from mineral pigments which produced colours of red, black, cream, purple, and white. Pottery decoration was most often geometric, with triangles, diamonds, checkered patterns, and thick parallel lines. In some instances the designs included people, animals, birds, and insects.

The *aryballus* jar was a characteristic shape in Inca pottery. It has a pointed base, and a long neck with flaring lips which could be topped by a flat lid. Used to transport and store liquids, the *aryballus* varied greatly in size. Some were as large as a person and others were quite small. Two small strap handles set low and vertically on the body of the *aryballus* helped make it easier to carry. The knob protruding below the neck made it possible to attach a rope for added balance.

Some Inca plates were moulded with small horizontal handles on each side. Others had a modelled handle on one side and a pair of lugs on the other. The modelled handle might take the form of a duck or a human head. The decoration on these plates consisted of a variety of painted designs.

The subjects of most Inca sculpture were llamas, alpacas, pumas, and humans. They were either carved from stone or cast in bronze, silver, or gold, polished with

Figure 24-13
An aryballus from the Sun Temple, Peru

sand and water. Llama and alpaca figurines might be made from stones of varying colours and textures. Holes cut into their backs were filled with coca or llama fat to be presented as offerings to the gods.

REFLECT AND ANALYZE

1. What features of Inca pottery were distinctive?
2. What influence did religion have upon the arts?
3. Create a short poem story that might have been created by an Inca storyteller recounting an event occurring between the arrival of the Spanish and the death of Atahuallpa.

THE SCIENCES

BRIDGE-CONSTRUCTION

The Incas became experts in bridge-construction out of necessity. The Andean rivers which ran through the steep mountain gorges were often subject to violent flooding, and the Inca needed to find a way around these. Bridges were the answer, but there was no timber at hand to construct bridges.

As a result, the Inca developed the technology for suspension bridges. *Cabuya* fibre was used to make cables as thick as a man's thigh. The cables were stretched across the gorge from one bank to another, anchored to stone pylons. Finer cords were used to join the cables and form the sides and floor of the bridge.

Citizens living near a bridge were responsible for its maintenance. Through this scrupulous attention to upkeep, many of the bridges were kept in operation for centuries. Although the Spanish admired the Incan ingenuity in constructing bridges, they were filled with trepidation whenever they crossed, because the bridge swayed in every wind and usually sagged dangerously in the middle.

RECORD-KEEPING

Since the Inca had no system of writing, records were kept on an instrument called a *quipu*. All young men of the upper class were trained in making a *quipu*. One who became an expert in the system was called a *quipu-mayoc*. Many of the *quipus* were destroyed by the Inca at the time of the Spanish Conquest so that their records would not fall into the hands of the enemy. The Spanish destroyed countless more. *Quipus* conveyed both historical and numerical information.

A *quipu* is a cord to which secondary cords of various colours are attached. Knots are tied in significant groups and at significant intervals in the cords, to convey specific information. Some *quipus* even had a third group of smaller cords or threads tied to the knots of the secondary cords. This third group of threads could also have various knots, and acted like a subordinate clause in a sentence, providing more detailed information.

TIME

The Inca had both a lunar calendar and a solar calendar. Even though they came to recognize that the solar calendar was more accurate, they maintained the lunar calen-

INNOVATIONS
Quipus

How did a *quipu-mayoc* use the *quipu* as both a mathematical and a historical record? Why do you think that the Spanish destroyed so many of the *quipus* that came into their possession?

If a *quipu-mayoc* was given an assignment to record statistical information concerning crop production, population, births, and deaths for a particular region of the empire, he would select different coloured cords for each area of his inquiry. For example, a white cord could be used to record information about crops, a green cord could be used for population statistics, a mauve cord for recording births, and a black cord for recording deaths.

Lesser cords containing a series of knots were attached to the white cord (crop information) to record the quantities of specific crop production. For example, a yellow cord would represent maize production, a pink cord would represent potato production, and a red cord

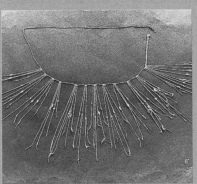

Figure 24-14 *A quipu*

would record the production of coca. In recording population statistics (the green cord), a blue knotted cord would be attached to the green cord to represent the male population and an orange cord would represent the female population.

A *quipu* could also be used to record historical information. For example, in recording history, a black cord represented time. A crimson cord tied halfway along a black cord stood for the emperor. A violet thread represented a chief, a blue thread represented the church, and small colourless knots represented people.

Imagine a crimson cord tied with a big knot in the centre of a black cord. Numerous colourless knots are attached to the right of the crimson cord but there are no other threads attached. The meaning of the *quipu* is: "The people before the first Inca, and during a very long time, had no king, no chief, and no religion."

dar because so many rituals were associated with the phases of the moon.

The twelve solar months were calculated from the sun's appearance on a number of stone towers built especially for this purpose on high locations to the east and west of Cuzco. On the first day of each month the rising of the sun from behind one of these towers was observed from the main square in Cuzco.

The Inca determined the time of day by observing the position of the sun in the sky. Their week contained ten days. There were three weeks in a month. An extra day or two were sometimes added to months by astronomers.

One of the great strengths of the Inca empire was its efficient and highly centralized government, headed by the Sapa Inca. He in turn was supported by a strong and efficient class of nobles who oversaw the administration of the empire. The Inca encouraged the development of skilled crafters and builders, and amassed a fabulous wealth in gold and silver that was the envy of the Spanish conquerors.

The Inca civilization is remembered for many significant achievements, such as paved roads, suspension bridges, roads, and posthouses, that extended over the wildest mountain ranges and throughout the coastal deserts. Inca farmers were the first to grow potatoes. Although the Inca had no form of writing, they maintained records through their use of a unique system of knotted cords called *quipus*. The work of Inca crafters in weaving, pottery, gold, and silver is considered to be extraordinarily artistic and exceptionally beautiful.

REFLECT AND ANALYZE

1. What makes the suspension bridges developed by the Inca such a remarkable technological achievement?

2. How do you think the Inca first developed the idea of the *quipu?*

3. The Inca system of record-keeping, although unique, was not as efficient as that used by other civilizations who had developed a written language. Do you agree or disagree? Explain the reasons for your answer.

LOOKING BACK

When Pizarro and the Spanish reached Peru in 1532, they encountered a vast empire which the Inca had conquered in less than a century. The rich Inca empire extended 4800 km along the Pacific coast from Ecuador to central Chile.

MAKING CONNECTIONS

1. Prepare a script for a scene representing the initial meeting between Atahuallpa's envoy and Pizarro.

2. Select a story about an event that is happening in your school or community. Design a Mayan codex to record it, creating simple glyphs to represent the sounds, words, and ideas you want to express. Keep in mind that others will need to be able to interpret your glyphs.

3. Using an organizer, compare the Spanish Conquest of the Maya under Hernando Cortez with the Spanish Conquest of Peru under Francisco Pizarro.

4. It has been said that the architecture of a people is the most accurate reflection of their culture and society. To what extent is this statement true of the Maya and the Inca?

5. Using an organizer, compare the political and social life of the Maya and the Inca. In what ways were they similar? In what ways were they different? Which culture would you have preferred to live in, and why?

6. Research the Maya and the Inca today. Where do they live? How do they make their living? To what extent are their traditional social and cultural values evident in their lives today?

DIGGING DEEPER

7. Research modern recipes used in Mexican cooking. To what extent are these recipes reminiscent of or influenced by the diet associated with the ancient Maya?

8. Do some research on the Mayan murals discovered in the vaulted rooms at Bonampak, Mexico. What can their study tell us about the lives of the Maya?

9. Research the architecture of a major city-state of the Maya such as Tikal or Chichen Itza. Construct a diagram or a model of the city-state, or develop a picture collage of the principal buildings that were the focus of the city.

10. Research the discovery and excavation of the Inca city of Machu Picchu further, and prepare a report. What has been discovered? What questions remain unanswered? Develop your own hypothesis on when the city was built and why it was abandoned. Provide evidence to support your position.

UNIT

5

OVERVIEW

11. Select one of the major technological achievements of either the Maya or the Inca. Do some research to find out how it worked and the benefits it provided. Make a model or prepare an illustrated report.

12. From the point of view of either a Maya or an Inca, write a story about the early years of Spanish rule. How did your life change? How did disease, cultural differences, and Spanish military strength affect you? Which affected you the most? Base your story on research into the early years of Spanish rule, and weave actual events into it.

SKILL DEVELOPMENT: DETECTING BIAS IN WRITTEN SOURCES

One of the more difficult tasks facing the historian is the detection of bias in written sources. Bias is usually defined as a tendency to hold one point of view over another without any factual evidence. Sometimes, bias is so obvious that you will have no difficulty detecting it. On many other occasions, however, bias is so subtle that you may never notice it unless you look for it. Most writers are not even aware that they have injected biased views into their writing.

Process
Step 1: The first step in detecting bias is to determine whether you are working with a primary source or a secondary source.

- Primary sources come directly from the people or the time period under study. They are records by participants which have survived the passage of time. Primary sources can consist of written records (a personal memoir, a public speech, census data, or a newspaper report), oral records (a folk tale, a myth, a song, or a poem), or visual records (a painting, a line drawing, or a political cartoon).

- Secondary sources are indirect records of past events, written long after the time period in which the people lived or the events took place.

Step 2: Find out who the author is. What is the author's background, experience, and social class? Does the author hold a political position or strong political views?

For example, is the author an eyewitness, or is the author reporting a second-hand view? Is the author personally involved or a dispassionate observer? Is the author an official upholding an official view? Is the author a member of a privileged elite, making it unlikely that his writing reflects the views of ordinary people? Similarly, is the author male, so that the views of women and children are seen through a male perspective? Is the author imposing twentieth-century standards on a much earlier time period by being too critical of the standards of another time? Is the author ethnocentric, regarding his or her own cultural values as superior to the cultural values of the people being studied and judging them on this basis?

Step 3: Find out what the author's purpose in writing was.

For example, is the author trying to provide a factual and impartial account? Is the author attempting to persuade the reader that a certain interpretation of events is the correct one? Is the author trying to flatter an important political figure?

Step 4: Determine the type of literature it is.

For example, is the author writing a form of literature intended to inform, or one intended to amuse and entertain from a personal, poetic, or dramatic viewpoint?

Step 5: Determine who the intended audience is.

For example, an official account of a battle may contain many detailed events, all depicted in the most favourable light to those in command. An account of the same battle written to a friend might diverge significantly from the official account.

APPLYING THE SKILL

A great deal of our knowledge of the Maya and the Inca comes from records and accounts from Spanish soldiers and priests. Assume that you are a Spanish soldier or priest and identify what biases might shape the way you view the Maya or the Inca upon first experiencing their civilization. How would these affect the way you might write or draw accounts of your experience?

SUGGESTED SOURCES FOR FURTHER RESEARCH

Humanity before Civilization

Cairns, T. *The Coming of Civilization*. Cambridge: Cambridge University Press, 1986.

Ceram, C. *Gods, Graves and Scholars*. New York: Knopf, 1967.

Gore, R. "Neandertals." *National Geographic*, vol. 189, no. 1 (January 1996).

Higham, C. *Life in the Stone Age*. Cambridge: Cambridge University Press, 1989.

Johanson, D. "The Dawn of Humans." *National Geographic*, vol. 189, no. 3 (March 1996).

Johanson, D. and J. Shreeve. *Lucy's Child: The Discovery of a Human Ancestor*. New York: William Morrow, 1989.

Leakey, M. "The Farthest Horizon: The Dawn of Humans." *National Geographic*, vol. 188, no. 3 (September 1995).

McIntosh, J. *The Practical Archaeologist*. New York: Facts on File Publications, 1986.

Roberts, M. *The Ancient World*. London: Macmillan, 1979.

Trueman, D. and J. Trueman. *The First Civilizers: From Cave to City*. Toronto: McGraw-Hill Ryerson, 1976.

Mesopotamia and Egypt

Cairns, T. *The Coming of Civilization*. Cambridge: Cambridge University Press, 1986.

Hobson, C. *The World of the Pharaohs*. London: Thames & Hudson, 1987.

Quirke, S. and J. Spencer. *The British Museum Book of Ancient Egypt*. London: British Museum Press, 1992.

Reade, J. *Mesopotamia*. London: British Museum Press, 1991.

Roberts, D. "Egypt's Old Kingdom." *National Geographic*, vol. 187, no. 1 (January 1995).

Roberts M. *The Ancient World*. London: Macmillan, 1979.

Rossini, S. *Egyptian Hieroglyphics*. New York: Dover Publications, 1989.

Sheppard, E. *Ancient Egypt*. Harlow, England: Longman, 1960.

Stead, M. *Egyptian Life*. London: British Museum Press, 1991.

Weeks, J. *The Pyramids*. New York: Cambridge University Press, 1971.

Wilson, E. *Ancient Egyptian Designs*. New York: Dover Publications, 1986.

The Mediterranean World

Amos, H. and A. Lang. *These Were the Greeks*. Bucks, England: Hulton, 1979.

Andrewes, A. *Greek Society*. Harmondsworth, England: Penguin, 1967.

Burn, A. *The Pelican History of Greece*. Harmondsworth, England: Penguin, 1965.

Gore, R. "When Ancient Greeks Went West." *National Geographic*, vol. 186, no. 5 (November 1994).

Grant, M. *The Founders of the Western World*. New York: Scribner's, 1991.

Hodge, P. *Roman Family Life*. Harlow, England: Longman, 1974.

Jenkins, I. *Greek and Roman Life*. London: British Museum, 1986.

Massey, M. *Roman Religion*. Harlow, England: Longman, 1979.

Sheppard, E. *Ancient Athens*. Harlow, England: Longman, 1967.

Sherwin-White, N. *Ancient Rome*. Harlow, England: Longman, 1978.

The Medieval World

Aries, P. and G. Duby. *A History of Private Life: Revelations of the Medieval World*. Cambridge: Belknap/Harvard University Press, 1988.

Bagley, J. *Medieval People*. London: Batsford, 1978.

Boyd, A. *Life in a Medieval Monastery*. Cambridge: Cambridge University Press, 1975.

Cairns, C. *Medieval Castles*. Cambridge: Cambridge University Press, 1987.

Cairns, T. *The Middle Ages*. Cambridge: Cambridge University Press, 1972.

——————*Renaissance and Reformation*. Cambridge: Cambridge University Press, 1975.

Chamberlain, E. *Florence in the Time of the Medici*. Harlow, England: Longman, 1974.

Cubitt, H. *Luther and the Reformation*. Harlow, England: Longman, 1976.

Duke, D. *The Growth of a Medieval Town*. Cambridge: Cambridge University Press, 1988.

Gies, J. and F. Gies. *Life in a Medieval Castle*. New York: Harper and Row, 1974.

Glubb, J. *The Life and Times of Muhammed*. New York: Stein and Day, 1970.

Haussig, H. *A History of Byzantine Civilization*. New York: Praeger, 1971.

Jones, J. *The Medieval World*. London: Macmillan, 1979.

——————*The Crusades*. London: Macmillan, 1984.

Lewis, B. *Islam and the Arab World*. New York: Knopf, 1976.

Lippman, T. *Understanding Islam: An Introduction to the Moslem World*. New York: New American Library, 1982.

Loverance, R. *Byzantium*. Cambridge, Mass.: Harvard University Press, 1988.

Morgan, G. *Life in a Medieval Village*. Cambridge. Cambridge University Press, 1975.

Norwich, J. *Byzantium: The Early Centuries*. New York: Viking, 1988.

Reeves, M. *The Medieval Village*. Harlow, England: Longman, 1954.

——————*The Medieval Castle*. Harlow, England: Longman, 1963.

Triggs, T. *The Black Death and the Peasants' Revolt*. London: Macmillan, 1985.

Trueman, D. and J. Trueman. *The Knight's Realm: The Castle*. Toronto, McGraw-Hill Ryerson, 1973.

——————*The Merchant's Domain:The Town*.

Toronto: McGraw-Hill Ryerson, 1973.
———*The Peasant's World: The Manor.*
Toronto: McGraw-Hill Ryerson, 1974.
———*The Peasant's World: The Monk's Community: The Monastery.* Toronto: McGraw-Hill Ryerson, 1974.
Walsh, M. "Michelangelo's Last Judgment." *National Geographic*, vol. 185, no. 5 (May 1994).
Williams, A. *The Crusades.* Harlow, England: Longman, 1975.

The Ancient Far East

Allen, T. "The Silk Road's Lost World." *National Geographic*, vol. 189, no. 3 (March 1996).
Basham, A. *The Wonder That Was India.* New York: Grove Press, 1954.
Cottrell, A. *China.* London: Pimlico, 1990.
Davis, D. and R. Davis. *Civilizations in History: Africa and Asia.* Toronto: Oxford University Press (Canada), 1992.
Kulke, H. and D. Rothermund. *A History of India.* London: Routledge, 1986.
Lewis, B. *Growing Up in Sumarai Japan.* London: Batsford, 1981.
Morton, W. *Japan: Its History and Culture.* New York: McGraw-Hill Ryerson, 1994.
Reza, "China's Buddhist Caves." *National Geographic*, vol. 189, no. 4 (April 1996).
Singhal, D. *A History of the Indian People.* London: Metheun, 1983.
Thorp, R. *Son of Heaven: Imperial Arts of China.* Seattle: Son of Heaven Press, 1988.
Wolpert, S. *India.* Los Angeles: University of California Press, 1991.

Central and South America

Bray, W. *Everyday Life of the Aztecs.* New York: Dorset Press, 1968.
Burlan, C. and W. Forman. *The Aztecs: Gods and Fate in Ancient Mexico.* London: Orbis, 1975.
Clendinnen, I. *Aztecs.* New York: Cambridge University Press, 1991.
Demarest. A. "Violent Saga of a Maya Kingdom." *National Geographic*, vol. 183, no. 2 (February 1993).
Dorner, J. *Cortes and the Aztecs.* Harlow, England: Longman, 1972.
Eagan, B. *Kingdoms of Gold, Kingdoms of Jade.* London: Thames & Hudson, 1991.
Gallenkamp, C. *Maya: The Riddle and Rediscovery of a Lost Civilization.* New York: Viking, 1985.
Hemming, J. "Pizarro, Conqueror of the Inca." *National Geographic*, vol. 181, no. 2 (February 1992).
Hyams, E. and G. Ordish. *The Last of the Incas.* New York: Dorset Press, 1963.
Kendall, A. *Everyday Life of the Incas.* New York: Dorset Press, 1963.
Loyn, H. *The Middle Ages: A Concise Encyclopaedia.* London: Thames & Hudson, 1989.
Matheny, R. "An Early Maya Metropolis Uncovered: El Mirado." *National Geographic*, vol. 172, no. 3 (September 1987).
McIntyre, L. *The Incredible Incas.* Washington: National Geographic Society, 1975.
Metraux, A. *The History of the Incas.* New York: Schoken Books, 1970.
Miller, M. "Maya Masterpiece Revealed at Bonampak." *National Geographic,* vol. 187, no. 2 (February 1995).
Morley, S. and G. Brainerd. *The Ancient Maya,* 4th ed. Stanford, CA: Stanford University Press, 1983.
Norton, J. *Ancient America.* New York: Time Life, 1967.
Reinhard, J. "Sacred Peaks of the Andes." *National Geographic*, vol. 181, no. 3 (March 1993).
Sabloff, J. *The Cities of Ancient Mexico.* London: Thames & Hudson, 1989.
Schele, L. and D. Freidel. *A Forest of Kings.* New York: Morrow, 1990.
Stuart, G. *The Mysterious Maya.* Washington: National Geographic, 1977.
———*The Mighty Aztecs.* Washington: National Geographic, 1981.
———"The Timeless Vision of Teotihuacan." *National Geographic*, vol. 188, no. 6 (December 1995).

GLOSSARY

alchemy: medieval chemistry that attempted to change worthless metals into gold

Allah: in Islam, the name of the Supreme Being or God

animistic: the attribution of living souls to plants, inanimate objects, and natural phenomena

ankh: an ancient Egyptian symbol of life in the form of a cross with of loop at the top

annulment: to make something void, as in marriage

anthropologist: a scientist who studies the social organization of a people

anthropomorphic: attributing human form or qualities to gods, animals, or other non-human forms

arabesque: an elaborate design of flowers, leaves, and geometrical figures

archaeologist: a scientist who studies the people, customs, and lifestyles of ancient times

archipelago: a group of islands

archon: a chief magistrate in ancient Athens

artifact: an object made through human skill or work, often associated with archaeology

bailiff: in the Middle Ages, the agent of a lord who managed the lord's smaller estates

Bedouin: a nomad of the desert and steppes of North Africa and the Middle East

Byzantine: having to do with the ancient city of Byzantium (later called Constantinople and now Istanbul)

capitalism: a free-market economic system in which the means of production are privately owned

caravan: a group of people travelling together

Catholic Reformation: reforms initiated by the Catholic church, beginning in the 1520s, that resulted in a renewed set of Catholic principles

charter: a written document guaranteeing the rights of citizens

city-state: an independent state consisting of a city and its surrounding territory

code of chivalry: a code of conduct in the Middle Ages that combined Christian qualities with warrior values

codices: ancient manuscript texts in book form

Common Law: in England, a system of law based on decisions of the royal courts that became accepted legal principles

consul: an official from the patrician class who administered laws in ancient Rome

corvée duty: unpaid work performed by a peasant for a feudal lord

Counter-Reformation: a movement launched in the Catholic church in the 1520s to stem the rising tide of Protestantism

Crusades: any of one of the Christian military expeditions between 1096 and 1272 designed to recover holy land from the Muslims

cuneiform: the wedge-shaped characters used in the writing of ancient Sumeria

Dark Ages: the Middle Ages, especially the early part

demotic: a simplified form of ancient Egyptian writing

dictator: a ruler with absolute power

diocese: a Christian administrative division over which a bishop has authority

direct democracy: a form of government in which the people participate directly rather than through representatives

divination: the act of seeing the unknown through supernatural means

doctrine: the teaching of the beliefs of a group, church, or nation

draconian: harsh or severe, especially of laws and their application; originating from *Draco*, an Athenian legislator of the seventh century BCE

dynasty: a succession of rulers belonging to the same family

epic: a long poem retelling the adventures of a great hero and expressing the ideals of a nation or race

Estates General: in medieval France, the three estates or social classes of the clergy, nobility, and townspeople that formed part of the government

excommunication: dismissal from the Roman Catholic church and its sacraments

fallow: land ploughed and left unseeded for one or more seasons

feudalism: a social system of rule by local lords in medieval Europe

fossil: the remains of a prehistoric plant or animal preserved in rock

frieze: a horizontal band forming part of the upper section of a wall, often adorned by sculpture

Gothic: an architectural style characterized by pointed arches and steep roofs developed in Europe in the Middle Ages

Gregorian calendar: the calendar introduced by Pope Gregory I in the sixteenth century, now used in most countries

guild: an association of merchants or craftspeople that governed a town or group in the Middle Ages

hadiths: the authorized records of Muhammad's saying and actions

harem: the part of a Muslim house where the women live

Hellenistic Age: a cultural age that blended eastern and western influences in Greece and other lands after the death of Alexander the Great

heresy: a belief that differs from the accepted beliefs of a church or other group

heretic: a person who holds a belief that is different from the accepted beliefs

hieratic: a simplified form of hieroglyphics used by early Egyptian priests

hieroglyphics: a system of writing developed in ancient Egypt that used pictures to represent words and sounds

hominid: any primate, including modern humans and their ancestors, that belongs to the family Hominidae

House of Commons: the elected members of Parliament in Britain

House of Lords: the upper, non-elective branch of Parliament in Britain

humanism: any system of thought or action mainly concerned with human activity

humours: various body fluids once thought to determine a person's health

icon: a sacred picture or image

iconoclasm: the breaking of images or attack of cherished beliefs and institutions, especially religious

iconoclast: a person who destroys images used in religious worship or who attacks established beliefs and institutions

ideographic: symbolizing the idea of a thing without indicating the sounds which make up its name; for example, a numeral or a Chinese character

illuminated manuscripts: books that have been decorated with gold, colours, pictures, and designs

Inquisition: a court established by the Roman Catholic church in the thirteenth century to suppress heresy and punish heretics

Islam: the Muslim religion that follows the teachings of Muhammad as the prophet of Allah

jousting: a combat between two knights on horseback who charge and try to unseat each other with their lances

kanun: in Islam, the body of law that regulates all citizens of a state

legend: a story retold from the past that is widely accepted as true

legion: a military formation of ancient Rome

magistrate: a government official appointed to preside over court cases

Magna Carta: the charter of 1215 guaranteeing personal and political liberties in England

Mandate of Heaven: a theory of government from Confucian philosophy, which placed ruling power in the descendants of the Sky God (China's first ruler), so long as they ruled benevolently

manor: in the Middle Ages, the village and surrounding land administered by a lord

martyr: a person who dies or suffers for his/her beliefs

medieval: having to do with the Middle Ages

meritocracy: a system based on merit rather than hereditary right

Messiah: the promised deliverer of the Jewish people from Roman rule, believed by Christians to have been Jesus Christ

monarchy: a government headed by a king or queen

monogamy: the practice of being married to only one person at a time

monotheistic: believing in only one god

mosaic: a picture or design created using chips of coloured stone inlaid together

mosque: a Muslim place of worship

mummification: the process of embalming and preserving a dead body to make of it a mummy, as in ancient Egypt

Muslim: a person who believes in the religion of Islam

mythology: a body of myths, or traditional stories, that relate to a particular culture or person

natural selection: the process by which the strongest plants and animals adapt to their environment and survive

nomarch: the official who governed a nome (province) in ancient Egypt

nomes: the provinces into which ancient Egypt was divided

oasis: a fertile place in a desert

oligarchy: a form of government in which power rests with a few people

oracle: divine or supernatural communication, or the place where such communication takes place

ostracism: in ancient Greece, a method of banishing a citizen by popular vote, without trial or formal accusation

paleoanthropologist: a scientist who studies ancient societies based on fossil evidence

paleontologist: a scientist who studies life forms from the fossil remains of earlier geological periods

parliament: the highest law-making body of certain governments

patriarch: in the Byzantine empire, the bishop of a major city

patrician: a member of the wealthy landowning class of ancient Rome

perspective: a mathematical technique for drawing three-dimensional objects on a two-dimensional surface

pharaoh: the title given to the rulers of ancient Egypt

philosophy: the study of the truth and principles that underlie all knowledge

pillars of Islam: the five essential duties every Muslim must carry out

plebeian: a member of the common class in ancient Rome

pogrom: an organized and violent raid on a Jewish community

polygamy: the practice of having more than one spouse at a time

polytheistic: the belief in or worship of more than one god

predestination: a Calvinist concept which claims that salvation is determined before birth and cannot be changed

primary document: an original document or first-hand account written by someone who directly participated in an event

primogeniture: the right of succession belonging to the first-born child (especially the eldest son)

Protestant: a member of certain churches that developed after breaking with the Roman Catholic church in the sixteenth century

purgatory: in the Roman Catholic church, a temporary condition in which the soul is purified of sin after death

Qur'an: the sacred book of Islam

Reformation: the religious movement in sixteenth-century Europe that began with Roman Catholic reforms and ended with the establishment of Protestant churches

regent: a person who rules in the name of an absent or child sovereign

relic: something which belonged to a holy person, kept as a sacred memorial

relief: a sculpture in which figures stand out from the surface on which they are cut

religious cult: a system of religious worship, especially as expressed in ritual

Renaissance: the great revival of classical art, literature, and learning in Europe from the fourteenth to sixteenth centuries

republic: a state in which elected representatives run the government, usually with a president as the formal head

Romanesque: an architectural style, characterized by round arches and vaults, which developed in Europe in the early Middle Ages

sacrament: a sacred rite in a formal religious ceremony in a Christian church

samurai: a class of warriors in feudal Japan which served provincial lords

sarcophagus: a stone coffin, often ornamented with sculpture or inscriptions

secondary account: a second-hand account written by someone not directly involved in an event

secular: concerned with the affairs of this world rather than with religious or sacred ones

serf: a peasant who worked for a lord on a feudal estate

shari'a: in Islam, the formal code of law dealing with doctrine and morality as well as religious practices and civil and criminal law

shawabto: funerary figurines

shogun: the title given to a succession of hereditary commanders-in-chief in ancient Japan whose regime lasted over 600 years

sunna: the practices of Muhammad

symposion: in ancient Greece a formal dinner party for male friends held in the late afternoon

theocracy: a form of government in which religious officials rule

tilting: a jousting match in which the competitors charge each other along opposite sides of a barrier

tithe: a payment to the church of 10 percent of a person's income

tribune: in ancient Rome, an official chosen by the plebeians to protect their rights

triumvirate: government by three people together

tyrant: a cruel or unjust ruler, usually with absolute power

usury: the practice of lending money and charging interest for it

vernacular: the everyday language used by the people of a certain country or place

wadi: a valley or stream through which a stream flows during the rainy season

wattle and daub: a network of rods and twigs plastered with mud or clay and used as a building material

ziggurat: an ancient Babylonian or Assyrian temple in the form of a pyramid of terraced towers

PHOTO CREDITS

(t) = top; (b) = bottom; (l) = left; (r) = right; (c) = centre
AAAC = Ancient Art and Architecture Collection
Art Resource = Art Resource, New York
Asian Art Museum of San Francisco= The Avery Brundage Collection/Asian Art Museum of San Francisco
Bettmann = Corbis-Bettmann Archive, New York
Granger = The Granger Collection, New York

3 (background) Granger, (tl) Bettmann, (tr) Kenneth Garrett, (b) Ronald Bowen/Robert Harding Picture Library; 4 Don Johanson/Institute of Human Origins; 6 John Reader/Science Photo Library; 8 Bettmann; 9 Bettmann; 11 Don Johanson/Institute of Human Origins; 16 (l) Ronald Bowen/Robert Harding Picture Library, (r) The Field Museum, Chicago, IL/Neg. 77811; 17 Granger; 18 Ronald Bowen/Robert Harding Picture Library; 20 Kenneth Garret/National Geographic; 22 Sonia Halliday; 29 (background) Granger, (tl) Granger, (tr) University of Pennsylvania/Neg S5-2319, (b) Ronald Sheridan/AAA; 30 University of Pennsylvania/Neg. S8-139328; 31 Robert Harding Picture Library; 32 (l) Granger, (c) University of Pennsylvania/Neg. S5-23191, (r) University of Pennsylvania/Neg. S5-133835; 36 Granger; 37 Bettmann; 39 Mansell Collection; 40 Ronald Sheridan/AAA; 41 Granger; 43 Ronald Sheridan/AAA; 44 (t) Granger, (b) Bettmann; 45 (t) Granger, (b) Ronald Sheridan/AAA; 50 Ronald Sheridan/AAA; 54 (t) Granger, (b) Bettmann; 55 Bettmann; 56 (l) Granger, (r) AAA; 59 Granger; 60 Robin White/Fotolex; 61 Mary Jelliffe/AAA; 64 Granger; 67 E. Hobson/AAA; 68 (t) Granger, (b) Robin White/Fotolex; 70 Alinari/Art Resource; 71 Borromeo/Art Resource; 73 Granger; 76 (l) Giraudon/Art Resource, (r) Bettmann; 77 Bettmann; 79 Corel CDROM; 80 Granger; 82 Bettmann; 85 Bettmann; 86 The Metropolitan Museum of Art (78119tfB); 90 (both) Ronald Sheridan/AAA; 91 Granger; 92 Robin White/Fotolex; 103 (background) Granger, (tl) Bettmann, (tr) British Museum/B209927, (b) Granger; 104 Granger; 105 Gary Braasch/Woodfin Camp; 107 Roger Sheridan/AAA; 112 (t) Geographical Visual Aids, (b) Bettmann; 116 Bettmann; 118 Bettmann; 121 British Museum/PS271245; 123 Bettmann; 124 (t) Bettmann, (b) G.T. Garvey/AAA; 130 Granger; 132 Foto Marburg/Art Resource; 134 Granger; 138 British Museum/B90751; 140 British Museum/B209927; 141 Granger; 142 British Museum/B90751; 144 (t) Giraudon/Art Resource, (b) Granger; 146 (tl) Granger, (tr) Granger, (b) Lauros-Giraudon/Art Resource; 147 Hulton-Deutsch; 148 Jean-Pierre Amet/Sygma/ Publiphoto; 150 Geographical Visual Aids; 153 Granger; 156 Bettmann; 157 Geographical Visual Aids; 159 Alinari/Art Resource; 163 Bettmann; 164 Mansell Collection; 168 Granger; 169 (t) Granger, (b) Bettmann;

174 Granger; 179 Bettmann; 180 Bettmann; 182 Granger; 186 (l, c) Bettmann, (r) Alinari/Art Resource; 187 Foto Marburg/Art Resource; 189 Mary Evans Picture Library; 190 Granger; 191 Hulton Deutsch; 193 Nimatallah/Art Resource; 196 Granger; 197 (t) Stevens/AAA, (bl) Scala/Art Resource, (br) Corel CDROM; 198 Alinari/Art Resource; 200 Geographical Visual Aids; 209 (background) Granger, (tl) Lauros-Giraudon/Art Resource, (tr) Christine Osborne Pictures, (b) Sonia Halliday; 210 Granger; 211 Snowden/Hoyer/ Focus/Woodfin Camp; 213 Granger; 218 (all) Granger; 219 Granger; 221 (t) Granger, (b) Giraudon/Art Resource; 222 Granger; 224 Granger; 225 Granger; 227 Granger; 228 Granger; 231 Granger; 235 Granger; 236 Granger; 237 Granger; 239 Erich Lessing/Art Resource; 242 British Library; 244 Alinari/Art Resource; 245 Lauros-Giraudon/Art Resource; 246 Granger; 248 Granger; 249 Granger; 251 Granger; 252 Granger; 254 D. Alix/Publiphoto; 257 Granger; 258 (both) Granger; 260 Granger; 261 Granger; 263 Scala/Art Resource; 265 Granger; 268 Granger; 270 (t) Granger, (b) Erich Lessing/Art Resource; 271 (both) Granger; 272 Alinari/ Art Resource, (b) Granger; 273 Granger; 275 Yves Beaulieu/Publiphoto; 276 (l) Granger, (r) J. Lauzon/ Publiphoto; 278 Granger; 279 Granger; 281 Art Resource; 282 Granger; 283 Granger; 284 Granger; 287 Sonia Halliday; 289 Granger; 290 Granger; 291 Granger; 294 Granger; 295 Alinari/Art Resource; 299 Sonia Halliday; 300 Scala/Art Resource; 302 Granger; 304 Sonia Halliday; 305 Sylvain Grandadam/Publiphoto; 306 Granger; 308 (l) Sonia Halliday, (r) British Library; 311 Granger; 313 (t) Granger, (b) Bettmann; 314 *The Meeting of Joseph and Potifar's Wife*, Cod.theol.graec. 31(Vienna Genesis), pag. 32/Austrian National Library; 316 (t) Granger, (b) Sonia Halliday; 317 Erich Lessing/ Art Resource; 318 (both) Sonia Halliday; 319 Alinari/Art Resource; 320 (t) Corel CDROM, (b) Jane Taylor/Sonia Halliday; 324 Granger; 325 D. Hudson/Publiphoto; 327 (t) Sonia Halliday, (b) Robert Azzi/Woodfin Camp; 330 Christine Osborne Pictures; 331 The British Library/Ms Add 259 00f.121v; 332 Israel Antiquities Authority; 334 Sonia Halliday; 335 G. Thouvenin/Explorer/Publiphoto; 337 Bettmann; 339 Giraudon/Art Resource; 341 Granger; 342 Christine Osborne Pictures; 343 Granger; 344 Corel CDROM; 345 Robert Azzi/Woodfin Camp; 347 J.P.H. Ruiz/Hoa-Qui/Publiphoto; 351 M. Shandiz/ Sygma/Publiphoto; 353 *View of Ankara*/Rijksmuseum-Stichting Amsterdam; 356 (t) A. Keler/Sygma/ Publiphoto, (b) Granger; 357 Laura Lushington/Sonia Halliday; 359 Christine Osborne Pictures; 360 (t) Victoria and Albert Museum, London/Art Resource, (b) Sonia Halliday; 363 Bettmann; 365 (t) The Metropolitan Museum of Art/The Cora Timken Burnett Collection of Persian miniatures and other Persian art objects/

Bequest of Cora Timken Burnett, 1957 (57.51.21), (b) Sonia Halliday; 373 (background) An Keren PPS/Photo Researchers, (tl) Granger, (tr) Chuck Fishman/Woodfin Camp, (b) Asian Museum of San Francisco; 374 Granger; 376 (t) Lowell Georgia/Photo Researchers, (b) Granger; 380 Brian Brake/Photo Researchers; 381 An Keren PPS/Photo Researchers; 383 Granger; 386 National Palace Museum, Taiwan; 388 Granger; 390 (l) Asian Art Museum of San Francisco (detail), (r) MacQuitty International Collection; 394 Palace Museum, Beijing; 395 Werner Forman Archive/Peking Palace Museum/Art Resource; 396 Freer Gallery of Art, Smithsonian Institution, Washington, D.C./36.6; 397 *Court Ladies Preparing Newly Woven Silk*/Chinese and Japanese Special Fund/Museum of Fine Arts, Boston; 398 Giraudon/Art Resource; 399 National Gallery of Canada, Ottawa; 400 Bibliotheque Nationale; 401 Oriental and India Office Collections/British Library; 405 Jed Share/First Light; 406 Karen Kasmauski/Woodfin Camp; 407 Asian Art Museum of San Francisco; 410 Asian Art Museum of San Francisco; 411 Granger; 412 Chuck Fishman/Woodfin Camp; 413 Asian Art Museum of San Francisco (detail); 415 Fenollosa-Weld Collection/Museum of Fine Arts, Boston; 417 Jed Share/First Light; 418 Barb and Ron Kroll; 419 Dallas and John Heaton/First Light; 420 Asian Museum of San Francisco (detail); 422 Tomomi Saito/Dunq/Photo Researchers; 423 Spencer Collection/The New York Public Library/Japanese Ms 165; 424 Orion Press/Tony Stone Images; 426 Granger; 427 Hiroshi Harada/Dunq/ Photo Researchers; 429 (t) Granger, (b) Hulton Deutsch; 435 (background) J. Belles/First Light, (tl) Kimbell Art Museum, Fort Worth, Texas, (tr) Robert Feldman, (b) N. Pecnik/Visuals Unlimited; 436 D. Donne Byrant/DDB Stock; 438 Peter Chartrand/DDB Stock; 439 D. Donne Bryant/DDB Stock; 443 (t) Simone Huber/Tony Stone Images, (b) Bibliotheque Nationale; 444 Peabody Museum, Harvard University/Photography by Hillel Burger/N26979; 445 N. Pecnik/Visuals Unlimited; 449 Carol Gracie; 450 Robert Fried/DDB Stock; 452 Dagli Orti; 454 D. Donne Byrant/DDB Stock; 457 (t) Kimbell Art Museum, Forth Worth, Texas, (b) Peabody Museum, Harvard University/N26980; 458 (l) D. Donne Bryant/ DDB Stock, (r) Granger; 459 Robert J. Walker; 460 D. Donne Bryant/DDB Stock; 465 Robert Fried/DDB Stock; 468 Det Kongelige Bibliotek; 471 (both) Granger; 472 Det Kongelige Bibliotek; 475 Granger; 476 (t) Robert Feldman, (b) Granger; 477 Virginia Ferrero/DDB Stock; 479 (l) Robert Feldman, (r) Inga Spence/DDB Stock; 481 J. Belles/First Light; 482 Det Kongelige Bibliotek; 483 Det Kongelige Bibliotek; 484 (l) Carolyn Kerson/DDB Stock, (r) Robert Feldman; 486 University of Pennsylvania Museum/S8-56203; 487 Museo Amano, Lima.

ACKNOWLEDGEMENTS OF SOURCES

4 From "Face-to-Face with Lucy's Family" by Donald C. Johanson from *National Geographic*, March 1996. Reprinted by permission. 5 "Earth's History" reprinted with the permission of Gage Educational Publishing Company from *Other Places, Other Times*, Rosemary Neering and Peter Grant. Copyright © 1986 Gage Educational Publishing Company. 14 Figure 1-8 from *Patterns in Prehistory*, Robert J. Wenke, (New York: Oxford University Press, 1990). Reprinted by permission of Oxford University Press, Inc. 15 Figure 1-9, from *Patterns in Prehistory*, Robert J. Wenke, (New York: Oxford University Press, 1990). Reprinted by permission of Oxford University Press, Inc. 20 "Tool Time Chart" reprinted with the permission of Gage Educational Publishing Company from *Other Places, Other Times*, Rosemary Neering and Peter Grant. Copyright © 1986 Gage Educational Publishing Company. 23 Figure 1-19 "Three squares" from *Patterns in Prehistory*, Robert J. Wenke (New York: Oxford University Press, 1990). Reprinted by permission of Oxford University Press, Inc. 39 "Plan of Babylon, sixth century B.C." reprinted from *Everyday Life in Babylonia & Assyria*, H.W.F. Saggs by permission of B.T. Batsford Limited. 50 Herodotus. Quote from *The Persian Wars*, translated by George Rawlinson, copyright, 1942, by Random House Inc. Reprinted by permission of Random House, Inc. 55 From *The Epic of Gilgamesh*, translated by N.K. Sandars, (Penguin Books, 1972) p92. 93 "Finding true north" from *The Pyramids*, John Weeks, (Cambridge University Press, 1971), © Cambridge University Press, 1971. Reprinted with the permission of Cambridge University Press; "Mining the limestone" from *The Pyramids*, John Weeks, (Cambridge University Press, 1971), © Cambridge University Press, 1971. Reprinted with the permission of Cambridge University Press. 94 "Transporting the stone to the building site" from *The Pyramids*, John Weeks, (Cambridge University Press, 1971), © Cambridge University Press, 1971. Reprinted with the permission of Cambridge University Press; "Constructing the pyramid" from *The Pyramids*, John Weeks, (Cambridge University Press, 1971), © Cambridge University Press, 1971. Reprinted with the permission of Cambridge University Press. 104 From *The Iliad of Homer*, translated by Ennis Rees, (Oxford University Press, 1991) pp453-454. 116 Herodotus

excerpt of the Battle of Salamis reprinted from *The Ancient World*, Martin Robert (Macmillan, 1979), pp142-143; Aeschylus excerpt of the Battle of Salamis from *Ancient Greece*, Margaret Killingray, World History Program, Greenhaven Press, San Diego, California. Reprinted by permission. 118-119 Thucydides, adaptation of Pericles Funeral Oration from *The Greek Commonwealth*, 5th edition, A. Zimmerman, (Clarendon Press, revised 1931). Reprinted by permission of Oxford University Press. 127 Excerpt from *The Republic*, Plato, translated by Desmond Lee, (Penguin Classics, 1955) copyright © H.D.P. Lee, 1955. Reproduced by permission of Penguin Books Ltd.; Aristotle, adapted excerpt from *The Politics*, edited and translated by Ernest Barker, (Clarendon Press, 1946). Reprinted by permission of Oxford University Press. 139 Excerpt from *The Republic*, Plato, translated by Desmond Lee (Penguin Classics, 1955) copyright © H.D.P. Lee, 1955. Reproduced by permission of Penguin Books Ltd. 140 Greek dress illustration from *Greek and Roman Life*, Ian Jenkins, (London: British Museum Press, 1986). Reprinted by permission of British Museum Press. 142 Ancient Greek town house illustration from *Greek and Roman Life*, Ian Jenkins, (London: British Museum Press, 1986). Reprinted by permission of British Museum Press. 149 From *The Odyssey*, Homer, translated by E.V. Rieu, (London: Penguin Books, 1946) pp149-150. 151 From "Ecclesiazusae", Aristophanes, translated by Jack Lindsay, from *The Complete Plays of Aristophanes*, edited by Moses Hadas, (New York: Bantam Books, 1962) pp 424-425. 182 From *The Annals of Imperial Rome*, Tacitus, translated by Michael Grant, (London: Penguin Books, 1956) p354. 195 From *Cicero Selected Letters*, translated by D.R. Shackleton Bailey, (Penguin Books, n.d.) p138. 196 From *The Aeneid of Virgil*, translated by C. Day Lewis, (London: The Hogarth Press, 1961) p139; from *The History of Rome: Volume 3*, Livy, from Everyman's Library, edited by Ernest Rhys, (J.M. Dent & Sons Ltd., 1931) pp3-4. 238 Reprinted from "The Murder of Thomas Becket" from *The Medieval Reader*, edited by Norman F. Cantor, (HarperCollins Publisher, 1994) pp186, 188. 266 From *The Prince*, Niccolo Machiavelli, translated by N.H.T., (London: Kegan Paul, Trench & Co., 1882) pp109, 110-111. 280 Excerpts reprinted by permission from

Martin Luther's Basic Theological Writings, edited by Timothy F. Lull, copyright © 1989 Augsburg Fortress. 287 Reprinted from *Great Ages of Man: Byzantium*, Philip Sherrard and the Editors of Time-Life Books, (Time-Life Books, 1966) p36. 301 "Unlucky Emperors" adapted from *Great Ages of Man: Byzantium*, Philip Sherrard and the Editors of Time-Life Books. © 1966 Time-Life Books Inc. 342 "The Exordium" from *The Koran*, translated by N.J. Dawood, (Penguin Classics, 1956, Fifth revised edition 1990) copyright © N.J. Dawood, 1956, 1959, 1966, 1968, 1974, 1990. Reprinted by permission of Penguin Books Ltd. 362 Poems from *A Garden Beyond Paradise: The Mystical Poetry of Rumi*, Jonathan Star and Shahram Shiva. Reprinted by permission of Shahram Shiva. 374 From *Cambridge Illustrated History: China*, P.B. Edbrey, (Cambridge University Press, 1966) p47. 385 From *Ancient China*, Schafer and the Editors of Time-Life Books, (New York: Time-Life Books, 1967) p84. 393 From *Translations from the Chinese*, Arthur Waley, (New York: Alfred A. Knopf, 1919, 1941) pp72-73. 411 From *Japan: Selected Readings*, edited by Hyman Kublin, (Houghton Mifflin Company, 1973) pp31-32, 33. 417 From "Man'Yoshu", translated by the Japanese Classics Translation Committee under the auspices of the Nippon Gakujutsu Shinkokai, in *Anthology of Japanese Literature*, edited by Donald Keene, (New York: Grove Press, 1955) pp37-38. 426 From *The Tale of Genji: A Novel in Six Parts* by Lady Murasaki, translated by Arthur Waley (London: George Allen & Unwin, 1935). Reprinted by permission of Harper Collins Publishers. 436 From *Incidents of Travel in South America, Chiapas and Yucatan*, 2 volumes, John Lloyd Stephen, (London, 1844) p82. 449 From *Maya* by Charles Gallenkamp. Copyright © 1959, 1976, 1981, 1985, renewed 1987 by Charles Gallenkamp. Used by permission of Viking Penguin, a division of Penguin Books USA Inc. 468 From *Ancient America*, John Guyatt, Appendix Document 16. Reprinted by permission of Greenhaven Press, San Diego. 472 From *Ancient America*, John Guyatt, Appendix Document 15. Reprinted by permission of Greenhaven Press, San Diego. 475 Reprinted from *Everyday Life of the Incas*, Ann Kendall, (Dorset Press, 1973), p47. 487 Quipu description based on *The Last of the Incas*, Edward Hyams and George Ordish, (New York: Dorset Press, 1963) pp76-87.

INDEX